The
Supreme Court
Yearbook
1991-1992

The
Supreme Court
Yearbook
1991-1992

Joan Biskupic

Congressional Quarterly Inc.
Washington, D.C.

Congressional Quarterly Inc.

Congressional Quarterly Inc., an editorial research service and publishing company, serves clients in the fields of news, education, business, and government. It combines specific coverage of Congress, government, and politics contained in the *Congressional Quarterly Weekly Report* with the more general subject range of an affiliated publication, *CQ Researcher.*

Congressional Quarterly publishes the *Congressional Quarterly Weekly Report* and a variety of books, including college political science textbooks under the CQ Press imprint and public affairs paperbacks on developing issues and events. CQ also publishes information directories and reference books on the federal government, national elections, and politics, such as the *Guide to the Presidency,* the *Guide to Congress,* the *Guide to the U.S. Supreme Court,* the *Guide to U.S. Elections,* and *Politics in America.* The *CQ Almanac,* a compendium of legislation for one session of Congress, is published each year. *Congress and the Nation,* a record of government for a presidential term, is published every four years. *Congress A to Z* and *The Presidency A to Z* are ready-reference encyclopedias providing essential information about the branches of U.S. government. The final volume in this set, *The Supreme Court A to Z,* will be available in June 1993.

CQ publishes the *Congressional Monitor,* a daily report on current and future activities of congressional committees, and several newsletters including *Congressional Insight,* a weekly analysis of congressional action.

An electronic online information system, Washington Alert, provides immediate access to CQ's databases of legislative action, votes, schedules, profiles, and analyses.

Cover design: Julie Booth

Photo credits: cover, pp. 31, 40, 180, 184 - R. Michael Jenkins; p. 3 - Ken Heinen; pp. 9, 206, 208, 212, 213, 215 - Supreme Court Historical Society/National Geographic Society; p. 21 - Teresa Zabala; pp. 51, 62, 203, 224 - Collection of the Curator, Supreme Court of the United States.

Copyright © 1993 Congressional Quarterly Inc.
1414 22nd St. N.W.
Washington, D.C. 20037

Published in the United States of America

ISBN 0-87187-716-3
ISBN 0-87187-715-5 (pbk.)
ISSN 1054-2701

Contents

Preface

The Supreme Court began its 1992-1993 term on October 5, 1992, and for the first time in three years, the nine sitting justices were the same as when the prior term ended. But few Court observers predicted that the makeup of the Court would remain unaltered for long. Because of the ages and bench tenure of some of the justices, the president elected in November 1992 could name as many as five new justices during his four-year term.

The Supreme Court Yearbook series is for people who are interested in the Court and the impact of the justices' decisions on public issues but who are not experts in the law. Although the books are intended to stand alone, they are used best with CQ's *Guide to the U.S. Supreme Court,* Second Edition, which covers 200 years of Supreme Court history.

This edition of the *Yearbook* provides an in-depth look at the 1991-1992 term. The opening chapter considers how today's Court increasingly is asked to render more decisions that affect the personal lives of Americans. Chapter 2 presents an overview of the 1991-1992 term and details ten major cases. Chapter 3 contains summaries of all 107 signed opinions for the term, arranged alphabetically by subject. Following that, in Chapter 4, are excerpts from the 1991-1992 term's major cases. Chapter 5 provides a preview of the 1992-1993 term and highlights a number of cases on the Court's docket. The final chapter explains the inner workings of the Court. Biographies of the justices and a glossary of legal terms are included in the Appendix.

The *Yearbook* series, named an Outstanding Reference Source by the American Library Association, has reached a wider audience with each edition. CQ Book Department director David R. Tarr and his colleagues deserve much credit for its success. For this edition, Colleen McGuiness provided especially thoughtful editing and Kerry V. Kern oversaw production. To all, I am grateful.

1 | The Contemporary Court

Moreso than at any other time in the history of the Supreme Court, the justices are confronting issues involving family problems and lifestyle questions. A generation ago the Court was known for taking an active and broad role in shaping American society—reordering the way people voted, where children went to school, and how police enforced the law; now it is occupied more by concerns that arise from personal, daily life.

Since 1988, for example, the Court has decided whether a family may cut off their comatose daughter's artificial life supports and if companies may exclude pregnant women from jobs that might harm a developing fetus. The justices considered the competing paternity rights of two men, one who was married to the child's mother and one who was the biological father. The Court also weighed whether a century-old civil rights law could be invoked when a social services agency fails to protect a child from abuse, when a foster child is not reunited with his family, or when a municipal sanitation worker dies while cleaning a sewer line.

The conservative majority under Chief Justice William H. Rehnquist, which coalesced during the late 1980s, generally opposed an expansive reading of the Constitution or statutes to address contemporary social dilemmas, deferring to Congress and state lawmakers on policy matters. But a reality of Court life is that, to a certain extent, a new majority lives within the boundaries set by its predecessors. In 1992, the Court's abortion decision in *Planned Parenthood of Southeastern Pennsylvania v. Casey* stressed court precedent and a regard for individual liberty in upholding most of *Roe v. Wade*, the 1973 decision that said women have a fundamental right to abortion.

Although the Rehnquist Court might want to be out of the fray on social policy, the docket continues to be filled with such cases. According to University of Virginia professor A. E. Dick Howard, "Once the court moves into an area—no matter if it rules conservatively or liberally—it doesn't abandon the field."

□□□

The Court began broadly expanding constitutional principles in response to social issues under Chief Justice Earl Warren (1953-1969). For example, the concept of equal protection for minorities was increased, notably in *Brown v. Board of Education* (1954), and due process of law meant more protection for criminal defendants. Under Chief Justice

Warren E. Burger (1969-1986), affirmative action was sanctioned through a reinterpretation of the Constitution's Equal Protection Clause and abortion became legal nationwide. In *Roe v. Wade*, the Court said a right to privacy, which derives from the Due Process Clause of the Fourteenth Amendment, encompasses and protects a woman's decision whether or not to bear a child.

The Court since has built on those landmark rulings, and today the ramifications continue to be felt as the justices are asked to apply equal protection and due process guarantees to a variety of situations.

□□□

The Court's involvement in virtually every area of human life arises from both its constitutional decisions and the interpretation of congressional statutes. For example, when the Court ruled in February 1992 that a student who was sexually harassed by a teacher could sue for money damages (*Franklin v. Gwinnett County Public Schools*), the decision was based on a broad reading of Title IX of the Education Amendments of 1972. A statute also was at the heart of the 1991 decision on the rights of pregnant women in performing hazardous jobs, *United Auto Workers v. Johnson Controls*. Based on an interpretation of the 1964 Civil Rights Act and the 1978 Pregnancy Discrimination amendments, the Court's unanimous ruling stated that companies may not exclude women from jobs that might harm a developing fetus. A five-justice majority then went on to say that Congress intended to forbid all hiring practices contingent upon a worker's ability to have children.

The Court's determinations on abortion and other areas of individual rights have prompted the greatest public anguish and debate. The 1990 case of Nancy Cruzan, who was in a persistent vegetative state after a car accident, involved the Fourteenth Amendment's implied right of privacy. The Court in 1976 avoided the question of who decides when life ends by refusing to review a New Jersey Supreme Court ruling that allowed Karen Ann Quinlan to be removed from a respirator. (She fell into a coma after taking tranquilizers and drinking alcoholic beverages.) But in *Cruzan v. Director, Missouri Department of Health*, the Court accepted that an individual has a constitutionally protected right to refuse lifesaving food and water. At the same time, a five-justice majority led by Rehnquist upheld Missouri legislation requiring clear evidence of a person's wish to die.

What in another generation might have been a routine personal injury case today can have civil rights overtones, mainly through the use of a federal law commonly known as Section 1983, in reference to its designation in Chapter 42 of the *United States Code*. Section 1983 provides money damages for people who prove their constitutional rights

The public may attend oral arguments, which are held in two-week sessions from the first Monday in October until mid-April.

were violated because of official government actions. Congress wrote the law in 1871 to stop state government abuse of blacks. As the Court adopted broader views of the Constitution and allowed the statute to be used against cities and other government entities, a wider range of litigants have invoked the law, with mixed results.

In 1989, the Court ruled that a county social services department is not liable under Section 1983 for failing to intervene in a child abuse case that ended with the death of the young boy (*DeShaney v. Winnebago County Department of Social Services*). The Court said the law is intended to protect people from the state, not from the conduct of others. But a year later, in *Wilder v. Virginia Hospital Association*, the Court said hospitals and nursing homes could use Section 1983 to pursue higher Medicaid reimbursement rates from the states. The Court said federal Medicaid law specifically created a right to sue to seek better rates to meet the costs of health care. During the 1991-1992 term, the justices rejected efforts to use Section 1983 in two key cases. In *Suter v.*

Artist M., the Court ruled that foster children may not cite the civil rights law to obtain money damages from states that fail to make reasonable efforts to unite families. The Court said the federal adoption law at the heart of the case did not create a clear right to sue as the Medicaid law had. In *Collins v. City of Harker Heights*, the Court said that a sewer worker's widow cannot sue the city based on a violation of due process of law because the city failed to train or warn the worker about job hazards. The justices said no due process right to a safe job environment exists.

□□□

To say that the Court is being drawn into decisions about personal lives is not to say that the justices want to be making them or want to be breaking new ground on individual rights.

In the 1989 paternity dispute *Michael H. v. Gerald D.*, a five-justice majority sided with a man who was married to a child's mother over the interests of a man who said he was the child's biological father. The splintered justices engaged in vigorous debate on what defines a family and traditional-versus-modern concepts of the liberty interests protected by the Due Process Clause of the Fourteenth Amendment.

Addressing Justice William J. Brennan, Jr.'s complaints about the Court's "pinched conception of the family," Justice Antonin Scalia responded: "The family unit accorded traditional respect in our society, which we have referred to as the 'unitary family,' is typified, of course, by the marital family, but also includes the household of unmarried parents and their children.

"Perhaps the concept can be expanded even beyond this, but this will bear no resemblance to traditionally respected relationships—and will thus cease to have any constitutional significance—if it is stretched so far as to include the relationship established between a married woman, her lover and their child during a three-month sojourn in St. Thomas, or during a subsequent 8-month period when, if he happened to be in Los Angeles, he stayed with her and the child."

The Rehnquist Court wants to extract itself from social issues. In the 1988-1989 term, for example, the Court narrowly read federal job discrimination law. The rulings affected Title VII of the 1964 Civil Rights Act, which bars employment discrimination based on race, color, religion, sex, or national origin. The Court also scaled back the reach of an 1866 law that permits damage awards for racial bias in making contracts. (Congress subsequently passed the 1991 Civil Rights Act to reverse the results of several antibias rulings under Rehnquist.) In both *Cruzan* and *Michael H.*, the Rehnquist Court resisted new interpretations of constitutional rights and deferred to state legislation and traditional concepts of family. Even in its decisions to uphold *Roe v. Wade*, the Court nevertheless allowed considerable legislative latitude for restrictions on abortion.

In terms of sheer numbers, the Rehnquist Court also is hearing fewer disputes. In the 1991-1992 term, it issued 107 signed opinions, down slightly from the 112 opinions in 1990-1991 term and 129 the term before that. The 1991-1992 total is almost a quarter less than the 151 cases decided in each of the terms ended in 1982 and 1983. During the 1970s, the court averaged 130 signed opinions a term.

The Court's docket is a byproduct of a changing society, where artificial life supports now are available, the women's movement continues to fight for reproductive rights, and the high incidence of divorce and growing acceptance of homosexual lifestyles challenge traditional notions of family. "Compared to even 50 years ago, the court makes many more rulings that are relevant to people's lives," said University of Chicago law professor Mary Becker.

2 | *The 1991–1992 Term*

After a half-decade of controversy and change, the Supreme Court in its 1991-1992 term made only an incremental difference in the law.

Consider what the Court has seen since 1987: the historic Senate fight over the nomination of Robert H. Bork and the eventual seating of Anthony M. Kennedy; the watershed 1988-1989 term in which a new conservative majority reinterpreted the nation's civil rights statutes and opened the door to restrictive abortion laws with its opinion in *Webster v. Reproductive Health Services;* the back-to-back resignations of liberal bulwarks William J. Brennan, Jr., and Thurgood Marshall, in 1990 and 1991, respectively; the subsequent appointment of David H. Souter and the unprecedented controversy over appointee Clarence Thomas; and the Court's own rulings in dozens of cases, displaying a vigorous new conservatism.

But the 1991-1992 term found the Court trying to steady itself. Justices Sandra Day O'Connor, Kennedy, and Souter formed a three-justice coalition that held sway in a number of decisions and that moderated the Court. Their opinions revealed an anxiety about the Court as an institution in American society and resisted the imposition of rapid change. In an unusual joint opinion (*Planned Parenthood of Southeastern Pennsylvania v. Casey*), they stressed the importance of precedent and the need to preserve the integrity of the Court.

The Court tempered its activism in the 1991-1992 term. In *Casey*, the majority affirmed most of *Roe v. Wade*, the 1973 landmark decision that made abortion legal nationwide. A narrow majority also resisted pressure from Chief Justice William H. Rehnquist, three other conservative justices, and the Bush administration to ease the separation between church and state. Adhering to precedent, the Court ruled against prayer at public school graduations (*Lee v. Weisman*). And in a major property rights case (*Lucas v. South Carolina Coastal Council*), the Court declined to broadly recast property law, although it opened the door to the possibility of greater rights for landowners at the cost of environmental protection statutes.

The Court also appeared to pull back from what only one term earlier observers had interpreted as an assault on the First Amendment (*Barnes v. Glen Theatre, Cohen v. Cowles Media, Gentile v. State Bar of Nevada,* and *Rust v. Sullivan*). The Court in 1991-1992 expansively interpreted the First Amendment to strike down laws that banned "hate speech" tied to race, color, creed, religion, or gender; that required authors of stories detailing their criminal acts to relinquish their publishing profits to a victims' fund; and that imposed a varying fee for parades in a Georgia county.

The Court, however, continued to take a strong hand against state court defendants seeking to challenge their cases in federal court. The Court restricted inmates' use of writs of habeas corpus, allowing states to have the final say on prisoner appeals in more situations. In the spring of 1992, the Court rejected the highly publicized pleas of two death row defendants to avoid execution. The Court allowed convicted murderer Robert Alton Harris to become the first person executed in California in twenty-five years and ignored an unprecedented media blitz on behalf of Virginian Roger Coleman, also convicted of murder, to escape the electric chair.

□□□

Two sets of alliances surfaced among justices in the 1991-1992 term.

The first was made up of O'Connor, Kennedy, and Souter, who, when they voted together, always were in the majority. The justices constituted an effective conservative-centrist bloc that controlled the outcomes of key cases, notably the *Casey* ruling and *Lee v. Weisman* school prayer dispute.

In recent terms, O'Connor had been gravitating toward the middle of the Court, likely in response to the unyielding conservatism of Chief Justice Rehnquist and, even more to the right, Justice Antonin Scalia. Although Souter during his first year on the bench regularly joined Rehnquist, he emerged as a swing vote and retained some of the voice of moderation that marked his testimony at his Senate confirmation hearings. Kennedy, however, was the surprise member of the triumvirate. In his first three full terms on the Court, Kennedy voted overwhelmingly with Chief Justice Rehnquist and Scalia. In the 1988-1989 term, for example, Kennedy voted with Scalia 93 percent of the time. By the 1991-1992 term, however, the percentage dropped to 76. Further, Kennedy's rulings in 1991-1992 on abortion and school prayer reversed or modified his previous, more conservative opinions.

The other alliance was between Justices Scalia and Thomas. The Court's newest justice enthusiastically joined Scalia in rejecting legislative history in the interpretation of statutes and emphasizing the original intent of the Framers for constitutional analysis. In many ways, Thomas took over Kennedy's position as a predictable fifth vote within the conservative wing on key issues.

Generally speaking, "conservative" in the judicial context means that the courts will not decide issues that are the province of legislators and, in a contest between government interest and individual rights, will enhance

The 1991-1992 Court: (seated, from left to right) John Paul Stevens, Byron R. White, Chief Justice William H. Rehnquist, Harry A. Blackmun, Sandra Day O'Connor, (standing, from left to right) David H. Souter, Antonin Scalia, Anthony M. Kennedy, and Clarence Thomas.

government power. Judicial liberals tend to have their priorities reversed, favoring individual interests and permitting courts to go beyond the bounds of a statute and past interpretations of the Constitution to decide social policy questions.

A clear conservative majority, led by Rehnquist, picked up a more activist pace in the 1990-1991 term. The majority overruled five criminal law precedents and in other cases took up constitutional issues that dissenting justices said did not have to be considered.

With a reconstituted Court in 1991-1992, however, the justices could not be neatly divided into liberal and conservative camps. Harry A. Blackmun was the most liberal justice, and he usually was joined by John Paul Stevens. Meanwhile, a spectrum of conservatism ranged from Scalia, Thomas, and Rehnquist on the far right; to Byron R. White, the court's most senior justice, who voted with the staunch conservatives more often than not but shifted to the middle on many key cases; to O'Connor, Kennedy, and Souter, in the newly formed middle, who were more likely than any of the other conservatives to sign an opinion with Blackmun and Stevens. Of the fourteen decisions with 5-4 splits, Blackmun, Stevens, O'Connor, Kennedy, and Souter were together most often as a majority— five times.

□□□

Following are ten major cases, listed chronologically as they were announced, from the 1991-1992 Supreme Court term:

Simon & Schuster, Inc. v. Members of New York State Crime Victims Board, decided by an 8-0 vote, December 10, 1991; O'Connor wrote the opinion; Thomas took no part in the case.

In a case affecting the popular genre of crime stories, the Court struck down a New York statute that redirected the book proceeds from criminals to a victims' fund. The unanimous Court said that New York's so-called "Son of Sam" law violated free speech guarantees of the First Amendment.

The law was aimed at ensuring that criminals do not profit from their exploits and that victims are compensated for their injuries. But the Court said New York lawmakers worded the statute too broadly. The law covered works on any subject that expressed an author's thoughts about his crime, however incidentally, and it applied to writers who admitted to crimes even if they never were charged or convicted.

Justice O'Connor said that at the outset the statute is flawed for singling out speech on a particular subject—crime. "[T]he statute plainly imposes a financial disincentive only on speech of a particular content." She was joined by Justices Rehnquist, White, Stevens, Scalia, and Souter. Blackmun and Kennedy concurred in the judgment. Thomas, who was not on the bench when the case was argued, did not participate.

The decision was a victory for free speech advocates, many of whom expected, because of previous recent rulings, that the conservative Court would take a different approach. In the 1990-1991 term, narrow majorities upheld a "gag" rule on abortion counseling at public clinics (*Rust v. Sullivan*), ruled that nude dancing was a form of expression that could be outlawed (*Barnes v. Glen Theatre*), decided that newspapers could be held liable when they break promises of confidentiality (*Cohen v. Cowles Media*), and curtailed trial lawyers' public comments (*Gentile v. State Bar of Nevada*).

But the First Amendment fared well in the 1991-1992 term. In addition to invalidating New York's "Son of Sam" law, which had become a model for other states' legislation, the Court used the Free Speech Clause to strike down a city "hate crime" ordinance (*R. A. V. v. St. Paul, Minn.*) and to reject a county's parade fee (*Forsyth County v. Nationalist Movement*).

At the center of the *Simon & Schuster* case was the 1986 book *Wiseguy: Life in a Mafia Family.* (It was turned into the highly acclaimed film "Goodfellas" in 1990.) The book was the fruit of a deal the publisher made with author Nicholas Pileggi, who contracted with organized crime figure Henry Hill. According to the Court opinion, Hill admitted to having been involved in many crimes, including the 1978-1979 Boston College basketball point-shaving scandal and the theft of $6 million from Lufthansa Airlines in 1978, reportedly the largest cash robbery in American history.

Under the "Son of Sam" law, money from works such as *Wiseguy* were to be put in an escrow account for five years, after which it then would go to victims and creditors of the criminal. The law was named after a serial killer, David Berkowitz, who terrorized New York in 1977 and called himself "Son of Sam."

According to the Court, the law, since enactment in 1977, was invoked mostly in well-publicized cases; for example, those involving Jean Harris, the convicted killer of "Scarsdale Diet" doctor Herman Tarnower; Mark David Chapman, the man convicted of assassinating John Lennon; and R. Foster Winans, the former *Wall Street Journal* columnist convicted of insider trading.

After the New York State Crime Victims Board went after Hill's proceeds, Simon & Schuster challenged the law. A federal district court ruled that the statute did not impinge on the First Amendment. An appeals court affirmed the decision, saying society's interests were served by not having criminals profit at the expense of their victims.

Reversing, the Supreme Court said the law is restrictive, "[w]hether the First Amendment 'speaker' is considered to be Henry Hill, whose income the statute places in escrow because of the story he has told, or Simon & Schuster, which can publish books about crime with the assistance of only those criminals willing to forgo remuneration for at least five years."

O'Connor highlighted in particular the problems with having the law cover authors irrespective of whether they ever were accused or convicted of a crime: "Should a prominent figure write his autobiography at the end of his career, and include in an early chapter a brief recollection of having stolen (in New York) a nearly worthless item as a youthful prank, the Board would control his entire income from the book for five years, and would make that income available to all of the author's creditors, despite the fact that the statute of limitations for this minor incident had long since run. That the Son of Sam law can produce such an outcome indicates that the statute is, to say the least, not narrowly tailored to achieve the state's objective of compensating crime victims from the profits of crime."

In his concurring opinion, Kennedy said that the Court need not have weighed the state's interest in compensating victims. He asserted that content-defined speech, such as outlawed in the "Son of Sam" statute, has the full protection of the First Amendment, which "is itself a full and sufficient reason for holding the statute unconstitutional."

Blackmun, also concurring only in the judgment, said the statute was too narrowly written and that the Court should have provided more guidance for states trying to rewrite laws.

□□□

Jacobson v. United States, decided by a 5-4 vote, April 6, 1992; White wrote the opinion; O'Connor, Rehnquist, Kennedy, and Scalia dissented.

Government sting operations took a hit when the Court ruled that prosecutors failed to show that a Nebraska farmer who ordered child pornography would have done so if not encouraged by undercover federal agents.

The narrow ruling reversed the conviction of Keith Jacobson, whom a jury had found guilty of receiving child pornography through the mails. Justice White wrote, "[T]he government overstepped the line between setting a trap for the 'unwary innocent' and the 'unwary criminal,' and as a matter of law failed to establish that [Jacobson] was independently predisposed to commit the crime for which he was arrested." The Court's most senior justice was joined by Blackmun, Stevens, Souter, and Thomas.

Dissenting justices insisted the majority instituted a difficult and possibly unworkable requirement for sting investigations. "Today, the Court holds that government conduct may be considered to create a predisposition to commit a crime, even before any government action to induce the commission of the crime," O'Connor wrote. "In my view, this holding changes entrapment doctrine. Generally, the inquiry is whether the suspect is predisposed before the government induces the commission of the crime, not before the government makes initial contact with him."

At the least, the ruling will require prosecutors to introduce evidence of a defendant's predisposition before any government contact.

This case began when Jacobson ordered two magazines, named *Bare Boys*, containing photographs of nude preteens and teenagers. Although those purchases were legal at the time—Congress since has made receiving sexually explicit depictions of children through the mail illegal— Jacobson's name ended up on a bookstore mailing list that government agents acquired. For more than two years, agents from the Postal Service and Customs Service tried to induce him to buy more child pornography as part of sting operations. Eventually he ordered a magazine, *Boys Who Love Boys*, which showed young boys engaged in sexual activities.

Jacobson claimed he had been entrapped and testified that he had not expected to receive photographs of minor boys. A jury found him guilty, and a federal appeals court affirmed the ruling.

The Supreme Court decision reversing the lower court stressed that when Jacobson received the original magazines, he was within the law;

that no other pornography was in his house other than the magazines from the original order and from the government; and that he testified he did not know the magazines would depict minors.

White said that prosecutors did not prove that Jacobson would have ordered the second magazine if not for government pressure. "In their zeal to enforce the law ... government agents may not originate a criminal design, implant in an innocent person's mind the disposition to commit a criminal act, and then induce commission of the crime so that the government may prosecute," he said.

"Had the agents in this case simply offered [Jacobson] the opportunity to order child pornography through the mails, and [Jacobson]—who must be presumed to know the law—had promptly availed himself of this criminal opportunity, it is unlikely that his entrapment defense would have warranted a jury instruction. But that is not what happened here. By the time [he] finally placed his order, he had already been the target of 26 months of repeated mailings and communications from government agents and fictitious organizations."

White noted that some of the government's enticing letters referred to the need to keep pornography free from censorship, and White said that Jacobson could have corresponded with the undercover agents simply out of a desire to fight censorship and preserve individual rights.

In her dissent, Justice O'Connor noted that both times that Jacobson was offered child pornography, he bought it. "He needed no government agent to coax, threaten or persuade him; no one played on his sympathies, friendship, or suggested that his committing the crime would further a greater good."

Rejecting the notion that Jacobson did not know that *Boys Who Love Boys* involved minors, she said that material was touted as "11 year old and 14 year old boys get it on in every way possible." Further, Jacobson sent this note with his order: "Will order other items later. I want to be discreet in order to protect you and me."

O'Connor was most concerned that the Court had jeopardized government sting operations by introducing new requirements for a suspect's predisposition to, and law enforcement's reasonable suspicion of, illegal activity—two fears that White said were unwarranted.

O'Connor, joined by Rehnquist, Scalia, and Kennedy, said, "This Court has held previously that a defendant's predisposition is to be assessed at the time the government first suggested the crime, not when the government agent first became involved." She added that the majority's rule could be read to say that the government must have sufficient evidence of a suspect's predisposition before it contacts him. "[T]he Court holds that the government must prove not only that a suspect was predisposed to commit the crime before the opportunity to commit it arose, but also before the government came on the scene."

O'Connor predicted that as a result of this case other defendants will assert that something the government did led them to commit a crime. "For example, a bribe taker will claim that the description of the amount of money available was so enticing that it implanted a disposition to accept the bribe later offered. A drug buyer will claim that the description of the drug's purity and effects was so tempting that it created the urge to try it for the first time.

"In short, the Court's opinion could be read to prohibit the government from advertising the seductions of criminal activity as part of its sting operation, for fear of creating a predisposition in its suspects. That limitation would be especially likely to hamper sting operations such as this one, which mimic the advertising done by genuine purveyors of pornography."

□□□

Keeney, Superintendent, Oregon State Penitentiary v. Tamayo-Reyes, decided by a 5-4 vote, May 4, 1992; White wrote the opinion; O'Connor, Blackmun, Stevens, and Kennedy dissented.

The Supreme Court continued trying to free the federal courts from hearing state prisoners' challenges to their cases. In this key decision, a five-justice majority overturned a Warren Court precedent and ruled that federal courts no longer must hold a hearing on a state case if the prisoner can show crucial facts were not presented in a state court appeal. The majority said it was seeking finality in state appellate rulings and efficiency in the criminal justice system.

At issue were inmate challenges to state court convictions through federal writs of habeas corpus. Latin for "you have the body," a habeas corpus writ is used to determine whether a person is lawfully imprisoned. Defendants who have exhausted direct appeals apply for a writ of habeas corpus on the ground that the conviction under which they are held is unconstitutional.

Until *Keeney v. Tamayo-Reyes*, when a prisoner challenged his case alleging that important facts had not been adequately presented to state courts, federal courts had to hold a hearing on the case. Now, a federal judge must hold a hearing only when a prisoner asserts a credible claim of "factual innocence."

This ruling is only one in a series of decisions in recent years cutting back on state prisoners' ability to obtain review of their convictions. During the 1990-1991 term, the Court said that death row prisoners may undergo only one round of federal court review through petitions for habeas corpus, barring extraordinary circumstances. That case, *McCleskey v. Zant*, involved a murder defendant who had been appealing his case for more than a decade. In *Teague v. Lane* (1989), the Court made filing habeas corpus petitions harder for prisoners when it restricted the situations under which a prisoner could establish an appeal based on a favorable court ruling issued in another case.

The Court in the 1991-1992 term also refused to intervene in two death row inmates' highly publicized eleventh-hour efforts to avoid execution. Both men, convicted murderers, were put to death. Robert Alton Harris became the first person executed in California in twenty-five years after the Supreme Court issued an unprecedented order to the federal appeals court in San Francisco not to cause any more delays in Harris's execution. The second case involved Virginian Roger Coleman, whose advocates engaged in a major media blitz to try to keep him from the electric chair.

In the June 1991 case of *Coleman v. Thompson*, the Court ruled that Coleman could not file a habeas corpus petition in federal court because he failed to abide by state court procedural rules. He missed a deadline for filing an appeal at the state level by three days. In 1992, the Court rejected Coleman's last-ditch efforts to appeal his sentence.

Keeney v. Tamayo-Reyes involved a Cuban immigrant with little education or ability to speak English. He alleged that he did not know what he was doing when he pled nolo contendere ("I will not contest it") to first degree manslaughter. He said the plea was invalid because his court-appointed translator had not translated accurately and completely the meaning of the mens rea element of the crime in question. Mens rea refers to the guilty knowledge and willfulness a defendant must have regarding the criminal act.

A state court dismissed the petition, the Oregon Court of Appeals affirmed, and the Oregon Supreme Court denied Tamayo-Reyes's appeal. A federal district court denied him habeas corpus relief.

However, a federal appeals court said the defendant was entitled to a federal evidentiary hearing on whether the mens rea element of the crime was properly explained to him, because a state appeals court had not examined whether the trial translation was adequate. The appeals court said Tamayo-Reyes's appeals lawyer's negligent failure to develop those facts in the state appeal did not constitute a "deliberate bypass" of the orderly procedure of the state courts, so he was entitled to federal court review.

The federal appeals court came to its conclusion by following a 1963 Supreme Court decision, *Townsend v. Sain*, that held that a federal court was required to hear a challenge if the facts were "not adequately developed" in state proceedings, unless the prisoner deliberately had bypassed the state court process. Congress wrote that holding into federal law in 1966.

But in *Keeney v. Tamayo-Reyes*, the Supreme Court said the appeals court used the wrong standard for determining whether an evidentiary hearing was required. The narrow Court majority held that instead of the "deliberate bypass" test, federal courts could hear the case only under a "cause-and-prejudice" standard.

Writing for the Court, White said, "Tamayo-Reyes is entitled to an evidentiary hearing if he can show cause for his failure to develop the facts in state-court proceedings and actual prejudice resulting from that failure." The so-called "cause-and-prejudice" standard is much harder for a defendant to meet than the "deliberate bypass" standard.

But the cause-and-prejudice standard has been adopted by the Court for federal appeals filed by state court defendants who fail to follow procedural rules or who have filed numerous previous challenges. White said using the same threshold standard for habeas corpus review was important for consistency. He was joined by Rehnquist, Scalia, Souter, and Thomas.

White, the Court's most senior justice, said state courts should resolve factual issues. He stressed the finality of state convictions and said he did not want to create incentives for "deferral of factfinding" to the federal courts. "The purpose of exhaustion [of state appeals] is not to create a procedural hurdle on the path to federal habeas court, but to channel claims into an appropriate forum, where meritorious claims may be vindicated and unfounded litigation obviated before resort to federal court," White wrote.

The case was remanded to a federal district court to give Tamayo-Reyes an opportunity to bring forward evidence under the cause-and-prejudice standard.

O'Connor, who sided with earlier Court rulings restricting habeas corpus, dissented. Joined by Justices Blackmun, Stevens, and Kennedy, she noted that the previous cases concerned procedural requirements that she believed should be the purview of states, not substantive issues of how a federal court should consider a legitimate claim. "[T]he balance of state and federal interests regarding whether a federal court will *consider* a claim raised on habeas cannot be simply lifted and transposed to the different question whether, once the court will consider the claim, it should hold an evidentiary hearing," O'Connor said. She said Tamayo-Reyes had alleged a fact that, if true, would entitle him to reversal of his conviction.

Kennedy's dissent also was a surprise. In the 1990-1991 term, he wrote the majority opinion in *McCleskey v. Zant.* Writing in a separate dissent in the *Keeney* case, Kennedy said *Townsend v. Sain* had been law for almost thirty years, and "there is no clear evidence that this particular classification of habeas proceedings has burdened the dockets of the federal courts." He said the majority opinion could lead to state courts ruling on a case without an accurate assessment of the facts.

□□□

United States v. Alvarez-Machain, decided by a 6-3 vote, June 15, 1992; Rehnquist wrote the opinion; Stevens, Blackmun, and O'Connor dissented.

The abduction of a Mexican citizen in Mexico implicated in the murder of a U.S. drug agent was not in violation of a U.S.-Mexico treaty. The treaty also does not bar the Mexican's trial on charges related to the murder.

The Court's opinion indicated how compelling U.S. officials believe the drug problem is in the United States and illustrated an extreme literal interpretation of treaty law. The ruling provoked outrage in the international community and may make U.S. citizens vulnerable to reciprocal actions by foreign governments.

The six-justice majority said that because neither the treaty's language nor the history of negotiations and practice under it specifically states that abductions are prohibited, they are not banned. Written by Chief Justice Rehnquist, the opinion relied on precedents that prosecutions are not prohibited simply because the defendant's presence was obtained through questionable means. He was joined by Justices White, Scalia, Kennedy, Souter, and Thomas.

Dissenting justices said the kidnapping "unquestionably constitutes a flagrant violation of international law."

In 1990, Humberto Alvarez-Machain was abducted from his home in Guadalajara, Mexico, and flown by private plane to Texas, where he was arrested. He was federally indicted for participating in the kidnapping and murder of Drug Enforcement Administration (DEA) special agent Enrique Camarena-Salazar and a Mexican pilot working with Camarena, Alfredo Zavala-Avelar.

The defendant is a medical doctor, and he was accused of taking part in the American drug agent's murder by prolonging the agent's life with drugs so that others could torture and interrogate him. U.S. officials reportedly directed the abduction of the doctor.

A district court dismissed the indictment, concluding that the kidnapping violated the Extradition Treaty between the United States and Mexico. The court ordered Alvarez-Machain returned to Mexico. A federal appeals court affirmed, noting that the United States had authorized the abduction and that the Mexican government had protested the treaty violation.

But the Supreme Court held that the treaty, signed in 1978, says nothing about either country refraining from forcibly abducting people from their homelands or the consequences if an abduction occurs. Further, Rehnquist wrote, general principles of international law offer no basis for interpreting the treaty to include an implication against international abductions.

The majority acknowledged that the abduction might have been "shocking" and "in violation of general international law principles," but it did not violate the Extradition Treaty between the United State and Mexico.

"Mexico has protested the abduction of respondent through diplomatic notes, and the decision of whether respondent should be returned to Mexico, as a matter outside of the Treaty, is a matter for the Executive Branch. We conclude, however, that respondent's abduction was not in violation of the Extradition Treaty between the United States and Mexico. . . . The fact of respondent's forcible abduction does not therefore prohibit his trial in a court in the United States for violations of the criminal laws of the United States."

Dissenting justices noted that Mexico said Alvarez-Machain would be prosecuted and punished.

Stevens scoffed at the notion that the absence of any express language in the treaty dictates its terms on abductions. "If the United States, for example, thought it more expedient to torture or simply to execute a person rather than to attempt extradition, these options would be equally available because they, too, were not explicitly prohibited by the Treaty." He called such an interpretation "highly improbable."

Joined by Blackmun and O'Connor, Stevens concluded, adopting language from court precedents: "Indeed, the desire for revenge exerts a kind of hydraulic pressure before which even well settled principles of law will bend, but it is precisely at such moments that we should remember and be guided by our duty to render judgment evenly and dispassionately according to law."

□□□

R. A. V. v. City of St. Paul, Minnesota, decided by a 9-0 vote, June 22, 1992; Scalia wrote the opinion.

This case began when three white teenagers burned a makeshift cross in the yard of a black family and were charged under the St. Paul, Minnesota, Bias-Motivated Crime Ordinance. While condemning the teenagers' conduct, the Court ruled that cities may not target "hate speech" tied to race, color, creed, religion, or gender.

The Court said the ordinance unconstitutionally prohibited speech on the basis of the speech's subject. Although the ruling striking down the ordinance was unanimous, the justices split sharply in their rationale.

A five-justice majority, in the voice of Justice Scalia, said "content-based regulations are presumptively invalid." He said governments may not ban speech "based on hostility—or favoritism—toward the underlying message expressed." The other four justices asserted that Scalia's opinion undermined the "fighting words" doctrine that allowed laws making content-based distinctions among speech.

The majority opinion said that, if a municipality wants to outlaw a particular kind of speech that would be considered fighting words, it must outlaw all fighting words, not just race-, religion-, or gender-based epithets. Fighting words was defined in a 1941 case as words that "by their very utterance inflict injury or tend to incite an immediate breach of the peace." Like defamation and obscenity, fighting words generally have no constitutional protection.

In a rebuke of the majority opinion, White noted that in past cases certain insults qualified as fighting words. He accused the majority of a "radical revision of First Amendment law" and of legitimatizing hate speech.

Overall, the outcome throws in doubt the validity of numerous laws and university codes aimed at acts and comments motivated by prejudice. The St. Paul Bias-Motivated Crime Ordinance outlawed the display of a symbol that one knows or has reason to know "arouses anger, alarm or resentment in others on the basis of race, color, creed, religion or gender." It was invoked in June 1990 after the teenagers made a cross by taping together broken chair legs and burned it on the lawn of a black family.

A state court dismissed the case, deciding that the ordinance was overbroad and impermissibly content-based. But the Minnesota Supreme Court reversed. It rejected the over-breadth claim, saying that the phrase "arouses anger, alarm or resentment in others" had been construed in earlier state cases to limit the ordinance's reach to fighting words unprotected by the First Amendment. The state court also concluded that the ordinance was not impermissibly content-based because it was tailored to serve a compelling governmental interest in protecting the community against bias-motivated threats to public safety and order.

Reversing, the U.S. Supreme Court said that the First Amendment does not allow legislation that targets certain subjects. "Selectivity of this sort creates the possibility that the city is seeking to handicap the expression of particular ideas," Scalia wrote. "Let there be no mistake about our belief that burning a cross in someone's front yard is reprehensible," Scalia said, joined by Rehnquist, Kennedy, Souter, and Thomas. "But St. Paul has sufficient means at its disposal to prevent such behavior without adding the First Amendment to the fire." In terms of First Amendment law, Scalia wrote that a state or city cannot favor or disfavor conduct within a category of prohibited speech. "Thus, the government may proscribe libel; but it may not make the further content discrimination of proscribing only libel critical of the government."

Justice White, joined by Blackmun, O'Connor, and, in most part, Stevens, said that government should have the discretion to discriminate among types of speech. "The Court announces that such content-based distinctions violate the First Amendment because 'the government may not regulate use based on hostility—or favoritism—toward the underlying message expressed.' Should the government want to criminalize certain fighting words, the Court now requires it to criminalize all fighting words."

White called the majority's method "a simplistic, all-or-nothing-at-all approach to First Amendment protection . . . at odds with common sense and with our jurisprudence as well." He said allowing government to prohibit an entire category of speech because the content of that speech is evil is inconsistent with then blocking government from targeting a subset of that category. "The content of the subset is by definition worthless and undeserving of constitutional protection," he maintained.

White, however, joined the judgment of the Court, finding the St. Paul ordinance too sweeping because, "[a]lthough the ordinance reaches conduct that is unprotected [by the First Amendment], it also makes criminal expressive conduct that causes only hurt feelings, offense, or resentment, and is protected by the First Amendment."

In a separate concurrence, Blackmun said, "If all expressive activity must be accorded the same protection, that protection will be scant. The simple reality is that the Court will never provide child pornography or cigarette advertising the level of protection customarily granted political speech. If we are forbidden from categorizing, as the Court has done here, we shall reduce protection across the board."

□□□

Cipollone, Individually and as Executor of the Estate of Cipollone v. Liggett Group, Inc., decided by a 7-2 vote, June 24, 1992; Stevens wrote the opinion; Scalia and Thomas dissented.

Cigarette manufacturers who lie about the dangers of smoking or otherwise misrepresent their products can be sued under state laws and potentially exposed to huge monetary awards. The Court opened the door to more litigation over cancer deaths by holding that federal law does not preempt all state common law liability lawsuits.

The family of a woman who died at age fifty-eight after smoking for forty-two years brought several claims in New Jersey state court, among them breach of express warranties contained in cigarette advertising; failure to warn consumers about smoking's hazards; fraudulent misrepresentation of the hazards of smoking to consumers; and conspiracy to deprive the public of medical and scientific information.

At issue was whether a federal cigarette labeling law preempted the state court claims. The federal law requires a conspicuous label warning of smoking's health hazards on every package of cigarettes. Originally passed in 1965, the law was amended in 1969 to say that "No requirement or prohibition based on smoking and health shall be imposed

The Court in June 1992 ruled that a federal cigarette labeling law does not protect cigarette manufacturers who misrepresent their products from all state liability lawsuits. The decision may encourage smokers to bring fraud and conspiracy charges and may result in companies having to pay large monetary awards.

under state law with respect to the advertising or promotion of any cigarettes the packages of which are [lawfully] labeled."

The Supreme Court ruled that federal law is the only avenue for allegations based on a failure to warn and for claims of omissions in the manufacturer's advertising or promotions. But the majority said a smoker can go to state court with allegations that manufacturers breached express warranties, that cigarette advertisements are fraudulent, that the companies hid the dangers of smoking from state authorities, or that manufacturers conspired to mislead smokers.

Stevens wrote the opinion. Chief Justice Rehnquist and Justices White and O'Connor signed all portions. Justices Blackmun, Kennedy, and Souter agreed that not all laws were preempted but would have gone further, allowing the Cipollone estate to press all of its claims in state court. Justices Scalia and Thomas dissented, saying that federal law was totally preemptory.

The troubled cigarette industry dismissed worries about the financial fallout of the decision, publicly predicting that a minimal number of lawsuits would be filed. But an estimated 390,000 Americans a year die from smoking-related diseases, including 143,000 from lung cancer, and lawyers speculated that smokers would be more likely to bring fraud and conspiracy lawsuits because of the Court's decision.

The case began when survivors of Rose Cipollone asserted that three cigarette manufacturers knew that cigarettes were dangerous but deceived smokers through their advertisements. (First, her husband/widower sued; when he died, her son took over the case.) The family maintained that actions by the companies violated New Jersey law. The manufacturers countered that the Federal Cigarette Labeling and Advertising Act preempted state liability claims.

A jury awarded the Cipollone family $400,000 against the Liggett Group and cleared the two other manufacturers. An appeals court reversed, saying the labeling act precludes state tort actions.

Under the Constitution's Supremacy Clause, the laws of Congress supersede those of the states. But the Supreme Court generally has held that preemption of state law needs to be clearly expressed in a statute. An exception arises when, according to Court rulings, federal regulation is "so pervasive as to make reasonable the inference that Congress left no room for the states to supplement it."

The Supreme Court held that the labeling law preempted only state laws requiring particular warnings on cigarette labels or in cigarette advertisements. Stevens said the express preemption provisions of the law dictate the scope of its preemption. That part of the opinion was decided by a 7-2 vote.

Then, a plurality of four justices concluded that, for the Cipollones, the act preempts the failure to warn and fraudulent misrepresentation claims but does not preempt lawsuits based on express warranty, intentional fraud, misrepresentation, or conspiracy. The test, according to Stevens, is whether the legal duty arises from a requirement concerning advertising or promotion.

The precluded claims are ones based on the theory that cigarette makers had a legal duty to go beyond the warning label requirements of federal law to more urgent warnings about the dangers of their products. However, Stevens said, "Congress offered no sign that it wished to insulate cigarette manufacturers from longstanding rules governing fraud."

Blackmun, joined by Kennedy and Souter, accused the Court of creating a "crazy quilt of preemption." He said the Court eliminated "a critical component of the States' traditional ability to protect the health and safety of their citizens."

Dissenting, Scalia, joined by Thomas, said he read the 1969 statute to have preempted all of the Cipollone common law claims. He said the majority read too narrowly the express preemption provisions. "[T]he result is extraordinary: The statute that says *anything* about preemption must say *everything*; and it must do so with great exactitude, as any ambiguity concerning its scope will be read in favor of preserving state power. If this is to be the law, surely only the most sporting of congresses will dare to say anything about preemption."

The two justices concurred in the part of the ruling saying that the failure-to-warn claims and certain of the fraudulent misrepresentation claims cannot be heard in state court.

□□□

Lee v. Weisman, personally and as a next friend of Weisman, decided by a 5-4 vote, June 24, 1992; Kennedy wrote the opinion; Scalia, Rehnquist, White, and Thomas dissented.

In an unanticipated affirmation of a clear separation between church and state, the Supreme Court ruled that allowing prayers as part of a public school graduation ceremony is unconstitutional. The Court, by one vote, sided with a Providence, Rhode Island, student who objected to the invocation and benediction by a rabbi at her junior high school graduation ceremony.

Under the First Amendment's Establishment Clause, government may not support religion. In his opinion for the majority, Kennedy noted that the Establishment Clause was inspired by the lesson "that in the hands of the government what might begin as a tolerant expression of religious views may end in a policy to indoctrinate and coerce." He said prayer exercises in elementary and secondary schools carry a particular risk of indirect coercion, and throughout the opinion he stressed the vulnerability of children.

In one respect, the ruling was a surprise because the Court's recent growing conservatism seemed to indicate a majority that could justify prayer in the schools, and because President Bush and his predecessor, Ronald Reagan, who sought a constitutional amendment to allow prayer in schools, together had appointed a majority of the sitting justices.

But in another respect, the ruling was consistent with Court precedent. Since 1962, the Court forbade prayer in school as a violation of the constitutional ban against establishment of religion. A new test for the separation of church and state would have been a landmark.

Kennedy was joined by Blackmun, Stevens, O'Connor, and Souter.

Dissenting, Scalia wrote that prayer at public ceremonies is rightly part of a national tradition. He derided Justice Kennedy for backing away from an earlier stand that would have altered Establishment Clause jurisprudence to allow greater government accommodation of religion than the *Lee v. Weisman* ruling seemed to indicate. In 1989, Kennedy dissented from a decision that invalidated the display of a nativity scene in a Pittsburgh courthouse and questioned the validity of the Court's test in religion cases (*Allegheny County v. American Civil Liberties Union*).

The new dispute arose when fourteen-year-old Deborah Weisman and her father challenged a rabbi's prayers at her 1989 graduation from Nathan Bishop Middle School, a public school in Providence. The principal of the school, who invited the rabbi, gave him a pamphlet prepared by the National Conference of Christians and Jews for guidance in his approach.

In his invocation, the rabbi said, "God of the Free, Hope of the Brave: For the legacy of America where diversity is celebrated and the rights of minorities are protected, we thank You. May these young men and women grow up to enrich it. For the liberty of America, we thank You. May these new graduates grow up to guard it. For the political process of America in which all its citizens may participate, for its court system where all may seek justice we thank You. May those we honor this morning always turn to it in trust. For the destiny of America we thank You. May the graduates of Nathan Bishop Middle School so live that they might help to share it." The rabbi also gave a benediction.

For its defense, the Providence school board asserted that prayers are an appropriate and important way for students and parents to seek spiritual guidance at an event such as graduation. The U.S. solicitor general backed the school board, also arguing that prayers are an essential part of graduation ceremonies.

When the case went before a federal district court, the judge applied the three-part Establishment Clause test from the Supreme Court's 1971 ruling in *Lemon v. Kurtzman*. Under that test, to satisfy the Establishment Clause a government practice must (1) show a clearly secular purpose, (2) have a primary effect that neither advances nor inhibits religion, and (3) avoid excessive government entanglement with religion.

The court ruled that the school's prayer policy failed the second part of test. The "effects" test is violated whenever government action "creates an identification of the state" with a religion or when the effect of the governmental action is to endorse one religion over another, or to endorse religion in general. An appeals court affirmed.

For its part, the Supreme Court's narrow majority said that the key facts that controlled the situation were that state officials directed the religious exercise and that the students' attendance in the graduation was in a real sense obligatory.

Rejecting a request by the Bush administration to revisit the *Lemon* test, the Court said that government involvement with religious activity in Providence creates outright a state-sponsored and state-directed religious exercise. "The question is not the good faith of the school in attempting to make the prayer acceptable to most persons, but the legitimacy of its undertaking that enterprise at all when the object is to produce a prayer to be used in a formal religious exercise which students, for all practical purposes, are obliged to attend," Kennedy wrote.

Emphasizing the need to protect freedom of conscience from the subtle coercive pressure in schools, Kennedy distinguished the case from the 1983 *Marsh v. Chambers* in which the Court condoned a prayer at the opening of a state legislature's daily session. "The atmosphere at the opening of a session of a state legislature where adults are free to enter and leave with little comment and for any number of reasons cannot compare with the constraining potential of the one school event most important for the student to attend," he said.

In a concurrence, Blackmun, joined by Stevens and O'Connor, said that application of the *Lemon* test is straightforward and that the invocation was a religious activity. "When the government arrogates to itself a role in religious affairs, it abandons its obligation as guarantor of democracy. Democracy requires the nourishment of dialogue and dissent, while religious faith puts its trust in an ultimate divine authority above all human deliberation."

Souter, joined by Stevens and O'Connor, wrote separately to stress that the Establishment Clause forbids not only state practices that endorse one religion over another but also those that generally support all religions.

Scalia, writing for the dissent, emphasized the unifying role of prayer in American celebrations. "The history and tradition of our Nation are replete with public ceremonies featuring prayers of thanksgiving and petition.... Most recently, President Bush, continuing the tradition established by President Washington, asked those attending his inauguration to bow their heads, and made a prayer his first official act as president."

Scalia, joined by Chief Justice Rehnquist and Justices White and Thomas, also said he did not find any element of coercion in the graduation prayers and scoffed at Kennedy's references to the social pressure on school children: "[I]nterior decorating is a rock-hard science compared to psychology practiced by amateurs."

□□□

United States v. Fordice, Governor of Mississippi; Ayers v. Fordice, Governor of Mississippi, decided by an 8-1 vote, June 26, 1992; White wrote the opinion; Scalia dissented.

Thirty-eight years after the Court's landmark ruling in *Brown v. Board of Education,* justices said that the state of Mississippi still had not done enough to desegregate its colleges and universities. The Court ruled that when students challenge a school system as discriminatory, the state must justify the potentially discriminatory practices.

The Court said that some 99 percent of Mississippi's white students were enrolled at five state schools, including the University of Mississippi, while some 71 percent of the state's black students attended three historically black schools. (All eight schools were in existence before *Brown* and were strictly segregated by law.) Justice White wrote for the majority, "If the State perpetuates policies and practices traceable to its prior system that continue to have segregative effects—whether by influencing student enrollment decisions or by fostering segregation in other facets of the university system—and such policies are without sound educational justification and can be practicably eliminated, the state has not satisfied its burden of" desegregation.

This lawsuit began in 1975 when citizens sued the state over its continued operation of the five almost completely white and three almost exclusively black universities. The United States intervened and charged that state officials failed to meet the requirements of the Equal Protection Clause of the Fourteenth Amendment and Title VI of the Civil Rights Act of 1964 to dismantle the dual system. Lower courts ruled that Mississippi was fulfilling its duty to break down the former de jure segregated system through "race-neutral" policies.

But the Supreme Court said that the lower courts did not apply the correct legal standard in assessing the school system. White said a court must ask whether the racial identity of a school stems from state policies and must examine a wide range of factors to determine whether the state has perpetuated its former segregation in any facet of the system. Under that standard, he said, several surviving aspects of Mississippi's prior dual system potentially violate the equal protection guarantee of the Fourteenth Amendment. Although the policies may be race neutral on their face, they substantially restrict a student's choice of schools and contribute to the racial identifiability of the eight public universities.

The Court specified four problem areas that the state would have to justify upon remand of the case: higher admission standards at the white universities; program duplication at black and white schools; institutional mission assignments, which provide more comprehensive programs at the white schools and effectively restrict black schools' programs; and continued operation of all eight public universities.

Justice O'Connor wrote a separate opinion "to emphasize that it is Mississippi's burden to prove that it has undone its prior segregation, and that the circumstances in which a State may maintain a policy or practice traceable to *de jure* segregation that has segregative effects are narrow." She referred to the "state's long history of discrimination."

Mississippi did not move to desegregate its higher education system until 1962, and then only under a court order that allowed James Meredith to enter the University of Mississippi.

In his first school desegregation case, Thomas, the Court's only black member, concurred with a cautionary note: "Although I agree that a State is not constitutionally *required* to maintain its historically black institutions as such, I do not understand our opinion to hold that a state is forbidden from doing so. It would be ironic, to say the least, if the institutions that sustained blacks during segregation were themselves destroyed in an effort to combat its vestiges."

Scalia filed the lone dissent. He said a university need only have ended discriminatory practices and put in place a neutral admissions standard to be constitutional. The majority's heightened standard, he said, was confusing, unrealistic, and effectively unsustainable.

Wrote Scalia, "What I do predict is a number of years of litigation-driven confusion and destabilization in the university systems of all the formerly *de jure* states, that will benefit neither blacks nor whites, neither predominantly black institutions nor white ones."

□□□

Lucas v. South Carolina Coastal Council, decided by a 6-3 vote, June 29, 1992; Scalia wrote the opinion; Blackmun, Stevens, and Souter dissented.

State regulations that effectively deny a property owner all value of his land constitute a "taking" under the Fifth Amendment and require compensation, the Court said, in a case demanding a balancing of property-owner rights and government's power to protect the environment.

The consequences from this decision could be great, if governments refuse to regulate land because they fear that they will have to make large compensatory payments to a landowner.

Overall, the ruling was modest compared with what some conservatives had sought: greater departure from pro-government precedents in favor of more protection for property rights. Still, because conservative justices—now a majority on the Court—typically endorse a broader view of what constitutes a taking, this case could be the first step toward more rights for property owners at the expense of environmental regulations.

At the heart of such disputes are local zoning ordinances, environmental protection laws, and other regulations of the use of private property. The South Carolina law at issue restricted beachfront development along the state's Atlantic coastline.

Writing for the majority, Justice Scalia said, "[R]egulations that leave the owner of land without economically beneficial or productive options for its use—typically, as here, by requiring land to be left substantially in its natural state—carry with them a heightened risk that private property is being pressed into some form of public service under the guise of mitigating serious harm."

The case was reversed and remanded to a lower court to determine whether the property lost all its value and the landowner must be paid.

Scalia was joined by Chief Justice Rehnquist and Justices White, O'Connor, and Thomas. Thomas wrote a separate concurring opinion. Blackmun, Stevens, and Souter dissented.

The Fifth Amendment of the Constitution prevents Congress from taking property without paying "just compensation" to the owner. The prohibition is extended to the states through the Fourteenth Amendment.

Two years after David H. Lucas bought two residential lots on a South Carolina barrier island, the state enacted its Beachfront Management Act. It barred Lucas from building any permanent dwellings on the land. He sued saying that the ban on construction deprived him of all "economically viable use" of his property.

The state trial court agreed, finding that the ban made Lucas's land "valueless" and awarding him more than $1.2 million. Reversing that order, the state supreme court ruled that when a regulation is designed to prevent "harmful or noxious uses" of property, similar to public nuisances, no compensation is required, regardless of the regulation's effect on the property's value.

But the U.S. Supreme Court said that standard for "harmful or noxious uses" does not apply in this case. The majority said regulations that deny the property owner all "economically viable use of his land" should be treated differently, without the usual case-specific inquiry into the public interest advanced by the regulation. Scalia said the other category of regulatory action that should be compensated without such inquiry is one that brings about a physical "invasion" of property.

Scalia then spelled out a "nuisance" exception to the Court's categorical rule that a "total taking" requires compensation. He said if a state bars property uses that would not be allowed under general principles of nuisance and property law, that is, "not part of his title to begin with," no compensation is owed. "This accords, we think, with our 'takings' jurisprudence, which has traditionally been guided by the understandings of our citizens regarding the content of, and the State's power over, the 'bundle of rights' that they acquire when they obtain title to property," he wrote. "The 'total taking' inquiry we require today will ordinarily entail (as the application of state nuisance law ordinarily entails) analysis of, among other things, the degree of harm to public lands and resources, or adjacent private property, posed by the claimant's proposed activities, the social value of the claimant's activities and their suitability to the locality in question and the relative ease with which the alleged harm can be avoided through measures taken by the claimant and the government (or adjacent private landowners) alike."

Kennedy concurred in the judgment and said the lower court should consider whether Lucas had the intent and capacity to develop the property and failed to do so before the regulation took effect. He also said, "Where a taking is alleged from regulations which deprive the property of all value, the test must be whether the deprivation is contrary to reasonable, investment-backed expectations."

Blackmun's dissent attacked the majority's ruling as too sweeping for the narrow issue: "Today the Court launches a missile to kill a mouse." He argued first that the case was not ripe for review because under the South Carolina law Lucas still had a chance to apply for an exemption to the construction ban and he, in effect, failed to exhaust an administrative remedy.

Blackmun, who wrote only for himself, went on to say, "Even if I agreed with the Court that there were no jurisdictional barriers to deciding this case, I still would not try to decide it. The Court creates its new taking jurisprudence based on the trial court's finding that the property had lost all economic value. This finding is almost certainly erroneous. Petitioner still can enjoy other attributes of ownership, such as the right to exclude others, 'one of the most essential sticks in the bundle of rights that are commonly characterized as property.'" He added that Lucas also could sell the property.

In a separate dissent, Stevens said the majority's rule was too rigid. "Admittedly, the economic impact of this regulation is dramatic and [Lucas's] investment-backed expectations are substantial. Yet, if anything, the costs to and expectations of the owners of developed land are even greater: I doubt, however, that the cost to owners of developed land of renourishing the beach and allowing their seawalls to deteriorate effects a taking. The costs imposed on the owners of undeveloped land, such as petitioner, differ from these costs only in degree, not in kind. . . .

"In view of all of these factors, even assuming that petitioner's property was rendered valueless, the risk inherent in investments of the sort made by petitioner, the generality of the Act, and the compelling purpose motivating the South Carolina Legislature persuade me that the Act did not effect a taking of petitioner's property."

Souter said the Court should not have accepted the case for review. He said the record did not show that the Lucas property had lost its economic value.

□□□

Planned Parenthood of Southeastern Pennsylvania v. Casey, Governor of Pennsylvania; Casey, Governor of Pennsylvania v. Planned Parenthood of Southeastern Pennsylvania, decided by 5-4 and 7-2 votes, June 29, 1992; O'Connor, Kennedy, and Souter wrote the opinion; Rehnquist, White, Scalia, and Thomas dissented from part of the opinion upholding a woman's right to an abortion; Blackmun and Stevens dissented from part of the opinion allowing Pennsylvania abortion restrictions to stand.

The most awaited opinion of the term, which was issued on the last day of the Court's regular session, defied conventional wisdom and upset the special interests on both sides of the debate, while, according to pollsters, pleasing the American public.

The Court basically affirmed the centerpiece of *Roe v. Wade* (1973), which established a constitutional right to abortion and said states may not prohibit abortions at least until a fetus becomes viable; that is, can live outside of the womb. But a plurality of justices instituted a new standard for testing whether state restrictions infringe on that right and allowed to stand Pennsylvania abortion regulations that in earlier years were found in conflict with *Roe v. Wade*'s "fundamental" right to abortion.

In an unusual joint effort, the opinion was written by Justices O'Connor, Kennedy, and Souter. Until this ruling, O'Connor wavered on abortion, believing *Roe v. Wade*'s legal framework "problematic" but sidestepping the question of whether it should be overruled. Souter, who joined the Court in 1990 after being nominated by an anti-abortion president, George Bush, never had decided an abortion rights case. Kennedy's vote was the most surprising. He had joined in the plurality opinion in the 1989 *Webster v. Reproductive Health Services*, which would have overturned *Roe v. Wade*. But in *Casey*, he sided with O'Connor and Souter to forge a moderate course.

The provisions that the Court upheld require a woman seeking an abortion to wait twenty-four hours after being given certain information about the medical procedure and alternatives; require minors to obtain permission from one parent or, alternatively, to go before a judge to get a

In the most controversial decision of the 1991-1992 term, the Court upheld a woman's right to abortion but put in place a new standard for testing whether state restrictions infringe on that right. The Court let stand Pennsylvania regulations requiring informed consent for minors and a twenty-four-hour waiting period.

waiver; impose reporting requirements on facilities providing abortions; and define a "medical emergency" that will excuse compliance with the foregoing requirements.

The Court struck down a provision requiring that a woman seeking an abortion sign a statement that she has notified her husband.

Justices Blackmun and Stevens joined the portion of the opinion saying that *Roe v. Wade* created a "rule of law and a component of liberty we cannot renounce." Blackmun, who was the author of *Roe v. Wade*, praised the three-justice opinion as an "act of personal courage and Constitutional principle." Dissenting from that portion and agreeing to the sections of the opinion upholding the Pennsylvania regulations were Chief Justice Rehnquist and Justices White, Scalia, and Thomas. Blackmun dissented from all the portions upholding the regulations. Stevens said only that the reporting requirements should be permitted.

In separate abortion action, the Court put off until the 1992-1993 term a decision in *Bray v. Alexandria Women's Health Clinic*. The Court asked for reargument in the case of whether anti-abortion protesters could be sued under a civil rights law for blocking medical clinics.

The *Casey* dispute was brought by five abortion clinics and a physician who provides abortion services. A district court held all the provisions unconstitutional and permanently enjoined their enforcement.

The court of appeals reversed in part and affirmed in part, allowing all the questionable provisions except the requirement for husband notification to stand.

The first paragraph of the Supreme Court's lengthy opinion affirming the appeals court noted that five times in the past decade presidents have asked the Court to overturn *Roe v. Wade*. The justices said, "Liberty finds no refuge in the jurisprudence of doubt," and they said the definition of liberty still is questioned.

The three-justice opinion first and foremost affirmed what it called the "essential holding" of *Roe v. Wade*. It said that landmark opinion had three key parts: a recognition of a woman's right to choose abortion before a fetus becomes viable and to obtain an abortion without undue interference from the state; a confirmation of the state's power to restrict abortions after viability, if the law contains exceptions for abortions necessary to save the mother's life or health; and the principle that the state has legitimate interests from the outset of a pregnancy in protecting the health of the woman and the life of the fetus that may become a child.

The plurality said *Roe v. Wade* needed to be addressed because past decisions, such as *Webster v. Reproductive Health Services*, have cast doubt on the *Roe* holding; because Chief Justice Rehnquist would strike down *Roe*; and because lower courts and governments need more guidance on the issue.

O'Connor, Kennedy, and Souter—all considered conservatives to some degree—said, "Some of us as individuals find abortion offensive to our most basic principles of morality, but that cannot control our decision. Our obligation is to define the liberty of all, not to mandate our own moral code."

They then went on to base their decision on regard for individual liberty and stare decisis, the policy of standing by precedent. They noted that *Roe v. Wade* held that a woman's decision to end her pregnancy is a "liberty" protected by the Due Process Clause of the Fourteenth Amendment. They said that although that 1973 ruling has generated opposition, it has worked in modern society.

They said *Roe* could not be overturned without serious social repercussions, because for the past twenty years people have lived with the idea that abortion is available if contraception fails. The plurality also said that women have achieved economic and social equality in part because of their ability to control their reproductive lives.

But the plurality changed the legal test for determining whether a state is interfering with an abortion choice. *Roe v. Wade* said that a state could interfere with a woman's "fundamental" right to an abortion only if it had a "compelling interest." Under that standard, virtually all restrictions on abortion through the first two trimesters—six months—of pregnancy were found invalid. The plurality in *Casey* said the standard now should be whether the regulation puts an "undue burden" on a woman seeking an abortion. An undue burden exists, and therefore a provision of law is invalid, if it places substantial obstacles in the path of a woman seeking an abortion before the fetus is viable. The Court said a state may put regulations in place to further the health or safety of a woman seeking an abortion but may not impose unnecessary health regulations.

Roe divided a state's interest into a trimester framework: During the first three months, a right to abortion was unconditional; during the second three months, a state could restrict abortions to protect a mother's health; during the last trimester, from month seven through nine, a state could prohibit abortions completely, except to save the life or health of the pregnant woman.

In the *Casey* ruling, the plurality rejected the trimester framework but said a state may not prohibit any woman from deciding to end her pregnancy before viability. The plurality also reaffirmed *Roe*'s holding that "subsequent to viability, the state in promoting its interest in the potentiality of human life may, if it chooses, regulate, and even proscribe, abortion except where it is necessary in appropriate medical judgment, for the preservation of the life or health of the mother." Under those standards, the Court concluded, only the Pennsylvania section requiring husband notification constitutes an undue burden. The justices said the provision reflects an outdated view of marriage.

Finally, the plurality acknowledged that it in effect was overruling two earlier abortion decisions that struck down "informed consent" provisions involving information about the abortion procedure and the state of the fetus. In the 1983 *City of Akron v. Akron Center for Reproductive Health*, the Court held invalid a law requiring women seeking abortions to wait at least twenty-four hours after receiving counseling, and in the 1986 *Thornburgh v. American College of Obstetricians and Gynecologists*, the Court rejected a Pennsylvania regulation requiring that women be given specific information intended to discourage abortions.

In his opinion dissenting in part, Blackmun said he believed none of the challenged regulations was constitutional. He also made a personal plea for the future of abortion rights generally, noting that by only the narrowest of majorities—one vote—had *Roe v. Wade* been upheld in *Casey*. "I am 83 years old," he wrote. "I cannot remain on this Court forever, and when I do step down, the confirmation process for my successor well may focus on the issue before us today."

At the other end of the spectrum, Rehnquist, White, Scalia, and Thomas said that *Roe* had gone too far and that the Court should have corrected it in this ruling. "Because abortion involves the purposeful termination of potential life, the abortion decision must be recognized as *sui generis*, different in kind from the rights protected in the earlier cases under the rubric of personal or family privacy and autonomy," Rehnquist wrote.

The chief justice predicted the undue burden standard would be unworkable and repeated the standard that the conservative plurality had sought in *Webster v. Reproductive Health Services*: "A woman's interest in having an abortion is a form of liberty protected by the Due Process Clause, but States may regulate abortion procedures in ways rationally related to a legitimate state interest." That test is comparatively easy for a state to meet.

In a separate dissent, Scalia said the abortion issue should be returned to state legislatures as it was before 1973. "[B]y foreclosing all democratic outlet for the deep passions this issue arouses, by banishing the issue from the political forum that gives all participants, even the losers, the satisfaction of a fair hearing and an honest fight, by continuing the imposition of a rigid national rule instead of allowing for regional differences, the Court merely prolongs and intensifies the anguish."

3 | *Case Summaries*

The Supreme Court issued 107 signed opinions during the 1991-1992 term. Twenty of those decisions were by unanimous vote with no separate opinions, the fewest unanimous rulings since William H. Rehnquist took over as chief justice in 1986. Although factions have developed among the seven conservative-leaning justices in recent years, causing the justices to concur in the judgment with different reasoning or to dissent altogether, this Court had comparatively few 5-4 votes.

The Court announced fourteen rulings that were decided by only one vote. That is slightly less than 15 percent of its total signed opinions, compared with the 1989-1990 term, when nearly 33 percent of the rulings were 5-4, and the 1990-1991 term, when 20 percent were decided by the narrowest of margins.

Of the fourteen cases, Justice Souter, who joined the Court in 1990 and has carved out a centrist role, was in the majority thirteen times. In those fourteen narrow votes, Chief Justice Rehnquist was in the majority the least.

Following are the case summaries for all signed opinions from the 1991-1992 term:

Business Law

Antitrust

Eastman Kodak Co. v. Image Technical Services, Inc., decided by a 6-3 vote, June 8, 1992; Blackmun wrote the opinion; Scalia, O'Connor, and Thomas dissented.

A district court should not have granted summary judgment (without a trial) against a claim that Kodak was restricting the sale of equipment parts to buyers who used Kodak's repair service, because sufficient evidence existed that Kodak might have violated antitrust law.

An independent firm that serviced photocopying equipment sued Kodak, alleging that Kodak engaged in "tying arrangements" under which a company agrees to sell one product on the condition that the buyer also purchases a different, or tied, product. Such deals violate the Sherman Act if the seller has appreciable economic power in the tying product market.

The Supreme Court majority said enough evidence had been presented to counter Kodak's argument that its lack of market power in the equipment market entitled it to summary judgment.

Federal Trade Commission v. Ticor Title Insurance Co., decided by a 6-3 vote, June 12, 1992; Kennedy wrote the opinion; Rehnquist, O'Connor, and Thomas dissented.

The rate-making activities of title insurance companies are not immune from antitrust liability when states have acquiesced in setting uniform rates.

The Court's decision stemmed from a Federal Trade Commission (FTC) complaint against six of the country's largest title insurance companies. The FTC alleged that the companies fixed their prices for title searches and title examinations. But the companies said they should be protected from antitrust liability under the doctrine of state-action immunity because the states, in effect, cleared the rates. The states in which the companies were based allowed rates to take effect within a stipulated time period unless specifically rejected by the state.

The Court said such arrangements, in which state officials do not actually scrutinize the rates, do not qualify for protection under state-action immunity doctrine.

Attorneys' Fees

City of Burlington v. Dague, decided by a 6-3 vote, June 24, 1992; Scalia wrote the opinion; Blackmun, Stevens, and O'Connor dissented.

The attorneys' fees provisions in two federal environmental laws do not allow fees to be paid beyond what would be a "reasonable rate" for the "reasonable hours" worked, even when an attorney took the case on a contingency basis and expected to earn a percentage of the court award.

In question were provisions of the Solid Waste Disposal Act and the Clean Water Act allowing courts to award "reasonable" fees to prevailing parties. The Court majority rejected a lower court ruling that enhanced the hourly rate attorneys' fees by 25 percent. The lower court said that without the extra money, individuals who bring environmental lawsuits against cities or large corporations will have trouble finding lawyers.

Bankruptcy

Barnhill v. Johnson, Trustee, decided by a 7-2 vote, March 25, 1992; Rehnquist wrote the opinion; Stevens and Blackmun dissented.

A transfer of funds made by a check occurs on the date the check is honored. Under federal bankruptcy law, a trustee generally is permitted to recover transfers of property made by the debtor within ninety days before the date the bankruptcy petition was filed. So the date funds are transferred is important for computing how much money can be recaptured for the estate.

A debtor wrote a check on November 18. The check was dated November 19 and was paid by the debtor's bank on November 20. The debtor later filed for bankruptcy; the ninetieth day before the bankruptcy filing was November 20. The Court rejected the contention by the person who received the check that the transfer date was November 18. Rehnquist said many events can intervene between delivery and presentment, such as the account being closed or subject to a lien.

Connecticut National Bank v. Germain, Trustee for the Estate of O'Sullivan's Fuel Oil Co., Inc., decided by a 9-0 vote, March 9, 1992; Thomas wrote the opinion.

Federal law allows a party to appeal an interim order issued by a district court sitting as a bankruptcy court of appeals. The unanimous Court ruling gives federal appeals courts more power to review bankruptcy disputes.

The case arose when a fuel oil company filed for bankruptcy and the court-appointed trustee sued a creditor of the bankrupt company over a contract dispute. After the contract case was transferred from Connecticut state court to a bankruptcy judge, the trustee requested a jury trial. The bankruptcy judge granted the jury trial motion, and a district judge, sitting as a designated bankruptcy court of appeals, affirmed.

The creditor then appealed the order to a federal appeals court, which said it lacked statutory authority to hear such an appeal. The Supreme Court, however, reversed the decision and returned the case for federal appeals court proceedings on the jury trial issue.

Dewsnup v. Timm, decided by a 6-2 vote, January 15, 1992; Blackmun wrote the opinion; Scalia and Souter dissented; Thomas took no part in the case.

This case involved a landowner who owed $120,000 from a loan secured by a lien on two parcels of Utah farmland. She sought to have the lien reduced because the $120,000 had come to exceed the fair market value of the parcels. (She wanted to redeem the property in return for paying the lender the estimated value of the land, $40,000.) But the Court said a debtor cannot "strip down" a creditor's lien on real property to the current value of the property when the value has become less than the amount of the claim secured by the lien.

The majority said the creditor's lien should be what was bargained for at the outset and should stay with the property until foreclosure.

Holywell Corp. v. Smith; United States v. Smith, decided by a 9-0 vote, February 25, 1992; Thomas wrote the opinion.

A bankruptcy trustee appointed to liquidate and distribute property must file income tax returns and pay taxes on the income attributable to the corporate debtor's property.

The unanimous Court said federal law requires a trustee to file a return as the "assignee" of the property of a corporation. It held that the trustee must pay the taxes due as the fiduciary of a trust.

Patterson, Trustee v. Shumate, decided by a 9-0 vote, June 15, 1992; Blackmun wrote the opinion.

Federal bankruptcy law allows a debtor's pension benefits to be excluded from the estate to be divided among creditors. The case required the Court to interpret the Employee Retirement Income Security Act (ERISA), a federal law intended to protect worker pensions, and how that law dovetails with the federal Bankruptcy Code.

The Code generally calls for all assets to become part of a debtor's estate, to be divided among creditors. But it exempts from the estate a debtor's interest in a trust "that is enforceable under applicable nonbankruptcy law." Blackmun read the exemption broadly, saying it means that pensions covered by ERISA are protected.

The case involved a former furniture company president who wanted to shield $250,000 in pension benefits from creditors.

Taylor v. Freeland & Kronz, decided by an 8-1 vote, April 21, 1992; Thomas wrote the opinion; Stevens dissented.

A bankruptcy trustee who missed a deadline for objecting to a debtor's effort to exempt certain funds from the estate waived access to the funds, even if the debtor lacked a good faith basis for the exemption.

A woman who filed for bankruptcy requested that her expected proceeds from a pending job discrimination lawsuit be exempt from creditors. (She was suing Trans World Airlines after being denied a promotion.) The trustee of her bankruptcy estate did not object to the claimed exemption within the thirty-day period required by bankruptcy rules. But when the trustee learned that the lawsuit was settled for $110,000, he filed a complaint in bankruptcy court.

The Court said even when no basis for the exemption exists—as apparently was the situation here—the thirty-day deadline must be enforced. "Deadlines may lead to unwelcome results, but they prompt parties to act and they produce finality," Thomas wrote for the majority. Stevens's dissent said innocent creditors would be harmed by the Court's ruling.

Union Bank v. Wolas, decided by a 9-0 vote, December 11, 1991; Stevens wrote the opinion.

A debtor's prior payments on long-term, as well as short-term, debt may qualify as payments made in "the ordinary course of business." As such, they are exempted from a bankruptcy trustee's effort to recover funds for an estate. The legal authority for recovery of funds is critical because the money regained is shared pro rata among similarly situated creditors.

The Court ruled that payments to a bank on a large business loan had been made in the ordinary course of business and therefore did not need to be returned to the estate.

United States v. Nordic Village, Inc., decided by a 7-2 vote, February 25, 1992; Scalia wrote the opinion; Stevens and Blackmun dissented.

A bankruptcy trustee trying to recover money that was paid to the Internal Revenue Service (IRS) without authority cannot sue the government. The Court said the bankruptcy law in question does not waive the sovereign immunity of the United States. Under the principle of sovereign immunity, the United States government is exempt from lawsuits unless Congress specifically waives immunity.

An officer of Nordic Village used funds from the bankrupt corporation to pay his individual taxes. The bankruptcy trustee tried to recover the money, and lower courts ruled that the IRS should return the funds.

But Scalia, writing for the majority, said the federal statute at issue does not contain "an unequivocal textual waiver" of the government's immunity from a bankruptcy trustee's claim. He said legislative history has no bearing on the issue.

Dissenting, Stevens said both the text and the legislative history of the bankruptcy code call for a contrary result, as does the interest in equitable treatment of creditors and shareholders of the corporation.

Securities

Holmes v. Securities Investor Protection Corporation, decided by a 9-0 vote, March 24, 1992; Souter wrote the opinion.

A plaintiff who sues under a federal racketeering law must show that his injury was caused by a specific conspiracy or other violation covered by the law. A federal agency that reimbursed defunct brokerage firms' customers tried to sue the brokerage firm under the Racketeer Influenced and Corrupt Organizations Act (RICO) to recover the money it paid out. The Court said that the connection between alleged fraud and those who lost money was too remote.

The agency alleged that a broker-dealer and others had conspired in a fraudulent stock manipulation scheme that prevented the broker-dealers from meeting obligations to customers. It said the brokers' acts amounted to a "pattern of racketeering activity" under RICO, which would have entitled the plaintiffs to recover triple money damages.

But the Supreme Court said that the agency could not sue because the alleged stock manipulation did not directly harm the brokerage customers; instead, it affected the investment companies.

The Supreme Court building is made primarily of marble and was designed in the Corinthian style of Greek architecture. The building, which opened in 1935, is across the street from the Capitol.

Taxes

Allied-Signal, Inc., as Successor-in-Interest to the Bendix Corp. v. Director, Division of Taxation, decided by 9-0 and 5-4 votes, June 15, 1992; Kennedy wrote the opinion; O'Connor, Rehnquist, Blackmun, and Thomas dissented in part.

States may not tax out-of-state businesses on the income derived from the sale of stock in separate in-state companies. The Court struck down a New Jersey assessment of an estimated $1.8 million in capital gains taxes on Bendix Corp. for its sale of shares in a New Jersey affiliate. Bendix since has become part of Allied-Signal Inc.

The justices unanimously upheld a rule, known as the unitary business principle, that allows a state to tax the investment income of an out-of-state firm doing business in the state only if certain relationships exist between the firm and the in-state entity whose securities produced the income. The unanimous Court said due process and the Commerce Clause generally prevent a state from taxing gains earned outside a state.

The justices then split 5-4 on whether the Bendix deal met certain criteria for state taxation. The majority said the relationship between the firms involved was not sufficient and that New Jersey could not tax the capital gain at issue.

Barker v. Kansas, decided by a 9-0 vote, April 21, 1992; White wrote the opinion.

The Court unanimously rejected a Kansas scheme that imposes income taxes on military retirements but not on the benefits received by retired state and local government employees.

The ruling reversed a Kansas Supreme Court conclusion that, for purposes of state taxation, military retirement benefits may be characterized and calculated as current compensation for reduced current services, instead of deferred pay for past services. The Court said no "significant differences" exist between military retirees and state and local government retirees for calculation of retirement benefits.

County of Yakima v. Confederated Tribes and Bands of the Yakima Indian Nation; Confederated Tribes and Bands of the Yakima Indian Nation v. County of Yakima, decided by an 8-1 vote, January 14, 1992; Scalia wrote the opinion; Blackmun dissented.

Yakima County may impose property taxes on Indian land, but it may not put an excise tax on sales of the land.

Yakima County, in Washington state, tried to foreclose on properties with past due ad valorem (general real estate taxes) and excise taxes, including a number of reservation parcels. The Yakima Nation sued, contending that federal law prohibited such taxes on lands held by the tribe or its members.

Scalia, writing for the majority, said states may tax reservation land if Congress made the authorization "unmistakably clear." He said the property taxes are allowed under the 1887 Indian General Allotment Act, which permits "taxation of . . . land" conveyed to Indians. The excise tax on land sales was disallowed because, the Court said, it is not a tax on the land itself.

INDOPCO, Inc. v. Commissioner of Internal Revenue, decided by a 9-0 vote, February 26, 1992; Blackmun wrote the opinion.

A corporation may not deduct from its income taxes as ordinary business expenses investment banking fees and expenses that it incurred during a friendly takeover. Here, the corporation, which was transformed from a publicly held, freestanding corporation into a wholly owned subsidiary of another company, wanted to write off the costs on its annual return as "ordinary and necessary business expenses."

But the Court said that such expenses, instead of being ordinary business expenses, are like capital expenditures, which generally are amortized over several years.

Rejecting the corporation's arguments, the Court said, "The fact that the expenditures do not create or enhance a separate and distinct additional asset is not controlling; the acquisition-related expenses bear the indicia of capital expenditures and are to be treated as such." The justices said the test is whether benefits will be realized beyond the year in which the expenditure is made.

Kraft General Foods, Inc. v. Iowa Department of Revenue and Finance, decided by a 7-2 vote, June 18, 1992; Stevens wrote the opinion; Rehnquist and Blackmun dissented.

States may not tax dividends businesses receive from foreign subsidiaries while exempting dividends from domestic subsidiaries.

Like the federal government, Iowa lets businesses deduct from net income all dividends received from domestic subsidiaries but not from foreign subsidiaries. But unlike the Internal Revenue Service, Iowa does not then give companies credit for foreign taxes they pay.

The Court said that because foreign dividends are treated less favorably, the Iowa statute discriminates against foreign commerce in violation of the Foreign Commerce Clause.

Nordlinger v. Hahn, in his capacity as Tax Assessor for Los Angeles County, decided by an 8-1 vote, June 18, 1992; Blackmun wrote the opinion; Stevens dissented.

California's Proposition 13 property tax assessment approach, which helps longtime property owners and hurts new home purchases, does not unconstitutionally discriminate. The property assessment is based on the value of a home when it was purchased, not the conventional current market value.

By allowing longtime owners to pay less in taxes than newer owners of comparable property, the Court said, the law's assessment scheme rationally furthers at least two legitimate state interests. First, justices said that neighborhood preservation and stability flows from a tax structure that discourages rapid home turnover. Second, they said that the state can conclude that a new owner does not have the same reliance interest warranting protection against higher taxes as does an existing owner. The existing owner already has bought and does not have the option of deciding not to purchase a home if taxes become prohibitively high.

Quill Corp. v. North Dakota, by and through its Tax Commissioner, Heitkamp, decided by an 8-1 vote, May 26, 1992; Stevens wrote the opinion; White dissented.

States may not force out-of-state mail order companies to pay taxes. The Court said while it no longer considered the taxes a violation of the constitutional guarantee of due process, the taxes do infringe on the Commerce Clause.

The Court said catalog sales companies may have "minimum contacts" with a taxing state as required by the Due Process Clause but lack the "substantial nexus" with the state required by the Commerce Clause. Concerns about the effects of state regulation on the national economy arise from the Commerce Clause protection, the Court said. Due process requirements may be met by continuous solicitation of business through mail order catalogs, but Commerce Clause conditions may be met only through a company's physical presence in the taxing state.

North Dakota filed an action in state court to require Quill Corp., an out-of-state mail order house with neither outlets nor sales representatives in the state, to collect and pay a tax on goods purchased for use in the state. All justices agreed that the taxes imposed did not violate due process. Only Justice White dissented on the Commerce Clause applicability question and would have allowed the North Dakota tax to stand.

Avoiding the North Dakota tax, the Court effectively turned the issue of whether states would be able to tax the thriving catalog business over to Congress, which has the constitutional authority to regulate interstate commerce. A reported $3 billion in annual taxes nationwide is at stake.

United States v. Burke, decided by a 7-2 vote, May 26, 1992; Blackmun wrote the opinion; O'Connor and Thomas dissented.

Backpay awards given to settle certain job discrimination claims are taxable to the recipient as gross income. The Court said the recipients of the money failed to show that recovery under Title VII of the 1964 Civil Rights Act was similar to relief in tort-like injuries and, as such, may be excluded from gross income under Internal Revenue Service law.

Blackmun, writing for the majority, said a hallmark of traditional tort liability is the availability of a broad range of damages to compensate an injured plaintiff. At the time of this lawsuit, however, Title VII permitted the award of only backpay, injunctions, and other equitable relief.

The parties had won the backpay as part of a settlement of a sex discrimination claim against the Tennessee Valley Authority.

United States v. Thompson/Center Arms Co., decided by a 5-4 vote, June 8, 1992; Souter wrote the opinion; White, Blackmun, Stevens, and Kennedy dissented.

When a "Contender" pistol and a conversion kit that would turn it into a rifle are packaged together and sold, it does not constitute the making of a short-barreled rifle, as taxable under federal law. The National Firearms Act imposes a $200 tax on anyone "making" such a firearm.

The Bureau of Alcohol, Tobacco and Firearms determined that when the Contender kit was possessed or distributed, it was a taxable firearm. A kit owner paid the tax but then sued for a refund.

The majority said the law was ambiguous about how much "making" must take place and at what stage of production a rifle is made. It said the statutory ambiguity should be resolved in favor of the gun owner under the rule of lenity.

The dissent, through Justice White, asserted, "When the components necessary to assemble a rifle are produced and held in conjunction with one another, a 'rifle' is, not surprisingly, the result."

Wisconsin Department of Revenue v. William Wrigley, Jr., Co., decided by a 6-3 vote, June 19, 1992; Scalia wrote the opinion; Kennedy, Rehnquist, and Blackmun dissented.

Wisconsin may levy an income tax on an Illinois chewing gum manufacturer who, in addition to seeking orders in Wisconsin, supplies gum for retail display racks, stores gum, and requires its sales representatives to replace stale gum in shops.

At issue was whether business activities by Wrigley Co., the world's largest chewing gum maker, should be protected by a federal law that bars a state from taxing the income of a corporation whose only business in a state is the "solicitation of orders" for tangible goods. The majority said Wrigley's activities went beyond mere solicitation of orders and constituted independent business functions.

O'Connor concurred in the judgment but disagreed that replacement of stale gum should be considered an independent business activity. Dissenting justices said the work in question was done in the the course of soliciting orders; they would have disallowed the taxes.

Trademarks

Two Pesos, Inc. v. Taco Cabana, Inc., decided by a 9-0 vote, June 26, 1992; White wrote the opinion.

A chain of Mexican restaurants should be able to successfully sue a similar chain for copying its festive motif, although no evidence is presented that consumers automatically associate the design with the original set of restaurants.

The Court said an inherently distinctive "trade dress" can be protected by federal trademark law without proof that it has acquired a so-called "secondary meaning." The trade dress of a product is its total image and appearance; secondary meaning signifies that a mark or dress has become uniquely associated with an entity.

The Trademark Act of 1946 (Lanham Act) protects distinctive trade dress, justices said, because such a motif is itself capable being associated with specific products or services. The Court affirmed an appeals court ruling that Two Pesos copied Taco Cabana's successful trade dress and tried to take over Taco Cabana's territory.

Civil Procedure

American National Red Cross v. S. G., decided by a 5-4 vote, June 19, 1992; Souter wrote the opinion; Scalia, Rehnquist, O'Connor, and Kennedy dissented.

In question was the charter of the American National Red Cross authorizing the organization "to sue and be sued in courts of law and equity, state or federal, within the jurisdiction of the United States." The Court ruled that the clause allows the Red Cross to have all lawsuits against the organization heard in federal court.

The Court's decision prohibited a New Hampshire couple from suing the American National Red Cross in state court. At issue was a blood transfusion allegedly tainted with the AIDS (acquired immune deficiency syndrome) virus.

The narrow majority said the charter created by Congress in 1905 and amended in 1947 allows the Red Cross to have all claims heard in federal courts. It said the provision's specific mention of federal courts confers such jurisdiction. Dissenting justices said the charter does not provide such an absolute right.

Ankenbrandt, as Next Friend and Mother of L. R. v. Richards, decided by a 9-0 vote, June 15, 1992; White wrote the opinion.

A federal court has jurisdiction to hear a civil case stemming from alleged child abuse when the parties are from different states. Generally, federal courts may not accept diversity lawsuits—disputes that go to federal court only because the litigants are from different states—when a domestic relations matter is at issue.

But the Court ruled unanimously that the abuse case does not fall into that exclusion. White said the rule only bars a judge from issuing divorce, alimony, or child custody decrees. The Court's decision reinstated a lawsuit by a Missouri woman who accused her ex-husband and his female companion of physically and sexually abusing the formerly married couple's two young daughters. The lawsuit sought money damages for the alleged injuries by the ex-husband.

Burlington Northern Railroad Co. v. Ford, decided by a 9-0 vote, June 12, 1992; Souter wrote the opinion.

A Montana law that allows railroad workers employed by out-of-state companies to sue their employers in any county in the state, but restricts workers suing a railroad that is incorporated in Montana to the county of its principal place of business, does not violate the Equal Protection Clause.

The Fourteenth Amendment forbids a state to "deny to any person within its jurisdiction the equal protection of the laws." But the unanimous Court said the state law neither deprives a railroad of a fundamental right nor favors an entity based on race, religion, or other category typically subject to Equal Protection complaints. The Court said the law flows from a legitimate state concern for balancing interests of parties to a lawsuit.

Rufo, Sheriff of Suffolk County v. Inmates of the Suffolk County Jail; Rapone, Commissioner of Correction of Massachusetts

v. Inmates of the Suffolk County Jail, decided by a 6-2 vote, January 15, 1992; White wrote the opinion; Stevens and Blackmun dissented; Thomas took no part in the case.

The Court eased the standard for challenging consent decrees, which are negotiated by the parties to a case and approved by a judge. A majority said a consent decree may be modified if one of the parties proves a "significant" change in law or fact.

Consent decrees often are used to settle prison and other institutional litigation when the government is a party. Civil rights abuses typically are at the core of such litigation. In this case, prisoners and officials in Massachusetts entered into a consent decree providing for construction of a new jail that would have single-occupancy cells for defendants awaiting trial. But officials later said increases in jail population had exceeded projections, and they sought to modify the consent decree forbidding double-celling of pretrial detainees.

A lower court denied the request, adopting a 1932 standard that "nothing less than a clear showing of grievous wrong evoked by new or unforeseen conditions should lead us to change what was decreed after years of litigation with the consent of all concerned."

The Supreme Court said a more flexible test was necessary. White wrote for the majority: "The upsurge in institutional reform litigation since *Brown v. Board of Education* [1954] has made the ability of a district court to modify a decree in response to changed circumstances all the more important. Because such decrees often remain in place for extended periods of time, the likelihood of significant changes occurring during the life of the decree is increased."

Still, White wrote for the Court, revising a decree should not be easy and the party seeking the modification bears the burden of establishing that a significant change in circumstances warrants it. Stevens and Blackmun supported the less rigid standard but said in a dissent that they would have affirmed the lower court order denying a change in the jail settlement agreement.

Smith v. Barry, decided by a 9-0 vote, January 14, 1992; O'Connor wrote the opinion.

A document filed as an appellate brief may qualify as the requisite notice of appeal under federal rules of appellate procedure. The key, the unanimous Court said, is that the document meet the deadline and content requirements of the federal rule for notice.

The decision stemmed from a prison inmate's appeal of a mixed verdict in a civil rights lawsuit. The inmate returned an "informal brief" to a court clerk with other requested information. The Supreme Court said the notice provided by a document, not the litigant's motivation in filing it, is what counts. Thus, many documents can be the "functional equivalent" of notice.

Willy v. Coastal Corp., decided by a 9-0 vote, March 3, 1992; Rehnquist wrote the opinion.

A federal district court's sanction of a party for frivolous filings should stand even when the court later is found to have lacked subject matter jurisdiction to hear the case. This lawsuit arose when a worker alleged he had been fired for refusing to be part of his employer's "violation" of environmental laws.

A district court dismissed the worker's case, saying he failed to state a claim. Also, because the worker had filed hundreds of pages in the case, the judge, saying the action "created a blur of absolute confusion," sanctioned the worker and his lawyer under a federal civil procedure rule. Rule 11 is intended to discourage frivolous court filings.

Subsequently, a federal appeals court ruled that the district court had lacked jurisdiction to hear the case because the worker's complaint raised no federal law claims. The appeals court said the case should be in state court. The appeals judge, however, allowed the Rule 11 penalties to stand. In its opinion affirming that decision, the unanimous Supreme Court said the Rule 11 sanction is important to keeping "orderly procedure" in the courts and irrespective to the merits of the case.

Criminal Law

Double Jeopardy

United States v. Felix, decided by 9-0 and 7-2 votes, March 25, 1992; Rehnquist wrote the opinion; Stevens and Blackmun dissented in part.

No double jeopardy violation occurs when, in the prosecution of a defendant of a drug conspiracy, a prosecutor uses evidence of overt acts that are based on substantive offenses for which the defendant previously had been convicted.

The Fifth Amendment says no one may be tried for the same offense twice. In this case, a defendant operated a drug facility in rural Oklahoma where he made methamphetamine. After federal agents raided and shut down the place, the defendant ordered chemicals and equipment to make methamphetamines and had them delivered to him in Joplin, Missouri. Federal agents caught and arrested him in that act.

He was prosecuted and convicted in Missouri for the offense of attempting to manufacture the illegal drug. The charge was based on the delivery of the materials to him in Joplin. He later was convicted in Oklahoma of conspiracy and other counts in connection with the operation of the facility in that state. An appeals court reversed most of the counts on which he had been found guilty, saying trial on these counts constituted double jeopardy because of the related Missouri prosecution.

But the Supreme Court held that none of the substantive offenses for which the defendant was prosecuted in Oklahoma was the same offense for which he was prosecuted in Missouri. The actual crimes charged in each case were different in both time and place, the justices said. Further, the majority held that a substantive crime and a conspiracy to commit that crime are not the "same offense" for double jeopardy purposes, even if they are based on the same underlying incidents. The Court said the key to the conspiracy offense is in the agreement to commit a crime. Stevens and Blackmun dissented from that part of the ruling.

Due Process

Estelle, Warden v. McGuire, decided by an 8-0 vote, December 4, 1991; Rehnquist wrote the opinion; O'Connor and Stevens dissented in part; Thomas took no part in the case.

The due process rights of a father on trial for murder of his child were not violated when evidence of the child's previous injuries was admitted at trial. The earlier injuries were not connected at trial to the father.

The defendant was found guilty of second-degree murder of his infant daughter. Two physicians testified that the infant was a battered child who had suffered other injuries. An appeals court ruled that the prior injury evidence was erroneously admitted, because no evidence linked the defendant to the prior injuries and no claim was made at trial that the child died accidentally.

Reversing that ruling, the Court said that although prosecutors did not relate the earlier injury evidence to the defendant, it likely established that the child had been beaten before and that the death was the result of an intentional act. O'Connor and Stevens dissented in part, saying that a jury instruction about the battered-child evidence was improper.

Foucha v. Louisiana, decided by a 5-4 vote, May 18, 1992; White wrote the opinion; Kennedy, Rehnquist, Thomas, and Scalia dissented.

A Louisiana statute that allows a defendant once judged to be insane to continue to be institutionalized, even when he no longer suffers from mental illness, violates constitutional due process. The statute said he could be held until he proved he was not dangerous to himself or to others.

The defendant, charged with aggravated burglary and illegal discharge of a firearm, was found not guilty by reason of insanity and was committed to an institution. A doctor later testified that the defendant had recovered from the drug induced psychosis from which he suffered upon commitment and was "in good shape" mentally. The doctor said, however, that the defendant had an antisocial personality and had several altercations at the institution.

Reversing a lower court ruling that the defendant remain confined, the Court said once an insanity acquitee has recovered his sanity, the basis for confinement no longer exists. Dissenting justices stressed that the defendant had committed a crime, with Thomas saying, "[I]t does not follow that, once the acquitee's sanity is 'restored,' the state is required to ignore his criminal act, and to renounce all interest in protecting society from him."

Griffin v. United States, decided by an 8-0 vote, December 3, 1991; Scalia wrote the opinion; Thomas took no part in the case.

A general guilty verdict stemming from a so-called multiple-object conspiracy need not be set aside even if the evidence is inadequate to support conviction on one of two or more objects or purposes. The justices unanimously said the Due Process Clause of the Fifth Amendment and Supreme Court precedents require only that the evidence be enough to support conviction on one of the objects.

The case began after a federal grand jury returned an indictment charging that the defendant conspired to defraud federal agencies. The unlawful conspiracy reportedly had two objects: impairing the efforts of the Internal Revenue Service to ascertain income taxes, and impairing the efforts of the Drug Enforcement Administration (DEA) to ascertain forfeitable assets. But at a jury trial, no evidence was presented to connect the defendant to the DEA forfeiture object. The judge told the jury it could return a guilty verdict against the defendant if it found she had participated in either one of the two objects of the conspiracy.

Upholding the conviction, the Supreme Court said it was settled law in England before the Declaration of Independence, and in the United States long afterwards, that a general guilty verdict is valid as long as it is legally supportable on one of the submitted grounds.

Medina v. California, decided by a 7-2 vote, June 22, 1992; Kennedy wrote the opinion; Blackmun and Stevens dissented.

A state may require a defendant who alleges he is mentally incompetent to stand trial to bear the burden of proving such by a preponderance of the evidence. The ruling affirmed a California Supreme Court opinion that a state statute's presumption of competency and burden of proof on the defendant did not violate a defendant's right to due process.

The defendant argued he was too mentally ill to stand trial and claimed that due process required the state to prove he was competent.

Dissenting justices noted that experts at the trial differed in their opinion of the defendant's competency and that the judge nonetheless told the jury to presume he was competent. Blackmun's dissent said, "I do not believe a Constitution that forbids the trial and conviction of an incompetent person tolerates the trial and conviction of a person about whom the evidence of competency is so equivocal and unclear."

Entrapment

Jacobson v. United States, decided by a 5-4 vote, April 6, 1992; White wrote the opinion; O'Connor, Rehnquist, Kennedy, and Scalia dissented.

In the case of a Nebraska farmer who was caught ordering child pornography magazines, prosecutors failed to provide evidence that the man was predisposed to buy the pornography and not encouraged by undercover government agents.

The defendant's trouble arose from a bookstore order he made for two *Bare Boys* magazines containing photographs of nude preteen and teenage boys. (At the time, the purchase was legal; Congress subsequently passed the Child Protection Act of 1984 making it illegal to receive through the mails sexually explicit depictions of children.) The defendant's name ended up on a mailing list that government agents obtained and used for a sting operation. The government tried for more than two years to persuade the man to buy more child pornography. Eventually the man ordered a magazine depicting young boys engaged in sexual activities and was arrested.

In overturning the conviction, the Court majority cited the government pressure and also noted that the defendant had not violated the law when he received the original magazines. Dissenting justices argued that the Court was changing entrapment doctrine and setting up unnecessarily high hurdles for government sting operations. *(See entry, p. 12; excerpts, p. 96)*

Evidence

United States v. Salerno, decided by an 8-1 vote, June 19, 1992; Thomas wrote the opinion; Stevens dissented.

A federal appeals court erroneously overturned the racketeering convictions of reputed mobsters, wrongly holding that certain grand jury testimony should have been included at trial. The case involved seven members of the criminal organization known as the Genovese Family of La Cosa Nostra in New York City. The family allegedly created a "club" of six concrete companies that gave it kickbacks in return for construction contracts.

The question was whether federal rules of evidence allow a criminal defendant to introduce the grand jury testimony of a witness who asserts the Fifth Amendment privilege at trial. The defendants here sought to use the grand jury testimony of two men who owned a construction company.

The panels of the bronze door at the main entrance of the Supreme Court building depict scenes on the development of the law.

The men, who testified to the grand jury under immunity, said they were not part of the club.

But at trial, government prosecutors argued that the two men were in on the kickback payments to defendants. When they would not testify at trial, the defendants sought to have their grand jury statements admitted as evidence.

Narrowly interpreting federal rules of evidence, the Supreme Court said the district court judge was correct to have excluded the immunized testimony before the grand jury. The Court remanded the case to determine whether the defendant could establish, according to the federal evidence rules, that the party against whom the testimony was offerered— the government—had a "similar motive" to develop the grand jury testimony at trial.

United States v. Williams, decided by a 5-4 vote, May 4, 1992; Scalia wrote the opinion; Stevens, Blackmun, O'Connor, and Thomas dissented.

Federal district courts may not dismiss an otherwise valid grand jury indictment because the government failed to disclose to the grand jury evidence that tended to clear the defendant. The narrow majority stressed that the grand jury is an institution separate from the courts and beyond the court's supervisory power.

A defendant who was charged with knowingly overstating his assets said prosecutors refused to give the grand jury ledgers, tax returns, and testimony in a bankruptcy proceeding that belied an intent to mislead the banks.

Scalia, writing for the majority, said that to require the prosecutor to present exculpatory evidence would alter the grand jury's historical role, transforming it from an accusatory body that sits to assess whether adequate basis exists for bringing a criminal charge into an adjudicatory one that determines guilt or innocence.

Dissenting justices said they agreed that a prosecutor need not provide all exculpatory evidence before the grand jury, "but that does not mean that the prosecutor may mislead the grand jury into believing that there is probable cause to indict by withholding clear evidence to the contrary." Stevens, writing for the dissent, said, "We do not protect the integrity and independence of the grand jury by closing our eyes to the countless forms of prosecutorial misconduct that may occur inside the secrecy of the grand jury room."

White v. Illinois, decided by a 9-0 vote, January 15, 1992; Rehnquist wrote the opinion.

The constitutional right of an accused person to face his accuser is not violated when, in a child abuse case, a jury considers out-of-court statements made by an alleged victim, even when the child is available to testify but has been excused. The child made statements about the alleged incident to her mother, a physician, and others.

Federal rules generally prohibit hearsay evidence unless accompanied by sufficient guarantees of reliability. In this case, the unanimous Court said that the child's statements qualified under an exception for spontaneous declarations or statements made in the course of a medical examination. Rehnquist said the factor that made the statements reliable cannot be recaptured by in-court testimony.

Habeas Corpus

Keeney, Superintendent, Oregon State Penitentiary v. Tamayo-Reyes, decided by a 5-4 vote, May 4, 1992; White wrote the opinion; O'Connor, Stevens, Blackmun, and Kennedy dissented.

A new, stricter standard should govern whether state court defendants who challenge their cases through a writ of habeas corpus may obtain evidentiary hearings before federal judges. The Court decided that federal courts no longer are required to hold a hearing to weigh evidence if important facts were not adequately presented in state court.

A Cuban immigrant said his plea of nolo contendere to first degree manslaughter was invalid because his court-appointed translator did not provide an accurate or complete explanation of the mens rea element of the crime. Mens rea refers to the guilty knowledge and willfulness a defendant must have regarding the criminal act.

A federal appeals court said a federal evidentiary hearing was warranted because a state appeals court had not determined whether the translation was adequate. The federal appeals court said the failure to develop those facts in the state appeal did not constitute a "deliberate bypass" of the orderly procedure of the state courts.

The Supreme Court said the appeals court should have used the "cause-and-prejudice" standard, not the "deliberate bypass" test, to determine whether an evidentiary hearing was required. White wrote, "[The defendant] is entitled to an evidentiary hearing if he can show cause for his failure to develop the facts in state-court proceedings and actual prejudice resulting from that failure." The case was remanded to a federal district court. *(See entry, p. 14; excerpts, p. 109)*

Sawyer v. Whitley, Warden, decided by a 6-3 vote, June 22, 1992; Rehnquist wrote the opinion; Blackmun, Stevens, and O'Connor dissented.

This case raised the standard for inmates trying to get a federal court to review the constitutionality of a state death sentence through a petition for writ of habeas corpus. The majority said that when a prisoner brings a second or subsequent petition, alleging he has new information in his case, he must prove by "clear and convincing evidence" that if the new information were presented "no reasonable juror would have found [the defendant] eligible for the death penalty."

The Court was unanimous that the defendant failed to cast sufficient doubt on his sentence, but justices split 6-3 on the standard for assessing whether a new claim should be heard.

Stringer v. Black, Commissioner, Mississippi Department of Corrections, decided by a 6-3 vote, March 9, 1992; Kennedy wrote the opinion; Souter, Scalia, and Thomas dissented.

Supreme Court opinions from 1988 and 1990 should be given retroactive effect for a defendant challenging the constitutionality of his 1982 death sentence. The 1988 and 1990 Court opinions said juries, deciding whether a convicted murderer deserves the death penalty, should not weigh whether the crime was "especially heinous, atrocious or cruel."

The defendant filed his petition for habeas corpus in 1987. The Supreme Court generally forbids inmates from benefiting in a habeas corpus petition from a "new rule" announced in another case after the defendant's conviction becomes final.

Kennedy, however, said that the 1988 and 1990 decisions did not embody "new rules" but were based on a 1980 decision, of which the defendant should have the benefit. The Court in 1980 found the jury instruction, allowing jurors to vote for the death penalty if the murder was "especially heinous, atrocious or cruel," unconstitutionally vague.

Wright, Warden, v. West, decided by a 9-0 vote, June 19, 1992; Thomas wrote the opinion.

The ten-year prison sentence of a Virginia man should be reinstated, the Court ruled, holding that the trial record contained more than enough evidence to support his grand larceny conviction.

The ruling reversed an appeals court decision that the evidence against the defendant was insufficient, under constitutional due process, to support his state court conviction.

Contrary to what was expected when the Court first accepted this case for review, the justices did not use the dispute to decide how much deference a federal court should give to state court findings when the federal court hears an inmate's habeas corpus petition. In this case, all justices agreed that under any standard the evidence was sufficient for conviction.

Imprisonment

Denton, Director of Corrections of California v. Hernandez, decided by a 7-2 vote, May 4, 1992; O'Connor wrote the opinion; Stevens and Blackmun dissented.

The Court lowered the threshold federal judges use to dismiss "frivolous" lawsuits filed under a federal law that allows poor people to

sue without paying court costs. A prisoner filed five civil rights suits against California officials alleging he was drugged and homosexually raped twenty-eight times by various inmates and prison officials at different institutions. A district court found the facts "fanciful," but an appeals court reversed, saying that a court cannot dismiss a complaint as factually frivolous if it is impossible to know whether the injuries—in this case, druggings and prison rapes—occurred.

Reversing the appeals court, the Supreme Court said a district court may dismiss only if the facts alleged are "clearly baseless."

Hudson v. McMillian, decided by a 7-2 vote, February 25, 1992; O'Connor wrote the opinion; Thomas and Scalia dissented.

The use of excessive physical force against a prison inmate may constitute cruel and unusual punishment under the Eighth Amendment, even if the prisoner does not suffer serious injury.

The Louisiana inmate who brought the lawsuit had been beaten by guards while handcuffed and shackled. A supervisor on duty watched and told the guards "not to have too much fun." The beating loosened the inmate's teeth, cracked his dental plate, and caused minor bruises and facial swelling.

The Supreme Court's ruling reversed a lower court decision that prisoners alleging excessive force in violation of the Eighth Amendment must prove "significant injury" and that this inmate could not prevail because his injuries were "minor," requiring no medical attention. The majority ruled that the test is whether the force was used in a "good-faith effort" to maintain or restore discipline, or whether it was "maliciously and sadistically" used to cause harm, which Justice O'Connor said was the situation here.

In a dissent, Thomas accused the majority of expanding the Constitution to "address all ills in our society." "[A] use of force that causes only insignificant harm to a prisoner may be immoral, it may be tortious, it may be criminal, and it may even be remediable under other provisions of the Federal Constitution, but it is not 'cruel and unusual punishment.' " Thomas, who was joined by Scalia, said the test should be whether the prisoner suffered a serious deprivation.

Blackmun and Stevens concurred in the Court's ruling but said they favored a less rigorous standard than whether the beating was committed maliciously and sadistically.

McCarthy v. Madigan, decided by a 9-0 vote, March 4, 1992; Blackmun wrote the opinion.

A federal inmate need not exhaust a prison's internal grievance procedure before filing a civil rights lawsuit for money damages in federal court. The Court said that, given the nature of the prisoner's claims of abuse and the time-consuming prison grievance process, the inmate's individual interests outweigh concerns favoring exhaustion of the grievance process, such as protecting agency authority and promoting judicial efficiency.

Three justices—Rehnquist, Scalia, and Thomas—joined in the judgment of the majority but said they did so only because the prison grievance procedure did not provide for any award of money damages. The inmate was seeking $300,000 in damages, alleging that the prison was indifferent to his medical problems associated with a back operation and a history of psychiatric troubles.

Jury Selection

Georgia v. McCollum, decided by a 7-2 vote, June 18, 1992; Blackmun wrote the opinion; O'Connor and Scalia dissented.

Lawyers for criminal defendants cannot eliminate prospective jurors based on their race. The Court extended an antidiscrimination rule it applied in 1986 to prosecutors and in 1991 to parties in civil litigation.

The majority said that any racially motivated approach to choosing a jury violates the constitutional guarantee of equal protection of the laws. At issue are so-called peremptory challenges allowed to both parties as they choose the jury. A certain number of the challenges may be used to exclude people without any stated reason.

Justice Blackmun wrote for the majority, "Be it at the hands of the state or the defense, if a court allows jurors to be excluded because of group bias, it is a willing participant in a scheme that could only undermine the very foundation of our system of justice—our citizens' confidence in it."

O'Connor's dissent raised concerns that black defendants might not get a fair trial if they end up with an all-white jury. "It is by now clear that conscious and unconscious racism can affect the way white jurors perceive minority defendants and the facts presented at their trials, perhaps determining the verdict of guilt or innocence."

In his dissent, Scalia defended the longstanding right of criminal defendants to choose their juries. "In the interest of promoting the supposedly greater good of race relations in the society as a whole (make no mistake that that is what underlies all of this), we use the Constitution to destroy the ages-old right of criminal defendants to exercise peremptory challenges as they wish, to secure a jury that they consider fair."

Morgan v. Illinois, decided by a 6-3 vote, June 15, 1992; White wrote the opinion; Scalia, Rehnquist, and Thomas dissented.

A criminal defendant has a constitutional right to ask potential jurors if they automatically would impose the death penalty if they found him guilty of murder. A potential juror answering in the affirmative rightfully can be excluded by the defendant.

The Court said the due process clause of the Fourteenth Amendment is intended to guarantee that a jury would consider any mitigating evidence that would offset imposition of the death penalty for a convicted murderer. "A juror who will automatically vote for the death penalty in every case [after conviction] will fail in good faith to consider the evidence of aggravating and mitigating circumstances as the [judge's] instructions require him to do so," White wrote.

Dissenting, Scalia said: "Today, obscured within the fog of confusion that is our annually improvised Eighth Amendment, 'death is different' jurisprudence, the Court strikes a further blow against the People in its [the Court's] campaign against the death penalty. Not only must mercy be allowed, but now only the merciful may be permitted to sit in judgment."

Sentencing

Dawson v. Delaware, decided by an 8-1 vote, March 9, 1992; Rehnquist wrote the opinion; Thomas dissented.

A murder defendant's First and Fourteenth Amendment rights were violated when evidence was admitted about the racist activities of the Aryan Brotherhood, because the evidence revealed only the defendant's abstract beliefs.

The Court said the evidence was not relevant. The defendant had the words "Aryan Brotherhood" tattooed on his hand, but the Court said that any racist beliefs were not tied to the murder because the defendant's victim was white, as was the defendant.

During sentencing, a prosecutor mentioned the defendant's membership in the Aryan Brotherhood and said it is "a white racist prison gang that began in the 1960s in California in response to other gangs of racial minorities. Separate gangs calling themselves the Aryan Brotherhood now exist in many state prisons including Delaware."

The Supreme Court said the sentencing jury wrongly took the membership into account. Racial hatred was not an issue in the case, and no "good" character evidence on race had been admitted. "The Aryan Brotherhood evidence presented in this case cannot be viewed as relevant 'bad' character evidence in its own right," Chief Justice Rehnquist wrote.

Sochor v. Florida, decided by a 5-4 vote, June 8, 1992; Souter wrote the opinion; Rehnquist, White, Thomas, and Scalia dissented.

When a court that is deciding whether a defendant should get the death penalty takes into consideration an invalid aggravating factor, an appeals court must determine whether it was a harmless error.

This case involved a murder defendant whose trial judge, following the recommendations of a jury, found four aggravating circumstances present, including that the crime was committed in a cold, calculating manner. The Florida Supreme Court later ruled that a "heightened" degree of premeditation, which allowed the coldness factor to be considered, was not shown.

Souter said the defendant's Eighth Amendment rights were violated when the trial judge weighed the coldness factor. Then, because the Florida Supreme Court did not explain or state that this error "was harmless beyond a reasonable doubt" in affecting the man's death sentence, the error was not corrected.

United States v. R. L. C., decided by a 7-2 vote, March 24, 1992; Souter wrote the opinion; O'Connor and Blackmun dissented.

The Juvenile Delinquency Act requires a prison sentence to be limited to "the maximum term of imprisonment that would be authorized if the juvenile had been tried and convicted as an adult." The Court ruled that the limitation refers to the maximum sentence that could be imposed if the juvenile were being sentenced after application of the U.S. Sentencing Guidelines.

This case involved a sixteen-year-old who while driving drunk fatally injured a small child. The maximum sentence for involuntary manslaughter is three years, but the guidelines take into account a defendant's criminal history. Given that "the lowest possible criminal history level" was involved, a similarly situated adult would have gotten a maximum term of only twenty-one months in prison for the offense. The Supreme Court agreed with an appeals court that the juvenile should have been sentenced to only twenty-one months, not to thirty-six months as a lower court ordered.

United States v. Wilson, decided by a 7-2 vote, March 24, 1992; Thomas wrote the opinion; Stevens and White dissented.

In a case involving an inmate who wanted credit for the time he spent in jail before he was sentenced, the Court said the attorney general of the United States computes the amount of the credit, not a district court judge. The inmate sought credit from a district court, which denied the request.

Under the federal law in question, a defendant may have a prison term shortened by the amount of time he already spent in either federal or state custody awaiting trial for his crime. At issue was whether a district court calculates the credit at the time of sentencing, as the defendant argued, or whether the attorney general computes it after the defendant began serving his sentence. The Supreme Court said the latter, reversing an appeals court. The dissent said the right to obtain jail credit is what is important, not who gives it out.

Wade v. United States, decided by a 9-0 vote, May 18, 1992; Souter wrote the opinion.

A federal district court may review the government's refusal to request a lower sentence for a defendant who aided government agents and may grant a remedy but only if the judge finds that the refusal was based on an unconstitutional motive. Neither a claim that a defendant provided substantial assistance nor general allegations of improper motive will entitle a defendant to a remedy, to discovery, or to an evidentiary hearing on the issue. A defendant must make a "substantial threshold showing" of a constitutional violation first.

After being arrested on federal drug charges, the defendant gave law enforcement officials information that led to the arrest of another drug dealer. The informant pleaded guilty to the charges, and the court sentenced him to the ten-year minimum sentence. The government did not move to have the sentence reduced below the statutory minimum. The Supreme Court said the defendant failed to show a constitutional violation on the government's part.

Williams v. United States, decided by a 7-2 vote, March 9, 1992; O'Connor wrote the opinion; White and Kennedy dissented.

When a district court relies on an improper ground in sentencing, an appeals court may not affirm a sentence based solely on its independent assessment of the reasonableness of the digression from the federal sentencing guidelines. The Supreme Court said the appeals court must conduct two separate inquiries, asking whether the sentence imposed violated the law or was an incorrect application of the guidelines, and whether the sentence is an unreasonably high or low departure from the relevant guideline range. At issue was a judge's departure from the guidelines, which had both invalid and arguably valid bases.

The defendant was convicted of possessing a firearm and was given three more months imprisonment than the maximum under the Sentencing Guidelines, an increase from twenty-four to twenty-seven months. The judge said the guidelines' category that the defendant fell into was not adequate because it did not allow for the inclusion of either two old convictions or several prior arrests that did not result in prosecution. The Supreme Court remanded the case for determination of whether the sentence was imposed as a result of the district court's improper consideration of those arrests.

Miscellaneous Criminal Cases

Doggett v. United States, decided by a 5-4 vote, June 24, 1992; Souter wrote the opinion; O'Connor, Thomas, Rehnquist, and Scalia dissented.

A delay of eight years between a defendant's indictment and arrest violated his Sixth Amendment right to a speedy trial, the majority ruled. The defendant was indicted on federal drug charges in 1980 but left the country before his arrest. He went on to serve time in Panama on drug charges, then moved to Colombia and eventually back to the United

States. In the United States, he married, earned a college degree, found steady employment, lived under his own name, and never got into any legal trouble.

The U.S. Marshals Service found the defendant during a routine credit check and arrested him. The Court said U.S. officials were negligent in tracking the defendant and noted that the man did not know of his indictment before he left the country eight years earlier.

Dissenting justices said that during the eight years the defendant did not face public accusations, experience any anxiety, or live with restricted liberty—all concerns of federal speedy trial law. They said the government should get a chance to prove its case.

Evans v. United States, decided by a 6-3 vote, May 26, 1992; Stevens wrote the opinion; Thomas, Rehnquist, and Scalia dissented.

Prosecutors trying to demonstrate that a public official is guilty of extortion need not prove that the official demanded a payoff. The Court said an affirmative act of inducement is not an element of extortion "under color of official right" prohibited by the Hobbs Act.

The ruling upheld the conviction of a Georgia county commissioner caught in an FBI investigation of property rezoning practices. The majority said that "the government need only show that a public official has obtained a payment to which he was not entitled, knowing that the payment was made in return for official acts."

In the 1990-1991 term, the Court held in *McCormack v. United States* that a public official violated the Hobbs Act if he was paid in return for a promise to perform or not perform a specific act, even if he never made good on the promise.

Riggins v. Nevada, decided by a 7-2 vote, May 18, 1992; O'Connor wrote the opinion; Thomas and Scalia dissented.

Forcing a defendant to take an antipsychotic drug during his murder trial violated the defendant's rights under the Sixth and Fourteenth Amendments. The Court said a state cannot force drugs on a mentally ill defendant without an "overriding justification."

The defendant admitted fighting with his victim but said that the individual was trying to kill him and that voices in his head said the killing would be justified. After the defendant's objections and without making any determination of the need or any findings about reasonable alternatives, the trial court allowed the defendant to be given high doses of the drug Mellaril. The defendant said the medication deprived him of a "full and fair" trial because he could not show jurors his true mental state when he offered an insanity defense.

The Supreme Court said the lower court failed to acknowledge the defendant's liberty interest in freedom from antipsychotic drugs. It said a state must show that the treatment is medically appropriate and "essential" for the safety of the defendant or others.

Elections

Burdick v. Takushi, Director of Elections of Hawaii, decided by a 6-3 vote, June 8, 1992; White wrote the opinion; Kennedy, Blackmun, and Stevens dissented.

A Hawaii ban on write-in voting is a limited and permissible infringement of citizens' First and Fourteenth Amendment rights. The Court said that because the state's election laws provide easy access to the primary ballot during a nomination period, any burden on the voters' rights falls only to those who failed to identify their choices until shortly before the primary.

The case was brought by a Honolulu man who said he wanted choices beyond the designated ballot, especially when candidates ran unopposed.

But the Court majority said Hawaii's asserted interest in avoiding "party raiding" during the primaries and unrestrained factionalism at the general election is legitimate and sufficient to outweigh the limited burden that the write-in voting ban imposes.

Franklin, Secretary of Commerce v. Massachusetts, decided by a 9-0 vote, June 26, 1992; O'Connor wrote the opinion.

In the wake of the 1990 census, when the president sent to Congress a statement showing the number of persons in each state and the number of representatives that would be apportioned, his action was not a "final agency action" subject to judicial review. The justices differentiated action by the commerce secretary in submitting the census count to the president.

The Court, through Justice O'Connor, also rejected a challenge to Census Bureau policy on how to count U.S. citizens living abroad. As a result of the ruling, the state of Massachusetts lost one of its eleven seats in the House of Representatives.

Presley v. Etowah County Commission, decided by a 6-3 vote, January 27, 1992; Kennedy wrote the opinion; Stevens, White, and Blackmun dissented.

State and local governments seeking to change the responsibilities of elected county commissioners do not need federal approval, even when the change adversely affects the political power of black county commissioners.

The 1965 Voting Rights Act requires state and local governments to obtain federal approval for changes "with respect to voting." The federal law was intended to make sure that states did not use literacy tests, poll taxes, and other excluding measures to keep minorities from voting.

The Court ruled the law applies only to modifications that bear a direct relation to voting itself. The majority said changes in the organization and functioning of government, as were at issue in this Alabama case, are not subject to the law.

"Contemplation of Justice" is one of two marble figures by James Earle Fraser that flank the main entrance to the Supreme Court.

United States Department of Commerce v. Montana, decided by a 9-0 vote, March 31, 1992; Stevens wrote the opinion.

A 1941 federal law for allocating members of the U.S. House of Representatives is constitutional, the Court ruled, rejecting a challenge by the state of Montana that the statute violates the constitutional guarantee of equal representation, known as "one person, one vote."

The Court said that principle is impossible to achieve because the Constitution guarantees each state at least one representative and prohibits House districts that cross state lines.

After redistricting following the 1990 census, Montana lost one of its two seats in the House. If it had kept both seats, each district would have been closer to the ideal size of a congressional district than the reapportioned single district.

The Court said that under the Constitution only three requirements exist for allocating House seats: the number of representatives must not exceed one for every thirty-thousand persons; each state must have at least one representative; and district boundaries may not cross state lines. Justices said those factors preclude the kind of precise equality that Montana sought in distribution of the 435 House seats. The Court said Congress has broad discretion in apportioning representatives.

Environmental

Arkansas v. Oklahoma; Environmental Protection Agency v. Oklahoma, decided by a 9-0 vote, February 26, 1992; Stevens wrote the opinion.

A U.S. Environmental Protection Agency (EPA) decision to issue a permit for an Arkansas sewage treatment plant was within the agency's authority, although the plant's discharge would not meet the water quality standards of a downstream state (Oklahoma). The Court noted that the EPA determined that the Arkansas discharge would not cause "detectable" harm to Oklahoma's water quality. The justices also said it was within EPA's authority to require that downstream state water standards generally prevail.

The Court said an appeals court exceeded its discretion for judicial review when the appeals court rejected an EPA interpretation of the Clean Water Act and decided that Oklahoma's water standards, which were federally approved, forbade any new pollution from the Arkansas sewerage plant.

Chemical Waste Management, Inc. v. Hunt, decided by an 8-1 vote, June 1, 1992; White wrote the opinion; Rehnquist dissented.

States may not discriminate against other states by imposing a special fee on out-of-state hazardous waste discarded at an in-state commercial facility. The Court rejected an Alabama law that set up a two-tier fee system for disposal of wastes generated in and outside the state.

White wrote that the Alabama law violated the Commerce Clause and that no state "may attempt to isolate itself from a problem common to the several states." He added that the state law interfered with the full financial operation of a waste company that accepted debris from both out-of-state and in-state companies.

The landfill in Emelle, Alabama, is a leading disposal site among fewer than twenty commercial hazardous waste landfills nationwide.

Department of Energy v. Ohio; Ohio v. Department of Energy, decided by a 6-3 vote, April 21, 1992; Souter wrote the opinion; White, Blackmun, and Stevens dissented.

Congress has not waived the federal government's sovereign immunity from civil penalties sought to be imposed by a state for pollution violations of the Clean Water Act and the Resource Conservation and Recovery Act of 1976. The Court said the federal acts did not contain the requisite unequivocal waivers, so the government was protected from lawsuits.

Ohio sued the U.S. Department of Energy over its operation of a uranium processing plant in Fernald, Ohio. Ohio officials charged that the plant's disposal of radioactive waste contaminated surface and ground water.

Fort Gratiot Landfill, Inc. v. Michigan Department of Natural Resources, decided by a 7-2 vote, June 1, 1992; Stevens wrote the opinion; Rehnquist and Blackmun dissented.

A Michigan statute that restricts the disposal of out-of-county waste discriminates against interstate commerce. The law barred private landfill operators from accepting solid waste generated in another county, state, or country unless officials of the county that would receive the waste explicitly authorized it.

Stevens said the statute encourages each county to isolate itself from the national economy and protects local waste producers from competition from out-of-state waste producers who want to use local landfills. Dissenting justices said the statute "is at least arguably directed to legitimate local concerns, rather than improper economic protectionism."

Gade, Director, Illinois Environmental Protection Agency v. National Solid Wastes Management Association, decided by a 5-4 vote, June 18, 1992; O'Connor wrote the opinion; Souter, Blackmun, Stevens, and Thomas dissented.

States cannot impose licensing and training requirements on hazardous waste site operators that are stricter than federal law. The Court ruled that regulations under the Occupational Safety and Health Act preempt Illinois laws regarding the licensing of workers at certain hazardous waste facilities.

The Illinois statutes in question required workers to meet higher training standards than federal law and were challenged by a group of hazardous waste businesses. The state asserted that because the statutes had the dual purpose of protecting employees and the general public, the laws should not be preempted by the federal employee safety statute.

But the Court majority said that the federal act preempts all state laws that directly and substantially regulate workers' health and safety. Dissenting justices said that the federal law had not clearly precluded such state safety laws and that, in the absence of clear preemption, the state legislation should stand.

Lujan, Secretary of the Interior v. Defenders of Wildlife, decided by a 7-2 vote, June 12, 1992; Scalia wrote the opinion; Blackmun and O'Connor dissented.

An environmental group does not have standing to sue the government over an interpretation of the Endangered Species Act because the group failed to show that it was sufficiently injured by the law.

The 1973 Endangered Species Act says that federal agencies must ensure that their activities do not jeopardize endangered or threatened species. Reversing a previous stance, the Interior Department in 1986 said the law did not apply to federally financed projects overseas.

The environmental group, which had sent representatives abroad, contended that the Interior Department policy was leading to increases in the rate of extinction of endangered animals. But the group failed to show sufficient activity abroad, according to Scalia, to demonstrate that its members would be hurt by U.S. practices overseas.

Stevens concurred in the judgment but differed in his reasoning, saying the act never was intended to apply to activities in foreign countries. Blackmun, with O'Connor, dissented, saying, "I cannot join the Court on what amounts to a slash-and-burn expedition through the law of environmental standing."

New York v. United States, decided by a 6-3 vote, June 19, 1992; O'Connor wrote the opinion; White, Blackmun, and Stevens dissented.

A key part of a federal law intended to make states responsible for the low-level radioactive waste they generate is unconstitutional. The provision in question says that a state failing to provide for the disposal of waste generated within its borders becomes the legal owner of the waste and assumes liability for any injuries the waste causes.

The case arose after New York state sued the federal government saying the 1985 law violated state sovereignty.

"Congress may not simply commandeer the legislative processes of the states by directly compelling them to enact and enforce a federal regulatory program," O'Connor wrote for the majority. Dissenting justices said Congress has an important role in the regulation among states in disposal of hazardous waste.

Robertson v. Seattle Audubon Society, decided by a 9-0 vote, March 25, 1992; Thomas wrote the opinion.

Congress's temporary suspension of certain environmental laws that were subject to dispute in pending court cases did not violate constitutional separation of powers. The question here was whether Congress interfered with the judicial proceedings in a 1989 mandate temporarily freeing timber sales from most court-ordered bans.

The directive for management of national forests containing northern spotted owls was adopted as part of an annual appropriations bill for the Department of Interior. The unanimous Supreme Court said Congress was effectively adopting a new law instead of ordering specific results under the old law.

Federal Regulation

Board of Governors of the Federal Reserve System v. MCorp Financial, Inc.; MCorp v. Board of Governors of the Federal Reserve System, decided by an 8-0 vote, December 3, 1991; Stevens wrote the opinion; Thomas took no part in the case.

Federal courts lack jurisdiction to hear a challenge to the Federal Reserve Board's controversial "source of strength" regulation while the board is conducting its own administrative enforcement proceedings. The source of strength policy requires bank holding companies to maintain adequate capital for their subsidiary banks and to be responsible for their financial viability.

The case began when the Federal Reserve Board alleged that MCorp was engaged in unsafe and unsound practices linked to capital problems at its subsidiary banks. Many of the banks were declared insolvent and eventually became part of one of the nation's largest commercial bank bailouts.

After the Federal Reserve Board charged MCorp with failing to act as a source of strength for subsidiary banks that had yet to be declared insolvent, MCorp initiated an adversary proceeding in the Bankruptcy Court to enjoin prosecution in the pending administrative proceedings. A district judge barred enforcement of the source of strength policy. Upholding the order, an appeals court ruled that the board's regulation exceeded its statutory authority.

But the Supreme Court reversed the lower courts. It said the 1966 Financial Institutions Supervisory Act forbids a court from affecting such administrative proceedings by injunction or otherwise.

Cipollone, Individually and as Executor of the Estate of Cipollone v. Liggett Group, Inc., decided by a 7-2 vote, June 24, 1992; Stevens wrote the opinion; Scalia and Thomas dissented.

Cigarette manufacturers who lie about the dangers of smoking or otherwise misrepresent their products can be sued under state laws and made to pay to large monetary awards.

The family of a woman who died of a smoking-related illness brought several claims in New Jersey state court against three cigarette manufacturers. The companies argued that the Federal Cigarette Labeling and Advertising Act preempted state liability claims. A jury awarded the family $400,000 against the Liggett Group; the two other manufacturers were cleared. Reversing, an appeals court held that the labeling act precludes state tort action.

Although the Supremacy Clause says federal laws supersede state laws, the Court usually has required that preemption of state laws be clearly expressed in statute. The majority in this case ruled that the federal labeling law preempted only state laws requiring particular warnings on cigarette labels or in cigarette advertising. A smoker could go to state court alleging that manufacturers breached express warranties, ran fraudulent cigarette advertisements, hid the dangers of smoking from state authorities, and conspired to mislead smokers.

The ruling was expected to encourage more litigation over smoking-related deaths. *(See entry, p. 20; excerpts, p. 130)*

Hilton v. South Carolina Public Railways Commission, decided by a 6-2 vote, December 16, 1991; Kennedy wrote the opinion; O'Connor and Scalia dissented; Thomas took no part in the case.

An injured railroad worker may sue a South Carolina public railways agency in state court under the Federal Employers' Liability Act (FELA).

The South Carolina Public Railways Commission was sued in state court under the Federal Employers' Liability Act by an employee alleging he was hurt on the job through the commission's negligence. A state court dismissed the suit, saying that the federal law does not cover state agencies.

The Supreme Court reversed the ruling, citing a twenty-eight-year-old precedent that said when Congress enacted the law and used the phrase "every common carrier by railroad" to describe the class of employers subject to its terms, Congress intended to include state-owned railroads. When lawsuits in state court are at issue, a statute need not provide a clear statement to abrogate states' Eleventh Amendment immunity from lawsuit, as required for federal court issues. The majority also said workers' compensation laws in many states specifically exclude railroad workers from their coverage, because of the assumption that the Federal Employers' Liability Act provides adequate protection for those workers. Therefore, without FELA coverage, a worker would have neither federal nor state protection.

Morales, Attorney General of Texas v. Trans World Airlines, Inc., decided by a 5-3 vote, June 1, 1992; Scalia wrote the opinion; Stevens, Rehnquist, and Blackmun dissented; Souter took no part in the case.

The federal Airline Deregulation Act of 1978 preempts states from regulating airline advertising to protect consumers from being misled about discount air fares. The Court said state interest in advertising practices is expressly superseded by the act's jurisdiction over laws relating to rates, routes, or services of any air carrier.

To stop false advertisements, the National Association of Attorneys General in 1987 proposed regulations on advertising, including purchase conditions that must be disclosed and the size of the type explaining special restrictions plus low-price seat availability. The airlines filed suit to block state enforcement of such general consumer protection regulations, saying federal law should govern any advertising.

Writing for the majority, Scalia said that a phrase in the federal law, "relating to rates," was broad enough to cover regulation of advertising of air fares. Dissenting justices argued that preemption was not clearly stated in the law's text and legislative history.

National Railroad Passenger Corporation v. Boston & Maine Corp.; Interstate Commerce Commission v. Boston & Maine Corp., decided by a 6-3 vote, March 25, 1992; Kennedy wrote the opinion; White, Blackmun, and Thomas dissented.

Amtrak was within its rights under federal law when it forced a private freight railroad to sell portions of its track and then turned the track over to a competitor of the original owner. (Amtrak's official name is the National Railroad Passenger Corporation.) This case arose from Interstate Commerce Commission (ICC) approval of a transaction that involved forty-nine miles of track in Vermont obtained from the Boston and Maine Corp. (B&M) railroad. Amtrak had track rights with B&M for its Montrealer train between Washington, D.C., and Montreal but claimed it was forced to discontinue the service because of B&M's poor maintenance of the track. When B&M and Amtrak failed to agree on terms for the acquisition of the track, Amtrak sought and obtained ICC approval to condemn it.

The Supreme Court said federal law includes a strong presumption that Amtrak will make reasonable business judgments on condemnation, and thus the ICC acted properly.

Nationwide Mutual Insurance Co. v. Darden, decided by a 9-0 vote, March 24, 1992; Souter wrote the opinion.

In a dispute over whether a worker qualified for pension benefits, the Court ruled that the term "employee" as used in the federal Employee Retirement Income Security Act (ERISA) derives from traditional agency law criteria for identifying master-servant relationships.

In question was the status of an insurance agent who sold policies for Nationwide Mutual Insurance Co. under a contractual agreement. The agent received pension benefits from the company, but they were cut off after his contract ended and he began competing with the company, contrary to a condition of his original contract. The agent wanted to sue under the federal pension law, which prohibits such benefit-forfeiture provisions. But Nationwide contended that the agent was an independent contractor not covered by the federal law.

Under the traditional "common law" test, the Court said, factors such as a company's right to control the worker, the location of the employee's work, his skill level, method of payment, and the duration of the business relationship would be weighed. The case was remanded for a ruling on the agent, but Souter suggested that independent agents probably do not qualify for ERISA protection.

United States v. Alaska, decided by a 9-0 vote, April 21, 1992; White wrote the opinion.

The secretary of the army may make approval of a plan to build a port and causeway in Nome conditional on Alaska's waiver of claims to any additional submerged land that might fall within the new port boundary. The port facilities would extend into Norton Sound, under federal jurisdiction, where the coastal waters have been the site of gold exploration for close to a century.

Alaska challenged the Army Corps of Engineers' authority to require the disclaimer that no change take place in the existing state-federal boundary. The unanimous Court said the army has broad discretion to grant or deny a permit for construction and had met the test of not having acted in an arbitrary or capricious manner.

United States Department of State v. Ray, decided by an 8-0 vote, December 16, 1991; Stevens wrote the opinion; Thomas took no part in the case.

Public disclosure of the names of Haitians who were deported from the United States, and later interviewed by the U.S. government to determine whether they were prosecuted in their homeland, would be an unwarranted invasion of the returnees' privacy.

This case stemmed from an assurance the United States won from the Haitian government in 1981 that it would not subject to prosecution for illegal departure undocumented Haitians interdicted and returned to Haiti. The U.S. government interviewed unsuccessful emigrants and said most reported no harassment or prosecution after their return.

Trying to disprove those findings, a Florida lawyer who represented undocumented Haitian nationals made requests for copies of the interview reports under the Freedom of Information Act. He received seventeen documents from which names and other identifying information had been blacked out.

The Supreme Court upheld the redaction under the act's exemption for "personnel and medical files and similar files the disclosure of which would constitute a clearly unwarranted invasion of personal privacy." The unanimous Court said the invasion of privacy from summaries containing personal details about particular returnees, while de minimis when the returnees' identities are unknown, is significant when the information is linked to particular individuals. The Court also said the disclosures could subject the returned Haitians to embarrassment or retaliation.

Immigration

Ardestani v. Immigration and Naturalization Service, decided by a 6-2 vote, December 10, 1991; O'Connor wrote the opinion; Stevens and Blackmun dissented; Thomas took no part in the case.

Administrative deportation proceedings are not adversary adjudications. As a result, they are not covered by a provision of the Equal Access to Justice Act allowing winning parties to receive attorneys' fees and costs.

An Iranian woman of the Bahai faith applied for asylum in the United States, saying that she feared persecution if deported to Iran. The State Department confirmed her fears, but the Immigration and Naturalization Service (INS) denied her application. The INS said the woman had reached a "safe haven" in Luxembourg and had established residence there. But she told the INS that she had been in Luxembourg only three days en route to the United States, that she had stayed only in a hotel, and that she never had applied for residency in Luxembourg. She eventually prevailed in a deportation proceeding but was denied attorneys' costs.

Justice O'Connor's majority opinion said that because the doctrine of sovereign immunity protects the United States from liability for attorneys' fees, any waiver must be clearly stated in the law. Any ambiguity in the fee recovery provision of the Equal Access to Justice Act is construed in favor of the government.

Immigration and Naturalization Service v. Doherty, decided by a 5-3 vote, January 15, 1992; Rehnquist wrote the opinion; Scalia, Stevens, and Souter dissented in part; Thomas took no part in the case.

A former leader of the Irish Republican Army must abide by the U.S. attorney general's ruling that he be deported to Great Britain, where he was convicted for the murder of a British officer in Northern Ireland. The Court ruled that Joseph Patrick Doherty exhausted his legal grounds for further hearing and that Attorney General Dick Thornburgh did not exceed his authority when he overturned a decision by the Board of Immigration Appeals that would have allowed Doherty to make new arguments for political asylum in the United States. The Court said the appropriate test was whether the attorney general abused his discretion.

Doherty was found guilty in 1981 in absentia by a Northern Ireland court. After the Immigration and Naturalization Service (INS) discovered him in the United States, arrested him, and began deportation proceedings, he applied for asylum. Doherty, a citizen of both Ireland and the United Kingdom, later withdrew that application and dropped his attempts to avoid deportation, designating Ireland as the country to which he was to be deported. An immigration judge, over an INS challenge to the designation, ordered deportation to Ireland and the Board of Immigration Appeals affirmed. Then, while an INS appeal to the attorney general was pending, Doherty moved to reopen his deportation proceedings and revoke election of Ireland on the basis that the 1987 Irish Extradition Act constituted new evidence requiring reopening of his claims for withholding of deportation and asylum. The act would have caused him to be extradited to Britain when he arrived in Ireland.

The Supreme Court said the attorney general did not abuse his discretion in denying reopening of the case.

Immigration and Naturalization Service v. Elias-Zacarias, decided by a 6-3 vote, January 22, 1992; Scalia wrote the opinion; Stevens, O'Connor, and Blackmun dissented.

A Guatemalan guerrilla organization's attempt to coerce a person into joining does not necessarily constitute "persecution on account of . . . political opinion" under federal immigration law, and therefore the individual is not eligible for asylum in the United States.

The Court endorsed a Board of Immigration Appeals finding that the man who fled Guatemala was not eligible for asylum because he did not have a well-founded fear of persecution. The majority said the record did not show that the guerrillas would persecute him because of his political opinions if he returned to his homeland. It stressed that the victim's political opinion, not the persecutor's, is at the core of a test for persecution.

Immigration and Naturalization Service v. National Center for Immigrants' Rights, Inc., decided by a 9-0 vote, December 16, 1991; Stevens wrote the opinion.

The U.S. attorney general has the authority to forbid the employment of foreigners who have been released on bond while awaiting rulings on whether they may remain in the United States. The federal regulation at issue allows the attorney general to arrest aliens and, pending a determination of their deportability, either to hold them in custody or to release them on bond containing numerous conditions.

A district court said the restriction concerning employment was beyond the attorney general's statutory authority.

The Supreme Court differed, saying the rule is consistent with the established concern of immigration law to preserve jobs for American workers and thus is squarely within the scope of the attorney general's statutory authority.

Individual Rights

Abortion Rights

Planned Parenthood of Southeastern Pennsylvania v. Casey, Governor of Pennsylvania; Casey, Governor of Pennsylvania v. Planned Parenthood of Southeastern Pennsylvania, decided by 5-4 and 7-2 votes, June 29, 1992; O'Connor, Kennedy, and Souter wrote the opinion; Rehnquist, White, Scalia, and Thomas dissented in part; Blackmun and Stevens dissented in part.

In the term's most controversial case, the Court reaffirmed that a woman has a constitutional right to an abortion, upholding the centerpiece of *Roe v. Wade* (1973). The Court, however, changed the legal test for determining whether a state is interfering with an abortion choice by ruling that the standard should be whether a regulation puts an "undue burden" on a woman seeking an abortion before the fetus is viable. *Roe v. Wade* said a state could interfere only if it had a "compelling interest," which made virtually all restrictions through the first two trimesters invalid.

In an unusual joint opinion written by three justices, the Court let stand Pennsylvania restrictions that required a twenty-four-hour waiting period and informed consent. The Court struck down a provision that said a woman seeking an abortion must sign a statement that she had notified her husband.

The case was brought by five abortion clinics and a physician who performed abortions. *(See entry, p. 30; excerpts, p. 159)*

Civil Rights

Collins v. City of Harker Heights, Texas, decided by a 9-0 vote, February 26, 1992; Stevens wrote the opinion.

A federal civil rights law that provides money damages for constitutional injuries done "under color of state law" cannot be invoked for a sanitation worker who died while cleaning a sewer line. The Court said municipalities have no constitutional obligation to create a safe workplace, even if their failure to warn workers about hazards arises from deliberate indifference.

Justices said that the failure to train or warn employees about known hazards in the workplace does not rise to a violation of the due process clause, as the worker's widow alleged. The Court also rejected a lower court test that such lawsuits can be brought only if "an abuse of governmental power" occurred. The Supreme Court said the proper analysis is whether the injury was caused by a constitutional violation and, if so, whether the city is responsible for that violation.

Franklin v. Gwinnett County Public Schools, decided by a 9-0 vote, February 26, 1992; White wrote the opinion.

Students who have been sexually harassed may sue for damages under a federal law barring sex discrimination in schools and colleges.

The Court adopted a broad view of Title IX of the Education Amendments of 1972 and rejected Bush administration arguments that the statute does not authorize money damages as a remedy for illegal discrimination. Congress had not specified the remedies available under the law, which covers any education program receiving federal aid.

A student contended that she had been sexually harassed by and forced to have intercourse with a teacher. The school discouraged the student from pressing charges, then dropped its investigation when the teacher quit.

After the student sued the school district for damages, a federal court dismissed the student's complaint, saying Title IX is limited to declaratory and injunctive relief and does not allow the award of money damages. But a unanimous Supreme Court said the general rule is that, when Congress has not spelled out the remedies, all appropriate relief is available in an action brought to vindicate a federal right.

Freeman v. Pitts, decided by an 8-0 vote, March 31, 1992; Kennedy wrote the opinion; Thomas took no part in the case.

While supervising a school desegregation plan, a district court has the authority to give up control of a school district in incremental stages before desegregation has been achieved in every area of school operations. The Court said a district court may decide not to order further remedies in areas where the school district is in compliance with the decree, at the same time retaining jurisdiction over the case.

School districts under court supervision must take all necessary steps to become desegregated or "unitary." The Court said the term "unitary" does not have a fixed meaning or content and does not confine a district court's discretion.

In this case involving Georgia schools, the Supreme Court also ruled that once the vestiges of de jure segregation have ended, school districts are not required to remedy racial disparities caused by demographic shifts.

Hafer v. Melo, decided by an 8-0 vote, November 5, 1991; O'Connor wrote the opinion; Thomas took no part in the case.

State officials may be held personally liable for actions taken in their official capacity. The Court's decision allowed workers who were fired by the Pennsylvania auditor general to continue seeking money damages from her under a federal civil rights law intended to redress improper conduct by persons acting "under color of state law."

Auditor Barbara Hafer vowed during her election campaign to fire workers who allegedly obtained their jobs through payoffs to a former worker in the auditor general's office. The incumbent auditor general cleared the workers of wrongdoing, but they were dismissed when he lost to Hafer. The workers sued, saying they had been denied due process of law because Hafer held no hearings. As supporters of Hafer's opponent, they also cited their free speech rights.

A district court dismissed the workers' claims, ruling that state officials who act in their official capacity are immune from personal monetary liability. But the unanimous Court said the auditor general, in effect, was sued in her individual capacity, not as a state official. It said the law in question was enacted to enforce due process against those who carry the badge of a state, whether they are acting under state authority. The capacity in which a person is sued, not the capacity in which he acted, determines the liability.

Suter v. Artist M., decided by a 7-2 vote, March 25, 1992; Rehnquist wrote the opinion; Blackmun and Stevens dissented.

Foster children may not use a federal civil rights law to sue states that fail to make reasonable efforts to prevent the removal of children from homes and to reunite families. The Court said the Adoption Assistance and Child Welfare Act of 1980 does not give its beneficiaries a private right of action under a Reconstruction-era civil rights law intended to redress constitutional violations "under color of law."

The adoption act provides for the federal government to reimburse states for expenses in administering foster care and adoption services. The question was whether the act's requirement that a state accepting federal funds make "reasonable efforts" to prevent the need for foster care placement and to reunify foster care children with their families is a privately enforceable right.

Writing for the majority, Rehnquist said states have broad discretion under the statute. Dissenting, Blackmun said that the Court in 1990 permitted such private civil rights lawsuits to enforce a Medicaid law requiring reasonable reimbursements for health care providers. "I cannot acquiesce in this unexplained disregard for established law. . . . After all, we are dealing here with children," Blackmun wrote. Rehnquist said that the statute in the 1990 case set out standards for whether states had adopted reasonable Medicaid reimbursement rates and that Congress had not given similar guidance in the 1980 adoption statute.

United States v. Fordice, Governor of Mississippi; Ayers v. Fordice, Governor of Mississippi, decided by an 8-1 vote, June 26, 1992; White wrote the opinion; Scalia dissented.

When a school system is charged with being discriminatory, the state bears the burden of justifying the potentially discriminatory practices.

This case began in 1975 when citizens sued the state of Mississippi over its continued operation of five almost completely white and three almost completely black universities. The United States then charged that state officials had not met the requirements of the Equal Protection Clause of the Fourteenth Amendment and Title VI of the 1964 Civil Rights Act to dismantle the dual system. Lower courts ruled that Mississippi was working to undo the former de jure segregated system through "race-neutral" policies.

The Supreme Court, however, said that the lower courts failed to apply the proper legal standard in assessing the school system. White said a court must ask whether the racial identity of a school stems from state policies and must examine a wide range of factors to determine whether the state perpetuated its former segregation in any facet of the system. Applying that standard, the Court held that several surviving aspects of Mississippi's dual system potentially violated the equal protection guarantee. *(See entry, p. 26; excerpts, p. 144)*

"Equal Justice Under Law" is carved across the front of the Supreme Court building.

First Amendment

Burson, Attorney General and Reporter for Tennessee v. Freeman, decided by a 5-3 vote, May 26, 1992; Blackmun wrote the opinion; Stevens, O'Connor, and Souter dissented; Thomas took no part in the case.

A Tennessee statute that bars the solicitation of votes and the distribution of campaign materials within 100 feet of the entrance to a polling place potentially encompassing streets and sidewalks does not violate political speech rights.

Writing for the Court, Blackmun said the key question was how large a restricted zone can be and how it is tailored to the state's interest. He said legislatures should be permitted to protect voters from interference and intimidation, provided the approach is reasonable and does not significantly impinge on free speech rights. He said the 100-foot boundary meets that test.

Stevens wrote for dissenting justices: "The hubbub of campaign workers outside a polling place may be a nuisance, but it is also the sound of vibrant democracy."

Forsyth County, Georgia v. Nationalist Movement, decided by a 5-4 vote, June 19, 1992; Blackmun wrote the opinion; Rehnquist, White, Scalia, and Thomas dissented.

A county ordinance requiring that organizers of a parade pay up to $1,000 for police protection violates the free speech guarantee of the First Amendment. The Forsyth County ordinance was adopted after police were called to intervene in civil rights rallies during which white counterdemonstrators became violent.

The Court majority was troubled by the broad discretion the ordinance gave to the county administrator to set the fee. It does not have "narrowly drawn, reasonable and definite standards" to guide the administrator, the majority said, noting that the administrator could decide not to assess the fee and is not obligated to provide an explanation for actions taken.

The justices also found the ordinance unconstitutionally content-based, because the administrator has to evaluate the message or purpose of marchers to determine security for the demonstration or parade.

Dissenting, Rehnquist wrote that the Constitution does not limit a parade license fee to a nominal amount. He also said municipalities need the discretion to keep order.

International Society for Krishna Consciousness, Inc. v. Lee, Superintendent of Port Authority Police, decided by a 6-3 vote, June 26, 1992; Rehnquist wrote the opinion; Souter, Blackmun, and Stevens dissented.

The Port Authority of New York and New Jersey, which operate three major airports in the New York City area, may forbid solicitations for money within airport terminals. The regulation was challenged by Krishnas, a religious group that has a ritual of "going into public places, disseminating religious literature and soliciting funds to support the religion," according to the Court opinion.

A majority said airports are not traditional forums for public speech, so the ban need only meet standards for reasonableness. Writing for the Court, Rehnquist said solicitation may have a disruptive effect on business by slowing the path of both those who must decide whether to contribute and those who would change their paths to avoid being solicited. Rehnquist was joined by White, O'Connor, Scalia, and Thomas. Kennedy concurred that solicitations could be banned, but he disagreed with the chief justice's reasoning that an airport was not a public forum.

A separate majority (Kennedy, O'Connor, Souter, Blackmun, and Stevens) ruled in *Lee v. International Society for Krishna Consciousness* that the airport authority's ban on distributing literature within the terminals was invalid.

Lee v. Weisman, personally and as a next friend of Weisman, decided by a 5-4 vote, June 24, 1992; Kennedy wrote the opinion; Scalia, Rehnquist, White, and Thomas dissented.

Allowing prayers as part of a public school graduation ceremony is unconstitutional.

In an unexpected decision reaffirming a clear separation between church and state, the Court supported a Providence, Rhode Island, student who objected to the invocation and benediction by a rabbi at her junior high school graduation ceremony. The majority said the Establishment Clause was meant to head off what might begin as a tolerant expression of religious views but end in a policy to indoctrinate and coerce. Prayer exercises in elementary and secondary schools carry a particular risk of coercion, the Court said. *(See entry, p. 23; excerpts, p. 137)*

Norman v. Reed; Cook County Officers Electoral Board v. Reed, decided by a 7-1 vote, January 14, 1992; Souter wrote the opinion; Scalia dissented; Thomas took no part in the case.

An Illinois election law that sought to keep a new party off the ballot in 1990 violated the First Amendment right of political association and Fourteenth Amendment right of equal protection of the laws.

Provisions of the Illinois statute in question set up stiff requirements for access to the ballot by new parties. One provision prevented a "new political party" in Cook County from using the name of a party already established in the city of Chicago. Another provision required that fifty thousand signatures were needed to run a slate of candidates in Cook County, which amounted to twice as many signatures as needed to field candidates for statewide office.

The Harold Washington party, which was established in Chicago in 1989 and named for the city's late mayor, challenged the law. The Court said a state may limit new parties' access to the ballot only to the extent that a sufficiently weighty state interest justifies the restriction. Here, the law was "inhospitable" to new parties, Justice Souter wrote for the majority, and violated the right of access to the ballot.

R. A. V. v. City of St. Paul, Minnesota, decided by a 9-0 vote, June 22, 1992; Scalia wrote the opinion.

Cities may not target "hate speech" based on race, color, creed, religion, or gender. Three white teenagers who burned a makeshift cross in the yard of a black family were charged under the St. Paul, Minnesota, Bias-Motivated Crime Ordinance, which the Court said unconstitutionally prohibited speech on the basis of the subject addressed in the speech.

Although the ruling was unanimous, the justices split sharply in their rationale. A five-justice majority said "content-based regulations are presumptively invalid." To ban a particular kind of speech that would be considered "fighting words"—words that "by their very utterance inflict injury or tend to incite an immediate breach of the peace"—a municipality must outlaw all fighting words.

White, meanwhile, found the ordinance unacceptably broad because "it also makes criminal expressive conduct that causes only hurt feelings, offense, or resentment." Writing for the four other justices, White said government should be able to categorize different types of speech. He said the majority opinion radically revises First Amendment law and legitimizes hate speech.

As a result of the decision, the validity of laws and university codes banning behavior and language elicited by prejudice may be in question. *(See entry, p. 18; excerpts, p. 124)*

Simon & Schuster, Inc. v. Members of New York State Crime Victims Board, decided by an 8-0 vote, December 10, 1991; O'Connor wrote the opinion; Thomas took no part in the case.

A New York law that prohibited paying criminals to tell their stories violates the First Amendment. The unanimous Court struck down the so-called "Son of Sam" law that required any money owed to the convict-writer be paid to a special fund to compensate the criminal's victims.

This suit arose after the New York State Crime Victims Board discovered that Simon & Schuster had signed an agreement with an author who had contracted with admitted organized crime figure Henry Hill. The Court said the law is too broad, because it applies to works on any subject that express the author's thoughts about his crime, however tangentially or incidentally, and because it covered authors who admit to committing a crime, whether or not they were accused or convicted.

The law was named after a serial killer who terrorized New York in 1977 and called himself "Son of Sam." *(See entry, p. 10; excerpts, p. 85)*

Labor

Estate of Cowart v. Nicklos Drilling Co., decided by a 6-3 vote, June 22, 1992; Kennedy wrote the opinion; Blackmun, Stevens, and O'Connor dissented.

This case required an interpretation of the Longshore and Harbor Workers' Compensation Act, under which workers injured or killed while employed on U.S. navigable waters are compensated. The act allows injured workers to pursue claims against third parties allegedly responsible for their injuries, without surrendering compensation from their employers. But a provision of the act states that a worker will forfeit all potential employer benefits, including medical benefits, if the worker settles with a third party without the written approval of his employer.

The Court ruled that this forfeiture provision applied to a worker whose employer was neither paying compensation to the worker nor subject to an order to pay under the act. The Court said even if a claim against an employer were not yet acknowledged nor adjudicated, it was covered.

General Motors Corp. v. Romein, decided by a 9-0 vote, March 9, 1992; O'Connor wrote the opinion.

A Michigan law forcing employers to pay retroactively workers' compensation benefits that they withheld under an old law is constitutional. The Court rejected a contention that the new law violated contractual and due process rights.

The case arose from a 1981 state law allowing employers to reduce workers' compensation payments by the amounts paid in other employee benefits, such as pension and disability plans. General Motors interpreted the law as allowing employers to offset other benefits against workers' compensation benefits even for accidents that occurred before the 1981 law took effect. The Michigan Supreme Court agreed in a 1985 case. But then the Michigan legislature in 1987 overturned the results of the state court ruling by passing a new law requiring employers to pay with interest and without offsets compensation they owed for work-related accidents to employees before the 1981 law took effect.

Writing for the unanimous Court, O'Connor said, "The retroactive repayment provision of the 1987 law was a rational means of meeting [a] legitimate objective" of making sure injured workers are not undercompensated or overcompensated.

Lechmere, Inc. v. National Labor Relations Board, decided by a 6-3 vote, January 27, 1992; Thomas wrote the opinion; White, Blackmun, and Stevens dissented.

An employer who bars nonemployee union organizers from distributing leaflets on the owner's property does not violate federal labor law. The case stemmed from a union campaign to organize Lechmere employees by occupying the retailer's parking lot and other property at the Newington, Connecticut, store.

The majority said the labor law in question protects only nonemployee union organizers in rare situations, such as logging camps, in which targeted workers cannot be reached by channels other than at the employer's property. The right of unions to organize would outweigh an employer's property rights, Justice Thomas said, only when a plant location and the employees' living quarters "place the employees beyond the reach of reasonable efforts to communicate with them."

Southwest Marine, Inc. v. Gizoni, decided by an 8-0 vote, December 4, 1991; White wrote the opinion; Thomas took no part in the case.

A maritime worker whose occupation is one of those covered by the Longshore and Harbor Workers' Compensation Act still may be a "seaman" within the meaning of the Jones Act and entitled to damages when he is injured.

The case arose after a rigging foreman, working on a floating platform, fell and disabled his leg and back. He received medical and compensation benefits from his employer, Southwest Marine, under the Longshore and Harbor Workers' Compensation Act. But he alleged he was injured because of Southwest Marine's negligence and sought money damages under the Jones Act.

To be a seaman qualifying for damages under the Jones Act, the Court said a maritime worker need only be doing a ship's work, which is not limited to only aiding in its navigation. Further, the Court said being a harbor worker or engaged in ship repair does not preclude someone from Jones Act protection.

Wooddell v. International Brotherhood of Electrical Workers, Local 71, decided by an 8-0 vote, December 4, 1991; White wrote the opinion; Thomas took no part in the case.

A union member alleging that the union discriminated against him in job referrals—a violation of the union's constitution and by-laws—has a federal cause of action against the union. The Court considered the electrical workers union's constitution a contract between the International Brotherhood of Electrical Workers and its local, and thus "between ... labor organizations" under federal law and subject to federal court jurisdiction.

The Court also said the union member is entitled to a jury trial in his effort to obtain money damages as well as injunctive relief under the Labor Management Relations Act. The Court said the injunctive relief, although typically not qualifying for a jury, may be heard by a jury when incidental to the lost wages and benefits being sought.

Property Law

Lucas v. South Carolina Coastal Council, decided by a 6-3 vote, June 29, 1992; Scalia wrote the opinion; Blackmun, Stevens, and Souter dissented.

State regulations that effectively deny a property owner all value of his land constitute a "taking" under the Fifth Amendment and require compensation, the Court said.

Two years after the petitioner in this case bought two residential lots on a South Carolina barrier island, the state enacted a law restricting beachfront development. As a result, no permanent dwellings could be built on the property owner's land. He sued saying the construction ban deprived him of all "economically viable use" of his property. The state trial court agreed, said his land was "valueless," and gave him a monetary award. The state supreme court, in overturning the ruling, maintained that, when a regulation is designed to prevent "harmful or noxious uses" of property, compensation is not required.

The U.S. Supreme Court said the "harmful or noxious uses" standard did not apply and reversed the decision. The case was remanded to a lower court to determine whether the property was valueless and the landowner had to be compensated. *(See entry, p. 27; excerpts, p. 155)*

Yee v. City of Escondido, California, decided by a 9-0 vote, April 1, 1992; O'Connor wrote the opinion.

The Takings Clause of the Fifth Amendment is not violated by the combination of a city rent control law and state restrictions on mobile home park owners that forces park owners to accept long-term below-market rents.

The Takings Clause requires compensation when the government authorizes a physical occupation of property or through some regulation deprives the owner of the property's value.

The city of Escondido's rent control ordinance keeps rents at 1986 levels and prohibits increases without the city council's approval. Further, under state law a park owner may cut off a mobile home owner's tenancy only if the rent is not paid or if the park owner changes the use of the land.

The Court said the laws at issue do not amount to a taking, but merely regulate the use of the land by directing the relationship between landlord and tenant. The justices noted that the park owners voluntarily rented their land to mobile home tenants and were not ordered to do so by either the city or the state.

Miscellaneous

Commerce Clause

Wyoming v. Oklahoma, decided by a 6-3 vote, January 22, 1992; White wrote the opinion; Scalia, Rehnquist, and Thomas dissented.

An Oklahoma state law requiring coal-fired electric utilities to use at least 10 percent Oklahoma-mined coal violates the Commerce Clause of the Constitution.

From 1981 to 1986, Wyoming provided virtually 100 percent of the coal purchased by four Oklahoma electric utilities. However, after the Oklahoma legislature passed an act requiring coal-fired electric utilities to burn a mixture containing at least 10 percent Oklahoma-mined coal, the utilities reduced their purchases of Wyoming coal in favor of Oklahoma coal, and Wyoming's revenues from its coal tax declined.

The Court said the Oklahoma law is invalid because it purports to exclude coal mined from other states based solely on its origin. White wrote for the majority that Wyoming had suffered a direct injury through the Oklahoma law in the loss of specific Wyoming tax revenues.

Employment Rights of Veterans

King v. St. Vincent's Hospital, decided by an 8-0 vote, December 16, 1991; Souter wrote the opinion; Thomas took no part in the case.

Federal law does not limit the time that a civilian employer must leave a job open for a worker going off on military duty. The worker in this case voluntarily accepted a three-year, full-time appointment with the National Guard and was seeking to have his employer, a hospital, hold his job for him until his return.

The law in question says an employer must grant an employee leave for active duty and then give him his old job when he returns. But the law does not provide any time limit on the protection it provides. Writing for the unanimous Court in ruling for the employee, Souter said, no "reasonableness" standard exists for the time limit. "We may grant that the congressionally mandated leave of absence can be an ungainly perquisite of military service," he said.

The decision reversed a lower court opinion that the three-year leave was per se unreasonable.

Immunity from Lawsuit

Wyatt v. Cole, decided by a 6-3 vote, May 18, 1992; O'Connor wrote the opinion; Rehnquist, Souter, and Thomas dissented.

Private defendants cannot invoke qualified immunity from lawsuits, as government officials may, when sued for actions they took under a state law later declared invalid.

The lawsuit stemmed from a cattle partnership gone bad. One partner sued another under a Mississippi replevin statute and obtained a court order for seizure of the other partner's property. The statute required only that he post a bond and swear to a state court that he was entitled to the property. The statute gave the judge no discretion to deny a writ of replevin.

When the first partner refused to comply with a subsequent court order to return the property seized under the statute, the other partner brought a federal lawsuit challenging the replevin statute's constitutionality and seeking injunctive relief and damages. A district court said the statute violated due process but that the first partner was entitled to qualified immunity from suit for conduct arising prior to the statute's invalidation.

But the Supreme Court held that private individuals cannot invoke qualified immunity from suit. Writing for the Court, O'Connor said, "The nexus between private parties and the historic purposes of qualified immunity is simply too attenuated to justify such an extension of our doctrine of immunity.... [Such an extension] would have no bearing on whether public officials are able to act forcefully and decisively in their jobs."

International Law

Republic of Argentina v. Weltover, Inc., decided by a 9-0 vote, June 12, 1992; Scalia wrote the opinion.

The Republic of Argentina's default on certain bonds issued as part of a plan to stabilize its currency was an act taken "in connection with a commercial activity" that had a "direct effect in the United States." As such, the Court said, Argentina was subject to being sued in a U.S. court under the Foreign Sovereign Immunities Act of 1976. Although the bondholders were all foreign corporations, Argentina had promised to repay the bonds in U.S. dollars.

The Court unanimously ruled that the district court properly asserted jurisdiction over the case. Argentina had tried to get the suit dismissed.

United States v. Alvarez-Machain, decided by a 6-3 vote, June 15, 1992; Rehnquist wrote the opinion; Stevens, Blackmun, and O'Connor dissented.

A U.S.-Mexico treaty was not violated when a Mexican citizen implicated in the murder of a U.S. drug agent was abducted in Mexico and flown to Texas, where he was arrested and indicted.

The Court said abductions were allowed because nothing in the Extradition Treaty between the United States and Mexico or its history prohibited them. Rehnquist wrote that the treaty cannot be interpreted to imply a ban against international abductions on the basis of principles of international law. The opinion relied on precedents that prosecution could take place even though the defendant's presence was obtained through questionable means.

A district court dismissed the indictment on the grounds that the abduction violated the Extradition Treaty. Affirming, a federal appeals court noted that the United States authorized the abduction and that the Mexican government protested the treaty violation.

The Court's ruling may open the door to abductions of U.S. citizens by foreign governments. *(See entry, p. 17; excerpts, p. 116)*

Torts

Molzof, Personal Representative of the Estate of Molzof v. United States, decided by a 9-0 vote, January 14, 1992; Thomas wrote the opinion.

Under the Federal Tort Claims Act, which exempts the United States from having to pay punitive damages, the term "punitive damages" should carry its traditional common law meaning. The Court said that the prohibition in question should not be read to bar a veterans hospital patient from recovering money damages for future medical expenses and loss of enjoyment of life. The man ended up in a coma after the ventilator tube that was providing him oxygen became disconnected, concededly through the negligence of hospital employees. The Court said that although the money for medical expenses and loss of life were not "compensatory," they were not necessarily "punitive."

The government had asserted that any damages other than those awarded for actual loss are "punitive." But Thomas rejected the government's limited reading of the forty-five-year-old law and said, "Legal dictionaries in existence when the [tort claims law] was drafted and enacted indicate that 'punitive damages' were commonly understood to be damages awarded to punish defendants for torts committed with fraud, actual malice, violence, or oppression."

Thomas said the damages the man's family sought are not punitive damages "because their recoverability does not depend upon any proof that the defendant has engaged in intentional or egregious misconduct."

Case Excerpts

Following are excerpts from some of the most important rulings of the Supreme Court's 1991-1992 term. They appear in the order in which they were announced.

No. 90-1059

Simon & Schuster, Inc., Petitioner v. Members of the New York State Crime Victims Board et al.

On writ of certiorari to the United States Court of Appeals
for the Second Circuit

[December 10, 1991]

JUSTICE O'CONNOR delivered the opinion of the Court.

New York's "Son of Sam" law requires that an accused or convicted criminal's income from works describing his crime be deposited in an escrow account. These funds are then made available to the victims of the crime and the criminal's other creditors. We consider whether this statute is consistent with the First Amendment.

I

A

In the summer of 1977, New York was terrorized by a serial killer popularly known as the Son of Sam. The hunt for the Son of Sam received considerable publicity, and by the time David Berkowitz was identified as the killer and apprehended, the rights to his story were worth a substantial amount. Berkowitz's chance to profit from his notoriety while his victims and their families remained uncompensated did not escape the notice of New York's Legislature. The State quickly enacted the statute at issue, N.Y. Exec. Law §632-a (McKinney 1982 and Supp. 1991). . . .

The Son of Sam law, as later amended, requires any entity contracting with an accused or convicted person for a depiction of the crime to submit a copy of the contract to respondent Crime Victims Board, and to turn over any income under that contract to the Board. This

requirement applies to all such contracts in any medium of communication:

> "Every person, firm, corporation, partnership, association or other legal entity contracting with any person or the representative or assignee of any person, accused or convicted of a crime in this state, with respect to the reenactment of such crime, by way of a movie, book, magazine article, tape recording, phonograph record, radio or television presentation, live entertainment of any kind, or from the expression of such accused or convicted person's thoughts, feelings, opinions or emotions regarding such crime, shall submit a copy of such contract to the board and pay over to the board any moneys which would otherwise, by terms of such contract, be owing to the person so accused or convicted or his representatives." N.Y. Exec. Law §632-a(1) (McKinney 1982)."

The Board is then required to deposit the payment in an escrow account "for the benefit of and payable to any victim . . . provided that such victim, within five years of the date of the establishment of such escrow account, brings a civil action in a court of competent jurisdiction and recovers a money judgment for damages against such [accused or convicted] person or his representatives." *Ibid.* After five years, if no actions are pending, "the board shall immediately pay over any moneys in the escrow account to such person or his legal representatives." §632-a(4). This 5-year period in which to bring a civil action against the convicted person begins to run when the escrow account is established, and supersedes any limitations period that expires earlier. §632-a(7).

Subsection (8) grants priority to two classes of claims against the escrow account. First, upon a court order, the Board must release assets "for the exclusive purpose of retaining legal representation." §632-a(8). In addition, the Board has the discretion, after giving notice to the victims of the crime, to "make payments from the escrow account to a representative of any person accused or convicted of a crime for the necessary expenses of the production of the moneys paid into the escrow account." *Ibid.* This provision permits payments to literary agents and other such representatives. Payments under subsection (8) may not exceed one-fifth of the amount collected in the account. *Ibid.*

Claims against the account are given the following priorities: (a) payments ordered by the Board under subsection (8); (b) subrogation claims of the State for payments made to victims of the crime; (c) civil judgments obtained by victims of the crime; and (d) claims of other creditors of the accused or convicted person, including state and local tax authorities. §632-a(11) (McKinney Supp. 1991).

Subsection (10) broadly defines "person convicted of a crime" to include "any person convicted of a crime in this state either by entry of a plea of guilty or by conviction after trial *and any person who has voluntarily and intelligently admitted the commission of a crime for which such person is not prosecuted.*" §632-a(10)(b) (emphasis added). Thus a person who has never been accused or convicted of a crime in the ordinary sense, but who admits in a book or other work to having committed a crime, is within the statute's coverage.

As recently construed by the New York Court of Appeals, however, the statute does not apply to victimless crimes. *Children of Bedford, Inc.* v. *Petromelis* (1991).

The Son of Sam law supplements pre-existing statutory schemes authorizing the Board to compensate crime victims for their losses, see N.Y. Civ. Prac. Law §§1310-1352 (McKinney Supp. 1991), providing for orders of restitution at sentencing, N.Y. Penal Law §60.27 (McKinney 1987); and affording prejudgment attachment procedures to ensure that wrongdoers do not dissipate their assets, N.Y. Civ. Prac. Law §§6201-6226 (McKinney 1980 and Supp. 1991). The escrow arrangement established by the Son of Sam law enhances these provisions only insofar as the accused or convicted person earns income within the scope of §632-a(1).

Since its enactment in 1977, the Son of Sam law has been invoked only a handful of times. As might be expected, the individuals whose profits the Board has sought to escrow have all become well known for having committed highly publicized crimes. These include Jean Harris, the convicted killer of "Scarsdale Diet" Doctor Herman Tarnower; Mark David Chapman, the man convicted of assassinating John Lennon; and R. Foster Winans, the former Wall Street Journal columnist convicted of insider trading. Ironically, the statute was never applied to the Son of Sam himself; David Berkowitz was found incompetent to stand trial, and the statute at that time applied only to criminals who had actually been convicted. N.Y. Times, Feb. 20, 1991, p. B8, col 4. According to the Board, Berkowitz voluntarily paid his share of the royalties from the book *Son of Sam*, published in 1981, to his victims or their estates. Brief for Respondents 8, n. 13.

This case began in 1986, when the Board first became aware of the contract between petitioner Simon & Schuster and admitted organized crime figure Henry Hill.

B

Looking back from the safety of the Federal Witness Protection Program, Henry Hill recalled: "At the age of twelve my ambition was to be a gangster. To be a wiseguy. To me being a wiseguy was better than being president of the United States." N. Pileggi, Wiseguy: Life in a Mafia Family 19 (1985) (hereinafter Wiseguy). Whatever one might think of Hill, at the very least it can be said that he realized his dreams. After a career spanning 25 years, Hill admitted engineering some of the most daring crimes of his day, including the 1978-1979 Boston College basketball point-shaving scandal, and the theft of $6 million from Lufthansa Airlines in 1978, the largest successful cash robbery in American history. Wiseguy 9. Most of Hill's crimes were more banausic: He committed extortion, he imported and distributed narcotics, and he organized numerous robberies.

Hill was arrested in 1980. In exchange for immunity from prosecution, he testified against many of his former colleagues. Since his arrest, he has lived under an assumed name in an unknown part of the country.

In August 1981, Hill entered into a contract with author Nicholas Pileggi for the production of a book about Hill's life. The following month, Hill and Pileggi signed a publishing agreement with Simon & Schuster. Under the agreement, Simon & Schuster agreed to make payments to both Hill and Pileggi. Over the next few years, according to Pileggi, he and Hill "talked at length virtually every single day, with not more than an occasional Sunday or holiday skipped. We spent more than three hundred hours together; my notes of conversations with Henry occupy more than six linear file feet." App. 27. Because producing the book required such a substantial investment of time and effort, Hill sought compensation. *Ibid.*

The result of Hill and Pileggi's collaboration was Wiseguy, which was published in January 1986. The book depicts, in colorful detail, the day-to-day existence of organized crime, primarily in Hill's first-person narrative. Throughout Wiseguy, Hill frankly admits to having participated in an astonishing variety of crimes. He discusses, among other things, his conviction of extortion and the prison sentence he served. In one portion of the book, Hill recounts how members of the Mafia received preferential treatment in prison:

> "The dorm was a separate three-story building outside the wall, which looked more like a Holiday Inn than a prison. There were four guys to a room, and we had comfortable beds and private baths. There were two dozen rooms on each floor, and each of them had mob guys living in them. It was like a wiseguy convention—the whole Gotti crew, Jimmy Doyle and his guys, 'Ernie Boy' Abbamonte and 'Joe Crow' Delvecchio, Vinnie Aloi, Frank Cotroni.
>
> "It was wild. There was wine and booze, and it was kept in bath-oil or after-shave jars. The hacks in the honor dorm were almost all on the take, and even though it was against the rules, we used to cook in our rooms. Looking back, I don't think Paulie went to the general mess five times in the two and a half years he was there. We had a stove and pots and pans and silverware stacked in the bathroom. We had glasses and an ice-water cooler where we kept the fresh meats and cheeses. When there was an inspection, we stored the stuff in the false ceiling, and once in a while, if it was confiscated, we'd just go to the kitchen and get new stuff.
>
> "We had the best food smuggled into our dorm from the kitchen. Steaks, veal cutlets, shrimp, red snapper. Whatever the hacks could buy, we ate. It cost

me two, three hundred a week. Guys like Paulie spent five hundred to a thousand bucks a week. Scotch cost thirty dollars a pint. The hacks used to bring it inside the walls in their lunch pails. We never ran out of booze, because we had six hacks bringing it in six days a week. Depending on what you wanted and how much you were willing to spend, life could be almost bearable." Wiseguy 150-151.

Wiseguy was reviewed favorably: The *Washington Post* called it an "amply detailed and entirely fascinating book that amounts to a piece of revisionist history," while New York Daily News columnist Jimmy Breslin named it "the best book on crime in America ever written." App. 5. The book was also a commercial success: Within 19 months of its publication, more than a million copies were in print. A few years later, the book was converted into a film called "Goodfellas", which won a host of awards as the best film of 1990.

From Henry Hill's perspective, however, the publicity generated by the book's success proved less desirable. The Crime Victims Board learned of Wiseguy in January 1986, soon after it was published.

C

On January 31, the Board notified Simon & Schuster: "It has come to our attention that you may have contracted with a person accused or convicted of a crime for the payment of monies to such person." The Board ordered Simon & Schuster to furnish copies of any contracts it had entered into with Hill, to provide the dollar amounts and dates of all payments to Hill in the future. Simon & Schuster complied with this order. By that time, Simon & Schuster had paid Hill's literary agent $96,250 in advances and royalties on Hill's behalf, and was holding $27,958 for eventual payment to Hill.

The Board reviewed the book and the contract, and on May 21, 1987, issued a Proposed Determination and Order. The Board determined that Wiseguy was covered by §632-a of the Executive Law, that Simon & Schuster had violated the law by failing to turn over its contract with Hill to the Board and by making payments to Hill, and that all money owed to Hill under the contract had to be turned over to the Board to be held in escrow for the victims of Hill's crimes. The Board ordered Hill to turn over the payments he had already received, and ordered Simon & Schuster to turn over all money payable to Hill at the time or in the future.

Simon & Schuster brought suit in August 1987, under 42 U.S.C. §1983, seeking a declaration that the Son of Sam law violates the First Amendment and an injunction barring the statute's enforcement. After the parties filed cross-motions for summary judgment, the District Court found the statute consistent with the First Amendment. A divided Court of Appeals affirmed.

Because the Federal Government and most of the States have enacted statutes with similar objectives, the issue is significant and likely to recur. We accordingly granted certiorari.

II

A

A statute is presumptively inconsistent with the First Amendment if it imposes a financial burden on speakers because of the content of their speech. As we emphasized in invalidating a content-based magazine tax, "official scrutiny of the content of publications as the basis for imposing a tax is entirely incompatible with the First Amendment's guarantee of freedom of the press." *Arkansas Writers' Project, Inc.* v. *Ragland* (1987).

This is a notion so engrained in our First Amendment jurisprudence that last Term we found it so "obvious" as to not require explanation. *Leathers* v. *Medlock* (1991). It is but one manifestation of a far broader principle: "Regulations which permit the Government to discriminate on the basis of the content of the message cannot be tolerated under the First Amendment." *Regan* v. *Time, Inc.* (1984). In the context of financial regulation, it bears repeating, as we did in *Leathers*, that the Government's ability to impose content-based burdens on speech raises the specter that the Government may effectively drive certain ideas or viewpoints from the marketplace. The First Amendment presumptively places this sort of discrimination beyond the power of the Government. As we reiterated in *Leathers*, "The constitutional right of free expression is . . . in the belief that no other approach would comport with the premise of individual dignity and choice upon which our political system rests."

The Son of Sam law is such a content-based statute. It singles out income derived from expressive activity for a burden the State places on no other income, and it is directed only at works with a specified content. Whether the First Amendment "speaker" is considered to be Henry Hill, whose income the statute places in escrow because of the story he has told, or Simon & Schuster, which can publish books about crime with the assistance of only those criminals willing to forgo remuneration for at least five years, the statute plainly imposes a financial disincentive only on speech of a particular content.

The Board tries unsuccessfully to distinguish the Son of Sam law from the discriminatory tax at issue in *Arkansas Writers' Project*. While the Son of Sam law escrows all of the speaker's speech-derived income for at least five years, rather than taxing a percentage of it outright, this difference can hardly serve as the basis for disparate treatment under the First Amendment. Both forms of financial burden operate as disincentives to speak; indeed, in many cases it will be impossible to discern in advance which type of regulation will be more costly to the speaker.

The Board next argues that discriminatory financial treatment is suspect under the First Amendment only when the legislature intends to suppress certain ideas. This assertion is incorrect; our cases have consistently held that "[i]llicit legislative intent is not the *sine qua non* of a violation of the First Amendment." [citing] *Minneapolis Star & Tribune Co.* v. *Minnesota Commissioner of Revenue* (1983). Simon & Schuster need adduce "no evidence of an improper censorial motive." [citing] *Arkansas Writers' Project, supra.*

Finally, the Board claims that even if the First Amendment prohibits content-based financial regulation specifically of the *media*, the Son of Sam law is different, because it imposes a general burden on any "entity" contracting with a convicted person to transmit that person's speech. . . .

This argument falters on both semantic and constitutional grounds. Any "entity" that enters into such a contract becomes by definition a medium of communication, if it wasn't one already. In any event, the characterization of an entity as a member of the "media" is irrelevant for these purposes. The Government's power to impose content-based financial disincentives on speech surely does not vary with the identity of the speaker.

The Son of Sam law establishes a financial disincentive to create or publish works with a particular content. In order to justify such differential treatment, "the State must show that its regulation is necessary to serve a compelling state interest and is narrowly drawn to achieve that end." *Arkansas Writers' Project.*

B

The Board disclaims, as it must, any state interest in suppressing descriptions of crime out of solicitude for the sensibilities of readers. As we have often had occasion to repeat, "[T]he fact that society may find speech offensive is not a sufficient reason for suppressing it. Indeed, if it is the speaker's opinion that gives offense, that consequence is a reason for according it constitutional protection." (quoting *FCC* v. *Pacifica Foundation* (1978)). "If there is a bedrock principle underlying the First Amendment, it is that the Government may not prohibit the expression of an idea simply because society finds the idea itself offensive or disagreeable." (quoting *Texas* v. *Johnson* (1989)). The Board thus does not assert any interest in limiting whatever anguish Henry Hill's victims may suffer from reliving their victimization.

There can be little doubt, on the other hand, that the State has a compelling interest in ensuring that victims of crime are compensated by those who harm them. Every State has a body of tort law serving exactly this interest. The State's interest in preventing wrongdoers from dissipating their assets before victims can recover explains the existence of the State's statutory provisions for prejudgment remedies and orders of restitution. We have recognized the importance of this interest before, in the Sixth Amendment context. See *Caplin & Drysdale, Chartered* v. *United States* (1989).

The State likewise has an undisputed compelling interest in ensuring that criminals do not profit from their crimes. . . .

The parties debate whether book royalties can properly be termed the profits of crime, but that is a question we need not address here. For the purposes of this case, we can assume without deciding that the income escrowed by the Son of Sam law represents the fruits of crime. We need only conclude that the State has a compelling interest in depriving criminals of the profits of their crimes, and in using these funds to compensate victims.

The Board attempts to define the State's interest more narrowly, as "ensuring that criminals do not profit from storytelling about their crimes before their victims have a meaningful opportunity to be compensated for their injuries." Here the Board is on far shakier ground. The Board cannot explain why the State should have any greater interest in compensating victims from the proceeds of such "storytelling" than from any of the criminal's other assets. Nor can the Board offer any justification for a distinction between this expressive activity and any other activity in connection with its interest in transferring the fruits of crime from criminals to their victims. Thus even if the State can be said to have an interest in classifying a criminal's assets in this manner, that interest is hardly compelling.

We have rejected similar assertions of a compelling interest in the past. In *Arkansas Writers' Project* and *Minneapolis Star*, we observed that while the State certainly has an important interest in raising revenue through taxation, that interest hardly justified selective taxation of the press, as it was completely unrelated to a press/non-press distinction. Likewise, in *Carey* v. *Brown* (1980), we recognized the State's interest in preserving privacy by prohibiting residential picketing, but refused to permit the State to ban only nonlabor picketing. This was because "nothing in the content-based labor-nonlabor distinction has any bearing whatsoever on privacy." Much the same is true here. The distinction drawn by the Son of Sam law has nothing to do with the State's interest in transferring the proceeds of crime from criminals to their victims.

Like the government entities in the above cases, the Board has taken the *effect* of the statute and posited that effect as the State's interest. If accepted, this sort of circular defense can sidestep judicial review of almost any statute, because it makes all statutes look narrowly tailored. . . .

In short, the State has a compelling interest in compensating victims from the fruits of the crime, but little if any interest in limiting such compensation to the proceeds of the wrongdoer's speech about the crime. We must therefore determine whether the Son of Sam law is narrowly tailored to advance the former, not the latter, objective.

C

As a means of ensuring that victims are compensated from the proceeds of crime, the Son of Sam law is significantly overinclusive. As counsel for the Board conceded at oral argument, the statute applies to works on *any* subject, provided that they express the author's thoughts or recollections about his crime, however tangentially or incidentally. In addition, the statute's broad definition of "person convicted of a crime" enables the Board to escrow the income of any author who admits in his work to having committed a crime, whether or not the author was ever actually accused or convicted.

These two provisions combine to encompass a potentially very large number of works. Had the Son of Sam law been in effect at the time and place of publication, it would have escrowed payment for such works as The Autobiography of Malcolm X, which describes crimes committed by the civil rights leader before he became a public figure; Civil Disobedience, in which there acknowledges his refusal to pay taxes and recalls his experience in jail; and even the Confessions of Saint Augustine, in which the author laments "my past foulness and the carnal corruptions of my soul," one instance of which involved the theft of pears from a neighboring vineyard. Association of American Publishers, Inc., has submitted a sobering bibliography listing hundreds of works by American prisoners and ex-prisoners, many of which contain descriptions of the crimes for which the authors were incarcerated, including works by such authors as Emma Goldman and Martin Luther King, Jr. A list of prominent figures whose autobiographies would be subject to the statute if written is not difficult to construct: The list could include Sir Walter Raleigh, who was convicted of treason after a dubiously conducted 1603 trial; Jesse Jackson, who was arrested in 1963 for trespass and resisting arrest after attempting to be served at a lunch counter in North Carolina; and Bertrand Russell, who was jailed for seven days at the age of 89 for participating in a sit-down protest against nuclear weapons. The argument that the statute like the Son of Sam law would prevent publication of *all* of these works is hyperbole—some would have been written without compensation—but the Son of Sam law clearly reaches a wide range of literature that does not enable a criminal to profit from his crime while a victim remains uncompensated.

Should a prominent figure write his autobiography at the end of his career, and include in an early chapter a brief recollection of having stolen (in New York) a nearly worthless item as a youthful prank, the Board would control his entire income from the book for five years, and would make that income available to all of the author's creditors, despite the fact that the statute of limitations for this minor incident had long since run. That the Son of Sam law can produce such an outcome indicates that the statute is, to say the least, not narrowly tailored to achieve the State's objective of compensating crime victims from the profits of crime.

III

The Federal Government and many of the States have enacted statutes designed to serve purposes similar to that served by the Son of Sam law. Some of these statutes may be quite different from New York's, and we have no occasion to determine the constitutionality of these other laws. We conclude simply that in the Son of Sam law, New York has singled out speech on a particular subject for a financial burden that it places on no other speech and no other income. The State's interest in compensating victims from the fruits of crime is a compelling one, but the Son of Sam law is not narrowly tailored to advance that objective. As a result, the statute is inconsistent with the First Amendment.

The judgment of the Court of Appeals is accordingly

Reversed.

JUSTICE THOMAS took no part in the consideration or decision of this case.

JUSTICE BLACKMUN, concurring in the judgment.

I am in general agreement with what the Court says in its opinion. I think, however, that the New York statute is underinclusive as well as overinclusive and that we should say so. Most other States have similar legislation and deserve from this Court all the guidance it can render in this very sensitive area.

JUSTICE KENNEDY, concurring in the judgment.

The New York statute we now consider imposes severe restrictions on authors and publishers, using as its sole criterion the content of what is written. The regulated content has the full protection of the First Amendment and this, I submit, is itself a full and sufficient reason for holding the statute unconstitutional. In my view it is both unnecessary and incorrect to ask whether the State can show that the statute "is necessary to serve a compelling state interest and is narrowly drawn to achieve that end." That test or formulation derives from our equal protection jurisprudence, and has no real or legitimate place when the Court considers the straightforward question whether the State may enact a burdensome restriction of speech based on content only, apart from any considerations of time, place, and manner or the use of public forums.

Here a law is directed to speech alone where the speech in question is not obscene, not defamatory, not words tantamount to an act otherwise criminal, not an impairment of some other constitutional right, not an incitement to lawless action, and not calculated or likely to bring about imminent harm the State has the substantive power to prevent. No further inquiry is necessary to reject the State's argument that the statute should be upheld.

Borrowing the compelling interest and narrow tailoring analysis is ill-advised when all that is at issue is a content-based restriction, for resort to the test might be read as a concession that States may censor speech whenever they believe there is a compelling justification for doing so. Our precedents and traditions allow no such inference.

This said, it must be acknowledged that the compelling interest inquiry has found its way into our First Amendment jurisprudence of late, even where the sole question is, or ought to be, whether the restriction is in fact content-based. Although the notion that protected speech may be restricted on the basis of content if the restriction survives what has sometimes been termed "the most exacting scrutiny," *Texas* v. *Johnson* (1989), may seem familiar, the Court appears to have adopted this formulation in First Amendment cases by accident rather than as the result of a considered judgment. . . .

The employment of the compelling interest test in the present context is in no way justified by my colleagues' citation of *Arkansas Writers' Project* v. *Ragland.* True, both *Ragland* and the case on which it relied, *Minneapolis Star & Tribune Co.* v. *Minnesota Commissioner of Revenue,* recite either the compelling interest test or a close variant, but neither is a case in which the State regulates speech for its content. . . .

The inapplicability of the compelling interest test to content-based restrictions on speech is demonstrated by our repeated statement that "above all else, the First Amendment means that government has no power to restrict expression because of its message, its ideas, its subject matter, or its content." *Police Dept. of Chicago* v. *Mosley* (1972).

There are a few legal categories in which content-based regulation has been permitted or at least contemplated. These include obscenity, or situations presenting some grave and imminent danger the government has the power to prevent. These are, however, historic and traditional categories long familiar to the bar, although with respect to the last category it is most difficult for the government to prevail. While it cannot be said with certainty that the foregoing types of expression are or will remain the only ones that are without First Amendment protection. . . . The use of these traditional legal categories is preferable to the sort of ad hoc balancing that the Court henceforth must perform in every case if the analysis here used becomes our standard test.

As a practical matter, perhaps we will interpret the compelling interest in cases involving content regulation so that the results become parallel to the historic categories I have discussed, although an enterprise such as today's tends not to remain *pro forma* but to take on a life of its own. When we leave open the possibility that various sorts of content regulations are appropriate, we discount the value of our precedents and invite experiments that in fact present clear violations of the First Amendment, as is true in the case before us.

To forgo the compelling interest test in cases involving direct content-based burdens on speech would not, of course, eliminate the need for difficult judgments respecting First Amendment issues. Among the questions we cannot avoid the necessity of deciding are: whether the restricted expression falls within one of the unprotected categories; whether some other constitutional right is impaired; whether, in the case of a regulation of activity which combines expressive with nonexpressive elements, the regulation aims at the activity or the expression; whether the regulation restricts speech itself or only the time, place, or manner of speech; and whether the regulation is in fact content-based or content-neutral. However difficult the lines may be to draw in some cases, here the answer to each of these questions is clear.

The case before us presents the opportunity to adhere to a surer test for content-based cases and to avoid using an unnecessary formulation, one with the capacity to weaken central protections of the First Amendment. I would recognize this opportunity to confirm our past holdings and to rule that the New York statute amounts to raw censorship based on content, censorship forbidden by the text of the First Amendment and well-settled principles protecting speech and the press. That ought to end the matter.

With these observations, I concur in the judgment of the Court holding the statute invalid.

□□□

No. 90-1124

Keith Jacobson, Petitioner v. United States

On writ of certiorari to the United States Court of Appeals for the Eighth Circuit

[April 6, 1992]

JUSTICE WHITE delivered the opinion of the Court.

On September 24, 1987, petitioner Keith Jacobson was indicted for violating a provision of the Child Protection Act of 1987 which criminalizes the knowing receipt through the mails of a "visual depiction [that] involves the use of a minor engaging in sexually explicit conduct.... " Petitioner defended on the ground that the Government entrapped him into committing the crime through a series of communications from undercover agents that spanned the 26 months preceding his arrest. Petitioner was found guilty after a jury trial. The Court of Appeals affirmed his conviction, holding that the Government had affirmed his conviction, holding that the Government had carried its burden of proving beyond reasonable doubt that petitioner was predisposed to break the law and hence has not entrapped.

Because the Government overstepped the line between setting a trap for the "unwary innocent" and the "unwary criminal," *Sherman* v. *United States* (1958), and as a matter of law failed to establish that petitioner was independently predisposed to commit the crime for which he was arrested, we reverse the Court of Appeals' judgment affirming his conviction.

I

In February 1984, petitioner [Keith Jacobson], a 56-year old veteran-turned-farmer who supported his elderly father in Nebraska, ordered two magazines and a brochure from a California adult bookstore. The magazines, entitled Bare Boys I and Bare Boys II, contained photographs of nude preteen and teenage boys. The contents of the magazines startled petitioner, who testified that he had expected to receive photographs of "young men 18 years or older." Tr. 425. On cross-examination, he explained his response to the magazines:

> "[PROSECUTOR]: [Y]ou were shocked and surprised that there were pictures of very young boys without clothes on, is that correct?
> "[JACOBSON]: Yes, I was.
> "[PROSECUTOR]: Were you offended?
> "[JACOBSON]: I was not offended because I thought these were a nudist type publication. Many of the pictures were out in a rural or outdoor setting. There was—I didn't draw any sexual connotation or connection with that." *Id.,* at 463.

The young men depicted in the magazines were not engaged in sexual activity, and petitioner's receipt of the magazines was legal under both federal and Nebraska law. Within three months, the law with respect to child pornography changed; Congress passed the Act illegalizing the receipt through the mails of sexually explicit depictions of children. In the very month that the new provision became law, postal inspectors found petitioner's name on the mailing list of California bookstore that had mailed him Bare Boys I and II. There followed over the next 2½ years, repeated efforts by two Government agencies, through five fictitious organizations and a bogus pen pal, to explore petitioner's willingness to break the new law by ordering sexually explicit photographs of children through the mail.

The Government began its efforts in January 1985 when a postal inspector sent petitioner a letter supposedly from the American Hedonist Society, which in fact was a fictitious organization. The letter included a membership application and stated the Society's doctrine: that members had the "right to read what we desire, the right to discuss similar interests with those who share our philosophy, and finally that we have the right to seek pleasure without restrictions being placed on us by outdated puritan morality." Record, Government Exhibit 7. Petitioner enrolled in the organization and returned a sexual attitude questionnaire that asked him to rank on a scale of one to four his enjoyment of various sexual materials, with one being "really enjoy," and four being "do not enjoy." Petitioner ranked the entry "[p]re-teen sex" as a two, but indicated that he was opposed to pedophilia. *Ibid.*

For a time, the Government left petitioner alone. But then a new "prohibited mail specialist" in the Postal Service found petitioner's name in a file, Tr. 328-331, and in May 1986, petitioner received a solicitation from a second fictitious consumer research company, "Midlands Data Research," seeking a response from those who "believe in the joys of sex and the complete awareness of those lusty and youthful lads and lasses of the neophite [*sic*] age." Record Government Exhibit 8. The letter never explained whether "neophite" referred to minors or young adults. Petitioner responded: "Please feel free to send me more information, I am interested in teenage sexuality. Please keep my name confidential." *Ibid.*

Petitioner then heard from yet another Government creation, "Heartland Institute for a New Tomorrow" (HINT), which proclaimed that it was "an organization founded to protect and promote sexual freedom and freedom of choice. We believe that arbitrarily imposed legislative sanctions restricting *your* sexual freedom should be rescinded through the legislative process." *Id.,* Defendant's Exhibit 102. The letter also enclosed a second survey. Petitioner indicated that his interest in "[p]reteen sex-homosexual" material was above average, but not high. In response to another question, petitioner wrote: "Not only sexual expression but freedom of the press is under attack. We must be ever vigilant to counter attack right wing fundamentalists who are determined to curtail our freedoms." *Id.,* Government Exhibit 9.

"HINT" replied, portraying itself as a lobbying organization seeking to repeal "all statutes which regulate sexual activities, except those laws which deal with violent behavior, such as rape. HINT is also lobbying to eliminate any legal definition of 'the age of consent'." *Id.,* at Defendant's Exhibit 113. These lobbying efforts were to be funded by sales from a catalog to be published in the future "offering the sale of various items which we believe you will find to be both interesting and stimulating." *Ibid.* HINT also provided computer matching of group members with similar survey responses; and, although petitioner was supplied with a list of potential "pen pals," he did not initiate any correspondence.

Nevertheless, the Government's "prohibited mail specialist" began writing to petitioner, using the pseudonym "Carl Long." The letters employed a tactic known as "mirroring," which the inspector described as "reflect[ing] whatever the interests are of the person we are writing to." Tr. 342. Petitioner responded at first, indicating that his interest was primarily in "male-male items." Record, Government Exhibit 9A. Inspector "Long" wrote back:

> "My interests too are primarily male-male items. Are you satisfied with the type of VCR tapes available? Personally, I like the amateur stuff better if its [sic] well produced as it can get more kinky and also seems more real. I think the actors enjoy it more." *Id.,* Government Exhibit 13.

Petitioner responded:

> "As far as my likes are concerned, I like good looking young guys (in their late teens and early 20's) doing their thing together." *Id.,* Government Exhibit 14.

Petitioner's letters to "Long" made no reference to child pornography. After writing two letters, petitioner discontinued the correspondence.

By March 1987, 34 months had passed since the Government obtained petitioner's name from the mailing list of the California bookstore, and 26 months had passed since the Postal Service had commenced its mailings to petitioner. Although petitioner had responded to surveys and letters, the Government had no evidence that petitioner had ever intentionally possessed or been exposed to child pornography. The Postal Service had not checked petitioner's mail to determine whether he was receiving questionable mailings from persons—other than the Government—involved in the child pornography industry.

At this point, a second Government agency, the Customs Service, included petitioner in its own child pornography sting, "Operation Borderline," after receiving his name on lists submitted by the Postal Service. *Id.,* at 71-72. Using the name of a fictitious Canadian company called "Produit Outaouais," the Customs Service mailed petitioner a brochure advertising photographs of young boys engaging in sex. Record, Government Exhibit 22. Petitioner placed an order that was never filled. *Id.,* Government Exhibit 24.

The Postal Service also continued its efforts in the Jacobson case, writing to petitioner as the "Far Eastern Trading Company Ltd." The letter began:

"As many of you know, much hysterical nonsense has appeared in the American media concerning 'pornography' and what must be done to stop it from coming across your borders. This brief letter does not allow us to give much comments; however, why is your government spending millions of dollars to exercise international censorship while tons of drugs, which makes yours the world's most crime ridden country are passed through easily." *Id.*, Government Exhibit 1.

The letter went on to say:

"[W]e have devised a method of getting these to you without prying eyes of U.S. Customs seizing your mail. . . . After consultations with American solicitors, we have been advised that once we have posted our material through your system, it cannot be opened for any inspection without authorization of a judge." *Ibid.*

The letter invited petitioner to send for more information. It also asked petitioner to sign an affirmation that he was "not a law enforcement officer or agent of the U.S. Government acting in an undercover capacity for the purpose of entrapping Far Eastern Trading Company, its agents or customers." Petitioner responded. *Ibid.* A catalogue was sent, *id.*, Government Exhibit 2, and petitioner ordered Boys Who Love Boys, *id.*, Government Exhibit 3, a pornographic magazine depicting young boys engaged in various sexual activities. Petitioner was arrested after a controlled delivery of a photocopy of the magazine.

When petitioner was asked at trial why he placed such an order, he explained that the Government has succeeded in piquing his curiosity:

"Well, the statement was made of all the trouble and the hysteria over pornography and I wanted to see what the material was. It didn't describe the—I didn't know for sure what kind of sexual action they were referring to in the Canadian letter. . . ." Tr. 427-428.

In petitioner's home, the Government found the Bare Boys magazines and materials that the Government had sent to him in the course of its protracted investigation, but no other materials that would indicate that petitioner collected or was actively interested in child pornography.

Petitioner was indicated for violating 18 U.S.C. §2552(a)(2)(A). The trial court instructed the jury on the petitioner's entrapment defense, petitioner was convicted, and divided Court of Appeals for the Eighth Circuit, sitting *en banc,* affirmed, concluding that "Jacobson was not entrapped as a matter of law." (1990). We granted certiorari. (1991).

II

There can be no dispute about the evils of child pornography or the difficulties that laws and law enforcement have encountered in eliminating it. See generally *Osborne* v. *Ohio* (1990); *New York* v. *Ferber* (1982). Likewise, there can be no dispute that the Government may use undercover agents to enforce the law. "It is well settled that the fact that officers or employees of the Government merely afford opportunities or facilities for the commission of the offense does not defeat the prosecution. Artifice and stratagem may be employed to catch those engaged in criminal enterprises." *Sorrells* v. *United States* (1932); *Sherman* v. *United States; United States* v. *Russell* (1973).

In their zeal to enforce the law, however, Government agents may not originate a criminal design, implant in an innocent person's mind the disposition to commit a criminal act, and then induce commission of the crime so that the Government may prosecute. *Sorrells, supra,* at 442; *Sherman, supra,* at 372. Where the Government has induced an individual to break the law and the defense of entrapment is at issue, as it was in this case, the prosecution must prove beyond reasonable doubt that the defendant was disposed to commit the criminal act prior to first being approached by Government agents. *United States* v. *Whoie* (1991).

Thus, an agent deployed to stop the traffic in illegal drugs may offer the opportunity to buy or sell drugs, and, if the offer is accepted, make an arrest on the spot or later. In such a typical case, or in a more elaborate "sting" operation involving government-sponsored fencing where the defendant is simply provided with the opportunity to commit a crime, the entrapment defense is of little use because the ready commission of the criminal act amply demonstrates the defendant's predisposition. See *United States* v. *Sherman* (CA2 1952). Had the agents in this case simply offered petitioner the opportunity to order child pornography through the mails, and petitioner—who must be presumed to know the law—had promptly availed himself of this criminal opportunity, it is unlikely that his entrapment defense would have warranted a jury instruction. *Mathews* v. *United States* (1988).

But that is not what happened here. By the time petitioner finally placed his order, he had already been the target of 26 months of repeated mailings and communications from Government agents and fictitious organizations. Therefore, although he had become predisposed to break the law by May 1987, it is our view that the Government did not prove that this predisposition was independent and not the product of the attention that the Government had directed at petitioner since January 1985. *Sorrells, supra,* at 442; *Sherman.*

The prosecution's evidence of predisposition falls into two categories: evidence developed prior to the Postal Service's mail campaign, and that developed during the course of the investigation. The sole piece of preinvestigation evidence is petitioner's 1984 order and receipt of the Bare Boys magazines. But this is scant if any proof of petitioner's predisposition to commit an illegal act, the criminal character of which a defendant is presumed to know. It may indicate a predisposition to view sexually-oriented photographs that are responsive to his sexual tastes; but evidence that merely indicates a generic inclination to act within a broad range, not all of which is criminal, is of little probative value in establishing predisposition.

Furthermore, petitioner was acting within the law at the time he received these magazines. Receipt through the mails of sexually explicit depictions of children for noncommercial use did not become illegal under federal law until May 1984, and Nebraska had no law that forbade petitioner's possession of such material until 1988. Neb Rev. Stat. §28-813.01 (1989). Evidence of predisposition to do what once was lawful is not, by itself, sufficient to show predisposition to do what is now illegal, for there is a common understanding that most people obey the law even when they disapprove of it. This obedience may reflect a generalized respect for legality or the fear of prosecution, but for whatever reason, the law's prohibitions are matters of consequence. Hence, the fact that petitioner legally ordered and received the Bare Boys magazines does little to further the Government's burden of proving that petitioner was predisposed to commit a criminal act. This is particularly true given petitioner's unchallenged testimony was that he did not know until they arrived that the magazines would depict minors.

The prosecution's evidence gathered during the investigation also fails to carry the Government's burden. Petitioner's responses to the many communications prior to the ultimate criminal act where at most indicative of certain personal inclinations, including a predisposition to view photographs of preteen sex and a willingness to promote a given agenda by supporting lobbying organizations. Even so, petitioner's responses hardly support an inference that he would commit the crime of receiving child pornography through the mails. Furthermore, a person's inclinations and "fantasies . . . are his own and beyond the reach of government. . . ." *Paris Adult Theatre I* v. *Slaton* (1973); *Stanley* v. *Georgia* (1969).

On the other hand, the strong arguable inference is that, by waving the banner of individual rights and disparaging the legitimacy and constitutionality of efforts to restrict the availability of sexually explicit materials, the Government not only excited petitioner's interest in sexually explicit materials banned by law but also exerted substantial pressure on petitioner to obtain and read such material as part of a fight against censorship and the infringement of individual rights. For instance, HINT described itself as "an organization founded to protect and promote sexual freedom and freedom of choice" and stated that "the most appropriate means to accomplish [its] objectives is to promote honest dialogue among concerned individuals and to continue its lobbying efforts with State Legislators." Record, Defendant's Exhibit 113. These lobbying efforts were to be financed through catalogue sales. *Ibid.* Mailings from the equally fictitious American Hedonist Society, *id.,* Government Exhibit 7, and the correspondence from the non-existent Carl Long, id., Defendant's Exhibit 5, endorsed these themes.

Similarly, the two solicitations in the spring of 1987 raised the spectre of censorship while suggesting that petitioner ought to be allowed to do what he had been solicited to do. The mailing from the Customs Service referred to "the worldwide ban and intense enforcement on this type of material," observed that "what was legal and commonplace is not an 'underground' and secretive service," and emphasized that "[t]his environment forces us to take extreme measures" to insure delivery. *Id.,* Government Exhibit 22. The Postal Service solicitation described the concern about child pornography as "hysterical nonsense," decried "international censorship," and assured petitioner, based on consultation with "American solicitors" that an order that had been posted could not be opened for inspection without authorization of a judge. *Id.,* Government Exhibit 1. It further asked petitioner to affirm that he was not a government agent attempting to entrap the mail order company or its customers. *Ibid.* In these particulars, both government solicitations suggested that receiving this material was something that petitioner ought to be allowed to do.

Petitioner's ready response to these solicitations cannot be enough to establish beyond reasonable doubt that he was predisposed, prior to the Government acts intended to create predisposition, to commit the crime of receiving child pornography through the mails. See *Sherman,* 356 U.S., at 374. The evidence that petitioner was ready and willing to commit the offense came only after the Government had devoted 2½ years to convincing him that he had or should have the right to engage in the very behavior proscribed by law. Rational jurors could not say beyond a reasonable doubt that petitioner possessed the requisite predisposition prior to the Government's investigation and that it existed independent of the Government's many and varied approaches to petitioner. As was explained in *Sherman,* where entrapment was found as a matter of law, "the Government [may not] pla[y] on the weakness of an innocent party and beguil[e] him into committing crimes which he otherwise would not have attempted." *Id.,* at 376.

Law enforcement officials go too far when they "implant in the mind of an innocent person the *disposition* to commit the alleged offense and induct its commission in order that they may prosecute." *Sorrels,* 287 U.S., at 442 (emphasis added). Like the *Sorrels* court, we are "unable to conclude that it was the intention of the Congress in enacting this statute that its processes of detection and enforcement should be abused by the instigation by government officials of an act on the part of persons otherwise innocent in order to lure them to its commission and to punish them." *Id.,* at 448. When the Government's quest for convictions leads to the apprehension of an otherwise law-abiding citizen who, if left to his own devices, likely would have never run afoul of the law, the courts should intervene.

Because we conclude that this is such a case and that the prosecution failed, as a matter of law, to adduce evidence to support the jury verdict that petitioner was predisposed, independent of the Government's acts and beyond a reasonable doubt, to violate the law by receiving child pornography through the mails, we reverse the Court of Appeals' judgment affirming the conviction of Keith Jacobson.

It is so ordered.

JUSTICE O'CONNOR, with whom THE CHIEF JUSTICE and JUSTICE KENNEDY join, and with whom JUSTICE SCALIA joins except as to Part II, dissenting.

Keith Jacobson was offered only two opportunities to buy child pornography through the mail. Both times, he ordered. Both times, he asked for opportunities to buy more. He needed no Government agent to coax, threaten, or persuade him; no one played on his sympathies, friendship, or suggested that his committing the crime would further a greater good. In fact, no Government agent even contacted him face-to-face. The Government contends that from the enthusiasm with which Mr. Jacobson responded to the chance to commit a crime, a reasonable jury could permissibly infer beyond a reasonable doubt that he was predisposed to commit the crime. I agree. . . .

The first time the Government sent Mr. Jacobson a catalog of illegal materials, he ordered a set of photographs advertised as picturing "young boys in sex action fun." He enclosed the following note with his order: "I received your brochure and decided to place an order. If I like your product, I will order more later." Record, Government Exhibit 24. For reasons undisclosed in the record, Mr. Jacobson's order was never delivered.

The second time the Government sent a catalog of illegal materials, Mr. Jacobson ordered a magazine called "Boys Who Love Boys," described as: "11 year old and 14 year old boys get it on in every way possible. Oral, anal sex and heavy masturbation. If you love boys, you will be delighted with this." *Id.,* Government Exhibit 2. Along with his order, Mr. Jacobson sent the following note: "Will order other items later. I want to be discreet in order to protect you and me." *Id.,* Government Exhibit 3.

Government agents admittedly did not offer Mr. Jacobson the chance to buy child pornography right away. Instead, they first sent questionnaires in order to make sure that he was generally interested in the subject matter. Indeed, a "cold call" in such a business would not only risk rebuff and suspicion, but might also shock and offend the uninitiated, or expose minors to suggestive materials. *Pacifica Foundation* (right to be free from offensive material in one's home); 39 U.S.C. §3010 (regulating the mailing of sexually explicit advertising materials). Mr. Jacobson's responses to the questionnaires gave the investigators reason to think he would be interested in photographs depicting preteen sex.

The Court, however, concludes that a reasonable jury could not have found Mr. Jacobson to be predisposed beyond a reasonable doubt on the basis of his responses to the Government's catalogs, even though it admits that, by that time, he was predisposed to commit the crime. The Government, the Court holds, failed to provide evidence that Mr. Jacobson's obvious predisposition at the time of the crime "was independent and not the product of the attention that the Government had directed at petitioner." *Ante,* at 9. In so holding, I believe the Court fails to acknowledge the reasonableness of the jury's inference from the evidence, redefines "predisposition," and introduces a new requirement that Government sting operations have a reasonable suspicion of illegal activity before contacting a suspect.

I

This Court has held previously that a defendant's predisposition is to be assessed as of the time the Government agent first suggested the crime, not when the Government agent first became involved. *Sherman* v. *United States.* See also, *United States* v. *Williams* (1983). Until the Government actually makes a suggestion of criminal conduct, it could not be said to have "implant[ed] in the mind of an innocent person the disposition to commit the alleged offense and induce its commission...." *Sorrells* v. *United States* (1932). Even in *Sherman* v. *United States, supra,* in which the Court held that the defendant had been entrapped as a matter of law, the Government agent had repeatedly and unsuccessfully coaxed the defendant to buy drugs, ultimately succeeding only by playing on the defendant's sympathy. The Court found lack of predisposition based on the Government's numerous unsuccessful attempts to induce the crime, not on the basis of preliminary contacts with the defendant.

Today, the Court holds that Government conduct may be considered to create a predisposition to commit a crime, even before any Government action to induce the commission of the crime. In my view, this holding changes entrapment doctrine. Generally, the inquiry is whether a suspect is predisposed before the Government induces the commission of the crime, not before the Government makes initial contact with him. There is no dispute here that the Government's questionnaires and letters were not sufficient to establish inducement; they did not even suggest that Mr. Jacobson should engage in any illegal activity. If all the Government had done was to send these materials, Mr. Jacobson's entrapment defense would fail. Yet the Court holds that the Government must prove not only that a suspect was predisposed to commit the crime before the opportunity to commit it arose, but also before the Government came on the scene. *Ante*, at 8.

The rule that preliminary Government contact can create a predisposition has the potential to be misread by lower courts as well as criminal investigators as requiring that the Government must have sufficient evidence of a defendant's predisposition *before it ever seeks to contact him.* Surely the Court cannot intend to impose such a requirement, for it would mean that the Government must have a reasonable suspicion of criminal activity before it begins an investigation, a condition that we have never before imposed. The Court denies that its new rule will affect run-of-the-mill sting operations, *ante*, at 8, and one hopes that it means what it says. Nonetheless, after this case, every defendant will claim that something the Government agent did before soliciting the crime "created" a predisposition that was not there before. For example, a bribe taker will claim that the description of the amount of money available was so enticing that it implanted a disposition to accept the bribe later offered. A drug buyer will claim that the description of the drug's purity and effects was so tempting that it created the urge to try it for the first time. In short, the Court's opinion could be read to prohibit the Government from advertising the seductions of criminal activity as part of its sting operation, for fear of creating a predisposition in its suspects. That limitation would be especially likely to hamper sting operations such as this one, which mimic the advertising done by genuine purveyors of pornography. No doubt the Court would protest that its opinion does not stand for so broad a proposition, but the apparent lack of a principled basis for distinguishing these scenarios exposes a flaw in the more limited rule the Court today adopts.

The Court's rule is all the more troubling because it does not distinguish between Government conduct that merely highlights the temptation of the crime itself, and Government conduct that threatens, coerces, or leads a suspect to commit a crime in order to fulfill some other obligation. For example, in *Sorrells,* the Government agent played on the defendant's sympathies, pretending to be going through drug withdrawal and begging the defendant to relieve his distress by helping him buy drugs. *Sherman, supra,* at 371.

The Government conduct in this case is not comparable. While the Court states that the Government "exerted substantial pressure on petitioner to obtain and read such material as part of a fight against censorship and the infringement of individual rights," *ante*, at 10, one looks at the record in vain for evidence of such "substantial pressure." The most one finds is letters advocating legislative action to liberalize obscenity laws, letters which could easily be ignored or thrown away. Much later, the Government sent separate mailings of catalogs of illegal materials. Nowhere did the Government suggest that the proceeds of the sale of the illegal materials would be used to support legislative reforms. While one of the HINT letters suggested that lobbying efforts would be funded by sales from a catalog, Record, Defendant's Exhibit 113, the catalogs actually sent, nearly a year later, were from different fictitious entities (Produit Outaouais and Far Eastern Trading Company), and gave no suggestion that money would be used for any political purposes. *Id.,* Government Exhibit 22, Government Exhibit 2. Nor did the Government claim to be organizing a civil disobedience movement, which would protect the pornography laws by breaking them. Contrary to the gloss given the evidence by the Court, the Government's suggestions of illegality may also have made buyers beware, and increased the mystique of the materials offered: "[f]or those of you who have enjoyed youthful material . . . we have devised a method of getting these to you without prying eyes of U.S. Customs seizing your mail." *Id.,* Government Exhibit 1. Mr. Jacobson's curiosity to see what " 'all the trouble and the hysteria' " was about, *ante,* at 6, is certainly susceptible of more than one interpretation. And it is the jury that is charged with the obligation of interpreting it. In sum, the Court fails to construe the evidence in the light most favorable to the Government, and fails to draw all reasonable inferences in the Government's favor. It was surely reasonable for the jury to infer that Mr. Jacobson was predisposed beyond a reasonable doubt, even if other inferences from the evidence were also possible.

II

The second puzzling thing about the Court's opinion is its redefinition of predisposition. The Court acknowledges that "[p]etitioner's responses to the many communications prior to the ultimate criminal act were . . . indicative of certain personal inclinations, including a predisposition to view photographs of preteen sex. . . ." *Ante,* at 10. If true, this should have settled the matter; Mr. Jacobson was predisposed to engage in the illegal conduct. Yet, the Court concludes, "petitioner's responses hardly support an inference that he would commit the crime of receiving child pornography through the mails." *Ibid.*

The Court seems to add something new to the burden of proving predisposition. Not only must the Government show that a defendant was predisposed to engage in the illegal conduct, here, receiving photographs of minors engaged in sex, but also that the defendant was predisposed to break the law knowingly in order to do so. The statute violated here, however, does not require proof of specific intent to break the law; it requires only knowing receipt of visual depictions produced by using minors engaged in sexually explicit conduct. See 18 U.S.C. §2552(a)(2); *United States* v. *Moncini,* 882 F.2d 401, 404-406 (CA9 1989). Under the Court's analysis, however, the Government must prove *more* to show predisposition than it need prove in order to convict.

The Court ignores the judgment of Congress that specific intent is not an element of the crime of receiving sexually explicit photographs of minors. The elements of predisposition should track the elements of the crime. The predisposition requirement is meant to eliminate the entrapment defense for those defendants who would have committed the crime anyway, even absent Government inducement. Because a defendant might very well be convicted of the crime here absent Government inducement even though he did not know his conduct was illegal, a specific intent requirement does little to distinguish between those who would commit the crime without the inducement and those who would not. In sum, although the fact that Mr. Jacobson's purchases of *Bare Boys I* and *Bare Boys II* were legal at the time may have some relevance to the question of predisposition, it is not, as the Court suggests, dispositive.

The crux of the Court's concern in this case is that the Government went too far and "abused" the "processes of detection and enforcement" by luring an innocent person to violate the law. *Ante,* at 12, quoting *Sorrels,* 287 U.S., at 448. Consequently, the Court holds that the Government failed to prove beyond a reasonable doubt that Mr. Jacobson was predisposed to commit the crime. It was, however, the jury's task, as the conscience of the community, to decide whether or not Mr. Jacobson was a willing participant in the criminal activity here or an innocent dupe. The jury is the traditional "defense against arbitrary law enforcement." *Duncan* v. *Louisiana* (1968). Indeed, in *Sorrells,* in which the Court was also concerned about overzealous law enforcement, the Court did not decide itself that the Government conduct constituted entrapment, but left the issue to the jury. *Sorrells, supra,* at 452. There is no dispute that the jury in this case was fully and accurately instructed in the law of entrapment, and nonetheless found Mr. Jacobson guilty. Because I believe there was sufficient evidence to uphold the jury's verdict, I respectfully dissent.

□□□

No. 90-1859

Keeney, Superintendent, Oregon State Penitentiary v. Tamayo-Reyes

On writ of certiorari to the United States Court of Appeals for the Ninth Circuit

[May 4, 1992]

JUSTICE WHITE delivered the opinion of the Court.

Respondent is a Cuban immigrant with little education and almost no knowledge of English. In 1984, he was charged with murder arising from the stabbing death of a man who had allegedly attempted to intervene in a confrontation between respondent and his girlfriend in a bar.

Respondent was provided with a defense attorney and interpreter. The attorney recommended to respondent that he plead *nolo contendere* to first-degree manslaughter. Respondent signed a plea form that explained in English the rights he was waiving by entering the plea. The state court held a plea hearing, at which the petitioner was represented by counsel and his interpreter. The judge asked the attorney and interpreter if they had explained to respondent the rights in the plea form and the consequences of his plea; they responded in the affirmative. The judge then explained to respondent, in English, the rights he would waive by his plea, and asked the interpreter to translate. Respondent indicated that he understood his rights and still wished to plead *nolo contendere*. The judge accepted his plea.

Later, respondent brought a collateral attack on the plea in a state-court proceeding. He alleged his plea had not been knowing and intelligent and therefore was invalid because his translator had not translated accurately and completely for him the *mens rea* element of manslaughter. He also contended that he did not understand the purposes of the plea form or the plea hearing. He contended that he did not know he was pleading no contest to manslaughter, but rather that he thought he was agreeing to be tried for manslaughter.

After a hearing, the state court dismissed respondent's petition, finding that the respondent was properly served by his trial interpreter and that the interpreter correctly, fully, and accurately translated the communications between respondent and his attorney. The State Court of Appeals affirmed, and the State Supreme Court denied review.

Respondent then entered Federal District Court seeking a writ of habeas corpus. Respondent contended that the material facts concerning the translation were not adequately developed at the state-court hearing, implicating the fifth circumstance of *Townsend* v. *Sain*, 372 U.S. 293, 313 (1963), and sought a federal evidentiary hearing on whether his *nolo contendere* plea was unconstitutional. The District Court found that the failure to develop the critical facts relevant to his federal claim was attributable to inexcusable neglect and that no evidentiary hearing was required. Respondent appealed.

The Court of Appeals for the Ninth Circuit recognized that the alleged failure to translate the *mens rea* element of first-degree manslaughter, if proved, would be a basis for overturning respondent's plea, and determined that material facts had not been adequately developed in the state postconviction court, apparently due to the negligence of postconviction counsel. The court held that *Townsend* v. *Sain,* and *Fay* v. *Noia,* 372 U.S. 391, 438 (1963), required an evidentiary hearing in the District Court unless respondent had deliberately bypassed the orderly procedure of the state courts. Because counsel's negligent failure to develop the facts did not constitute a deliberate bypass, the Court of Appeals ruled that respondent was entitled to an evidentiary hearing on the question whether the *mens rea* element of first-degree manslaughter was properly explained to him.

We granted certiorari to decide whether the deliberate bypass standard is the correct standard for excusing a habeas petitioner's failure to develop a material fact in state-court proceedings. We reverse.

Because the holding of *Townsend* v. *Sain* that *Fay* v. *Noia*'s deliberate bypass standard is applicable in a case like this had not been reversed, it is quite understandable that the Court of Appeals applied that standard in this case. However, in light of more recent decisions of this Court, *Townsend*'s holding in this respect must be overruled. *Fay* v. *Noia* was itself a case where the habeas petitioner had not taken advantage of state remedies by failing to appeal—a procedural default case. Since that time, however, this Court has rejected the deliberate bypass standard in state procedural default cases and has applied instead a standard of cause and prejudice.

In *Francis* v. *Henderson,* 425 U.S. 536 (1976), we acknowledged a federal court's power to entertain an application for habeas even where the claim has been procedurally waived in state proceedings, but nonetheless examined the appropriateness of the exercise of that power and recognized, as we had in *Fay,* that considerations of comity and concerns for the orderly administration of criminal justice may in some circumstances require a federal court to forgo the exercise of its habeas corpus power. We held that a federal habeas petitioner is required to show cause for his procedural default, as well as actual prejudice.

In *Wainwright* v. *Sykes,* 433 U.S. 72 (1977), we rejected the application of *Fay*'s standard of "knowing waiver" or "deliberate bypass" to excuse a petitioner's failure to comply with a state contemporaneous-objection rule, stating that the state rule deserved more respect than the *Fay* standard accorded it. We observed that procedural rules that contribute to error-free state trial proceedings are thoroughly desirable. We applied a cause-and-prejudice standard to a petitioner's failure to object at trial and limited *Fay* to its facts. We have consistently reaffirmed that the "cause and prejudice" standard embodies the correct accommodation between the competing concerns implicated in a federal court's habeas power.

In *McCleskey* v. *Zant,* 499 U.S. _____ (1991), we held that the same standard used to excuse state procedural defaults should be applied in habeas corpus cases where abuse of the writ is claimed by the government. This conclusion rested on the fact that the two doctrines are similar in purpose and design and implicate similar concerns. The writ strikes at finality of a state criminal conviction, a matter of particular importance in a federal system. Federal habeas litigation also places a heavy burden on scarce judicial resources, may give litigants incentives to withhold claims for manipulative purposes, and may create disincentives to present claims when evidence is fresh.

Again addressing the issue of state procedural default in *Coleman* v. *Thompson,* 501 U.S. _____ (1991), we described *Fay* as based on a conception of federal/state relations that undervalued the importance of state procedural rules, and went on to hold that the cause-and-prejudice standard applicable to failure to raise a particular claim should apply as well to failure to appeal at all. "All of the State's interests—in channeling the resolution of claims to the most appropriate forum, in finality, and in having an opportunity to correct its own errors—are implicated whether a prisoner defaults one claim or all of them." We therefore applied the cause and prejudice standard uniformly to state procedural defaults, eliminating the "irrational" distinction between *Fay* and subsequent cases. In light of these decisions, it is similarly irrational to distinguish between failing to properly assert a federal claim in state court and failing in state court to properly develop such a claim, and to apply to the latter a remnant of a decision that is no longer upheld with regard to the former.

The concerns that motivated the rejection of the deliberate bypass standard in *Wainwright, Coleman,* and other cases are equally applicable to this case. As in cases of state procedural default, application of the cause-and-prejudice standard to excuse a state prisoner's failure to develop material facts in state court will appropriately accommodate concerns of finality, comity, judicial economy, and channeling the resolution of claims into the most appropriate forum.

Applying the cause-and-prejudice standard in cases like this will obviously contribute to the finality of convictions, for requiring a federal evidentiary hearing solely on the basis of a habeas petitioner's negligent failure to develop facts in state-court proceedings dramatically increases the opportunities to relitigate a conviction.

Similarly, encouraging the full factual development in state court of a claim that state courts committed constitutional error advances comity by allowing a coordinate jurisdiction to correct its own errors in the first instance. It reduces the "inevitable friction" that results when a federal habeas court "overturn[s] either the factual or legal conclusions reached by the state-court system."

Also, by ensuring that full factual development takes place in the earlier, state-court proceedings, the cause-and-prejudice standard plainly serves the interest of judicial economy. It is hardly a good use of scarce judicial resources to duplicate factfinding in federal court merely because a petitioner has negligently failed to take advantage of opportunities in state-court proceedings.

. . . Exhaustion means more than notice. In requiring exhaustion of a federal claim in state court, Congress surely meant that exhaustion be serious and meaningful.

The purpose of exhaustion is not to create a procedural hurdle on the path to federal habeas court, but to channel claims into an appropriate forum, where meritorious claims may be vindicated and unfounded litigation obviated before resort to federal court. Comity concerns dictate that the requirement of exhaustion is not satisfied by the mere statement of a federal claim in state court. . . .

Finally, it is worth noting that applying the cause-and-prejudice standard in this case also advances uniformity in the law of habeas corpus. There is no good reason to maintain in one area of habeas law a standard that has been rejected in the area in which it was principally enunciated. And little can be said for holding a habeas petitioner to one standard for failing to bring a claim in state court and excusing the petitioner under another, lower standard for failing to develop the factual basis of that claim in the same forum. A different rule could mean that a habeas petitioner would not be excused for negligent failure to object to the introduction of the prosecution's evidence, but nonetheless would be excused for negligent failure to introduce any evidence of his own to support a constitutional claim.

Respondent Tamayo-Reyes is entitled to an evidentiary hearing if he can show cause for his failure to develop the facts in the state-court proceedings and actual prejudice resulting from that failure. We also adopt the narrow exception to the cause-and-prejudice requirement: A habeas petitioner's failure to develop a claim in state-court proceedings will be excused and a hearing mandated if he can show that a fundamental miscarriage of justice would result from failure to hold a federal evidentiary hearing.

The State concedes that a remand to the District Court is appropriate in order to afford respondent the opportunity to bring forward evidence establishing cause and prejudice, and we agree that the respondent should have that opportunity. Accordingly, the decision of the Court of Appeals is reversed, and the cause is remanded to the District Court for further proceedings consistent with this opinion.

So ordered.

JUSTICE O'CONNOR, with whom JUSTICE BLACKMUN, JUSTICE STEVENS, and JUSTICE KENNEDY join, dissenting.

Under the guise of overruling "a remnant of a decision," and achieving "uniformity in the law," the Court has changed the law of habeas corpus in a fundamental way by effectively overruling cases decided long before *Townsend* v. *Sain.* I do not think this change is supported by the line of our recent procedural default cases upon which the Court relies: In my view, the balance of state and federal interests regarding whether a federal court will *consider* a claim raised on habeas cannot be simply lifted and transposed to the different question whether, once the court will consider the claim, it should hold an evidentiary hearing. Moreover I do not think the Court's decision can be reconciled with 28 U.S.C. §2254(d), a statute Congress enacted three years after *Townsend.*

I

Jose Tamayo-Reyes' habeas petition stated that because he does not speak English he pleaded *nolo contendere* to manslaughter without any understanding of what "manslaughter" means. If this assertion is true, his conviction was unconstitutionally obtained, Tamayo-Reyes would be entitled to a writ of habeas corpus. Despite the Court's attempt to characterize his allegation as a technical quibble—"his translator had not translated accurately and completely for him the *mens rea* element of manslaughter," this much is not in dispute. Tamayo-Reyes has alleged a fact that, if true, would entitle him to the relief he seeks.

Tamayo-Reyes initially, and properly, challenged the voluntariness of his plea in a petition for postconviction relief in state court. The court held a hearing, after which it found that "[p]etitioner's plea of guilty was knowingly and voluntarily entered." Yet the record of the postconviction hearing hardly inspires confidence in the accuracy of this determination. Tamayo-Reyes was the only witness to testify, but his attorney did not ask him whether his interpreter had translated "manslaughter" for him. Counsel instead introduced the deposition testimony of the interpreter, who admitted that he had translated "manslaughter" only as "less than murder." No witnesses capable of assessing the interpreter's performance were called; the attorney instead tried to direct the court's attention to various sections of the interpreter's deposition and attempted to point out where the interpreter had erred. When the prosecutor objected to this discussion on the ground that counsel was not qualified as an expert witness, his "presentation of the issue quickly disintegrated." The state court had no other relevant evidence before it when it determined that Tamayo-Reyes actually understood the charge to which he was pleading.

Contrary to the impression conveyed by this court's opinion, the question whether a federal court should defer to this sort of dubious "factfinding" in addressing a habeas corpus petition is one with a long history behind it, a history that did not begin with *Townsend* v. *Sain.* . . .

The Court today holds that even when the reliability of state factfinding is doubtful because crucial evidence was not presented to the state trier of fact, a habeas petitioner is ordinarily not entitled to an opportunity to prove the facts necessary to his claim. This holding, of course, directly overrules a portion of *Townsend,* but more than that, I think it departs significantly from the pre-*Townsend* law of habeas corpus. Even before *Townsend,* when a habeas petitioner's claim was properly before a federal court, and when the accurate resolution of that claim depended on proof of facts that had been resolved against the petitioner in an unreliable state proceeding, the petitioner was entitled to his day in federal court. As Justice Holmes wrote for the Court, in a case where the state courts had rejected—under somewhat suspicious circumstances—the petitioner's allegation that his trial had been dominated by an angry mob, "it does not seem to us sufficient to allow a Judge of the United States to escape the duty of examining the facts for himself when if true as alleged they make the trial absolutely void." The class of petitioners eligible to present claims on habeas may have been narrower in days gone by, and the class of claims one might present may have been smaller, but once the claim was properly before the court, the right to a hearing was not construed as narrowly as the Court construes it today.

Instead of looking to the history of the right to an evidentiary hearing, the Court simply borrows the cause and prejudice standard from a series of our recent habeas corpus cases. All but one of these cases address the question of when a habeas claim is properly before a federal court despite the petitioner's procedural default. . . .

The question we are considering here is quite different. Here, the Federal District Court has already determined that it will consider the claimed constitutional violation; the only question is how the court will go about it. When it comes to determining whether a hearing is to be held to resolve a claim that is already properly before a federal court, the federalism concerns underlying our procedural default cases are diminished somewhat. By this point, our concern is less with encroaching on the territory of the state courts than it is with managing the territory of the federal courts in a manner that will best implement their responsibility to consider habeas petitions. Our adoption of a cause and prejudice standard to resolve the first concern should not cause us reflexively to adopt the same standard to resolve the second. Federalism, comity, and finality are all advanced by declining to permit relitigation of claims in federal court in certain circumstances; these interests are less significantly advanced, once relitigation properly occurs, by permitting district courts to resolve claims based on an incomplete record.

The Court's decision today cannot be reconciled with subsection (d) of 28 U.S.C. §2254, which Congress only enacted three years after we decided *Townsend*. Subsection (d) provides that state court factfinding "shall be presumed to be correct, unless the applicant shall establish" one of eight listed circumstances. Most of these circumstances are taken word for word from *Townsend*, including the one at issue here; §2254(d)(3) renders the presumption of correctness inapplicable where "the material facts were not adequately developed at the State court hearing." The effect of the presumption is to augment the habeas petitioner's burden of proof. . . .

In enacting a statute that so closely parallels *Townsend*, Congress established a procedural framework that relies upon *Townsend*'s continuing validity. In general, therefore, overruling *Townsend* would frustrate the evident intent of Congress that the question of when a hearing is to be held should be governed by the same standards as the question of when a federal court should defer to state court factfinding. In particular, the Court's adoption of a "cause and prejudice" standard for determining whether the material facts were adequately developed in state proceedings will frustrate Congress' intent with respect to that *Townsend* circumstance's statutory analog, §2254(d)(3). . . .

Jose Tamayo-Reyes alleges that he pleaded *nolo contendere* to a crime he did not understand. He has exhausted state remedies, has committed no procedural default, has properly presented his claim to a federal district court in his first petition for a writ of habeas corpus, and would be entitled to a hearing under the standard set forth in *Townsend*. Given that his claim is properly before the district court, I would not cut off his right to prove his claim at a hearing. I respectfully dissent.

JUSTICE KENNEDY, dissenting.

By definition, the cases within the ambit of the court's holding are confined to those in which the factual record developed in the state-court proceedings is inadequate to resolve the legal question. I should think those cases will be few in number. *Townsend* v. *Sain* has been the law for almost 30 years and there is no clear evidence that this particular classification of habeas proceedings has burdened the dockets of the federal courts. And in my view, the concept of factual inadequacy comprehends only those petitions with respect to which there is a realistic possibility that an evidentiary hearing will make a difference in the outcome. This serves to narrow the number of cases in a further respect and to insure that they are the ones, as JUSTICE O'CONNOR points out, in which we have valid concerns with constitutional error.

Our recent decisions in *Coleman* v. *Thompson, McCleskey* v. *Zant,* and *Teague* v. *Lane* serve to protect the integrity of the writ, curbing its abuse and insuring that the legal questions presented are ones which, if resolved against the State, can invalidate a final judgment. So we consider today only those habeas actions which present questions federal courts are bound to decide in order to protect constitutional rights. We ought not to take steps which diminish the likelihood that those courts will base their legal decision on an accurate assessment of the facts. For these reasons and all those set forth by JUSTICE O'CONNOR, I dissent from the opinion and judgment of the Court.

□□□

No. 91-712

United States, Petitioner v. Humberto Alvarez-Machain

On writ of certiorari to the United States Court of Appeals for the Ninth Circuit

[June 15, 1992]

THE CHIEF JUSTICE delivered the opinion of the Court.

The issue in this case is whether a criminal defendant, abducted to the United States from a nation with which it has an extradition treaty, thereby acquires a defense to the jurisdiction of this country's courts. We hold that he does not, and that he may be tried in federal district court for violations of the criminal law of the United States.

Respondent, Humberto Alvarez-Machain, is a citizen and resident of Mexico. He was indicted for participating in the kidnap and murder of United States Drug Enforcement Administration (DEA) special agent Enrique Camarena-Salazar and a Mexican pilot working with Camarena, Alfredo Zavala-Avelar. The DEA believes that respondent, a medical doctor, participated in the murder by prolonging agent Camarena's life so that others could further torture and interrogate him. On April 2, 1990, respondent was forcibly kidnapped from his medical office in Guadalajara, Mexico, to be flown by private plane to El Paso, Texas, where he was arrested by DEA officials. The District Court concluded that DEA agents were responsible for respondent's abduction, although they were not personally involved in it.

Respondent moved to dismiss the indictment, claiming that his abduction constituted outrageous governmental conduct, and that the

District Court lacked jurisdiction to try him because he was abducted in violation of the extradition treaty between the United States and Mexico. The District Court rejected the outrageous governmental conduct claim, but held that it lacked jurisdiction to try respondent because his abduction violated the Extradition Treaty. The district court discharged respondent and ordered that he be repatriated to Mexico.

The Court of Appeals affirmed the dismissal of the indictment and the repatriation of respondent, relying on its decision in *United States* v. *Verdugo-Urquidez* (1991). In *Verdugo,* the Court of Appeals held that the forcible abduction of a Mexican national with the authorization or participation of the United States violated the Extradition Treaty between the United States and Mexico. Although the Treaty does not expressly prohibit such abductions, the Court of Appeals held that the "purpose" of the Treaty was violated by a forcible abduction, which, along with a formal protest by the offended nation, would give a defendant the right to invoke the treaty violation to defeat jurisdiction of the district court to try him. The Court of Appeals further held that the proper remedy for such a violation would be dismissal of the indictment and repatriation of the defendant to Mexico.

In the instant case, the Court of Appeals affirmed the district court's finding that the United States had authorized the abduction of respondent, and that letters from the Mexican government to the United States government served as an official protest of the Treaty violation. Therefore, the Court of Appeals ordered that the indictment against respondent be dismissed and that respondent be repatriated to Mexico. We granted certiorari and now reverse.

Although we have never before addressed the precise issue raised in the present case, we have previously considered proceedings in claimed violation of an extradition treaty, and proceedings against a defendant brought before a court by means of a forcible abduction. We addressed the former issue in *United States* v. *Rauscher* (1886); more precisely, the issue of whether the Webster-Ashburton Treaty of 1842, 8 Stat. 576, which governed extraditions between England and the United States, prohibited the prosecution of defendant Rauscher for a crime other than the crime for which he had been extradited. Whether this prohibition, known as the doctrine of specialty, was an intended part of the treaty had been disputed between the two nations for some time. Justice Miller delivered the opinion of the Court, which carefully examined the terms and history of the treaty; the practice of nations in regards to extradition treaties; the case law from the states; and the writings of commentators, and reached the following conclusion:

> "[A] person who has been brought within the jurisdiction of the court *by virtue of proceedings under an extradition treaty,* can only be tried for one of the offences described in that treaty, and for the offence with which he is charged in

the proceedings for his extradition, until a reasonable time and opportunity have been given him, after his release or trial upon such charge, to return to the country from whose asylum he had been forcibly taken under those proceedings." (emphasis added).

In addition, Justice Miller's opinion noted that any doubt as to this interpretation was put to rest by two federal statutes which imposed the doctrine of specialty upon extradition treaties to which the United States was a party. Unlike the case before us today, the defendant in *Rauscher* had been brought to the United States by way of an extradition treaty; there was no issue of a forcible abduction.

In *Ker* v. *Illinois* (1886), also written by Justice Miller and decided the same day as *Rauscher,* we addressed the issue of a defendant brought before the court by way of a forcible abduction. Frederick Ker had been tried and convicted in an Illinois court for larceny; his presence before the court was procured by means of forcible abduction from Peru. A messenger was sent to Lima with the proper warrant to demand Ker by virtue of the extradition treaty between Peru and the United States. The messenger, however, disdained reliance on the treaty processes, and instead forcibly kidnapped Ker and brought him to the United States. We distinguished Ker's case from *Rauscher,* on the basis that Ker was not brought into the United States by virtue of the extradition treaty between the United States and Peru, and rejected Ker's argument that he had a right under the extradition treaty to be returned to this country only in accordance with its terms. We rejected Ker's due process argument more broadly, holding in line with "the highest authorities" that "such forcible abduction is no sufficient reason why the party should not answer when brought within the jurisdiction of the court which has the right to try him for such an offence, and presents no valid objection to his trial in such court." . . .

The only differences between *Ker* and the present case are that *Ker* was decided on the premise that there was no governmental involvement in the abduction, and Peru, from which Ker was abducted, did not object to his prosecution. Respondent finds these differences to be dispositive, as did the Court of Appeals in *Verdugo,* contending that they show that respondent's prosecution, like the prosecution of Rauscher, violates the implied terms of a valid extradition treaty. The Government, on the other hand, argues that *Rauscher* stands as an "exception" to the rule in *Ker* only when an extradition treaty is invoked, and the terms of the treaty provide that its breach will limit the jurisdiction of a court. Therefore, our first inquiry must be whether the abduction of respondent from Mexico violated the extradition treaty between the United States and Mexico. If we conclude that the Treaty does not prohibit respondent's abduction, the rule in *Ker* applies, and the court need not inquire as to how respondent came before it.

In construing a treaty, as in construing a statute, we first look to its terms to determine its meaning. The Treaty says nothing about the obligations of the United States and Mexico to refrain from forcible abductions of people from the territory of the other nation, or the consequences under the Treaty if such an abduction occurs. Respondent submits that Article 22(1) of the Treaty which states that it "shall apply to offenses specified in Article 2 [including murder] committed before and after this Treaty enters into force," evidences an intent to make application of the Treaty mandatory for those offenses. However, the more natural conclusion is that Article 22 was included to ensure that the Treaty was applied to extraditions requested after the Treaty went into force, regardless of when the crime of extradition occurred.

More critical to respondent's argument is Article 9 of the Treaty which provides:

"1. Neither Contracting Party shall be bound to deliver up its own nationals, but the executive authority of the requested Party shall, if not prevented by the laws of that Party, have the power to deliver them up if, in its discretion, it be deemed proper to do so.

"2. If extradition is not granted pursuant to paragraph 1 of this Article, the requested Party shall submit the case to its competent authorities for the purpose of prosecution, provided that Party has jurisdiction over the offense."

According to respondent, Article 9 embodies the terms of the bargain which the United States struck: if the United States wishes to prosecute a Mexican national, it may request that individual's extradition. Upon a request from the United States, Mexico may either extradite the individual, or submit the case to the proper authorities for prosecution in Mexico. In this way, respondent reasons, each nation preserved its right to choose whether its nationals would be tried in its own courts or by the courts of the other nation. This preservation of rights would be frustrated if either nation were free to abduct nationals of the other nation for the purposes of prosecution. More broadly, respondent reasons, as did the Court of Appeals, that all the processes and restrictions on the obligation to extradite established by the Treaty would make no sense if either nation were free to resort to forcible kidnapping to gain the presence of an individual for prosecution in a manner not contemplated by the Treaty.

We do not read the Treaty in such a fashion. Article 9 does not purport to specify the only way in which one country may gain custody of a national of the other country for the purposes of prosecution. In the absence of an extradition treaty, nations are under no obligation to surrender those in their country to foreign authorities for prosecution. . . .

The history of negotiation and practice under the Treaty also fails to show that abductions outside of the Treaty constitute a violation of the Treaty. As the Solicitor General notes, the Mexican government was made aware, as early as 1906, of the *Ker* doctrine, and the United States' position that it applied to forcible abductions made outside of the terms of the United States-Mexico extradition treaty. Nonetheless, the current version of the Treaty, signed in 1978, does not attempt to establish a rule that would in any way curtail the effect of *Ker.* Moreover, although language which would grant individuals exactly the right sought by respondent had been considered and drafted as early as 1935 by a prominent group of legal scholars sponsored by the faculty of Harvard Law School, no such clause appears in the current treaty.

Thus, the language of the Treaty, in the context of its history, does not support the proposition that the Treaty prohibits abductions outside of its terms. The remaining question, therefore, is whether the Treaty should be interpreted so as to include an implied term prohibiting prosecution where the defendant's presence is obtained by means other than those established by the Treaty.

Respondent contends that the Treaty must be interpreted against the backdrop of customary international law, and that international abductions are "so clearly prohibited in international law" that there was no reason to include such a clause in the Treaty itself. The international censure of international abductions is further evidenced, according to respondent by the United Nations Charter and the Charter of the Organization of American States. Respondent does not argue that these sources of international law provide an independent basis for the right respondent asserts not to be tried in the United States, but rather that they should inform the interpretation of the Treaty terms.

The Court of Appeals deemed it essential, in order for the individual defendant to assert a right under the Treaty, that the affected foreign government had registered a protest. Respondent agrees that the right exercised by the individual is derivative of the nation's right under the Treaty, since nations are authorized, notwithstanding the terms of an extradition treaty, to voluntarily render an individual to the other country on terms completely outside of those provided in the Treaty. The formal protest, therefore, ensures that the "offended" nation actually objects to the abduction and has not in some way voluntarily rendered the individual for prosecution. Thus the Extradition Treaty only prohibits gaining the defendant's presence by means other than those set forth in the Treaty when the nation from which the defendant was abducted objects. . . .

In sum, to infer from this Treaty and its terms that it prohibits all means of gaining the presence of an individual outside of its terms goes beyond established precedent and practice. In *Rauscher,* the implication of a doctrine of specialty into the terms of the Webster-Ashburton treaty which, by its terms, required the presentation of evidence establishing probable cause of the crime of extradition before extradition was required, was a small step to take. By contrast, to imply from the terms of this

Treaty that it prohibits obtaining the presence of an individual by means outside of the procedures the Treaty establishes requires a much larger inferential leap, with only the most general of international law principles to support it. The general principles cited by respondent simply fail to persuade us that we should imply in the United States-Mexico Extradition Treaty a term prohibiting international abductions. . . .

The judgment of the Court of Appeals is therefore reversed, and the case is remanded for further proceedings consistent with this opinion.

So ordered.

JUSTICE STEVENS, with whom JUSTICE BLACKMUN and JUSTICE O'CONNOR join, dissenting.

The Court correctly observes that this case raises a question of first impression. The case is unique for several reasons. It does not involve an ordinary abduction by a private kidnaper, or bounty hunter, as in *Ker* v. *Illinois*. . . . Rather, it involves this country's abduction of another country's citizen; it also involves a violation of the territorial integrity of that other country, with which this country has signed an extradition treaty.

A Mexican citizen was kidnaped in Mexico and charged with a crime committed in Mexico; his offense allegedly violated both Mexican and American law. Mexico has formally demanded on at least two separate occasions that he be returned to Mexico and has represented that he will be prosecuted and punished for his alleged offense. It is clear that Mexico's demand must be honored if this official abduction violated the 1978 Extradition Treaty between the United States and Mexico. In my opinion, a fair reading of the treaty in light of our decision in *United States* v. *Rauscher,* and applicable principles of international law, leads inexorably to the conclusion that the District Court and the Court of Appeals for the Ninth Circuit correctly construed that instrument.

I

The Extradition Treaty with Mexico is a comprehensive document containing 23 articles and an appendix listing the extraditable offenses covered by the agreement. The parties announced their purpose in the preamble: The two Governments desire "to cooperate more closely in the fight against crime and, to this end, to mutually render better assistance in matters of extradition." From the preamble, through the description of the parties' obligations with respect to offenses committed within as well as beyond the territory of a requesting party, the delineation of the procedures and evidentiary requirements for extradition, the special provisions for political offenses and capital punishment, and other details, the Treaty appears to have been designed to cover the entire subject of extradition. Thus, Article 22, entitled "Scope of Application" states that the "Treaty shall apply to offenses specified in Article 2 committed before and after this Treaty enters into force," and Article 2 directs that "[e]xtradition shall take place, subject to this treaty, for willful acts which fall within any of [the extraditable offenses listed in] the clauses of the Appendix." Moreover, as noted by the Court, Article 9 expressly provides that neither Contracting Party is bound to deliver up its own nationals, although it may do so in its discretion, but if it does not do so, it "shall submit the case to its competent authorities for purposes of prosecution."

Petitioner's claim that the Treaty is not exclusive, but permits forcible governmental kidnaping, would transform these, and other, provisions into little more than verbiage. . . .

It is true, as the Court notes, that there is no express promise by either party to refrain from forcible abductions in the territory of the other Nation. Relying on that omission, the Court, in effect, concludes that the Treaty merely creates an optional method of obtaining jurisdiction over alleged offenders, and that the parties silently reserved the right to resort to self help whenever they deem force more expeditious than legal process. If the United States, for example, thought it more expedient to torture or simply to execute a person rather than to attempt extradition, these options would be equally available because they, too, were not explicitly prohibited by the Treaty. That, however, is a highly improbable interpretation of a consensual agreement, which on its face appears to have been intended to set forth comprehensive and exclusive rules concerning the subject of extradition. In my opinion, "the manifest scope and object of the treaty itself" plainly imply a mutual undertaking to respect the territorial integrity of the other contracting party. That opinion is confirmed by a consideration of the "legal context" in which the Treaty was negotiated.

[II omitted]
III

A critical flaw pervades the Court's entire opinion. It fails to differentiate between the conduct of private citizens, which does not violate any treaty obligation, and conduct expressly authorized by the Executive Branch of the Government, which unquestionably constitutes a flagrant violation of international law, and in my opinion, also constitutes a breach of our treaty obligations. Thus, at the outset of its opinion, the Court states the issue as "whether a criminal defendant, abducted to the United States from a nation with which it has an extradition treaty, thereby acquires a defense to the jurisdiction of this country's courts." That, of course, is the question decided in *Ker* v. *Illinois;* it is not, however, the question presented for decision today.

The importance of the distinction between a court's exercise of jurisdiction over either a person or property that has been wrongfully seized by a private citizen, or even by a state law enforcement agent, on the one hand, and the attempted exercise of jurisdiction predicated on a seizure by federal officers acting beyond the authority conferred by treaty, on the other hand, is explained by Justice Brandeis in his opinion for the Court in *Cook* v. *United States* (1933). That case involved a construction of a prohibition era treaty with Great Britain that authorized American agents to board certain British vessels to ascertain whether they were engaged in importing alcoholic beverages. A British vessel was boarded 11½ miles off the coast of Massachusetts, found to be carrying unmanifested alcoholic beverages, and taken into port. The Collector of Customs assessed a penalty which he attempted to collect by means of libels against both the cargo and the seized vessel.

The Court held that the seizure was not authorized by the treaty because it occurred more than 10 miles off shore. The Government argued that the illegality of the seizure was immaterial because, as in *Ker,* the court's jurisdiction was supported by possession even if the seizure was wrongful. Justice Brandeis acknowledged that the argument would succeed if the seizure had been made by a private party without authority to act for the Government, but that a different rule prevails when the Government itself lacks the power to seize. . . .

The Court's failure to differentiate between private abductions and official invasions of another sovereign's territory also accounts for its misplaced reliance on the 1935 proposal made by the Advisory Committee on Research in International Law. As the text of that proposal plainly states, it would have rejected the rule of the *Ker* case. The failure to adopt that recommendation does not speak to the issue that the Court decides today. The Court's admittedly "shocking" disdain for customary and conventional international law principles is thus entirely unsupported by case law and commentary.

As the Court observes at the outset of its opinion, there is reason to believe the respondent participated in an especially brutal murder of an American law enforcement agent. That fact, if true, may explain the Executive's intense interest in punishing respondent in our courts. Such an explanation, however, provides no justification for disregarding the Rule of Law that this Court has a duty to uphold. That the Executive may wish to reinterpret the Treaty to allow for an action that the Treaty in no way authorizes should not influence this Court's interpretation. Indeed, the desire for revenge exerts "a kind of hydraulic pressure . . . before which even well settled principles of law will bend" (1904), but it is precisely at such moments that we should remember and be guided by our duty "to render judgment evenly and dispassionately according to law, as each is given understanding to ascertain and apply it" [cites omitted]. The way that we perform that duty in a case of this kind sets an example that other tribunals in other countries are sure to emulate.

□□□

No. 90-7675

R.A.V., Petitioner v. City of St. Paul, Minnesota

On writ of certiorari to the Supreme Court of Minnesota

[June 22, 1992]

JUSTICE SCALIA delivered the opinion of the Court.

In the predawn hours of June 21, 1990, petitioner and several other teenagers allegedly assembled a crudely-made cross by taping together broken chair legs. They then allegedly burned the cross inside the fenced yard of a black family that lived across the street from the house where the petitioner was staying. Although this conduct could have been punished under any number of laws, one of the two provisions under which respondent city of St. Paul chose to charge petitioner (then a juvenile) was the St. Paul Bias-Motivated Crime Ordinance. . . .

I

In construing the St. Paul ordinance, we are bound by the construction given to it by the Minnesota court. Accordingly, we accept the Minnesota Supreme Court's authoritative statement that the ordinance reaches only those expressions that constitute "fighting words" within the meaning of *Chaplinsky* [v. *New Hampshire*, 1942]. Petitioner . . . urge[s] us to modify the scope of the *Chaplinsky* formulation, thereby invalidating the ordinance as "substantially overbroad." We find it unnecessary to consider this issue. Assuming, *arguendo*, that all of the expression reached by the ordinance is proscribable under the "fighting words" doctrine, we nonetheless conclude that the ordinance is facially unconstitutional in that it prohibits otherwise permitted speech solely on the basis of the subjects the speech addresses.

The First Amendment generally prevents government from proscribing speech, *Cantwell* v. *Connecticut* (1940) or even expressive conduct, see *Texas* v. *Johnson* (1989), because of disapproval of the ideas expressed. Content-based regulations are presumptively invalid. *Simon & Schuster,*

Inc. v. *Members of N.Y. State Crime Victims Bd.* (1991). From 1791 to the present, however, our society, like other free but civilized societies, has permitted restrictions upon the content of speech in a few limited areas, which are "of such slight social value as a step to truth that any benefit that may be derived from them is clearly outweighed by the social interest in order and morality." *Chaplinsky.* We have recognized that "the freedom of speech" referred to by the First Amendment does not include a freedom to disregard these traditional limitations. See, *e.g., Roth* v. *United States* (1957) (obscenity); *Beauharnais* v. *Illinois* (1952) (defamation); *Chaplinsky* v. *New Hampshire* ("fighting words"). Our decisions since the 1960's have narrowed the scope of the traditional categorical exceptions for defamation and for obscenity, but a limited categorical approach has remained an important part of our First Amendment jurisprudence.

We have sometimes said that these categories of expression are "not within the area of constitutionally protected speech" or that the "protection of the First Amendment does not extend" to them. Such statements must be taken in context, however, and are no more literally true than is the occasionally repeated shorthand characterizing obscenity "as not being speech at all." What they mean is that these areas of speech can, consistently with the First Amendment, be regulated *because of their constitutionally proscribable content* (obscenity, defamation, etc.)—not that they are categories of speech entirely invisible to the Constitution, so that they may be made the vehicles for content discrimination unrelated to their distinctively proscribable content. Thus, the government may proscribe libel; but it may not make the further content discrimination of proscribing *only* libel critical of the government. We recently acknowledged this distinction in [*New York* v.] *Ferber* [1982], where, in upholding New York's child pornography law, we expressly recognized that there was no "question here of censoring a particular literary theme. . . ."

Our cases surely do not establish the proposition that the First Amendment imposes no obstacle whatsoever to regulation of particular instances of such proscribable expression, so that the government "may regulate [them] freely." That would mean that a city council could enact an ordinance prohibiting only those legally obscene works that contain criticism of the city government or, indeed, that do not include endorsement of the city government. Such a simplistic, all-or-nothing-at-all approach to First Amendment protection is at odds with common sense and with our jurisprudence as well. It is not true that "fighting words" have at most a *"de minimis"* expressive content, or that their content is *in all respects* "worthless and undeserving of constitutional protection"; sometimes they are quite expressive indeed. We have not said that they constitute *"no* part of the expression of ideas," but only that they constitute "no *essential* part of any exposition of ideas."

The proposition that a particular instance of speech can be proscribable on the basis of one feature (*e.g.*, obscenity) but not on the basis of another (*e.g.*, opposition to the city government) is commonplace, and has found application in many contexts. We have long held, for example, that nonverbal expressive activity can be banned because of the action it entails, but not because of the ideas it expresses—so that burning a flag in violation of an ordinance against outdoor fires could be punishable, whereas burning a flag in violation of an ordinance against dishonoring the flag is not. . . .

In other words, the exclusion of "fighting words" from the scope of the First Amendment simply means that, for purposes of that Amendment, the unprotected features of the words are, despite their verbal character, essentially a "nonspeech" element of communication. Fighting words are thus analogous to a noisy sound truck: Each is, as Justice Frankfurter recognized, a "mode of speech"; both can be used to convey an idea; but neither has, in and of itself, a claim upon the First Amendment. As with the sound truck, however, so also with fighting words: The government may not regulate use based on hostility—or favoritism—towards the underlying message expressed.

The concurrences describe us as setting forth a new First Amendment principle that prohibition of constitutionally proscribable speech cannot be "underinclusiv[e]"—a First Amendment "absolutism" whereby "within a particular 'proscribable' category of expression, . . . a government must either proscribe *all* speech or no speech at all." That easy target is of the concurrences' own invention. In our view, the First Amendment imposes not an "underinclusiveness" limitation but a "content discrimination" limitation upon a State's prohibition of proscribable speech. There is no problem whatever, for example, with a State's prohibiting obscenity (and other forms of proscribable expression) only in certain media or markets, for although that prohibition would be "underinclusive," it would not discriminate on the basis of content.

Even the prohibition against content discrimination that we assert the First Amendment requires is not absolute. It applies differently in the context of proscribable speech than in the area of fully protected speech. The rationale of the general prohibition, after all, is that content discrimination "rais[es] the specter that the Government may effectively drive certain ideas or viewpoints from the marketplace." *Simon & Schuster.* But content discrimination among various instances of a class of proscribable speech often does not pose this threat.

When the basis for the content discrimination consists entirely of the very reason the entire class of speech at issue is proscribable, no significant danger of idea or viewpoint discrimination exists. Such a reason, having been adjudged neutral enough to support exclusion of the entire class of speech from First Amendment protection, is also neutral enough to form the basis of distinction within the class. To illustrate: A State might choose to prohibit only that obscenity which is the most patently offensive *in its prurience*—*i.e.,* that which involves the most lascivious displays of sexual activity. But it may not prohibit, for example, only that obscenity which includes offensive *political* messages. . . .

Another valid basis for according differential treatment to even a content-defined subclass of proscribable speech is that the subclass happens to be associated with particular "secondary effects" of the speech, so that the regulation is *"justified* without reference to the content of the . . . speech." A State could, for example, permit all obscene live performances except those involving minors. Moreover, since words can in some circumstances violate laws directed not against speech but against conduct (a law against treason, for example, is violated by telling the enemy the nation's defense secrets), a particular content-based subcategory of a proscribable class of speech can be swept up incidentally within the reach of a statute directed at conduct rather than speech. Thus, for example, sexually derogatory "fighting words," among other words, may produce a violation of Title VII's general prohibition against sexual discrimination in employment practices. Where the government does not target conduct on the basis of its expressive content, acts are not shielded from regulation merely because they express a discriminatory idea or philosophy.

These bases for distinction refute the proposition that the selectivity of the restriction is "even arguably 'conditioned upon the sovereign's agreement with what a speaker may intend to say.' " There may be other such bases as well. Indeed, to validate such selectivity (where totally proscribable speech is at issue) it may not even be necessary to identify any particular "neutral" basis, so long as the nature of the content discrimination is such that there is no realistic possibility that official suppression of ideas is afoot. (We cannot think of any First Amendment interest that would stand in the way of a State's prohibiting only those obscene motion pictures with blue-eyed actresses.) Save for that limitation, the regulation of "fighting words," like the regulation of noisy speech, may address some offensive instances and leave other, equally offensive, instances alone.

II

Applying these principles to the St. Paul ordinance, we conclude that, even as narrowly construed by the Minnesota Supreme Court, the ordinance is facially unconstitutional. Although the phrase in the ordinance, "arouses anger, alarm or resentment in others," has been limited by the Minnesota Supreme Court's construction to reach only those symbols or displays that amount to "fighting words," the remaining, unmodified terms make clear that the ordinance applies only to "fighting words" that insult, or provoke violence, "on the basis of race, color, creed, religion or gender." Displays containing abusive invective, no matter how vicious or severe, are permissible unless they are addressed to one of the specified disfavored topics. Those who wish to use "fighting words" in connection with other ideas—to express hostility, for example, on the basis of political affiliation, union membership, or homosexuality—are not covered. The First Amendment does not permit St. Paul to impose special prohibitions on those speakers who express views on disfavored subjects.

In its practical operation, moreover, the ordinance goes even beyond mere content discrimination, to actual viewpoint discrimination. Displays containing some words—odious racial epithets, for example—would be prohibited to proponents of all views. But "fighting words" that do not themselves invoke race, color, creed, religion, or gender—aspersions upon a person's mother, for example—would seemingly be usable *ad libitum* in the placards of those arguing *in favor* of racial, color, etc. tolerance and equality, but could not be used by that speaker's opponents. One could hold up a sign saying, for example, that all "anti-Catholic bigots" are misbegotten; but not that all "papists" are, for that would insult and provoke violence "on the basis of religion." St. Paul has no such authority to license one side of a debate to fight freestyle, while requiring the other to follow Marquis of Queensbury Rules.

What we have here, it must be emphasized, is not a prohibition of fighting words that are directed at certain persons or groups (which would be *facially* valid if it met the requirements of the Equal Protection Clause); but rather, a prohibition of fighting words that contain (as the Minnesota Supreme Court repeatedly emphasized) messages of "bias-motivated" hatred and in particular, as applied to this case, messages "based on virulent notions of racial supremacy." One must wholeheartedly agree with the Minnesota Supreme Court that "[i]t is the responsibility, even the obligation, of diverse communities to confront such notions in whatever form they appear," but the manner of that confrontation cannot consist of selective limitations upon speech. St. Paul's brief asserts that a general "fighting words" law would not meet the city's needs because only a content-specific measure can communicate to minority groups that the "group hatred" aspect of such speech "is not condoned by the majority." The point of the First Amendment is that majority preferences must be expressed in some fashion other than silencing speech on the basis of its content. . . .

The content-based discrimination reflected in the St. Paul ordinance comes within neither any of the specific exceptions to the First Amendment prohibition we discussed earlier, nor within a more general exception for content discrimination that does not threaten censorship of ideas. It assuredly does not fall within the exception for content discrimination based on the very reasons why the particular class of speech at issue (here, fighting words) is proscribable. . . . [T]he reason why fighting words are categorically excluded from the protection of the First Amendment is not that their content communicates any particular idea, but that their content embodies a particularly intolerable (and socially unnecessary) *mode* of expressing *whatever* idea the speaker wishes to convey. St. Paul has not singled out an especially offensive mode of expression—it has not, for example, selected for prohibition only those fighting words that communicate ideas in a threatening (as opposed to a merely obnoxious) manner. Rather, it has proscribed fighting words of whatever manner that communicate messages of racial, gender, or religious intolerance. Selectivity of this sort creates the possibility that the city is seeking to handicap the expression of particular ideas. That possibility would alone be enough to render the ordinance presumptively invalid, but St. Paul's comments and concessions in this case elevate the possibility to a certainty.

St. Paul argues that the ordinance comes within another of the specific exceptions we mentioned, the one that allows content discrimination aimed only at the "secondary effects" of the speech. According to St. Paul, the ordinance is intended, "not to impact on [*sic*] the right of free expression of the accused," but rather to "protect against the victimization of a person or persons who are particularly vulnerable because of their membership in a group that historically has been discriminated against." Even assuming that an ordinance that completely proscribes, rather than merely regulates, a specified category of speech can ever be considered to be directed only to the secondary effects of such speech, it is clear that the St. Paul ordinance is not directed to secondary effects within the meaning of *Renton.* . . .

It hardly needs discussion that the ordinance does not fall within some more general exception permitting *all* selectivity that for any reason is beyond the suspicion of official suppression of ideas. The statements of St. Paul in this very case afford ample basis for, if not full confirmation of, that suspicion.

Finally, St. Paul . . . defend[s] the conclusion of the Minnesota Supreme Court that, even if the ordinance regulates expression based on hostility towards its protected ideological content, this discrimination is nonetheless justified because it is narrowly tailored to serve compelling state interests. Specifically, they assert that the ordinance helps to ensure the basic human rights of members of groups that have historically been subjected to discrimination, including the right of such group members to live in peace where they wish. We do not doubt that these interests are compelling, and that the ordinance can be said to promote them. But the "danger of censorship" presented by a facially content-based statute requires that that weapon be employed only where it is "*necessary* to serve the asserted [compelling] interest.". . . The dispositive question in this case, therefore, is whether content discrimination is reasonably necessary to achieve St. Paul's compelling interests; it plainly is not. An ordinance not limited to the favored topics, for example, would have precisely the same beneficial effect. In fact the only interest distinctively served by the content limitation is that of displaying the city council's special hostility towards the particular biases thus singled out. That is precisely what the First Amendment forbids. The politicians of St. Paul are entitled to express that hostility—but not through the means of imposing unique limitations upon speakers who (however benightedly) disagree.

Let there be no mistake about our belief that burning a cross is someone's front yard is reprehensible. But St. Paul has sufficient means at its disposal to prevent such behavior without adding the First Amendment to the fire.

The judgment of the Minnesota Supreme Court is reversed, and the case is remanded for proceedings not inconsistent with this opinion.

It is so ordered.

No. 90-1038

Thomas Cipollone, Individually and as Executor of the Estate of Rose D. Cipollone, Petitioner v. Liggett Group, Inc., et al.

On writ of certiorari to the United States Court of Appeals for the Third Circuit

[June 24, 1992]

JUSTICE JOHN PAUL STEVENS delivered the opinion of the Court. . . .

"WARNING: THE SURGEON GENERAL HAS DETERMINED THAT CIGARETTE SMOKING IS DANGEROUS TO YOUR HEALTH." A federal statute enacted in 1969 requires that warning (or a variation thereof) to appear in a conspicuous place on every package of cigarettes sold in the United States. The questions presented to us by this case are whether that statute, or its 1965 predecessor which required a less alarming label, pre-empted petitioner's common law claims against respondent cigarette manufacturers. . . .

[I omitted]
II

Although physicians had suspected a link between smoking and illness for centuries, the first medical studies of that connection did not appear until the 1920s. The ensuing decades saw a wide range of epidemiologic and laboratory studies on the health hazards of smoking. Thus, by the time the Surgeon General convened an advisory committee to examine the issue in 1962, there were more than 7,000 publications examining the relationship between smoking and health.

In 1964, the advisory committee issued its report, which stated as its central conclusion: "Cigarette smoking is a health hazard of sufficient importance in the United States to warrant appropriate remedial action." Relying in part on that report, the Federal Trade Commission (FTC), which had long regulated unfair and deceptive advertising practices in the cigarette industry, promulgated a new trade regulation rule. That rule, which was to take effect January 1, 1965, established that it would be a violation of the Federal Trade Commission Act "to fail to disclose, clearly and prominently, in all advertising and on every pack, box, carton, or container [of cigarettes] that cigarette smoking is dangerous to health and may cause death from cancer and other diseases." Several States also moved to regulate the advertising and labeling of cigarettes. Upon a congressional request, the FTC postponed enforcement of its new regulation for six months. In July 1965, Congress enacted the Federal Cigarette Labeling and Advertising Act. The 1965 Act effectively adopted half of the FTC's regulation: the Act mandated warnings on cigarette packages (§ 5(a)), but barred the requirement of such warnings in cigarette advertising (§ 5(b)).

Section 2 of the Act declares the statute's two purposes: (1) adequately informing the public that cigarette smoking may be hazardous to health, and (2) protecting the national economy from the burden imposed by diverse, nonuniform and confusing cigarette labeling and advertising regulations. In furtherance of the first purpose, § 4 of the Act made it unlawful to sell or distribute any cigarettes in the United States unless the package bore a conspicuous label stating: "CAUTION: CIGARETTE SMOKING MAY BE HAZARDOUS TO YOUR HEALTH." In furtherance of the second purpose, § 5, captioned "Preemption," provided in part:

> "(a) No statement relating to smoking and health, other than the statement required by section 4 of this Act, shall be required on any cigarette package.
> "(b) No statement relating to smoking and health shall be required in the advertising of any cigarettes the packages of which are labeled in conformity with the provisions of this Act."

Although the Act took effect January 1, 1966, § 10 of the Act provided that its provisions affecting the regulation of advertising would terminate on July 1, 1969.

As that termination date approached, federal authorities prepared to issue further regulations on cigarette advertising. The FTC announced the reinstitution of its 1964 proceedings concerning a warning requirement for cigarette advertisements. The Federal Communications Commission (FCC) announced that it would consider "a proposed rule which would ban the broadcast of cigarette commercials by radio and television stations." State authorities also prepared to take actions regulating cigarette advertisements.

It was in this context that Congress enacted the Public Health Cigarette Smoking Act of 1969, which amended the 1965 Act in several ways. First, the 1969 Act strengthened the warning label, in part by requiring a statement that cigarette smoking "is dangerous" rather than that it "may be hazardous." Second, the 1969 Act banned cigarette advertising in "any medium of electronic communication subject to [FCC] jurisdiction." Third, and related, the 1969 Act modified the pre-emption provision by replacing the original § 5(b) with a provision that reads:

> "(b) No requirement or prohibition based on smoking and health shall be imposed under State law with respect to the advertising or promotion of any cigarettes the packages of which are labeled in conformity with the provisions of this Act." . . .

III

Article VI of the Constitution provides that the laws of the United States "shall be the supreme Law of the Land; . . . any Thing in the Constitution or Laws of any state to the Contrary notwithstanding." Art. VI, cl. 2. Thus, since our decision in *McCulloch* v. *Maryland* (1819), it has been settled that state law that conflicts with federal law is "without effect." Consideration of issues arising under the Supremacy Clause "start[s] with the assumption that the historic police powers of the States [are] not to be superseded by . . . Federal Act unless that [is] the clear and manifest purpose of Congress." *Rice* v. *Santa Fe Elevator Corp.* (1947). Accordingly, " '[t]he purpose of Congress is the ultimate touchstone' " of preemption analysis.

Congress' intent may be "explicitly stated in the statute's language or implicitly contained in its structure and purpose." In the absence of an express congressional command, state law is pre-empted if that law actually conflicts with federal law, or if federal law so thoroughly occupies a legislative field " 'as to make reasonable the inference that Congress left no room for the States to supplement it.' " . . .

In our opinion, the pre-emptive scope of the 1965 Act and the 1969 Act is governed entirely by the express language in § 5 of each Act. When Congress has considered the issue of pre-emption and has included in the enacted legislation a provision explicitly addressing that issue, and when that provision provides a "reliable indicium of congressional intent with respect to state authority, there is no need to infer congressional intent to pre-empt state laws from the substantive provisions" of the legislation.

Such reasoning is a variant of the familiar principle of *expressio unius est exclusio alterius:* Congress' enactment of a provision defining the preemptive reach of a statute implies that matters beyond that reach are not pre-empted. In this case, the other provisions of the 1965 and 1969 Acts offer no cause to look beyond § 5 of each Act. Therefore, we need only identify the domain expressly pre-empted by each of those sections. As the 1965 and 1969 provisions differ substantially, we consider each in turn.

IV

In the 1965 pre-emption provision regarding advertising (§ 5(b)), Congress spoke precisely and narrowly: "No *statement* relating to smoking and health shall be required *in the advertising* of [properly labeled] cigarettes." Section 5(a) used the same phrase ("No *statement* relating to smoking and health") with regard to cigarette labeling. As § 5(a) made clear, that phrase referred to the sort of warning provided for in § 4, which set forth verbatim the warning Congress determined to be appropriate. Thus, on their face, these provisions merely prohibited state and federal rule-making bodies from mandating particular cautionary statements on cigarette labels (§ 5(a)) or in cigarette advertisements (§ 5(b)).

Beyond the precise words of these provisions, this reading is appropriate for several reasons. First, as discussed above, we must construe these provisions in light of the presumption against the preemption of state police power regulations. This presumption reinforces the appropriateness of a narrow reading of § 5. Second, the warning required in § 4 does not by its own effect foreclose additional obligations imposed under state law. That Congress requires a particular warning label does not automatically pre-empt a regulatory field. Third, there is no general, inherent conflict between federal pre-emption of state warning requirements and the continued vitality of state common law damages actions. . . . All of these considerations indicate that § 5 is best read as having superseded only positive enactments by legislatures or administrative agencies that mandate particular warning labels. . . .

For these reasons, we conclude that § 5 of the 1965 Act only preempted state and federal rulemaking bodies from mandating particular cautionary statements and did not pre-empt state law damages actions.

V

Compared to its predecessor in the 1965 Act, the plain language of the pre-emption provision in the 1969 Act is much broader. First, the later Act bars not simply "statements" but rather "requirement[s] or prohibition[s] ... imposed under State law." Second, the later Act reaches beyond statements "in the advertising" to obligations "with respect to the advertising or promotion" of cigarettes.

... The 1969 Act worked substantial changes in the law: rewriting the label warning, banning broadcast advertising, and allowing the FTC to regulate print advertising. ...

Petitioner ... contends that § 5(b), however broadened by the 1969 Act, does not pre-empt *common law* actions. He offers two theories for limiting the reach of the amended § 5(b). First, he argues that common law damages actions do not impose "requirement[s] or prohibition[s]" and that Congress intended only to trump "state statute[s], injunction[s], or executive pronouncement[s]." We disagree; such an analysis is at odds both with the plain words of the 1969 Act and with the general understanding of common law damages actions. ... As we noted in another context, "[state] regulation can be as effectively exerted through an award of damages as through some form of preventive relief. The obligation to pay compensation can be, indeed is designed to be, a potent method of governing conduct and controlling policy." ...

Petitioner's second argument for excluding common law rules from the reach of § 5(b) hinges on the phrase "imposed under State law." This argument fails as well. At least since *Erie R.* v. *Tompkins* (1938), we have recognized the phrase "state law" to include common law as well as statutes and regulations. ...

That the pre-emptive scope of § 5(b) cannot be limited to positive enactments does not mean that that section pre-empts all common law claims. ...

Nor does the statute indicate that any familiar subdivision of common law claims is or is not pre-empted. ... Instead we must fairly but—in light of the strong presumption against pre-emption—narrowly construe the precise language of § 5(b) and we must look to each of petitioner's common law claims to determine whether it is in fact pre-empted. The central inquiry in each case is straightforward: we ask whether the legal duty that is the predicate of the common law damages action constitutes a "requirement or prohibition based on smoking and health ... imposed under State law with respect to ... advertising or promotion," giving that clause a fair but narrow reading. As discussed below, each phrase within that clause limits the universe of common law claims pre-empted by the statute.

We consider each category of damages actions in turn. ...

Failure to Warn

... In this case, petitioner offered two closely related theories concerning the failure to warn: first, that respondents "were negligent in the manner [that] they tested, researched, sold, promoted, and advertised" their cigarettes; and second, that respondents failed to provide "adequate warnings of the health consequences of cigarette smoking."

Petitioner's claims are pre-empted to the extent that they rely on a state law "requirement or prohibition . . . with respect to . . . advertising or promotion." Thus, insofar as claims under either failure to warn theory require a showing that respondents' post-1969 advertising or promotions should have included additional, or more clearly stated, warnings, those claims are pre-empted. The Act does not, however, pre-empt petitioner's claims that rely solely on respondents' testing or research practices or other actions unrelated to advertising or promotion.

Breach of Express Warranty

Petitioner's claim for breach of an express warranty arises under N.J. Stat. Ann. § 12A:2-313(1)(a), which provides:

> "Any affirmation of fact or promise made by the seller to the buyer which relates to the goods and becomes part of the basis of the bargain creates an express warranty that the goods shall conform to the affirmation or promise."

Petitioner's evidence of an express warranty consists largely of statements made in respondents' advertising. . . .

That the terms of the warranty may have been set forth in advertisements rather than in separate documents is irrelevant to the pre-emption issue . . . because although the breach of warranty claim is made "with respect to advertising" it does not rest on a duty imposed under state law. Accordingly, to the extent that petitioner has a viable claim for breach of express warranties made by respondents, that claim is not pre-empted by the 1969 Act.

Fraudulent Misrepresentation

Petitioner alleges two theories of fraudulent misrepresentation. First, petitioner alleges that respondents, through their advertising, neutralized the effect of federally mandated warning labels. Such a claim is predicated on a state-law prohibition against statements in advertising and promotional materials that tend to minimize the health hazards associated with smoking. Such a *prohibition,* however, is merely the converse of a state law *requirement* that warnings be included in advertising and promotional materials. Section 5(b) of the 1969 Act pre-empts both requirements and prohibitions; it therefore supersedes petitioner's first fraudulent misrepresentation theory. . . .

Petitioner's second theory . . . alleges intentional fraud and misrepresentation both by "false representation of a material fact [and by] conceal[ment of] a material fact." The predicate of this claim is a state law duty not to make false statements of material fact or to conceal such facts. . . .

Section 5(b) pre-empts only the imposition of state law obligations "with respect to the advertising or promotion" of cigarettes. Petitioner's claims that respondents concealed material facts are therefore not pre-empted insofar as those claims rely on a state law duty to disclose such facts through channels of communication other than advertising or promotion. . . .

Moreover, petitioner's fraudulent misrepresentation claims that do arise with respect to advertising and promotions (most notably claims based on allegedly false statements of material fact made in advertisements) are not pre-empted by § 5(b). Such claims are not predicated on a duty "based on smoking and health" but rather on a more general obligation—the duty not to deceive. . . . Congress offered no sign that it wished to insulate cigarette manufacturers from longstanding rules governing fraud. To the contrary, both the 1965 and the 1969 Acts explicitly reserved the FTC's authority to identify and punish deceptive advertising practices—an authority that the FTC had long exercised and continues to exercise. This indicates that Congress intended the phrase "relating to smoking and health" (which was essentially unchanged by the 1969 Act) to be construed narrowly, so as not to proscribe the regulation of deceptive advertising.

. . . Accordingly, petitioner's claim based on allegedly fraudulent statements made in respondents' advertisements are not pre-empted by § 5(b) of the 1969 Act.

Conspiracy to Misrepresent or Conceal Material Facts

Petitioner's final claim alleges a conspiracy among respondents to misrepresent or conceal material facts concerning the health hazards of smoking. The predicate duty underlying this claim is a duty not to conspire to commit fraud. For the reasons stated in our analysis of petitioner's intentional fraud claim, this duty is not pre-empted by § 5(b) for it is not a prohibition "based on smoking and health" as that phrase is properly construed. Accordingly, we conclude that the 1969 Act does not pre-empt petitioner's conspiracy claim.

VI

To summarize our holding: The 1965 Act did not pre-empt state law damages actions; the 1969 Act pre-empts petitioner's claims based on a failure to warn and the neutralization of federally mandated warnings to the extent that those claims rely on omissions or inclusions in respondents' advertising or promotions; the 1969 Act does not pre-empt petitioner's claims based on express warranty, intentional fraud and misrepresentation, or conspiracy.

The judgment of the Court of Appeals is accordingly reversed in part and affirmed in part, and the case is remanded for further proceedings consistent with this opinion.

It is so ordered.

□□□

No. 90-1014

Robert E. Lee, Individually and as Principal of Nathan Bishop Middle School, et al., Petitioners v. Daniel Weisman etc.

On writ of certiorari to the United States Court of Appeals for the First Circuit

[June 24, 1992]

JUSTICE KENNEDY delivered the opinion of the Court.

School principals in the public school system of the city of Providence, Rhode Island, are permitted to invite members of the clergy to offer invocation and benediction prayers as part of the formal graduation ceremonies for middle schools and for high schools. The question before us is whether including clerical members who offer prayers as part of the official school graduation ceremony is consistent with the Religion Clauses of the First Amendment, provisions the Fourteenth Amendment makes applicable with full force to the States and their school districts. . . .

[I omitted]
II

These dominant facts mark and control the confines of our decision: State officials direct the performance of a formal religious exercise at promotional and graduation ceremonies for secondary schools. Even for those students who object to the religious exercise, their attendance and participation in the state-sponsored religious activity are in a fair and real sense obligatory, though the school district does not require attendance as a condition for receipt of the diploma.

This case does not require us to revisit the difficult questions dividing us in recent cases, questions of the definition and full scope of the principles governing the extent of permitted accommodation by the State for the religious beliefs and practices of many of its citizens. See *Allegheny County* v. *Greater Pittsburgh ACLU* (1989); *Wallace* v. *Jaffree* (1985); *Lynch* v. *Donnelly* (1984). For without reference to those principles in other contexts, the controlling precedents as they relate to prayer and religious exercise in primary and secondary public schools compel the holding here that the policy of the city of Providence is an unconstitutional one. We can decide the case without reconsidering the general constitutional framework by which public schools' efforts to accommodate religion are measured. Thus we do not accept the invitation of petitioners and *amicus* the United States to reconsider our decision in *Lemon* v. *Kurtzman* [1971]. The government involvement with religious activity in this case is pervasive, to the point of creating a state-sponsored and state-directed religious exercise in a public school. Conducting this formal religious observance conflicts with settled rules pertaining to prayer exercises for students, and that suffices to determine the question before us.

The principle that government may accommodate the free exercise of religion does not supersede the fundamental limitations imposed by the Establishment Clause. It is beyond dispute that, at a minimum, the Constitution guarantees that government may not coerce anyone to support or participate in religion or its exercise, or otherwise act in a way which "establishes a [state] religion or religious faith, or tends to do so." *Lynch,* quoting *Everson* v. *Board of Education of Ewing* (1947). The State's involvement in the school prayers challenged today violates these central principles.

That involvement is as troubling as it is undenied. A school official, the principal, decided that an invocation and a benediction should be given; this is a choice attributable to the State, and from a constitutional perspective it is as if a state statute decreed that the prayers must occur. The principal chose the religious participant, here a rabbi, and that choice is also attributable to the State. . . .

The State's role did not end with the decision to include a prayer and with the choice of clergyman. Principal Lee provided Rabbi Gutterman with a copy of the "Guidelines for Civic Occasions," and advised him that his prayers should be nonsectarian. Through these means the principal directed and controlled the content of the prayer. Even if the only sanction for ignoring the instructions were that the rabbi would not be invited back, we think no religious representative who valued his or her continued reputation and effectiveness in the community would incur the State's displeasure in this regard. It is a cornerstone principle of our Establishment Clause jurisprudence that "it is no part of the business of government to compose official prayers for any group of the American people to recite as a part of a religious program carried on by government," *Engel* v. *Vitale* (1962), and that is what the school officials attempted to do. . . .

We are asked to recognize the existence of a practice of nonsectarian prayer, prayer within the embrace of what is known as the Judeo-Christian tradition, prayer which is more acceptable than one which, for example, makes explicit references to the God of Israel, or to Jesus Christ, or to a patron saint. There may be some support, as an empirical observation, to the statement of the Court of Appeals for the Sixth Circuit, picked up by Judge Campbell's dissent in the Court of Appeals in this case, that there has emerged in the country a civic religion, one which is tolerated when sectarian exercises are not. If common ground can be defined which permits once conflicting faiths to express the shared conviction that there is an ethic and a morality which transcend human invention, the sense of community and purpose sought by all decent societies might be advanced. But though the First Amendment does not allow the government to stifle prayers which aspire to these ends, neither does it permit the government to undertake that task for itself. . . .

The degree of school involvement here made it clear that the graduation prayers bore the imprint of the State and thus put school-age children who objected in an untenable position. We turn our attention now to consider the position of the students, both those who desired the prayer and she who did not.

To endure the speech of false ideas or offensive content and then to counter it is part of learning how to live in a pluralistic society, a society which insists upon open discourse towards the end of a tolerant citizenry. And tolerance presupposes some mutuality of obligation. It is argued that our constitutional vision of a free society requires confidence in our own ability to accept or reject ideas of which we do not approve, and that prayer at a high school graduation does nothing more than offer a choice. By the time they are seniors, high school students no doubt have been required to attend classes and assemblies and to complete assignments exposing them to ideas they find distasteful or immoral or absurd or all of these. Against this background, students may consider it an odd measure of justice to be subjected during the course of their educations to ideas deemed offensive and irreligious, but to be denied a brief, formal prayer ceremony that the school offers in return. This argument cannot prevail, however. It overlooks a fundamental dynamic of the Constitution.

The First Amendment protects speech and religion by quite different mechanisms. Speech is protected by insuring its full expression even when the government participates, for the very object of some of our most important speech is to persuade the government to adopt an idea as its own. The method for protecting freedom of worship and freedom of conscience in religious matters is quite the reverse. In religious debate or expression the government is not a prime participant, for the Framers deemed religious establishment antithetical to the freedom of all. The Free Exercise Clause embraces a freedom of conscience and worship that has close parallels in the speech provisions of the First Amendment, but the Establishment Clause is a specific prohibition on forms of state intervention in religious affairs with no precise counterpart in the speech provisions. The explanation lies in the lesson of history that was and is the inspiration for the Establishment Clause, the lesson that in the hands of government what might begin as a tolerant expression of religious views may end in a policy to indoctrinate and coerce. A state-created orthodoxy puts at grave risk that freedom of belief and conscience which are the sole assurance that religious faith is real, not imposed.

The lessons of the First Amendment are as urgent in the modern world as in the 18th Century when it was written. One timeless lesson is that if citizens are subjected to state-sponsored religious exercises, the State disavows its own duty to guard and respect that sphere of inviolable conscience and belief which is the mark of a free people. To compromise that principle today would be to deny our own tradition and forfeit our standing to urge others to secure the protections of that tradition for themselves.

As we have observed before, there are heightened concerns with protecting freedom of conscience from subtle coercive pressure in the elementary and secondary public schools. Our decisions in *Engle* v. *Vitale* (1962), and *Abington School District* [v. *Schempp*, 1963] recognize, among other things, that prayer exercises in public schools carry a particular risk of indirect coercion. The concern may not be limited to the context of schools, but it is most pronounced here. See *Allegheny County* v. *Greater Pittsburgh ACLU* (KENNEDY, J., concurring in judgment in part and dissenting in part). What to most believers may seem nothing more than a reasonable request that the nonbeliever respect their religious practices, in a school context may appear to the nonbeliever or dissenter to be an attempt to employ the machinery of the State to enforce a religious orthodoxy.

We need not look beyond the circumstances of this case to see the phenomenon at work. The undeniable fact is that the school district's supervision and control of a high school graduation ceremony places public pressure, as well as peer pressure, on attending students to stand as a group or, at least, maintain respectful silence during the Invocation and Benediction. This pressure, though subtle and indirect, can be as real as any overt compulsion. Of course, in our culture standing or remaining silent can signify adherence to a view or simple respect for the views of others. And no doubt some persons who have no desire to join a prayer have little objection to standing as a sign of respect for those who do. But for the dissenter of high school age, who has a reasonable perception that she is being forced by the state to pray in a manner her conscience will not allow, the injury is no less real. There can be no doubt that for many, if not most, of the students at the graduation, the act of standing or remaining silent was an expression of participation in the Rabbi's prayer. That was the very point of the religious exercise. It is of little comfort to a dissenter, then, to be told that for her the act of standing or remaining in silence signifies mere respect, rather than participation. What matters is that, given our social conventions, a reasonable dissenter in this milieu could believe that the group exercise signified her own participation or approval of it.

Finding no violation under these circumstances would place objectors in the dilemma of participating, with all that implies, or protesting. We do not address whether that choice is acceptable if the affected citizens are mature adults, but we think the State may not, consistent with the Establishment Clause, place primary and secondary school children in this position. Research in psychology supports the common assumption that adolescents are often susceptible to pressure from their peers towards conformity, and that the influence is strongest in matters of social convention. To recognize that the choice imposed by the State constitutes an unacceptable constraint only acknowledges that the government may no more use social pressure to enforce orthodoxy than it may use more direct means.

The injury caused by the government's action, and the reason why Daniel and Deborah Weisman object to it, is that the State, in a school setting, in effect required participation in a religious exercise. It is, we concede, a brief exercise during which the individual can concentrate on joining its message, meditate on her own religion, or let her mind wander. But the embarrassment and the intrusion of the religious exercise cannot be refuted by arguing that these prayers, and similar ones to be said in the future, are of a *de minimis* character. To do so would be an affront to the Rabbi who offered them and to all those for whom the prayers were an essential and profound recognition of divine authority. And for the same reason, we think that the intrusion is greater than the two minutes or so of time consumed for prayers like these. Assuming, as we must, that the prayers were offensive to the student and the parent who now object, the intrusion was both real and, in the context of a secondary school, a violation of the objectors' rights. That the intrusion was in the course of promulgating religion that sought to be civic or nonsectarian rather than pertaining to one sect does not lessen the offense or isolation to the objectors. At best it narrows their number, at worse increases their sense of isolation and affront.

There was a stipulation in the District Court that attendance at graduation and promotional ceremonies is voluntary. Petitioners and the United States, as *amicus,* made this a center point of the case, arguing that the option of not attending the graduation excuses any inducement or coercion in the ceremony itself. The argument lacks all persuasion. Law reaches past formalism. And to say a teenage student has a real choice not to.attend her high school graduation is formalistic in the extreme. True, Deborah could elect not to attend commencement without renouncing her diploma; but we shall not allow the case to turn on this point. Everyone knows that in our society and in our culture high school graduation is one of life's most significant occasions. A school rule which excuses attendance is beside the point. Attendance may not be required by official decree, yet it is apparent that a student is not free to absent herself from the graduation exercise in any real sense of the term "voluntary," for absence would require forfeiture of those intangible benefits which have motivated the student through youth and all her high school years. Graduation is a time for family and those closest to the student to celebrate success and express mutual wishes of gratitude and respect, all to the end of impressing upon the young person the role that it is his or her right and duty to assume in the community and all of its diverse parts.

... The Constitution forbids the State to exact religious conformity from a student as the price of attending her own high school graduation. This is the calculus the Constitution commands.

The Government's argument gives insufficient recognition to the real conflict of conscience faced by the young student. The essence of the Government's position is that with regard to a civic occasion of this importance it is the objector, not the majority, who must take unilateral and private action to avoid compromising religious scruples, here by electing to miss the graduation exercise. This turns conventional First Amendment analysis on its head. It is a tenet of the First Amendment that the State cannot require one of its citizens to forfeit his or her rights and benefits as the price of resisting conformance to state-sponsored religious practice. To say that a student must remain apart from the ceremony at the opening invocation and closing benediction is to risk compelling conformity in an environment analogous to the classroom setting, where we have said the risk of compulsion is especially high. Just as in *Engel* v. *Vitale* and *Abington School District* v. *Schempp,* we found that provisions within the challenged legislation permitting a student to be voluntarily excused from attendance or participation in the daily prayers did not shield those practices from invalidation; the fact that attendance at the graduation ceremonies is voluntary in a legal sense does not save the religious exercise.

Inherent differences between the public school system and a session of State Legislature distinguish this case from *Marsh* v. *Chambers* (1983). The considerations we have raised in objection to the invocation and benediction are in many respects similar to the arguments we considered in *Marsh*. But there are also obvious differences. The atmosphere at the opening of a session of a state legislature where adults are free to enter and leave with little comment and for any number of reasons cannot compare with the constraining potential of the one school event most important for the student to attend. The influence and force of a formal exercise in a school graduation are far greater than the prayer exercise we condoned in *Marsh*. The *Marsh* majority in fact gave specific recognition to this distinction and placed particular reliance on it in upholding the prayers at issue there. Today's case is different. At a high school graduation, teachers and principals must and do retain a high degree of control over the precise contents of the program, the speeches, the timing, the movements, the dress, and the decorum of the students. In this atmosphere the state-imposed character of an invocation and benediction by clergy selected by the school combine to make the prayer a state-sanctioned religious exercise in which the student was left with no alternative but to submit. This is different from *Marsh* and suffices to make the religious exercise a First Amendment violation. Our Establishment Clause jurisprudence remains a delicate and fact-sensitive one, and we cannot accept the parallel relied upon by petitioners and the United States between the facts of *Marsh* and the case now before us. Our decisions in *Engel* v. *Vitale* and *Abington School District* v. *Schempp* require us to distinguish the public school context.

We do not hold that every state action implicating religion is invalid if one or a few citizens find it offensive. People may take offense at all manner of religious as well as nonreligious messages, but offense alone does not in every case show a violation. We know too that sometimes to endure social isolation or even anger may be the price of conscience or nonconformity. But, by any reading of our cases, the conformity required of the student in this case was too high an exaction to withstand the test of the Establishment Clause. The prayer exercises in this case are especially improper because the State has in every practical sense compelled attendance and participation in an explicit religious exercise at an event of singular importance to every student, one the objecting student had no real alternative to avoid. . . .

Our society would be less than true to its heritage if it lacked abiding concern for the values of its young people, and we acknowledge the profound belief of adherents to many faiths that there must be a place in the student's life for precepts of a morality higher even than the law we today enforce. We express no hostility to those aspirations, nor would our oath permit us to do so. A relentless and all-pervasive attempt to exclude religion from every aspect of public life could itself become inconsistent with the Constitution. We recognize that, at graduation time and throughout the course of the educational process, there will be instances when religious values, religious practices, and religious persons will have some interaction with the public schools and their students. But these matters, often questions of accommodation of religion, are not before us. The sole question presented is whether a religious exercise may be conducted at a graduation ceremony in circumstances where, as we have found, young graduates who object are induced to conform. No holding by this Court suggests that a school can persuade or compel a student to participate in a religious exercise. That is being done here, and it is forbidden by the Establishment Clause of the First Amendment.

For the reasons we have stated, the judgment of the Court of Appeals is

Affirmed.

□□□

Nos. 90-1205 and 90-6588

United States, Petitioner v. Kirk Fordice, Governor of Mississippi, et al.

Jake Ayers, et al., Petitioners v. Kirk Fordice, Governor of Mississippi, et al.

On writs of certiorari to the United States Court of Appeals for the Fifth Circuit

[June 26, 1992]

JUSTICE WHITE delivered the opinion of the Court.

In 1954, this Court held that the concept of " 'separate but equal' " has no place in the field of public education. *Brown* v. *Board of Education (Brown I)* (1954). The following year, the Court ordered an end to segregated public education "with all deliberate speed." *Brown* v. *Board of Education (Brown II)* (1955). Since these decisions, the Court has had many occasions to evaluate whether a public school district has met its affirmative obligation to dismantle its prior *de jure* segregated system in elementary and secondary schools. In this case we decide what standards to apply in determining whether the State of Mississippi has met this obligation in the university context.

I

Mississippi launched its public university system in 1848 by establishing the University of Mississippi, an institution dedicated to higher education exclusively of white persons. In succeeding decades, the State erected additional post-secondary, single-race educational facilities. Alcorn State University opened its doors in 1871 as "an agricultural college for the education of Mississippi's black youth." Creation of four more exclusively white institutions followed: Mississippi State University (1880), Mississippi University for Women (1885), University of Southern Mississippi (1912), and Delta State University (1925). The State added two more solely black institutions in 1940 and 1950: in the former year,

Jackson State University, which was charged with training "black teachers for the black public schools," and in the latter year, Mississippi Valley State University, whose functions were to educate teachers primarily for rural and elementary schools and to provide vocational instruction to black students.

Despite this Court's decisions in *Brown I* and *Brown II*, Mississippi's policy of *de jure* segregation continued. The first black student was not admitted to the University of Mississippi until 1962, and then only by court order. For the next 12 years the segregated public university system in the State remained largely intact. Mississippi State University, Mississippi University for Women, University of Southern Mississippi, and Delta State University each admitted at least one black student during these years, but the student composition of these institutions was still almost completely white. During this period, Jackson State and Mississippi Valley State were exclusively black; Alcorn State had admitted five white students by 1968.

In 1969, the United States Department of Health, Education and Welfare (HEW) initiated efforts to enforce Title VI of the Civil Rights Act of 1964. HEW requested that the State devise a plan to disestablish the formerly *de jure* segregated university system. In June 1973, the Board of Trustees of State Institutions of Higher Learning submitted a Plan of Compliance, which expressed the aims of improving educational opportunities for all Mississippi citizens by setting numerical goals on the enrollment of other-race students at State universities, hiring other-race faculty members, and instituting remedial programs and special recruitment efforts to achieve those goals. HEW rejected this Plan as failing to comply with Title VI because it did not go far enough in the areas of student recruitment and enrollment, faculty hiring, elimination of unnecessary program duplication, and institutional funding practices to ensure that "a student's choice of institution or campus, henceforth, will be based on other than racial criteria." The Board reluctantly offered amendments, prefacing its reform pledge to HEW with this statement: "With deference, it is the position of the Board of Trustees . . . that the Mississippi system of higher education is in compliance with Title VI of the Civil Rights Act of 1964." At this time, the racial composition of the State's universities had changed only marginally from the levels of 1968, which were almost exclusively single-race. Though HEW refused to accept the modified Plan, the Board adopted it anyway. But even the limited effects of this Plan in disestablishing the prior *de jure* segregated system were substantially constricted by the state legislature, which refused to fund it until Fiscal Year 1978, and even then at well under half the amount sought by the Board.

Private petitioners initiated this lawsuit in 1975. They complained that Mississippi had maintained the racially segregative effects of its prior dual system of post-secondary education in violation of the Fifth, Ninth,

Thirteenth, and Fourteenth Amendments, and Title VI of the Civil Rights Act of 1964. Shortly thereafter, the United States filed its complaint in intervention, charging that State officials had failed to satisfy their obligation under the Equal Protection Clause of the Fourteenth Amendment and Title VI to dismantle Mississippi's dual system of higher education.

After this lawsuit was filed, the parties attempted for 12 years to achieve a consensual resolution of their differences through voluntary dismantlement by the State of its prior separated system. The Board of Trustees implemented reviews of existing curricula and program "mission" at each institution. In 1981, the Board issued "Mission Statements" that identified the extant purpose of each public university. These "missions" were clustered into three categories: comprehensive, urban, and regional. "Comprehensive" universities were classified as those with the greatest existing resources and program offerings. All three such institutions (University of Mississippi, Mississippi State, and Southern Mississippi) were exclusively white under the prior *de jure* segregated system. The Board authorized each to continue offering doctoral degrees and to assert leadership in certain disciplines. Jackson State, the sole urban university, was assigned a more limited research and degree mission, with both functions geared toward its urban setting. It was exclusively black at its inception. The "regional" designation was something of a misnomer, as the Board envisioned those institutions primarily in an undergraduate role, rather than a "regional" one in the geographical sense of serving just the localities in which they were based. Only the universities classified as "regional" included institutions that, prior to desegregation, had been either exclusively white—Delta State and Mississippi University for Women—or exclusively black—Alcorn State and Mississippi Valley.

By the mid-1980's, 30 years after *Brown,* more than 99 percent of Mississippi's white students were enrolled at University of Mississippi, Mississippi State, Southern Mississippi, Delta State, and Mississippi University for Women. The student bodies at these universities remained predominantly white, averaging between 80 and 91 percent white students. Seventy-one percent of the State's black students attended Jackson State, Alcorn State, and Mississippi Valley, where the racial composition ranged from 92 to 99 percent black.

II

By 1987, the parties concluded that they could not agree on whether the State had taken the requisite affirmative steps to dismantle its prior *de jure* segregated system. They proceeded to trial. Both sides presented voluminous evidence on a full range of educational issues spanning admissions standards, faculty and administrative staff recruitment, program duplication, on-campus discrimination, institutional funding disparities, and satellite campuses. Petitioners argued that in various ways the State continued to reinforce historic, race-based distinctions among the universities. Respondents argued generally that the State had fulfilled its duty to disestablish its state-imposed segregative system by implementing and maintaining good-faith, nondiscriminatory race-neutral policies and practices in student admission, faculty hiring, and operations. Moreover, they suggested, the State had attracted significant numbers of qualified black students to those universities composed mostly of white persons. Respondents averred that the mere continued existence of racially identifiable universities was not unlawful given the freedom of students to choose which institution to attend and the varying objectives and features of the State's universities.

At trials' end, based on the testimony of 71 witnesses and 56,700 pages of exhibits, the District Court entered extensive findings of fact. The court first offered a historical overview of the higher education institutions in Mississippi and the developments in the system between 1954 and the filing of this suit in 1975. It then made specific findings recounting post-1975 developments, including a description at the time of trial, in those areas of the higher education system under attack by plaintiffs: admission requirements and recruitment; institutional classification and assignment of missions; duplication of programs; facilities and finance; the land grant institutions; faculty and staff; and governance.

The court's conclusions of law followed. As an overview, the court outlined the common ground in the case: "Where a state has previously maintained a racially dual system of public education established by law, it assumes an 'affirmative duty' to reform those policies and practices which required or contributed to the separation of the races.". . . [T]he court stated: "While student enrollment and faculty and staff hiring patterns are to be examined, greater emphasis should instead be placed on current state higher education policies and practices in order to insure that such policies and practices are racially neutral, developed and implemented in good faith, and do not substantially contribute to the continued racial identifiability of individual institutions."

When it addressed the same aspects of the university system covered by the fact-findings in light of the foregoing standard, the court found no violation of federal law in any of them. "In summary, the court finds that current actions on the part of the defendants demonstrate conclusively that the defendants are fulfilling their affirmative duty to disestablish the former *de jure* segregated system of higher education."

The Court of Appeals reheard the case en banc and affirmed the decision of the District Court. With a single exception, it did not disturb the District Court's findings of fact or conclusions of law. . . .

III

The District Court, the Court of Appeals, and respondents recognize and acknowledge that the State of Mississippi had the constitutional duty to dismantle the dual school system that its laws once mandated. Nor is there any dispute that this obligation applies to its higher education system. If the State has not discharged this duty, it remains in violation of the Fourteenth Amendment. *Brown* v. *Board of Education* and its progeny clearly mandate this observation. Thus, the primary issue in this case is whether the State has met its affirmative duty to dismantle its prior dual university system. . . .

Like the United States, we do not disagree with the Court of Appeals' observation that a state university system is quite different in very relevant respects from primary and secondary schools. Unlike attendance at the lower level schools, a student's decision to seek higher education has been a matter of choice. The State historically has not assigned university students to a particular institution. . . .

We do not agree with the Court of Appeals or the District Court, however, that the adoption and implementation of race-neutral policies alone suffice to demonstrate that the State has completely abandoned its prior dual system. That college attendance is by choice and not by assignment does not mean that a race-neutral admissions policy cures the constitutional violation of a dual system. In a system based on choice, student attendance is determined not simply by admissions policies, but also by many other factors. Although some of these factors clearly cannot be attributed to State policies, many can be. Thus, even after a State dismantles its segregative *admissions* policy, there may still be state action that is traceable to the State's prior *de jure* segregation and that continues to foster segregation. . . . If policies traceable to the *de jure* system are still in force and have discriminatory effects, those policies too must be reformed to the extent practicable and consistent with sound educational practices. We also disagree with respondents that the Court of Appeals and District Court properly relied on our decision in *Bazemore* v. *Friday* (1986). *Bazemore* neither requires nor justifies the conclusions reached by the two courts below.

Bazemore raised the issue whether the financing and operational assistance provided by a state university's extension service to voluntary 4-H and Homemaker Clubs was inconsistent with the Equal Protection Clause because of the existence of numerous all-white and all-black clubs. Though prior to 1965 the clubs were supported on a segregated basis, the District Court had found that the policy of segregation had been completely abandoned and that no evidence existed of any lingering discrimination in either services or membership; any racial imbalance resulted from the wholly voluntary and unfettered choice of private individuals. In this context, we held inapplicable the *Green* [v. *New Kent County School Bd.,* 1968] Court's judgment that a voluntary choice program was insufficient to dismantle a *de jure* dual system in public primary and secondary schools, but only after satisfying ourselves that the State had not fostered segregation by playing a part in the decision of which club an individual chose to join.

Bazemore plainly does not excuse inquiry into whether Mississippi has left in place certain aspects of its prior dual system that perpetuate the racially segregated higher education system. If the State perpetuates policies and practices traceable to its prior system that continue to have segregative effects—whether by influencing student enrollment decisions or by fostering segregation in other facets of the university system—and such policies are without sound educational justification and can be practicably eliminated, the State has not satisfied its burden of proving that it has dismantled its prior system. Such policies run afoul of the Equal Protection Clause, even though the State has abolished the legal requirement that whites and blacks be educated separately and has established racially neutral policies not animated by a discriminatory purpose. Because the standard applied by the District Court did not make these inquiries, we hold that the Court of Appeals erred in affirming the District Court's ruling that the State had brought itself into compliance with the Equal Protection Clause in the operation of its higher education system.

IV

Had the Court of Appeals applied the correct legal standard, it would have been apparent from the undisturbed factual findings of the District Court that there are several surviving aspects of Mississippi's prior dual system which are constitutionally suspect; for even though such policies may be race-neutral on their face, they substantially restrict a person's choice of which institution to enter and they contribute to the racial identifiability of the eight public universities. Mississippi must justify these policies or eliminate them.

It is important to state at the outset that we make no effort to identify an exclusive list of unconstitutional remnants of Mississippi's *de jure* system. . . . With this caveat in mind, we address four policies of the present system: admission standards, program duplication, institutional mission assignments, and continued operation of all eight public universities.

We deal first with the current admissions policies of Mississippi's public universities. As the District Court found, the three flagship historically white universities in the system—University of Mississippi,

Mississippi State University, and University of Southern Mississippi—enacted policies in 1963 requiring all entrants to achieve a minimum composite score of 15 on the American College Testing Program (ACT). The court described the "discriminatory taint" of this policy, an obvious reference to the fact that, at the time, the average ACT score for white students was 18 and the average for blacks was 7. The District Court concluded, and the en banc Court of Appeals agreed, that present admissions standards derived from policies enacted in the 1970's to redress the problem of student unpreparedness. Obviously, this mid-passage justification for perpetuating a policy enacted originally to discriminate against black students does not make the present admissions standards any less constitutionally suspect.

The present admission standards are not only traceable to the *de jure* system and were originally adopted for a discriminatory purpose, but they also have present discriminatory effects. Every Mississippi resident under 21 seeking admission to the university system must take the ACT. Any applicant who scores at least 15 qualifies for automatic admission to any of the five historically white institutions except Mississippi University for Women, which requires a score of 18 for automatic admission unless the student has a 3.0 high school grade average. Those scoring less than 15 but at least 13 automatically qualify to enter Jackson State University, Alcorn State University, and Mississippi Valley State University. Without doubt, these requirements restrict the range of choices of entering students as to which institution they may attend in a way that perpetuates segregation. . . .

The segregative effect of this automatic entrance standard is especially striking in light of the differences in minimum automatic entrance scores among the regional universities in Mississippi's system. The minimum score for automatic admission to Mississippi University for Women (MUW) is 18; it is 13 for the historically black universities. Yet MUW is assigned the same institutional mission as two other regional universities, Alcorn State and Mississippi Valley—that of providing quality undergraduate education. The effects of the policy fall disproportionately on black students who might wish to attend MUW; and though the disparate impact is not as great, the same is true of the minimum standard ACT score of 15 at Delta State University—the other "regional" university—as compared to the historically black "regional" universities where a score of 13 suffices for automatic admission. The courts below made little if any effort to justify in educational terms those particular disparities in entrance requirements or to inquire whether it was practicable to eliminate them.

We also find inadequately justified by the courts below or by the record before us the differential admissions requirements between universities with dissimilar programmatic missions. We do not suggest that absent a discriminatory purpose different programmatic missions accompanied by different admissions standards would be constitutionally suspect simply because one or more schools are racially identifiable. But here the differential admission standards are remnants of the dual system with a continuing discriminatory effect, and the mission assignments "to some degree follow the historical racial assignments." Moreover, the District Court did not justify the differing admission standards based on the different mission assignments. It observed only that in the 1970's, the Board of Trustees justified a minimum ACT score of 15 because too many students with lower scores were not prepared for the historically white institutions and that imposing the 15 score requirement on admissions to the historically black institutions would decimate attendance at those universities. The District Court also stated that the mission of the regional universities had the more modest function of providing quality undergraduate education. Certainly the comprehensive universities are also, among other things, educating undergraduates. But we think the 15 ACT test score for automatic admission to the comprehensive universities, as compared with a score of 13 for the regionals, requires further justification in terms of sound educational policy.

Another constitutionally problematic aspect of the State's use of the ACT test scores is its policy of denying automatic admission if an applicant fails to earn the minimum ACT score specified for the particular institution, without also resorting to the applicant's high school grades as an additional factor in predicting college performance. The United States produced evidence that the American College Testing Program (ATCP), the administering organization of the ACT, discourages use of ACT scores as the sole admissions criterion on the ground that it gives an incomplete "picture" of the student applicant's ability to perform adequately in college. . . . The record also indicated that the disparity between black and white students' high school grade averages was much narrower than the gap between their average ACT scores, thereby suggesting that an admissions formula which included grades would increase the number of black students eligible for automatic admission to all of Mississippi's public universities. . . .

A second aspect of the present system that necessitates further inquiry is the widespread duplication of programs. "Unnecessary" duplication refers, under the District Court's definition, "to those instances where two or more institutions offer the same nonessential or noncore program. Under this definition, all duplication at the bachelor's level of nonbasic liberal arts and sciences course work and all duplication at the master's level and above are considered to be unnecessary." The District Court found that 34.6 percent of the 29 undergraduate programs at historically black institutions are "unnecessarily duplicated" by the historically white universities, and that 90 percent of the graduate programs at the historically black institutions are unnecessarily duplicated at the historically white institutions. In its conclusions of law on this point, the District Court nevertheless determined that "there is no proof" that such duplication "is directly associated with the racial identifiability of institutions," and that "there is no proof that the elimination of unnecessary program duplication would be justifiable from an educational standpoint or that its elimination would have a substantial effect on student choice."

The District Court's treatment of this issue is problematic from several different perspectives. First, the court appeared to impose the burden of proof on the plaintiffs to meet a legal standard the court itself acknowledged was not yet formulated. It can hardly be denied that such duplication was part and parcel of the prior dual system of higher education—the whole notion of "separate but equal" required duplicative programs in two sets of schools—and that the present unnecessary duplication is a continuation of that practice. *Brown* and its progeny, however, established that the burden of proof falls on the *State,* and not the aggrieved plaintiffs, to establish that it has dismantled its prior *de jure* segregated system. The court's holding that petitioners could not establish the constitutional defect of unnecessary duplication, therefore, improperly shifted the burden away from the State. Second, implicit in the District Court's finding of "unnecessary" duplication is the absence of any educational justification and the fact that some if not all duplication may be practicably eliminated. Indeed, the District Court observed that such duplication "cannot be justified economically or in terms of providing quality education." Yet by stating that "there is no proof" that elimination of unnecessary duplication would decrease institutional racial identifiability, affect student choice, and promote educationally sound policies, the court did not make clear whether it had directed the parties to develop evidence on these points, and if so, what that evidence revealed. Finally, by treating this issue in isolation, the court failed to consider the combined effects of unnecessary program duplication with other policies, such as differential admissions standards, in evaluating whether the State had met its duty to dismantle its prior *de jure* segregated system.

We next address Mississippi's scheme of institutional mission classification, and whether it perpetuates the State's formerly *de jure* dual system. The District Court found that, throughout the period of *de jure* segregation, University of Mississippi, Mississippi State University, and University of Southern Mississippi were the flagship institutions in the state system. They received the most funds, initiated the most advanced and specialized programs, and developed the widest range of curricular functions. At their inception, each was restricted for the education solely of white persons. The missions of Mississippi University for Women and Delta State University (DSU), by contrast, were more limited than their other all-white counterparts during the period of legalized segregation. MUW and DSU were each established to provide undergraduate education solely for white students in the liberal arts and such other fields as music, art, education, and home economics. When they were founded, the three exclusively black universities were more limited in their assigned academic missions than the five all-white institutions. Alcorn State, for example, was designated to serve as "an agricultural college for the education of Mississippi's black youth.". . . .

In 1981, the State assigned certain missions to Mississippi's public universities as they then existed. It classified University of Mississippi, Mississippi State, and Southern Mississippi as "comprehensive" universities having the most varied programs and offering graduate degrees. Two of the historically white institutions, Delta State University and Mississippi University for Women, along with two of the historically black institutions, Alcorn State University and Mississippi Valley State University, were designated as "regional" universities with more limited programs and devoted primarily to undergraduate education. Jackson State University was classified as an "urban" university whose mission was defined by its urban location.

The institutional mission designations adopted in 1981 have as their antecedents the policies enacted to perpetuate racial separation during the *de jure* segregated regime. . . . That different missions are assigned to the universities surely limits to some extent an entering student's choice as to which university to seek admittance. . . . We do not suggest that absent discriminatory purpose the assignment of different missions to various institutions in a State's higher education system would raise an equal protection issue where one or more of the institutions become or remain predominantly black or white. But here the issue is whether the State has sufficiently dismantled its prior dual system; and when combined with the differential admission practices and unnecessary program duplication, it is likely that the mission designations interfere with student choice and tend to perpetuate the segregated system. On remand, the court should inquire whether it would be practicable and consistent with sound educational practices to eliminate any such discriminatory effects of the State's present policy of mission assignments.

Fourth, the State attempted to bring itself into compliance with the Constitution by continuing to maintain and operate all eight higher educational institutions. The existence of eight instead of some lesser number was undoubtedly occasioned by State laws forbidding the mingling of the races. And as the District Court recognized, continuing to maintain all eight universities in Mississippi is wasteful and irrational. The District Court pointed especially to the facts that Delta State and Mississippi Valley are only 35 miles apart and that only 20 miles separate Mississippi State and Mississippi University for Women. It was evident to the District Court that "the defendants undertake to fund more institutions of higher learning than are justified by the amount of financial resources available to the state," but the court concluded that such fiscal irresponsibility was a policy choice of the legislature rather than a feature of a system subject to constitutional scrutiny.

Unquestionably, a larger rather than a smaller number of institutions from which to choose in itself makes for different choices, particularly when examined in the light of other factors present in the operation of the system, such as admissions, program duplication, and institutional mission designations. Though certainly closure of one or more institutions would decrease the discriminatory effects of the present system, based on the present record we are unable to say whether such action is constitutionally required. Elimination of program duplication and revision of admissions criteria may make institutional closure unnecessary. However, on remand this issue should be carefully explored by inquiring and determining whether retention of all eight institutions itself affects student choice and perpetuates the segregated higher education system, whether maintenance of each of the universities is educationally justifiable, and whether one or more of them can be practicably closed or merged with other existing institutions.

Because the former *de jure* segregated system of public universities in Mississippi impeded the free choice of prospective students, the State in dismantling that system must take the necessary steps to ensure that this choice now is truly free. The full range of policies and practices must be examined with this duty in mind. That an institution is predominantly white or black does not in itself make out a constitutional violation. But surely the State may not leave in place policies rooted in its prior officially-segregated system that serve to maintain the racial identifiability of its universities if those policies can practicably be eliminated without eroding sound educational policies. . . .

Because the District Court and the Court of Appeals failed to reconsider the State's duties in their proper light, the cases must be remanded. To the extent that the State has not met its affirmative obligation to dismantle its prior dual system, it shall be adjudged in violation of the Constitution and Title VI and remedial proceedings shall be conducted. The decision of the Court of Appeals is vacated, and the cases are remanded for further proceedings consistent with this opinion.

It is so ordered.

No. 91-453

David H. Lucas, Petitioner v. South Carolina Coastal Council

On writ of certiorari to the Supreme Court of South Carolina

[June 29, 1992]

JUSTICE SCALIA delivered the opinion of the Court.

[I and II omitted]
III

A

Prior to Justice Holmes' exposition in *Pennsylvania Coal Co.* v. *Mahon* (1922), it was generally thought that the Takings Clause reached only a "direct appropriation" of property or the functional equivalent of a "practical ouster of [the owner's] possession." Justice Holmes recognized in *Mahon*, however, that if the protection against physical appropriations of private property was to be meaningfully enforced, the government's power to redefine the range of interests included in the ownership of property was necessarily constrained by constitutional limits. If, instead, the uses of private property were subject to unbridled, uncompensated qualification under the police power, "the natural tendency of human nature [would be] to extend the qualification more and more until at last private property disappear[ed]." These considerations gave birth in that case to the oft-cited maxim that, "while property may be regulated to a certain extent, if regulation goes too far it will be recognized as a taking."

Nevertheless, our decision in *Mahon* offered little insight into when, and under what circumstances, a given regulation would be seen as going "too far" for purposes of the Fifth Amendment. . . . We have, however, described at least two discrete categories of regulatory action as compensable without case-specific inquiry into the public interest advanced in support of the restraint. The first encompasses regulations that compel the property owner to suffer a physical "invasion" of his property. In general (at least with regard to permanent invasions), no matter how minute the intrusion, and no matter how weighty the public purpose behind it, we have required compensation. . . .

The second situation in which we have found categorical treatment appropriate is where regulation denies all economically beneficial or productive use of land. As we have said on numerous occasions, the Fifth Amendment is violated when land-use regulation "does not substantially advance legitimate state interests *or denies an owner economically viable use of his land.*" . . .

We think . . . that there are good reasons for our frequently expressed belief that when the owner of real property has been called upon to sacrifice *all* economically beneficial uses in the name of the common good, that is, to leave his property economically idle, he has suffered a taking.

B

The trial court found Lucas's two beachfront lots to have been rendered valueless by respondent's enforcement of the coastal-zone construction ban. Under Lucas's theory of the case, which rested upon our "no economically viable use" statements, that finding entitled him to compensation. . . . The South Carolina Supreme Court, however, thought otherwise. In its view, the Beachfront Management Act was no ordinary enactment, but involved an exercise of South Carolina's "police powers" to mitigate the harm to the public interest that petitioner's use of his land might occasion. . . .

It is correct that many of our prior opinions have suggested that "harmful or noxious uses" of property may be proscribed by government regulation without the requirement of compensation. For a number of reasons, however, we think the South Carolina Supreme Court was too quick to conclude that that principle decides the present case. The "harmful or noxious uses" principle was the Court's early attempt to describe in theoretical terms why government may, consistent with the Takings Clause, affect property values by regulation without incurring an obligation to compensate—a reality we nowadays acknowledge explicitly with respect to the full scope of the State's police power. . . . "Harmful or noxious use" analysis was, in other words, simply the progenitor of our more contemporary statements that "land-use regulation does not effect a taking if it 'substantially advance[s] legitimate state interests'. . . ."

The transition from our early focus on control of "noxious" uses to our contemporary understanding of the broad realm within which government may regulate without compensation was an easy one, since the distinction between "harm-preventing" and "benefit-conferring" regulation is often in the eye of the beholder. It is quite possible, for example, to describe in *either* fashion the ecological, economic, and aesthetic concerns that inspired the South Carolina legislature in the present case. One could say that imposing a servitude on Lucas's land is necessary in order to prevent his use of it from "harming" South Carolina's ecological resources; or, instead, in order to achieve the "benefits" of an ecological preserve. . . . Whether Lucas's construction of single-family residences on his parcels should be described as bringing "harm" to South Carolina's adjacent ecological resources thus depends principally upon whether the describer believes that the State's use interest in nurturing those resources is so important that *any* competing adjacent use must yield.

When it is understood that "prevention of harmful use" was merely our early formulation of the police power justification necessary to sustain (without compensation) *any* regulatory diminution in value; and that the distinction between regulation that "prevents harmful use" and that which "confers benefits" is difficult, if not impossible, to discern on an objective, value-free basis; it becomes self-evident that noxious-use logic cannot serve as a touchstone to distinguish regulatory "takings"—which require compensation—from regulatory deprivations that do not require compensation. *A fortiori* the legislature's recitation of a noxious-use justification cannot be the basis for departing from our categorical rule that total regulatory takings must be compensated. If it were, departure would virtually always be allowed. . . .

Where the State seeks to sustain regulation that deprives land of all economically beneficial use, we think it may resist compensation only if the logically antecedent inquiry into the nature of the owner's estate shows that the proscribed use interests were not part of his title to begin with. This accords, we think, with our "takings" jurisprudence, which has traditionally been guided by the understandings of our citizens regarding the content of, and the State's power over, the "bundle of rights" that they acquire when they obtain title to property. It seems to us that the property owner necessarily expects the uses of his property to be restricted, from time to time, by various measures newly enacted by the State in legitimate exercise of its police powers; "[a]s long recognized, some values are enjoyed under an implied limitation and must yield to the police power." And in the case of personal property, by reason of the State's traditionally high degree of control over commercial dealings, he ought to be aware of the possibility that new regulation might even render his property economically worthless (at least if the property's only economically productive use is sale or manufacture for sale). In the case of land, however, we think the notion pressed by the Council that title is somehow held subject to the "implied limitation" that the State may subsequently eliminate all economically valuable use is inconsistent with the historical compact recorded in the Takings Clause that has become part of our constitutional culture.

Where "permanent physical occupation" of land is concerned, we have refused to allow the government to decree it anew (without compensation), no matter how weighty the asserted "public interests" involved. . . . We believe similar treatment must be accorded confiscatory regulations, *i.e.,* regulations that prohibit all economically beneficial use of land: Any limitation so severe cannot be newly legislated or decreed (without compensation), but must inhere in the title itself, in the restrictions that background principles of the State's law of property and nuisance already place upon land ownership. A law or decree with such an effect must, in other words, do no more than duplicate the result that could have been achieved in the courts—by adjacent landowners (or other uniquely affected persons) under the State's law of private nuisance, or by the State under its complementary power to abate nuisances that affect the public generally, or otherwise.

On this analysis, the owner of a lake bed, for example, would not be entitled to compensation when he is denied the requisite permit to engage in a landfilling operation that would have the effect of flooding others' land. Nor the corporate owner of a nuclear generating plant, when it is directed to remove all improvements from its land upon discovery that the plant sits astride an earthquake fault. Such regulatory action may well have the effect of eliminating the land's only economically productive use, but it does not proscribe a productive use that was previously permissible under relevant property and nuisance principles. The use of these properties for what are now expressly prohibited purposes was *always* unlawful, and (subject to other constitutional limitations) it was open to the State at any point to make the implication of those background principles of nuisance and property law explicit.... When, however, a regulation that declares "off-limits" all economically productive or beneficial uses of land goes beyond what the relevant background principles would dictate, compensation must be paid to sustain it.

The "total taking" inquiry we require today will ordinarily entail (as the application of state nuisance law ordinarily entails) analysis of, among other things, the degree of harm to public lands and resources, or adjacent private property, posed by the claimant's proposed activities, the social value of the claimant's activities and their suitability to the locality in question, and the relative ease with which the alleged harm can be avoided through measures taken by the claimant and the government (or adjacent private landowners) alike. The fact that a particular use has long been engaged in by similarly situated owners ordinarily imports a lack of any common-law prohibition (though changed circumstances or new knowledge may make what was previously permissible no longer so). So also does the fact that other landowners, similarly situated, are permitted to continue the use denied to the claimant.

It seems unlikely that common-law principles would have prevented the erection of any habitable or productive improvements on petitioner's land; they rarely support prohibition of the "essential use" of land. The question, however, is one of state law to be dealt with on remand. We emphasize that to win its case South Carolina must do more than proffer the legislature's declaration that the uses Lucas desires are inconsistent with the public interest, or the conclusory assertion that they violate a common-law maxim.... As we have said, a "State, by *ipse dixit,* may not transform private property into public property without compensation. . . ." Instead, as it would be required to do if it sought to restrain Lucas in a common-law action for public nuisance, South Carolina must identify background principles of nuisance and property law that prohibit the uses he now intends in the circumstances in which the property is presently found. Only on this showing can the State fairly claim that, in proscribing all such beneficial uses, the Beachfront Management Act is taking nothing.

The judgment is reversed and the cause remanded for proceedings not inconsistent with this opinion.

So ordered.

□□□

Nos. 91-744 and 91-902

Planned Parenthood of Southeastern Pennsylvania, et al., Petitioners v. Robert P. Casey, et al., etc.

Robert P. Casey, et al., etc., Petitioners v. Planned Parenthood of Southeastern Pennsylvania, et al.

On writs of certiorari to the United States Court of Appeals for the Third Circuit

[June 29, 1992]

JUSTICE O'CONNOR, JUSTICE KENNEDY, and JUSTICE SOUTER announced the judgment of the Court [JUSTICE STEVENS joins, concurring in part and dissenting in part]. . . .

I

Liberty finds no refuge in a jurisprudence of doubt. Yet 19 years after our holding that the Constitution protects a woman's right to terminate her pregnancy in its early stages, *Roe* v. *Wade* (1973), that definition of liberty is still questioned. Joining the respondents as *amicus curiae*, the United States, as it has done in five other cases in the last decade, again asks us to overrule *Roe*. . . .

. . . And at oral argument in this Court, the attorney for the parties challenging the statute took the position that none of the enactments can be upheld without overruling *Roe* v. *Wade*. We disagree with that analysis; but we acknowledge that our decisions after *Roe* cast doubt upon the meaning and reach of its holding. Further, the Chief Justice admits that he would overrule the central holding of *Roe* and adopt the rational relationship test as the sole criterion of constitutionality. State and federal courts as well as legislatures throughout the Union must have guidance as they seek to address this subject in conformance with the Constitution. Given these premises, we find it imperative to review once more the principles that define the rights of the woman and the legitimate authority of the State respecting the termination of pregnancies by abortion procedures.

After considering the fundamental constitutional questions resolved by *Roe,* principles of institutional integrity, and the rule of *stare decisis,* we are led to conclude this: the essential holding of *Roe* v. *Wade* should be retained and once again reaffirmed.

It must be stated at the outset and with clarity that *Roe*'s essential holding, the holding we reaffirm, has three parts. First is a recognition of the right of the woman to choose to have an abortion before viability and to obtain it without undue interference from the State. Before viability, the State's interests are not strong enough to support a prohibition of abortion or the imposition of a substantial obstacle to the woman's effective right to elect the procedure. Second is a confirmation of the State's power to restrict abortions after fetal viability, if the law contains exceptions for pregnancies which endanger a woman's life or health. And third is the principle that the State has legitimate interests from the outset of the pregnancy in protecting the health of the woman and the life of the fetus that may become a child. These principles do not contradict one another; and we adhere to each.

II

... Men and women of good conscience can disagree, and we suppose some always shall disagree, about the profound moral and spiritual implications of terminating a pregnancy, even in its earliest stage. Some of us as individuals find abortion offensive to our most basic principles of morality, but that cannot control our decision. Our obligation is to define the liberty of all, not to mandate our own moral code. The underlying constitutional issue is whether the State can resolve these philosophic questions in such a definitive way that a woman lacks all choice in the matter, except perhaps in those rare circumstances in which the pregnancy is itself a danger to her own life or health, or is the result of rape or incest.

It is conventional constitutional doctrine that where reasonable people disagree the government can adopt one position or the other. That theorem, however, assumes a state of affairs in which the choice does not intrude upon a protected liberty. Thus, while some people might disagree about whether or not the flag should be saluted, or disagree about the proposition that it may not be defiled, we have ruled that a State may not compel or enforce one view or the other.

Our law affords constitutional protection to personal decisions relating to marriage, procreation, contraception, family relationships, child rearing, and education. . . . These matters, involving the most intimate and personal choices a person may make in a lifetime, choices central to personal dignity and autonomy, are central to the liberty protected by the Fourteenth Amendment. At the heart of liberty is the right to define one's own concept of existence, of meaning, of the universe, and of the mystery of human life. Beliefs about these matters could not define the attributes of personhood were they formed under compulsion of the State.

These considerations begin our analysis of the woman's interest in terminating her pregnancy but cannot end it, for this reason: though the abortion decision may originate within the zone of conscience and belief, it is more than a philosophic exercise. Abortion is a unique act. It is an act fraught with consequences for others: for the woman who must live with the implications of her decision, for the persons who perform and assist in the procedure; for the spouse, family, and society which must confront the knowledge that these procedures exist, procedures some deem nothing short of an act of violence against innocent human life; and, depending on one's beliefs, for the life or potential life that is aborted. Though abortion is conduct, it does not follow that the State is entitled to proscribe it in all instances. That is because the liberty of the woman is at stake in a sense unique to the human condition and so unique to the law. The mother who carries a child to full term is subject to anxieties, to physical constraints, to pain that only she must bear. That these sacrifices have from the beginning of the human race been endured by woman with a pride that ennobles her in the eyes of others and gives to the infant a bond of love cannot alone be grounds for the State to insist she make the sacrifice. Her suffering is too intimate and personal for the State to insist, without more, upon its own vision of the woman's role, however dominant that vision has been in the course of our history and our culture. The destiny of the woman must be shaped to a large extent on her conception of her spiritual imperatives and her place in society.

It should be recognized, moreover, that in some critical respects the abortion decision is of the same character as the decision to use contraception, to which *Griswold* v. *Connecticut, Eisenstadt* v. *Baird,* and *Carey* v. *Population Services International,* afford constitutional protection. We have no doubt as to the correctness of those decisions. They support the reasoning in *Roe* relating to the woman's liberty because they involve personal decisions concerning not only the meaning of procreation but also human responsibility and respect for it. . . .

It was this dimension of personal liberty that *Roe* sought to protect, and its holding invoked the reasoning and the tradition of the precedents we have discussed, granting protection to substantive liberties of the person. *Roe* was, of course, an extension of those cases and, as the decision itself indicated, the separate States could act in some degree to further their own legitimate interests in protecting pre-natal life. The extent to which the legislatures of the States might act to outweigh the interests of the woman in choosing to terminate her pregnancy was a subject of debate both in *Roe* itself and in decisions following it.

While we appreciate the weight of the arguments made on behalf of the State in the case before us, arguments which in their ultimate formulation conclude that *Roe* should be overruled, the reservations any of us may have in reaffirming the central holding of *Roe* are outweighed by the explication of individual liberty we have given combined with the force of *stare decisis*. We turn now to that doctrine.

III

A

The obligation to follow precedent begins with necessity, and a contrary necessity marks its outer limit. With Cardozo, we recognize that no judicial system could do society's work if it eyed each issue afresh in every case that raised it. See B. Cardozo, The Nature of the Judicial Process (1921). Indeed, the very concept of the rule of law underlying our own Constitution requires such continuity over time that a respect for precedent is, by definition, indispensable. At the other extreme, a different necessity would make itself felt if a prior judicial ruling should come to be seen so clearly as error that its enforcement was for that very reason doomed. . . .

So in this case we may inquire whether *Roe*'s central rule has been found unworkable; whether the rule's limitation on state power could be removed without serious inequity to those who have relied upon it or significant damage to the stability of the society governed by the rule in question; whether the law's growth in the intervening years has left *Roe*'s central rule a doctrinal anachronism discounted by society; and whether *Roe*'s premises of fact have so far changed in the ensuing two decades as to render its central holding somehow irrelevant or unjustifiable in dealing with the issue it addressed.

1

Although *Roe* has engendered opposition, it has in no sense proven "unworkable," representing as it does a simple limitation beyond which a state law is unenforceable. While *Roe* has, of course, required judicial assessment of state laws affecting the exercise of the choice guaranteed against government infringement, and although the need for such review will remain as a consequence of today's decision, the required determinations fall within judicial competence.

2

The inquiry into reliance counts the cost of a rule's repudiation as it would fall on those who have relied reasonably on the rule's continued application. Since the classic case for weighing reliance heavily in favor of following the earlier rule occurs in the commercial context, where advance planning of great precision is most obviously a necessity, it is no cause for surprise that some would find no reliance worthy of consideration in support of *Roe*.

While neither respondents nor their *amici* in so many words deny that the abortion right invites some reliance prior to its actual exercise, one can readily imagine an argument stressing the dissimilarity of this case to one involving property or contract. Abortion is customarily chosen as an unplanned response to the consequence of unplanned activity or to the failure of conventional birth control, and except on the assumption that no intercourse would have occurred but for *Roe*'s holding, such behavior may appear to justify no reliance claim. Even if reliance could be claimed on that unrealistic assumption, the argument might run, any reliance interest would be *de minimis*. This argument would be premised on the hypothesis that reproductive planning could take virtually immediate account of any sudden restoration of state authority to ban abortions.

To eliminate the issue of reliance that easily, however, one would need to limit cognizable reliance to specific instances of sexual activity. But to do this would be simply to refuse to face the fact that for two decades of economic and social developments, people have organized intimate relationships and made choices that define their views of themselves and their places in society, in reliance on the availability of abortion in the event that contraception should fail. The ability of women to participate equally in the economic and social life of the Nation has been facilitated by their ability to control their reproductive lives. The Constitution serves human values, and while the effect of reliance on *Roe* cannot be exactly measured, neither can the certain cost of overruling *Roe* for people who have ordered their thinking and living around that case be dismissed.

3

No evolution of legal principle has left *Roe*'s doctrinal footings weaker than they were in 1973. No development of constitutional law since the case was decided has implicitly or explicitly left *Roe* behind as a mere survivor of obsolete constitutional thinking.

It will be recognized, of course, that *Roe* stands at an intersection of two lines of decisions, but in whichever doctrinal category one reads the case, the result for present purposes will be the same. The *Roe* Court itself placed its holding in the succession of cases most prominently exemplified by *Griswold* v. *Connecticut* (1965). When it is so seen, *Roe* is clearly in no jeopardy, since subsequent constitutional developments have neither disturbed, nor do they threaten to diminish, the scope of recognized protection accorded to the liberty relating to intimate relationships, the family, and decisions about whether or not to beget or bear a child.

Roe, however, may be seen not only as an exemplar of *Griswold* liberty but as a rule (whether or not mistaken) of personal autonomy and bodily integrity, with doctrinal affinity to cases recognizing limits on governmental power to mandate medical treatment or to bar its rejection. If so, our cases since *Roe* accord with *Roe's* view that a State's interest in the protection of life falls short of justifying any plenary override of individual liberty claims.

Finally, one could classify *Roe* as *sui generis*. If the case is so viewed, then there clearly has been no erosion of its central determination. The original holding resting on the concurrence of seven Members of the Court in 1973 was expressly affirmed by a majority of six in 1983, see *Akron* v. *Akron Center for Reproductive Health, Inc.* (1983) *(Akron I)*, and by a majority of five in 1986, see *Thornburgh* v. *American College of Obstetricians and Gynecologists* (1986), expressing adherence to the constitutional ruling despite legislative efforts in some States to test its limits. More recently, in *Webster* v. *Reproductive Health Services* (1989), although two of the present authors questioned the trimester framework in a way consistent with our judgment today, a majority of the Court either decided to reaffirm or declined to address the constitutional validity of the central holding of *Roe*. . . .

4

We have seen how time has overtaken some of *Roe's* factual assumptions: advances in maternal health care allow for abortions safe to the mother later in pregnancy than was true in 1973, and advances in neonatal care have advanced viability to a point somewhat earlier. But these facts go only to the scheme of time limits on the realization of competing interests, and the divergences from the factual premises of 1973 have no bearing on the validity of *Roe's* central holding, that viability marks the earliest point at which the State's interest in fetal life is constitutionally adequate to justify a legislative ban on nontherapeutic abortions. The soundness or unsoundness of that constitutional judgment in no sense turns on whether viability occurs at approximately 28 weeks, as was usual at the time of *Roe*, at 23 to 24 weeks, as it sometimes does today, or at some moment even slightly earlier in pregnancy, as it may if fetal respiratory capacity can somehow be enhanced in the future. Whenever it may occur, the attainment of viability may continue to serve as the critical fact, just as it has done since *Roe* was decided; which is to say that no change in *Roe*'s factual underpinning has left its central holding obsolete, and none supports an argument for overruling it.

5

The sum of the precedential inquiry to this point shows *Roe*'s underpinnings unweakened in any way affecting its central holding. While it has engendered disapproval, it has not been unworkable. An entire generation has come of age free to assume *Roe*'s concept of liberty in defining the capacity of women to act in society, and to make reproductive decisions; no erosion of principle going to liberty or personal autonomy has left *Roe*'s central holding a doctrinal remnant; *Roe* portends no developments at odds with other precedent for the analysis of personal liberty; and no changes of fact have rendered viability more or less appropriate as the point at which the balance of interests tips. Within the bounds of normal *stare decisis* analysis, then, and subject to the considerations on which it customarily turns, the stronger argument is for affirming *Roe*'s central holding, with whatever degree of personal reluctance any of us may have, for not overruling it.

B

In a less significant case, *stare decisis* analysis could, and would, stop at the point we have reached. . . .

C

. . . Our analysis would not be complete, however, without explaining why overruling *Roe*'s central holding would not only reach an unjustifiable result under principles of *stare decisis,* but would seriously weaken the Court's capacity to exercise the judicial power and to function as the Supreme Court of a Nation dedicated to the rule of law. To understand why this would be so it is necessary to understand the source of this Court's authority, the conditions necessary for its preservation, and its relationship to the country's understanding of itself as a constitutional Republic.

The root of American governmental power is revealed most clearly in the instance of the power conferred by the Constitution upon the Judiciary of the United States and specifically upon this Court. As Americans of each succeeding generation are rightly told, the Court cannot buy support for its decisions by spending money and, except to a minor degree, it cannot independently coerce obedience to its decrees. The Court's power lies, rather, in its legitimacy, a product of substance and perception that shows itself in the people's acceptance of the Judiciary as fit to determine what the Nation's law means and to declare what it demands.

The underlying substance of this legitimacy is of course the warrant for the Court's decisions in the Constitution and the lesser sources of legal principle on which the Court draws. That substance is expressed in the Court's opinions, and our contemporary understanding is such that a decision without principled justification would be no judicial act at all. But even when justification is furnished by apposite legal principle, something more is required. Because not every conscientious claim of principled justification will be accepted as such, the justification claimed must be beyond dispute. The Court must take care to speak and act in ways that allow people to accept its decisions on the terms the Court claims for them, as grounded truly in principle, not as compromises with social and political pressures having, as such, no bearing on the principled choices that the Court is obliged to make. Thus, the Court's legitimacy depends on making legally principled decisions under circumstances in which their principled character is sufficiently plausible to be accepted by the Nation.

The need for principled action to be perceived as such is implicated to some degree whenever this, or any other appellate court, overrules a prior case. This is not to say, of course, that this Court cannot give a perfectly satisfactory explanation in most cases. People understand that some of the Constitution's language is hard to fathom and that the Court's Justices are sometimes able to perceive significant facts or to understand principles of law that eluded their predecessors and that justify departures from existing decisions. However upsetting it may be to those most directly affected when one judicially derived rule replaces another, the country can accept some correction of error without necessarily questioning the legitimacy of the Court.

In two circumstances, however, the Court would almost certainly fail to receive the benefit of the doubt in overruling prior cases. There is, first, a point beyond which frequent overruling would overtax the country's belief in the Court's good faith. Despite the variety of reasons that may inform and justify a decision to overrule, we cannot forget that such a decision is usually perceived (and perceived correctly) as, at the least, a statement that a prior decision was wrong. There is a limit to the amount of error that can plausibly be imputed to prior courts. If that limit should be exceeded, disturbance of prior rulings would be taken as evidence that justifiable reexamination of principle had given way to drives for particular results in the short term. The legitimacy of the Court would fade with the frequency of its vacillation.

That first circumstance can be described as hypothetical; the second is to the point here and now. Where, in the performance of its judicial duties, the Court decides a case in such a way as to resolve the sort of intensely divisive controversy reflected in *Roe* and those rare, comparable cases, its decision has a dimension that the resolution of the normal case does not carry. It is the dimension present whenever the Court's interpretation of the Constitution calls the contending sides of a national controversy to end their national division by accepting a common mandate rooted in the Constitution.

The Court is not asked to do this very often, having thus addressed the Nation only twice in our lifetime, in the decisions of *Brown* and *Roe*. But when the Court does act in this way, its decision requires an equally rare precedential force to counter the inevitable efforts to overturn it and to thwart its implementation. Some of those efforts may be mere unprincipled emotional reactions; others may proceed from principles worthy of profound respect. But whatever the premises of opposition may be, only the most convincing justification under accepted standards of precedent could suffice to demonstrate that a later decision overruling the first was anything but a surrender to political pressure, and an unjustified repudiation of the principle on which the Court staked its authority in the first instance. So to overrule under fire in the absence of the most compelling reasons to reexamine a watershed decision would subvert the Court's legitimacy beyond any serious question. . . .

The Court's duty in the present case is clear. In 1973, it confronted the already-divisive issue of governmental power to limit personal choice to undergo abortion, for which it provided a new resolution based on the due process guaranteed by the Fourteenth Amendment. Whether or not a new social consensus is developing on that issue, its divisiveness is no less today than in 1973, and pressure to overrule the decision, like pressure to retain it, has grown only more intense. A decision to overrule *Roe*'s essential holding under the existing circumstances would address error, if error there was, at the cost of both profound and unnecessary damage to the Court's legitimacy, and to the Nation's commitment to the rule of law. It is therefore imperative to adhere to the essence of *Roe*'s original decision, and we do so today.

IV

From what we have said so far it follows that it is a constitutional liberty of the woman to have some freedom to terminate her pregnancy. We conclude that the basic decision in *Roe* was based on a constitutional analysis which we cannot now repudiate. The woman's liberty is not so unlimited, however, that from the outset the State cannot show its concern for the life of the unborn, and at a later point in fetal development the State's interest in life has sufficient force so that the right of the woman to terminate the pregnancy can be restricted.

That brings us, of course, to the point where much criticism has been directed at *Roe,* a criticism that always inheres when the Court draws a specific rule from what in the Constitution is but a general standard. We conclude, however, that the urgent claims of the woman to retain the ultimate control over her destiny and her body, claims implicit in the meaning of liberty, require us to perform that function. Liberty must not be extinguished for want of a line that is clear. And it falls to us to give some real substance to the woman's liberty to determine whether to carry her pregnancy to full term.

We conclude the line should be drawn at viability, so that before that time the woman has a right to choose to terminate her pregnancy. We adhere to this principle for two reasons. First, as we have said, is the doctrine of *stare decisis.* Any judicial act of line-drawing may seem somewhat arbitrary, but *Roe* was a reasoned statement, elaborated with great care. We have twice reaffirmed it in the face of great opposition. Although we must overrule those parts of *Thornburgh* and *Akron I* which, in our view, are inconsistent with *Roe's* statement that the State has a legitimate interest in promoting the life or potential life of the unborn, the central premise of those cases represents an unbroken commitment by this Court to the essential holding of *Roe.* It is that premise which we reaffirm today.

The second reason is that the concept of viability, as we noted in *Roe,* is the time at which there is a realistic possibility of maintaining and nourishing a life outside the womb, so that the independent existence of the second life can in reason and all fairness be the object of state protection that now overrides the rights of the woman. Consistent with other constitutional norms, legislatures may draw lines which appear arbitrary without the necessity of offering a justification. But courts may not. We must justify the lines we draw. And there is no line other than viability which is more workable. To be sure, as we have said, there may be some medical developments that affect the precise point of viability, but this is an imprecision within tolerable limits given that the medical community and all those who must apply its discoveries will continue to explore the matter. The viability line also has, as a practical matter, an element of fairness. In some broad sense it might be said that a woman who fails to act before viability has consented to the State's intervention on behalf of the developing child.

The woman's right to terminate her pregnancy before viability is the most central principle of *Roe v. Wade.* It is a rule of law and a component of liberty we cannot renounce. . . .

Yet it must be remembered that *Roe v. Wade* speaks with clarity in establishing not only the woman's liberty but also the State's "important and legitimate interest in potential life." That portion of the decision in *Roe* has been given too little acknowledgement and implementation by the

Court in its subsequent cases. Those cases decided that any regulation touching upon the abortion decision must survive strict scrutiny, to be sustained only if drawn in narrow terms to further a compelling state interest. Not all of the cases decided under that formulation can be reconciled with the holding in *Roe* itself that the State has legitimate interests in the health of the woman and in protecting the potential life within her. In resolving this tension, we choose to rely upon *Roe,* as against the later cases.

Roe established a trimester framework to govern abortion regulations. Under this elaborate but rigid construct, almost no regulation at all is permitted during the first trimester of pregnancy; regulations designed to protect the woman's health, but not to further the State's interest in potential life, are permitted during the second trimester; and during the third trimester, when the fetus is viable, prohibitions are permitted provided the life or health of the mother is not at stake. Most of our cases since *Roe* have involved the application of rules derived from the trimester framework. . . .

We reject the trimester framework, which we do not consider to be part of the essential holding of *Roe*. Measures aimed at ensuring that a woman's choice contemplates the consequences for the fetus do not necessarily interfere with the right recognized in *Roe,* although those measures have been found to be inconsistent with the rigid trimester framework announced in that case. A logical reading of the central holding in *Roe* itself, and a necessary reconciliation of the liberty of the woman and the interest of the State in promoting prenatal life, require, in our view, that we abandon the trimester framework as a rigid prohibition on all previability regulation aimed at the protection of fetal life. The trimester framework suffers from these basic flaws: in its formulation it misconceives the nature of the pregnant woman's interest; and in practice it undervalues the State's interest in potential life, as recognized in *Roe*.

As our jurisprudence relating to all liberties save perhaps abortion has recognized, not every law which makes a right more difficult to exercise is *ipso facto,* an infringement of that right. An example clarifies the point. We have held that not every ballot access limitation amounts to an infringement of the right to vote. Rather, the States are granted substantial flexibility in establishing the framework within which voters choose the candidates for whom they wish to vote.

The abortion right is similar. Numerous forms of state regulation might have the incidental effect of increasing the cost or decreasing the availability of medical care, whether for abortion or any other medical procedure. The fact that a law which serves a valid purpose, one not designed to strike at the right itself, has the incidental effect of making it more difficult or more expensive to procure an abortion cannot be enough to invalidate it. Only where state regulation imposes an undue burden on a woman's ability to make this decision does the power of the State reach into the heart of the liberty protected by the Due Process Clause. . . .

The concept of an undue burden has been utilized by the Court as well as individual members of the Court, including two of us, in ways that could be considered inconsistent. Because we set forth a standard of general application to which we intend to adhere, it is important to clarify what is meant by an undue burden.

A finding of an undue burden is a shorthand for the conclusion that a state regulation has the purpose or effect of placing a substantial obstacle in the path of a woman seeking an abortion of a nonviable fetus. A statute with this purpose is invalid because the means chosen by the State to further the interest in potential life must be calculated to inform the woman's free choice, not hinder it. And a statute which, while furthering the interest in potential life or some other valid state interest, has the effect of placing a substantial obstacle in the path of a woman's choice cannot be considered a permissible means of serving its legitimate ends. To the extent that the opinions of the Court or of individual Justices use the undue burden standard in a manner that is inconsistent with this analysis, we set out what in our view should be the controlling standard. . . . Understood another way, we answer the question, left open in previous opinions discussing the undue burden formulation, whether a law designed to further the State's interest in fetal life which imposes an undue burden on the woman's decision before fetal viability could be constitutional. The answer is no.

Some guiding principles should emerge. What is at stake is the woman's right to make the ultimate decision, not a right to be insulated from all others in doing so. Regulations which do no more than create a structural mechanism by which the State, or the parent or guardian of a minor, may express profound respect for the life of the unborn are permitted, if they are not a substantial obstacle to the woman's exercise of the right to choose. Unless it has that effect on her right of choice, a state measure designed to persuade her to choose childbirth over abortion will be upheld if reasonably related to that goal. Regulations designed to foster the health of a woman seeking an abortion are valid if they do not constitute an undue burden.

Even when jurists reason from shared premises, some disagreement is inevitable. That is to be expected in the application of any legal standard which must accommodate life's complexity. We do not expect it to be otherwise with respect to the undue burden standard. We give this summary:

(a) To protect the central right recognized by *Roe* v. *Wade* while at the same time accommodating the State's profound interest in potential life, we will employ the undue burden analysis as explained in this opinion. An undue burden exists, and therefore a provision of law is invalid, if its purpose or effect is to place a substantial obstacle in the path of a woman seeking an abortion before the fetus attains viability.

(b) We reject the rigid trimester framework of *Roe* v. *Wade.* To promote the State's profound interest in potential life, throughout pregnancy the State may take measures to ensure that the woman's choice is informed, and measures designed to advance this interest will not be invalidated as long as their purpose is to persuade the woman to choose childbirth over abortion. These measures must not be an undue burden on the right.

(c) As with any medical procedure, the State may enact regulations to further the health or safety of a woman seeking an abortion. Unnecessary health regulations that have the purpose or effect of presenting a substantial obstacle to a woman seeking an abortion impose an undue burden on the right.

(d) Our adoption of the undue burden analysis does not disturb the central holding of *Roe* v. *Wade,* and we reaffirm that holding. Regardless of whether exceptions are made for particular circumstances, a State may not prohibit any woman from making the ultimate decision to terminate her pregnancy before viability.

(e) We also affirm *Roe*'s holding that "subsequent to viability, the State in promoting its interest in the potentiality of human life may, if it chooses, regulate, and even proscribe, abortion except where it is necessary, inappropriate medical judgment, for the preservation of the life or health of the mother."

These principles control our assessment of the Pennsylvania statute, and we now turn to the issue of the validity of the challenged provisions.

V

The Court of Appeals applied what it believed to be the undue burden standard and upheld each of the provisions except for the husband notification requirement. We agree generally with this conclusion, but refine the undue burden analysis in accordance with the principles articulated above. We now consider the separate statutory sections at issue. . . .

[A omitted]
B

. . . Except in a medical emergency, the statute requires that at least 24 hours before performing an abortion a physician inform the woman of the nature of the procedure, the health risks of the abortion and of childbirth, and the "probable gestational age of the unborn child."...

In *Akron I* (1983), we invalidated an ordinance which required that a woman seeking an abortion be provided by her physician with specific information "designed to influence the woman's informed choice between abortion or childbirth." As we later described the *Akron I* holding in *Thornburgh* v. *American College of Obstetricians and Gynecologists,* there were two purported flaws in the Akron ordinance: the information was designed to dissuade the woman from having an abortion and the ordinance imposed "a rigid requirement that a specific body of information be given in all cases, irrespective of the particular needs of the patient...."

To the extent *Akron I* and *Thornburgh* find a constitutional violation when the government requires, as it does here, the giving of truthful, nonmisleading information about the nature of the procedure, the attendant health risks and those of childbirth, and the "probable gestational age" of the fetus, those cases go too far, are inconsistent with *Roe*'s acknowledgment of an important interest in potential life, and are overruled....

We also see no reason why the State may not require doctors to inform a woman seeking an abortion of the availability of materials relating to the consequences to the fetus, even when those consequences have no direct relation to her health. An example illustrates the point. We would think it constitutional for the State to require that in order for there to be informed consent to a kidney transplant operation the recipient must be supplied with information about risks to the donor as well as risks to himself or herself.... In short, requiring that the woman be informed of the availability of information relating to fetal development and the assistance available should she decide to carry the pregnancy to full term is a reasonable measure to insure an informed choice, one which might cause the woman to choose childbirth over abortion. This requirement cannot be considered a substantial obstacle to obtaining an abortion, and, it follows, there is no undue burden....

Our analysis of Pennsylvania's 24-hour waiting period between the provision of the information deemed necessary to informed consent and the performance of an abortion under the undue burden standard requires us to reconsider the premise behind the decision in *Akron I* invalidating a parallel requirement. In *Akron I* we said: "Nor are we convinced that the State's legitimate concern that the woman's decision be informed is reasonably served by requiring a 24-hour delay as a matter of course." We consider that conclusion to be wrong. The idea that important decisions will be more informed and deliberate if they follow some period of reflection does not strike us as unreasonable, particularly where the statute directs that important information become part of the background of the decision. The statute, as construed by the Court of Appeals, permits avoidance of the waiting period in the event of a medical emergency and the record evidence shows that in the vast majority of cases, a 24-hour delay does not create any appreciable health risk. In theory, at least, the waiting period is a reasonable measure to implement the State's interest in protecting the life of the unborn, a measure that does not amount to an undue burden.

Whether the mandatory 24-hour waiting period is nonetheless invalid because in practice it is a substantial obstacle to a woman's choice to terminate her pregnancy is a closer question. The findings of fact by the District Court indicate that because of the distances many women must travel to reach an abortion provider, the practical effect will often be a delay of much more than a day because the waiting period requires that a woman seeking an abortion must make at least two visits to the doctor. The District Court also found that in many instances this will increase the exposure of women seeking abortions to "the harassment and hostility of anti-abortion protesters demonstrating outside a clinic." As a result, the District Court found that for those women who have the fewest financial resources, those who must travel long distances, and those who have difficulty explaining their whereabouts to husbands, employers, or others, the 24-hour waiting period will be "particularly burdensome."

These findings are troubling in some respects, but they do not demonstrate that the waiting period constitutes an undue burden. . . .

We are left with the argument that the various aspects of the informed consent requirement are unconstitutional because they place barriers in the way of abortion on demand. Even the broadest reading of *Roe,* however, has not suggested that there is a constitutional right to abortion on demand. Rather, the right protected by *Roe* is a right to decide to terminate a pregnancy free of undue interference by the State. Because the informed consent requirement facilitates the wise exercise of that right it cannot be classified as an interference with the right *Roe* protects. The informed consent requirement is not an undue burden on that right.

C

Section 3209 of Pennsylvania's abortion law provides, except in cases of medical emergency, that no physician shall perform an abortion on a married woman without receiving a signed statement from the woman that she has notified her spouse that she is about to undergo an abortion. . . .

. . . The American Medical Association (AMA) has published a summary of the recent research . . . which indicates that in an average 12-month period in this country, approximately two million women are the victims of severe assaults by their male partners. In a 1985 survey, women reported that nearly one of every eight husbands had assaulted their wives during the past year. The AMA views these figures as "marked underestimates," because the nature of these incidents discourages women from reporting them, and because surveys typically exclude the very poor, those who do not speak English well, and women who are homeless or in institutions or hospitals when the survey is conducted. . . .

Other studies fill the rest of this troubling picture. Physical violence is only the most visible form of abuse. Psychological abuse, particularly forced social and economic isolation of women, is also common. Many victims of domestic violence remain with their abusers, perhaps because they perceive no superior alternative. . . .

The limited research that has been conducted with respect to notifying one's husband about an abortion, although involving samples too small to be representative, also supports the District Court's findings of fact. The vast majority of women notify their male partners of their decision to obtain an abortion. In many cases in which married women do not notify their husbands, the pregnancy is the result of an extramarital affair. Where the husband is the father, the primary reason women do not notify their husbands is that the husband and wife are experiencing marital difficulties, often accompanied by incidents of violence. . . .

This information . . . reinforce[s] what common sense would suggest. In well-functioning marriages, spouses discuss important intimate decisions such as whether to bear a child. But there are millions of women in this country who are the victims of regular physical and psychological abuse at the hands of their husbands. Should these women become pregnant, they may have very good reasons for not wishing to inform their husbands of their decision to obtain an abortion. . . .

The spousal notification requirement is thus likely to prevent a significant number of women from obtaining an abortion. It does not merely make abortions a little more difficult or expensive to obtain; for many women, it will impose a substantial obstacle. We must not blind ourselves to the fact that the significant number of women who fear for their safety and the safety of their children are likely to be deterred from procuring an abortion as surely as if the Commonwealth had outlawed abortion in all cases. . . .

Section 3209 embodies a view of marriage consonant with the common-law status of married women but repugnant to our present understanding of marriage and of the nature of the rights secured by the Constitution. Women do not lose their constitutionally protected liberty when they marry. The Constitution protects all individuals, male or female, married or unmarried, from the abuse of governmental power, even where that power is employed for the supposed benefit of a member of the individual's family. These considerations confirm our conclusion that § 3209 is invalid.

D

We next consider the parental consent provision. . . .

We have been over most of this ground before. Our cases establish, and we reaffirm today, that a State may require a minor seeking an abortion to obtain the consent of a parent or guardian, provided that there is an adequate judicial bypass procedure. In our view, the one-parent consent requirement and judicial bypass procedure are constitutional. . . .

E

Under the recordkeeping and reporting requirements of the statute, every facility which performs abortions is required to file a report stating its name and address as well as the name and address of any related entity, such as a controlling or subsidiary organization. In the case of state-funded institutions, the information becomes public. . . .

In *Danforth* we held that recordkeeping and reporting provisions "that are reasonably directed to the preservation of maternal health and that properly respect a patient's confidentiality and privacy are permissible." We think that under this standard, all the provisions at issue here except that relating to spousal notice are constitutional. Although they do not relate to the State's interest in informing the woman's choice, they do relate to health. The collection of information with respect to actual patients is a vital element of medical research, and so it cannot be said that the requirements serve no purpose other than to make abortions more difficult. Nor do we find that the requirements impose a substantial obstacle to a woman's choice. At most they might increase the cost of some abortions by a slight amount. While at some point increased cost could become a substantial obstacle, there is no such showing on the record before us.

Subsection (12) of the reporting provision requires the reporting of, among other things, a married woman's "reason for failure to provide notice" to her husband. This provision in effect requires women, as a condition of obtaining an abortion, to provide the Commonwealth with the precise information we have already recognized that many women have pressing reasons not to reveal. Like the spousal notice requirement itself, this provision places an undue burden on a woman's choice, and must be invalidated for that reason.

VI

Our Constitution is a covenant running from the first generation of Americans to us and then to future generations. It is a coherent succession.

Each generation must learn anew that the Constitution's written terms embody ideas and aspirations that must survive more ages than one. We accept our responsibility not to retreat from interpreting the full meaning of the covenant in light of all of our precedents. We invoke it once again to define the freedom guaranteed by the Constitution's own promise, the promise of liberty. . . .

It is so ordered.

JUSTICE BLACKMUN, concurring in part, concurring in the judgment in part, and dissenting in part.

Three years ago in *Webster* v. *Reproductive Health Serv.* (1989), four Members of this Court appeared poised to "cas[t] into darkness the hopes and visions of every woman in this country" who had come to believe that the Constitution guaranteed her the right to reproductive choice. All that remained between the promise of *Roe* and the darkness of the plurality was a single, flickering flame. Decisions since *Webster* gave little reason to hope that this flame would cast much light. But now, just when so many expected the darkness to fall, the flame has grown bright.

I do not underestimate the significance of today's joint opinion. Yet I remain steadfast in my belief that the right to reproductive choice is entitled to the full protection afforded by this Court before *Webster*. And I fear for the darkness as four Justices anxiously await the single vote necessary to extinguish the light.

Make no mistake, the joint opinion of JUSTICES O'CONNOR, KENNEDY, and SOUTER is an act of personal courage and constitutional principle. In contrast to previous decisions in which JUSTICES O'CONNOR and KENNEDY postponed reconsideration of *Roe* v. *Wade* (1973), the authors of the joint opinion today join JUSTICE STEVENS and me in concluding that "the essential holding of *Roe* should be retained and once again reaffirmed." In brief, five Members of this Court today recognize that "the Constitution protects a woman's right to terminate her pregnancy in its early stages.". . .

In one sense, the Court's approach is worlds apart from that of THE CHIEF JUSTICE and JUSTICE SCALIA. And yet, in another sense, the distance between the two approaches is short—the distance is but a single vote.

I am 83 years old. I cannot remain on this Court forever, and when I do step down, the confirmation process for my successor well may focus on the issue before us today. That, I regret, may be exactly where the choice between the two worlds will be made.

CHIEF JUSTICE REHNQUIST, with whom JUSTICE WHITE, JUSTICE SCALIA, and JUSTICE THOMAS join, concurring in the judgment in part and dissenting in part.

The joint opinion, following its newly-minted variation on *stare decisis,* retains the outer shell of *Roe* v. *Wade,* but beats a wholesale retreat from the substance of that case. We believe that *Roe* was wrongly decided, and that it can and should be overruled consistently with our traditional approach to *stare decisis* in constitutional cases. We would adopt the approach of the plurality in *Webster* v. *Reproductive Health Services* and uphold the challenged provisions of the Pennsylvania statute in their entirety.

JUSTICE SCALIA, with whom THE CHIEF JUSTICE, JUSTICE WHITE, and JUSTICE THOMAS join, concurring in the judgment in part and dissenting in part.

My views on this matter are unchanged from those I set forth in my separate opinions in *Webster* v. *Reproductive Health Services.* . . . The States may, if they wish, permit abortion-on-demand, but the Constitution does not *require* them to do so. The permissibility of abortion, and the limitations upon it, are to be resolved like most important questions in our democracy: by citizens trying to persuade one another and then voting. As the Court acknowledges, "where reasonable people disagree the government can adopt one position or the other." The Court is correct in adding the qualification that this "assumes a state of affairs in which the choice does not intrude upon a protected liberty," but the crucial part of that qualification is the penultimate word. A State's choice between two positions on which reasonable people can disagree is constitutional even when (as is often the case) it intrudes upon a "liberty" in the absolute sense. Laws against bigamy, for example—which entire societies of reasonable people disagree with—intrude upon men and women's liberty to marry and live with one another. But bigamy happens not to be a liberty specially "protected" by the Constitution.

That is, quite simply, the issue in this case: not whether the power of a woman to abort her unborn child is a "liberty" in the absolute sense; or even whether it is a liberty of great importance to many women. Of course it is both. The issue is whether it is a liberty protected by the Constitution of the United States. I am sure it is not. I reach that conclusion not because of anything so exalted as my views concerning the "concept of existence, of meaning, of the universe, and of the mystery of human life." Rather, I reach it for the same reason I reach the conclusion that bigamy is not constitutionally protected—because of two simple facts: (1) the Constitution says absolutely nothing about it, and (2) the longstanding traditions of American society have permitted it to be legally proscribed. . . .

There is a poignant aspect to today's opinion. Its length, and what might be called its epic tone, suggest that its authors believe they are bringing to an end a troublesome era in the history of our Nation and of our Court. "It is the dimension" of authority, they say, to "cal[l] the contending sides of national controversy to end their national division by accepting a common mandate rooted in the Constitution."

There comes vividly to mind a portrait by Emanuel Leutze that hangs in the Harvard Law School: Roger Brooke Taney, painted in 1859, the 82d year of his life, the 24th of his Chief Justiceship, the second after his opinion in *Dred Scott*. He is all in black, sitting in a shadowed red armchair, left hand resting upon a pad of paper in his lap, right hand hanging limply, almost lifelessly, beside the inner arm of the chair. He sits facing the viewer, and staring straight out. There seems to be on his face, and in his deep-set eyes, an expression of profound sadness and disillusionment. Perhaps he always looked that way, even when dwelling upon the happiest of thoughts. But those of us who know how the lustre of his great Chief Justiceship came to be eclipsed by *Dred Scott* cannot help believing that he had that case—its already apparent consequences for the Nation—burning on his mind. I expect that two years earlier he, too, had thought himself "call[ing] the contending sides of national controversy to end their national division by accepting a common mandate rooted in the Constitution."

It is no more realistic for us in this case, than it was for him in that, to think that an issue of the sort they both involved—an issue involving life and death, freedom and subjugation—can be "speedily and finally settled" by the Supreme Court, as President James Buchanan in his inaugural address said the issue of slavery in the territories would be. Quite to the contrary, by foreclosing all democratic outlet for the deep passions this issue arouses, by banishing the issue from the political forum that gives all participants, even the losers, the satisfaction of a fair hearing and an honest fight, by continuing the imposition of a rigid national rule instead of allowing for regional differences, the Court merely prolongs and intensifies the anguish.

We should get out of this area, where we have no right to be, and where we do neither ourselves nor the country any good by remaining.

5 | *Preview of the 1992–1993 Term*

The 1992-1993 Supreme Court term picked up where the prior term ended, with keen interest in how permanent the newly emerged coalition of Justices Sandra Day O'Connor, Anthony M. Kennedy, and David H. Souter will be on the Court. In the 1991-1992 term, the three formed a moderate conservative bloc that resisted the conservatism of Chief Justice William H. Rehnquist and Justices Antonin Scalia and Clarence Thomas.

Major opinions joined by O'Connor, Kennedy, and Souter were marked by a regard for precedent and the institutional integrity of the Court. The three justices dictated the outcome of two of the Court's most controversial cases of the term: In *Planned Parenthood of Southeastern Pennsylvania v. Casey*, the Court voted, 5-4, to uphold a woman's right to end a pregnancy; and in *Lee v. Weisman*, the Court affirmed, 5-4, a clear separation between church and state by ruling that allowing prayers as part of a public school graduation ceremony is unconstitutional. They made the difference in striking down as First Amendment violations a Georgia county's parade fee (*Forsyth County v. Nationalist Movement*) and a ban on leafletting at New York area airports (*International Society for Krishna Consciousness v. Lee*). The three also helped block Rehnquist from winning a long-advocated change in how federal courts review state rulings on prisoners' cases (*Wright v. West*). Rehnquist wanted federal judges to defer more to state courts' application of the law to the particular facts of a case.

Whenever O'Connor, Kennedy, and Souter voted together, they were in the majority. If this alliance continues to hold, it could be a significant force in shaping the direction of the Court. All three justices are comparatively young (O'Connor is sixty-two; Kennedy, fifty-six; and Souter, fifty-three), and a voting bloc of three has a strong hand in deciding any case.

In the 1992-1993 docket, the three could play a decisive role in a key constitutional case involving a city ordinance that bans animal sacrifice (*Church of the Lukumi Babalu Aye v. Hialeah, Florida*). The Santeria church, which engages in animal slaughter as part of its birth, marriage, and death rituals, has challenged the Hialeah ordinance as an affront to the First Amendment guarantee of free exercise of religion. The city says the prohibition is necessary for public safety and animal welfare.

The Court could use the case to modify a controversial 1990 ruling. In that case (*Employment Division v. Smith*), the Court abandoned a test used in earlier free exercise cases that required a local government to prove it had a "compelling interest" in enforcing a statute that incidentally infringed on religious freedom. Since then, a bipartisan coalition in Congress, supported by a broad spectrum of religious groups, had been trying to reverse the results of the opinion, asserting that the Court undermined First Amendment protections by allowing governments more easily to erect laws that encroach on religious practices.

Although O'Connor joined in the 6-3 judgment on the *Smith* case, saying that the state of Oregon had an interest in outlawing the use of the drug peyote, even when used in religious ceremonies by American Indians, she disagreed with Justice Scalia's majority opinion lessening the test for local laws. Souter testified during his 1990 confirmation hearings that he agreed with O'Connor's position.

The question is whether Kennedy, who also voted with the majority in *Smith*, will be interested in modifying the *Smith* doctrine in the face of potential persuasion by O'Connor and Souter. Kennedy's votes in the abortion and school prayer cases in 1992 were reversals of positions he had held, and he appears sympathetic to arguments that the Court should not upset precedent. Members of Congress have asserted that that is

In a controversial case held over from 1991-1992, the Court will decide whether women seeking abortions can use a Reconstruction-era civil rights law to sue protesters blocking their access to health clinics.

exactly what the Court did in *Smith* and that the ruling could have broad implications for religious rights in the future. The Court also could avoid revisitng *Smith*, if it decides that the Hialeah law specifically targeted the Santeria church instead of incidentally infringing on its practices through an otherwise neutral law. Laws aimed specifically at religious practices have required more court scrutiny and justification than those that secondarily affect religion.

Also on the docket is the controversial case of *Bray v. Alexandria Women's Health Clinic* that will test whether the three justices will determine the outcome of another abortion-related matter. This dispute, focusing on the rights of women seeking abortions in the face of protesters' blockades, was argued in the 1991-1992 term. However, the Court's newest justice, Clarence Thomas, had yet to join the Court and, because the eight sitting justices could not reach a conclusion, because an unusual alliance on another abortion case was in the works, or because of unstated reasons, the Court rescheduled the matter for the 1992-1993 term. As is typical, the Court provided no explanation for holding over the case. An overriding question is how the justices who staked out the center in 1991-1992 to ensure a right to abortion will assess the exercise of the right when protesters block health clinics.

O'Connor, Kennedy, and Souter also could be pivotal in new cases involving prisoners' appeals. All three justices, but most vigorously O'Connor, signaled in 1991-1992 that the Court's conservative wing might be going too far in restricting state prisoners' challenges to their convictions in federal courts.

The key case of *Herrara v. Collins* asks whether an inmate's claim of innocence entitles him to federal court review after he exhausted the usual appeals process. The prisoner is on Texas's death row for the killing of two state police officers. He says he has evidence that his now-deceased brother confessed to the killings.

A federal appeals court held that a claim of innocence alone is not sufficient to win federal court review. At the most basic level, the prisoner has asked the Court to decide whether it is constitutional to execute an innocent man.

□□□

Following are summaries of some of the major cases on the Supreme Court's docket for the term that began October 5, 1992:

Church of the Lukumi Babalu Aye v. Hialeah, Florida. This case involves 1987 Hialeah ordinances that bar the slaughter of animals for any type of ritual. After a challenge by members of the Santeria religion, a lower court ruled that the ordinances do not violate the First Amendment's guarantee of free exercise of religion because of city interests in public health and animal welfare. The question before the Court is whether a city may constitutionally enact a law that restricts animal slaughter for religious reasons, while permitting slaughters for secular reasons (at slaughterhouses, for example). The Court is expected to look at whether this was deliberate or incidental discrimination and just how great a city's interest must be when an ordinance infringes on a religious practice.

Nixon v. United States. In 1989, when the Senate was about to hear the impeachment case of former U.S. district judge Walter L. Nixon, Jr., senators appointed a special committee, as they had done in other impeachments, to listen to witnesses and take evidence. The former Mississippi judge said the Senate violated a constitutional requirement "to try all impeachments" because eighty-eight of the one-hundred members of the Senate did not hear the witnesses called by prosecutors from the House of Representatives and by Nixon.

A threshold issue to be resolved is whether the justices should be ruling on the merits of Nixon's claim at all. An appeals court said that the federal judiciary could not hear the case because it involves a political question and because any ruling would lead to court infringement on congressional powers. The U.S. solicitor general's office agrees, asserting that the Constitution grants the Senate "sole power" over impeachment trials and that the Senate alone may decide how to hear a case.

Bray v. Alexandria Women's Health Clinic. The dispute arose from blockades organized by Operation Rescue at Washington, D.C., area health clinics that performed abortion. Women seeking abortions want to use a Reconstruction-era civil rights law to sue protesters blocking their access to clinics. The law, the 1871 Ku Klux Klan Act, originally was intended to protect blacks. Among the questions the justices will address is whether women who want abortions constitute a valid "class" for protection under the law and whether the protesters, acting as purely private individuals, violate the constitutional right to interstate travel when a would-be clinic patron comes from out of state. The Bush administration supports the anti-abortion group Operation Rescue in this case.

Herrera v. Collins. The case is among a number of arguments the justices will hear in the 1992-1993 term on prisoners' rights to challenge their state convictions in federal court. Defendants who have exhausted direct appeals apply for a writ of habeas corpus by claiming that the conviction under which they are held is unconstitutional. The Rehnquist Court in recent years has restricted the grounds on which a prisoner may seek a writ of habeas corpus. The Court will decide whether a death row prisoner may file a petition based on a claim of innocence, arising from newly discovered evidence. (The prisoner's brother supposedly confessed to the slaying before he died.) An appeals court ruled that such a claim,

In a case involving the 1989 impeachment trial of former U.S. district judge Walter L. Nixon, Jr., a threshold issue is whether the justices should make a ruling at all. An appeal court said any decision would lead to court infringement on congressional powers.

standing alone, does not require habeas relief when a prisoner already had been through federal court review.

Withrow v. Williams. A murder suspect made incriminating statements to police while in custody but before he had been read his so-called Miranda rights. His statements were admitted at trial. The question is whether federal courts have jurisdiction to review the case after a state court found that no violation occurred of the *Miranda v. Arizona* rule. (The suspect was at the police station when he was questioned, but he had not been formally arrested.)

Montana v. Imlay. The defendant's prison sentence, arising from the sexual assault of a seven-year-old girl, was suspended on the condition that he enroll in a therapy program. But the defendant refused to admit guilt, could not complete a sex offender program, and his suspended sentence was revoked. The question is whether his Fifth Amendment privilege against self-incrimination was violated.

Commissioner of Internal Revenue v. Soliman. An anesthesiologist who practiced at a number of hospitals wanted to claim a business tax deduction for his home, where he kept patient records, billing information, and medical texts. He said that his McLean, Virginia, condominium was his "principal place of business" and listed on his income tax return deductions for condominium fees, utilities, and depreciation arising from the home office.

The U.S. Tax Court ruled in favor of the anesthesiologist after asking whether the "taxpayer's home office is essential to his business, he spends substantial time there, and there is no other location available to perform the office functions of the business." But the Internal Revenue Service (IRS) asserts that federal tax law does not allow a taxpayer to deduct home office expenses when the home is "the principal *office* of the business," but instead when the home office is "the principal *place* of business." The IRS says that, of all the hospitals he visits, the doctor spends most of his time working in a Bethesda, Maryland, hospital.

Helling v. McKinney. In this case, an inmate argues that tobacco smoke from the smoking of other prisoners exposes him to an unreasonable health risk, in violation of his Eighth Amendment protection from cruel and unusual punishment. The Nevada state prison inmate shared a cell with a heavy smoker. In a 1991 case, *Wilson v. Seiter,* the Supreme Court ruled that a prisoner who claims that the conditions of his confinement violate the Eighth Amendment must show a culpable state of mine, "deliberate indifference," on the part of prison officials. In the new

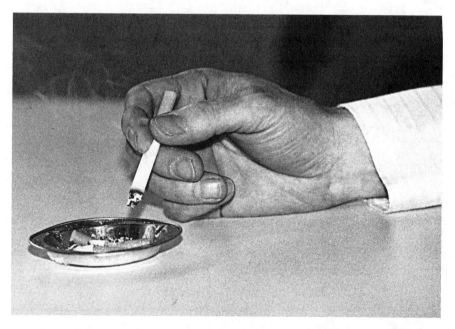

In 1992-1993, the Court will examine whether an inmate's forced exposure to secondary cigarette smoke is a violation of his Eighth Amendment protection from cruel and unusual punishment. The Court also is scheduled to hear numerous arguments on prisoners' rights to challenge state convictions in federal court.

case, justices will examine whether forced exposure to secondary smoke is unconstitutional and under what standard prison officials' conduct should be judged.

Alexander v. United States. The owner of an adult entertainment business was convicted on federal racketeering and obscenity charges based on the sale of four magazines and three videotapes. After a forfeiture proceeding, millions of dollars in property, inventory, and proceeds from his book and video stores were seized. At issue is whether the seizure—allowed under the Racketeer Influenced and Corrupt Organizations Act (RICO)—violated the First Amendment, or, combined with a six-year prison term and more than $200,000 in fines, breached Eighth Amendment protection against excessive punishment.

Voinovich v. Quilter. The case involves an Ohio reapportionment plan that allegedly "packed" black voters into an electoral district without the proper legal justification under a key 1986 case, *Thornburg v. Gingles.* A lower court ruled that Ohio could not create such a minority district unless, prior to redistricting, it had shown an existing violation of federal law protecting minority voting rights. The U.S. solicitor general argues in an amicus curiae brief that the 1986 ruling does not require a proven violation of the Voting Rights Act. Instead, a minority group only must show it is sufficiently large and geographically compact to be a majority of the population in a single-member district; it is politically cohesive; and the white majority votes as a bloc, usually defeating the minority's preferred candidate.

Growe v. Emison. Minnesota officials are challenging redistricing plans for both state legislative and congressional districts ordered by a federal court. The question for the justices is whether, when parallel redistricting proceedings are under way, a federal court should defer to the state court's resolution. A group made up of members of Congress and state legislators has submitted an amicus curiae brief, arguing that the power to redraw congressional and legislative districts is reserved for the states and that the federal intervention compromises the integrity of elections within a state's borders.

6 | *How the Court Works*

The Constitution makes the Supreme Court the final arbiter in "cases" and "controversies" arising under the Constitution or the laws of the United States. As the interpreter of the law, the Court often is viewed as the least mutable and most tradition-bound of the three branches of the federal government.

The Court has undergone innumerable changes in its history, some of which have been mandated by law. Almost all of the changes, however, were made because the justices thought they would provide a more efficient or a more equitable way of dealing with the Court's responsibilities. Some of the changes are embodied in Court rules; others are informal adaptations to needs and circumstances.

The Schedule of the Term

The Court's annual schedule reflects both continuity and change. During its formal annual sessions, certain times are set aside for oral argument, for conferences, for the writing of opinions, and for the announcement of decisions. Given the number of cases they face each year, the justices are confronted with a tremendous amount of work during the regular term, which now lasts nine months. Their work does not end when the session is finished, however. During the summer recess, the justices receive new cases to consider. About a fourth of the applications for review filed during the term are read by the justices and their law clerks during the summer interim.

Annual Terms

By law, the Supreme Court begins its regular annual term on the first Monday in October and may hold a special term whenever necessary. The regular session, known as the October term, lasts nine months. The summer recess, which is not determined by statute or Court rules, generally begins in late June or early July of the following year.

In the past the Court adjourned when the summer recess began. The chief justice would announce in open court, "All cases submitted and all business before the Court at this term in readiness for disposition having been disposed of, it is ordered by this Court that all cases on the docket be, and they are hereby, continued to the next term." Since 1979, however, the Court has been in continuous session throughout the year, marked by periodic recesses. This system makes it unnecessary to convene a special term to deal with matters arising in the summer.

Opening Day

Opening day ceremonies of the new term have changed considerably since the Court first met on February 1, 1790. Chief Justice John Jay was forced to postpone the first formal session for a day because some of the justices were unable to reach New York City—at that time the nation's capital and home of the Court. Proceedings began the next day in a crowded courtroom and with an empty docket.

Beginning in 1917 and until 1975, the opening day and week were spent in conference. The justices discussed cases that had not been disposed of during the previous term and some of the petitions that had reached the Court during the summer recess. The decisions arrived at during this initial conference on which cases to accept for oral argument were announced on the second Monday of October.

At the beginning of the October 1975 term, this practice was changed. The justices reassembled for the initial conference during the last week in September. When the justices formally convened on the first Monday in October, oral arguments began.

Arguments and Conferences

At least four justices must request that a case be argued before it can be accepted. Arguments are heard on Monday, Tuesday, and Wednesday for seven two-week sessions, beginning in the first week in October and ending in mid-April. Two-week or longer recesses are held between the sessions of oral arguments during which the justices consider the cases and deal with other Court business.

The schedule for oral arguments—10:00 a.m. to noon and 1 p.m. to 3 p.m.—began during the 1969 term. Since most cases receive one hour apiece for argument, the Court can hear twelve cases a week.

The Court holds conferences on the Friday just before the two-week oral argument periods and on Wednesday and Friday during the weeks when oral arguments are scheduled. The conferences are designed for consideration of cases already heard in oral argument and for resolving other business.

Prior to each of the Friday conferences, the chief justice circulates a "discuss" list—a list of cases deemed important enough for discussion and a vote. Appeals (of which there now are only a small number) are placed on the discuss list almost automatically, but as many as three-quarters of the petitions for certiorari are summarily denied a place on the list and

On the bench, the chief justice sits in the center, with the most senior associate justice on his right and the second senior associate justice on his left. The remaining seats are occupied alternately by the other justices in order of seniority.

simply disappear. No case is denied review during conference, however, without an initial examination by the justices and their law clerks. Any one of the justices can have a case placed on the Court's conference agenda for review. Most of the cases scheduled for the discuss list also are denied review in the end, but only after discussion by the justices during the conference.

Although the last oral arguments have been heard by mid-April each year, the conferences of the justices continue until the end of the term to consider cases remaining on the Court's agenda.

All conferences are held in secrecy, with no legal assistants or other staff present. The attendance of six justices constitutes a quorum. Conferences begin with handshakes all around. In discussing a case, the chief justice speaks first, followed by each justice in order of seniority.

Decision Days

In the Court's early years, conferences were held whenever the justices decided one was necessary—sometimes in the evening or on weekends. Similarly, decisions were announced whenever they were ready. No formal or informal schedule existed for conferences or for the announcement of decisions.

Visiting the Supreme Court

The Supreme Court building has six levels, two of which are accessible to the public. The basement contains a parking garage, a printing press, and offices for security guards and maintenance personnel. A public information office is on the ground floor, and the courtroom is on the main floor. The second floor contains the justices' offices, dining rooms, library, and various other offices; the third floor, the Court library; and the fourth floor, the gym and storage areas.

From October to mid-April, the Court hears oral arguments Monday through Wednesday for about two weeks a month. These sessions begin at 10 a.m. and continue until 3 p.m., with a one-hour recess starting at noon. They are open to the public on a first-come, first-served basis.

Visitors may inspect the Supreme Court chamber any time the Court is not in session. Historical exhibits and a free motion picture on how the Court works also are available throughout the year. The Supreme Court building is open from 9 a.m. to 4:30 p.m. Monday through Friday, except for legal holidays. When the Court is not in session, lectures are given in the courtroom every hour on the half hour between 9:30 a.m. and 3:30 p.m.

The tradition of releasing decisions on Monday—"Decision Monday"—began in 1857. This practice continued until the Court said on April 5, 1965, that "commencing the week of April 26, 1965, it will no longer adhere to the practice of reporting its decisions only at Monday sessions and that in the future they will be reported as they become ready for decision at any session of the Court." At present, opinions are released on Tuesdays and Wednesdays during the weeks that the Court is hearing oral arguments; during other weeks, they are released on Mondays.

In addition to opinions, the Court also releases an "orders" list—the summary of the Court's action granting or denying review. The orders list is posted at the beginning of the Monday session. It is not announced orally but can be obtained from the clerk and the public information officer. When urgent or important matters arise, the Court's summary orders may be made available on a day other than Monday.

Unlike its orders, decisions of the Court are announced orally in open Court. The justice who wrote the opinion announces the Court's decision, and justices writing concurring or dissenting opinions may state their views as well. When more than one decision is to be rendered, the justices who wrote the opinion make their announcements in reverse order of seniority. Rarely, all or a large portion of the opinion is read aloud. More often, the author will summarize the opinion or simply announce the result and state that a written opinion has been filed.

Reviewing Cases

In determining whether to accept a case for review, the Court has considerable discretion, subject only to the restraints imposed by the Constitution and Congress. Article III, Section 2, of the Constitution provides that "In all Cases affecting Ambassadors, other public Ministers and Consuls, and those in which a State shall be Party, the supreme Court shall have original Jurisdiction. In all the other Cases ... the supreme Court shall have appellate Jurisdiction, both as to Law and Fact, with such Exceptions, and under such Regulations as the Congress shall make."

Original jurisdiction refers to the right of the Supreme Court to hear a case before any other court does. Appellate jurisdiction is the right to review the decision of a lower court. The vast majority of cases reaching the Supreme Court are appeals from rulings of the lower courts; generally only a handful of original jurisdiction cases are filed each term.

After enactment of the Judiciary Act of 1925, the Supreme Court had broad discretion to decide for itself what cases it would hear. Since Congress in 1988 virtually eliminated the Court's mandatory jurisdiction through which it was obliged to hear most appeals, that discretion has been virtually unlimited.

Methods of Appeal

Cases come to the Supreme Court in several ways: through petitions for writs of certiorari, appeals, and requests for certification.

In petitioning for a writ of certiorari, a litigant who has lost a case in a lower court sets out the reasons why the Supreme Court should review the case. If a writ is granted, the Court requests a certified record of the case from the lower court.

Supreme Court rules state:

> Whenever a petition for writ of certiorari to review a decision of any court is granted, the clerk shall enter an order to that effect and shall forthwith notify the court below and counsel of record. The case will then be scheduled for briefing and oral argument. If the record has not previously been filed, the Clerk of this Court shall request the clerk of the court possessed of the record to certify it and transmit it to this Court. A formal writ shall not issue unless specially directed.

The main difference between the certiorari and appeal routes is that the Court has complete discretion to grant a request for a writ of certiorari but is under more obligation to accept and decide a case that comes to it on appeal.

Most cases reach the Supreme Court by means of the writ of certiorari. In the relatively few cases to reach the Court by means of appeal, the appellant must file a jurisdictional statement explaining why the case qualifies for review and why the Court should grant it a hearing. Often the justices dispose of these cases by deciding them summarily, without oral argument or formal opinion.

Those whose petitions for certiorari have been granted must pay the Court's standard $300 fee for docketing the case. The U.S. government does not have to pay these fees, nor do persons too poor to afford them. The latter may file in forma pauperis (in the character or manner of a pauper) petitions. Another, seldom used, method of appeal is certification, the request by a lower court—usually a court of appeals—for a final answer to questions of law in a particular case. The Supreme Court, after examining the certificate, may order the case argued before it.

Process of Review

Each year the Court is asked to review some five thousand cases. All petitions are examined by the staff of the clerk of the Court; those found to

The Supreme Court library is paneled in hand-carved oak. The Court's collection contains about 300,000 titles.

be in reasonably proper form are placed on the docket and given a number. All cases, except those falling within the Court's original jurisdiction, are placed on a single docket, known simply as "the docket." Only in the numbering of the cases is a distinction made between prepaid and in forma pauperis cases on the docket. Beginning with the 1971 term, prepaid cases were labeled with the year and the number. The first case filed in 1992, for example, would be designated 92-1. In forma pauperis cases contain the year and begin with the number 5001. The second in forma pauperis case filed in 1992 would thus be number 92-5002.

Each justice, aided by law clerks, is responsible for reviewing all cases on the docket. In recent years a number of justices have used a "cert pool" system in this review. Their clerks work together to examine cases, writing a pool memo on several petitions. The memo then is given to the justices who determine if more research is needed. (Other justices prefer to use a system in which they or their clerks review each petition themselves.) Justice William O. Douglas (1939-1975) called the review of cases on the docket "in many respects the most important and interesting of all our functions." Others have found it time-consuming and tedious and support the cert pool as a mechanism to reduce the burden on the justices and their staffs.

Petitions on the docket vary from elegantly printed and bound documents, of which multiple copies are submitted to the Court, to single sheets of prison stationery scribbled in pencil. All are considered by the justices, however, in the process of deciding which merit review. The decisions to grant or deny review of cases are made in conferences, which are held in the conference room adjacent to the chief justice's chambers. Justices are summoned to the conference room by a buzzer, usually between 9:30 and 10:00 a.m. They shake hands with each other, take their appointed seats, and the chief justice begins the discussion.

Discuss and Orders Lists

A few days before the conference convenes, the chief justice compiles the discuss list of cases deemed important enough for discussion and a vote. As many as three-quarters of the petitions for certiorari are denied a place on the list and thus rejected without further consideration. Any justice can have a case placed on the discuss list simply by requesting that it be placed there.

Only the justices attend conferences, and no legal assistants or staff are present. The junior associate justice acts as doorkeeper and messenger, sending for reference material and receiving messages and data. Unlike other parts of the federal government, few leaks have occurred about what transpires during the conferences.

At the start of the conference, the chief justice makes a brief statement outlining the facts of each case. Then each justice, beginning with the senior associate justice, comments on the case, usually indicating in the course of the comments how he intends to vote. A traditional but unwritten rule specifies that it takes four affirmative votes to have a case scheduled for oral argument.

Petitions for certiorari, appeal, and in forma pauperis that are approved for review or denied review during conference are placed on a certified orders list to be released the following Monday in open court.

Arguments

Once the Court announces it will hear a case, the clerk of the Court arranges the schedule for oral argument. Cases are argued roughly in the order in which they were granted review, subject to modification if more time is needed to acquire all the necessary documents. Cases generally are heard not sooner than three months after the Court has agreed to review them. Under special circumstances, the date scheduled for oral argument can be advanced or postponed.

Well before oral argument takes place, the justices receive the briefs and records from counsel in the case. The measure of attention the brief receives—from a thorough and exhaustive study to a cursory glance—depends both on the nature of the case and the work habits of the justice.

As one of the two public functions of the Court, oral arguments are viewed by some as very important. Justice William J. Brennan, Jr., (1956-1990) said, "Oral argument is the absolute indispensable ingredient of appellate advocacy. . . . Often my whole notion of what a case is about crystallizes at oral argument. This happens even though I read the briefs before oral argument." Others dispute the significance of oral arguments, contending that by the time a case is heard most of the justices already have made up their minds.

Time Limits

The time allowed each side for oral argument is thirty minutes. Since the time allotted must accommodate any questions the justices may wish to ask, the actual time for presentation may be considerably shorter than thirty minutes. Under the current rules of the Court, effective January 1, 1990, one counsel only will be heard for each side, except by special permission.

An exception is made for an amicus curiae—a person who volunteers or is invited to take part in matters before a court but is not a party in the case. Counsel for an amicus curiae may participate in oral argument if the party supported by the amicus allows use of part of its argument time or the Court grants a motion permitting argument by counsel for the "friend of the court." The motion must show, the rules state, that the amicus's argument "is thought to provide assistance to the Court not otherwise available."

Because the Court is reluctant to extend the time that each side is given for oral argument and because amicus curiae participation in oral argument often would necessitate such an extension, the Court generally is unreceptive to such motions. And counsel in a case usually is equally unreceptive to a request to give an amicus counsel any of the precious minutes allotted to argue the case.

Court rules provide advice to counsel presenting oral arguments before the Court: "Oral argument should emphasize and clarify the written arguments appearing in the briefs on the merits." That same rule warns—with italicized emphasis—that the Court "looks with disfavor on oral argument read from a prepared text." Most attorneys appearing before the Court use an outline or notes to make sure they cover the important points.

Circulating the Argument

The Supreme Court has tape-recorded oral arguments since 1955. In 1968 the Court, in addition to its own recording, began contracting with private firms to tape and transcribe all oral arguments. The contract stipulates that the transcript "shall include everything spoken in argument, by Court, counsel, or others, and nothing shall be omitted from the transcript unless the Chief Justice or Presiding Justice so directs." But "the names of Justices asking questions shall not be recorded or transcribed; questions shall be indicated by the letter 'Q.' "

The marshal of the Court keeps the Court's tapes during the term when oral arguments are presented. During that time use of these tapes usually is limited to the justices and their law clerks. At the end of the term, the tapes are sent to the National Archives. Persons wishing to listen to the tapes or buy a copy of a transcript can apply to the Archives for permission to do so.

Transcripts made by a private firm can be acquired more quickly. These transcripts usually are available a week after arguments are heard. Those who purchase the transcripts from the firm must agree that they will not be photographically reproduced. Transcripts usually run from forty to fifty pages for one hour of oral argument.

Proposals have been made to tape arguments for television and radio use. To date, the Court has shown little enthusiasm for these proposals.

Use of Briefs

Supreme Court Rule 28 states, "Counsel should assume that all Justices of the Court have read the briefs in advance of oral argument." Nonetheless, justices vary considerably in the attention they personally give to an attorney's briefs. If the brief has been thoroughly digested by the justices, the attorney can use his arguments to highlight certain elements. But if it merely has been scanned—and perhaps largely forgotten—in the interval between the reading and the oral argument, the attorney will want to go into considerable detail about the nature of the case and the facts involved. Most lawyers therefore prepare their argument on the assumption that the justices know relatively little about their particular case but are well-acquainted with the general principles of relevant law.

The brief of the petitioner or appellant must be filed within forty-five days of the Court's announced decision to hear the case. Except for in forma pauperis cases, forty copies of the brief must be filed with the Court. For in forma pauperis proceedings, the Court requires only that documents be legible. The opposing brief from the respondent or appellee is to be filed within thirty days of receipt of the brief of the petitioner or appellant. Either party may appeal to the clerk for an extension of time in filing the brief.

Court Rules 24 sets forth the elements that a brief should contain. These are: the questions presented for review; a list of all parties to the proceeding; a table of contents and table of authorities; citations of the opinions and judgments delivered in the lower courts; "a concise statement of the grounds on which the jurisdiction of this Court is invoked"; constitutional provisions, treaties, statutes, ordinances, and regulations involved; "a concise statement of the case containing all that is material to the consideration of the questions presented"; a summary of argument; the argument, which exhibits "clearly the points of fact and of law being presented and citing the authorities and statutes relied upon"; and a conclusion "specifying with particularity the relief which the party seeks."

The form and organization of the brief are covered by rules 33 and 34 of the Court. The rules limit the number of pages in various types of briefs. The rules also set out a color code for the covers of different kinds of briefs. Petitions are white; motions opposing them are orange. Petitioner's briefs on the merits are light blue, while those of respondents are red. Reply briefs are yellow; amicus curiae, green; and documents filed by the United States, gray.

Questioning

During oral argument the justices may interrupt with questions or remarks as often as they wish. On the average, questions consume about a third of counsel's allotted half-hour of argument. Unless counsel has been granted special permission extending the thirty-minute limit, he can continue talking after the time has expired only to complete a sentence.

The frequency of questioning, as well as the manner in which questions are asked, depends on the style of the justices and their interest in a particular case. Chief Justice Warren E. Burger (1969-1986) asked very few questions. Justice Antonin Scalia has from his first day on the bench peppered attorneys with questions, sparking more active interrogation from a number of his colleagues.

Questions from the justices may upset and unnerve counsel by interrupting a well-rehearsed argument and introducing an unexpected element. Nevertheless, questioning has several advantages. It serves to alert counsel about what aspects of the case need further elaboration or more information. For the Court, questions can bring out weak points in an argument—and sometimes strengthen it.

Conferences

Cases for which oral arguments have been heard then are dealt with in conference. During the Wednesday afternoon conference, the four cases that were argued the previous Monday are discussed and decided. At the all-day Friday conference, the eight cases argued on the preceding Tuesday and Wednesday are discussed and decided. Justices also consider new motions, appeals, and petitions while in conference.

Conferences are conducted in complete secrecy. No secretaries, clerks, stenographers, or messengers are allowed into the room. This practice began many years ago when the justices became convinced that decisions were being disclosed prematurely.

The justices meet in an oak-paneled, book-lined conference room adjacent to the chief justice's suite. Nine chairs surround the large rectangular table, each chair bearing the nameplate of the justice who sits there. The chief justice sits at the east end of the table, and the senior associate justice at the west end. The other justices take their places in order of seniority. The junior justice is charged with sending for and receiving documents or other information the Court needs.

On entering the conference room the justices shake hands with each other, a symbol of harmony that began in the 1880s. The chief justice begins the conference by calling the first case to be decided and discussing it. When the chief justice is finished, the senior associate justice speaks, followed by the other justices in order of seniority.

The justices can speak for as long as they wish, but they practice restraint because of the amount of business to be completed. By custom each justice speaks without interruption. Other than these procedural

In conference, the justices consider cases heard in oral argument and discuss other Court business. Meetings are held in private, with no legal assistants or staff present.

arrangements, little is known about what transpires in conference. Although discussions generally are said to be polite and orderly, occasionally they can be acrimonious. Likewise, consideration of the issues in a particular case may be full and probing, or perfunctory, leaving the real debate on the question to go on in the written drafts of opinions circulating up and down the Court's corridors between chambers.

Generally the discussion of the case clearly indicates how a justice plans to vote on it. A majority vote is needed to decide a case—five votes if all nine justices are participating.

Opinions

After the justices have voted on a case, the writing of the opinion or opinions begins. An opinion is a reasoned argument explaining the legal issues in the case and the precedents on which the opinion is based. Soon after a case is decided in conference, the task of writing the majority opinion is assigned. When in the majority, the chief justice designates the writer.

When the chief justice is in the minority, the senior associate justice voting with the majority assigns the job of writing the majority opinion.

Any justice may write a separate opinion. If in agreement with the Court's decision but not with some of the reasoning in the majority opinion, the justice writes a concurring opinion giving his reasoning. If in disagreement with the majority, the justice writes a dissenting opinion or simply goes on record as a dissenter without an opinion. More than one justice can sign a concurring opinion or a dissenting opinion.

The amount of time consumed between the vote on a case and the announcement of the decision varies from case to case. In simple cases where few points of law are at issue, the opinion sometimes can be written and cleared by the other justices in a week or less. In more complex cases, especially those with several dissenting or concurring opinions, the process can take six months or more. Some cases may have to be reargued or the initial decision reversed after the drafts of opinions have been circulated.

The assigning justice may consider the points made by majority justices during the conference discussion, the workload of the other justices, the need to avoid the more extreme opinions within the majority, and expertise in the particular area of law involved in a case.

The style of writing a Court opinion—majority, concurring, or dissenting—depends primarily on the individual justice. In some cases, the justice may prefer to write a restricted and limited opinion; in others, a broader approach to the subject. The decision likely is to be influenced by the need to satisfy the other justices in the majority.

When a justice is satisfied that the written opinion is conclusive or "unanswerable," it goes into print. In the past this process occurred at a print shop in the Court's basement, where the draft was printed under rigid security, with each copy numbered to prevent the removal of copies from the premises. In the 1980s, however, high technology arrived at the Court; draft opinions are circulated, revised, and printed on a computerized typesetting system.

The circulation of the drafts—whether computer-to-computer or on paper—provokes further discussion in many cases. Often the suggestions and criticisms require the writer to juggle opposing views. To retain a majority, the author of the draft opinion frequently feels obliged to make major emendations to satisfy justices who are unhappy with the initial draft. Some opinions have to be rewritten several times.

One reason for the secrecy surrounding the circulation of drafts is that some of the justices who voted with the majority may find the majority draft opinion so unpersuasive—or one or more of the dissenting drafts so convincing—that they change their vote. If enough justices alter their votes, the majority may shift, so that a former dissent becomes the majority opinion. When a new majority emerges from this process, the task of writing, printing, and circulating a new majority draft begins all over again.

In the past few decades considerable concern has arisen about the lack of unanimity in Court decisions and the frequent use of dissenting and concurring opinions. The chief argument in favor of greater unanimity is that it increases the authority of—and hence the respect for—the Court's decisions. A dissenting justice, however, may hope that the dissent will convince a majority of the other justices that his opinion is the correct one or that a later Court will adopt the view. Moreover, the dissenter generally has only himself to please, a fact that makes many well-reasoned and well-written dissents more memorable or more enjoyable to read than the majority opinion. A concurring opinion indicates that the justice who wrote it agrees in general with the majority opinion but has reservations about the way it was written, the reasoning behind it, or specific points in it. When the drafts of an opinion—including dissents and concurring views—have been written, circulated, discussed, and revised, if necessary, the final versions then are printed. Before the opinion is produced the reporter of decisions adds a "headnote" or syllabus summarizing the decision and a "lineup" at the end showing how the justices voted.

One hundred seventy-five copies of the "bench opinion" are made. As the decision is announced in Court, the bench opinion is distributed to journalists and others in the public information office. Another copy, with any necessary corrections noted on it, is sent to the U.S. Government Printing Office, which prints 4,444 "slip" opinions, which are distributed to federal and state courts and agencies. The Court receives 400 of these, and they are available to the public free through the Public Information Office as long as supplies last. The Government Printing Office also prints the opinion for inclusion in *United States Reports*, the official record of Supreme Court opinions.

The public announcement of opinions in Court probably is the Court's most dramatic function. It also may be the most expendable. Depending on who delivers the opinion and how, announcements can take a considerable amount of the Court's time. Opinions are given simultaneously to the public information officer for distribution. Nevertheless, those who are in the courtroom to hear the announcement of a ruling are participating in a very old tradition. The actual delivery may be tedious or exciting, depending on the nature of the case, the eloquence of the opinion, and the style of its oral delivery.

In the twentieth century, the Court has reduced the amount of time spent in delivering opinions. Before 1930 the Court generally read long opinions word for word; some opinions took days to announce. As the workload increased, this practice came to be regarded as a waste of the Court's time. The justice who has written the majority opinion now generally delivers only a summary, and dissenting justices often do the same with their opinions.

Appendix

Brief Biographies

William Hubbs Rehnquist

President Ronald Reagan's appointment of William H. Rehnquist as chief justice of the United States in 1986 clearly indicated that the president was hoping to shift the Court to the right. Since his early years as an associate justice in the 1970s, Rehnquist has been one of the Court's most conservative justices.

Rehnquist, the fourth associate justice to become chief, argues that the original intent of the framers of the Constitution and the Bill of Rights is the proper standard for interpret-
ing those documents today. He also takes a literal approach to individual rights. These beliefs have led him to dissent from the Court's rulings protecting a woman's privacy-based right to abortion, to argue that no constitutional barrier exists to school prayer, and to side with police and prosecutors on questions of criminal law. In 1991, he wrote the Court's decision upholding an administration ban on abortion counseling at publicly financed clinics and, in 1992, vigorously dissented from the Court's af-
firmation of *Roe v. Wade*, the 1973 opinion that made abortion legal nationwide.

Born in Milwaukee, Wisconsin, October 1, 1924, Rehnquist went west to college. At Stanford University, where he received both his undergraduate and law degrees, classmates recalled him as an intelligent student whose already well-entrenched conservative views set him apart from his more liberal classmates.

After graduating from law school in 1952, Rehnquist came to Washington, D.C., to serve as a law clerk to Supreme Court justice Robert H. Jackson. There, he wrote a memorandum that later would come back to haunt him during his Senate confirmation hearings. In the memo, Rehnquist favored separate but equal schools for blacks and whites. Asked about those views by the Senate Judiciary Committee in 1971, Rehnquist repudiated them, declaring that they were Justice Jackson's—not his own.

Following his clerkship, Rehnquist decided to practice law in the Southwest. He moved to Phoenix and immediately became immersed in Arizona Republican politics. From his earliest days in the state, he was associated with the party's conservative wing. A 1957 speech denouncing the liberalism of the Warren Court typified his views at the time.

During the 1964 presidential race, Rehnquist campaigned ardently for Barry Goldwater. It was then that Rehnquist met and worked with Richard G. Kleindienst, who later, as President Richard Nixon's deputy attorney general, would appoint Rehnquist to head the Justice Department's Office of Legal Counsel as an assistant attorney general. In 1971 the once-obscure Phoenix lawyer was nominated by President Nixon to the Supreme Court.

Controversy surrounded Rehnquist's 1986 nomination as chief justice. He was accused of harassing voters and challenging their right to vote years earlier when he was a GOP poll watcher in Phoenix. Accusations of racial bias also were raised against him. His views on civil rights were questioned, and he was found to have accepted anti-Semitic restrictions in a property deed to a Vermont home.

Before Clarence Thomas's 1991 nomination battle, more votes were cast against Rehnquist for chief justice (thirty-three nays to sixty-five ayes) than against any other successful Supreme Court nominee in the twentieth century. In 1971 Rehnquist had tied for the second-highest number of negative votes (twenty-six nays to sixty-eight ayes) when he was confirmed as an associate justice.

Rehnquist was married to Natalie Cornell, who died in 1991. They had two daughters and a son.

Born October 1, 1924, Milwaukee, Wisconsin; Stanford University B.A. (1948); Phi Beta Kappa; Harvard University M.A. (1949); Stanford University Law School LL.B. (1952); law clerk to Justice Robert H. Jackson, U.S. Supreme Court 1952-1953; married Natalie Cornell 1953; two daughters, one son; practiced law 1953-1969; assistant U.S. attorney general, Office of Legal Counsel 1969-1971; nominated as associate justice of the U.S. Supreme Court by President Nixon October 21, 1971; confirmed December 10, 1971; nominated as chief justice of the United States by President Reagan June 17, 1986; confirmed September 17, 1986.

Byron Raymond White

Since 1991, Byron R. White has been the most senior justice. After spending years ensconced on the conservative side of the Court, he began emerging as a swing vote as Reagan and Bush justices stepped in far to his right. In 1992, White wrote the Court's 5-4 opinion finding that government agents had pressured a Nebraska farmer to buy pornographic magazines. The case imposed tougher standards for government sting operations. White also in 1992 was the author of a major school desegregation decision, in which the Court held that Mississippi had not gone far enough to rid its higher education system of discriminatory practices.

White is noted for his quick and precise legal mind and his incisive questioning during oral argument. He was born June 8, 1917, in Fort Collins, Colorado, and grew up in Wellington, a small town in a sugar beet growing area of the state. Ranking first in his high school class, White won a scholarship to the University of Colorado, which he entered in 1934.

At the university White earned a reputation as an outstanding scholar-athlete. He was first in his class, a member of Phi Beta Kappa, and the winner of three varsity letters in football, four in basketball, and three in baseball. By the end of his college career in 1938 he had been nicknamed "Whizzer" for his outstanding performance as a football player, a performance that earned him not only a national reputation but also a one-year contract with the Pittsburgh Pirates (now the Steelers). White already had accepted a coveted Rhodes Scholarship for study at Oxford but decided to postpone his year in England.

Despite his success as a professional player, at the end of the football season White sailed for England to attend Oxford. When the European war broke out in September 1939, White returned to the United States and entered Yale Law School. But during 1940 and 1941 he alternated law study with playing football for the Detroit Lions.

After the United States entered the war, White served in the Navy in the South Pacific. There he renewed an old acquaintance with John F. Kennedy, whom he had met in England and who later would nominate White to the Supreme Court. After the war, White returned to Yale, earning his law degree magna cum laude in 1946. Following graduation, White served as law clerk to U.S. Chief Justice Fred M. Vinson. In 1947 White returned to his native Colorado, where for the next fourteen years he practiced law with the Denver law firm of Lewis, Grant, and Davis.

White renewed his contact with Kennedy during the 1960 presidential campaign, leading the nationwide volunteer group Citizens for Kennedy. After the election, Kennedy named White to the post of deputy attorney general, a position he held until his Supreme Court appointment in 1962.

White has been married since 1946 to Marion Stearns. They have one son and one daughter.

Born June 8, 1917, Fort Collins, Colorado; University of Colorado B.A. (1938); Phi Beta Kappa; Rhodes scholar, Oxford University; Yale University Law School LL.B. magna cum laude (1946); married Marion Stearns 1946; one son, one daughter; law clerk to Chief Justice Fred M. Vinson, U.S. Supreme Court 1946-1947; practiced law, Denver, 1947-1960; U.S. deputy attorney general 1961-1962; nominated as associate justice of the U.S. Supreme Court by President Kennedy March 30, 1962; confirmed April 11, 1962.

Harry Andrew Blackmun

During his first years on the Court, Harry A. Blackmun frequently was described as one of the "Minnesota Twins" along with the Court's other Minnesota native, Chief Justice Warren E. Burger. Blackmun and Burger, who retired in 1986, were friends who initially voted together on important decisions.

However, Blackmun, who originally impressed observers as a modest, even meek, addition to the Court's conservative bloc, has written some of the Court's most controversial, liberally oriented decisions, among them its 1973 ruling upholding a woman's right to an abortion. He since has become the liberal pole.

Blackmun was born in Nashville, Illinois, November 12, 1908, but spent most of his early years in Minneapolis-St. Paul, where his father

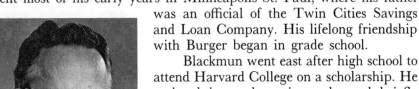

was an official of the Twin Cities Savings and Loan Company. His lifelong friendship with Burger began in grade school.

Blackmun went east after high school to attend Harvard College on a scholarship. He majored in mathematics and toyed briefly with the idea of becoming a physician.

But he chose the law instead. After graduating from Harvard in 1929, Phi Beta Kappa, Blackmun entered Harvard Law School, from which he graduated in 1932. During his law school years Blackmun supported himself with a variety of odd jobs, including tutoring in math and driving the launch for the college crew team.

Following law school Blackmun returned to St. Paul, where he served for a year and a half as a law clerk to United States Circuit Court judge John B. Sanborn, whom Blackmun succeeded twenty years later.

He left the clerkship at the end of 1933 and joined the Minneapolis law firm of Dorsey, Colman, Barker, Scott, and Barber. At the same time he taught for a year at William Mitchell College of Law in St. Paul, Burger's alma mater. In addition to his practice, Blackmun taught for two years during the 1940s at the University of Minnesota Law School.

In 1950 he accepted a post as "house counsel" for the world-famous Mayo Clinic in Rochester, Minnesota. Among his colleagues at the clinic, Blackmun quickly developed a reputation as a serious man, totally engrossed in his profession. The reputation followed him to the bench of the U.S. Court of Appeals for the Eighth Circuit, to which Blackmun was appointed by President Dwight D. Eisenhower in 1959. As a judge, Blackmun was known for his scholarly and thorough opinions.

Blackmun's total devotion to the law leaves little time for outside activities. He is an avid reader, delving primarily into judicial tomes. Over the years he also has been active in Methodist church affairs. Before he developed knee problems, Blackmun was a proficient squash and tennis player. It was on the tennis court that Blackmun met his future wife, Dorothy E. Clark. They were married in 1941 and have three daughters.

Born November 12, 1908, Nashville, Illinois; Harvard College B.A. (1929); Phi Beta Kappa; Harvard University Law School LL.B. (1932); law clerk to John Sanborn, U.S. Court of Appeals for the Eighth Circuit, St. Paul, 1932-1933; practiced law, Minneapolis, 1934-1950; married Dorothy E. Clark 1941; three daughters; resident counsel, Mayo Clinic, Rochester, Minnesota, 1950-1959; judge, U.S. Court of Appeals for the Eighth Circuit 1959-1970; nominated as associate justice of the U.S. Supreme Court by President Nixon April 14, 1970; confirmed May 12, 1970.

John Paul Stevens

When President Gerald R. Ford nominated federal appeals court judge John Paul Stevens to the Supreme Court seat vacated by veteran liberal William O. Douglas in 1975, Court observers struggled to pin an ideological label on the new nominee. The consensus that finally emerged was that Stevens was neither a doctrinaire liberal nor conservative, but a judicial centrist. His subsequent opinions bear out this description, although in recent years he has leaned more toward the liberal side.

A soft-spoken, mild-mannered man who occasionally sports a bow tie under his judicial robes, Stevens had a long record of excellence in scholarship. A member of a prominent Chicago family, Stevens graduated Phi Beta Kappa from the University of Chicago in 1941. After a wartime stint in the Navy, during which he earned the Bronze Star, he returned to Chicago to enter Northwestern University Law School, from which he graduated magna cum laude in 1947. From there, Stevens left for Washington, where he served as a law clerk to Supreme Court justice Wiley Rutledge. He returned to Chicago to join the prominent law firm of Poppenhusen, Johnston, Thompson, and Raymond, which specialized in

antitrust law. Stevens developed a reputation as a preeminent antitrust lawyer, and after three years with Poppenhusen he left in 1952 to form his own firm, Rothschild, Stevens, Barry, and Myers. He remained there, engaging in private practice and teaching part time at Northwestern and the University of Chicago law schools, until his appointment by President Richard Nixon in 1970 to the U.S. Court of Appeals for the Seventh Circuit.

Stevens developed a reputation as a political moderate during his undergraduate days at the University of Chicago, then an overwhelmingly liberal campus. Although he is a registered Republican, he has never been active in partisan politics.

Nevertheless, Stevens did serve as Republican counsel in 1951 to the House Judiciary Subcommittee on the Study of Monopoly Power. He also served from 1953 to 1955, during the Eisenhower administration, as a member of the Attorney General's National Committee to Study the Antitrust Laws.

In 1942 Stevens married Elizabeth Jane Sheeren. They have four children. They were divorced in 1979. Stevens subsequently married Maryan Mulholland Simon, a longtime neighbor in Chicago.

Born April 20, 1920, Chicago, Illinois; University of Chicago B.A. (1941); Phi Beta Kappa; Northwestern University School of Law J.D. magna cum laude (1947); married Elizabeth Jane Sheeren 1942; three daughters, one son; divorced 1979; married Maryan Mulholland Simon 1980; law clerk to Justice Wiley Rutledge, U.S. Supreme Court 1947-1948; practiced law, Chicago, 1949-1970; judge, U.S. Court of Appeals for the Seventh Circuit 1970-1975; nominated as associate justice of the U.S. Supreme Court by President Ford November 28, 1975; confirmed December 17, 1975.

Sandra Day O'Connor

Sandra Day O'Connor was the Court's first woman justice, and in 1992, after a decade on the Court, she emerged as a coalition builder in the Court's legal doctrine on abortion and other controversial issues.

Pioneering came naturally to O'Connor. Her grandfather left Kansas in 1880 to take up ranching in the desert land that eventually would become the state of Arizona. O'Connor, born in El Paso, Texas, where her mother's parents lived, was raised on the Lazy B Ranch, the 162,000-acre spread that her grandfather founded in southeastern Arizona near Duncan. She spent her school years in El Paso, living with her grandmother. She graduated from high school at age sixteen and then entered Stanford University.

Six years later, in 1952, Sandra Day had won degrees, with great distinction, both from the university, in economics, and from Stanford Law School. At Stanford, she met John J. O'Connor III, her future husband, and William H. Rehnquist, a future colleague on the Supreme Court. While in law school, Sandra Day was an editor of the *Stanford Law Review* and a member of Order of the Coif, both reflecting her academic leadership.

But despite her outstanding law school record, she found securing a job as an attorney difficult in 1952 when relatively few women were practicing law. She applied, among other places, to the firm in which William French Smith—first attorney general in the Reagan administration—was a partner, only to be offered a job as a secretary.

After she completed a short stint as deputy county attorney for San Mateo County (California) while her new husband completed law school at Stanford, the O'Connors moved with the U.S. Army to Frankfurt, Germany. There Sandra O'Connor worked as a civilian attorney for the Army, while John O'Connor served his tour of duty.

In 1957 they returned to Phoenix. In the next eight years their three sons were born, and O'Connor's life was a mix of mothering, homemaking, volunteer work, and some "miscellaneous legal tasks" on the side.

In 1965 she resumed her legal career full time, taking a job as an assistant attorney general for Arizona. After four years in that post she was appointed to fill a vacancy in the state Senate, where she served on the judiciary committee. In 1970 she was elected to the same body and two years later was chosen its majority leader, the first woman in the nation to hold such a post.

O'Connor was active in Republican party politics and was co-chairman of the Arizona Committee for the Re-election of the President in 1972.

In 1974 she was elected to the Superior Court for Maricopa County, where she served for five years. Then in 1979 Gov. Bruce Babbitt—

acting, some said, to remove a potential rival for the governorship—appointed O'Connor to the Arizona Court of Appeals. It was from that seat that President Ronald Reagan chose her as his first nominee to the Supreme Court, succeeding Potter Stewart, who had retired. Reagan described her as "a person for all seasons."

By a vote of 99-0 the Senate confirmed O'Connor September 21, 1981, as the first woman associate justice of the U.S. Supreme Court.

Born March 26, 1930, El Paso, Texas; Stanford University B.A. magna cum laude (1950); Stanford University Law School LL.B. with high honors (1952); married John J. O'Connor III 1952; three sons; deputy county attorney, San Mateo, California, 1952-1953; assistant attorney general, Arizona, 1965-1969; Arizona state senator 1969-1975; Arizona Senate majority leader 1972-1975; judge, Maricopa County Superior Court 1974-1979; judge, Arizona Court of Appeals 1979-1981; nominated as associate justice of the U.S. Supreme Court by President Reagan August 19, 1981; confirmed September 21, 1981.

Antonin Scalia

After Warren E. Burger resigned from the Court and Ronald Reagan named William H. Rehnquist to succeed him as chief justice, the president's next move—appointing Antonin Scalia as associate justice—was not surprising. On issues dear to Reagan, Scalia clearly met the president's tests for conservatism. Scalia, whom Reagan had named to the U.S. Court of Appeals for the District of Columbia in 1982, became the first Supreme Court justice of Italian ancestry. A Roman Catholic, he has nine children and opposes abortion. He also has expressed opposition to "affirmative action" preferences for minorities.

Deregulation, which Reagan pushed as president, was a subject of considerable interest to Scalia, a specialist in administrative law. From 1977 to 1982 he was editor of the magazine *Regulation*, published by the American Enterprise Institute for Public Policy Research.

In sharp contrast to the hours of floor debate over Rehnquist's nomination as chief justice, only a few moments of speeches were given in opposition to the equally conservative Scalia before he was confirmed, 98-0. He has since become the scourge of some members of Congress because of his suspicion of committee reports, floor speeches, and other artifacts of legislative history that courts traditionally relied on in interpreting a statute.

Born in Trenton, New Jersey, March 11, 1936, Scalia grew up in Queens, New York. He graduated from Georgetown University in 1957 and from Harvard Law School in 1960. He worked for six years for the firm of Jones, Day in Cleveland and then taught contract, commercial, and comparative law at the University of Virginia Law School.

Scalia served as general counsel of the White House Office of Telecommunications Policy from 1971 to 1972. He then headed the Administrative Conference of the United States, a group that advises the government on questions of administrative law and procedure. From 1974 through the Ford administration he headed the Justice Department's Office of Legal Counsel, a post Rehnquist had held three years earlier. Scalia then returned to academia, to teach at the University of Chicago Law School.

Scalia showed himself to be a hard worker, an aggressive interrogator, and an articulate advocate. On the appeals court he was impatient with what he saw as regulatory or judicial overreaching. In 1983 he dissented from a ruling requiring the Food and Drug Administration (FDA) to consider whether drugs used for legal injections met FDA standards as safe and effective. The Supreme Court agreed, reversing the appeals court in 1985.

Scalia was thought to be the principal author of an unsigned decision in 1986 that declared major portions of the Gramm-Rudman-Hollings budget-balancing act unconstitutional. The Supreme Court upheld the decision later in the year.

Born March 11, 1936, Trenton, New Jersey; Georgetown University A.B. (1957); Harvard University Law School LL.B. (1960); practiced law, Cleveland, 1960-1967; married Maureen McCarthy 1960; five sons, four daughters; taught at the University of Virginia 1967-1971; general counsel, White House Office of Telecommunications Policy 1971-1972; chairman, Administrative Conference of the United States 1972-1974; head, Office of Legal Counsel 1974-1977; taught at the University of Chicago Law School 1977-1982; judge, U.S. Court of Appeals for the District of Columbia 1982-1986; nominated as associate justice of the U.S. Supreme Court by President Reagan June 17, 1986; confirmed September 17, 1986.

Anthony McLeod Kennedy

Anthony M. Kennedy, President Reagan's third choice for his third appointment to the Supreme Court, made all the difference when the Court's conservative majority began coalescing in 1989.

Kennedy proved to be a crucial fifth vote for the Court's conservative wing in civil rights cases, a firm supporter of state authority over defendants' rights in criminal cases, and a strict constructionist in the mode of Chief Justice William H. Rehnquist in most cases. Kennedy's presence effectively ushered in a new era on the Court. Both of Reagan's earlier appointees, Sandra Day O'Connor and Antonin Scalia, were somewhat more conservative than the men they replaced, Potter Stewart and Warren E. Burger, but they did not shift the balance on the Court.

That role fell to Kennedy, who succeeded Lewis F. Powell, Jr., a moderate conservative and a critical swing vote. On a range of issues where Powell often joined the Court's four liberals, Kennedy has gone the other way.

Kennedy, however, broke with the hardline conservatives in 1992. He voted to disallow prayer at public school graduations and to uphold a woman's right to abortion.

Before Kennedy's nomination in November 1987, the Senate and the country agonized through Reagan's two unsuccessful attempts to replace Powell, first with Robert H. Bork and then with Douglas H. Ginsburg. The Senate rejected Bork's nomination after contentious hearings, and Ginsburg withdrew his name amid controversy about his qualifications and admitted past use of marijuana.

A quiet sense of relief came to pass when Reagan finally selected a nominee who could be confirmed without another wrenching confrontation. Later, Republicans would note the irony in that the man who anti-Bork Democrats so willingly called a moderate conservative tipped the balance on the Court.

Kennedy spent twelve years as a judge on the U.S. Court of Appeals for the Ninth Circuit. But unlike Bork, who wrote and spoke extensively for twenty years, Kennedy's record was confined mostly to his approximately five hundred judicial opinions. His views thus were based in large part on issues that were distilled at the trial level and further refined by legal and oral arguments. Furthermore, Kennedy sought to decide issues narrowly instead of using his opinions as a testing ground for constitutional theories. He continued this approach in the decisions he has written on the high Court.

Confirmed by the Senate 97-0 February 3, 1988, Kennedy was sworn in February 18.

A native Californian, Kennedy attended Stanford University from 1954 to 1957 and the London School of Economics from 1957 to 1958. He received an A.B. from Stanford in 1958 and an LL.B. from Harvard Law

School in 1961. Admitted to the California bar in 1962, he was in private law practice until 1975, when President Gerald R. Ford appointed him to the appeals court. From 1965 to 1988 he taught constitutional law at McGeorge School of Law, University of the Pacific.

He and his wife, Mary Davis, have three children.

Born July 23, 1936, Sacramento, California; Stanford University A.B. (1958); Phi Beta Kappa; Harvard University Law School LL.B. (1961); California Army National Guard 1961; married Mary Davis 1963; two sons, one daughter; associate, Thelen, Marrin, John & Bridges, San Francisco, 1961-1963; sole practitioner, Sacramento, 1963-1967; partner, Evans, Jackson & Kennedy, Sacramento, 1967-1975; professor of constitutional law, McGeorge School of Law, University of the Pacific 1965-1988; judge, U.S. Court of Appeals for the Ninth Circuit 1975-1988; nominated as associate justice of the U.S. Supreme Court by President Reagan November 11, 1987; confirmed February 3, 1988.

David Hackett Souter

At first, the Senate did not know what to make of David H. Souter, a cerebral, button-down nominee who was President Bush's first appointment to the Court. Souter was little known outside of his home state of New Hampshire, where he had been attorney general (1976-1978), a trial judge (1978-1983), and a state supreme court justice (1983-1990).

Unlike Antonin Scalia and Anthony M. Kennedy, his immediate predecessors on the Court, Souter had virtually no scholarly writings to dissect and little federal court experience to scrutinize. Only three months earlier Bush had appointed him to the U.S. Court of Appeals for the First Circuit. Souter had yet to write a legal opinion on the appeals court.

And during Souter's first year on the Supreme Court he remained a mystery. He was a tenacious questioner during oral argument but was reserved in the opinions he authored.

He, however, could be counted on to side with the conservative wing of the Court. In the 1989-1990 term, before Souter replaced Justice William J. Brennan, Jr., one-third of the Court's decisions were 5-4 rulings. In 1990-1991, only one-fifth were so narrowly decided, and many controversial disputes were settled by 6-3 votes.

Souter, in the 1991-1992 term, staked out a more middle ground with Justices Sandra Day O'Connor and Kennedy.

During his confirmation hearings, the Harvard graduate and former Rhodes scholar demonstrated intellectual rigor and a masterly approach to constitutional law. Souter was able to recognize where a particular questioner was headed and to deflect most tough inquiries. He took refuge in the history of legal principles.

His earlier work as state attorney general and as a New Hampshire Supreme Court justice had a conservative bent, but Souter came across as more moderate in the hearings, winning over both Democrats and Republicans with his knowledge of judicial precedent. Senators predicted he would be a swing vote, but in his first year that was not the case.

Souter was approved by the Senate 90-9; dissenting senators cited his reluctance to take a stand on abortion. During his confirmation hearings, Souter refused to say how he would vote if the question of overruling *Roe v. Wade* arose.

Souter is known for his intensely private, ascetic life. He was born September 17, 1939, in Melrose, Massachusetts. An only child, he moved with his parents to Weare, New Hampshire, at age eleven. Except for college, he had lived in Weare since.

Souter graduated from Harvard College in 1961. He attended Oxford University on a Rhodes Scholarship from 1961 to 1963, then returned to Cambridge for Harvard Law School. Graduating in 1966, he worked for two years in a Concord law firm. In 1968 he became an assistant attorney general, rose to deputy attorney general in 1971, and in 1976 was appointed attorney general. Under conservative governor Meldrim Thomson, Jr., Attorney General Souter defended a number of controversial orders, including the lowering of state flags to half-staff on Good Friday to observe the death of Jesus. He prosecuted Jehovah's Witnesses who obscured the state motto "Live Free or Die" on their license plates.

Souter served as attorney general until 1978, when he was named to the state's trial court. Five years later, Gov. John H. Sununu appointed Souter to the state Supreme Court. Sununu was Bush's chief of staff when Souter was named to the U.S. Supreme Court.

Souter, a bachelor, is a nature enthusiast and avid hiker.

Born September 17, 1939, Melrose, Massachusetts; Harvard College B.A. (1961); Rhodes scholar, Oxford University 1961-1963; Harvard University Law School LL.B. (1966); private law practice, Concord, New Hampshire, 1966-1968; assistant attorney general, New Hampshire, 1968-1971; deputy attorney general, New Hampshire, 1971-1976; attorney general, New Hampshire, 1976-1978; associate justice, New Hampshire Superior Court 1978-1983; associate justice, New Hampshire Supreme Court 1983-1990; judge, U.S. Court of Appeals for the First

Circuit 1990; nominated as associate justice of the U.S. Supreme Court by President Bush July 23, 1990; confirmed October 2, 1990.

Clarence Thomas

The Senate's 52-48 vote on Clarence Thomas was the closest Supreme Court confirmation vote in more than a century and followed a tumultuous nomination process that culminated in accusations against Thomas of sexual harassment. The charges, brought out in nationally televised hearings, were never proved and led the black nominee to accuse the Senate of a "high-tech lynching."

Thomas, who took his judicial oath on October 23, 1991, succeeded Thurgood Marshall, the Court's last consistent liberal and a man whose six-decade legal career shaped the country's civil rights struggle. Marshall was the first black justice and Thomas became the second.

Thomas also was the fifth conservative appointment by a Republican president in ten years, a historic record that raised the stakes for the Democratically controlled Senate and led in part to the politics surrounding the confirmation. Thomas was a forty-three-year-old federal appeals court judge when named by President Bush, and senators noted that Thomas likely would be affecting the outcome of major constitutional rulings well into the twenty-first century. His confirmation also solidified the conservative majority on the Court that began asserting itself in the late 1980s.

Most difficult for Thomas were the eleventh-hour allegations from a former employee that he had sexually harassed her when he was assistant secretary of education for civil rights and then chairman of the Equal Employment Opportunity Commission (EEOC). In an unprecedented move, senators abruptly postponed a scheduled confirmation vote and reconvened hearings to take testimony from accuser Anita F. Hill, a University of Oklahoma law professor; Thomas; and witnesses for both.

In the end, most senators said Hill's charges and Thomas's defense—a categorical denial—were inconclusive. Senators fell back on their previous positions based on Thomas's judicial philosophy or his determined character and rise from poverty in rural Georgia.

In Thomas's first year on the Court, he voted most often with Antonin Scalia. Thomas was with dissenting justices when the Court upheld a constitutional right to abortion and prohibited prayer at public school graduations.

After Thomas graduated from Yale Law School in 1974, he worked as an assistant attorney general of Missouri and later was a staff attorney for Monsanto Co. He worked for Sen. John C. Danforth, R-Mo., as a legislative assistant and served in the Department of Education as assistant secretary for civil rights for one year before being named to the EEOC.

Born June 23, 1948, Savannah, Georgia; Immaculate Conception Seminary 1967-1968; Holy Cross College B.A. cum laude 1971; Yale University Law School J.D. 1974; assistant attorney general, Missouri, 1974-1977; one son from first marriage; attorney, Monsanto Co. 1977-1979; legislative assistant to Sen. John C. Danforth, R-Mo., 1979-1981; assistant secretary of education for the civil rights division 1981-1982; chairman, Equal Employment Opportunity Commission 1982-1990; married Virginia Bess Lamp 1987; judge, U.S. Court of Appeals for the District of Columbia 1990-1991; nominated as associate justice of the U.S. Supreme Court by President Bush July 1, 1991; confirmed October 15, 1991.

Glossary of Legal Terms

Accessory. In criminal law, a person not present at the commission of an offense who commands, advises, instigates, or conceals the offense.

Acquittal. A person is acquitted when a jury returns a verdict of not guilty. A person also may be acquitted when a judge determines that insufficient evidence exists to convict him or that a violation of due process precludes a fair trial.

Adjudicate. To determine finally by the exercise of judicial authority, to decide a case.

Affidavit. A voluntary written statement of facts or charges affirmed under oath.

A fortiori. With stronger force, with more reason.

Amicus curiae. A friend of the court; a person, not a party to litigation, who volunteers or is invited by the court to give his views on a case.

Appeal. To take a case to a higher court for review. Generally, a party losing in a trial court may appeal once to an appellate court as a matter of right. If the party loses in the appellate court, appeal to a higher court is within the discretion of the higher court. Most appeals to the U.S. Supreme Court are within its discretion.

However, when the highest court in a state rules that a U.S. statute is unconstitutional or upholds a state statute against the claim that it is unconstitutional, appeal to the Supreme Court is a matter of right.

Appellant. The party who appeals a lower court decision to a higher court.

Appellee. One who has an interest in upholding the decision of a lower court and is compelled to respond when the case is appealed to a higher court by an appellant.

Arraignment. The formal process of charging a person with a crime, reading that person the charge, asking whether he pleads guilty or not guilty, and entering the plea.

Attainder, Bill of. A legislative act pronouncing a particular individual guilty of a crime without trial or conviction and imposing a sentence.

Bail. The security, usually money, given as assurance of a prisoner's due appearance at a designated time and place (as in court) to procure in the interim the prisoner's release from jail.

Bailiff. A minor officer of a court usually serving as an usher or a messenger.

Brief. A document prepared by counsel to serve as the basis for an argument in court, setting out the facts of and the legal arguments in support of the case.

Burden of proof. The need or duty of affirmatively providing a fact or facts that are disputed.

Case law. The law as defined by previously decided cases, distinct from statutes and other sources of law.

Cause. A case, suit, litigation, or action, civil or criminal.

Certiorari, Writ of. A writ issued from the Supreme Court, at its discretion, to order a lower court to prepare the record of a case and send it to the Supreme Court for review.

Civil law. Body of law dealing with the private rights of individuals, as distinguished from criminal law.

Class action. A lawsuit brought by one person or group on behalf of all persons similarly situated.

Code. A collection of laws, arranged systematically.

Comity. Courtesy, respect; usually used in the legal sense to refer to the proper relationship between state and federal courts.

Common law. Collection of principles and rules of action, particularly from unwritten English law, that derive their authority from longstanding usage and custom or from courts recognizing and enforcing these customs. Sometimes used synonymously with case law.

Consent decree. A court-sanctioned agreement settling a legal dispute and entered into by the consent of the parties.

Contempt (civil and criminal). Civil contempt arises from a failure to follow a court order for the benefit of another party. Criminal contempt occurs when a person willfully exhibits disrespect for the court or obstructs the administration of justice.

Conviction. Final judgment or sentence that the defendant is guilty as charged.

Criminal law. The branch of law that deals with the enforcement of laws and the punishment of persons who, by breaking laws, commit crimes.

Declaratory judgment. A court pronouncement declaring a legal right or interpretation but not ordering a specific action.

De facto. In fact, in reality.

Defendant. In a civil action, the party denying or defending itself against charges brought by a plaintiff. In a criminal action, the person indicted for commission of an offense.

De jure. As a result of law, as a result of official action.

De novo. Anew; afresh; a second time.

Deposition. Oral testimony from a witness taken out of court in response to written or oral questions, committed to writing, and intended to be used in the preparation of a case.

Dicta. *See* Obiter dictum.

Dismissal. Order disposing of a case without a trial.

Docket. A calendar prepared by the clerks of the court listing the cases set to be tried.

Due process. Fair and regular procedure. The Fifth and Fourteenth Amendments guarantee persons that they will not be deprived of life, liberty, or property by the government until fair and usual procedures have been followed.

Error, Writ of. A writ issued from an appeals court to a lower court requiring it to send to the appeals court the record of a case in which it has entered a final judgment and which the appeals court will review for error.

Ex parte. Only from, or on, one side. Application to a court for some ruling or action on behalf of only one party.

Ex post facto. After the fact; an ex post facto law makes an action a crime after it already has been committed, or otherwise changes the legal consequences of some past action.

Ex rel. Upon information from; usually used to describe legal proceedings begun by an official in the name of the state, but at the instigation of, and with information from, a private individual interested in the matter.

Grand jury. Group of twelve to twenty-three persons impanelled to hear, in private, evidence presented by the state against an individual or persons accused of a criminal act and to issue indictments when a majority of the jurors find probable cause to believe that the accused has committed a crime. Called a "grand" jury because it comprises a greater number of persons than a "petit" jury.

Grand jury report. A public report, often called "presentments," released by a grand jury after an investigation into activities of public officials that fall short of criminal actions.

Guilty. A word used by a defendant in entering a plea or by a jury in returning a verdict, indicating that the defendant is legally responsible as charged for a crime or other wrongdoing.

Habeas corpus. Literally, "you have the body"; a writ issued to inquire whether a person is lawfully imprisoned or detained. The writ demands that the persons holding the prisoner justify the detention or release the prisoner.

Immunity. A grant of exemption from prosecution in return for evidence or testimony.

In camera. In chambers. Refers to court hearings in private without spectators.

In forma pauperis. In the manner of a pauper, without liability for court costs.

In personam. Done or directed against a particular person.

In re. In the affair of, concerning. Frequent title of judicial proceedings in which there are no adversaries, but instead where the matter itself—such as a bankrupt's estate—requires judicial action.

In rem. Done or directed against the thing, not the person.

Indictment. A formal written statement, based on evidence presented by the prosecutor, from a grand jury. Decided by a majority vote, an indictment charges one or more persons with specified offenses.

Information. A written set of accusations, similar to an indictment, but filed directly by a prosecutor.

Injunction. A court order prohibiting the person to whom it is directed from performing a particular act.

Interlocutory decree. A provisional decision of the court before completion of a legal action that temporarily settles an intervening matter.

Judgment. Official decision of a court based on the rights and claims of the parties to a case that was submitted for determination.

Jurisdiction. The power of a court to hear a case in question, which exists when the proper parties are present and when the point to be decided is within the issues authorized to be handled by the particular court.

Juries. *See* Grand jury; Petit jury.

Magistrate. A judicial officer having jurisdiction to try minor criminal cases and conduct preliminary examinations of persons charged with serious crimes.

Mandamus. "We command." An order issued from a superior court directing a lower court or other authority to perform a particular act.

Moot. Unsettled, undecided. A moot question also is one that no longer is material; a moot case is one that has become hypothetical.

Motion. Written or oral application to a court or a judge to obtain a rule or an order.

Nolo contendere. "I will not contest it." A plea entered by a defendant at the discretion of the judge with the same legal effect as a plea of guilty, but it may not be cited in other proceedings as an admission of guilt.

Obiter dictum. Statements by a judge or justice expressing an opinion and included with, but not essential to, an opinion resolving a case before the court. Dicta are not necessarily binding in future cases.

Parole. A conditional release from imprisonment under conditions that, if the prisoner abides by the law and other restrictions that may be imposed, the prisoner will not have to serve the remainder of the sentence.

Per curiam. "By the court." An unsigned opinion of the court, or an opinion written by the whole court.

Petit jury. A trial jury, originally a panel of twelve persons who tried to reach a unanimous verdict on questions of fact in criminal and civil proceedings. Since 1970 the Supreme Court has upheld the legality of state juries with fewer than twelve persons. Fewer persons serve on a "petit" jury than on a "grand" jury.

Petitioner. One who files a petition with a court seeking action or relief, including a plaintiff or an appellant. But a petitioner also is a person who files for other court action where charges are not necessarily made; for example, a party may petition the court for an order requiring another person or party to produce documents. The opposite party is called the respondent.

When a writ of certiorari is granted by the Supreme Court, the parties to the case are called petitioner and respondent in contrast to the appellant and appellee terms used in an appeal.

Plaintiff. A party who brings a civil action or sues to obtain a remedy for injury to his rights. The party against whom action is brought is termed the defendant.

Plea bargaining. Negotiations between a prosecutor and the defendant aimed at exchanging a plea of guilty from the defendant for concessions by the prosecutor, such as reduction of charges or a request for leniency.

Pleas. *See* Guilty; Nolo contendere.

Presentment. *See* Grand jury report.

Prima facie. At first sight; referring to a fact or other evidence presumably sufficient to establish a defense or a claim unless otherwise contradicted.

Probation. Process under which a person convicted of an offense, usually a first offense, receives a suspended sentence and is given freedom, usually under the guardianship of a probation officer.

Quash. To overthrow, annul, or vacate; as to quash a subpoena.

Recognizance. An obligation entered into before a court or magistrate requiring the performance of a specified act—usually to appear in court at a later date. It is an alternative to bail for pretrial release.

Remand. To send back. When a decision is remanded, it is sent back by a higher court to the court from which it came for further action.

Respondent. One who is compelled to answer the claims or questions posed in court by a petitioner. A defendant and an appellee may be called respondents, but the term also includes those parties who answer in court during actions where charges are not necessarily brought or where the Supreme Court has granted a writ of certiorari.

Seriatim. Separately, individually, one by one.

Stare decisis. "Let the decision stand." The principle of adherence to settled cases, the doctrine that principles of law established in earlier judicial decisions should be accepted as authoritative in similar subsequent cases.

Statute. A written law enacted by a legislature. A collection of statutes for a particular governmental division is called a code.

Stay. To halt or suspend further judicial proceedings.

Subpoena. An order to present oneself before a grand jury, court, or legislative hearing.

Subpoena duces tecum. An order to produce specified documents or papers.

Tort. An injury or wrong to the person or property of another.

Transactional immunity. Protects a witness from prosecution for any offense mentioned in or related to his testimony, regardless of independent evidence against the witness.

Use immunity. Protects a witness from the use of his testimony against the witness in prosecution.

Vacate. To make void, annul, or rescind.

Writ. A written court order commanding the designated recipient to perform or not perform specified acts.

Constitution of the United States

We the People of the United States, in Order to form a more perfect Union, establish Justice, insure domestic Tranquility, provide for the common defence, promote the general Welfare, and secure the Blessings of Liberty to ourselves and our Posterity, do ordain and establish this Constitution for the United States of America.

Article I

Section 1. All legislative Powers herein granted shall be vested in a Congress of the United States, which shall consist of a Senate and House of Representatives.

Section 2. The House of Representatives shall be composed of Members chosen every second Year by the People of the several States, and the Electors in each State shall have the Qualifications requisite for Electors of the most numerous Branch of the State Legislature.

No Person shall be a Representative who shall not have attained to the age of twenty five Years, and been seven Years a Citizen of the United States, and who shall not, when elected, be an Inhabitant of that State in which he shall be chosen.

[Representatives and direct Taxes shall be apportioned among the several States which may be included within this Union, according to their respective Numbers, which shall be determined by adding to the whole Number of free Persons, including those bound to Service for a Term of Years, and excluding Indians not taxed, three fifths of all other Persons.][1] The actual Enumeration shall be made within three Years after the first Meeting of the Congress of the United States, and within every subsequent Term of ten Years, in such Manner as they shall by Law direct. The Number of Representatives shall not exceed one for every thirty Thousand, but each State shall have at Least one Representative; and until such enumeration shall be made, the State of New Hampshire shall be entitled to chuse three, Massachusetts eight, Rhode-Island and Providence Plantations one, Connecticut five, New-York six, New Jersey four, Pennsylvania eight, Delaware one, Maryland six, Virginia ten, North Carolina five, South Carolina five, and Georgia three.

When vacancies happen in the Representation from any State, the

Executive Authority thereof shall issue Writs of Election to fill such Vacancies.

The House of Representatives shall chuse their Speaker and other Officers; and shall have the sole Power of Impeachment.

Section 3. The Senate of the United States shall be composed of two Senators from each State, [chosen by the Legislature thereof,][2] for six Years; and each Senator shall have one Vote.

Immediately after they shall be assembled in Consequence of the first Election, they shall be divided as equally as may be into three Classes. The Seats of the Senators of the first Class shall be vacated at the Expiration of the second Year, of the second Class at the Expiration of the fourth Year, and of the third Class at the Expiration of the sixth Year, so that one third may be chosen every second Year; [and if Vacancies happen by Resignation, or otherwise, during the Recess of the Legislature of any State, the Executive thereof may make temporary Appointments until the next Meeting of the Legislature, which shall then fill such Vacancies.][3]

No Person shall be a Senator who shall not have attained to the Age of thirty Years, and been nine Years a Citizen of the United States, and who shall not, when elected, be an Inhabitant of that State for which he shall be chosen.

The Vice President of the United States shall be President of the Senate, but shall have no Vote, unless they be equally divided.

The Senate shall chuse their other Officers, and also a President pro tempore, in the Absence of the Vice President, or when he shall exercise the Office of President of the United States.

The Senate shall have the sole Power to try all Impeachments. When sitting for that Purpose, they shall be on Oath or Affirmation. When the President of the United States is tried, the Chief Justice shall preside: And no Person shall be convicted without the Concurrence of two thirds of the Members present.

Judgment in Cases of Impeachment shall not extend further than to removal from Office, and disqualification to hold and enjoy any Office of honor, Trust or Profit under the United States: but the Party convicted shall nevertheless be liable and subject to Indictment, Trial, Judgment and Punishment, according to Law.

Section 4. The Times, Places and Manner of holding Elections for Senators and Representatives, shall be prescribed in each State by the Legislature thereof; but the Congress may at any time by Law make or alter such Regulations, except as to the Places of chusing Senators.

The Congress shall assemble at least once in every Year, and such Meeting shall [be on the first Monday in December],[4] unless they shall by Law appoint a different Day.

Section 5. Each House shall be the Judge of the Elections, Returns and Qualifications of its own Members, and a Majority of each shall constitute a Quorum to do Business; but a smaller Number may adjourn from day to day, and may be authorized to compel the Attendance of absent Members, in such Manner, and under such Penalties as each House may provide.

Each House may determine the Rules of its Proceedings, punish its Members for disorderly Behaviour, and, with the Concurrence of two thirds, expel a Member.

Each House shall keep a Journal of its Proceedings, and from time to time publish the same, excepting such Parts as may in their Judgment require Secrecy; and the Yeas and Nays of the Members of either House on any question shall, at the Desire of one fifth of those Present, be entered on the Journal.

Neither House, during the Session of Congress, shall, without the Consent of the other, adjourn for more than three days, nor to any other Place than that in which the two Houses shall be sitting.

Section 6. The Senators and Representatives shall receive a Compensation for their Services, to be ascertained by Law, and paid out of the Treasury of the United States. They shall in all Cases, except Treason, Felony and Breach of the Peace, be privileged from Arrest during their Attendance at the Session of their respective Houses, and in going to and returning from the same; and for any Speech or Debate in either House, they shall not be questioned in any other Place.

No Senator or Representative shall, during the Time for which he was elected, be appointed to any civil Office under the Authority of the United States, which shall have been created, or the Emoluments whereof shall have been encreased during such time; and no Person holding any Office under the United States, shall be a Member of either House during his Continuance in Office.

Section 7. All Bills for raising Revenue shall originate in the House of Representatives; but the Senate may propose or concur with Amendments as on other Bills.

Every Bill which shall have passed the House of Representatives and the Senate, shall, before it become a Law, be presented to the President of the United States; If he approve he shall sign it, but if not he shall return it, with his Objections to that House in which it shall have originated, who shall enter the Objections at large on their Journal, and proceed to reconsider it. If after such Reconsideration two thirds of that House shall agree to pass the Bill, it shall be sent, together with the Objections, to the other House, by which it shall likewise be reconsidered, and if approved by two thirds of that House, it shall become a Law. But in all such Cases the Votes of both Houses shall be determined by yeas and Nays, and the Names of the Persons voting for and against the Bill shall be entered on the Journal of each House respectively. If any Bill shall not be returned by the President within ten Days (Sundays excepted) after it shall have been presented to him, the Same shall be a Law, in like Manner as if he had signed it, unless the Congress by their Adjournment prevent its Return, in which Case it shall not be a Law.

Every Order, Resolution, or Vote to which the Concurrence of the Senate and House of Representatives may be necessary (except on a question of Adjournment) shall be presented to the President of the United States; and before the Same shall take Effect, shall be approved by him, or being disapproved by him, shall be repassed by two thirds of the Senate and House of Representatives, according to the Rules and Limitations prescribed in the Case of a Bill.

Section 8. The Congress shall have Power To lay and collect Taxes, Duties, Imposts and Excises, to pay the Debts and provide for the common Defence and general Welfare of the United States; but all Duties, Imposts and Excises shall be uniform throughout the United States;

To borrow Money on the credit of the United States;

To regulate Commerce with foreign Nations, and among the several States, and with the Indian Tribes;

To establish an uniform Rule of Naturalization, and uniform Laws on the subject of Bankruptcies throughout the United States;

To coin Money, regulate the Value thereof, and of foreign Coin, and fix the Standard of Weights and Measures;

To provide for the Punishment of counterfeiting the Securities and current Coin of the United States;

To establish Post Offices and post Roads;

To promote the Progress of Science and useful Arts, by securing for limited Times to Authors and Inventors the exclusive Right to their respective Writings and Discoveries;

To constitute Tribunals inferior to the supreme Court;

To define and punish Piracies and Felonies committed on the high Seas, and Offences against the Law of Nations;

To declare War, grant Letters of Marque and Reprisal, and make Rules concerning Captures on Land and Water;

To raise and support Armies, but no Appropriation of Money to that Use shall be for a longer Term than two Years;

To provide and maintain a Navy;

To make Rules for the Government and Regulation of the land and naval Forces;

To provide for calling forth the Militia to execute the Laws of the Union, suppress Insurrections and repel Invasions;

To provide for organizing, arming, and disciplining, the Militia, and for governing such Part of them as may be employed in the Service of the United States, reserving to the States respectively, the Appointment of the Officers, and the Authority of training the Militia according to the discipline prescribed by Congress;

To exercise exclusive Legislation in all Cases whatsoever, over such District (not exceeding ten Miles square) as may, by Cession of particular States, and the Acceptance of Congress, become the Seat of the Government of the United States, and to exercise like Authority over all Places purchased by the Consent of the Legislature of the State in which the Same shall be, for the Erection of Forts, Magazines, Arsenals, dock-Yards, and other needful Buildings;—And

To make all Laws which shall be necessary and proper for carrying into Execution the foregoing Powers, and all other Powers vested by this Constitution in the Government of the United States, or in any Department or Officer thereof.

Section 9. The Migration or Importation of such Persons as any of the States now existing shall think proper to admit, shall not be prohibited by the Congress prior to the Year one thousand eight hundred and eight, but a Tax or duty may be imposed on such Importation, not exceeding ten dollars for each Person.

The Privilege of the Writ of Habeas Corpus shall not be suspended, unless when in Cases of Rebellion or Invasion the public Safety may require it.

No Bill of Attainder or ex post facto Law shall be passed.

No Capitation, or other direct, Tax shall be laid, unless in Proportion to the Census or Enumeration herein before directed to be taken.[5]

No Tax or Duty shall be laid on Articles exported from any State.

No Preference shall be given by any Regulation of Commerce or Revenue to the Ports of one State over those of another; nor shall Vessels bound to, or from, one State, be obliged to enter, clear, or pay Duties in another.

No Money shall be drawn from the Treasury, but in Consequence of Appropriations made by Law; and a regular Statement and Account of the Receipts and Expenditures of all public Money shall be published from time to time.

No Title of Nobility shall be granted by the United States: And no Person holding any Office of Profit or Trust under them, shall, without the Consent of the Congress, accept of any present, Emolument, Office, or Title, of any kind whatever, from any King, Prince, or foreign State.

Section 10. No State shall enter into any Treaty, Alliance, or Confederation; grant Letters of Marque and Reprisal; coin Money; emit

Bills of Credit; make any Thing but gold and silver Coin a Tender in Payment of Debts; pass any Bill of Attainder, ex post facto Law, or Law impairing the Obligation of Contracts, or grant any Title of Nobility.

No State shall, without the Consent of the Congress, lay any Imposts or Duties on Imports or Exports, except what may be absolutely necessary for executing it's inspection Laws: and the net Produce of all Duties and Imposts, laid by any State on Imports or Exports, shall be for the Use of the Treasury of the United States; and all such Laws shall be subject to the Revision and Controul of the Congress.

No State shall, without the Consent of Congress, lay any Duty of Tonnage, keep Troops, or Ships of War in time of Peace, enter into any Agreement or Compact with another State, or with a foreign Power, or engage in War, unless actually invaded, or in such imminent Danger as will not admit of delay.

Article II

Section 1. The executive Power shall be vested in a President of the United States of America. He shall hold his Office during the Term of four Years, and, together with the Vice President, chosen for the same Term, be elected, as follows

Each State shall appoint, in such Manner as the Legislature thereof may direct, a Number of Electors, equal to the whole Number of Senators and Representatives to which the State may be entitled in the Congress: but no Senator or Representative, or Person holding an Office of Trust or Profit under the United States, shall be appointed an Elector.

[The Electors shall meet in their respective States, and vote by Ballot for two Persons, of whom one at least shall not be an Inhabitant of the same State with themselves. And they shall make a List of all the Persons voted for, and of the Number of Votes for each; which List they shall sign and certify, and transmit sealed to the Seat of the Government of the United States, directed to the President of the Senate. The President of the Senate shall, in the Presence of the Senate and House of Representatives, open all the Certificates, and the Votes shall then be counted. The Person having the greatest Number of Votes shall be the President, if such Number be a Majority of the whole Number of Electors appointed; and if there be more than one who have such Majority, and have an equal Number of Votes, then the House of Representatives shall immediately chuse by Ballot one of them for President; and if no Person have a Majority, then from the five highest on the list the said House shall in like Manner chuse the President. But in chusing the President, the Votes shall be taken by States, the Representation from each State having one Vote; A quorum for this Purpose shall consist of a Member or Members from two thirds of the States, and a Majority of all the States shall be necessary to a Choice. In every Case, after the Choice of the President, the Person having the greatest Number of Votes of the Electors shall be the Vice President. But if there should remain two or more who have equal Votes, the Senate shall chuse from them by Ballot the Vice President.][6]

The Congress may determine the Time of chusing the Electors, and the Day on which they shall give their Votes; which Day shall be the same throughout the United States.

No Person except a natural born Citizen, or a Citizen of the United States, at the time of the Adoption of this Constitution, shall be eligible to the Office of President; neither shall any Person be eligible to that Office who shall not have attained to the Age of thirty five Years, and been fourteen Years a Resident within the United States.

In Case of the Removal of the President from Office, or of his Death, Resignation, or Inability to discharge the Powers and Duties of the said Office,[7] the Same shall devolve on the Vice President, and the Congress may by Law provide for the Case of Removal, Death, Resignation or Inability, both of the President and Vice President, declaring what Officer shall then act as President, and such Officer shall act accordingly, until the Disability be removed, or a President shall be elected.

The President shall, at stated Times, receive for his Services, a Compensation, which shall neither be encreased nor diminished during the Period for which he shall have been elected, and he shall not receive within that Period any other Emolument from the United States, or any of them.

Before he enter on the Execution of his Office, he shall take the following Oath or Affirmation:—"I do solemnly swear (or affirm) that I will faithfully execute the Office of President of the United States, and will to the best of my Ability, preserve, protect and defend the Constitution of the United States."

Section 2. The President shall be Commander in Chief of the Army and Navy of the United States, and of the Militia of the several States, when called into the actual Service of the United States; he may require the Opinion, in writing, of the principal Officer in each of the executive Departments, upon any Subject relating to the Duties of their respective Offices, and he shall have Power to grant Reprieves and Pardons for Offences against the United States, except in Cases of Impeachment.

He shall have Power, by and with the Advice and Consent of the Senate, to make Treaties, provided two thirds of the Senators present concur; and he shall nominate, and by and with the Advice and Consent of the Senate, shall appoint Ambassadors, other public Ministers and Consuls, Judges of the supreme Court, and all other Officers of the United States, whose Appointments are not herein otherwise provided for, and which shall be established by Law: but the Congress may by Law vest the Appointment of such inferior Officers, as they think proper, in the President alone, in the Courts of Law, or in the Heads of Departments.

The President shall have Power to fill up all Vacancies that may happen during the Recess of the Senate, by granting Commissions which shall expire at the End of their next Session.

Section 3. He shall from time to time give to the Congress Information of the State of the Union, and recommend to their Consideration such Measures as he shall judge necessary and expedient; he may, on extraordinary Occasions, convene both Houses, or either of them, and in Case of Disagreement between them, with Respect to the Time of Adjournment, he may adjourn them to such Time as he shall think proper; he shall receive Ambassadors and other public Ministers; he shall take Care that the Laws be faithfully executed, and shall Commission all the Officers of the United States.

Section 4. The President, Vice President and all civil Officers of the United States, shall be removed from Office on Impeachment for, and Conviction of, Treason, Bribery, or other high Crimes and Misdemeanors.

Article III

Section 1. The judicial Power of the United States, shall be vested in one supreme Court, and in such inferior Courts as the Congress may from time to time ordain and establish. The Judges, both of the supreme and inferior Courts, shall hold their Offices during good Behaviour, and shall, at stated Times, receive for their Services, a Compensation, which shall not be diminished during their Continuance in Office.

Section 2. The judicial Power shall extend to all Cases, in Law and Equity, arising under this Constitution, the Laws of the United States, and Treaties made, or which shall be made, under their Authority;—to all Cases affecting Ambassadors, other public Ministers and Consuls;—to all Cases of admiralty and maritime Jurisdiction;—to Controversies to which the United States shall be a Party;—to Controversies between two or more States;—between a State and Citizens of another State;[8]—between Citizens of different States;—between Citizens of the same State claiming Lands under Grants of different States, and between a State, or the Citizens thereof, and foreign States, Citizens or Subjects.[8]

In all Cases affecting Ambassadors, other public Ministers and Consuls, and those in which a State shall be Party, the supreme Court shall have original Jurisdiction. In all the other Cases before mentioned, the supreme Court shall have appellate Jurisdiction, both as to Law and Fact, with such Exceptions, and under such Regulations as the Congress shall make.

The Trial of all Crimes, except in Cases of Impeachment, shall be by Jury; and such Trial shall be held in the State where the said Crimes shall have been committed; but when not committed within any State, the Trial shall be at such Place or Places as the Congress may by Law have directed.

Section 3. Treason against the United States, shall consist only in levying War against them, or in adhering to their Enemies, giving them Aid and Comfort. No Person shall be convicted of Treason unless on the Testimony of two Witnesses to the same overt Act, or on Confession in open Court.

The Congress shall have Power to declare the Punishment of Treason, but no Attainder of Treason shall work Corruption of Blood, or Forfeiture except during the Life of the Person attainted.

Article IV

Section 1. Full Faith and Credit shall be given in each State to the public Acts, Records, and judicial Proceedings of every other State. And the Congress may by general Laws prescribe the Manner in which such Acts, Records and Proceedings shall be proved, and the Effect thereof.

Section 2. The Citizens of each State shall be entitled to all Privileges and Immunities of Citizens in the several States.

A Person charged in any State with Treason, Felony, or other Crime, who shall flee from Justice, and be found in another State, shall on Demand of the executive Authority of the State from which he fled, be delivered up, to be removed to the State having Jurisdiction of the Crime.

[No Person held to Service or Labour in one State, under the Laws thereof, escaping into another, shall, in Consequence of any Law or Regulation therein, be discharged from such Service or Labour, but shall be delivered up on Claim of the Party to whom such Service or Labour may be due.][9]

Section 3. New States may be admitted by the Congress into this Union; but no new State shall be formed or erected within the Jurisdiction of any other State; nor any State be formed by the Junction of two or more States, or Parts of States, without the Consent of the Legislatures of the States concerned as well as of the Congress.

The Congress shall have Power to dispose of and make all needful Rules and Regulations respecting the Territory or other Property belonging to the United States; and nothing in this Constitution shall be so construed as to Prejudice any Claims of the United States, or of any particular State.

Section 4. The United States shall guarantee to every State in this Union a Republican Form of Government, and shall protect each of them against Invasion; and on Application of the Legislature, or of the Executive (when the Legislature cannot be convened) against domestic Violence.

Article V

The Congress, whenever two thirds of both Houses shall deem it necessary, shall propose Amendments to this Constitution, or, on the Application of the Legislatures of two thirds of the several States, shall call a Convention for proposing Amendments, which, in either Case, shall be valid to all Intents and Purposes, as Part of this Constitution, when ratified by the Legislatures of three fourths of the several States, or by Conventions in three fourths thereof, as the one or the other Mode of Ratification may be proposed by the Congress; Provided [that no Amendment which may be made prior to the Year One thousand eight hundred and eight shall in any Manner affect the first and fourth Clauses in the Ninth Section of the first Article; and][10] that no State, without its Consent, shall be deprived of its equal Suffrage in the Senate.

Article VI

All Debts contracted and Engagements entered into, before the Adoption of this Constitution, shall be as valid against the United States under this Constitution, as under the Confederation.

This Constitution, and the Laws of the United States which shall be made in Pursuance thereof; and all Treaties made, or which shall be made, under the Authority of the United States, shall be the supreme Law of the Land; and the Judges in every State shall be bound thereby, any Thing in the Constitution or Laws of any State to the Contrary notwithstanding.

The Senators and Representatives before mentioned, and the Members of the several State Legislatures, and all executive and judicial Officers, both of the United States and of the several States, shall be bound by Oath or Affirmation, to support this Constitution; but no religious Test shall ever be required as a Qualification to any Office or public Trust under the United States.

Article VII

The Ratification of the Conventions of nine States, shall be sufficient for the Establishment of this Constitution between the States so ratifying the Same.

Done in Convention by the Unanimous Consent of the States present the Seventeenth Day of September in the Year of our Lord one thousand seven hundred and Eighty seven and of the Independence of the United States of America the Twelfth. IN WITNESS whereof We have hereunto subscribed our Names,

George Washington,
President and
deputy from Virginia.

New Hampshire: John Langdon,
Nicholas Gilman.

Massachusetts: Nathaniel Gorham,
Rufus King.

Connecticut: William Samuel Johnson,
Roger Sherman.

New York: Alexander Hamilton.

New Jersey: William Livingston,
David Brearley,
William Paterson,
Jonathan Dayton.

Pennsylvania: Benjamin Franklin,
Thomas Mifflin,
Robert Morris,
George Clymer,
Thomas FitzSimons,
Jared Ingersoll,
James Wilson,
Gouverneur Morris.

Delaware: George Read,
Gunning Bedford Jr.,
John Dickinson,
Richard Bassett,
Jacob Broom.

Maryland:	James McHenry, Daniel of St. Thomas Jenifer, Daniel Carroll.
Virginia:	John Blair, James Madison Jr.
North Carolina:	William Blount, Richard Dobbs Spaight, Hugh Williamson.
South Carolina:	John Rutledge, Charles Cotesworth Pinckney, Charles Pinckney, Pierce Butler.
Georgia:	William Few, Abraham Baldwin.

[The language of the original Constitution, not including the Amendments, was adopted by a convention of the states on September 17, 1787, and was subsequently ratified by the states on the following dates: Delaware, December 7, 1787; Pennsylvania, December 12, 1787; New Jersey, December 18, 1787; Georgia, January 2, 1788; Connecticut, January 9, 1788; Massachusetts, February 6, 1788; Maryland, April 28, 1788; South Carolina, May 23, 1788; New Hampshire, June 21, 1788.

Ratification was completed on June 21, 1788.

The Constitution subsequently was ratified by Virginia, June 25, 1788; New York, July 26, 1788; North Carolina, November 21, 1789; Rhode Island, May 29, 1790; and Vermont, January 10, 1791.]

Amendments

Amendment I

(First ten amendments ratified December 15, 1791.)

Congress shall make no law respecting an establishment of religion, or prohibiting the free exercise thereof; or abridging the freedom of speech, or of the press; or the right of the people peaceably to assemble, and to petition the Government for a redress of grievances.

Amendment II

A well regulated Militia, being necessary to the security of a free State, the right of the people to keep and bear Arms, shall not be infringed.

Amendment III

No Soldier shall, in time of peace be quartered in any house, without the consent of the Owner, nor in time of war, but in a manner to be prescribed by law.

Amendment IV

The right of the people to be secure in their persons, houses, papers, and effects, against unreasonable searches and seizures, shall not be violated, and no Warrants shall issue, but upon probable cause, supported by Oath or affirmation, and particularly describing the place to be searched, and the persons or things to be seized.

Amendment V

No person shall be held to answer for a capital, or otherwise infamous crime, unless on a presentment or indictment of a Grand Jury, except in cases arising in the land or naval forces, or in the Militia, when in actual service in time of War or public danger; nor shall any person be subject for the same offence to be twice put in jeopardy of life or limb; nor shall be compelled in any criminal case to be a witness against himself, nor be deprived of life, liberty, or property, without due process of law; nor shall private property be taken for public use, without just compensation.

Amendment VI

In all criminal prosecutions, the accused shall enjoy the right to a speedy and public trial, by an impartial jury of the State and district wherein the crime shall have been committed, which district shall have been previously ascertained by law, and to be informed of the nature and cause of the accusation; to be confronted with the witnesses against him; to have compulsory process for obtaining witnesses in his favor, and to have the Assistance of Counsel for his defence.

Amendment VII

In Suits at common law, where the value in controversy shall exceed twenty dollars, the right of trial by jury shall be preserved, and no fact tried by a jury, shall be otherwise re-examined in any Court of the United States, than according to the rules of the common law.

Amendment VIII

Excessive bail shall not be required, nor excessive fines imposed, nor cruel and unusual punishments inflicted.

Amendment IX

The enumeration in the Constitution, of certain rights, shall not be construed to deny or disparage others retained by the people.

Amendment X

The powers not delegated to the United States by the Constitution, nor prohibited by it to the States, are reserved to the States respectively, or to the people.

Amendment XI

(Ratified February 7, 1795)

The Judicial power of the United States shall not be construed to extend to any suit in law or equity, commenced or prosecuted against one of the United States by Citizens of another State, or by Citizens or Subjects of any Foreign State.

Amendment XII

(Ratified June 15, 1804)

The Electors shall meet in their respective states and vote by ballot for President and Vice-President, one of whom, at least, shall not be an inhabitant of the same state with themselves; they shall name in their ballots the person voted for as President, and in distinct ballots the person voted for as Vice-President, and they shall make distinct lists of all persons voted for as President, and of all persons voted for as Vice-President, and of the number of votes for each, which lists they shall sign and certify, and transmit sealed to the seat of the government of the United States, directed to the President of the Senate;—The President of the Senate shall, in the presence of the Senate and House of Representatives, open all the certificates and the votes shall then be counted;— The person having the greatest number of votes for President, shall be the President, if such number be a majority of the whole number of

Electors appointed; and if no person have such majority, then from the persons having the highest numbers not exceeding three on the list of those voted for as President, the House of Representatives shall choose immediately, by ballot, the President. But in choosing the President, the votes shall be taken by states, the representation from each state having one vote; a quorum for this purpose shall consist of a member or members from two-thirds of the states, and a majority of all the states shall be necessary to a choice. [And if the House of Representatives shall not choose a President whenever the right of choice shall devolve upon them, before the fourth day of March next following, then the Vice-President shall act as President, as in the case of the death or other constitutional disability of the President.—][11] The person having the greatest number of votes as Vice-President, shall be the Vice-President, if such number be a majority of the whole number of Electors appointed, and if no person have a majority, then from the two highest numbers on the list, the Senate shall choose the Vice-President; a quorum for the purpose shall consist of two-thirds of the whole number of Senators, and a majority of the whole number shall be necessary to a choice. But no person constitutionally ineligible to the office of President shall be eligible to that of Vice-President of the United States.

Amendment XIII

(Ratified December 6, 1865)

Section 1. Neither slavery nor involuntary servitude, except as a punishment for crime whereof the party shall have been duly convicted, shall exist within the United States, or any place subject to their jurisdiction.

Section 2. Congress shall have power to enforce this article by appropriate legislation.

Amendment XIV

(Ratified July 9, 1868)

Section 1. All persons born or naturalized in the United States, and subject to the jurisdiction thereof, are citizens of the United States and of the State wherein they reside. No State shall make or enforce any law which shall abridge the privileges or immunities of citizens of the United States; nor shall any State deprive any person of life, liberty, or property, without due process of law; nor deny to any person within its jurisdiction the equal protection of the laws.

Section 2. Representatives shall be apportioned among the several States according to their respective numbers, counting the whole number of persons in each State, excluding Indians not taxed. But when the right to vote at any election for the choice of electors for President and Vice President of the United States, Representatives in Congress, the Executive and Judicial officers of a State, or the members of the Legislature thereof, is denied to any of the male inhabitants of such State, being twenty-one years of age,[12] and citizens of the United States, or in any way abridged, except for participation in rebellion, or other crime, the basis of representation therein shall be reduced in the proportion which the number of such male citizens shall bear to the whole number of male citizens twenty-one years of age in such State.

Section 3. No person shall be a Senator or Representative in Congress, or elector of President and Vice President, or hold any office, civil or military, under the United States, or under any State, who, having previously taken an oath, as a member of Congress, or as an officer of the United States, or as a member of any State legislature, or as an executive or judicial officer of any State, to support the Constitution of the United States, shall have engaged in insurrection or rebellion against the same, or given aid or comfort to the enemies thereof. But Congress may by a vote of two-thirds of each House, remove such disability.

Section 4. The validity of the public debt of the United States, authorized by law, including debts incurred for payment of pensions and bounties for services in suppressing insurrection or rebellion, shall not be questioned. But neither the United States nor any State shall assume or pay any debt or obligation incurred in aid of insurrection or rebellion against the United States, or any claim for the loss or emancipation of any slave; but all such debts, obligations and claims shall be held illegal and void.

Section 5. The Congress shall have power to enforce, by appropriate legislation, the provisions of this article.

Amendment XV

(Ratified February 3, 1870)

Section 1. The right of citizens of the United States to vote shall not be denied or abridged by the United States or by any State on account of race, color, or previous condition of servitude.

Section 2. The Congress shall have power to enforce this article by appropriate legislation.

Amendment XVI

(Ratified February 3, 1913)

The Congress shall have power to lay and collect taxes on incomes, from whatever source derived, without apportionment among the several States, and without regard to any census or enumeration.

Amendment XVII

(Ratified April 8, 1913)

The Senate of the United States shall be composed of two Senators from each State, elected by the people thereof, for six years; and each Senator shall have one vote. The electors in each State shall have the qualifications requisite for electors of the most numerous branch of the State legislatures.

When vacancies happen in the representation of any State in the Senate, the executive authority of such State shall issue writs of election to fill such vacancies: *Provided,* That the legislature of any State may empower the executive thereof to make temporary appointments until the people fill the vacancies by election as the legislature may direct.

This amendment shall not be so construed as to affect the election or term of any Senator chosen before it becomes valid as part of the Constitution.

[Amendment XVIII

(Ratified January 16, 1919)

Section 1. After one year from the ratification of this article the manufacture, sale, or transportation of intoxicating liquors within, the importation thereof into, or the exportation thereof from the United States and all territory subject to the jurisdiction thereof for beverage purposes is hereby prohibited.

Section 2. The Congress and the several States shall have concurrent power to enforce this article by appropriate legislation.

Section 3. This article shall be inoperative unless it shall have been ratified as an amendment to the Constitution by the legislatures of the several States, as provided in the Constitution, within seven years from the date of the submission hereof to the States by the Congress.][13]

Amendment XIX

(Ratified August 18, 1920)

The right of citizens of the United States to vote shall not be denied or abridged by the United States or by any State on account of sex.

Congress shall have power to enforce this article by appropriate legislation.

Amendment XX

(Ratified January 23, 1933)

Section 1. The terms of the President and Vice President shall end at noon on the 20th day of January, and the terms of Senators and Representatives at noon on the 3d day of January, of the years in which such terms would have ended if this article had not been ratified; and the terms of their successors shall then begin.

Section 2. The Congress shall assemble at least once in every year, and such meeting shall begin at noon on the 3d day of January, unless they shall by law appoint a different day.

Section 3.[14] If, at the time fixed for the beginning of the term of the President, the President elect shall have died, the Vice President elect shall become President. If a President shall not have been chosen before the time fixed for the beginning of his term, or if the President elect shall have failed to qualify, then the Vice President elect shall act as President until a President shall have qualified; and the Congress may by law provide for the case wherein neither a President elect nor a Vice President elect shall have qualified, declaring who shall then act as President, or the manner in which one who is to act shall be selected, and such person shall act accordingly until a President or Vice President shall have qualified.

Section 4. The Congress may by law provide for the case of the death of any of the persons from whom the House of Representatives may choose a President whenever the right of choice shall have devolved upon them, and for the case of the death of any of the persons from whom the Senate may choose a Vice President whenever the right of choice shall have devolved upon them.

Section 5. Sections 1 and 2 shall take effect on the 15th day of October following the ratification of this article.

Section 6. This article shall be inoperative unless it shall have been ratified as an amendment to the Constitution by the legislatures of three-fourths of the several States within seven years from the date of its submission.

Amendment XXI

(Ratified December 5, 1933)

Section 1. The eighteenth article of amendment to the Constitution of the United States is hereby repealed.

Section 2. The transportation or importation into any State, Territory, or possession of the United States for delivery or use therein of intoxicating liquors, in violation of the laws thereof, is hereby prohibited.

Section 3. This article shall be inoperative unless it shall have been ratified as an amendment to the Constitution by conventions in the several States, as provided in the Constitution, within seven years from the date of the submission hereof to the States by the Congress.

Amendment XXII

(Ratified February 27, 1951)

Section 1. No person shall be elected to the office of the President more than twice, and no person who has held the office of President, or acted as President, for more than two years of a term to which some other person was elected President shall be elected to the office of the President more than once. But this Article shall not apply to any person holding the office of President when this Article was proposed by the Congress, and shall not prevent any person who may be holding the office of President, or acting as President, during the term within which this Article become operative from holding the office of President or acting as President during the remainder of such term.

Section 2. This article shall be inoperative unless it shall have been ratified as an amendment to the Constitution by the legislatures of three-fourths of the several States within seven years from the date of its submission to the States by the Congress.

Amendment XXIII

(Ratified March 29, 1961)

Section 1. The District constituting the seat of Government of the United States shall appoint in such manner as the Congress may direct:

A number of electors of President and Vice President equal to the whole number of Senators and Representatives in Congress to which the District would be entitled if it were a State, but in no event more than the least populous State; they shall be in addition to those appointed by the States, but they shall be considered, for the purposes of the election of President and Vice President, to be electors appointed by a State; and they shall meet in the District and perform such duties as provided by the twelfth article of amendment.

Section 2. The Congress shall have power to enforce this article by appropriate legislation.

Amendment XXIV

(Ratified January 23, 1964)

Section 1. The right of citizens of the United States to vote in any primary or other election for President or Vice President, for electors for President or Vice President, or for Senator or Representative in Congress, shall not be denied or abridged by the United States or any State by reason of failure to pay any poll tax or other tax.

Section 2. The Congress shall have power to enforce this article by appropriate legislation.

Amendment XXV

(Ratified February 10, 1967)

Section 1. In case of the removal of the President from office or of his death or resignation, the Vice President shall become President.

Section 2. Whenever there is a vacancy in the office of the Vice President, the President shall nominate a Vice President who shall take office upon confirmation by a majority vote of both Houses of Congress.

Section 3. Whenever the President transmits to the President pro tempore of the Senate and the Speaker of the House of Representatives his written declaration that he is unable to discharge the powers and duties of his office, and until he transmits to them a written declaration to the contrary, such powers and duties shall be discharged by the Vice President as Acting President.

Section 4. Whenever the Vice President and a majority of either the principal officers of the executive departments or of such other body as Congress may by law provide, transmit to the President pro tempore of the Senate and the Speaker of the House of Representatives their written declaration that the President is unable to discharge the powers and duties of his office, the Vice President shall immediately assume the powers and duties of the office as Acting President.

Thereafter, when the President transmits to the President pro tempore of the Senate and the Speaker of the House of Representatives his written declaration that no inability exists, he shall resume the powers and duties of his office unless the Vice President and a majority of either the principal officers of the executive department or of such other body as Congress may by law provide, transmit within four days to the President pro tempore of the Senate and the Speaker of the House of Representatives their written declaration that the President is unable to discharge the powers and duties of his office. Thereupon Congress shall decide the issue, assembling within forty-eight hours for that purpose if not in session. If the Congress, within twenty-one days after receipt of the latter written declaration, or, if Congress is not in session, within twenty-one days after Congress is required to assemble, determines by two-thirds vote of both Houses that the President is unable to discharge the powers and duties of his office, the Vice President shall continue to discharge the same as Acting President; otherwise, the President shall resume the powers and duties of his office.

Amendment XXVI

(Ratified July 1, 1971)

Section 1. The right of citizens of the United States, who are eighteen years of age or older, to vote shall not be denied or abridged by the United States or by any State on account of age.

Section 2. The Congress shall have power to enforce this article by appropriate legislation.

Amendment XXVII

(Ratified May 7, 1992)

No law varying the compensation for the services of the Senators and Representatives shall take effect, until an election of Representatives shall have intervened.

Notes

1. The part in brackets was changed by section 2 of the Fourteenth Amendment.
2. The part in brackets was changed by the first paragraph of the Seventeenth Amendment.
3. The part in brackets was changed by the second paragraph of the Seventeenth Amendment.
4. The part in brackets was changed by section 2 of the Twentieth Amendment.
5. The Sixteenth Amendment gave Congress the power to tax incomes.
6. The material in brackets has been superseded by the Twelfth Amendment.
7. This provision has been affected by the Twenty-fifth Amendment.
8. These clauses were affected by the Eleventh Amendment.
9. This paragraph has been superseded by the Thirteenth Amendment.
10. Obsolete.
11. The part in brackets has been superseded by section 3 of the Twentieth Amendment.
12. See the Nineteenth and Twenty-sixth Amendments.
13. This Amendment was repealed by section 1 of the Twenty-first Amendment.
14. See the Twenty-fifth Amendment.

Source: House Committee on the Judiciary, *The Constitution of the United States of America, as Amended,* H. Doc. 100-94, 100th Cong., 1st sess., 1987.

Index

The New Rule... ...ive text for
any organiza... ...ts as green
or sustainabl...

...Capitalism

Jacquelyn wil... ...g not only to
generate grow... ...r as you help
improve the l...

...EOs, method

A must-read... ...and moving
markets tow...

   Cathy L. H... ...ket Diffusion
                    ...M. Huntsman
                    ...te University

. . . Jacquely... ...l advocate of
the green m... ...sity to develop
greener pro... ...pt a more sustainable lif... ...eting students
and profes... ...is right for the
establishm...

   Dr l... ...lustrial Design
and Design for Sustainability Professor, Delft University of Technology

This is a must-read for every marketer in their quest to add value to their existing business flow.

Hiro Motoki, Deputy Chief Executive, E-Square Inc.; Lecturer, Tohoku University Graduate School of Environmental Studies,

Jacquie Ottman has always been at the forefront in bridging the gap between the sustainable marketing theorists and visionaries, and the practical marketing world of competitive pressures and constraints. With her new book she has taken that bridge-building ability to a whole new level.

Professor Ken Peattie, Director, BRASS Research Centre, Cardiff University

Ms. Ottman's books and articles have been some of the key go-to works I have used to serve my clients and students for over a decade.

Wendy Jedlicka, author of *Packaging Sustainability*

Green marketing is the future and Jacquie Ottman is our guide. A high-energy, straight-talking book filled with useful pointers for anyone interested in smart, sustainable brand communications.

Brian Dougherty, author of *Green Graphic Design*

Every entrepreneur involved in sustainable consumer products should read this book.

CJ Kettler, Entrepreneur, Founder and CEO of LIME Media

Green marketing pioneer Jacquelyn Ottman delivers the "New Rules" in a comprehensive, engaging, and readable book sure to become another classic . . . Everything a green marketing professor (and her students) could ask for!

Fredrica Rudell, Associate Professor and Chair of Marketing, Hagan School of Business, Iona College

From the guru of green marketing, Jacquelyn Ottman's *New Rules of Green Marketing* provides an indispensable strategy for the marketing of products and services in the critical times ahead.

Jon Naar, author of *Design for a Livable Planet*

Jacquie Ottman is still the oracle on the subject . . . Jacquie continues to teach us all where responsible green marketing has come from. And, more importantly, where it will be in the next 20 years. Enjoy.

Sol Salinas, Former Director of Marketing and Planning, ENERGY STAR; Federal Sustainability Lead, Accenture Sustainability Services NA

In this new volume, [Jacquie] has once again integrated compelling data and keen observations into an engaging and insightful treatise on the topic.

Michael V. Russo, author, *Companies on a Mission*

Jacquie's latest book provides a highly readable, thoughtful, yet practical route map through often complex and challenging issues.

Martin Charter, Director, The Centre for Sustainable Design, UK

. . . in her new book Jacquie shows us what the next big thing is in the green marketplace.

Ichin Cheng, Director & Partner, Sustainable Innovation Lab, UK

Jacquelyn Ottman has yet again written an indispensable book about green marketing . . . *The New Rules of Green Marketing* is a must-read for every marketer.

Jennifer Kaplan, author of *Greening Your Small Business*

Finally, the book that we need for a 21st-century approach to marketing.

Mary McBride, Design Management Graduate Program, Pratt Institute

This book will become a key reference "rule book" for anyone who wants to participate in this new Green World reality.

Tukee Nemcek, Director, New Brand Initiative, BISSELL Homecare Inc.

Everyone who wants to participate in the sustainability space should read this book.

Ron Buckhalt, Manager USDA BioPreferred program

The New Rules of Green Marketing should be the compass for the business navigating on the odyssey of sustainability.

Jay Fang, CEO, Green Consumers' Foundation, Taiwan

Jacquie Ottman takes her 25 years of experience in green marketing and gives insightful data and helpful checklists for practitioners in the field.

Shelley Zimmer, Environmental Initiatives Manager, HP

The New Rules of Green Marketing is brilliant. A must-read for anyone interested in sustainability.

Laurie Tema-Lyn, Principal, Practical Imagination Enterprises

Ottman's *The New Rules of Green Marketing* is a wonderful, highly valuable resource.

Valerie L. Vaccaro, Associate Professor of Marketing, Kean University

Anyone who buys, designs, or sells *anything* can use this book to make better choices for a lasting and prosperous future.

Pamela J. Gordon, author of *Lean and Green*

Ottman's done it again. Jacquelyn doesn't just have her finger on the pulse of green marketing: she is the pulse.

John Rooks, author of *More Than Promote*

Other books by the author

Environmental Consumerism: What Every Marketer Needs to Know (with Eric Miller; Alert Publishing, 1991)

Green Marketing: Challenges and Opportunities for the New Marketing Age (NTC Business Books, 1993)

Green Marketing: Opportunity for Innovation (McGraw Hill, 1998)

JACQUELYN A. OTTMAN

THE
NEW RULES
OF
GREEN
MARKETING

Strategies, Tools, and Inspiration
for Sustainable Branding

785266 000297

Greenleaf
PUBLISHING

$\overline{\text{BK}}$

Berrett–Koehler Publishers, Inc.
San Francisco
a BK Business book

© 2011 J. Ottman Consulting, Inc. All rights reserved.

Published in the United States and Canada by
Berrett-Koehler Publishers, Inc.
235 Montgomery Street, Suite 650
San Francisco, California 94104-2916, USA
Tel: +1 415 288-0260 Fax: +1 415 362-2512 www.bkconnection.com

Published in the UK by
Greenleaf Publishing Limited
Aizlewood's Mill
Nursery Street
Sheffield S3 8GG
UK
www.greenleaf-publishing.com

Cataloging information is available from the Library of Congress.
    ISBN-13: 978-1-60509-866-1

British Library Cataloguing in Publication Data:
    A catalogue record for this book is available from the British Library.
    ISBN-13: 978-1-906093-44-0

Printed in the United Kingdom
Printed on acid-free paper using vegetable-based inks by
CPI Antony Rowe, Chippenham and Eastbourne

Cover by LaliAbril.com

**For my Geoff,
the original recycler**

Contents

Foreword

Over the past decade few marketing topics have been more dynamic than that of "green" or "sustainability". In a few short years we have witnessed consumers shift from being highly skeptical about the performance of green products to the commoditization of green in many categories.

The recent explosion of green media, products, services, and marketing has brought with it a sea of confusion and a lack of trust, all of which risk undermining the entire green movement and returning us to an era of consumer apathy.

Further complicating the green movement is the arrival of Gen Y who, now in their twenties, are taking center stage in the arena of consumerism. This generation's formative years were the prosperous '90s where they had so many choices that values often became the brand differentiator. Sustainability and green values are a generational characteristic for this 80-million-strong cohort that will influence their lifetime brand loyalty. Not only do they bring these deeply rooted values to the forefront of our economy, but also the tools to support or expose companies in the form of social media.

As this book goes to press we are seeing some of the world's largest polluters also rank high as some of the most "environmental" companies, according to consumer perception. This misalignment between public perception and true environmental impact is being fostered by mass marketing that frequently highlights a handful of "green halo" products or initiatives. But this won't last. The transparency of the Internet and the openness of social media tools will ruthlessly expose the differences between a company's private and public face. With this will come a shift in green marketing from what you say . . . to what you do.

As we move to a future where green marketing cannot remain separate from a business's operations, the role of the marketing team and its internal influence will evolve as well. At the heart of green marketing is a mission bigger than your own brand – the planet. It's about a higher purpose that will require marketers to change their role in an organization to one that influences the organization's actions and accurately reflects its true environmental impact. Is there a difference between green marketing and a green company? Today? Yes. Tomorrow? No.

Jacquelyn Ottman's *The New Rules of Green Marketing* is a timely arrival that will enable us to navigate this changing world. She will help you move from "green" as a niche opportunity to its being a core part of any company's marketing and overall corporate philosophy. Jacquelyn will inspire you about the potential of green marketing not only to generate growth but to feel better about yourself and your career as you help improve the health of the planet.

As we built the *method* brand over the past few years we undertook a pioneering journey bringing green home care into the mainstream. We have navigated these shifts within "green" by maintaining at the heart of our organization a true dedication to building a green and sustainable company called "People Against Dirty". At *method* we do not sell a product; we sell a philosophy. By following our values and beliefs we have created not only a financially rewarding brand, but a higher level of satisfaction and happiness in work – knowing that we are part of something bigger than ourselves. After all, who wants to just make soap when you can save a planet? We hope you find yourselves on a similar journey.

Adam Lowry and Eric Ryan
Co-founders and CEOs, **method**
San Francisco, California

Preface

This book is about the new rules of green marketing that increasingly characterize the purchasing sensibilities of billions of consumers around the world. It took over 20 years of my career advising leading businesses on green marketing strategies (and 15 more years than I had projected), but few would now question the facts that green is mainstream and the rules of the game for marketers are rapidly changing. Is every consumer making every purchase decision a green one? No. Far from it. But are awareness, concern, and intent to purchase the right thing squarely on the radar screens of most consumers in the developed world today? Is green also changing the agendas of the manufacturers and service companies that meet consumers' needs, as well as shaping the agendas of government officials, NGOs, church leaders, the news media, educators, Hollywood celebrities, and every other important force in society? The answer to both of these questions is an emphatic Yes!

This book is also about the strategies needed to play by the new rules. Reflecting the changing attitudes and behaviors of today's consumers, these strategies cover greening current products and inventing sustainable ones; communicating credibly and impactfully, and working proactively with a variety of stakeholders in order to extend one's resources and address consumer needs authentically and thoroughly. I illustrate these strategies by telling the stories of the sustainability leaders – brands with green ingrained in their DNA. Included are stories from Seventh Generation, Timberland, and Stonyfield Farm, companies that are swiftly growing their businesses by extending their appeal from a once very fringe audience to now mainstream consumers. Also included are the stories of the big multinational brands such as GE, HSBC, Starbucks, Nike, Procter & Gamble, Toyota, and Wal-Mart who are quickly adapting to the new rules. This book is also about these two forces coming together to open the doors for young, innovative upstarts such as Method to go green *and* mainstream from their very beginnings – and what everyone can learn by studying their ingeniously unique strategies.

Driven by fears for the future, consumer demand for sustainable products is built on trust. Unfortunately, as I write, the term "green marketing" bears the perceptual brunt of "greenwashing" – players within the industry who overstate or otherwise mislead consumers about the environmental attributes of their offerings. I personally believe that much so-called greenwashing is unintentional and even understandable in a fast-growing industry still finding its sea legs. Green marketers today largely operate without the light of a strong governmental sun or established self-governance. (The U.S. Federal Trade Commission executed zero cases of green claims during the Bush Administration of 2000–2008!) There is no form of certification for green marketing practitioners, and few, if any, courses about sustainable branding are available in community colleges, business schools, or corporate training programs. Nevertheless, I am encouraged by the many sincere efforts to communicate the benefits of legitimate sustainable products that are on the market today; it is these stories and strategies that I recount and celebrate from my many years deeply involved in this industry.

The goal of this book is to help every well-intended marketer to understand the strategies needed to adapt to the new rules of green marketing and to find a profitable, low-risk path to meeting consumer needs in a truly sustainable fashion – indeed, to be inspired to become a leader in his or her own right. Written primarily from the perspective of my native U.S., it nonetheless contains rich content from around the world. I wrote this book for sustainability directors and brand executives at consumer product manufacturers and service providers and their advertising and PR staff and agencies. It is also a valuable tool for entrepreneurs and venture capitalists, professors and students, and representatives of trade associations, NGOs, and government agencies.

I start by making the case for the mainstreaming of green and the ways in which the rules are quickly changing (Chapter 1). In Chapter 2, I describe two ways for segmenting green consumers before characterizing their swiftly changing buyer motives and psychology. Then I describe the new green marketing paradigm (Chapter 3) and provide an in-depth look at one company that superbly exemplifies this paradigm, Method. I move on to discuss what it takes to address the new green marketing paradigm, starting with the strategies for greening one's products (Chapter 4). This is followed by an introduction to sustainable innovation together with five practical strategies for forging an exciting path for significantly reducing one's environmental and sustainability impacts while improving one's top line far into the future (Chapter 5).

With legitimately greener products in hand, readers will be ready to learn about the new strategies of green consumer communications and how to deliver the benefits of their wares with impact (Chapter 6). An entire chapter (Chapter 7) follows devoted to the full complement of strategies for establishing trust and avoiding greenwash. I then offer in Chapter 8 the new strategies for collaborating with various key stakeholders – an essential step in ensuring the legitimacy and completeness of one's efforts in a complex world where one company cannot possibly garner the resources and the expertise necessary for the task.

I close with Chapter 9, which encompasses the in-depth stories and strategies of two sustainability leaders, Starbucks and Timberland, which exemplify a deep understanding of the new rules of green marketing and are laudably showing the way toward integrating environmental and social considerations successfully and profitably into their businesses. I then conclude (Chapter 10), followed by a full complement of resources from around the globe.

Enjoy reading this book and the examples of successful green marketing efforts being conducted by many sustainability leaders including, I am proud to say, some of our clients. I hope you find, as intended, that you will keep it within reach as a useful resource, practical guide, and source of ongoing inspiration.

I'd love to hear your comments, your questions, and the details of your own journey and successes. Send them to me via our company's website, www.greenmarketing.com, and indicate if you'd like to be added to our mailing list. Use the many articles and links there, as well as my blog, www.greenmarketing.com/blog, as supplementary guidance for your efforts and as updates to the material contained within this book.

I wish you much success addressing the **new rules of green marketing**.

Jacquelyn A. Ottman
New York, New York
Fall 2010

Acknowledgments

In the same way it takes a village to raise a child, it took an army of colleagues and associates whom I've met over my 22 years as a green marketing consultant to write this book.

At J. Ottman Consulting we regularly track the most successful greener products and campaigns for our clients. Several interns and other colleagues helped to further research and write many case examples referred to throughout this book. They include: David Aigner, Ann Amarga, James Blackburn, Catie Carter, Brynne Cochran, Marjorie Dunlap, JC Darne, Ling Feng Fu, Laura Gardner, Alana Gerson, Laura Kortebein, Lisa Martin, Isabelle Mills-Tannenbaum, Michael Mintz, Emily-Anne Rigal, Kyle Weatherholtz, and Margot Wood. Veronica Gordon, Sydnee Grushak, Sarah McGrath, Candela Montero, Alexandra San Romàn, and especially Elizabeth Weisser need to be singled out for particularly significant contributions to the text.

In addition, I am grateful to the many representatives of the sustainable corporate leaders, including some of our clients, who reviewed passages of this book for their accuracy. They include: Steve Davies of Natureworks, Clifford Henry and Laura Thaman of Procter & Gamble, Kate Lewis of the USDA's BioPreferred program, Steven Mojo of BPI, Katie Molinari of Method, Anastasia O'Rourke of Ecolabel Index, Ben Packard of Starbucks, David Rinard of Steelcase, Nicole Rousseau of HSBC, Cara Vanderbeck of Timberland, Jill Vohr of the U.S. EPA's ENERGY STAR program, and Shelley Zimmer of HP.

Special thanks to Gwynne Rogers of the Natural Marketing Institute who provided several proprietary charts, and Martin Wolf of Seventh Generation who guided the passages on life-cycle assessment as he has so ably done in my two previous books.

Several esteemed colleagues reviewed sections of the manuscript and provided valuable input and critique including: Martin Charter, Fred Curtis, Joy Fournier, Ann Graham, Wendy Jedlicka, Byron Kennard, John Paul Kusz, Birgitte Racine, Inês Sousa, Edwin Stafford, Pamela van Orden, Rudy Vetter, and particularly John Laumer. Special thanks to Mark Eisen who painstakingly made one last thorough edit towards the completion of the manuscript, and Stephanie Tevonian for her invaluable design assistance.

A final note of thanks goes to my publishers, Greenleaf Publishing in the UK and Berrett-Koehler in the U.S., and in particular to Dean Bargh, Jeevan Sivasubramaniam, and Johanna Vondeling for their significant contributions. Finally, my especial appreciation to John Stuart of Greenleaf for embracing this project with enthusiasm, intelligence, and grace.

The 20 New Rules of Green Marketing

1 Green is mainstream. Not too long ago, just a small group of deep green consumers existed. Today, 83% of consumers – representing every generation, from Baby Boomers to Millennials and Gen Ys – are some shade of green. Moreover, there are now finely defined segments of green consumers.

2 Green is cool. Once a faddish preoccupation of the fringe, green is not only mainstream, it's chic. In fact, green consumers are early adopters and leaders who influence purchasing behavior. Celebrities and other cool types generally are espousing green causes. People show off (and self-actualize) by tooling around in a Toyota Prius (or soon, we predict, in a Nissan LEAF electric), and carry cloth shopping bags to look the part.

3 Greener products work equally or better – and are often worth a premium price. Thanks to advances in technology, we've come a long way since the days when greener products gathered dust on health food store shelves because they didn't work as well and were not a good value. Organics, hybrid cars, and safer cleaning products now command a price premium.

4 Green inspires innovative products and services that can result in better consumer value, enhanced brands, and a stronger company. Savvy managers no longer consider the environment to be a burden that represents added cost and overhead – but an investment that can pay back handsomely.

5 Values guide consumer purchasing. Historically, consumers bought solely on price, performance, and convenience. But today, how products are sourced, manufactured, packaged, disposed of – and even such social aspects as how factory and farm workers are treated – all matter.

6 A life-cycle approach is necessary. Single attributes such as recyclable, organic, or energy-efficient matter greatly, but don't mean a product is green overall. Recycled products still create waste, organic strawberries can travel thousands of miles, and CFLs contain mercury. So a more thorough, life-cycle or carbon-based approach to greening is necessary.

7 **Manufacturer and retailer reputation count now more than ever.** In addition to looking for trusted brand names on supermarket shelves, consumers are now flipping over packages, saying, "Who makes this brand? Did they produce this product with high environmental and social standards?"

8 **Save me!** Scrap the images of planets! Bag the daisies! Nix the babies! Even the greenest consumers no longer buy products just to "save the planet." Today's consumers buy greener brands to help protect their health, save money, or because they simply work better. That's why products such as organics, natural personal care and pet care, and energy-efficient products are leading the way in sales.

9 **Businesses are their philosophies.** It used to be that companies were what they made. International Business Machines. General Foods. General Motors. Now, businesses and brands are what they stand for. Method. Starbucks. Timberland.

10 **Sustainability represents an important consumer need, and is now an integral aspect of product quality.** Green is no longer simply a market position. Products need to be green. Brands need to be socially responsible. Period.

11 **The greenest products represent new concepts with business models with significantly less impact.** If we simply keep greening up the same old "brown" products we've been using forever, we're never going to get to sustainability. With time running out, we've got to "leap" to service replacements for products, and adopt entirely new ways of doing business.

12 **Consumers don't necessarily need to own products; services can meet their needs, perhaps even better.** Consumers historically met their needs by owning products, but concepts like Zipcar and ebooks are starting to prove that utility and service are what really matters.

13 **The brands consumers buy and trust today educate and engage them in meaningful conversation through a variety of media, especially via websites and online social networks.** Talking "at" consumers through traditional media and paid advertising can't build loyalty among empowered consumers in a connected world.

14 **Green consumers are strongly influenced by the recommendations of friends and family, and trusted third parties.** With rampant cynicism about traditional forms of advertising and a backlash in place against perceived greenwashing, savvy marketers leverage purchase influencers and third parties like NGOs and especially eco-labelers.

15   Green consumers trust brands that tell all. BP, ExxonMobil, and SIGG learned this lesson the hard way. It's no longer enough to have a well-known name. Today's brands become trusted by practicing "radical transparency," disclosing the good – and the bad.

16   Green consumers don't expect perfection. Just like there's no more whitest whites, there's no greenest of the green. Consumers expect that you'll set high goals (i.e., perform beyond mere compliance), keep improving, and report on progress.

17   Environmentalists are no longer the enemy. Recognizing the power of the marketplace to effect change, many environmental advocates willingly partner with industry, offering useful guidance and expertise.

18   Nearly everyone is a corporate stakeholder. No longer confined to just customers, employees, and investors, publics of all stripes are now corporate stakeholders: environmentalists, educators, and children – even the unborn.

19   Authenticity. It's not enough to slap on a recycling logo or make a biodegradability claim. Brands viewed as the most genuine integrate relevant sustainability benefits into their products. That's why HSBC and Stonyfield Farm aim to reduce the carbon impacts of their operations.

20   Keep it simple. Plato was an environmentalist: "Simplicity is elegance." Today's consumers are cutting out the needless purchases, and getting rid of the gadgets and gizmos that don't add value to their lives. That's why they are migrating to brands that help express these values – Method, Starbucks, Timberland. It's just that simple.

785266 000297

Green is now mainstream

Back in the 1960s, trying to lead an environmentally conscious lifestyle, and especially integrating green into one's shopping, was a very fringe phenomenon. But it's now decidedly mainstream – and changing the rules of the marketing game in a very big way. Set in motion by Rachel Carson's seminal book *Silent Spring* (1962), the clichéd forerunners of today's green consumers lived off the nation's electric grid, installed solar-powered hot-water heaters on their roofs, crunched granola they baked themselves, and could be spotted wearing hemp clothing, Birkenstocks, and driving a Volkswagen bus. Whatever greener products were available – mostly from fringe businesses, and sometimes manufactured in basements and garages – gathered dust on the bottom shelves of health food stores for good reason: they didn't work, they were pricey, and they sported brand names no one had ever heard of. Not surprisingly, there was little demand for them. The natural laundry powders that were introduced in response to the phosphate scare of 1970 left clothes looking dingy, first-generation compact fluorescent light bulbs sputtered and cast a green haze, and multigrain cereals tasted like cardboard. If you were motivated to recycle, you lugged your bottles and daily newspapers to a drop-off spot inconveniently located on the far side of town. Green media was limited to treasured copies of *National Geographic*, PBS specials of Jacques Cousteau's underwater adventures, and the idealist and liberal *Mother Jones, Utne Reader*, and *New Age* magazines.

That was then. Times have changed – a lot, and with them the rules of green marketing. Today, mirroring their counterparts around the world, 83% of today's American adults can be considered at least some "shade" of green.[1] They enjoy a lifestyle where sustainable choices are highly accessible, attractive and expected. Thanks to advances in materials and technology, today's "greener" products (defined as having a lighter impact on the planet than alternatives) and today's more "sustainable" products (those that add a social dimension, e.g., fair trade) now not only work well, they likely work better and more efficiently than their "brown" counterparts.

Moreso, the channels of distribution have changed. Today, sustainable products are readily available in conventional supermarkets such as Fred Meyer and Safeway, brightly lit emporiums such as Trader Joe's and Whole Foods Market, and of course online. Once confined to rooftops, solar power is now mobile, fueling a modern-day, on-the-go lifestyle embedded in cellphone chargers, backpacks, and even the latest fleet of powerboats. Once confined to the tissue boxes or wrappers of days gone by, recycled content is now good enough for Kimberly-Clark's own Scott Naturals line of tissue products and Staples' EcoEasy office paper, not to mention an exciting range of many other kinds of products from Patagonia's Synchilla PCR (post-consumer recycled) T-shirts made from recycled soda bottles, and even cosmetics packaging like that made from recycled newsprint which embellishes Aveda's Uruku brand, to name just a few.

The green market is not just here to stay, it will also grow and mature, evolving the rules of engagement even further. Knowing how best to cater to today's green consumers will bring significant opportunities to grow your top-line sales and revenue growth and increase your market share among the fast-growing numbers of green consumers, as well as to save money, enhance employee morale, and recruit and retain the brightest minds. As we'll discuss throughout this book, it will also stimulate game-changing innovation, and the ability to enhance your corporate reputation. Embrace sustainability – defined as acting today so that future generations can meet their needs – and enjoy long-term markets for your products, while safeguarding the sources of raw materials on which your very business depends.

Everyone is worried

Green has gone mainstream because more people are worried about sustainability-related issues than ever before. Reflecting awareness that has been steadily building over the past 20 years, the general public is beginning to comprehend the impact these issues will have on their lives now, and in the years ahead – and is starting to act.

Figure 1.1 **Top environmental issues of concern**
% U.S. adults indicating that the following issues concern them

		2009 %	2005–09 % change
Water quality		67	–1%
Hazardous, toxic, and nuclear waste		61	–6%
Pollution from cars and trucks		54	+2%
Water conservation		53	+10%
Deforestation		52	+8%
Global warming or climate change		50	+2%
Overpopulation		50	+28%
Reliance on fossil fuels		47	+18%
Lack of open space or urban sprawl		37	+42%

Source: © Natural Marketing Institute (NMI), 2009 LOHAS Consumer Trends Database®
All Rights Reserved

Historically, green marketers believed that people worried about the environment because they felt the planet was hurting – and their communications reflected as much. (Recall all the ads of days gone by featuring babies, daisies, and planets.) But today's marketers increasingly realize that consumers really fear the planet is losing its ability to sustain human life; they fret about their own immediate health, and that of their children. (Keep in mind that the planet will always be here!) That's why health-related issues such as water quality, hazardous waste and air pollution, water availability, global warming, and overpopulation top the list of environmental concerns consumers fear most (see Fig. 1.1).

This fear has been building for a long time. Toxic waste poisoning the water and community of Love Canal in New York State and the Cuyahoga River's catching fire in Cleveland, Ohio in 1972 put air and water quality at the top of Americans' worry list. Throw in the plight of the Mobro garbage barge that in 1987 searched in vain for a port, and packaging became a worry, too. The devastation wrought by Hurricane Katrina to New Orleans in the summer of 2005, Al Gore's 2006 Oscar-winning movie *An Inconvenient Truth*, and a steady stream of news reports that the Earth is warming and the ice caps are melting introduced the frightening prospect of climate change into living rooms. As I write, America deals with the aftermath of the BP oil spill in the Gulf of Mexico with projections of devastation worse than the *Exxon Valdez* oil spill of 1989.

Toxics – whether they are generated far away in industrial plants or reside in cleaning products tucked under the kitchen sink – are firmly planted on the list, too, fanned by a steady spate of scares over such chemicals as asbestos, PCBs and their dioxin and hormonal effects, perchloroethylene ("perc") used in dry cleaning, polyvinyl chloride (PVC), phthalates, the softening agent in plastic toys, and, most recently, bisphenol A (BPA), which was linked to fetal developmental problems, a discovery that led water bottles and baby products to be whisked from retailer shelves.

Limited supplies of natural resources and rapid population growth bring up the rear on the list of top scares. Save a watt! Save a tree! Save a drop! Consumers fret about dwindling resources of fossil fuels and increased dependence on foreign sources, depleting supplies of fresh water, and deforestation and, increasingly, its link to climate change. Gas prices in the U.S. spiked to over $4 a gallon during the summer of 2008 and many drivers fear such price increases may be just the beginning.

Every generation is green

One's behavior reflects one's values, and "sustainability" – caring for nature and the planet and the people who live here now and in the future – is now a core value of every living generation, starting with the Baby Boomers who led the green charge back in the mid to late 1960s. As important as Baby Boomers are to environmental activism as the nation's primary household shoppers and societal leaders, the potential impact to be made by the Internet-savvy Generations X, Y, and Z may be the most significant yet.

Baby Boomers: The first modern green generation

The heads of millions of U.S. households, the Baby Boomers, have long led the green movement through the values and attitudes they have instilled upon society and have imparted to their children and grandchildren. Born between 1946 and 1964, and ranging in age from 46 to 64 in 2010, the oldest Boomers, as college students and young adults, led the anti-Vietnam war, anti-big business, and pro-environment activist movements of the late 1960s and early 1970s. The brainchild of the then senator Gaylord Nelson, Earth Day was first celebrated by the Baby Boomers in 1970 followed by the first Solar Day in 1971. Their demonstrations of concern gave rise to the National Environmental Policy Act of 1969, the founding of the U.S. Environmental Protection Agency in 1970, the Clean Air and the Clean Water Acts that same year, and the Endangered Species Act of 1973.

Then came the Middle East oil embargo, marking the beginning of the energy crisis of 1973–75, which sharpened the Baby Boomers' focus on the need for smaller, more fuel-efficient cars and renewable forms of energy. In 1979 the release of the fictional *The China Syndrome*, a movie about safety cover-ups at a nuclear power plant, serendipitously opened two weeks prior to the partial core meltdown at the Three Mile Island nuclear-generating station near Harrisburg, Pennsylvania. Today, over half (54%) of Baby Boomers are considered to be "socially conscious shoppers."[2] That's 40 million green Boomers who choose organics, pluck resource-conserving products off the shelf, boycott the products of companies that pollute, and "pro-cott" the products of companies that give back to the community.

Generation X: Eyes on the world

Raised during the emergence of CNN which brought global issues into living rooms 24/7, Generation Xers (Gen Xers, also known as the Baby Bust generation) were born between 1964 and 1977 and are 33–46 years old as of 2010. Counting among them actors Leonardo DiCaprio and Cameron Diaz as two of the most outspoken environmentalists of their generation, Gen Xers see environmental concerns through a lens that aligns social, educational, and political issues.

In 1984, the Gen Xers witnessed the fire in a Union Carbide plant in Bhopal, India, which took over 3,000 lives and is thought to be still causing serious health problems today.[3] In 1985, the Live Aid concert organized by musicians Bob Geldof and Midge Ure broadcast the need for famine relief in a desperate Ethiopia to an unprecedented 400 million worldwide – and opened the eyes of millions of Gen Xers residing in developed nations to the horrors taking place in developing countries. In 1986, Gen Xers also experienced the aftermath of the explosion in the Chernobyl nuclear power plant. And in 1989, their same televisions showcased the devastation wrought by the *Exxon Valdez* oil spill in Prince William Sound, Alaska, and they were likely aware of events such as the Rio Summit of 1992.[4]

Generation Y: Digital media at their command

The likely new leaders of the modern-day green movement are the Generation Ys, born between the early 1980s and the early 1990s, and in 2010 ranging in age from 20 to 30 years old. This tech-savvy generation of Gen Ys (also known as Millennials) grew up with computers and the Internet. Distrustful of government and authority, they are quick to challenge marketing practices they deem to be unauthentic or untruthful. With the ability to express their opinions through blogging, texting, and social networks, they are capable of mustering immediate responses from millions around the globe. The offspring of the Baby Boomers whose social and environmental values they share, today's young adults lived through the Hurricane Katrina in 2005 and the BP Oil Spill in the Gulf of Mexico in 2010, and share awareness of the Great Pacific Garbage Patch, a mass of plastic trash whose exact size is estimated to be bigger than the state of Texas. Like their counterparts in other generations, Gen Ys believe that global climate change is caused by human activities and they are almost twice as likely to buy more green products than those consumers who think climate change is occurring naturally.[5]

Green is an integral part of this generation's college experience. Many schools have signed the American College & University President's Climate Commitment,[6] and legions of students are engaged in newly created environmental studies programs and in campus sustainability initiatives. Reusable water bottles and coffee mugs are ubiquitous on college campuses where many savvy companies are reaching out with sustainability messages to students who will soon become householders with significant incomes. Not content to sacrifice all for the almighty dollar, Gen Ys seek to balance "quality of life" and the "quest for wealth";[7] they seek to work for socially conscious employers.

Generation Z: Green is a natural part of their lives

Suggesting that green is here to stay are Generation Z; the first generation to be brought up in an environmentally conscious world, green is a part of their everyday life. Generation Zs, those currently under the age of 16, think nothing of living in solar-powered homes with a hybrid car in the driveway. Learning about environmental issues in school, they were likely exposed to *The Story of Stuff*, a 20-minute animated video that divulges the environmental impact of our daily consumption. For Gen Zs, sorting paper and plastic for recycling is as natural a daily activity as taking out the trash was for their parents. In school and at home the 3Rs of waste management, "reduce, reuse, and recycle," are as common as the 3Rs of "reading, writing, and 'rithmetic." Environmentally sensitive cleaning aids, locally grown produce, and recycled-paper goods top their parents' shopping lists. Clothes made from organically grown cotton and biobased fibers are part of the Gen Z uniform.

Green behavior: A daily phenomenon

With every generation now espousing sustainable values, environmentally considerate behavior is becoming the norm. As detailed in Figure 1.2, in 2009 nearly all (95%) of Americans are involved in various types of, albeit mostly easy, environmental activities they can do at home, from dropping empties in the recycling bin (recycling is now accessible to 87% of Americans),[8] to replacing an incandescent light bulb with a compact fluorescent lamp (CFL), or light-emitting diode (LED). (A scheduled phase-out of incandescent bulbs will begin in the U.S. in 2012.) They turn off the lights, nudge the thermometer down a degree or two, and turn off the tap when brushing their teeth.

Driven by higher gas prices and corporate carpooling programs, as of 2009, 23% of U.S. adults now claim to share rides to work (thanks in part to corporate rideshare programs), nearly one in four consumers takes the bus or subway, and 31% now claim to walk or ride a bike instead of driving a car. Thanks to new awareness of the harm caused by plastic shopping bags that choke marine life or wind up as litter, and incentivized by monetary rewards at the checkout, peer pressure, and even a desire to make a fashion statement), as of 2009, nearly half (48%) of U.S. adults claim to regularly take reusable shopping bags to the grocery store, up 30% from 2006. Importantly, almost half (46%) of consumers maintain that they regularly boycott a brand or company that has environmental or social practices they do not like, up

Figure 1.2 **Top consumer environmental behaviors**

% U.S. adult population indicating they regularly (daily/weekly/monthly) do the following:

	2009 %	2006–09 % change
Conserve energy by turning off lights	95	NC
Turn off electronics when not in use	90	−1%
Conserve water	85	+2%
Recycle all or most plastic bottles, jars, etc.*	65	+9%
Recycle all or most paper (e.g., newspapers)*	61	+3%
Take own bag to the grocery store	48	+30%
Boycott a brand or company that has practices I don't like	46	+17%
Walk or ride bike instead of driving a vehicle	31	+5%
Compost kitchen scraps and garden waste	27	+2%
Carpool	23	+8%
Take public transportation (e.g., bus, train, etc.)	17	+4%

* Change versus 2007. Recycling behavior measured in quantity not in frequency.

Source: © Natural Marketing Institute (NMI), 2009 LOHAS Consumer Trends Database®
All Rights Reserved

17% since 2006. Big-name companies have become easy targets for activist groups. Exxon, McDonald's, Coca-Cola, Wal-Mart, and Kimberly-Clark are just a few of the big brands that have all been castigated by Greenpeace and other activists for deficient environmental or social practices, including excess packaging, high sugar content, unfair labor practices, and unsustainable forestry operations. Once negative perceptions are created, they are almost impossible to reverse. Who still fails to link Nike to unfair labor practices or Exxon to the Alaskan oil spill?

Green voters and citizens

Concern over the state of the environment has swayed an unprecedented number of voters and has prompted citizens to volunteer in their communities. Broad swaths of citizens voted with the environment in mind when they supported Barack Obama in 2008 for taking even greener positions at the heart of his platform than had Al Gore. Support for such issues as mitigating global warming, curbing nuclear power, limiting offshore drilling, reducing ethanol production, and improving food and product safety have helped to propel green Congressional candidates in both the 2006 and 2008 elections.[9] To boot, since 2006, over 80% of candidates endorsed by the League of Conservation Voters have won seats in the House or Senate, while 43 out of 67 candidates identified as anti-environmental were defeated.[10]

Earth-shattering events that have occurred since the start of the new millennium such as the terrorist attack on 9/11, Hurricane Katrina, the wars in Iraq and Afghanistan, and the Indian Ocean tsunami have led to a skyrocketing number of applications to service organizations such as AmeriCorps and the Peace Corps – and the BP oil spill in the Gulf of Mexico now materializing will likely trigger a similar outpouring. Applications to Teach for America, an organization that serves neglected urban and rural areas, reached almost 19,000 in 2006, almost triple the number in 2000; in 2005 the Peace Corps added almost 8,000 volunteers (the largest group in 30 years), from 11,500 applications, up 20% over the year 2000; and AmeriCorps VISTA (Volunteers in Service to America) had a 50% increase in job applicants from 2004 to 2006.[11]

Shopping goes green

The rules are changing – and shopping lists along with them. An overwhelming majority (84%) of shoppers are now buying some green products from time to time, fueling mass markets for clothing made from organically grown fibers; organically produced foods; cold-water and ultra-concentrated detergents; natural cleaning, personal-care, and pet-care products; air- and water-filtration devices; low-VOC (volatile organic compounds) paints; portable bottled water containers; and biological pesticides and fertilizers. Thanks to a massive campaign from Wal-Mart during 2007 and intensive promotion by local utilities, purchases of CFLs top the list, followed by energy-efficient electronics and appliances, and natural/organic foods and cleaning products.

As of 2008, U.S. consumers invested an estimated $290 billion in a wide range of products and services representing such sectors as organic foods,

Figure 1.3 **Green purchasing behavior**

% U.S. adult population indicating they have purchased products within the last 3 years,[1] 12 months,[2] 6 months,[3] 3 months,[4] and those that own/lease a hybrid vehicle.[5]

	General population %
Any	84
CFLs[2]	51
Energy-efficient electronics and appliances[1]	34
Rechargeable batteries[3]	33
Natural foods/beverages[4]	29
Organic foods/beverages[4]	26
Natural/organic personal care[3]	25
Natural household cleaning products[2]	21
Natural/organic pet food[2]	19
Home water purifiers[1]	18
Low-flow toilets[1]	16
Energy-efficient windows[1]	15
Non-toxic or low fume paint[1]	12
Solar-powered lights[1]	11
Clothing made from organic cotton[3]	10
Eco-friendly lawn and garden[2]	9
Hybrid vehicle[5]	3
Furniture made with sustainable materials[1]	2
Environmentally friendly carpet[1]	2
Solar panels for my house[1]	1

Source: © Natural Marketing Institute (NMI), 2009 LOHAS Consumer Trends Database®

natural personal care, ENERGY STAR-labeled appliances, hybrid cars, eco-tourism, green home furnishings and apparel, and renewable power, up from $219 billion in 2005.[12] This market will only magnify over time, reflecting further advancements in design and technology and an ever-expanding range of high-quality green products with trusted brand names that are readily accessible at mass merchandisers and supermarkets.

Interest in green shopping holds steady, even in a recession; indeed, some recession-driven behaviors are making green downright fashionable: 67% of Americans agree that "even in tough economic times, it is important to purchase products with social and environmental benefits."[13] It's one thing to express interest verbally, and another to demonstrate interest with one's credit card. While all shopping, including green, has been hit hard by the recession, many classes of green products have fared remarkably well, thanks in part to the health and cost-saving benefits that they bestow. For instance, according to the Organic Trade Association, in 2008 organic food sales grew by 15.8% to reach $22.9 billion (accounting for 3.5% of all food products sales in the U.S., up from 2.8% in 2006). Sales of organic non-foods (organic fibers, personal-care products, and pet foods) grew by 39.4% to $1.6 billion.[14] Burt's Bees, the line of natural cosmetics now owned by Clorox, continued to rack up annual sales of $200 million despite recessionary times.[15] During its 2008 market debut, Clorox's Green Works line of natural cleaning products grabbed $123 million in sales, representing a leading share of this burgeoning market, while Seventh Generation's sales of household products grew by more than 20% in 2009 over the previous year to $150 million – and will only multiply with distribution in Wal-Mart, announced in the summer of 2010. Toyota's fuel-efficient Prius sold at a brisk 140,000 vehicles in the U.S. in 2009, while Honda, who make a fuel cell vehicle and a natural gas Civic, reintroduced the Insight during fall 2009 with the goal of selling 500,000 units worldwide by early next decade.[16] And in 2008, General Electric saw a 21% gain in revenue for its portfolio of environmentally sustainable consumer and industrial products, to $17 billion.

Sensing the opportunities are now ripe for picking (and likely fearing that greener competitors will steal their lunch), mainstream consumer-products giants are introducing new green brands. They are skewing advertising dollars, beefing up their websites and quickly getting up to speed on the latest social media networks to educate their own eco-aware consumers about the environmental benefits of their products. Some notable examples include: Kimberly-Clark's Scott Naturals (household paper products made from recycled material), Reynolds Wrap foil made from 100% recycled aluminum, and Church & Dwight's Arm & Hammer Essentials laundry products. Having spent the past 20 years addressing consumer concerns mostly via reduced packaging, the mighty Procter & Gamble (P&G) have themselves started to play by the new green rules. They have pledged to develop and market by 2012 at least $20 billion in cumulative sales of "sustainable innovation products," which they define as "products with a significantly reduced environmental footprint versus previous alternative products."[17] Toward that end, in spring 2010, they inaugurated in the U.S. a multi-brand, multi-platform green campaign dubbed "Future Friendly." Its goal is to place their greenest offerings in 50 million U.S. homes by year-end. The effort, started in the UK and Canada in 2007, will be bolstered by educational messages conducted with conservation groups and will feature P&G brands such as Duracell Rechargeable batteries, Tide HE (high-efficiency) laundry powder and Tide Coldwater, and PUR water filtration products.[18] As the manufacturer of several billion-dollar brands, P&G's campaign builds on research showing that consumers are looking to understand how the brands they already know and trust can help them reduce their impact on the environment.

Another sign that the rules are rapidly changing: well-established mass marketers are also now acquiring leading sustainable brands with the adjudged potential for mass-market expansion. Just a few examples include The Body Shop (acquired by L'Oréal), Stonyfield Farm (now 40% owned by Danone), Tom's of Maine natural personal-care products (Colgate-Palmolive), Aveda cosmetics (Estée Lauder), Green & Black's organic chocolates (Cadbury, now part of Kraft), Ben & Jerry's ice cream (Unilever), Cascadian Farm cereals (General Mills) and Burt's Bees personal-care line and Brita water filters (Clorox).

Expect more supermarket shelves to be lined with green choices in the future. In 2007, the U.S. Patent and Trademark Office saw more than 300,000 applications for green-related brand names, logos, and tag lines. According to Datamonitor, as of April 2009, there were more than 450 sustainable product launches for the year, on track to represent triple the number of launches in 2008, which was in itself more than double those in 2007.[19] Retailers are demanding greener alternatives from their suppliers and are giving greener products preferential shelf treatment. Leading the charge is the Sustainability Consortium Wal-Mart announced during the summer of 2009, and formed in conjunction with the University of Arkansas and Arizona State University. The Consortium is tasked to understand the best way to label products with life-cycle-based data to inform consumer purchase decisions – no doubt raising the green bar for the products they stock in the future.

Finally, over $4 billion in venture capital – more than ever before – is being invested in the cleantech industry to support the development of solar and wind, biofuel, geothermal, and other renewable alternatives to fossil fuels.[20] More money is being invested in renewable energy than for conventional power, and cleantech is now the largest U.S. venture capital category, representing 27% of all venture funds.

Media turns green

Green stories now run in all sections of the *New York Times* and the *Washington Post* and other major dailies each day, and are featured on the covers of *Vanity Fair, Newsweek, Wired,* and the *Sunday New York Times Magazine,* among many others. Big-budget ad campaigns such as those for Apple's "Greenest Laptops," Kashi cereals' "Seven Whole Grains on a Mission," and Scott Naturals' "Green Done Right" run on primetime television. Discovery Channel, Planet Green, Sundance, and other eco-cable channels target the sustainability-aware viewer. At NBC, attention is paid to green via the special programming and "Green is Universal" campaign. With nearly five million subscribers, *Good Housekeeping* magazine has even introduced its own green seal accompaniment to its venerable Good Housekeeping seal. Such organizations are not only committed to addressing the green interests of their viewers and readers, they are greening themselves, some through the Open Media and Information Companies (Open MIC) initiative dedicated to making corporate management practices of the media industry more transparent and responsible.[21]

Many of the uncountable daily messages and images that fan the mainstream consumer's green lifestyle are supported behind the scenes by the Environmental Media Association (EMA), a Hollywood-based nonprofit group with the goal of securing primetime television and movie exposure for the environment. Helping EMA to paint green as cool, accessible, and something people want to emulate, are many Hollywood celebrities including Bette Midler, Brad Pitt, Julia Louis Dreyfus, Cameron Diaz, Leonardo DiCaprio, and the father of Hollywood green, Ed Begley Jr., who among other celebrities walked the green carpet from his Toyota Prius into the Academy Awards in 2006.

Meanwhile the Internet is fast changing the media landscape, becoming the interactive medium for information-seeking aware consumers. Websites such as Discovery's treehugger.com and greenamerica.org empower visitors with the latest new green products and green living tips. Do an Internet search of the words, "green," "environment," or "eco" and you will find that entire communities of tweeters and bloggers are passing along trusted recommendations about which products to buy and which companies to trust. Is your sustainable brand part of this digital conversation? (See the Further Information section on page 199 for the names of more consumer-focused websites and media.) Finally, according to J.D. Power & Associates, conversations on sustainability-related blog posts and discussion boards more than doubled between January 2007 and December 2008. By the end of 2008, more than 70% of online contributors indicated that they were concerned about the environment and nearly half reported that they were actively doing something about it: e.g., driving less, recycling – and buying green products.[22]

Governments take action

Any politician who believes that green is inconsistent with a robust economy may soon be unelectable. In stark contrast to the Bush administration, which failed to lead on global climate change and many other key environmental matters, the Obama administration is fast changing the green rules by making green jobs, green energy, and green infrastructure a focal point of its national agenda. Among its first out-of-the-box initiatives: the 2009 Economic Stimulus Package, which included more than $30 billion in funding focused on energy efficiency grants for state and local budgets, weatherization for low-income housing, retrofitting and modernization of federal buildings, investments in the "smart grid" for electrical power, and "clean coal" carbon capture and sequestration projects. The highly successful Cash for Clunkers program launched in July 2009 aimed to take inefficient, high-emission cars off the road and to stimulate the struggling automobile industry through the purchase of newer, more fuel-efficient cars. A special White House office for green jobs spearheads a national initiative that actively works to educate, train, and prepare a labor force prepared for tomorrow's green technologies.

Although mostly symbolic in nature, it is still telling that in one of her first acts as First Lady, Michelle Obama planted a "slow food" garden at the White House to help educate Americans about the benefits of healthy, locally grown fruits and vegetables.

In response to Americans' sustainability concerns, leaders at the municipal, state, and federal levels are creating more sustainable cities and towns characterized by more green spaces for city dwellers and reduced inner-city congestion (e.g., closing Broadway to traffic in New York City); bike paths and hiking trails built over old railroad tracks (including New York City's new High Line); mandated hybrid taxis and natural gas "clean air" buses; composting by residents (in San Francisco among others); and giving a boost to farmers' markets and community-supported agriculture.

With a history of internal mandates on green purchasing, governments at all levels are now taking steps to skew the mammoth consumer economy toward a greener shade by creating (or promoting more established) eco-labels that favor energy-efficient (ENERGY STAR), organic (USDA [U.S. Department of Agriculture] Organic), and water-efficient (WaterSense) goods; and as of this writing, the USDA is readying a voluntary consumer label to accompany its BioPreferred program for federal purchasing of biobased products. If California's Senator Dianne Feinstein has her way, the U.S. will one day soon have a multi-attribute eco-label resembling Europe's Eco Flower, Japan's EcoMark, and Brazil's "Qualidade Ambiental."

The specter of rising sea levels is fast changing the rules in the many cities that have banned bottled water (whose transportation-related fuel use is now linked to global warming), from government meetings or are incentivizing the construction or upgrade of green buildings and the products (office equipment, carpeting, etc.) that furnish them. With an eye toward reducing greenhouse gas emissions linked to energy generation, many government buildings must now be benchmarked according to the EPA's ENERGY STAR building guidelines or meet the U.S. Green Building Council's Leadership in Energy and Environmental Design (LEED) certification.

Far-reaching business opportunities

Consumer demand for greener products and services creates opportunities for businesses to promote their greener offerings, and introduce profitable new ones, all the while building their top-line sales, enhancing their image, and bolstering the morale of employees newly engaged in a higher purpose.

Higher profits

Polls indicate that consumers are willing to pay a premium for green. However, empirical evidence is demanded by skeptical businesspeople to justify the investments in new technology, special materials or ingredients, and high start-up costs of introducing new greener products. A key new rule of green marketing: people will now pay a premium for such brands as Aveda, Burt's Bees, Method, Stonyfield Farm, and Toyota Prius, all discussed in this book, indicating that today's consumers have higher expectations for the products they buy and that environmental soundness is a new dimension of quality. To the extent that businesses can meet or exceed these new consumer expectations, they will enhance their products' image and ability to command a premium.

According to the old rules, consumers didn't expect ecologically preferable products to work well. However, as will be demonstrated throughout this book, and specifically in Chapter 4, thanks to advances in technology, today's greener products work far better than their predecessors that languished on health food retailer shelves; by definition, the current crop of greener products are perceived as healthier, less toxic, and capable of saving time and money, as well as contributing to a sustainable future. Just a few examples: faucet aerators and water-saving showerheads help slash water and energy bills, concentrated laundry detergents can be carried and stored with greater ease, and non-toxic cleaning products, pest control, and garden products are viewed as safer for children and pets.

Some greener products appeal to consumers for many reasons, suggesting the potential to win over more than one segment of the now enormous

Figure 1.4 **Green products offer mainstream benefits**

Product category	Consumer benefits
CFL lightbulbs	Save money, last longer
Hybrid cars	Quiet ride, fewer fill-ups, status
Natural cleaners	Safety, peace of mind
Organic produce	Safety, better taste
Recycled paper	Save money
Car sharing	Convenience, save money
Solar-powered cellphones	Extended use

Chart: J. Ottman Consulting, Inc.

market for green. Own a hybrid? You might because it's more fuel-efficient, but chances are you want to eventually save money (beyond the purchase premium) or to make fewer trips to the filling station. You may also want to drive in the HOV (High Occupancy Vehicle) or just to look good while tooling around town. And so it goes with so many other greener products, as demonstrated in Figure 1.4.

Expect the genuine value-added benefits of superior performance, convenience, cost savings, and increased health and safety to continue to propel the mass market for eco-inspired products in the years and decades ahead.

New source of innovation

Historically, going green helped to unearth efficiencies that beefed up a company's bottom line. Under the new rules, businesses are discovering the even more attractive eco-opportunity for innovation that boosts top-line revenues. That's because green means doing things differently. As will be demonstrated in Chapter 5, proactive companies are inventing new greener technologies, new business models, and new designs that are capturing media attention, grabbing new customers, and establishing a competitive advantage – if not changing the rules of the game altogether. Examples abound. Zipcar, the new time-sharing scheme for cars, is changing the models for vehicle ownership, leasing, and rental. Toyota's Prius has reawakened a truck- and SUV-focused Detroit to the future-saving possibilities of hybrid-engine vehicles, and a new generation of electric cars and fuel cells is right on Toyota's tail. Cargill's NatureWorks is proving that plastics don't have to rely on fossil fuels and can be recyclable and compostable as well. And "smart grid" technology, coupled with in-home energy meters and web-based monitoring systems, is creating exciting new business opportunities springing from increased consumer awareness about the ability to save money through efficient resource management.

The time for marketers to act is now

The condition of the environment is expected to worsen in the years and decades ahead. Despite conflicting reports and opinions, most scientists still predict that the average temperature will rise between 1.8 and 4.0 degrees Celsius during the 21st century due solely to the burning of fossil fuels.[23] By 2030, climate-change-induced calamities alone are projected to account for 500,000 deaths and $340 billion in damages, up from 315,000 and $125 billion today.[24] The fast-developing BRIC economies of Brazil, Russia, India, and China now attempt to meet their own escalating resource demands and will no doubt put further pressure on commodities. Over the past 50 years, fresh water consumption around the world has tripled;[25] it is projected that, by 2025, two-thirds of the world's people will not have access to potable water.[26]

Green touches the lives of all people around the globe. Businesses cater to myriad stakeholders, including customers, investors, and employees; so industry leaders that are sensitized to the new rules are greening up their products and processes. They know that projecting a company's image as a leader and an innovator, as well as being socially and environmentally aware, can only be positive. Influential customers want to do business with companies that have established their green credentials, so companies are launching hefty advertising and web campaigns, publishing extensively documented sustainability reports, cooperating with external sources to communicate transparently, and communicating their efforts internally.

Pick up any copy of *Fortune* or *BusinessWeek* or tune into a TV news program and you will likely see advertisements for multinational companies that are spending millions to project their commitment to sustainability and to create awareness for exciting new products and technologies: Dow Chemical's The Human Element campaign portrays its ability to address pressing global economic, social, and environmental concerns. Chevron's Human Energy campaign advocates for energy efficiency. General Electric's Ecomagination campaign underscores its commitment to solve pressing environmental problems while driving profitable growth through the development of more efficient jet engines, wind turbines, major appliances, and other technologies. Underscoring social benefits, SC Johnson takes great pains to let you know it is A Family Company while Toyota communicates its interest in enriching the community and being a good neighbor via its campaign We See Beyond Cars. Although some campaigns may be questionable (should General Electric be advocating "clean coal" technology? And few would argue now that BP's Beyond Petroleum campaign was markedly premature in light of the Gulf Oil spill and other recent environmental transgressions), the fact remains that companies now recognize opportunities and are attempting to seize them.

Communicating a company's embrace of sustainability can enhance corporate equity since investors seek to reduce risk and many "socially responsible" investors want to align their values with their savings. Recognizing the opportunity, more and more companies are communicating their green mission and progress. For example, according to a study conducted by SIRAN, a working group of the Social Investment Forum, as of 2007, 49 of the Standard & Poor's 100 issued sustainability reports, up 26% from 2005; and by 2008, 86 out of 100 had special websites detailing their efforts to address the triple bottom line – social, environmental, and economic – of sustainability, compared to 58 in 2005.[27] These reports often detail progress related to sustainability performance aligned with standards produced by the Global Reporting Initiative, along with glowing mentions of coveted green awards – credible third-party demonstrations of environmental and sustainable excellence. For instance, a list of winners of the World Environment Center's annual Gold Medal Award reads like a Who's Who of Corporate America: the Coca-Cola Company, Starbucks Coffee Company, S.C. Johnson & Son Inc., the Procter & Gamble Company, and IBM number among their ranks. Dozens of companies representing over 50 product categories have cherished their nod as U.S. EPA's "ENERGY STAR Partner of the Year," indicating their willingness to work positively with government to foster energy efficiency. Some companies, like our client Bissell ("Get a Little Greener" site), Patagonia ("ecofootprint" site), and IKEA Canada ("The IKEA Way"), have special websites with detailed information for consumers.[28]

On the product front, the Industrial Designers Society of America (IDSA) bestows special Industrial Design Excellence Award (IDEA) prizes that have been won by Nike, Timberland, Herman Miller, and many other leaders for eco-innovative product designs. Some examples are listed in Figure 1.5.

Figure 1.5 **IDEA award winners for design excellence**

Company	Product
Dell	Studio hybrid eco-conscious PC
Herman Miller	Leaf Lamp energy-efficient LED light
Nike	Trash Talk recycled shoe
Tesla	Roadster electric car
Timberland	Mion footwear
Tricycle	SIM carpet sample simulator

Chart: J. Ottman Consulting, Inc.

Finally, special green "Effies" – the advertising industry's Oscar equivalent for campaign effectiveness – have been awarded to General Electric (GE) ("Ecomagination"), our client HSBC ("There's No Small Change"), Wal-Mart ("Personal Sustainability Project"), and Frito-Lay's SunChips ("Compostable Bag").

Personal rewards, too

The rules are also changing as to what constitutes personal satisfaction at work. With customers and stakeholders of all stripes, from employees and plant neighbors to legislators and NGOs, clamoring for businesses to embrace sustainability in their products and their processes, smart CEOs know that sustainability offers a rare opportunity to integrate one's own values and vision into the workplace – and, as demonstrated by the ardor of the Gen Ys for work that balances making a living with making a difference, this is becoming essential in recruiting future generations of capable employees. Sustainable branding helps take that vision to one's customers through the prism of products that are more in sync with nature and via communications that are more in tune with consumers' own evolving values – all the while affording the unique opportunity to personally contribute to a brighter future for our children and grandchildren and sustain human life on the planet for generations to come.

Grasping the new rules of green marketing starts with an in-depth understanding of how today's mainstream green consumers differ markedly from yesterday's fringe activists in attitudes, behaviors, lifestyle, and corporate expectations. Let's start by discussing the full range of issues that concern today's consumers, their green purchasing motivations and behavior, and how this total broad swatch of consumers can be segmented for green marketing purposes – the subjects of the next chapter.

The *New Rules* Checklist

Use the following checklist to test your understanding of the mainstreaming of green and the need for your business to respond now.

○ Is there an awareness within our company of the true extent of environmentalism within society today?

○ What are the top environmental issues of concern to our consumers? Shareholders? Employees? Suppliers? Retailers? Community?

○ What is our top environmental risk? Is there a PVC, BPA, or other chemical scare lurking in our brand's future?

○ What are the natural resources that our brands depend on – and what are the long-term projections for their availability?

○ To which generations do our consumers belong and what are the unique ways in which they express their environmental and social concerns?

○ To what extent do environmental issues affect the way consumers engage with our brand and the products in our category in general?

○ To what extent are our consumers politically and socially active about environmental issues?

○ How has environmentalism affected the shopping habits of our consumers? What types of greener products and services are our consumers buying these days?

○ What are our competitors' key sustainability-oriented initiatives? To what extent are they introducing or possibly acquiring new sustainable brands?

○ What are the key sources of sustainability-related information on which our consumers rely?

○ Which environment-oriented legislators and legislative initiatives affect our business?

○ What opportunities do we have to grow our sales and enhance our image through greener products and green marketing campaigns?

○ What personal rewards in going green might be meaningful in enlisting the support of colleagues and stakeholders in our company's sustainability efforts?

785266 000297

We are all green consumers

Since it was first ignited during the 1970s, the green consumer revolution has been led by women aged between 30 and 49 with children and with better-than-average education. They are motivated by a desire to keep their loved ones free from harm and to secure their future. That women have historically been in the forefront of green purchasing cannot be underestimated. They still do most of the shopping and make most of the brand purchasing decisions (albeit aided by tiny eco-cops riding in the front seat of shopping carts), and they naturally exhibit a nurturing instinct for the health and welfare of the next generation. Poll after poll shows that women weigh environmental and social criteria more heavily in their purchasing decisions than do men. This may also reflect the fact that men in general feel less vulnerable and more in control than women, and thus feel relatively less threatened by news of environmental gloom and doom.

However, with the mainstreaming of green, we are *all* green consumers now. Yesterday's activist moms have been joined by teen daughters searching out Burt's Bees lip balm made from beeswax while their "twenty-something" nephews opt to clean their new digs with Method cleaning products. Husbands boast of higher mileage, fewer fill-ups, and the peppy look of their new Mini Coopers or diesel-powered Jettas that get 50-plus miles to the gallon. The incidence of green purchasing is so prevalent throughout the U.S. population (and I would venture to guess the populations of all countries where greening is prevalent), that consumers need to be segmented psychographically, i.e., by lifestyle orientation and commitment to green, in order to zero in on one's most appropriate target customers. One such segmentation is provided by the Natural Marketing Institute (NMI) of Harleysville, Pennsylvania. Their research, based on interviews with over 4,000 U.S. adults and entitled *The LOHAS Report: Consumers and Sustainability*, is excerpted below.

Five shades of green consumers

According to the NMI, the vast majority of today's consumers – a whopping 83% of the U.S. population – can be classified as some shade of green, signifying their involvement in green values, activities, and purchasing. The balance, an estimated 17%, however unconcerned they may be about the planet, can be viewed as inadvertent greens if only because they must abide

Figure 2.1 **NMI's 2009 green consumer segmentation model**
% U.S. adults

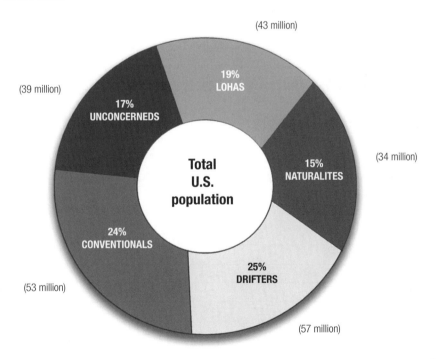

Figure 2.2 Demographic composition of five NMI consumer segments

Capital letters indicate significant difference between groups at 95%.
Percentages rounded.

	Total U.S. adults %	LOHAS (A) %	Naturalites (B) %	Drifters (C) %	Conventionals (D) %	Unconcerneds (E) %
Gender						
Male	48	39	40	49 ^{AB}	57 ^{ABC}	54 ^{AB}
Female	52	61 ^{CDE}	60 ^{CDE}	51 ^{D}	43	46
Age						
Mean (years)	47.3	48.6 ^{CE}	46.6	46.3	49.1 ^{BCE}	45.5
Generation						
Gen Y	24	21	27 ^{AD}	26 ^{AD}	19	30 ^{AD}
Gen X	20	19	19	22	22	18
Booomers	37	40 ^{C}	36	33	39	36
Seniors	19	19	18	19	21	17
Race						
White	78	80 ^{B}	72	77	82 ^{BC}	80 ^{B}
African-American	11	8	23 ^{ACDE}	10	7	11 ^{D}
Asian	2	2	1	4 ^{ABDE}	2	2
Latino	4	4 ^{B}	1	4 ^{B}	4 ^{B}	3
Employment status						
Employed	51	54 ^{B}	45	51	52 ^{B}	51
Retired	23	20	24	23	25 ^{AE}	20
Children in the household						
Children under 18	28	23	31 ^{AE}	33 ^{ADE}	26	25
Age 0–4	10	7	11 ^{A}	13 ^{AD}	8	9
Age 5–12	15	13	19 ^{ADE}	16	14	14
Age 12–17	12	10	13	14 ^{AE}	12	9
Education						
High School or less	44	33	53 ^{AD}	47 ^{AD}	39 ^{A}	50 ^{AD}
Less than College Grad	29	33 ^{C}	27	26	29	28
College and Post Grad	28	34 ^{BCE}	20	27 ^{BE}	32 ^{BCE}	21
Annual household income						
Median (US$000)	$59.6	$68.6	$43.3	$60.5	$69.4	$50.8
Geography						
Northeast	21	27	13	25	25	10
Midwest	22	21	23	20	23	27
South	33	29	48	27	26	45
West	23	24	16	28	26	19

by local laws requiring green behavior – and the consuming that goes with it, such as recycling. Led by the LOHAS (Lifestyles of Health and Sustainability)[1] segment (the deep greens), the NMI's segmentation of U.S. adult consumers into five distinct and mutually exclusive groups makes targeted marketing of mainstream consumers possible (see Fig. 2.1).

LOHAS

As their name suggests, the LOHAS (Lifestyles of Health and Sustainability) segment represents the most environmentally conscious, holistically oriented, and active of all consumers. Representing 19% of all U.S. adults or 43 million people in 2009, they see a universal connection between health and global preservation and use products that support both personal and planetary well-being. The segment that historically has held the most cachet for sustainable marketers, the typical LOHAS consumer, as depicted in Figure 2.2, tends to be a married, educated, middle-aged female. With the second highest income of all five segments, these consumers tend to be less sensitive to price than the other segments, and particularly so for greener products.

Active at home and in their communities, they readily pluck environmentally sustainable products off the shelf, support advocacy programs for a variety of eco and social causes, and are conscious stewards of the environment. They lead the pack in such behaviors as energy and water conservation, toting cloth shopping bags, and lobbying elected officials to pass environmentally protective laws (see Fig. 2.3). A great consumer for any marketer to snag, they are early adopters of greener technologies. Nearly twice as likely to associate their own personal values with companies and their brands, they are more loyal to companies that mirror their values than their counterparts in other segments. Influential in their communities, they recommend greener brands to friends and family.

Representing a change in the rules for their own purchasing, LOHAS consumers energetically seek out information to ensure the products they purchase synchronize with their discerning environmental and social standards. They scrutinize food and beverage labels, opt for foods with minimal processing, and consume more organically grown produce than any other segment. They also study up on corporate sustainability policies; an astonishing 71% will boycott a brand or company that has practices they do not like, almost twice as high as that of their cousins in other segments. Distrustful of paid media, they will consult the Internet and social among other sources of information. According to the NMI, 14% of the LOHAS segment reports that they purchase hard-to-find greener products online.

Naturalites

About one in six U.S. adults, or 34 million consumers, falls into the Naturalites segment. Assuming a very personal approach to the environment, Naturalites aim to achieve a healthy lifestyle and believe in mind–body–spirit philosophies in addition to the power of prayer. Motivated by buzzwords such as "antibacterial," "free of synthetic chemicals," and "natural," Naturalites are concerned about the harmful effects of chemicals in such products as paint, cosmetics, and food. They are quick to select what they perceive to be safer alternatives for themselves and their children. They are also more likely than any of the other segments (aside from LOHAS) to find it important for their stores to carry organic food, with 19% purchasing natural cleaning products in the past year.

Naturalites see themselves as committed to sustainability, but in reality, they are not as dedicated to green purchasing or behaviors including even recycling as their LOHAS or even Drifter cousins. Nevertheless, Naturalites do want to learn more and become more active in environmental protection and are receptive to education in this regard, especially when there is a personal connection to their health. Demographically, Naturalites are the least likely to be college-educated, and have the lowest incomes. Half of Naturalites live in the South (where recycling is not as prevalent as in other areas) and are much more likely to be African-American.

Drifters

Driven by trends more than by deeply held beliefs, Drifters are the second largest segment of the population, representing 25% of all U.S. adults or 57 million consumers. Younger and concentrated in coastal cities, unlike their LOHAS counterparts they have not yet integrated their values and ethics with their lifestyles. With green considered to be "in," catch Drifters making the scene at a Whole Foods lunch bar with a trendy cloth sack in hand, or driving a hybrid not to save money on gas, but for how they will look driving about town. They will boycott companies with questionable environmental reputations, but yield to information culled from the media rather than through their own research. Eager to pitch in on simple green activities they understand – they are avid recyclers and energy conservers – they are less apt than their LOHAS counterparts to engage in more nuanced eco-behaviors such as taking steps to reduce carbon emissions.

Demographically, Drifters tend to have larger household sizes with a third having children under the age of 18. Because Drifters are somewhat conscious of the effects that their actions have on the environment, and earn

Figure 2.3 **Consumer behavior by NMI segment**

% of each segment that regularly (daily/weekly/monthly) does the following:

Activity on a regular (daily/weekly/monthly) basis	LOHAS %	Naturalites %	Drifters %	Conventionals %	Unconcerneds %
Conserve energy by turning off the lights	99	94	95	96	92
Turn off electronics when not in use	96	88	90	90	84
Make extra efforts to reduce heating and cooling costs	95	85	85	89	74
Control thermostat to conserve energy	93	83	85	86	77
Conserve water	96	81	88	86	68
Recycle all/most newspapers	87	29	78	79	24
Slow down when I drive to save gas	79	67	67	66	47
Turn off my car when it's idle to save gas	74	66	64	61	50
Take my own bag to the grocery store or other stores I shop frequently	71	38	50	50	26
Boycott a brand or company that has practices I don't like	71	44	45	40	29
Walk or ride my bike instead of driving a vehicle	43	26	34	31	19
Encourage my elected officials to pass laws to protect the environment	43	23	19	17	8
Compost kitchen scraps and garden waste	41	21	30	28	12
Carpool	31	19	26	23	15
Take public transportation (bus, train, etc.)	21	15	19	16	10

a moderate income, they represent an attractive segment for green market-ers. According to NMI, nearly one-fifth think it's too difficult to consider the environmental impacts of their actions and nearly one-half of Drifters wish they did more to advance sustainability. Marketers who are able to commu-nicate the camaraderie and a sense of belonging that a green lifestyle brings to Drifters will enjoy exceptional returns.

Conventionals

Picture a practical dad directing his kids to pull on a sweater instead of turn-ing up the heat and constantly badgering them to turn off the lights and you get a feel for the Conventionals, the second largest segment represent-ing 53 million consumers who are driven to green for practical reasons. For instance, if LOHAS consumers spend the green for the sake of green, Con-ventionals will spend more for an ENERGY STAR-labeled fridge knowing it will slash their utility bills.

Characterized by good old Yankee ingenuity or midwestern values, Con-ventionals are adept at recycling, and they reuse and repurpose things in an effort to reduce waste and pinch pennies. They are aware of environmental issues but are not as motivated to purchase organic foods or other health-re-lated products as their LOHAS cousins for health or environmental reasons. Likely to be males in their mid-to-late forties with the highest incomes of all the segments, 25% of Conventionals are retired, more than other segments, and a sensible group: 45% of them always pay the entire balance on their credit cards every month.

Unconcerneds

In contrast to their LOHAS, Drifter, and Conventional counterparts, 17% of the population representing 39 million consumers, called the Uncon-cerneds, demonstrate the least environmental responsibility of all the seg-ments. Just over one-quarter will boycott brands made by manufacturers they do not approve of, versus upwards of 40% for their counterparts in other segments; and while 61% say they care about protecting the environ-ment, only 24% recycle. Demographically, the Unconcerneds skew towards younger males living in the South with slightly below-average incomes and lower education levels.

Segmenting by green interests

The rules for addressing the fears of green consumers just got tougher and more complicated. Whereas their counterparts in an earlier day fretted over a rather short list of eco issues topped by clean air and water, recycling, and conserving energy, today's green consumers fear a much wider range of environmental, social, and economically related ills that include carbon emissions and global climate change, fair trade, and labor rights. No one, of course, has the mental and psychological bandwidth, time, or resources to act on all of these issues. So, even the most eco-aware consumers tend to prioritize their environmental concerns, making it necessary to further divide green consumers into four sub-segments characterized by specific issues and causes: resources, health, animals, and the great outdoors. My colleagues and I at J. Ottman Consulting derived the segmentation depicted

Figure 2.4 **Segmenting by green interests**

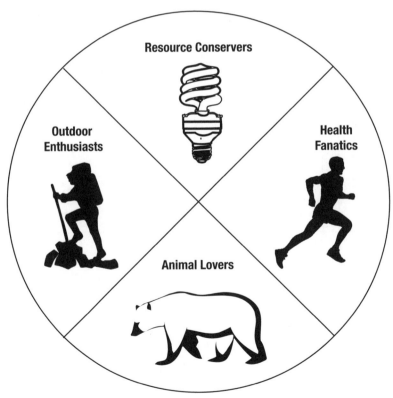

Figure 2.5 **Segmenting by green interests: in depth**

Resource Conservers	Health Fanatics	Animal Lovers	Outdoor Enthusiasts
Likely belong to:	**Likely belong to:**	**Likely belong to:**	**Likely belong to:**
American Rivers	Beyond Pesticides	Wildlife Conservation Society	Sierra Club
Green America	Organic Consumers Association	Defenders of Wildlife	Surfrider Foundation
Center for the New American Dream	Slow Food	People for the Ethical Treatment of Animals (PETA)	American Hiking Society
Likely environmental behavior:	**Likely environmental behavior:**	**Likely environmental behavior:**	**Likely environmental behavior:**
Conserve energy, water	Buy organic foods	Vegetarian/vegan	Use durable, reusable bottles and bags
Recycle bottles, cans, newspapers	Buy natural cosmetics	Boycott tuna, ivory	Avoid excessive packaging
Buy compact fluorescent bulbs	Buy natural cleaning aids	Boycott products tested on animals	Buy natural/biodegradable products for easy camping/hiking clean up
Use reusable shopping bags	Use sunscreens	Avoid fur	Purchase outdoor gear and clothing made with recycled materials
Likely read or visit:	**Likely read or visit:**	**Likely read or visit:**	**Likely read or visit:**
www.treehugger.com	HealthyStuff.org	*Animal Fair Magazine*	*Sierra magazine*
www.greenerchoices.org	*Natural Life magazine*	*Veg News Magazine*	*Backpackers Magazine*
www.earth911.com	*Natural Awakenings magazine*	*The Animals Voice magazine*	*Outdoors Magazine*

Chart: J. Ottman Consulting, Inc.

in Figure 2.4, with further depth provided in Figure 2.5, from empirical evidence, and offer it as a supplement to the NMI segmentation described above to help you add relevance and precision to efforts targeting the deeper green consumers.

Resource Conservers

Resource Conservers (author included) hate waste. Wearing classic styles that last for years, they can be spotted carrying canvas shopping bags and sipping water from reusable bottles. They take their used printer cartridges and electronics to the drop-off center at Best Buy. Once avid newspaper recyclers, they switched to online news services long ago. At home, they reuse their plastic food storage bags and aluminum foil. Ever watchful of saving their "drops" and "watts," they install water-saving toilets and showerheads and faucet aerators. They shun over-packaged products, knowing they will cost them more in "pay as you throw" municipal waste systems. They've swapped their incandescent lamps for CFLs long ago, and they plug their lamps and appliances into power strips, allowing them to save more watts while at work or during a weekend away.

Given the means to do so, they buy home composters to process food waste and install solar panels to save money on electricity. Resource Conservers relish the financial savings that result from these behaviors (it makes them feel smart), and share their experiences with their friends and family to help cut down on more waste. Organizations such as Green America and Center for the New American Dream keep them supplied with ever more tips on eliminating waste.

Health Fanatics

The rule of thumb for Health Fanatics is the consequences of environmental maladies on one's personal health. These are the folks who worry about sun-induced skin cancer, fear the long-term impacts on their children's health from pesticide residues on produce, and perk up to news articles about lead and other contaminants in children's toys and school supplies. Health Fanatics apply sunscreen, pay a premium for organic foods, non-toxic cleaning products, and natural pet care. Catch them bookmarking websites such as the Ecology Center's HealthyStuff.org and HealthyToys.org to keep abreast of the latest on toxic substances in such recently spotlighted products as school supplies, car seats, toys, automobiles, and pet products.

Animal Lovers

As their name suggests, Animal Lovers are passionate about all animals, whether it be their own pets or those in shelters, as well as those in the wild. Likely to be vegetarian or vegan, Animal Lovers are committed to a pro-animal lifestyle. They belong to People for the Ethical Treatment of Animals (PETA), boycott tuna and fur, and only buy products labeled as "cruelty-free" (not tested on animals). They perk up to news stories featuring animals in need, whether it be manatees or polar bears in faraway sites to strays in their neighborhood, and are most likely to volunteer at the local animal shelter. Out of concern for marine life, they eschew plastic bags. This group would favor the cause-related campaign currently being run by Dawn dishwashing liquid, discovered to be an excellent cleaner of oil-soaked wildlife.

Outdoor Enthusiasts

Outdoor Enthusiasts love the outdoors and spend much of their time actively engaged in such activities as camping, "bouldering" (rock climbing without the aid of ropes), skiing, and hiking. They vacation in national parks and enjoy reading about natural destinations around the world. Outdoor Enthusiasts are also actively involved in such organizations as the Sierra Club and the American Hiking Society, which preserve the pristine spaces they value so highly. Whether it's purchasing Dr. Bronner's castile soap to reduce the impact of washing dishes while camping, or reusing bottles and bags to avoid littering the trail, Outdoor Enthusiasts are serious about minimizing the environmental impact of their recreational activities. Their new purchasing criteria includes outdoor gear made from recycled materials, such as Synchilla PCR polyester from Patagonia, Timberland's Earthkeepers boots, and reusable water bottles from Klean Kanteen.

Green consumer motives and buying strategies

Although they express their environmental concerns in individual ways, all green consumers, no matter how "deep" or "light," are motivated by universal needs (see Fig. 2.6) that translate into new purchasing strategies with implications for the way authentic sustainable brands are developed and marketed.

Figure 2.6 **Green consumer motives and buying strategies**

Chart: J. Ottman Consulting, Inc.

Take control

At least one fundamental rule of green consumerism has not changed and likely will not: consumers are looking to control a world they see as spinning out of control. Driven zealously to protect their health and that of their families, sustainability-minded consumers take control in the marketplace, scrutinizing products and their packaging and ingredients with a vengeance; as an added precaution, they also note the reputations of product manufacturers for eco and social responsibility. A key reason consumers are taking things into their own hands is because they tend not to trust manufacturers or retailers – the historical polluters – to provide them with credible information on environmental matters. (see Fig. 2.7).

Today's consumers are doing more at the shelf than just checking prices and looking for familiar brand names. They turn over packages in search of such descriptors as "pesticide-free," "recycled," and "petroleum-free." As depicted in Figure 2.8, the various buzzwords that consumers now use to guide their decision-making represent every phase of the product life-cycle. This suggests that, momentously, while such attributes as performance, price and convenience – once the only things consumers considered when shopping – continue to be important, today's consumers now want to know about the specifics of a product's full panoply of green bona fides such as where raw materials were procured, how a product was manufactured, how much energy is required during use, and whether a product and its packaging can be safely disposed of. Remarkably, as a result of green as well as social concerns (e.g., child labor, fair trade), today's shopping agendas now encompass factors consumers can't feel or see!

Figure 2.7 **Whom do consumers trust for information on global warming?**

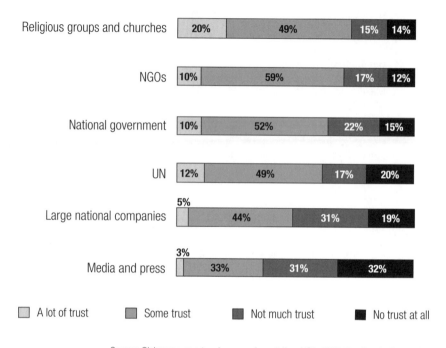

Source: Globescan report on issues and reputation, USA, 2009. Reprinted with permission

Figure 2.8 also references manufacturers – for good reason. Reflecting the deep-seated loyalties of the LOHAS segment, according to the new rules of green marketing, sustainability-aware consumers now look to see if branded product manufacturers can be trusted for eco and socially conscious practices. Consumers are asking such new questions as: Do they treat their workers well? Pay fair wages? Have a low carbon footprint? If the answers are "yes," the vast majority of consumers claim they will "pro-cott" or reward such companies. In a 2008 survey, 57% of respondents said they were likely to trust a company after finding out that it is environmentally considerate, and 60% said they were likely to purchase its products.[2]

Manufacturer (and retailer) reputations for environmental and social responsibility are also critical to consumers' purchasing decisions in another important way. In the absence of information on the package or shelf identifying a specific product as environmentally responsible in one way or another, today's consumers defer to their perceptions of a manufacturer's or retailer's eco and social track records as de facto eco-labels. The fact that

Figure 2.8 **Green purchasing buzzwords**

Raw materials

Sustainably harvested
Biobased
Fair trade

Marketing

Ethical
Cause-related
Transparent

**Manufacturing/
production**

Unbleached
Pesticide-free
Carbon neutral

In-use

Low-fume
Resource-efficient
Durable

Packaging

Recycled
Non-aerosol
Minimal

After-use

Recyclable
Refillable
Reusable

Manufacturer

Socially responsible
Low carbon footprint

Distribution

Fuel-efficient
Local
Reusable packaging

Disposal

Landfill-safe
Compostable
Biodegradable

Chart: J. Ottman Consulting, Inc.

there are so many corporate ads with green themes suggests that business leaders recognize this new reality and are responding accordingly.

As discussed in Chapter 1, following in the tradition of the Baby Boomers who first boycotted companies that invested in South Africa (and hence enabled apartheid social policies), today's greener and social-leaning consumers will also boycott suspected polluters, so a questionable reputation for environmental and social practices can also drive consumers away at the shelf.

Get information

Yesterday's consumers cared mostly about a product's performance and price. To help them take control of a world they increasingly see as risky, today's consumers are asking more penetrating questions. They are finding the answers offered in plentiful supply from a broad array of sources. For example, eco-shoppers can now consult any number of trusted environmental groups, including Green America and Center for the New American Dream. They can log onto favorite Internet sites and get the answers to frequently asked questions such as "What's all the fuss about bamboo?" and "What are some ways that I can save energy in my home?"[3] Consumers can also link to any number of other electronic sources, too, including the very detailed GoodGuide.com website and iPhone application for a peek into the health, environmental, and social impacts of over 70,000 food, toys, personal care, and household products; scores reflect data from nearly 200 sources, including government databases, nonprofits, academia institutions, and scientists on the Good Guide staff.

However, not all of this information is consistent, and consumers are having trouble sorting through it in their quest to tell the greener products from their "brown" counterparts, and find out which products and packages can be recycled or composted in their community. Confusion and distrust are setting in, and the reasons are understandable and many: greener alternatives don't always sport eco-sounding brand names – how can consumers tell by its name that the Method line-up of cleaning products may be greener than Palmolive or Mr. Clean? Alternative cleaners such as baking soda and vinegar may be even greener than Method but are not labeled as such.

As will be discussed in more detail in Chapter 7, today's greener consumers seek out trusted eco-labels such as ENERGY STAR and USDA Organic. In fact, at last count, there are more than 400 eco-labels and certifications in existence. However, only a small percentage of greener products actually carries an eco-label, and if they do, there's no guarantee that consumers will recognize or understand it. As depicted in Figure 2.9, awareness is high for such terms as "global warming" and "biodegradable," but falls off for newer concepts such as "carbon offset" and "socially responsible investments."

Figure 2.9 **Consumer awareness of environmental terms**
% U.S. adult population indicating which of the following terms they are aware of:

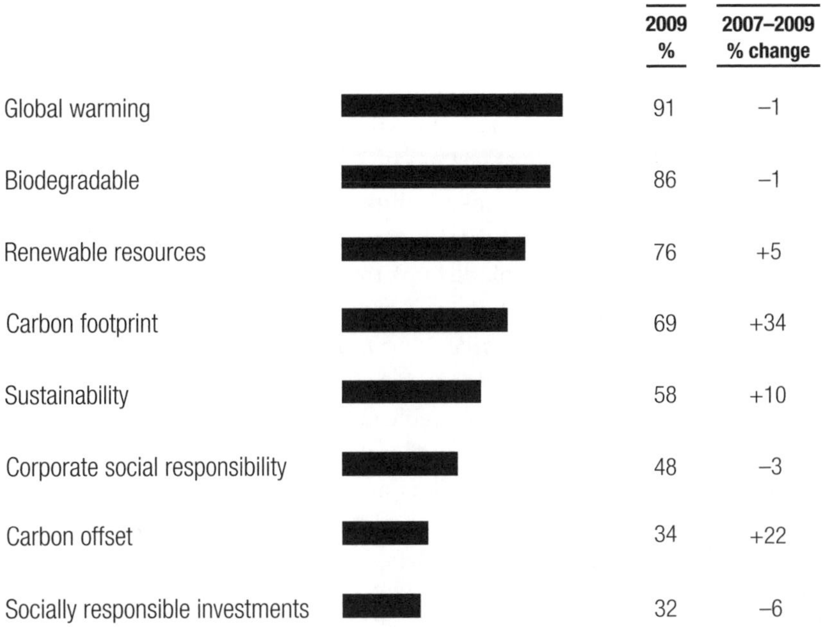
2009 %
2007–2009 % change
Global warming 91 –1
Biodegradable 86 –1
Renewable resources 76 +5
Carbon footprint 69 +34
Sustainability 58 +10
Corporate social responsibility 48 –3
Carbon offset 34 +22
Socially responsible investments 32 –6

Source: © Natural Marketing Institute (NMI), 2009 LOHAS Consumer Trends Database®

Making things worse, sometimes labels can be misleading – or even wrong. Products and packages marked "biodegradable" or "compostable" may be compostable in municipal composting programs, but may not in fact be compostable in backyard composters; those marked "recyclable" may not in fact be recyclable in one's own community if no facilities exist. (Some of this information is the result of intended or unintentional "greenwashing" by businesses looking to put their best green foot forward. See Chapter 7 for more details about greenwashing.)

Although environmental concern runs high and consumers say they are trying to educate themselves, there are still many issues that they don't fully comprehend. For instance, most consumers – and even many well-intentioned green marketers – still believe that anything "biodegradable" simply "disappears" – and will even do so in a landfill – rather than decomposing into soil or other nutrients under controlled conditions in a municipal composting facility, when the truth is that trash in landfills is simply entombed.

Make a difference/alleviate guilt

With the world seen as spinning out of control, green consumers want to feel that they can make a difference either as single shoppers or in concert with all the other users of the products they buy. Acutely aware of how humans are compromising their own health and that of the planet, an increasing number of consumers are now reassessing their own consumption and asking, "Do I really need another widget?" For those looking to pitch in, the mantra becomes, "What can I do to make a difference?" This is called "empowerment," and it underlies such bestsellers as *50 Simple Things You Can Do to Save the Earth*, the groundbreaking book that was revamped in 2006. It is now joined on the shelf by *It's Easy Being Green: A Handbook for Earth-Friendly Living*; *Gorgeously Green: 8 Simple Steps to an Earth-Friendly Life*; and *The Lazy Environmentalist: Your Guide to Easy, Stylish, Green Living*. And they're watching new television shows on cable such as those produced by Animal Planet, The Science Channel, and National Geographic Channel.

Electronically inclined consumers are also linking to other greens via social networks such as MakeMeSustainable.com, Care2.com, Zerofootprint.net, Carbonrally.com, Change.org, Celsias.com, and Worldcoolers.org. Care2.com, for instance, has a Care2 Green Living section and the Care2 News Network where members can post the latest green news stories.

As demonstrated in Figure 2.10, over half (56%) of consumers believe they are doing their bit to protect the environment and indeed perceive themselves as leading other societal groups in this regard, especially government and business. Yet a nearly identical amount (55%) think they should be doing even more – a sentiment that has been trending upward. Consumers' need to make a difference stems as much from a desire for control as from a corresponding need to alleviate guilt, so their greener purchases can make aware consumers feel good about themselves.

Figure 2.10 **Who should be doing more?**

% U.S. adult population stating the following organizations are either currently acting
as a leader in protecting the environment or should be doing more:

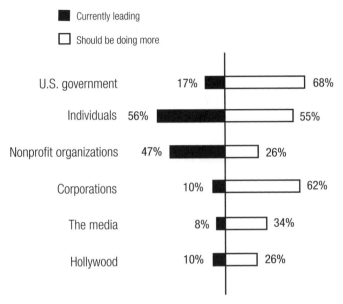

■ Currently leading

☐ Should be doing more

	Currently leading	Should be doing more
U.S. government	17%	68%
Individuals	56%	55%
Nonprofit organizations	47%	26%
Corporations	10%	62%
The media	8%	34%
Hollywood	10%	26%

Source: © Natural Marketing Institute (NMI), 2009 LOHAS Consumer Trends Database®
All Rights Reserved

Maintain lifestyle

The environment may be on every consumer's shopping list, but it's rarely
at the top – for a very understandable reason. Greener products still need to
be effective, tasty, safe, sanitary, attractive, and easy to find in mainstream
outlets – just like the "brown" counterparts consumers have been dropping
into their shopping carts for decades. Although they are concerned about
the planet, at the end of the day, shoppers of any stripe, green or not, will –
and should – always prefer the laundry detergent that gets their clothes clean
over the one that simply promises to "save the Earth." So it's imperative that,
to be successful, sustainable brands deliver on performance, and why new
entries from established brands (e.g., Clorox GreenWorks) perceived by consumers as treading lightly will always win the green day over the proverbial
"Happy Planet" brand from an unknown entity.

Despite recessions that bring them back to stark reality, American consumers have been traditionally loath to save for a rainy day, preferring to
spend today on short-term gains and pleasures. The same holds true for the

environment. Consumers in general are more involved in buying products that will save them money or protect their health today, rather than seeking products that can ameliorate "big picture" issues such as global warming.

Similarly, it is not surprising that price tops the list of barriers to green purchasing (see Fig. 2.11). Likely sharing this with many types of products (most consumers cannot afford to pay premiums for any products, green or not), resistance to paying a premium for green is exacerbated by the facts that many greener products rely on untested materials, ingredients or technology, have unfamiliar brand names, and, in general, carry perceptual baggage left over from the 1970s when many greener products didn't work. So ensuring that products work as well as conventional ones, while pricing competitively with alternatives or justifying a premium price with a compelling value proposition, is the name of the game when attempting to meet the needs of the new mainstream green consumer.

Figure 2.11 **Barriers to green purchasing**

% U.S. adults indicating each of the following prevents them from using environmentally responsible products and services:

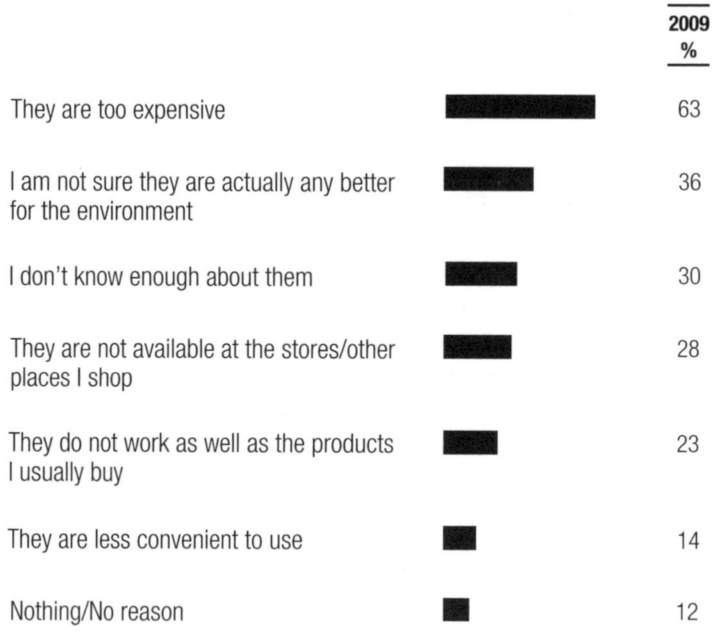

	2009 %
They are too expensive	63
I am not sure they are actually any better for the environment	36
I don't know enough about them	30
They are not available at the stores/other places I shop	28
They do not work as well as the products I usually buy	23
They are less convenient to use	14
Nothing/No reason	12

Source: © Natural Marketing Institute (NMI), 2009 LOHAS Consumer Trends Database®
All Rights Reserved

Despite the aforementioned, are there times when consumers *will* pay a premium for green? The answer to this $64,000 question of green marketing is a resounding "Yes!" Consumers will pay a premium if they know a product will save them money. That's why CFLs are flying off the shelves at Wal-Mart despite their significant premiums over 75¢ incandescent bulbs, and why Americans state they are three times more likely to pay more upfront for energy-efficient electronic equipment than they are to pay less for an energy-guzzling model upfront.[4] Consumers will also spend more for their health. Organic. Natural. PVC- and BPA-free. These are the reasons why sales of organic foods and clothing, natural personal care and pet care, and green cleaning products are growing so dramatically.

Lastly, consumers need to believe that brands are genuinely attempting to be more sustainable, a challenge for marketers with implications for education and efforts with the goal of establishing credibility for their messages, discussed throughout this book.

Look smart

It's the early 21st century. Green is trendy, and as such is part of many consumers' identity projection. There is a cachet in being green. Green is cool. Celebrities are into sustainability, and the fashionistas enjoy making stylish new clothes out of organic cotton, recycled soda bottles, and other hot materials perceived as greener. Method's teardrop-shaped bottle and the now iconic Anya Hindmarch "I'm not a plastic bag" reusable tote help outwardly focused Greens (read: Drifters, see above) project their values. Even with record levels of concern over climate change, a study of Prius owners conducted in 2007 found the number one reason why they bought their vehicle was "because of the statement it makes about me,"[5] rather than high fuel economy or lower emissions.

Environmental concerns have found their way into consumers' shopping decisions, and, in turn, are affecting all areas of marketing. Manufacturers and marketers looking to cater to aware and active consumers must adopt a new paradigm for green marketing, detailed in the next chapter.

The *New Rules* Checklist

Ask the following questions to assess the environment- and social-related issues that affect your products, branding, marketing, and corporate reputation.

- Which segment(s) do our consumers fall into? Which consumer segment(s) likely represent the best target audience for our new sustainable brand?

- What are the chief environment-related interests of our consumers? Are they motivated most by issues such as health? Saving resources? Protecting animals? Enjoying the outdoors and wildlife?

- What are the chief environment-related behaviors of our consumers?

- To what extent are our consumers likely to read labels? Take preventive measures? Switch brands or stores? Buy greener alternatives that fit their lifestyle? Buy "conspicuous" green goods?

- To what extent are our consumers actively using the Internet to find environment-related product and corporate information?

- Which product-related life-cycle issues concern our consumers? Raw materials? Manufacturing? Packaging? In-use consumption? Disposal?

- To what extent are our consumers willing to boycott or pro-cott our own company's brands?

- To what extent do our consumers believe that they should be doing more to help the environment? In what ways might they want to express this environmentalism?

- What can we learn for our brand from all the various ways that environmentally conscious consumers act on their concerns?

The new green marketing paradigm

Conventional marketing is out. Green marketing and what is increasingly being called "sustainable branding" is in. According to the new rules of green marketing, effectively addressing the needs of consumers with a heightened environmental and social consciousness cannot be achieved with the same assumptions and formulae that guided consumer marketing since the post-war era. Times have changed. A new paradigm has emerged requiring new strategies with a holistic point of view and eco-innovative product and service offering.

Historically, marketers developed products that met consumers' needs at affordable prices and then communicated the benefits of their brands in a memorable way. Paid media campaigns characterized by ads with catchy slogans were de rigueur. Green or "sustainable" marketing and branding is more complex. It addresses consumers' new heightened expectations for businesses to operate and requires two strategies:

1. Develop products that balance consumers' needs for quality, performance, affordability, and convenience with the lowest impact possible on the environment, and with due concern for social considerations, e.g., labor, community.

2. Create demand for the resulting brands through credible, values-laden communications that offer practical benefits while empowering and

engaging consumers in meaningful ways about important environmental and social issues. These communications represent value to consumers for what they provide functionally and what they represent, and often positively reinforce the manufacturer's track record for sustainability as well.

The new rules being laid down by today's eco-conscious consumers cannot be addressed with conventional marketing strategies and tactics. Brand builders in the 21st century are accountable to tough new standards. Sustainability represents deep psychological and sociological shifts – not to mention seismically important issues – as did one of its predecessors, feminism, which forced marketers to develop more convenient products in step with two-income lifestyles and to portray women with a new respect. Meeting the challenges of today's level of green consumerism presents its own mandates for corporate processes, branding practices, product quality, price, and promotion.

To realize that the rules of the game have changed in a big way, one need only recall the unsavory backlash that is now occurring over what is perceived by environmentalists, regulators, and the press as inconsistent and often misleading eco-labels and messages. The resulting deluge of skepticism, confusion, and regulatory nightmares that spurious green claims – dubbed "greenwash" – are spawning in the marketplace proves that environmental marketing involves more than tweaking one or two product attributes and dressing up packages with meaningless and often misleading claims. Too many marketers are learning the hard way that leveraging environment-related opportunities and addressing sustainability-related challenges requires a total commitment to greening one's products and communications. Green marketing done according to the new rules also affects how a corporation manages its business and brands and interacts with all of its stakeholders who may be affected by its environmental and social practices (see Chapter 7 for more on this).

The new green marketing paradigm

A new paradigm is being forged by sustainability leaders that are creatively, authentically, and distinctively addressing the new rules of green marketing. Basic assumptions about how to best cater to consumer needs are being shattered. To successfully market to environmentally and socially aware consumers credibly and with impact requires first that one no longer view people as mere "consumers" with insatiable appetites for material goods, but as human beings looking to lead full, healthy lives. To follow the new rules means to project one's values, and to be sensitive to how one's customers, employees, and other stakeholders interact with nature; to be cognizant of how the production and consumption of material goods impacts lives positively as well as negatively, short-term as well as long-term (see Fig. 3.1).

In the age of sustainability, products are ideally designed to travel in endless loops; when their useful lives end, materials are not heedlessly disposed of in a landfill, but thoughtfully recaptured for recycling, reuse, or remanufacturing. Consciousness is growing for the benefits of sourcing one's materials locally, and about products that do a better job of fitting regional environmental considerations or the specific environmental needs of different segments of consumers. Under the new rules of green marketing, yesterday's resource-intensive products are being replaced by eco-innovative ones with radical new designs and technologies. Some products are even being shunted aside by services representing exciting new business models that allow forward-looking businesses to be profitable and ecologically responsible while increasing value and convenience for consumers.

Today's more sustainable product and service brands are marketed with communications that derive added value from the empowering educational messages that they impart, the values they project, and the communities – increasingly online as well as offline – of users they build. Many ecologically sound brands are so appreciated by consumers in the vanguard of environmental and social consciousness, they do not have to be advertised at all; rather, they make their way to the top of influential consumers' shopping lists based solely on the power of word of mouth. Goodwill propels many sustainable brands; today's consumers feel empowered when they reward companies they see as positively impacting people and the planet; and environmentally and socially aware consumers who spot gross infractions of this new paradigm will be quick to boycott as well.

The new rules of green marketing call for businesses to excel by being proactive. Aiming to surpass minimal compliance standards, they set the standards by which they and their competitors will be judged; they are not afraid of disclosing their ingredients and swinging open the doors of their factories in order to build a lasting relationship with green consumers ready to reward them with their loyalty.

Ecologically and socially responsible corporations are akin to nature's processes – interdependent. They ally with the panoply of corporate envi-

Figure 3.1 **The new green marketing paradigm**

	Conventional marketing	**Green marketing**
Consumers	Consumers with lifestyles	People with lives
Products	"Cradle to grave"	"Cradle to cradle"
	Products	Services
	Globally sourced	Locally sourced
	One size fits all	Regionally tailored
Marketing and communications	Product end-benefits	Values
	Selling	Educating and empowering
	One-way communication	Creating community
	Paid advertising	Word of mouth
Corporate	Secretive	Transparent
	Reactive	Proactive
	Independent and autonomous	Interdependent/ allied with stakeholders
	Competitive	Cooperative
	Departmentalized	Holistic
	Short term-oriented/ profit-maximizing	Long term-oriented/ triple bottom line

Source: J. Ottman Consulting, Inc.

ronmental stakeholders in cooperative, positive alliances and work hand in hand with suppliers, retailers, and local governments to manage environmental and social issues throughout their products' value chain. Cross-functional corporate teams convene with a web of external stakeholders to find the best possible holistic solution to sustainability challenges. These stakeholders are willing partners in the quest to innovate, communicate, and challenge the company to achieve ever-higher levels of sustainability. Long-term rather than short-term in orientation, these companies manage with an eye on a triple bottom line – one each for profits, the company's contribution to society, and the planet.

The seven strategies for green marketing success

Under the new rules, the currency of sustainable branding is innovation, flexibility, and heart. I have formulated seven strategies which I believe can help businesses address these deep-seated and lasting changes in consumer sensibility. Reflecting our learning from working with sustainability leaders over the past 20-plus years, they can be summarized as follows:

Ottman's seven winning strategies for green marketing

1. Understand the deeply held environmental and social beliefs and values of your consumers and other stakeholders and develop a long-term plan to align with them.
2. Create new products and services that balance consumers' desires for quality, convenience, and affordability with minimal adverse environmental and social impacts over the life of the product.
3. Develop brands that offer practical benefits while empowering and engaging consumers in meaningful ways about the important issues that affect their lives.
4. Establish credibility for your efforts by communicating your corporate commitment and striving for complete transparency.
5. Be proactive. Go beyond what is expected from stakeholders. Proactively commit to doing your share to solve emerging environmental and social problems – and discover competitive advantage in the process.
6. Think holistically. Underscore community with users and with the broad array of corporate environmental and societal stakeholders.
7. Don't quit. Promote responsible product use and disposal practices. Continuously strive for "zero" impact.

Source: J. Ottman Consulting, Inc.

Many enlightened companies, too numerous to mention, have already awoken to this new green marketing paradigm. They are putting these seven winning strategies into practice in their own ways, thus forging their own brands to fit the new consumer sensibility. Many of their stories illustrate the strategies described later in this book. One such story focuses on eco-entrepreneurs Eric Ryan and Adam Lowry, founders and co-CEOs of Method, who have created a much-talked-about sustainable brand and set a greener pace that others must follow.

Addressing the New Rules

Method makes a difference by being different

The Method difference

In 1999, in what they considered the dirtiest apartment in San Francisco, long-time friends Adam Lowry and Eric Ryan, both under 30, decided to clean up their act – and everyone else's. Sensing the opportunity to transform household cleaning from a chore to something fun, Lowry and Ryan combined their expertise – Lowry in chemical engineering and Ryan in marketing – and founded Method. Their goal: create "a line of environmentally friendly cleaning and personal-care products that are safe for every home and every body." Today, with a loyal and growing following among engaged young adults, and an enlightened approach to sustainability, they are proving themselves as deliberate change agents in a sleepy category with such entrenched entries as Tide, Wisk, and Palmolive.

With a fast-growing line of household and personal-care products that spans body lotions and hand sanitizers to air fresheners and mops, and distribution in over 25,000 retail locations such as Lowe's, Target, and Whole Foods Market, they have achieved over $100 million in revenues despite prices that can be up to 30% more than their well-known competitors. In 2008, their market share increased in all product categories, most notably a near 18% growth in sales over the previous year for the all-purpose cleaner, one of their most popular products, representing $5 million in sales alone.

In stark contrast to the big "soapers," P&G, Unilever, and Colgate-Palmolive, who follow the old rules and just sell *products* – and even the drudgery associated with cleaning one's home and dishes – Method serves up an entire cleaning *experience*, characterized by fun and social awareness. Eye-catching, museum-quality design – previously unheard of in their industry

– draws in their youthful customers; an appreciation of Method's demonstrated commitment to sustainability, and their other brand hallmarks of efficacy, safety, environment, and fragrance, keep them coming back for more.

Customers who want more than clean

Lowry and Ryan know their customers won't settle for positive reinforcement for a job well done (you won't catch them admiring their reflections in plates made shiny by Joy liquid). Unlike the customers of "Madge the manicurist," the historical television spokesperson for Palmolive dishwashing liquid, Method users are hip, young, aware, and desirous of solving problems in the world. In contrast to clunky bottles of conventional dishwashing liquids that are typically hidden under the kitchen sink, Method's sleekly designed bottles stay perched on the countertops, adding to the kitchen decor and helping to project their consumers' values to others.

According to Method, its users are young, professional females whom they dub "progressive domestics." Whereas the venerable Seventh Generation brand attracts a loyal following of "deep green" (LOHAS) consumers, Method draws from the larger band of light green, the "Drifters" who view eco-awareness as popular and hip; to them, Method represents something easy to do about issues they care about. The Method brand makes them feel good about their purchases and themselves. In Method they find everything they want in a personal-care or household-cleaning aid – efficacy, fragrance, and chic design in addition to a lighter environmental footprint and low toxicity. Even the name "Method" doesn't sound deep green like "Seventh Generation" (reflecting an Iroquois slogan about preserving the Earth for the next seven generations), but is non-specific yet provocative, even scientific, ensuring mainstream appeal.

A company with a conscience

The company's deep-seated environmental and social values have translated into state-of-the-art green operating and manufacturing processes with the accolades to prove it. For starters, they have green offices (including one that's certified to the U.S. Green Building Council's LEED standards) and a factory that doesn't emit a drop of waste-water. They achieve a lofty goal of carbon neutrality in all manufacturing, office operations, and employee travel through a combination of energy efficiency, biodiesel fuel in transport trucks, and use of renewable energy such as wind and solar; their remaining carbon is offset by buying Renewable Energy Certificates (RECs)[1] (from

*Native*Energy, a nonprofit that supports projects to capture methane and energy from three Pennsylvania dairy farms).

Method's environmental consciousness is partnered with a social one, marked by support for numerous service projects that help to foster good community relations. Employees get three paid days per year to volunteer, enabling them to pitch in on projects like Park(ing) Day, an annual event where volunteers transform parking spaces in cities around the world into parks for the day; Save the Bay, removing litter, testing the water's phosphate levels, and planting native seedlings in the San Francisco Bay Area; and cleaning, repainting, and installing new furniture at the local family shelter run by San Francisco nonprofit Compass Community Services.

To help monitor their progress, in June 2007 Method underwent certification as a B Corporation by the B Lab, a Philadelphia-based nonprofit organization that provides third-party audit ratings of a company's commitment to social and environmental issues.

Figure 3.2 **Method's B Impact Report**

Summary		Certified: June 2007
	Points earned	**% Points available**
Environment	36.9	80%
Employees	33.6	80%
Community	14.4	33%
Consumers	29.2	60%
Leadership	14.4	75%
Composite B Score	128.5	66%

▷ 80 out of 200 is eligible for certification
▷ 60% points available = Area of excellence

Source: BCorporation.net. Reprinted with permission from Method

Companies that score highly in the ratings are eligible for B Corporation certification (which also includes a legal expansion of corporate responsibilities to include consideration of stakeholder interests). B Impact Reports for all Certified B Corporations are publicly available on B Lab's website. One

thousand other progressive companies in 54 industries, including Seventh Generation, Numi Tea, and Dansko footwear are also rated.[2] Publishing these results shows customers that Method values transparency and is willing to receive constructive criticism on the functioning of its company. Method's B Corp rating (Fig. 3.2) reflected a composite score of 128.5 placing it in the top 10% of all B Corporations (the bar for eligibility is 80 points, and B Corporations have an average score of about 100 points). Method's high scores reflect the company's wide-ranging social and environmental commitments; the relatively lower scores for "Community" and "Leadership" do not indicate that the company is not doing good things, but rather that Method has not chosen those topics as a focus of its business.

Figure 3.3 **Method "teardrop" bottle**

Reprinted with permission from Method

Five product hallmarks

In tune with their desire to make cleaning fun, Method products step out from the cobwebbed cleaning products category and claim a strong aesthetic sensibility. To meet their youthful customers' demands, they strike a balance for efficacy, environment, safety, design, and fragrance – and fun. As one example, the Method baby + kid line features hypoallergenic, pediatrician-tested, and "never tested on rubber duckies" bath-time formula in penguin-shaped bottles.

Packaging is sleek and trendy – and easy to spot on the retail shelf. In keeping with a Method moral that each product has a past, present, and future, packaging is minimal and uses recycled or recyclable materials. For example, as of 2008 all packaging for surface cleaners, floor cleaners, specialty sprays, and other cleaning products is made from 100% recycled and recyclable PET (polyethylene terephthalate) plastic – with the goal of extending this recycled and recyclable plastic packaging to all Method products.

Naturally appealing fragrances and colors such as pink grapefruit and lime-green cucumber distinguish the Method experience by reinforcing the natural aura of the products and making them fun to use. The line is spiced up during the holiday season with special scents such as winterberry and frosted fir.

When choosing ingredients, Method follows a paraphrased "precautionary principle": "if there's a chance it's bad, don't use it." Product formulations start with the non-toxic and biodegradable ingredients on Method's "clean list"; their "dirty list" includes items they will never use such as phosphates and chlorine.

Method's bottles are sculpted by noted designers to make the brand stand apart from competitors and help to reach a wider group of consumers than simply the deep greens. One, a now-famous "teardrop" bottle, is shown in Figure 3.3.

At Method, good design is very much a deliberate "added plus" to a focus on sustainability – that element that helps to distinguish their brands from competitors. (As discussed in Chapter 6, this strategy is known as "bundling" additional benefits to add value to sustainable products. As co-founder Adam Lowry explains:

> One of the big goals with Method, and why design and sustainability are inextricably linked in our brand, is that if you don't have the design element, you're only going to appeal to people who are already green, so you're not actually going to create any real environmental change . . . To us, "sustainability" and "green" are just aspects of the quality of our product – they are not a marketing positioning . . . I mean everything should be that way. Just build it into the quality of the product and let the experience of the product be the real hero.[3]

Credible, impactful green marketing

In stark contrast to the old rules for marketing household products, Method's marketing platform is built on three essential hallmarks: limited or no paid advertising, transparency, and community. All three work synergistically to create loyal followers.

Unlike the primary focus on paid advertising invested by their competitors each year, Lowry and Ryan have historically targeted their users through direct consumer education and engagement that reinforces the fun experience of using the brand and underscores Method's credibility. To demonstrate the inherent safety of their products and underscore fun, sales brochures feature models cleaning a house in the buff. Bold package design gets noticed on the shelves and reinforces the brand within the home. Indeed, the quality of the experience of using, owning – even discovering – the product, generates word of mouth among excited users who immediately link the brand to fun and authenticity.

Method's first paid media campaign, launched in 2010 to support their revolutionary 8X concentrated laundry liquid, takes direct aim at mainstream laundry aids that, in their words, feed a household's heinous "jug habit."[4] Cheeky-tone ads executed in print and online attempt to provoke change and begin a new conversation by imploring presumably "addicted" consumers to "Say no to jugs" or to support a "jug-free America," position the brand as a David to Tide's Goliath, and encourage consumers to rethink ingrained habits.

Pluck a bottle of any major brand of dishwashing liquid off the shelf and you might find a statement indicating that the product is phosphate-free or possibly packaged in recycled plastic. But Method, in line with its commitment to transparency, discloses its ingredients on its website. As the nude campaigners photographed in their sales brochures prove, it is clear that Method has nothing to hide!

In addition, Lowry and Ryan have opened their doors to outside auditors. Their products are certified by the EPA's Design for the Environment (DfE) label and the Cradle to Cradle (C2C) certification. DfE has assessed over 50 Method product formulas to date to ensure that the company uses only environmentally responsible ingredients. Method has already earned C2C certification on 20 of its products and, as of this writing, is in the process of certifying 20 more.

Have you ever seen anyone wearing a T-shirt that has the brand name of a popular brand of household cleaning products on it? Of course not! But some fiercely loyal Method consumers gladly sport T-shirts that they buy on the company website with the Method brand name emblazoned on the front, accompanied by silly slogans such as "Cleans like a mother."

An important aspect of Method's approach to green marketing is engaging their users, which the company does offline and, increasingly, online. Facebook page fans make suggestions about products and practices, and participate in contests to win free Method products. At last count, over 6,000 users were following "methodtweet" on Twitter, while Flickr visitors keep up to date on goings-on inside the company – on moving day, employees were pictured walking down the street with office supplies in hand, followed by a mariachi band.

One of Method's most popular outreach activities is their People Against Dirty campaign, with over 5,300 advocates united in a common passion for Method and its cleaning mission. A blog informs readers of topics related to design, sustainability, and environmental awareness. After signing up on the Method website, and uploading their photo, members receive updates, previews of new Method products, and even an "Advocacy Kit," including three individual pass-along kits they can give to friends and family. Method is now working on ways that users can interact with one another through the site.

To equip consumers with the information they seek to make responsible product choices Lowry and Ryan wrote *Squeaky Green: The Method Guide to Detoxing Your Home*, giving home-cleaning tips and exposing the "dirty little secrets" of traditional cleaning products. Method also runs Cleaning Tours in Chicago, Boston, New York, and other cities, setting up pop-up shops on street corners where customers can swap an old toxic cleaning product for a free Method one. While on tour, staffers throw "detox parties" in consumer homes. Guests receive a "plastic bag rehab" tote filled with Method products.

Cleaning up at the checkout

Method's rule-breaking approach to cleaning not only builds fierce brand loyalty and free word-of-mouth advertising, it also helps it clean up at the cash register – while sprucing up their competitors.

Besides fast-growing sales and extensive retail distribution, Method's proverbial trophy shelf is crammed with such accolades as being named in November 2008 a "Champion" of the Safer Detergents Stewardship Initiative of the DfE program, commending Method for its voluntary commitment to use safer surfactants (ingredients that help remove dirt from surfaces and do no harm to aquatic life). In 2006, Method was ranked seventh on *Inc.* magazine's annual list of the 500 fastest-growing private companies in the U.S.; that year, too, annual revenues grew 80% in an industry that is normally lucky if it sees 4% growth, and PETA named Lowry and Ryan as "Persons of the Year" for creating a revolutionary line of home-cleaning supplies that are free of animal-derived ingredients and are not tested on animals.

Perhaps Lowry and Ryan's biggest gold star relates to achieving the goal they set for themselves at their company's founding: to revolutionize and provoke change in the cleaning-products industry. No longer content to follow age-old rules, key competitors now offer their own greener cleaning products: Palmolive's pure + clear range contains "no unnecessary chemicals and no heavy fragrances," while P&G's Pure Essentials Dawn dishwashing liquid has no added dyes or superfluous ingredients and is packaged in a bottle made with 25% post-consumer recycled plastic. Madge has finally cleaned up her act. What a nice reflection on Method.[5]

The rules have changed. A new green marketing paradigm has arrived, characterized by my seven strategies that will be integral to consumer products marketing for decades to come. Successfully adapting to the new rules and executing the strategies outlined as part of this new green marketing paradigm starts with taking a life-cycle approach to one's product offering – the subject of the next chapter.

The *New Rules* Checklist

Use the following checklist to assess how well your organization understands and addresses the new green marketing paradigm.

- ○ Do we strive to offer a product that balances consumers' traditional needs with minimal impact on the environment and addresses social considerations?

- ○ Do our communications offer practical benefits while empowering and engaging consumers in meaningful ways about important issues that affect their lives?

- ○ Do we have a short- and long-term plan of environmental and social-related improvements for our products?

- ○ Do we view our consumers with respect as human beings concerned about their health and the state of the world around them?

- ○ In what ways can we express our sensitivity to how our customers, employees, and other stakeholders interact with nature?

- ○ Do we know how the production and consumption of our products impacts human lives negatively as well as positively? Long-term as well as short-term?

- ○ Are we taking pains to ensure that our products are designed for an afterlife versus a landfill? Materials are sourced locally? Our products address regional considerations?

- ○ Are we taking advantage of opportunities to use eco-innovative designs and technologies? Are we looking at new business models?

- ○ How do our consumers feel about our brand? Do they reward us with their loyalty (pro-cott)? To what extent are they willing to boycott?

- ○ Are we sufficiently aware of and linked with our various environmental and social stakeholders?

- ○ Are we taking advantage of opportunities to engage employees to help manage and magnify the sustainability aspects of our brand?

- ○ Do we have our eyes sufficiently on the longer-term sustainability aspects of our brand?

785266 000297

Designing greener products
A life-cycle approach

It used to be that consumers simply expected the products they bought to work well, sport a familiar brand name, be sold in a nearby store, and be affordably priced. The rules have changed. Today, that once seemingly short checklist includes minimizing the environmental impacts of those products at every phase of their life-cycle, starting with the impacts associated with mining, growing, or otherwise processing the raw materials right through to the impacts linked to a product's eventual disposal. And now, throw in for good measure a number of social considerations such as fair working conditions and whether or not laborers receive a living wage (even perhaps in some equitable proportion to the salaries of the highest-paid managers), use of child labor, whether prices paid to producers are deemed fair (can coffee growers afford to send their children to school?), and whether the manufacturer is a good member of the community. This presents to businesses looking to develop highly marketable and legitimately sustainable brands the need to juggle traditional product considerations with an extremely varied and highly complex list of issues involving the entire supply chain.

These issues also include the harnessing and consumption of natural resources such as water and energy, as well as the protection of natural habitats and endangered species. It is generally not the brand manager's job to be responsible for a product's environmental and social impacts. However, given that they sit on cross-functional teams, and their consumers are increasingly favoring brands based on their track records for managing these issues, this chapter is included as a primer on green product design. Its relevance to marketers is illustrated with numerous examples of how green product benefits can be associated with business success; in successive chapters we will deal with the strategies for communicating these various benefits with credibility and impact.

Consider the entire life-cycle

Designing products and packaging for minimal impact can be tricky. What may appear to be an ecological benefit may actually result in little or no added environmental value. Some plastic plates made from cornstarch, for example, may decompose in a municipal composting facility but not in backyard composters, where conditions are not likely to be so hot and steamy. Hybrid cars save energy but the batteries they contain represent a potentially significant source of hazardous waste.

Sometimes the presumed greening of a product can actually increase overall environmental impact. CPC, the makers of Mueller's pasta, found that converting to recycled carton material would actually add about 20% to the width of their package material and this would at least partially offset savings to the environment, considering the extra energy needed to ship the new boxes. Because of the energy it takes to transport recyclables to a processing facility, it may be that a product with a very high degree of recycled content may represent greater impact than one with less recycled content.

It can even be argued that there is no such thing as a truly "green" product, because every product, no matter how thoughtfully designed, uses resources and creates waste. Therefore, "green" is a relative term, with some products being greener for certain reasons or in certain circumstances (and hence my preference for the term "green*er* products" throughout this book).

So, in order to address consumers' various sustainability-related product concerns discussed in Chapter 2, and to prevent backlash from consumers, environmental groups, and other stakeholders, all of whom may be quick to point out the shortcomings of products and packaging touted as green, a thorough approach to improving the environmental profile of one's products/services and processes is required. A tool called life-cycle assessment (LCA) can help by examining all the environmental issues involved in designing a greener product:

Green product design issues

Raw materials acquisition and processing

- Conservation of natural resources
- Use of renewable resources; sustainable use of resources
- Use of recycled and recyclable materials
- Protection of natural habitats and endangered species
- Water conservation
- Energy conservation
- Waste minimization and pollution prevention, especially the use of toxics and release of toxics to air, water, and land
- Transportation

Manufacturing and distribution

- Minimal use of materials
- Waste minimization and pollution prevention, especially the use of toxics and release of toxics to air, water, and land
- By-product management
- Energy conservation
- Water conservation

Product use and packaging

- Conservation of natural resources
- Energy efficiency
- Water efficiency
- Consumer health and environmental safety
- Packaging efficiency
- Packaging recycled content
- Packaging recycle rates

After-use/disposal

- Recyclability; ease of reuse, remanufacture, and repair
- Waste minimization
- Durability
- Biodegradability/compostability
- Safety when incinerated or landfilled

Source: Martin Wolf, Seventh Generation Inc. Printed with permission

The first step in conducting a full life-cycle analysis of a product is to define the functional unit and the product system. For instance, in conducting an LCA of a toothbrush, you need to decide whether to analyze just the toothbrush, or include the package, too. What about the water and toothpaste used throughout the life of the toothbrush? Conducting an LCA also requires you to set boundaries on the data to be collected for analysis; for instance, should you consider the environmental impacts associated with making the trucks needed to transport the toothbrushes to stores? Likely not! But factoring in the energy used in transportation would be totally appropriate.

Your study may encompass the product's complete life-cycle, from raw material extraction to disposal ("cradle-to-grave" analysis), or it may be limited to the processes from raw materials extraction to product production ("cradle-to-gate" analysis). Ideally, it would look at the impacts associated with a "cradle-to-cradle" point of view,[1] and take into account various options for recycling or otherwise responsibly turning your product into useful new material or energy.

Your study may take into account the materials, energy, and emissions to produce a kilogram of product, or to produce enough product for 1,000 uses.

Once the boundaries and assumptions are determined, quantify the use of energy, resources, and emissions associated with raw-material procurement, manufacturing and production, packaging, distribution, and in-use (e.g., use of energy, water, or other consumables) straight through to after-use (e.g., recycling and recovery) or final disposal. Then, analyze the data, identify problems and opportunities, and allocate the resources to address them in priority.

An LCA of a washing machine, for example, would quantify the environmental impacts associated with fabricating the metal, along with pollutants and energy from the mining process (which can be significant). It would consider the energy needed to manufacture the machines and transport them to stores. Then it would factor in the water, energy, and detergent needed to run the washer over an estimated lifetime (likely measured in years), making assumptions regarding such things as number of washings per week, water temperatures, and size of loads. Finally, it would consider the impacts associated with collecting and recycling the machines, and/or eventual disposal in a landfill or incinerator.

LCAs can help assess particular impacts: for instance, energy, which is often a key component in all products. The Procter & Gamble Company has conducted life-cycle assessments of many of their company's products. Some of their results through 2006 are summarized in Figure 4.1. As can be seen, areas of greatest energy usage vary greatly by life-cycle stage and product category. An LCA of a laundry detergent, for instance, shows that the greatest energy impacts by far occur during the usage stage, considering all the energy needed to heat the water. It was this type of assessment that spurred P&G to introduce Tide Coldwater (discussed in Chapter 6), a product that P&G estimates could help to save the equivalent of 3% of total U.S. energy consumption, and over 8% of the CO_2 reduction target for the U.S. set in the Kyoto Protocol.[2]

Figure 4.1 **Product energy usage from a life-cycle perspective**

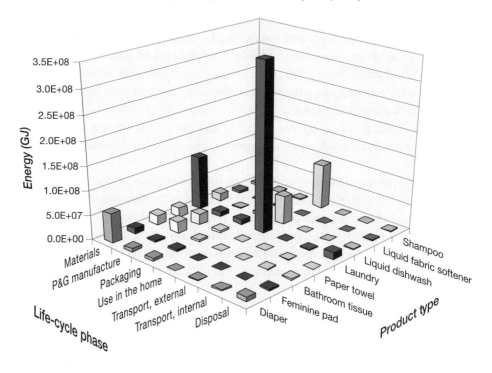

Energy's contribution to so many products during use represents a key reason why the U.S. government has devoted so much attention to the ENERGY STAR label (discussed in more detail in Chapter 7). It was an LCA, too, that prompted the move by makers of soft drinks in the 1970s to save energy by shifting from returnable glass bottles that required two-way transport by grocers to one-way disposable PET (polyethylene terephthalate) bottles.

LCA is a valuable tool for addressing the new rules of green marketing, as it can be very useful for:

- Comparing the costs associated with energy and resource usage and environmental emissions associated with existing product designs, manufacturing and packaging methods and their alternatives

- Identifying significant areas for reducing energy use, water use, and waste

- Comparing energy and resource usage and environmental emissions associated with competitive products, i.e., as the basis for manufacturing claims.

Many organizations around the world have performed LCAs in industries ranging from automotive, paper, paperboard, glass, steel, lighting, energy, aluminum, plastic beverage containers, and delivery systems to building materials and transportation products. Many different methodologies have evolved, both quantitative and qualitative; some allow businesses to conduct their own LCAs with the aid of sophisticated software tools such as SimaPro, GaBi, and Umberto programmed with estimates of the environmental impacts for various materials and processes.

Use caution when attempting to use life-cycle assessment as a marketing tool! The transparency afforded by LCA is highly desirable but challenges abound. For instance, it's one thing to report to consumers the results of an LCA conducted on one's own product, as Timberland does with its Green Index (see Chapter 9), but comparisons with competitors' products can be tricky. Comparisons that favor a study sponsor can easily be criticized – and held suspect. Besides, it is not easy obtaining accurate data on competitors' products!

Moreover, try comparing the environmental impacts of two different concepts that meet the same consumer need. Take diapers as an example. What's more important to society: landfill space or water and energy associated with laundering cloth? Also tricky – LCAs of two products based on the same technology can yield very dissimilar results, making comparisons for marketing purposes unfair. For instance, two competitive products might have been made in different countries (or even different states or provinces) with different types of energy, each with their respective pollutants. For instance, an LCA of a washing machine conducted in the U.S. may likely be based on coal, the predominant type of energy used in the U.S., whereas in France it may be nuclear. Consumers, at least for now, are not knowledgeable enough about LCA to ask the right questions when presented with comparative results.

Experts in industry, government, and academia are working to legitimize the use of LCA and other approaches as marketing tools. The EPA has created an online resource called LCAccess, designed to "promote the use of LCA to make more informed decisions through a better understanding of the human health and environmental impacts of products, processes, and activities."[3] Businesses looking to use LCA data to more easily compare competitors and alternatives may want to consider a standardized system of analysis such as the economic input–output LCA software developed by Carnegie Mellon University's Green Design Initiative and available on the web (www.eiolca.net).

Among its shortcomings, LCA does not adequately address certain environmental and social concerns. According to Martin Wolf, Director of Product and Environmental Technology, Seventh Generation, an expert on life-cycle inventory and green product development, an LCA must be augmented with a holistic evaluation of a product's total environmental and social impacts. Renewable or sustainable resource use, habitat destruction, biodiversity depletion, odors, visual pollution, noise pollution, toxicity, biodegradability, and social issues such as fair trade, labor practices, and community responsibility of import to environmentalists, consumers, and others in society cannot be evaluated by the quantitative approach of LCA and must be considered separately.

Representing a new development in product LCA, carbon footprinting has emerged as an alternative to LCA. Given the fact that LCAs can be extremely complex, and that energy can represent a good proxy for an LCA given that so much of any product's life-cycle impacts are energy-related, calculating the carbon footprint of a product, rather than conducting a full LCA, is becoming popular. Similar to conducting an LCA, one would determine a product's carbon footprint by calculating the amount of energy consumed at each stage of the product life-cycle, then converting it into the amount of emissions associated with each stage, before arriving at a total carbon footprint.

One product that is watching its carbon footprint these days is PepsiCo's Walkers Crisps, a brand of potato chip sold in the UK. Since 2007, the Walkers package has sported a Carbon Reduction Label developed by the Carbon Trust (see Chapter 7 for more detail). Pepsi worked with the UK-based not-for-profit to develop the carbon footprint of Walkers Crisps – and learned a lot in the process. From 2007 to 2009, PepsiCo has been able to reduce the carbon footprint of Walkers Crisps by 7%, saving about 4,800 tons of emissions. This has paid off at the point of sale, with about 52% of those polled in the UK saying they were more likely to buy a product carrying the Carbon Reduction Label. Pepsi has since put the label on UK-based packages of Quaker Oats, as well as Oatso Simple Original and Oatso Simple Golden Syrup.[4]

Strategies for sustainable product design

Many marketers now grow their businesses and attempt to minimize their environmental and health-related risks by addressing the specific environmental and social issues most relevant to their consumers and other stakeholders. Proactive green marketers keep an eye on the future with a phased plan for managing potential risks 5–15 years hence. In the process, they often save money and enhance brand image while ensuring future sales for existing and new products. A plethora of strategies, ideally considered as part of a holistic effort to manage one's brand rather than incorporated in isolation, exist to inspire profitable new and improved products and packages that address the new rules of balancing consumers' needs with sustainability considerations. These are examined below.

15 strategies for sustainable product design

1. Sustainable harvesting and mining practices
2. Recycled content
3. Source reduce
4. Organically grown
5. Fair trade
6. Reduce toxicity
7. Think global, grow local
8. Responsible manufacturing practices
9. Energy- and fuel-efficient
10. Water-efficient
11. Extend product life
12. Reusable and refillable
13. Recyclable
14. Compostable
15. Safe for disposal

1 Sustainable harvesting and mining practices

Sustainability has established itself as a buzzword in the business world, but it has become particularly important for manufacturers whose supplies of raw material are threatened. What is abundant today may become scarce tomorrow, wreaking havoc for manufacturers whose designs are dependent on specific types of raw materials. Herman Miller's Eames lounge chair and ottoman, the design icon introduced in 1956, originally featured Brazilian rosewood which is now endangered; however, taking great care to protect its authentic design sensibility, since 1991 Herman Miller has produced the chair with cherry and walnut wood from sustainably managed forests.

C.F. Martin & Company

With supplies of rosewood, spruce, and mahogany all scarcer in recent years due to unsustainable logging practices, Christian F. Martin IV is the first generation of Nazareth, Pennsylvania-based guitar makers C.F. Martin & Company, to worry that his family company's supply of wood would soon become exhausted. With an eye on the future, in 2007 Martin teamed up with three other leading U.S. producers of guitars and Greenpeace to form the Music Wood Coalition to promote better logging practices in the areas where these rare woods are grown. One thing the coalition learned was that the last old-growth Sitka spruce tree from a temperate rainforest in Alaska, which had been an important source of wood for the guitar industry, would be harvested within the decade. So, C.F. Martin led the industry in the use of more plentiful, alternative woods such as birch and cherry.[5]

Tiffany & Company

Blood diamonds, meet dirty gold. Gold mining can wreak havoc with water supplies, violate human rights and decimate an area's natural surroundings. Production of just one gold ring can generate 20 tons of waste.[6]

Tiffany & Co., the legendary jewelers, recognized the issue of dirty gold early on and took out a full-page ad in the *Washington Post* asking the Federal Government to halt construction of a controversial silver mine that threatened Montana's Cabinet Mountains Wilderness and called for important mining reforms.[7] The first jeweler to respond to NGO Earthworks' call for responsible mining, Tiffany embraced the DC-based environmental group's No Dirty Gold campaign calling for jewelers to pledge to work only with those mining companies that adhered to Earthworks' high standards of social and environmental responsibility.[8]

By taking an early definitive stance against destructive mining, Tiffany has defended its sterling reputation and protected market share among its discriminating customers. Michael J. Kowalski, Tiffany's chairman and CEO, says it best in Tiffany & Co.'s sustainability report: "Tiffany & Co. is committed to obtaining precious metals and gemstones and crafting our jewelry in ways that are socially and environmentally responsible. It is simply the right thing to do: Our customers expect and deserve nothing less."[9]

2 Recycled content

Recycling is the most popular eco-design strategy, and for good reasons. It can save the energy needed to mine, ship, and produce new materials, in turn preventing the air pollution associated with the generation of new energy. For instance, creating aluminum cans from recycled content uses 95% less energy than constructing new ones from virgin material. Some materials, such as glass and aluminum, can be recycled in a theoretically endless loop while most plastics and paper are simply "downcycled" into less valuable uses. Recycling also spares valuable materials from ending up in a landfill and prevents toxins from leaching into underground water. Along with these environmental benefits, recycling can save businesses money, so it is great for the bottom line, too. And, of course, it's relatively easy for consumers to pitch in.

HP inkjet cartridges

Materials such as newspapers, packaging, magazines, books, clothes, and toys – what we all throw away every day – are considered "post-consumer waste." This includes the 700 million inkjet and toner printer cartridges that are used yearly across the U.S.[10] Uncomfortable with these numbers (which represent future risk), Hewlett-Packard now makes more than 200 million of its inkjet cartridges with post-consumer plastics. Their process combines various kinds of recycled plastics, from used inkjet cartridges to common water bottles, with a variety of chemical additives. HP used 12 million pounds of recycled plastic in 2008, more than double what it used the previous year.[11] Helping consumers to close the loop, HP includes a pre-paid return envelope in its packages; they have also arranged for consumers to take used cartridges to recycling centers and many office supply stores such as Staples, Office Depot, and OfficeMax.

Recycline

Recycline Inc. of Waltham, Massachusetts, founded in 1996, manufactures the Preserve brand of toothbrushes, razors, tongue cleaners, and tableware made exclusively from recycled feedstocks. The Preserve toothbrush, Recycline's premier product, is made of 100% recycled polypropylene plastic, the majority of which comes from Stonyfield Farm's yogurt containers as well as old or broken grocery store carts and toys.

Until 2007, Recycline's products were sold principally at specialty green-type stores, but with mainstream consumers ready for a recycling step forward, Recycline's Preserve toothbrushes are now sold by Wal-Mart and on Amazon.com, as well as by their primary retailer, Whole Foods Market. In 2007, Recycline won Forbes.com's Boost Your Business contest over nearly 1,000 other small businesses from around the country.[12]

3 Source reduce

Recycling has much to recommend it ecologically, but does have its drawbacks. It still takes energy to transport the recyclables to a processing facility, topped off by the energy used to recycle those materials. Sometimes such factors weigh *against* recycling. While recycling is most often preferable to landfilling, source reduction and reuse of products usually have less environmental impact than recycling – hence the mantra "Reduce, Reuse, and Recycle." In assessing the feasibility of recycling polystyrene clamshells, for example, McDonald's found that the amount of energy needed to transport the super-lightweight yet bulky materials (requiring multiple trucks) made the operation infeasible. They decided against recycling in favor of very thin "quilt wraps" – a form of source reduction – which were landfilled after one use.

Source reduction, a strategy most often associated with packaging, was originally referenced in the U.S. Pollution Prevention Act of 1990 with a statement that "pollution should be prevented or reduced at its source whenever feasible." Since the cost savings derived from source reduction are often parallel to the amount of materials eliminated, the tenets of this law are not only good for the environment, they are good for business.

Dropps dissolvable laundry capsules

Many large corporations are seizing opportunities to source reduce, prodded by a Wal-Mart pledge to skim 5% of all packaging from its supply chain by 2013, along with nearly 700,000 metric tons of carbon emissions and $3.4 billion. Accordingly, Wal-Mart is giving preferential shelf treatment to such innovations as Sun Products' "All small & mighty," a detergent that is three times more concentrated than traditional All. The environmental benefits? Smaller bottles requiring less plastic to produce, fewer boxes to ship, less water – and less weight for the same number of loads – as well as fewer trucks to ship them. Such benefits are desirable in and of themselves, but Dropps, a Philadelphia-based start-up, has an even better idea.

Instead of a bulky plastic container, the folks at Dropps have decided to sell their laundry detergent packed inside dissolvable one-inch square capsules dubbed "Dropps," packed 20 in a stand-up pouch. According to the company, the collapsible plastic pouches are so thin, it would take 292 of them to equal the plastic represented by one empty jug of All. Representing pre-measured portions of six-times concentrated detergent, tossed into the wash, they leave behind nothing but clean clothes. In addition, the super-concentrated formula means that there is very little water being shipped with the detergent, reducing transportation costs and maximizing the retailer's shelf space efficiency. Beyond its own formula for super source reduction, Dropps' low-suds formula is free of chlorine, NPE (nonylphenol ethoxylate – a stain-fighting additive found to be an endocrine disruptor[13]) and phosphate. A sure-to-be-rising star of the concentrated detergents market, Dropps can now be found on the shelves of Publix, Safeway, and Target stores.

4 Organically grown

Since the deadly effects of DDT were first publicized in Rachel Carson's 1962 watershed book *Silent Spring*, society has fretted about the potential health threats of using pesticides and fertilizers in crops. So started the organic foods movement over 40 years ago. Today, organic is everywhere. Hershey makes organic chocolate. The Gap produces organic clothing. Even Target, Wal-Mart, and 7-Eleven stock a huge range of organic foods, cleaning products, and make-up. Free of artificial preservatives, coloring, irradiation, pesticides, fungicides, and hormones, organic products chalked up $24.6 billion in consumer purchases in the U.S. in 2008, an increase of 17.1% over 2007.[14] The organic movement even has its own government seal. (To learn about the USDA Organic seal, see Chapter 7.)

Safeway's O organics line

Safeway's USDA-certified "O" brand line, with 300 organic products in more than 30 categories, and thus appealing to a wide array of consumers, has enjoyed such success that the products are now carried by other food chains.

In addition to milk, bread, and other staples, the line consists of frozen dinners, snacks such as popcorn and chips, and even ice cream bars. The line is especially targeted at new mothers seeking to provide their children with healthier food without spending much more. With prices comparable to conventional alternatives, James White, president of Safeway's Lucerne Foods division, says the brand is "making organics available to everyone," and with the spread of the line into other supermarkets, this may soon be true. In its first year, 2005, the line brought in $150 million, sales doubled to $300 million in 2007,[15] and were projected to be $400 million for 2008.[16]

Earth's Best organic baby food

New mothers are especially concerned about how synthetic pesticides can affect the development of young children. One company offering an alternative to conventional baby foods is Earth's Best, an organic baby food launched in 1985 and now in the hands of Hain Celestial Group, the largest manufacturer of natural food products with brands that are increasingly being embraced by mainstream consumers such as Celestial Seasonings Tea, Arrowhead Mills, Health Valley, and Terra Chips, Earth's Best is USDA-certified organic and delivers flavorful taste without any preservatives, salt, refined sugar, or modified starches.

With a product line-up including jarred food, cookies, frozen meals, cereal, and body care, sales in 2006 were up almost 50% from the previous year.[17] According to Philip Tasho, manager of the Aston/TAMO Small Cap Fund that owns Hain shares, "The natural and organic food industry is broadening and becoming more mainstream. Overall consumer spending may decline, but consumers aren't going to scrimp on products for their health."[18]

Nike Organics

Although 100% cotton may suggest 100% natural or 100% organic, both are far from true. For starters, producing 2.5 pounds of cotton takes anywhere from 2,000 to 8,000 gallons of water.[19] Cotton also requires the extensive use of herbicides and pesticides – more than any single crop. And if that's not enough, cotton crops are sprayed with a chemical defoliant to prevent leaf staining, and the resulting fiber is saturated with bleach or dyed with any number of potentially toxic chemicals.

All of this impact is not lost on Nike, one of the world's largest manufacturers of cotton clothing. To address this issue, Nike has become the world's largest buyer of organic cotton and, in 2005, they launched Nike Organics, a full line of clothing made from 100% organic cotton in the spirit that "one shouldn't have to decide between style and nature." The USDA certifies Nike's cotton as organic, documenting the process all the way from the farm to the finished garment. Nike's commitment stretches further than this one line: 9% of all the cotton they used in 2007 was organic – no small amount at 11 million pounds[20] – and the company aims to blend 5% organic cotton in all of its cotton garments by 2010.[21] Nike is not alone in playing by different cotton rules. According to the Organic Exchange, a trade organization, global organic cotton sales rose from $245 million in 2001 to $4.3 billion in 2009. Riding a 40% average annual growth rate since 2001, projections for 2010 are close to $5.1 billion.[22]

5 Fair trade

The rules of the game are fast changing when it comes to labor practices and resulting in favorable impacts on worker wages and living standards, and none too soon. According to UNICEF, one-sixth of the world's children aged 5–14, 158 million in all, are engaged in child labor, vulnerable to exploitation and the poverty that accompanies a lack of education.[23] Such conditions can persist throughout a lifetime, especially for women, who account for 70% of the more than one billion people living in extreme poverty worldwide.[24]

Several certification programs run at the national/regional levels by groups such as Oakland, California-based TransFair USA and the UK-based Fairtrade Foundation have sprung up to address the issue. Progress is being made. According to the World Trade Organization, over 7.5 million disadvantaged producers and their families are estimated to benefit from fair-trade-funded infrastructure and community development projects.[25] In 2008, worldwide sales of fair trade products such as coffee, cocoa, tea, herbs, spices, fruit, and sugar skyrocketed to over $4 billion, an increase of 22% over 2007.[26] One of the top volume sellers of Fair Trade Certified coffee in the U.S. is Starbucks, whose Café Estima brand helps to create a positive impact on the lives of farmers in Latin America and Africa.

Divine Chocolate Limited

"Heavenly Chocolate with a Heart" is the slogan of Divine Chocolate Limited, a fair trade chocolate manufacturer that is owned (45%) by the members of the Kuapa Kokoo cooperative in Ghana, who not only receive fair trade prices for their cocoa but also sit on the board of directors and share in the profits.[27]

Launched in the UK in 1998, Divine Chocolate is now available in many U.S. grocery stores including Wegmans, Fairway, and Whole Foods in addition to specialty chocolate stores throughout the country. Representing U.S. sales of $2 million in 2008, Divine Chocolate has won accolades for its socially conscious practices, winning the Social Enterprise Coalition (the UK's national body for social enterprise) award for Best Social Enterprise in 2007 and UK *Observer* newspaper's Best Ethical Business award in 2008, as well as *Good Housekeeping*'s Favorite Fair Trade Product in 2008.[28]

Following the example of committed companies such as Divine, chocolate industry leaders are beginning to follow new rules themselves. UK-based Cadbury, one of the world's largest confectioners (now owned by U.S. conglomerate Kraft), purchased the organic chocolate company Green & Black's in 2005 and launched its own fair trade product in July 2009 as the new Cadbury Dairy Milk chocolate – a commitment that translates to tripling the amount of fair trade cocoa bought from Ghana. Not to be left behind, a month after Cadbury's announcement, competitor Mars Inc. publicized its goal to produce candy from only sustainable sources by 2020.[29]

Ben & Jerry's Fair Trade Certified Chunks and Swirls

Since 1978, Ben & Jerry's, the Vermont-based wholly owned subsidiary of Unilever known for its super-premium ice cream, has been operating its business on a three-part mission which emphasizes product quality, economic reward, and a responsibility to the community. In 2010, Fair Trade Certified ingredients became part of that mission, when the company announced its decision to go fully Fair Trade across its entire global flavor portfolio by the end of 2013.

Ben & Jerry's Fair Trade commitment, the first in its industry, means that every ingredient in its ice creams and confections that can be sourced Fair Trade Certified, now or in the future, is Fair Trade Certified. Globally, this involves working across diverse ingredients such as cocoa, banana, vanilla, and other flavorings, fruits, and nuts. It also means coordinating with Fair Trade cooperatives representing a combined membership of over 27,000 farmers.

Rob Cameron, Chief Executive of Fairtrade Labelling Organizations International, believes Fair Trade Certified is consistent with the Ben & Jerry's brand. In his words, "Ben & Jerry's, like all of us in the Fair Trade movement, believe that people can have fun standing up to injustice and campaigning against poverty while enjoying some of Ben & Jerry's best-selling favorites like Phish Food and Chocolate Fudge Brownie, how cool is that."[30]

Clarins beauty products

Taking an alternative approach to fair trade certification, Clarins, the France-based manufacturer of upscale skin care, make-up and perfumes, opts to rigorously screen their suppliers of precious botanical ingredients themselves, and commit to fair trade agreements and hands-on community development projects in indigenous communities. [31]

In Madagascar, Clarins supports over 2,500 families by offering agricultural jobs for harvesters. Additionally, Clarins reinvests 5% of all of its profit from a harvest back into local community projects.[32] For example, they helped to install an infrastructure system to supply a village in Marovay with clean drinking water and renovated a village school. Clarins also pledged to replant 10,000 native Katafray trees, and to teach local farmers how to remove the bark used in their products, sustainably.[33]

In Vietnam, Clarins has set up fair trade agreements to purchase Vu Sua, a fruit used for Clarins firming lotions, which is the main source of revenue for the village of Vin Kim.[34] Clarins also helped to finance and remodel one of the area's schools.

To help promote further socially responsible projects and protect the sources of its brand-distinguishing botanicals, Clarins recognizes outstanding individuals with company-sponsored service awards, such as the Dynamic Woman Award[35] started in 1997, and the ClarinsMen Environment Award, first given to Jean-Pierre Nicolas, an ethnopharmacologist, in 2004 for his organization Jardins du Monde, which brings alternative medicine to communities where conventional medicine is unavailable or too expensive.[36]

6 Reduce toxicity

Toxicity affects products at every stage of their life-cycle: for example, chemical spills on highways, fires and lethal toxin leaks at chemical plants such as the one in Bhopal, India, in 1984, and such issues as asbestos risks to workers and arsenic-laden mine tailings. Phthalates, a compound used as a plastics softener in children's toys, is believed to have adverse effects on the endocrine system and to be linked to birth defects in males.[37] Mercury and other toxic metals leach from batteries and cell phones as they languish in landfills long after their useful lives. Some chemical agents in common cleaning products, such as butyl, are also thought to pose a significant risk to children and pets.

Heeding consumer demand for healthier products, governments and corporations are taking action. The U.S. Congress passed the Consumer

Product Safety Improvement Act in August 2008 banning phthalates in children's toys. Wal-Mart, Target, and Toys R Us began requiring suppliers to follow similar standards for all children's products by January 2009.[38]

Reducing toxicity is good for business. It reduces the liability associated with risks to workers, and safer alternatives can enhance productivity and cut workers' compensation claims. Less (or non-) toxic materials save money on handling costs, while speeding time to market since there may be fewer legal hurdles to navigate. And, of course, there's the opportunity to market to the growing number of mainstream consumers looking for safer alternatives.

Nike's Considered shoe line

Working toward the elimination of noxious adhesives needed to join uppers and lowers on its sports shoes, in 2005 Nike launched its Considered line. A unique weaving process now holds the pieces together while lending the boot a unique moccasin-like aesthetic – and helping it to earn a coveted gold IDEA award from the Industrial Designers Society of America. Targeted toward "deep green" consumers, Considered helped illustrate Nike's commitment to sustainability – as exemplified through its impressive reductions of 61% in manufacturing waste, 35% in energy consumption, and 89% in the use of solvents.[39]

Nike has since sought to make the concept more universally appealing. The new Air Jordan XX3 is constructed using material from old recycled sneakers, manufacturing scraps, and jigsaw-like components resulting in an inner construction that uses less glue. This shoe even inspired the invention of a sewing machine designed to produce sneakers using more stitching and fewer chemical-based glues. Testament to the universal appeal of green, the new Air Jordan is targeted toward the same audience as the rest of the Air Jordan line, with the emphasis placed on performance. The green factor is included as an added bonus for those who are interested. Consumers are buying. Nike brand chief Charles Denson reported that during the first quarter of 2009, the company's basketball shoe division grew by double digits, propelled by Air Jordan sales.[40]

Marmoleum flooring from Forbo

For over half a century, vinyl has been the cheapest, easiest-to-install kind of flooring. However, it fades and scuffs and eventually needs to be replaced and sent to landfills. If incinerated, the scrapped vinyl (short for polyvinyl chloride – PVC) releases dioxins into the air. The vinyl manufacturing process also creates dioxin, one of the deadliest toxins on the planet, so constantly replacing vinyl exacerbates the situation.

Propelled by growing awareness for the environmental drawbacks of vinyl, old-fashioned natural linoleum is making a comeback. Produced from linseed oil, rosins, wood flour, and natural pigments with a backing made from jute, linoleum is an ecological alternative to vinyl. Leading the charge is Forbo Flooring, the industry leader, headquartered near Zurich, Switzerland. Its star product, Marmoleum, is helping to reinvent the image of linoleum. The company asserts that Marmoleum comes in an array of colors and styles and installs as easily as vinyl, but mounts using a safe water-based adhesive. To help combat the fact that the linoleum tiles are significantly costlier than vinyl, usually about $6 to $8 per square foot as opposed to prices that can run as low as $0.99 per square foot, the company emphasizes the fact that linoleum is healthier, antistatic, and does not promote the growth of bacteria, mold, or mildew. Also notable is the longer life of Marmoleum, which the company maintains does not sustain water damage, rip, gouge, or develop gaps, but ages gracefully, staying more richly colored, cushiony, and quieter than vinyl.[41] Someone is listening, as Forbo rides the green building and green home wave, enjoying net sales of over US$1.8 billion worldwide in 2009.[42]

Seventh Generation household cleaning products

Typical household cleaning products contain any number of synthetic chemicals including ammonia, chlorine, and parabens.[43] However, with the Burlington, Vermont-based Seventh Generation line-up, there is less worry about child-proofing the kitchen cabinet: although some of the company's products require trace amounts of preservatives, Seventh Generation products typically use plant-based ingredients that are biodegradable as well as chlorine- and phosphate-free, and the resulting products are just as effective as their conventional counterparts. Seventh Generation's cleaning products are also "not acutely toxic" as defined by the Consumer Products Safety Commission, by oral, dermal, or inhalation exposure.[44]

To reinforce their safer stance, Seventh Generation's product labels and website include ingredient lists for every product, as well as Material Safety Data Sheets. The website also includes a Corporate Responsibility Report and a blog by CEO Jeffrey Hollender on all things green. Thanks to this combination of safety, efficacy, and transparency, since 1989 Seventh Generation has grown from a catalog founded to serve the green niche directly, to one of the most trusted names in cleaning products found on the shelves of Whole Foods, Target, and many mainstream supermarkets.[45]

7 Think global, grow local

On average, commercially produced meals travel from 8 to 92 times farther from field to plate than locally grown meals,[46] and much of that food is carried on airplanes – the most carbon-intensive form of transportation.[47] Today, in a world watching its carbon consumption, buying and producing locally helps to minimize transportation costs and impacts, while supporting local farmers and strengthening communities. Mainstream consumers are starting to get the point. According to the NMI, in 2009 39% of U.S. consumers noted "buying products that are made locally" as an area of concern, up from 31% three years before.[48]

All across the U.S. the number of local farmers' markets is growing in response to consumers' desire for local produce, and gourmet chefs are writing new rules for their menus, promoting high-quality local produce. According to the USDA, the number of farmers' markets in the U.S. was 6,132 in 2010, versus 1,755 in 1994, and up 16% from 2009 alone.[49] Local purveyors such as Oregon-based New Seasons Market, a grocery store chain with seven locations throughout the state, to the 280-unit Whole Foods chain now make local sourcing a priority. Whole Foods even runs special Native Growers and Producers Events where local growers and producers of products including artisan snacks, vegan treats, and small batch soaps can learn about packaging and labeling guidelines, operations, and logistics support, as well as a local loan program. This is not just confined to the U.S.: UK supermarkets are increasingly bringing local food in, with one of the latest entrants being Waitrose, who as, this book was going to print, started a trial of local suppliers in its Saxmundham, Suffolk branch.

Wal-Mart

Even Wal-Mart is demonstrating a commitment to local sourcing, racking up annual sales of $400 million in locally grown produce from farmers throughout the country in 2008, making the retail giant the largest single purchaser of local produce in the United States. In 2008, the company increased local partnerships by 50% over 2006, and purchased more than 70% of its produce from U.S.-based suppliers.

Senior Vice President Pam Kohn says that this commitment saves on fuel costs and enables Wal-Mart to offer fresh products at low prices.[50] Demonstrating the potential to eliminate thousands of food miles that contribute to greenhouse gas emissions and air pollution, in 2008, by expanding their peach sourcing from just South Carolina and Georgia to 18 different states and selling locally, Wal-Mart slashed 672,000 food miles – translating to savings of 112,000 gallons of diesel fuel and more than $1.4 million.[51]

8 Use responsible manufacturing practices

Sometimes it's what consumers don't see that can have the most impact: the energy use and emissions from the manufacturing plant being a case in point. Recognizing this, a number of manufacturers are taking steps to reduce their plant emissions, green their energy sources, and curb their use of water, among other measures.

Kettle Foods

In keeping with its commitment to using all-natural ingredients, Kettle Foods makes its full line of snacks including potato chips, tortilla chips, nuts, and trail mix with an eye toward minimizing impact on the environment. "Walking their talk" as a producer of healthy snacks, Kettle Foods cooks its chips in sunflower and safflower oils; afterwards it converts 100% of the waste vegetable oil into biodiesel, which in turn runs a growing fleet of company vehicles and prevents 8 tons of CO_2 from being emitted each year.

In 2003 Kettle Foods Inc. partnered with Portland General Electric and Energy Trust of Oregon, a nonprofit organization, to install 600 solar panels atop their manufacturing plant, representing one of the largest arrays in the Pacific Northwest. The 120,000 kWh of electricity per year that is generated is enough power to produce 250,000 bags of Kettle Chips each year and eliminates 65 tons of CO_2 emissions per year when compared with fossil-fuel-based methods. Kettle Foods also offsets 100% of the plant's electricity use through wind power, which is the equivalent of taking 1,000 cars off the road or planting 1,600 acres of trees.

In 2000, when Kettle Foods Inc. moved its headquarters and production to its five-acre Mill Creek site in Salem, Oregon, it chose to restore the wetlands on the property. It introduced native and aquatic plants and built a two-acre trail system for people in the community to enjoy. They now see herons that faithfully return each year. In 2007, Kettle opened a second factory in Beloit, Wisconsin. It was the first U.S. food manufacturing facility to earn LEED gold certification. The factory has 18 wind turbines on its roof and is surrounded by prairie land that the company is restoring to its native state.[52]

Kettle Foods Inc.'s all-natural product produced in a natural way has helped the company generate a loyal following among consumers around the world who are prepared to pay premium prices versus more mainstream chips.[53]

9 Energy- and fuel-efficient

Electricity is needed to heat and light buildings and streets as well as to power all kinds of products, from those that plug into the wall to those that are fueled by batteries. However, the generation of electricity represents the single largest source of air pollution and greenhouse gas emissions in the United States. Nationally, power plant emissions are responsible for spewing significant amounts of carbon dioxide (CO_2), sulfur dioxide (SO_2), nitrogen oxides (NO_x), and mercury (Hg) into the air, not to mention particulate emissions that can be particularly harmful to athsmatics and other sensitive individuals. These four pollutants are the major cause of such serious environmental problems as acid rain, smog, mercury contamination, and global climate change.

Happily, much of this pollution can be avoided through simple actions and intelligent design. For example, "standby power," which enables televisions to be turned on instantly, accounts for approximately 5% of total residential electricity consumption in America, adding up to over $3 billion in annual energy costs.[54] Cutting down on standby power is one benefit of the ENERGY STAR label (see Chapter 7), which can now be found on more than 50 kinds of energy-using product, including homes and commercial buildings.

Bosch appliances

German-based Bosch is the only manufacturer selling appliances in the U.S. to have an ENERGY STAR label on all of its models. Bosch received ENERGY STAR recognition in 2008 and 2009, and was named ENERGY STAR's Partner of the Year in 2010. Bosch appliances, including the Nexxt clothes washer and Evolution dishwasher, are also competitively priced, ensuring their appeal to the mass market.

Bosch's "Nexxt" clothing washers benefit from multiple new technologies: a computer sensor that optimizes the water level for each wash, an internal water heater that monitors water temperature for efficiency, an inclined drum that cleans clothes with less water, and a final washer spin at 1,200 rpm that quickens the drying process. Using these washers which exceed ENERGY STAR guidelines by 102%[55] instead of top-loader washers, can save $150 a year in water and energy bills.[56]

The company's EcoSense Wash Management System for dishwashers provides similar sensors that cut energy use by 20%; dishwashers also offer effective water heating systems, condensation drying techniques, and the option for users to select an energy- and water-sipping half-load wash. At 190 kWh per year, the SH_98M model is the most efficient available in the U.S.[57]

Smart-Grid-enabled appliances

Many electric utilities, electrical product manufacturers, government, software manufacturers, and other organizations including Google and Microsoft are now working jointly to transform the nation's power grid into one digitally controlled "Smart-Grid" network that can convey electricity to consumers more efficiently, cutting pollution and electric bills in the process.

General Electric and Whirlpool are even readying "smart appliances" that are Smart-Grid-compliant: that is, they can be controlled from afar by the power company, who can lower thermostats, switch into energy-saver mode, or shut them down entirely during times of peak demand. Whirlpool predicts it will put one million smart clothes dryers on the market during 2011. Offering the potential for significant energy and cost savings, a smarter clothes dryer may help Whirlpool climb out of recession-induced sales slump, while also benefiting the environment: an electric dryer that tumbles without heat uses only about 200 watts of electricity, in comparison to the 500 watts used by one that's set on maximum heat. Multiplied by one million, this results in the equivalent of six big coal-fired power plants.[58]

Nokia's mobile phones

Approximately two-thirds of the energy used to power mobile phones is wasted when the charger remains plugged in or when the phone has finished charging but energy is still flowing – the "no-load" mode. To combat this, Nokia has reduced the no-load demand of its chargers by 70% over the decade preceding 2006, and aims to further reduce the demand by an additional 50% by 2010. Their most efficient charger uses just 0.03 W, beating the ENERGY STAR requirement by 94%.

In 2007, Nokia was the first cell phone manufacturer to build in alerts to encourage users to unplug when the phones are fully charged. The potential energy savings? If the owners of all one billion Nokia phones in use around the world unplugged their chargers when alerted, it would save enough energy to power 100,000 homes.[59] To save even more energy, users can turn off extraneous sounds such as keypad tones, dim the screen, and set backlight standby time to a minimum.

Toyota Prius

Representing a now iconic greener product, the now globally distributed Toyota Prius hybrid sedan combines smart design and a new brand of marketing (discussed in more detail in Chapter 6) with an exceptional rate of fuel efficiency gauged at 50 miles-per-gallon overall (city 51/highway 48). All of this adds up to fewer trips to the gas pump, less money spent on gasoline, and less pollution than competitive sedans.[60] Indeed, many U.S. states allow hybrid cars to use High Occupancy Vehicle (HOV) lanes even if there is only one person in the car, offering a competitive edge against popular sedans such as the Nissan Altima and Honda's Accord. To Toyota's credit, the Prius dashboard even includes a feedback display that promotes more efficient driving. Anecdotal reports indicate that Prius drivers have fun challenging themselves to get way beyond the estimated 50 mpg in fuel efficiency every time they drive. (The device has been so successful that Ford recently unveiled its own dashboard device, Smart Gauge, which is set to debut in its gas-electric hybrid cars in 2010.)[61]

10 Water-efficient

The United Nations Environment Programme predicts that 1.8 billion people will be living in places with severe water shortages by 2025, and two-thirds of the world's population could be subject to some water scarcity.[62] Due to a near tripling of per capita water usage in the past few decades, General Accounting Office anticipates water shortages in 36 U.S. states by 2013,[63] likely leading to price spikes and treacherous implications for crops, livestock, and other water-intensive industries.

In an effort to spur the market toward water-conserving showerheads, faucets, toilets, urinals, and even landscape irrigation practices and newly built homes, the EPA offers the WaterSense label, the H_2O-saving counterpart to its ENERGY STAR label. With the availability of xeriscaping, a water-efficient landscape that has been found to use up to 75% less water, the amount of turf grass allowed on newly built homes could be government's next target.[64] Meanwhile, if the San Francisco-based Carbon Disclosure Project, a nonprofit group that has persuaded major corporations to disclose greenhouse gas emissions, has its way, water-intensive industries, such as auto manufacturing, electric utilities, food and beverage manufacturing, mining, and pharmaceuticals, will become water-efficient. The group is now surveying major corporations about their water use and discharges into nearby water bodies, as well as water-related risks, opportunities, and strategies.

Caroma dual-flush toilets

The average household uses 350 gallons of water per day, over 40% of which is used in the bathroom.[65] The latest development from Brisbane, Australia-based Caroma, one of the world's leading plumbing product companies, is a new dual-flush toilet that is a pioneer in water-saving technology. The toilet has two different buttons – one for liquid waste and one for solid, using 0.8

and 1.6 gallons of water per flush, respectively. This single product with its half-flush and full-flush technology reduces water usage by up to 67% compared with traditional toilets, which use almost 3 gallons per flush.[66] Caroma toilets are distributed all across the world and bearing the EPA's WaterSense logo they are used by universities, hotels, companies, and homes throughout North America.[67]

A new rule in the making: product water-footprints. As reflected throughout this book, water efficiency is usually referred to about products in use. But a lot of water goes into the making of many consumer products. For instance, because of the water consumed in cotton growing, it takes 10,855 gallons of water to make a pair of jeans, and 15,5000 for a kilogram of beef.[68] With expected pressure on water supplies in the not-too-distant future, expect consumers to start to demand information about your product's water footprint, similar to the nascent carbon footprint.

11 Extend product life

Consumers have long valued brands such as Maytag, Volvo, and Zippo for their high quality and long life. With the mainstreaming of green, durable products are being valued anew for their low environmental impact, eliminating the stigma often associated with used products. As just one example, Lexus gives their high-end cars a second life as "certified, pre-owned" cars, attracting a clientele usually in the market for new cars.

Stokke Tripp Trapp chair

Smart designers have created cribs that transform into regular beds as the child grows. Stokke, a Norwegian-based furniture manufacturer specializing in versatile baby products, has designed a highchair that grows with the child. With an adjustable seat and footrest, their Tripp Trapp chair evolves over time from a safe seat for a small child to comfortable seating for an adult. Constructed primarily of sustainably harvested beech wood with formaldehyde-free varnish, the chair is durable and easily cleaned with a damp cloth. Underscoring the company's commitment to durability, the Tripp Trapp Chair comes with a seven-year warranty on all the wooden components.[69]

12 Reusable and refillable

Reusable materials and refillable packaging reduce waste and save businesses money. Mainstream shoppers are getting the hang of reusability, thanks to the efforts of eco-conscious retailers that sell reusable bags in their stores rewarding consumers who bring their own bags, and penalizing those who don't. IKEA and Whole Foods Market encourage shoppers to bring their own tote bags by giving them five and ten cents off their purchase, respectively.

Reusable water bottles

Advertising for bottled water often showcases pristine springs bubbling up from deep within the earth, but behind the scenes loom the environmental impacts associated with its transportation and packaging, which together consume about 17 million barrels of oil per year.[70] In 2006, over 30 billion bottles of water were consumed in the United States[71] – 86% of the bottles subsequently became litter or sent to landfills; when incinerated, they create chlorine gas and harmful by-products.[72] A backlash is already in place among local governments and concerned consumers, creating opportunities for Nalgene and Klean Kanteen among other manufacturers touting a reusable solution. Nalgene has teamed up with Brita water filter company in an innovative partnership to promote the benefits of bottling one's purified water at home. Meanwhile, sales of Klean Kanteen's sleek stainless steel water bottles have skyrocketed from $2.5 million in 2007 to $18 million in 2008.

ecoEnvelopes

Online bill paying is fast becoming the norm, but each year, more than 81 billion return envelopes are still enclosed in utility bills, credit card statements, and other mailings.[73] Ann DeLaVergne, a former organic farmer based in Minnesota, is attempting to rewrite the rules for assisting in bill collection: she has invented the ecoEnvelope, a reusable mail solution, which in February 2008 was approved by the U.S. Postal Service. Users zip open the ecoEnvelope by lifting a tab and pulling along a perforated strip. They then insert their response, moisten, and close the flap.

ecoEnvelopes are manufactured exclusively on FSC- and SFI (Sustainable Forestry Initiative)-certified recycled paper from sustainably managed forests, and use soy and water-based inks. Not only do ecoEnvelopes cut down on waste, they can also help companies project an ecologically conscious image to their customers and save 15% to 45% on mailing costs.[74] Companies such as the Land Stewardship Foundation, Fresh Energy, and Renewable Choice Energy are already using ecoEnvelopes, saving money while literally sending a message to their customers about their commitment to sustainability.

13 Recyclable

It's great if products are made from recycled content, but those same products need to be easy to disassemble in order to keep labor costs down so recycling can be economically feasible. Done correctly, designing for disassembly can lead to business success.

Herman Miller Mirra work chair

Introduced in 2003, the Mirra work chair from Herman Miller has it all. It is made from a high percentage of post-consumer and post-industrial aluminum. With a minimum number of parts – and taking all of 15 minutes with normal household tools – it is easy to disassemble for recycling. Parts are coded for recycling according to American Society for Testing and Materials standards. Because it is easy to disassemble, the chair is also a cinch to repair.

Representing a holistic approach to environmental design, the Mirra chair eschews PVC. It is made in a manufacturing plant that is LEED-certified and powered by 100% renewable energy, and it comes with a 12-year warranty. The design has received positive publicity, as well as accolades for environmental and ergonomic performance, not to mention being well on its way toward becoming a design icon.

Patagonia Common Threads recycling program

A product designed for easy disassembly and made of recyclable content must also be easy for consumers to return for recycling, whether by bringing used products back to store or sent to another location, or picked up, or handed over to a retailer or other third party who will recycle them.

Patagonia's Synchilla PCR fleece and Capilene fabrics are made using recyclable fibers that are easily broken down to their original monomers, a process that eventually results in new fibers equal in quality to the originals. Seizing an opportunity to make new garments from old ones and satisfy customer demands for recycling, in 2005, Patagonia launched the Common Threads Recycling Program, a garment take-back program driven by in-store collection of used garments made from polyester. Reusing old garments to manufacture new Capilene (polyester) garments saves 76% of the energy associated with making a new garment from scratch.[75] Representing a true closing of the loop, since spring 2007 Capilene fabrics have included old Capilene garments which have been recycled into virgin-grade polyester collected through the Common Threads Recycling Progam.[76] With the instigation of a new chemical recycling process in the summer of 2008, Patagonia can now collect and recycle nylon products, too.[77]

14 Compostable

In nature, everything is recycled – waste for one organism becomes food for another. According to the EPA, approximately 30% of solid waste, mostly food, is biodegradable material that can be effectively composted into humus, an organic matter that can enrich gardens and agricultural soils, but only a small amount of consumers have access to municipal or backyard composters. So most waste winds up in landfills, where it will be entombed forever or, even worse, slowly degrade, creating methane gas, which is highly flammable and 21 times more powerful than CO_2 as a global warming gas. Composting, which typically involves the use of new biobased materials, will need to play a big part in future waste disposal scenarios. Happily, a number of new products and packages designs are appearing in the market, encouraging more composting activity. Innovative designers are now developing compostable products and packages with this idea in mind.

VerTerra dinnerware

Sometimes the inspiration for a new material can come from an existing material that may be old or overlooked. Michael Dwork, founder and CEO of VerTerra, Ltd., an enterprising firm located in New York City, on a trip to Asia saw that fallen palm leaves from plantations were being burned. He noticed that a woman had taken some of the fallen palm leaves, soaked them and pressed them into shape with a crude waffle iron and used them as plates.[78] That provided the inspiration to repurpose the plates on a larger scale as the basis of attractive, functional, and compostable line of plates, bowls, and trays.

The leaves, which otherwise would have been burned, are steamed, heated, and pressed in a local factory. No chemicals, glues, lacquers, or bonding agents are used in the manufacture of the products. In 2008, VerTerra salvaged 1.5 tons of leaves per month. In 2009 that monthly average jumped to nearly 12 tons; annual production and sales tracked in similar fashion up nearly eight times. The waste from the process is powdered and traded back to the farmers as mulch in exchange for more leaves. Compostable and biodegradable, VerTerra's food service line has earned the BPI logo, and is currently used by major universities such as Columbia University in the City of New York, by major sports stadiums such as that of the Dallas Cowboys, and by Evelyn Hill Inc., concessionaire for the Statue of Liberty and the Playboy Mansion. In early 2009 VerTerra launched a retail line that is now available at natural and specialty stores across the country such as Whole Foods Markets and numerous health food stores and Internet websites; a set of eight plates starts at $3.99.[79]

Frito-Lay SunChips packaging

Launched in 1991, SunChips, a multigrain snack made with sunflower and with 30% less fat than potato chips, has appealed to consumers looking for healthier alternatives. But after the brand team realized that its health-conscious clientele care seriously about the environment as well, they launched a program propelled by greener marketing, production, and packaging strategies – and once-flagging sales have nearly doubled from $172 million in 2007 to $308 million in 2009.[80]

As part of its synergistic strategy of "healthy for me" and "healthy for the planet," the SunChips plant in Modesto, California, which cranks out 145,000 snack bags daily, is powered by the sun, and all of Frito-Lay's carbon emissions in the U.S. are offset by the purchase of green energy credits.[81] In 2010, Frito-Lay rolled out across the U.S. new chip bags made largely of Ingeo by Natureworks LLC. Made from polylactic acid (PLA) derived from corn fermentation, it is compostable in industrial composting facilities and, since it is quite thin, over a longer period of time in backyard composters, thus representing the potential to reduce landfill waste and the greenhouse gases associated with the production of petroleum-based packaging.[82] The bags are noisier than conventional chip bags – an issue the brand is working through as this book goes to press – but judging by nearly 50,000 YouTube views of a SunChips 30-second commercial showing time-lapsed decomposition, consumers are excited by the bag's compostability, and Frito-Lay is demonstrating a firm commitment to perfecting this innovative new material and disposal method.

Harvest Collection by GenPak

As the use of disposable cutlery and tableware has become more common in the home as well as at picnics, parties, and other gatherings, compostable products are emerging to replace the tons of plastic cutlery that end up in landfills. One such line is the Harvest Collection by GenPak, which includes compostable plates, cups, and food containers. These products are made from renewable resources such as corn, rice, and wheat, which are either grown or recovered as crop residue. All Harvest Collection cutlery and dinnerware is completely heat- and water-resistant and will break down within months of being composted.[83]

Compostable products are beginning to appear more frequently on store shelves, but, as mentioned above, not all products that claim to be so are actually compostable. To deal with this issue, the Biodegradable Products Institute (BPI) created a eco-label to help consumers and compost facility operators easily identify plastic products that will actually compost completely and safely in the proper facilities.[84] BPI's label is designed to facilitate composting by eliminating the need to sort food scraps from tableware. This is especially useful for picking up after large gatherings. The entire waste stream – food, tableware, and cutlery – can be composted, rather than land-filled.[85] In addition to finished products, BPI certifies producers of resins, the raw materials that can be converted into a plethora of products including bags, food serviceware, and packaging.

Figure 4.2 **BPI logo**

Source: Reprinted with permission from BPI

15 Safe for disposal

With the potential for disposable batteries, cell phones, iPods, and other ubiquitous electronic equipment to contain toxic substances that can leach into underground water supplies from landfills, the call for reduced toxicity is fast changing the rules for business. In 2006, the European Union passed the Restriction of Hazardous Substances (ROHS) directive prohibiting sales of new electrical and electronic equipment containing more than agreed-on levels of lead, cadmium, mercury, hexavalent chromium, polybrominated biphenyl (PBB), and polybrominated diphenyl ether (PBDE) flame retardants. As Sony learned the hard way, not complying with such legislation is one game with very high stakes. In December 2001, the Sony Playstation was rejected for sale in the European Union and $162 million worth of merchandise was impounded because the power cord exceeded the allowable amount of cadmium, causing Sony to miss the all-important Christmas sales season.[86]

Philips Alto II fluorescent lamps

Even though CFLs represent a game-changing step forward in energy efficiency, all compact fluorescents contain a tiny, yet highly toxic amount of mercury. Once in landfills, it can contaminate underground water supplies.

Indeed, many states prohibit the disposal of CFLs (and all fluorescent lighting) in regular trash. Even without laws, the value of this mercury, as well as the energy embodied in CFLs, behooves lamp manufacturers to collect the bulbs for recycling.

One bulb that is raising the bar for product disposal is Philips Alto fluorescent lamps. Easily spotted by their bright green end caps, the Alto II fluorescents have the lowest mercury content on the market, and use a lead-free solder.[87] They pass the EPA's Toxicity Characteristic Leaching Procedure (TCLP) test, thus classifying the bulbs as non-hazardous waste and relieving commercial customers of regulatory burdens associated with disposing of fluorescent bulbs. Their longer life saves money on bulbs and labor-intensive change-outs. There are over half a billion Alto lamps in operation.[88]

As demonstrated in this chapter, the new rules of green marketing now require businesses to adopt a life-cycle approach to their products and packages. Doing so not only minimizes environmental and social impacts and risks, and helps to meet consumer needs, but it can be also be a sure route to innovation. However, greening can present even greater opportunities for businesses that want to change the rules of the game to innovate further. Many of the strategies and tools being used by sustainability leaders for "sustainable product innovation" are discussed in the next chapter.

The *New Rules* Checklist

Use the following checklist to explore the myriad opportunities for refining your products or developing new ones to environmental imperatives and satisfy consumers' primary demands for quality/performance and affordability.

- Do we know the full range of environmental and social issues that are associated with our product or service? Can we consider a "cradle-to-gate" or "cradle-to-grave" or even a "cradle-to-cradle" life-cycle assessment for our products?

- How do our products' environmental and social impacts compare to our competitors?

- Do we have a short- and long-term plan of environmental and social-related improvements for our products?

○ What environmental improvements do we anticipate competitors introducing? Are we prepared with a response?

○ In what ways do environmental enhancements improve our product or service's overall performance and quality?

○ Are there opportunities to use environmental enhancements to extend our brand?

Raw material use and procurement

○ Are we using the minimum amount of raw materials possible, i.e., taking advantage of opportunities for source reduction?

○ Are we ensuring that procurement processes for our raw materials avoids tropical deforestation? Clear-cutting? Land stripping? Oil spills?

○ Can we use renewable resources or resources that are sustainably managed and harvested? Organically grown?

○ Can we use locally procured raw materials to keep energy shipping costs to a minimum and assist local farmers?

○ Are our suppliers certified by such organizations as TransFair, Rainforest Alliance, or the Fairtrade Foundation for sustainable harvesting and fair labor practices?

○ What steps are we taking for reducing the use of toxic chemicals in our products?

Manufacturing and distribution

○ What steps can we take to prevent or otherwise reduce the production of solid and hazardous waste in our manufacturing processes? How can we reduce our use of water? How can we reduce our emissions to air and releases to waterways?

○ Can we use solar or wind or other forms of renewable energy to power our manufacturing plants?

○ Are we manufacturing close to our markets so as to create local jobs and minimize transportation energy and costs?

Packaging

○ Can we redesign our packages to reduce materials? Make them from recycled content? Make them recyclable?

○ Can we use alternative materials such as bioplastics to make them compostable?

Use

○ Can we redesign our products to make them more energy- fuel- or water-efficient and thereby reduce consumers' operating costs and carbon footprint?

○ Might we provide real-time information that informs consumers of their environmental impact as it relates to a product?

○ Can we use alternative ingredients that help to minimize risks to health and the environment?

After-use

○ Can we design our products to be durable? Refillable? Reusable? Repairable? Remanufacturable? Rechargeable?

○ Can we design our products so they can be easily disassembled for recycling?

○ Are we designing our products from materials that are easily recyclable and do facilities exist for recycling in consumers' communities?

○ Can we take back our products for recycling? Can we create reverse distribution logistics and strategies?

Disposal

○ Can we use materials and ingredients that are biodegradable or compostable?

○ Can we make our products and packaging safer to landfill or incinerate?

Innovate for sustainability

Almost daily, new scientific data become available, suggesting that humans will need to tread significantly more lightly on the planet to meet our future needs sustainably. In short, all signs point toward present modes of production and consumption being unsustainable. This issue is especially critical for U.S. consumers whose lifestyles are the least sustainable on the planet and, to boot, are emulated or aspired to by billions of other consumers in emerging economies and developing nations. According to the U.S. EPA, in 2006 American households threw away more than 251 million tons of trash. The bulk of this waste ended up in landfills, consuming vast quantities of energy to transport and potentially adding toxic leachate to underground water supplies, not to mention using millions of pounds of raw materials that will take untold quantities of new resources and energy to replace. Some experts go so far as to estimate that, to achieve significant reductions in our energy and natural resource use over the next several decades, we will need to radically alter our entire means of production and consumption by a factor of four. One way to address this critical problem is through innovation.

Innovating for sustainability brings with it exciting opportunities for businesses to help grow their top-line sales and even evolve and transform their business models – indeed, their entire company – to better compete within the rules of a more sustainable future. That this represents a opportunity for marketers to lead the way is unquestioned. Brand managers and marketers – those responsible for the development and communications of products and services – are closest to their brands and often the lead the way toward creative new products that can best meet their consumers' needs. This chapter is aimed at managers and marketers who want to understand how the quest for sustainability can help them discover the next big idea leading to meaningful new products and more satisfied consumers.

Beyond eco-design to eco-innovation

It is one thing to use the most authentic green design principles, such as those described in Chapter 4, to create products with a lower impact. But the rules are quickly changing. To stay competitive and meet the challenges of sustainable development, forward-thinking businesses will need to combine innovation with ecology, through the power of what's known (especially in Europe) as "eco-innovation." Eco-innovation can be defined as innovating at the concept stage, or developing entirely new products and services (including materials and technologies) capable of performing the same function as existing ones only with significantly less environmental impact. As will be seen in many of the examples to follow, it represents the opportunity to at once solve pressing environmental issues while superbly meeting consumer needs, and even to transform one's company – profitably.

Figure 5.1 **Sustainable product innovation**

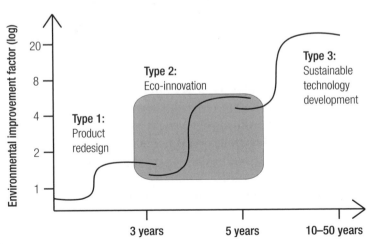

Source: TNO Science and Industry, The Netherlands

As can be seen in Figure 5.1, denoting the progression of three "S" curves of sustainable product innovation, existing products can only be tweaked (eco-designed) so much before it becomes necessary to leap to an entirely new product concept in order to meet the same consumer need with significantly reduced environmental impact. At the end of even the most thoroughly executed process, greening a product by making adjustments in raw materials, packaging, and so forth, leaves you, by definition, with pretty much the same concept as when you started. Your toothbrush is still a toothbrush, but now uses recycled materials. Your water bottle is still a water bottle, only the shoulders are a little shaved off, or it is made from aluminum instead of plastic. Even at the end of a series of multiple iterations aimed at greening, at some point you will find yourself at the end of the first "S" curve labeled "Type 1: Product redesign," unable to achieve greater environmental improvement; you are limited by your product concept.

In order to achieve significant, not just incremental, reductions in eco-impact, you must jump-shift to an entirely new product concept. This is called "eco-" or "functional innovation," represented by the second "S" curve labeled "Type 2: Eco-innovation." To develop new product concepts that perform the same function as existing products but with significantly less impact, start by questioning fundamental assumptions. For instance, to further reduce the environmental impact of a toothbrush, first consider modifying the task from merely "greening a toothbrush" to, let's say, "cleaning teeth without a toothbrush." This might trigger a new product concept such as a specially treated chewing gum that will clean teeth without the need for a toothbrush (and also the toothpaste, water, and the packaging!).

To proceed from the second to the third "S" curve labeled "Type 3: Sustainable technology development," you must redefine your task more radically – for instance, from "cleaning teeth" to "preventing the plaque from forming in the first place." This might lead to developing, say, a benign food additive that would accomplish the task. Moving up and across the three "S" curves in this graph starting with a product concept of a toothbrush made of recycled materials, then evolving to chewing gum, and finally to a food additive, shows how eco-innovation can inspire new products and new business models with significantly reduced environmental impact – and economic benefit as well.

Among its many attractive business and green marketing opportunities, eco-innovation represents the potential for significantly enhanced consumer benefits. In the case of the chewing gum, one can imagine significant cost, convenience, and even efficacy plusses (not to mention ending the problem of getting the kids to brush). Rather than simply focusing on eco-efficiency and its desirable but less exciting effect on the bottom line, moving along these "S" curves of sustainable innovation represents the potential for changing the rules of the game, and, as GE experienced with its Ecomagination initiative, the ability to project an image as a leader, innovator, and socially responsible corporate citizen, all rolled into one. Finally, many sustainably innovative companies gain competitive advantage by anticipating future changes in the market. Innovating for sustainability before it reaches the radar screens of others in your industry allows companies to anticipate market changes. Eco-innovative products, such as the ones described in this chapter, put their developers, designers, and producers way ahead of the curve, often yielding a first-mover advantage that neatly translates into a better brand image for their products and companies.

Five strategies for eco-innovation

There are several strategies that forward-looking companies can use to eco-innovate. Let's take a closer look at five of them.

Five strategies for eco-innovation

1. Innovate at the system level
2. Develop new materials
3. Develop new technologies
4. Develop new business models
5. Restore the environment

1 Innovate at the system level

No one is an island, and no product stands alone, either. Products are part of a larger system from which they draw resources and deposit by-products and wastes. The most successful businesses understand, appreciate, and leverage the system in which their products operate. Changing the system in which products are developed and/or delivered allows innovators to expand their business and redefine their industry. Following are three of many ways to change a product's system in order to minimize its environmental impact: changing the elements in a product system, dematerializing the product, and creating a new product system.

Change individual elements within an existing product system

Changing a product system is a big task – but starting small and rethinking the individual elements of an existing product system not only gets you started, it can also achieve some pretty big results in and of itself. For example, a lot of water is still used even if consumers use low-flush toilets and turn off the water while brushing their teeth or washing their hands. But if one first considers the fixtures in a bathroom as working together in one unified system, rather than as individual standalone units, exciting new business opportunities arise.

AQUS greywater recycling system

Take the AQUS system by WaterSaver Technologies of Louisville, Kentucky. This ingenious technology makes use of a concept called "greywater". Runoff water from the bathroom sink feeds into the toilet, and is then used for flushing. The water works twice at no additional cost! Given that about 40% of all water used in households is used to flush toilets, combining the sink and toilet in such a unique new product system saves the typical two-person household between 10 and 20 gallons a day, or about 5,000 gallons per year.

Soladey toothbrush

Japanese company Soladey took a step back and decided that the toothbrushing system as we know it didn't need as many elements. So they built a photocatalytic titanium dioxide rod into the handle of their toothbrush. Brushing teeth with this toothbrush in a bright room causes chemical reactions to break down tooth plaque, eliminating the need for toothpaste.[1] By combining two elements of the toothbrush product system, Soladey has created a streamlined system with the potential for significantly reduced environmental impact.[2]

gDiapers

According to the EPA, in 2005 approximately 3.5 million tons of diaper waste, representing about 20 billion disposable diapers, were dumped in U.S. landfills, where they will take an estimated 500 years to decompose.[3] Two concerned parents invented the gDiaper, capitalizing on new materials and a systems-oriented product view to invent a radically new alternative.

Conventional disposable diapers are composed of an inner diaper made from wood pulp and an outer lining made of plastic, both of which are thrown away with every diaper change. The gDiaper's advantage is that the inner and outer components are detachable, so that the outer lining can be washed and reused while the inner diaper can be flushed down the toilet. This ensures that the bacteria-laden human waste winds up in the sewage treatment system where it belongs, rather than in a landfill where it can leach into the underground water.[4] Representing a feasible and convenient alternative to both cloth and disposable diapers with a measurably reduced environmental and material impact, the gDiaper is poised to take significant market share from conventional disposables.

Dematerialize

Reconceive a product so that it requires significantly fewer material inputs (and, consequently, outputs). Ask: can a product perform the same function by using only a fraction of its original materials? In many cases, the answer is yes.

Tricycle's SIM simulated carpet sample

One company that is taking a swipe at the estimated 1 million pounds of carpet samples that end up in American landfills each year[5] is Tricycle, a Chattanooga, Tennessee-based design firm. Most carpet swatches used by designers and showrooms are discarded after a single use – and since an average order of carpet samples uses more than seven gallons of oil, the environmental and financial impacts of these swatches can really add up.[6]

Thinking outside the box, Tricycle devised SIM, which relies on an inventive technology that prints images on swatch-sized pieces of paper that simulate the exact colors and textures of a particular section of carpet, but with 95% less water and energy and 100% less oil than conventional swatches. Add to that, traditionally produced swatches may take days or weeks to be delivered from carpet factories, but SIM reduces the wait time to less than 24 hours.[7]

In 2005, SIM clients were shipped about 34,000 paper samples[8] – saving manufacturers 70% of the costs associated with samples, or about $5 million per year.[9] For its efforts, Tricycle won a Gold IDEA from the Industrial Designers Society of America for 2006.

E-readers

Suddenly they are everywhere. Amazon's Kindle, Barnes & Noble's Nook, Sony's Reader, and Apple's iPad. People are fast abandoning newspapers and books and turning to these and other exciting new e-readers – handheld devices that electronically deliver the content of printed books but with many additional features. With a screen about the size of a paperback book and wireless connectivity that allows users to read their favorite newspapers, magazines, and blogs within moments of publication, users can wirelessly purchase new releases at a significant discount from hardcovers. Books take less than 60 seconds to download, and more than 1,500 titles can be stored at a time, making an e-reader an attractive option whether traveling, commuting, or at home. And the environmental benefits of using e-readers to read electronic books (ebooks) are compelling: the Cleantech Group projects that in 2012, 5.27 billion kilograms of carbon dioxide emissions will be prevented due by ebooks.[10]

Create a new system

Sometimes the most effective way to cut down on eco-impacts is to abandon a product concept altogether and create an entirely new system. This requires a business to learn from the larger environment in which its products function. It takes the efforts of cross-functional product development and marketing teams that can interpret information from the full range of product life-cycle phases and synthesize new ideas.

Holistic to the core, systems thinking holds that every employee and citizen has something significant to contribute. It may also entail cooperating with manufacturers of complementary products, reaching out beyond one's corporate borders to stakeholders in the local community, and even bringing perspectives as diverse as those of children into the process. But the rewards are potentially the most significant because of the inherent potential to change the rules of the game.

Admittedly, the challenge of creating a new system can be daunting if stakeholders feel the ultimate eco-innovation may threaten an existing business; for these reasons, eco-innovative activity needs the full support of the CEO and others responsible for long-term strategy. It is best carried out in a "spin-off" or "incubator" mode or by a start-up with no pre-existing stake in the current system. Within established businesses, potential enemies need to be converted into allies by demonstrating how they can benefit.

Better Place recharging stations

Demand for plug-in hybrid vehicles like Chevy's Volt and Nissan's LEAF is projected to skyrocket to 600,000 vehicles by 2015. The drivers of all of those new cars will benefit from an innovation being pioneered by the start-up Better Place, based in Palo Alto, California. They have invented an entirely new system that overcomes the range limitations of electric vehicles.

Rather than making drivers of electric cars wait to recharge their batteries at home overnight, Better Place shifts the paradigm, offering multiple "fill-up" stations where drivers can either exchange their battery for a newly charged one, or opt to charge their battery within the network of charging stations, wired parking lots, and battery replacement stations that Better Place has built throughout their Israeli test market. By the end of 2010, there will be a station every 25 miles – and Better Place also sells the electric cars that can be charged at those stations.[11] The company aims to have tens of thousands of electric cars on Israel's roads by 2011. With the projected costs of battery-powered car ownership as much as 50% lower than a comparable gasoline-powered car, Better Place provides an alternative that is convenient and cost-effective – as well as environmentally sensible.

2 Develop new materials

There are currently thousands of different materials on the market for consumer, commercial, and industrial use, from the softest fibers to bulletproof plastics and metals and everything in between. Each of these materials is particularly suited to meet specific needs or functions – and each bears an environmental impact. Promising new materials are in development, leading to sustainable advances and an ever-growing opportunity for innovation. One particularly exciting material with the potential for a wide range of applications is bioplastics. Now growing in volume between 20% and 30% each year, bioplastics are derived from renewable resources such as corn or sugar cane, contain no toxins (unlike petroleum-based plastics), and are generally compostable in municipal facilities and often backyard composters. Considering that only about 5% of the 30 million tons of plastic used in the U.S. annually is recycled, biodegradable bioplastics have emerged in recent years as a viable method to reduce waste from petroleum-based plastics.[12]

Coke's PlantBottle

One exciting application for bio-plastics is Coca-Cola's "PlantBottle," made from a combination of traditional petroleum-based plastic and up to 30% plant-based materials such as sugar cane and molasses, a by-product of sugar production. A life-cycle analysis conducted by Imperial College London shows the "PlantBottle" represents up to 25% reduced carbon emissions compared with 100% petroleum-based PET. Also, unlike some other plant-based plastics, it can be recycled without contaminating traditional PET.[13]

Metabolix's Mirel bioplastic

If two big companies have their way, we'll see a lot more plant-based bottles in the future. Metabolix, a joint venture with Archer Daniels Midland called

Telles, and NatureWorks, a Cargill subsidiary, are both staking our big positions in bioplastics. As of this writing, Telles is about to start shipping its Mirel plastic pellets from a new plant in Clinton, Iowa. One of the first products is resin for a $1.25 biodegradable Paper Mate pen made by Newell Rubbermaid. Paper Mate says advance demand is strong. The pen, however, does cost more to make. Metabolix charges about $2.50 a pound for its green plastic, around twice that of traditional feedstock. The good news is that Paper Mate's pens use so little plastic that the pen maker needs to reduce its margins by only a couple of percentage points compared with its regular pens.[14]

Natureworks's Ingeo bioplastic

Natureworks's Ingeo brand of bioplastics is made from 100% polylactic acid (PLA) produced by the fermentation of corn. Ingeo's versatile functionality – like traditional, petroleum-based plastics it can be molded into a variety of forms: opaque, clear, flexible, or rigid – is already being leveraged for a variety of food packaging. Catch it keeping muffins fresh at Target, in use for food serviceware, and in the lining of the Ecotainer, a compostable paper-based cold drink cup, a joint initiative between Coca-Cola and International Paper.[15] Other sustainable brands who have incorporated Ingeo into their products include Noble Juices, for the first juice bottle and shrink sleeve label made from Ingeo, Method's compostable cleaning wipes, and Green Mountain Coffee Roasters' compostable coffee bags. Ingeo polymer can also be converted into a fiber-like polyester, which can be used as fiberfill bedding for use in pillows and comforters. Most recently, it is being used in baby diapers such as the Huggies Natural line.[16]

Like all greener products, however, Ingeo has its trade-offs. It is compostable, but will typically only readily break down in industrial composters – taking much longer in backyard compost piles if at all, and there are only about 100 such facilities in the entire United States. Also, PLA products can contaminate the recycling stream when mixed with products made from PET, a look-alike petrochemical resin, thus requiring special labeling and sorting at the PLA products' end-of-life stage and educating mainstream consumers about proper disposal techniques.[17] A collection and composting system is being developed by the Bioplastics Recycling Consortium to address these issues.[18]

3 Develop new technologies

Many people argue that most of our modern-day environmental woes are a direct result of industrialization. However, new eco-innovative technologies can mitigate the problems of the past and pave the way to a more sustainable future. Such technologies can be high-tech, expensive, and complicated, but they can also represent simple, low-tech solutions of comparable efficacy. Three particularly good opportunities exist in the areas of high-efficiency lighting, portable renewable energy, and alternative automotives.

Light-emitting diodes (LEDs)

Just as consumers are getting used to CFLs as a replacement for incandescent lamps, an even more exciting alternative is here to take its place: light-emitting diodes (LEDs). Projected to represent 46% of the $4.4 billion U.S. market for lamps in the commercial, industrial, and outdoor stationary sectors by 2020, LEDs are more efficient and last twice as long – typically 50,000 hours – as CFLs.[19] Also, in contrast to CFLs, LEDs do not need a ballast and do not contain toxic mercury, so they are safer to dispose of.

Historically, prices for these wonder bulbs were an impediment to market acceptance, but thanks to recent innovations affordable LEDs are fast making their way to retail shelves. One standout is EcoSmart LED light bulbs sold exclusively in Home Depot. Retailing for $19.97, compared to over $50 for other 40 watt incandescents, the bulb uses about 80% less energy and is expected to last more than 22 years. Also, it is dimmable, completely recyclable, and offers outstanding quality of light – and will pay back its initial investment in less than two years, accounting for energy and replacement savings.[20]

Distributed renewable energy

Demand for alternative energy is exploding, and will continue to rise along with consumer concern over climate change and other threats. Thanks to advances in technology, the cost of wind power has fallen by 80% over the past 30 years to between 4 and 6 cents per kWh,[21] making it competitive to oil (5 cents per kWh) and natural gas (3 cents per kWh).[22] In fact, wind power now provides 1% of energy in the U.S., or about enough energy to power 4.5 million homes.[23]

Solio solar-powered charger

Long confined to rooftop solar panels and windmills, renewable energy sources are ready to hit the road. They are now accessible via hip, portable consumer products such as Solio, a hand-held, solar-powered charger for small electronic devices such as cell phones, iPods, and digital cameras. Fully charged after a bath in direct sunlight for 8–10 hours, a Solio can run an MP3 player for up to 56 hours.[24] Working on the same principle, tote bags and backpacks produced by Voltaic Systems[25] and Reware[26] power small electronic devices such as cell phones and even laptops via solar panels woven onto the bags.

Swift wind turbine

Who needs the grid? Some consumers are producing clean, renewable energy themselves with the Swift Wind Turbine, designed by the UK-based company Renewable Devices, and produced in the U.S. by Cascade Engineering of Grand Rapids, Michigan. Perched on a rooftop, this small $10,000 turbine sends the 2,000 kilowatts of free electricity it generates each year directly to the consumer's electric system. Considering that the typical American household consumes between 6,500 and 10,000 kWh of electricity per year, the Swift Wind Turbine can cut a home's electrical demand from the grid by one-fifth to one-third. A $1,000 federal renewable energy tax credit can defray part of that already reduced cost.[27]

Human-powered products

A limitless and clean energy resource that is literally available at our fingertips is kinetic energy – and it's powering a growing number of products. Referred to as human-powered products, these items can be conveniently small – for example, the Ventura digital watch that is powered by the motions of the wearer's wrist[28] – and they can put the power of charging small electronic devices literally into your hands. Consider the Aladdin hand generator that charges cell phones, iPods, or even a portable DVD player with just a few squeezes of a handle.[29]

Just think about all the kinetic energy produced by bicycles and treadmills! This notion dawned on the owner of a string of gyms in Hong Kong, who rigged cycling and cross-training machines to power a gym's lights and store extra energy in batteries for later use.[30] The Human Power Trainer, made by Windstream Power LLC of North Ferrisburg, Vermont, works on the same concept. It mounts a bicycle on a frame so that the rear tire can turn a turbine that generates power, which is stored in a 12-volt battery which, in turn, powers household appliances. An average person can produce between 100 and 150 watts over the course of a typical workout[31] – enough power to run a pair of speakers, an electric hand mixer, or a small television.

Alternative automotives

Watch out, Toyota Prius! Gasoline–electric hybrids are getting the attention now, but eco-innovative electric cars with zero direct emissions are driving into town. General Motors hopes to reinvent itself behind the Chevy Volt, a plug-in hybrid electric vehicle that will be released in the U.S. for the 2011 model year.[32] With a range of 40 miles from a single charge, it can successfully navigate the average (33 mile) daily round-trip commute of most Americans – using zero gasoline and producing zero direct emissions. Unlike a conventional hybrid vehicle that has a second, gasoline-powered engine, the Volt has a gasoline-powered engine that powers a electric generator which kicks in after the battery is drained, so the car is powered exclusively by electric motor.[33] Priced at a hefty $41,000 base cost, up to $7,500 in federal tax credits are available to jumpstart the mainstream market.

What may surpass even electric cars in the long term are vehicles powered by fuel cells. Although electric cars are emission-free, they are still responsible for indirect atmospheric emissions generated by coal- and gas-fired power plants. However, cars that run on hydrogen fuel cells, such as Honda's FCX Clarity, have the potential if the hydrogen can be generated without emissions, since its production requires natural gas. (Experiments going on in Iceland are currently producing hydrogen using geothermal energy.) Hydrogen fuel cells harness the power created by a chemical reaction between hydrogen gas and the oxygen found in ambient air. The sole by-product of this reaction is pure water.[34] The biggest limitation to widespread adoption of fuel cell cars is the lack of hydrogen filling stations, so when Honda rolled out the Clarity in late 2007 it did so only in Southern California, where it had also built refueling facilities.[35] Honda has calculated the Clarity's fuel consumption to be the equivalent of 68 miles per gallon in a gasoline-powered car. With a travel range of 270 miles,[36] test drivers report that the Clarity is also a dream to drive.[37]

**Addressing
the New Rules**

Nissan's innovative drive toward sustainability

Nissan, the Japanese auto giant, is revving up a holistic approach to sustainable transportation that goes beyond cranking out greener cars. Since 1992, they have been on a mission to bring forth a "Symbiosis of People, Vehicles and Nature,"[38] and have been integrating innovative design, proactive life-cycle management, and government partnerships with the goal of keeping the environmental impact caused by their operations and their vehicles within the Earth's "natural ability to absorb that impact."[39] In attempting to reduce carbon and other emissions, and promote the 3Rs (Reduce, Reuse, Recycle), Nissan demonstrates how sustainability can drive innovation and business success.

Nissan's sustainability commitment starts by making their traditional gas-guzzling vehicles more fuel-efficient via clean-diesel engines and more resourceful catalysts. Next, attempts at bringing electric, fuel-cell, and hybrid vehicles to mainstream drivers in Japan, North America, and Europe are paying off with the X-Trail FCV (fuel cell vehicle), now available in Japan for limited lease agreements, and more fuel cell vehicles are expected.[40]

On the hybrid front, in 2007 Nissan introduced the Altima Hybrid, its first hybrid car, and the Infiniti Hybrid is in the offing.[41] Nissan's LEAF, a medium-sized hatchback introduced in 2009, is slated to be the world's first affordable electric, zero-emission car. The LEAF, an acronym for Leading, Environmentally friendly, Affordable, Family car, is on track for a full rollout in Japan, Europe and the U.S. by 2012.[42] Unlike the Prius and the Volt, which combine electric batteries and gasoline engines, albeit in different ways, the Nissan LEAF is solely powered by its electric battery. Making clear that its commitment to producing electric vehicles will continue over the long term, the company plans to build a plant in Tennessee that will produce more than 100,000 electric cars annually by 2013.[43] Helping drivers conserve fuel further, Nissan empowers Japanese drivers with CARWINGS, a GPS system that uses real-time traffic information and data from other CARWINGS users to guide them towards the fastest route.[44] Nissan also lets CARWINGS members compare fuel consumption and eco-driving rankings. To notch fuel efficiency up to 10%, Nissan crafted the "Eco-Pedal System," which monitors pressure on the accelerator and alerts the driver when the car is burning more fuel than needed.[45]

With a lofty goal of attaining a 100% recovery rate, Nissan is focusing on the three Rs of Reduce, Reuse, and Recycle throughout the vehicle life-cycle. This includes reducing the use of harmful materials, incorporating more recycled plastic parts from end-of-life cars, using recycled plastics and renewable biomaterials, and improving recyclability and dismantling efficiency. Nissan certifies dealerships in Japan as Nissan Green Shops, which ensure that end-of-life vehicles are handled properly.[46] Most admirably, as of 2006, all new Nissan models in Japan and Europe claim a recoverability rate of 95% – almost ten years ahead of Japan's Automobile Recycling Law's recoverability rate target as a result of changes in the production and development.[47]

The final component of Nissan's drive toward sustainability consists of partnerships with community groups and government agencies. In Beijing, China, Nissan works with the Beijing Transportation Information Center to relieve bumper-to-bumper traffic and improve traffic patterns. With the help of French automaker Renault, Nissan has established partnership agreements with governments in Israel, Portugal, Yohoma (Japan), and Tennessee and Oregon aimed at creating settings for the integration of electric vehicles.[48]

4 Develop new business models

Eco-innovative products and services can end up being more expensive than their conventional counterparts because they lack economy of scale, or because they use new materials or technologies. But new business models can surmount these hurdles to acceptance, creating a win–win–win situation for businesses, the environment, and consumers.

Manufacturers and retailers sell products to consumers, who usually assume responsibility for maintenance and eventual disposal. One exciting alternative business model that is currently finding favor is selling the actual service provided by a product, as opposed to simply selling the product outright. Consumers already meet many of their needs through services: they think nothing of doing laundry at a laundromat, renting a car, or borrowing DVDs from Netflix. Take a moment to look at your product through a service lens. Can it be delivered partially or completely by a service? If it can, you may have an opportunity to significantly reduce costs and environmental impacts of your product. Consumers can enjoy the benefits they seek without the need for maintenance, and are assured access to the latest and cleanest technologies. A service-based business model helps businesses retain ownership of the materials and energy that are embodied in the products they design and produce. This helps facilitate repair, reuse, and recycling, whether prompted by regulation or manufacturing economies. Keep in mind that there are trade-offs involved with providing services, like the energy it takes to power an ebook, and, more importantly, to deliver the digital content.

Services can be offered in many innovative ways: providing the product as part of a service; replacing a product, partially or completely with an electronic service; or substituting knowledge, wholly or in part, for a physical product.

Offer the product as part of a service

Zipcar car-sharing service

Consumers don't need to *own* a product per se – they just need access to the service (the functionality) that the product represents. Many car owners don't want to give up the independence afforded by driving their own car, but they would like to skip the hassle of parking and maintenance. These are the principles that underpin the largest car-sharing company in the world, Boston-based Zipcar. For as little as an annual membership fee of $50 and about $8 per hour or $77 per day – gas and insurance included – members can pick up a car, run their errands, and return it to a designated parking spot ready to go for the next member (ever try to find a parking space in Paris or Tokyo at midday?) without the worry of insurance, loans, maintenance, or filling up the tank.[49]

By promoting car sharing as a popular and hip way to avoid the hassles of car ownership, Zipcar, serving 13 cities in the U.S., Canada, and London, England, is becoming the car of choice for urban dwellers, college students, and even corporate fleets – and it has myriad environmental and social benefits, too. Projecting that they have the potential to reduce the number of cars on the road by one million, the company reports that 65% of Zipcar members give up their cars or delay the purchase of a new one.[50] Furthermore, the company estimates that each Zipcar replaces over 15 privately owned vehicles.[51] Taking cars off the road can translate to less pollution, less dependence on oil, and more green space not needed for parking. And Zipcar members save money, too. According to the company, Zipcar members save more than $500 per month over the cost of car ownership.[52] As of June 2009, the company had 300,000 members and 6,500 vehicles in urban areas and college campuses throughout 26 North American states and provinces as well as in London, England.[53]

Vélib bicycle-sharing service

Representing the biking equivalent of car sharing, in 2007 the city of Paris, France, launched Vélib, a pay-as-you-go bicycle rental program. With over 20,000 bicycles in about 1,500 self-service rental kiosks, the bicycles are a convenient, cheap, trendy, and emission-free way for locals and tourists to get around town. Bikes can be rented for pre-paid amounts of time ranging from 30 minutes up to one week, and then dropped off at any kiosk. In the first year alone, more than 27.5 million trips – an average of 120,000 trips per day – significantly reduced car congestion and earned the city more than

$31 million in revenue.[54] The concept is being emulated around the world in Barcelona, Mexico City, and London.

College textbook rentals

Product sharing isn't limited to transportation; Cengage Learning, one of the largest textbook publishers in America, has recently adopted it. In August 2009, the company announced that it would begin renting textbooks to college students, who, upon purchase, will receive immediate access electronically to the first chapter, then receive the physical book by mail. They can then either return or sell the book after a set rental period.[55] At 40% to 70% of the sale price, the option to rent textbooks promises to defer the often-bemoaned cost of college textbooks, and is environmentally sound. Through its iChapters service, Cengage is also one of a growing list of companies who will sell students downloadable PDF chapters of textbooks, for a complete digital learning experience.

Power purchase agreements

Solar power is a clean energy source that is attractive because sunlight is free – but the time it takes to recoup the initial investment prevents wider adoption among homeowners. That's where the power purchase agreement (PPA) comes in. Under a PPA, a provider installs (at its own expense or usually with the help of a third-party lender or a bank) solar panels on a residential rooftop or commercial property. The customer then purchases the resulting power at a fixed rate for the term of the contract, often at a lower rate than power generated by the local electric company.[56] Launched by California's SunEdison LLC, SunPower, and REC Solar,[57] the PPA provider is responsible for maintaining the solar panel system for a set period, usually 15 years, when the customer can purchase the system or extend the PPA.

Substitute an electronic service for a product, wholly or in part

Digital media represents untold opportunity for eco-innovation by replacing material products with electronic services with superior performance. Surface mail has quickly evolved into email, newspaper content is delivered on a BlackBerry or iPhone, and a single CD-ROM can carry 90 million phone numbers. Digital product delivery lies at the heart of Apple's iPod, one of the most successful new product introductions ever, with its iTunes database of music selections. Similarly, Netflix members rent movies online and receive DVDs through the mail, or stream movies directly from the Internet. Netflix recently signed up its tenth million member and delivered its two billionth DVD.[58]

Zonbu computer service

Is there a virtual desktop in your future? If Zonbu computer has its way, traditional computer ownership will be replaced by a subscription service. In 2007, Silicon Valley's Zonbu began selling a simplified desktop computer for $99. Users pay a monthly subscription fee of about $15 for access to Zonbu's centralized Web-based programs, operating system, storage space, and virus protection. Should you lose your laptop or the computer malfunctions, your files are safe on Zonbu's servers and accessible from another Zonbu computer, eliminating the hassles of computer maintenance tasks such as software updates and virus and spyware protection. Zonbu's desktop computer (the company launched a laptop in 2008) was the first consumer-oriented computer to earn a "Gold" rating by the Electronic Product Environment Assessment Tool (EPEAT), which evaluates electronic products in relation to 51 total environmental criteria.[59]

Substitute knowledge for a physical product, wholly or in part

Integrated pest management

Why make a product when your brain can do the job with no environmental impact at all? Take pest control. Integrated pest management (IPM) relies on information about the life-cycles of pests and their interaction with the environment, keeping the use of chemical pesticides to a minimum. Pest control companies use IPM to monitor pest populations and determine if and when pest control action must be taken. Most importantly, IPM programs help manage crops, lawns, and indoor areas to prevent pests from becoming a threat in the first place. IPM represents the opportunity for a profitable contract management business model; get paid to keep pests away, rather than simply apply costly and toxic chemicals once they appear.

5 Restore the environment

Eco-design and eco-innovation share a worthy goal: minimizing environmental impact. But what if one were to consider new products or services based on revolutionary new materials and technologies that could actually restore the social, environmental, and economic systems that sustain us?

BASF PremAir ozone catalyst

Consider all the pollution a car generates. Gasoline combustion creates ground-level ozone, the main component of smog that can aggravate respiratory problems such as asthma. Enter the BASF PremAir ozone catalyst, which, when attached to car radiators, converts to oxygen up to 80% of the ground-level ozone that comes into contact with the device.[60] The PremAir catalyst purifies the air as you drive, and is now standard in several auto- mobiles, including all Volvo models and certain BMW, Mercedes, Mitsubishi, and Hyundai cars.[61]

PUR water purifier

Procter & Gamble's PUR brand water purifier is a small satchel filled with powder. When stirred into a bucket of dirty water and filtered out, it removes dirt, microbial cysts (such as cryptosporidium) and pollutants, and kills viruses and bacteria, leaving safe, drinkable water.[62] Distributed by 70 non- profits in developing countries where it has helped to purify more than 1.6 billion gallons of water, it has now found a new market in the United States and Canada as a camping/emergency preparedness tool.

Chapters 4 and 5 discussed several strategies for greening one's existing products (eco-design) and offered several strategies for eco-innovating – developing the next generation of products and services with the ability to significantly minimize environmental impact. With greener products and eco-innovations in hand, green marketers are prepared to develop credible impactful branding and communications, the subject of the next two chapters.

The *New Rules* Checklist

Ask the following questions to help inspire you and your team to uncover creative opportunities to innovate for sustainability.

- ○ What policy changes do we need to prepare for? Can we get a jump on these changes by eco-innovating now?

- ○ Where along the innovation curve is our product? How much more opportunity is there to minimize environmental impact? Might we be better off, strategically, to eco-innovate?

- ○ What do we have to do differently to deliver our product with signifi- cantly reduced – or even zero – environmental and material impacts?

- ○ What opportunities exist for us to eco-innovate around our product's system? Can we change individual elements within our product's system?

○ In what ways might we engage with other manufacturers to reduce the environmental impacts of the total system in which our product exists? What opportunities exist to collaborate with manufacturers of complementary products to develop new products or even systems?

○ In what ways might we dematerialize our product or service? Use electronic technology? Create a new system altogether?

○ What opportunities exist to use new materials such as bioplastics?

○ What ways exist for us to make renewable energy more affordable and portable?

○ What opportunities exist for us to use new business models to grow our business with less environmental impact? Is there an opportunity to make our greener product or service more affordable or accessible by adopting a new business model?

○ Can we offer services as a replacement for our products? Or, can we lease our product to customers? Can our products be shared?

○ Can we replace our products with smarter alternatives (knowledge or more targeted products)?

○ What business model might we need to adopt to make services affordable for consumers and profitable for our business?

○ Are there opportunities to replace our product wholly or in part with an electronic service?

○ Can we provide a knowledge-based service instead of a physical product?

○ Can we offer products that might actually restore the environment?

Communicating sustainability with impact

Hertz promised to get you out of airports faster. Tide guaranteed to get clothes whiter than white. Keds sneakers assured kids that they would run faster and jump higher. But with environmentalism now a core societal value, consumers want to see green themes in marketing messages in addition to traditional promises associated with a better life. Indeed, communicating environmental and social initiatives with authenticity and impact can help establish one's brand in the vanguard of this important trend. Indeed, such messaging can even ward off legislative threats and potentially protect one's corporate reputation when things go wrong. Also, with stakeholders of all types – employees, investors, and consumers among them – wanting to know about the sustainability of products at every phase of their life-cycles, communicating the environmental and social advantages of one's brands is now critical to running a well-managed business.

Although there are many opportunities associated with communicating one's sustainability initiatives, challenges abound – and not communicating one's environmentally and socially oriented product and corporate initiatives may be riskier still. Marketers who don't tout the sustainability achievements of their brands may find that consumers and other stakeholders assume their products and processes are not ecologically sound; this is a sure way to be replaced on the shelf by a competitor with recognized green credentials! Fail to get on the radar screens of the sustainability-aware and lose opportunities to increase market share among the growing number of influential and affluent LOHAS consumers. Address the new rules of green marketing and expect to enjoy such rewards as enhanced brand equity and a stronger emotional bond with stakeholders.

Challenges of communicating sustainability

Convinced that you need to communicate the sustainable advantages of your brand? Not sure where to begin? Begin your planning process by considering the challenges. For starters, environmental and social benefits can be indirect, intangible, or even insignificant to the consumer. Consumers can't see the emissions being reduced at the power plant when they use energy-saving appliances. (They may not even immediately notice the savings on their power bill.) Similarly, they can't see the capacity increase in the landfill when they recycle, and they have to take it on faith that you pay a fair (living) wage to your employees (and your suppliers are doing likewise).

Trade-offs are a factor, too. Although many greener products are cheaper, faster, or more convenient, some are more expensive, slower, or not as attractive. Toilet paper made from 100% recycled content may be cheaper, but it may not be as soft as virgin counterparts. Taking the bus or train or carpooling saves money over driving one's car and allows one to read, socialize, work, or snooze, but these ecologically preferable options fall short on the flexibility demanded by working parents who have to pick up the kids, a take-out dinner, and the dry-cleaning along a circuitous commute home.

Getting your sustainability-oriented campaign in front of the right people can be a challenge. Demographics-based markets such as homeowners living in the parched Southwest or new mothers with extra pennies to spend on organically grown baby food are easy to pinpoint through conventional media, but lifestyle-based targets such as wildlife lovers or the chemically sensitive, while being easier to reach these days thanks to the Internet, are still pretty hard to pin down.

Sustainable branding is complex – and can be pricey to do well. In addition to underscoring consumer benefits, the historical focus of marketing communications, today's green consumers must be educated on the benefits of new, often technically sophisticated materials, technologies, and designs. New brand names must be established. Corporate green credentials must be put forth. Such tasks can overwhelm the budgets of start-ups with big green ideas. Compounding these tasks, sought-after benefits change with the times. In the past, organic produce was favored because of its perceived health benefits, but today, a wider audience scoops it up because they think it tastes better. Some homeowners install rooftop solar panels to keep up with the technologically savvy neighbors, while others simply want to save money on their energy bill.

And then there's the question of credibility. As discussed in Chapter 2, industry is found to be far less trustworthy on environmental matters than other groups such as NGOs or government. As discussed further in Chapter 7, myriad eco-labels exist, but products are often expensive to certify to, and it is difficult to wade through the clutter. Get it wrong and a backlash can occur. Green communications that appear insignificant or insincere often invite criticism from environmentalists, bloggers, and citizen journalists who are quick to sniff out perceived "greenwashers"; and U.S. state attorneys general and the Federal Trade Commission (FTC), as well as counterpart organizations in such countries as the UK (Advertising Standards Authority), Canada (Advertising Standards Canada), and Australia (Australian Competition and Consumer Commission), can be quick to take action against marketers who make deceptive environmental claims.

Finally, consumers can tire of the same green messages and imagery. Planets, babies, and daisies eventually wear thin with skeptical consumers. "Green fatigue" is brewing due to the plethora of green campaigns in so many consumer media. How many messages have you seen asking you to "do it for Mother Earth" or because "your kids will thank you for it"?

Ottman's fundamentals of good green marketing

Sustainability-oriented marketing communications targeted to mainstream consumers work best when they address the new rules of green marketing head on. As alluded to in Chapter 2, if you want to communicate green benefits to consumers, you should keep in mind that the following conditions, fundamental to all green marketing efforts, must be met:

- Consumers are aware of and concerned about the issues your product or service professes to address.

- The consumer feels, as one person or in concert with others, that he or she can make a difference by using your product or service. This is "empowerment" and it lies at the heart of green marketing. (If consumers didn't feel they would make a difference by using a greener product, they wouldn't buy it in the first place.) This assumes that the sustainability benefits of a product or service can be clearly communicated.

- The product provides tangible, direct benefits to a meaningful number of consumers. In other words, green can't be the only (or even main) benefit a more sustainable product provides. Consumers still need to be attracted to your product or service for the primary reasons why they would buy any product in that category, e.g., getting clothes clean, providing dependable transportation.

- Your product performs equally well or better than your competitors' green or still "brown" alternative. Consumers will not give up quality or performance in order to secure a greener product. Said another way, greener products must perform their intended function first; environmental benefits are viewed as a new source of added value. What's more, often the environmental benefits actually enhance a product's ability to perform its intended function, and, as described more fully in Chapter 1, in these instances, marketers can expect to earn a premium! For example, organic produce tastes better, and Samsung's new solar-power cell phone provides the important benefits of protecting one from running out of battery power.

- Premium pricing needs to be justified through superior performance or another benefit. Keep in mind that many consumers can't afford premiums for many products, including green ones, especially in times of austerity.

- Consumers believe you. This means that your sustainability-related claims can be backed up by data or other evidence. Product-related efforts are reinforced by substantive corporate progress.

- Your products are accessible. To succeed with mainstream consumers, greener products must be available on the websites or shelves at popular supermarkets and mass merchandisers, right next to the "browner" products they are designed to replace.

Ottman's fundamentals of good green marketing

Consumers must:

- Be aware of and concerned about the issues
- Feel empowered to act
- Must know what's in it for *them*
- Afford any premiums – and feel they are worth it
- Believe you
- Find your brand easily

Source: J. Ottman Consulting, Inc.

Once you're fully aware of these fundamentals, take advantage of the following strategies being forged by sustainability leaders around the globe to overcome the challenges and take advantage of the many opportunities afforded by green communications.

Six strategies of sustainable marketing communication

Six strategies of sustainable marketing communication

1. Know your customer
2. Appeal to consumers' self-interest
3. Educate and empower
4. Reassure on performance
5. Engage the community
6. Be credible

Source: J. Ottman Consulting, Inc.

1 Know your customer

In selecting the right consumer to target, keep in mind the complexity of green consumer segments. As described in detail in Chapter 2, consumers can be segmented psychographically into the five NMI segments: LOHAS, Naturalites, Drifters, Conventionals, and Unconcerneds. They can be further segmented according to specific area of personal interest: natural resource conservation, health, animals, and the outdoors.

Just as there are many different types of green consumers, there are many different kinds of environmental and social issues of concern. Figure 1.1 on page 3 showed that water quality, hazardous waste, and pollution from cars and trucks top the list, but there are literally dozens of other issues ranging from endangered species to graffiti and noise pollution that concern even the most mainstream of consumers. Not all consumers will likely be aware of or concerned about all sustainability-related issues, so it is important to pinpoint the consumers who will be most receptive to your message, and to provide any additional education that's needed to bring consumers on board.

One marketer who learned the hard way about the need to measure consumer awareness for the issues that affected their business is Whirlpool. In the early 1990s they won a $30 million "Golden Carrot" award that was put up by the U.S. Department of Energy and a consortium of electrical utilities for being first to market with a chlorofluorocarbon (CFC)-free refrigerator. But they misjudged consumers' willingness to pay a 10% premium for a product with an environmental benefit that many did not appreciate. Likely many consumers, not even knowing what a CFC was, thought the appliance to be deficient, suggesting the need to educate consumers as part of one's marketing; many examples are provided throughout this chapter.

2 Appeal to consumers' self-interest

Many readers will approach this chapter thinking the focus will be on the best ways to highlight the ecological benefits of one's products. You may have visions of ads showcasing the now tiresome images of babies, daisies, and planets that are associated so strongly with green ads. Although the environment is important to consumers – indeed, it may have been the primary reason the product was created in the first place – they will likely *not* be the primary motivation to buy your brand in preference to that of your competitors. In other words, don't commit the fatal sin of green marketing myopia! As my colleagues, Ed Stafford and Cathy Hartman of the Huntsman Business School of Utah State, and I point out in our much-quoted article, "Avoiding Green Marketing Myopia,"[1] remember that consumers buy products to meet basic needs – not altruism. When they enter a grocery, they don their consumer caps – looking to find the products that will get their clothes clean, that will taste great, or that will make themselves look attractive to others; environmental and social benefits are best positioned as an important plus that can help sway purchase decisions, particularly between two otherwise comparable products.

Keep in mind that with environmental issues a threat to health above all else, the number one reason why consumers buy greener products is not to "save the planet" (which isn't in danger of going away anytime soon) but to protect their own health. So it is important to make sure that superior delivery of primary benefits are underscored in design and marketing. Focus too heavily on environmental benefits at the expense of primary benefits like saving money or getting the clothes clean – and expect your brand to wind up in the green graveyard, buried in good intentions.

Underscoring the primary reasons why consumers purchase your brand – sometimes referred to as "quiet green" – can broaden the appeal of your greener products and services way beyond the niche of deepest green consumers and help overcome a premium price hurdle. Demonstrate how consumers can protect their health, save money, or keep their home and community safe and clean. Show busy consumers how some environmentally inclined behaviors can save time and effort. To be clear, this does not mean focusing exclusively on such benefits – to do so would be to go back to conventional marketing altogether. Today's consumers want to know your whole story, so focus on primary benefits in context of a full story that incorporates the environment as a desirable *extra* benefit; better yet, integrate relevant environmental and social benefits within your brand's already established market positioning, and you've got the stuff for a meaningful sale.

Does your green product promise to protect or enhance health? You're in luck. Categories most closely aligned with health are growing the fastest and tend to command the highest premiums. Consider a print ad for AFM Safecoat featuring 16 buckets of paint; 15 of the buckets are painted red and bear labels such as "Gorgeous Paints," "100% Pure," "Low Odor," and "Sustainable." However, the last bucket stands out in green and announces "The Only Paint that is Doctor Recommended." While the ad highlights the health aspects of the low-VOC paint, the website delves more into the "eco" in Safecoat, stating that it is "the leading provider of environmentally responsible, sustainable and non-polluting paints, stains, wood finishes, sealers and related green building products."[2]

Does your product appeal to the style-conscious? American Apparel was created as a brand proud to be made in the United States, provides excellent working conditions for its employees, and uses organic cotton. But, in 2004, when its "sweatshop free" label did not bring in the numbers that CEO Dov Charney was hoping for, he switched to promoting a sexy, youthful image for his company – complete with racy, controversial ads featuring scantily clad girls. Three years later, the company has 180 stores and revenue around $380 million.[3] (Sounds heretical? Keep in mind that the same sustainably responsible clothing is still being sold to consumers, together with all the same benefits to society and the environment; mainstream consumers simply need to hear a message that underscores the primary reason why they buy clothes in the first place.)

Does your product save consumers money? Ads for Kenmore's HE5t steam washer state that it uses 77% less water and 81% less energy than older models. The headline grabs readers with the compelling promise, "You pay for the washer. It pays for the dryer."

Is your product quieter, too? Television commercials for Bosch appliances spotlight energy efficiency and quiet performance. In one, a gentle deer walking through a forest meanders past an operating Bosch Nexxt washer and dryer tandem and never notices the appliance. A second ad highlights an owl swooping through an orange canyon to rest on the working Bosch Evolution dishwasher. Positive environmental impacts, obliquely referenced by situating the products in a forest setting and using animals, are tertiary to the silence and energy efficiency. Among its accolades is an Excellence in ENERGY STAR Promotion Award bestowed by the EPA.

When it comes to identifying the primary consumer benefits your greener alternatives can deliver, many brands like the ones described above find that their products' green benefits neatly translate into something direct and meaningful to the customer; energy savings translating into cost savings is an excellent example. (See Fig. 1.5 on page 19 for more examples.) However, when direct consumer benefits are not readily apparent, green marketers can use what my colleagues Ed Stafford and Cathy Hartman have dubbed "bundling," i.e., adding in desirable benefits.[4] An excellent example is the award-winning and highly successful Whirlpool Duet, a front-loading washing machine and dryer that bundled a highly appealing design with energy and water savings. It may be safe to say by bundling design with the environmental benefits, Whirlpool was able to fetch a higher premium for their offering.

In choosing the combination of primary and sustainability benefits to communicate, strive to *integrate* the two in order to ensure relevance. As examples, greener benefits such as recycled content or energy saving can add fresh life to the messaging of value brands, as is the case with Elmwood Park, New Jersey-based Marcal's Small Steps campaign which positions the use of 100%-recycled-content household paper products as an easy measure to take for the environment and save money. Our client, Austria-based Lenzing, makes Modal brand fiber from reconstituted cellulose from beech trees.

The resulting fabrics are touted as "dreamy soft" by Eileen West in their legendary nightgowns heralded for quality and comfort. Forbo promises that its Marmoleum linoleum flooring "Creates better environments." Synergies can come from surprising places; the cause marketing campaign mentioned later in this chapter for Dawn's dishwashing liquid relating to Dawn's role in cleaning oil-despoiled waterfowl acts as a subtle demonstration of the product's efficacy.

Understanding the specific interests of your green consumers can also add relevance to marketing communications programs in other ways. For example, segmenting green consumers can enhance targeting and relevance. In planning your green marketing campaign, ask such questions about your consumers as: To which environmental organizations do members of our target audience belong (the Appalachian Mountain Club or Greenpeace)? Which types of vacations do they take (hiking or the beach)? Which environmental magazines and websites do they read or visit (*Sierra* or *Animal Fair*)? Which types of products do they buy? (green fashions or energy-sipping light bulbs)? Which eco-labels do they seek out (Renewable "e" Energy or Cruelty-free)?

3 Educate and empower consumers with solutions

Consumers want to line up their shopping choices with their green values, and they applaud marketers' efforts to provide the information they need to make informed purchasing decisions as well as to use and dispose of the products responsibly. Especially effective are emotion-laden messages that help consumers acquire a sense of control over their lives and their world. For advertisers that make the effort to teach, educational messages represent special opportunities to boost purchase intent, enhance imagery, and bolster credibility. So demonstrate how environmentally superior products and services can help consumers safeguard their health, preserve the environment for their grandkids, or protect the outdoors for recreation and wildlife. Make environmental benefits tangible through compelling illustrations and statistics and make consumers feel as if their choices make a difference.

In 2008 Pepsi launched an empowering Have We Met Before? recycling campaign. It featured fun fact-based messages from the National Recycling Coalition that underscored the difference recycling can make, and it encouraged consumers to make recycling a part of their daily routine. Two facts emblazoned on specially designed cans included: "Recycling could save 95% of the energy used to make this can" and "The average person has the opportunity to recycle 25,000 cans in a lifetime."[5]

Increasingly, consumers are turning to the Internet for information. Opportunities abound to provide additional information on one's own website or a third party's website, in addition to conventional places such as advertising and packaging. Yahoo!'s 18Seconds.org website, named for the time it takes a person to change a light bulb, ranks states and cities according to their CFL purchases and describes CFLs and the difference it makes to use them. Also included are facts about where energy comes from and opportunities to spread the word by emailing friends or linking to the page from one's own website.[6]

Sensing an opportunity to home in on sales of the beleaguered bottled water industry, in 2007 Brita and Nalgene teamed up to co-promote their Brita filters and Nalgene water bottles as a cheaper and greener alternative to bottled water. A special website, www.filterforgood.com, described the carbon costs of producing and shipping bottled water as well as the environmental strain associated with plastic bottle waste. Visitors were invited to "take the pledge" to reduce bottled water usage. Displaying power in numbers, a map of all the pledges made across the country depicted how many bottles were saved.[7] Appealing to the "online generation," filterforgood.com also created a Facebook application that allows users to track how many bottles they have saved, and gives them a chance to win a $100 prize pack.[8]

Dramatize environmental benefits

Make your environmental achievements tangible and compelling to your target by citing statistics and using visuals that help dramatize the potential benefits. To help them reach their goal in 2007 of selling 100 million CFL light bulbs, Wal-Mart underscored the facts that, by changing out all the bulbs in an average home, customers could save up to $350 per year, and that the environmental savings represented the equivalent of taking 700,000 cars off the road or conserving the energy needed to power 450,000 single-family homes.

Similarly, Netflix markets its DVD-rental and video-streaming service on the convenience it provides; yet on its website it also points out that, if Netflix members had to drive to video rental stores, they would consume 800,000 gallons of gasoline and release more than 2.2 million tons of carbon dioxide emissions annually.[9]

**Addressing
the New Rules**

HSBC empowers big change with its There's No Small Change campaign

HSBC, the global banking giant headquartered in the UK, has many reasons to be concerned about global climate change, principal among them its many office buildings and thousands of branches around the world that need to be lit, heated, cooled, and ventilated, as well as running the millions of computers, printers, copiers, and other office equipment they contain. For 20 years, the bank made steady, significant investments in what eventually became an industry-leading Carbon Management Plan which helped the company achieve carbon neutrality in 2006. In recognition of its efforts, HSBC won the EPA's Climate Protection Award in 2007; and for two years straight, in 2005 and 2006, the EPA and U.S. Department of Energy named the company "Green Power Partner of the Year."

With this strong track record of environmental achievement on an issue relevant to a broad swath of consumers, we thought HSBC was ready to make a powerful message: with 120 million customers worldwide, the bank could champion the power of small changes. Hence was born HSBC's There's No Small Change marketing campaign, which we had the pleasure to work on with them. Run in the U.S. during spring 2007, it gave consumers empowering tips for reducing their own carbon footprint through various steps including HSBC's new paperless checking and statements.

Newspaper ads, in-branch posters, and other collateral developed by our partner, the New York office of JWT, the global advertising agency with support from my firm, J. Ottman Consulting, suggested ways customers could make a difference in all aspects of their lives: for instance, "get green power," "reduce paper waste," and "bank wisely." Carbon calculators provided by a leading environmental group, handed out inside the branches and made available through a special website, helped customers measure savings from such actions as powering down computers and copiers at night. New customers were presented with "Green Living Kits" packed with such enviro-goodies as CFLs, a Chicobag reusable shopping bag, coupons for organic flowers, and a free issue of *The Green Guide* magazine. For every new account opened, HSBC donated money to local environmental charities, totaling $1 million by the end of the campaign. To extend reach to small business and "premier" customers, HSBC worked with local nonprofit groups to sponsor green business seminars, an Earth Day event in Central Park, New York, and a Green Drinks networking event.

Partnering with credible organizations was critical to the campaign strategy. In the words of JWT SVP, Linda Lewi, "When we developed the creative platform for 'There's No Small Change' we knew how the brand behaved as it executed the campaign would be as important as what it said, and so we developed a grassroots communications plan that partnered with green organizations to provide the everyday sustainable solutions and outreach efforts to our target consumers."

By adopting a strategy focused on credible education and empowerment, HSBC energized its employees, earned credibility among its audience of green consumers and businesspeople, and built its business: the effort yielded 46,420 new accounts (103% of goal and for only 65% of the acquisition cost of a typical customer) – with a 50% uplift in online bill paying, higher deposit balances in both Personal and Premier accounts, with three times the standard cross-sell ratio (people who opened a checking account and bought another product).

To boot, I'm proud to report the campaign won one of the first ever Green Effie awards from the American Marketing Association, sponsored by Discovery Communications' Planet Green network, honoring effective eco-marketing.[10]

Be optimistic

In the midst of a national energy crisis in 1978, U.S. president Jimmy Carter took to the airwaves in a cardigan sweater encouraging Americans to conserve energy by turning down the thermostat to 68°. His campaign failed because of its link to deprivation (and the cardigan sweater industry is still reeling from its effects). Like the entire "back to basics" green movement of which it was a part, President Carter's well-intended initiative failed because it represented a threat to the upward mobility and prosperity that is America. While some may question the idea that "bigger is better" and "growth is necessary for a healthy economy," most Americans have not historically been willing to reverse their hard-won struggles to "have" for a future characterized by "have not."

Happily this mind-set is already changing for the better in some advanced environmentally aware countries such as Germany and in Scandinavia, and ideally will in the rest of the world. But for now businesses need to play by one of the fundamental new rules of green marketing: consumers believe that technology, coupled with cooperative efforts on the part of all key players in society, will safeguard their future. So, invite consumers' participation via simple actions and the prospect of a better future – not by leveraging fear tactics, playing to pessimism, or pressing guilt buttons. That's why we guided our client, Epson, towards an more hopeful, integrated corporate positioning, "Better Products for a Better Future," and why TV commercials for Kashi cereals showcase vignettes of healthy people and end with the tagline, "Seven Whole Grains on a Mission."

Londonderry, New Hampshire-based Stonyfield Farm, makers of organic yogurt and other popular dairy products, manages to keep its messages refreshingly upbeat and fun. A visit to their "Yogurt on a Mission"-themed website lets fans meet Gary Hirshberg, the "CE-Yo," view lighthearted videos about how they make yogurt, even "Have-A-Cow" by learning about some of the specific family farms from where it sources its ingredients.[11]

Finally, offering the opportunity to "test drive a low-car and less expensive lifestyle," the Zipcar car-sharing service, in June of 2009, playfully announced the "Low-Car Diet," asking participants from all 13 Zipcar cities in the U.S., Canada, and England to swap their personal car for a Zipcar membership, supplemented by the use of bikes, public transportation, and walking. Positioning the program as a step up in lifestyle for participants, the company asserted that the "Monthlong program gives urban residents the opportunity to experience the economic, environmental and health benefits of a low-car lifestyle."[12]

Address the underlying motivations of consumers

In line with the segmentations of green consumers outlined in Chapter 2, focus your messaging on concepts that are understood by the consumers who are most important to your business. Empower the disenfranchised. Reward those consumers who are trying to make a difference.

- Motivate the deep green LOHAS consumers by demonstrating how they can make a contribution. Reward their initiative, leadership, and commitment to high standards.

- Show Naturalites (and my Health Fanatics) that environmental benefits are consistent with healthy lifestyles. Demonstrate how natural products can benefit adults, children, and pets.

- Provide Drifters with easy, even fashionable ways to make a contribution that doesn't cost a lot. Enlist the support of celebrities and help them show off their eco-consciousness on favorite social networking sites.

- Encourage Conventionals (and my Resource Conservers) with practical, cost-effective reasons for choosing greener products and behaviors. Underscore opportunities to save money immediately or over the lifetime of a product. Communicate how long a product may last, or that it is reusable.

- Help Unconcerneds understand how all individuals can make a difference. Underscore that small actions performed by many people can make big changes.

 **Addressing
the New Rules**

Toyota Prius appeals to mainstream consumers one segment at a time

On launching its Prius sedan in 2001, Toyota opted first to target not the green-leaning drivers one might expect, but rather tech-savvy, "early adopter" consumers. Featuring a beauty shot of a shiny new car parked at a stoplight and illustrated by the provocative headline, "Ever heard the sound a stoplight makes?" an introductory print ad emphasized the hybrid car's quiet ride (and specifically the fact that the motor, switched into electric gear, did not idle at stop lights like combustion engines). Putting primary benefits first, the key visual was a big, bold beauty shot of the car itself set off against a backdrop of the Golden Gate Bridge while the body copy explained the revolutionary technology. Environmental benefits appeared at the top right corner of the ad – in mouseprint – in the form of compelling statistics about the car's fuel economy and emissions. To establish its green bona fides and get a buzz going among influential greens, a supplemental campaign, "Genius," spotlighted the car's lighter environmental touch and activist group endorsements.

Spiked gasoline prices subsequently triggered a new campaign highlighting the car's fuel efficiency, no doubt bringing price-conscious Conventionals on board. Today, its distinctive styling makes the Prius a rolling billboard of one's environmental values and forward thinking. A successful public relations campaign, including stunts like celebrities rolling up to the Academy Awards in a Prius, bestow the car with a "coolness" factor – the reason why, anecdotally, many people buy a Prius.

The potential to motivate the large mass of passive greens with the promise of fitting in cannot be overstated. That's because environmental issues are inherently social – your gas-guzzling car pollutes my air; my wastefulness clogs our landfill. Today, the "cool" people care about the environment – the influential LOHAS consumers whom many emulate and, of course, so many Hollywood celebrities. Intentionally, "cool" underpinned the most successful anti-litter campaign in history. It was created for the Texas Department of Transportation by our friends at the Austin-based GSD&M advertising agency in 1985 and is still running. When research showed that slogans like "Pitch In" were having no effect on habitual litterers (men 18–34), advertising enlisted popular Texas celebrities such as Willie Nelson, Lance Armstrong, and Jennifer Love Hewitt to demonstrate that it is "uncool" to litter.[14] The Don't Mess with Texas campaign has helped to significantly reduce visible roadside litter, from 1 billion pieces of trash tossed onto Texas roads in 2001 to 827 million pieces in 2005.[15]

4 Reassure on performance

Environmentally preferable technologies are new to consumers and often look or perform differently than their brown counterparts. Carried over from the days when CFLs sputtered and cast a green haze and when natural laundry detergents left clothes dingy, as pointed out in Figure 2.11 on page 40, "Barriers to green purchasing," greener products are still perceived by some as less effective or not having the same value as the more familiar brown alternatives. And, although these perceptions are declining, it still deters some potential customers from purchasing greener products.[16] Remove this potential barrier to purchase by addressing the issue head on.

Seventh Generation (see Chapter 4) brand dishwashing liquid, which competes with Palmolive and Dawn – brands with long-established track records for cutting grease – underscores its efficacy by stressing in print ads spotlighting an adorable youngster, "Because you don't have to choose between safety and spotless dishes," while Reynolds Wrap addresses the myth that recycled content is somehow inferior to virgin, by emphasizing its Reynolds Wrap 100% recycled aluminum foil is "100% Recycled, 100% Reynolds."[17]

5 Engage the community

As underscored earlier in this book, green consumers tend to be well educated, and quite reliant on their own research. As demonstrated in Figure 6.2, they increasingly tend to trust the recommendations of friends and family even more than traditional forms of paid media; hence the astronomical rise in importance of social media in the past few years.

Figure 6.2 **Whom do consumers trust for information?**

Consumer trust in advertising by channel (trust somewhat/completely), 2009 compared to 2007

		2009 %	2007–09 % change
Recommendations from people I know		90	+15%
Brand websites		70	+17%
Consumer opinions posted online		70	+15%
Brand sponsorships		63	+29%
Ads on TV		61	+9%
Ads in newspapers		61	−3%
Ads in magazines		59	+5%
Ads on radio		55	+2%
Emails I signed up for		55	+12%
Ads before movies		52	+37%
Ads served in search engine results		41	+21%
Online banner ads		33	+27%
Text ads on mobile phones		24	+33%

Source: The Nielsen Company, *Trust in Advertising*, October 2009
Reprinted with permission

This suggests rather than simply communicating green benefits in traditional ways, take the opportunity to use your brand to educate and engage your consumers about the issues they are concerned about: the values that guide their lives and purchasing. Acknowledge the consumer's new role as co-creator of your brand and vigorously stoke the conversation. Offer credible, in-depth information and tell meaningful stories that extend beyond paid advertisements in broadcast and print, and on pack messages, to include sponsorships and information on websites and social media. Given consumers' propensity to trust others like themselves, educate them on the details of your products and packaging and provide infrastructure and content that makes it easy for them to share information about your brand with each other.

Engage in cause-related marketing

Best known as promotional efforts in which businesses donate a portion of product revenues to popular nonprofit groups, cause-related marketing can enhance brand image while boosting sales, and allows businesses to have an impact that goes far beyond that associated with just writing a tax-deductible check (philanthropy). With cause-related marketing, everybody wins. Consumers can contribute to favorite sustainability causes with little or no added expense or inconvenience; nonprofit partners enjoy broadened publicity and the potential to attract new members and financial support; and business sponsors and their retailers and distributors can distinguish themselves in a cluttered marketplace, enhance brand equity, and build sales.

No longer viewed as a short-term promotional tactic, all signs point to cause-related marketing as a mature, long-term strategic business practice approached with increasing sophistication by organizations large and small. International Events Group (IEG) Sponsorship Report predicts that cause marketing will rise by 6.1% to $1.61 billion in 2010, up from $1.51 billion in 2009.[19]

Confirming that cause-related marketing represents the power to build one's business, the 2008 Cone Cause Evolution Study revealed record high levels of positive response from consumers to cause-related campaigns, specifically:

- 85% of Americans say they have a more positive image of a product or company when it supports a cause they care about (remains unchanged from 1993)

- 85% feel it is acceptable for companies to involve a cause in their marketing (compared to 66% in 1993)

- 79% say they would be likely to switch from one brand to another, when price and quality are about equal, if the other brand is associated with a good cause (compared to 66% in 1993)

- 38% have bought a product associated with a cause in the last 12 months (compared to 20% in 1993).[20]

Cause-marketing campaigns conducted by organizations worldwide span a range of environmental and social topics. One of the most visible in the history of cause-related marketing is Project (RED). Launched in 2006 by Bono of rock group U2 and Bobby Shriver of Debt, AIDS, Trade in Africa (DATA), multiple high-profile partners including American Express, Apple, Converse, Dell, Gap, Giorgio Armani, Hallmark, Motorola, and Starbucks raise money for the Global Fund to Fight AIDS, Tuberculosis and Malaria (the Global Fund) by donating 50% of profits from products labeled as (RED). Funds generated to date have provided more than 825,000 HIV-positive people with a year's worth of antiretroviral therapy, provided 3.2 million AIDS orphans with basic care, and supported programs that have prevented more than 3.5 millions deaths.[21]

IKEA partnered with UNICEF on a promotion to benefit children in Angola and Uganda. IKEA agreed to donate $2.00 from every sale of their BRUM teddy bears to UNICEF's "Children's Right to Play" program, which uses play-based interaction to educate and empower children in need. The promotion was called "A Bear that Gives," and between 2003 and 2005 it raised $2.2 million, which went to the education of 80,000 street children in Angola and 55,000 children in displacement camps in Uganda, put 38,000 Ugandan children in daycare centers and reunited 200 of them with their families.[22]

Opportunities exist for even small businesses to get meaningfully involved in cause-marketing. Consider 1% for the Planet, founded by the environmentally passionate Yvon Chouinard (founder of Patagonia) and Craig Mathews (owner of Blue Ribbon Flies) to connect businesses and their consumers with philanthropy. Currently, more than 700 environmentally conscious companies contribute 1% of their sales to a growing list of more than 1,500 environmental groups around the world.[23] Participating organizations, ranging from Galaxy Granola in California and our client, Modo, makers of E(arth) C(onscious) O(ptics) eyewear in New York, to Natural Technology in France, benefit from the marketing boost that accrues from being listed on the 1% for the Planet website and the ability to differentiate their businesses from their competition by using the 1% for the Planet logo on their packages and promotions.

Lastly, and perhaps with important implications for the future, some brands have made causes central to their business. Consider the enormously successful Newman's Own brand, which through the Newman's Own Foundation donates all profits to charitable causes, and TOMS One for One campaign which gives a pair of shoes to a child in need for every pair of their rubber-soled alpargatas shoes they sell.

Before embarking on your own cause-marketing effort, realize that there are some rules of the road. Consumers are attracted to causes that put them in the driver's seat, and they will turn on a misguided campaign. Examples abound. Some Sierra Club members created a stir – and some even pulled out of the organization – in response to breaking news that the Sierra Club was receiving an undisclosed amount of money for what they perceived as an endorsement of Clorox's Green Works cleaning products. Sierra Club members' objections to the partnership included the fact that Clorox manufactured chlorine and that 98% of Clorox products were still made from synthetic chemicals. (Green Works only accounted for 2% of Clorox's total sales).[24] Both organizations now disclose the financial compensation that Sierra Club receives for its support, and, likely prompted more by pending legislation than by the Sierra Club, as of late 2009, Clorox announced it would no longer make bleach out of chlorine and sodium hydroxide.[25]

Reflecting its ability to gently but effectively clean waterfowl affected by oil spills, Dawn dishwashing liquid is running a cause-related campaign with the Marine Mammal Center and the International Bird Rescue Research Center in which it will donate $1 for every specially marked package bought by consumers. However, some visitors to its Facebook page and YouTube commercial have protested at the promotion, citing that Procter & Gamble tests its products on animals, forcing the company to defend its policies and remind its detractors that it has invested more than $250 million developing alternative testing methods.[26]

Finally, Ethos Water, co-owned by Pepsi and Starbucks, donates 5 cents for every unit sold to help people in underdeveloped regions to get clean water. Environmentalists question this approach, maintaining that clean, drinkable water should be a human right and not a function of corporate profits. They also maintain that promoting bottled water for environmental benefits is inconsistent with the related impacts of plastic recycling, energy expended to transport the product, and potential depletion of natural water supplies.[27]

To reap the benefits amply demonstrated over 15 years of cause-related marketing, follow these guidelines for success suggested by Cone's 2008 Cause Evolution Study:[28]

- Allow consumers to select their own cause

- Ensure that the cause you pick is both personally relevant to consumers and makes strategic sense to your business

- Choose a trusted, established not-for-profit organization

- Provide practical incentives for involvement, such as saving money or time

- Provide emotional incentives for involvement, such as it making them feel good or alleviating shopping guilt.

Get creative

Many sustainable brand leaders including Whole Foods, Seventh Generation, Ben & Jerry's Homemade, Burt's Bees, and Stonyfield Farm, have built their reputations and continue to establish goodwill credibly and affordably through such creative publicity-generating efforts as sponsoring worthy causes, adopting local charities, protecting small dairy farmers, or donating profits to charity. They have spoken out against bovine growth hormone (in the case of Ben & Jerry's and Stonyfield Farm) or supported organic and fair trade products, organizing special events targeted at younger demographics such as Ben & Jerry's One World One Heart music festival, or Burt's Bees' Beautify Your World tour, allowing consumers to try products first-hand.

With the mainstreaming of green, larger companies are starting to get creative, too. In 2007, Philips, for example, partnered with the Alliance for Climate Protection and the global Live Earth concerts to promote the use of energy-efficient lighting via their A Simple Switch campaign to combat climate change.[29] Companies such as Sprint and Coca-Cola's Odwalla brand are sponsoring signs and trail maps at parks and ski resorts, a very direct way to reach outdoor enthusiasts.[30]

Without paid media advertising how did Stonyfield Farm become the third largest yogurt brand in the U.S.? The answer is its unconventional marketing, most of it on the pack – what founder Gary Hirshberg calls "mini billboards." Packaging and lids highlight Stonyfield Farm's environmental practices and the environmental and social causes it supports, in addition to facts that educate consumers about the benefits of adopting a sustainable lifestyle. The company even offers a "Have-a-Cow" program where consumers sponsor a dairy cow, thus bringing them closer to the farmers providing the yogurt they eat.[31]

With nearly 2 billion users worldwide – more than a quarter of the population – the Internet represents an efficient means of reaching consumers with information and advice on greener products.[32] Spending on online and mobile advertising, including search and lead generation, online classifieds, and consumer-generated ads, reached almost $30 billion in 2007, up 29% from the year before.[33]

Many environmental groups have created websites in order to share information on global environmental problems, and a few sites now have microsites where consumers can shop and/or obtain information about greener products, companies, and behavior. Some good examples include GreenHome.com and Buygreen.com.

Sustainability leaders are now devising creative ways to get closer to their consumers and generate a positive buzz about their brands via blogging and social networking sites and by creating communities through their own websites. For example, Yahoo, GM, Crest, and Eden Organic are just a few of the brands that advertise to the seven million members of the Care2.com social networking site. No Sweat Apparel uses online blogs and sponsorship to create a buzz about their clothing, which is produced in factories throughout the world where all workers are paid a living wage.[34] Consumers know that greener products and services are still relatively rare, and when they find an exciting new brand which is also sustainable, they will likely tell their friends about it, sometimes with support from the brand itself. Consumers can "friend" Method on Facebook to learn about new product offerings and leave positive testimonials, and thousands of fans of the "Seventh Generation Nation" network Facebook page leave feedback and even suggest new product ideas.

Out of the 110 million Americans (making up 60% of Internet users) who use social networking sites such as Facebook, Twitter, LinkedIn, or MySpace, 52% have "friended" or become a fan of at least one brand on a social networking site.[35] One of the biggest users of such social networking sites is Whole Foods Market. To help celebrate their one millionth Twitter follower, Whole Foods held a contest that asked followers to tweet their food philosophies in five words. The ten most creative tweets received a $50 Whole Foods gift card.[36] To engage their Facebook followers in conversation, throughout the summer of 2010, Whole Foods invited them to share some of their fondest high school tunes, how hot it was where lived, and their favorite party recipes.[37] It's time to plan for their next millionth addition; as of August 2010, Whole Foods had 1,792,404 followers on Twitter in addition to 310,638 Facebook fans.

The web and social media are creating opportunities for exciting new forms of experiential marketing including YouTube videos, product placement, mobile advertising, iPhone and BlackBerry applications, and pop-up stores – all just beginning to be explored.

**Addressing
the New Rules**

Tide Coldwater warms up consumers with engaging website

Procter & Gamble's Tide Coldwater is specially designed to clean clothes in cold water as effectively as the leading competitive detergent does in warm water. Tide Coldwater is a concentrated formula (reducing packaging as well as energy costs) that may save consumers up to 80% of the energy they would use per load in a traditional warm/cold cycle of a hot water top-loading machine.

To assuage doubters, P&G assures customers that its cold-water formula works just as well as traditional products to wash clothes. With both a regular and high-efficiency (HE) formula, it also works with all washing machines and traditional laundry additives such as bleach and fabric softeners.

In 2005, P&G launched Tide Coldwater by announcing the Tide Coldwater Challenge. On a special website (www.coldwaterchallenge.com), this interactive challenge incentivized mainstream consumers to test the product and share the results with friends. An interactive map charted the spread of participants throughout the U.S. – at one time showing upwards of 1 million participants. Other areas of the website underscored the product's efficacy and associated the brand with energy-efficient products and programs.

The Alliance to Save Energy, an independent not-for-profit group, actively partnered with Tide Coldwater – they have sent email promotions and offer tips on the website on ways consumers can save energy and money. Such direct marketing early on and follow-up efforts, including free samples and opportunities to inform friends through email, set the stage for a successful launch.

A later Tide Coldwater campaign dramatizes how much energy consumers can save by switching from hot and warm water washes. For example, a TV ad promises, "if everyone washed in cold water, we could save enough energy to power all the households in 1,000 towns," while a more hard-hitting value-oriented pitch claims to "save up to $10 on your energy bill with every 100 oz. bottle."[38]

This chapter discussed five of six strategies for successful sustainable brand communications: among them, empowering consumers to act on the issues they care most about, integrating sustainability messages with primary consumer benefits, and underscoring the inherent value of one's sustainable offerings. None of these objectives can be met if green marketers don't meet my sixth strategy of sustainable communications, "Be credible" – a subject so important, I devote the entire next chapter to it.

The *New Rules* Checklist

Ask the following questions to uncover opportunities to add impact to your sustainable branding and communications.

- Does our customer know and care about the environmental issues our brand attempts to solve? How do we know? What types of education might be necessary?

- Who is the primary purchaser of our brand? Primary influencer? What role do children play in influencing the purchase of our environmentally oriented brand?

- Is our environmental technology, material, etc. legitimate?

- Are we asking our customer to trade off on quality/performance, convenience, aesthetics, etc. and asking for a premium price? Are we underscoring primary benefits that our brand can deliver on?

- Are we taking advantage of opportunities to target specific segments of green consumers with customized messages?

- Do our customers know what's in it for them (versus just the environment, society, or economy)? Does our brand offer any direct, tangible benefits to consumers? For instance, do they help consumers save money? Save time? Protect health? Enhance self-esteem and status?

- Are we tailoring our messages to the specific lifestyles and green interests of our consumers?

- Are the environment-related benefits of our brand well understood by our consumers? What types of education might we need to provide? To which consumers would our brand's environmentally oriented benefits appeal most?

- In what ways can our brand and marketing communications empower consumers to solve environmental problems? Does it save energy? Conserve water? Cut down on toxics? In what ways? By how much?

In what ways might we dramatize the sustainable benefits of our products to make our message more tangible and compelling?

○ Are our messages upbeat and empowering, and do they use positive imagery? Do we stay away from trite imagery and jargon?

○ Are there opportunities to engage consumers via a cause-related marketing campaign?

○ Do we need to reassure consumers about the quality/performance or our product or service?

○ In what ways can we generate a buzz among influential consumers?

○ What mix of media represents the best fit with our consumers and our message?

○ How can we use interactive Web vehicles or social media such as a customized website, Facebook, or Twitter? How might we use You-Tube, mobile advertising, iPhone and BlackBerry apps, and other kinds of experiential marketing?

785266 000297

Establishing credibility and avoiding greenwash

In 1990 Sam Walton promised that Wal-Mart would reward the Procter & Gambles and Unilevers of the world with special shelf talkers (the signs that appeal alongside a given product), if they could prove that their products had greener features. Respond they did, and soon Wal-Mart's shelves were emblazoned with all sorts of messages about the greener features of various products including dubious ones such as household paper towels where the cardboard core was made of recycled content but not the paper towels. Not surprisingly, environmental activists called the effort a sham, on two counts: the features had been there all along, so no real progress was being made, and the presence of one green feature didn't necessary mean a product was green overall. This example and others like it represented the very first, likely unintentional, case of greenwashing, and it set the stage for new standards of eco-communications firmly rooted in genuine progress and transparency.

Greenwash!

With green awareness now squarely mainstream, many companies cater to newly eco-aware consumers by launching products and services that may, intentionally or not, be less than legitimately "green." The popular term for such activity is "greenwashing." Coined by environmentalist Jay Westerveld to criticize hotels that encouraged guests to reuse towels for environmental reasons but made little or no effort to recycle waste, accusations of green-washing can emanate from many sources including regulators, environmentalists, the media, consumers, competitors, and the scientific community, and it can be serious, long-lasting, and hugely detrimental to a brand's reputation. With an eye toward making headlines and creating an example for everyone else to heed, advocates tend to target the most trusted and well-known companies. BP, for one, received heaps of criticism on launching its $200 million Beyond Petroleum campaign touting its commitment to renewable energy which, in fact, represented less than 1% of total global sales; and that criticism was only compounded by the oil spill in the Gulf of Mexico, an estimated 18 times the size of the epic Exxon oil spill in Prince William Sound in spring 1989.

Bill Ford Jr.'s reputation – and that of his family's venerable company – was tarnished when as chairman of the Ford Motor Company he was unable to fulfill his pledge to build greener cars and follow through on an otherwise laudable Heroes of the Planet campaign. Instead, with the company falling on hard times, he bent to the collective will of senior associates who advocated continuing to crank out gas-guzzling SUVs – and wound up paying dearly for the consequences.[1] Relatedly, in the summer of 2008 General Motors got flack from advocate bloggers for announcing plans to "reinvent the automobile" while continuing to manufacture perhaps the most environmentally unfriendly car on the planet – the soon-to-be-defunct Hummer.[2] Meanwhile, its Chevrolet division compounded the PR trouble by running ads heralding a "gas friendly" Volt electric car that was not yet in production.

Greenwashers: consumers are on to you! According to a survey conducted in December 2007 at the UN Climate Change Conference, nearly nine out of ten delegates and participants agreed with the statement, "Some companies are advertising products and services with environmental claims that would be considered false, unsubstantiated, and/or unethical."[3] In January 2007, British Telecom found only 3% of UK consumers think businesses are honest about their actions to become more environmentally or socially responsible, with 33% believing businesses exaggerate what they are doing.[4]

The risks of backlash are high. Using resources and energy and forever creating waste, no company and no product can ever be 100% green. Corporate efforts hinting at aspirations to be green often attract critics. And warm-hearted depictions of furry animals that strike emotional chords with consumers may simultaneously incite the wrath of environmentalists (another reason to lead with primary benefits!). Among other credibility hurdles, consumers perceive that it is not in industry's interest to promote environmental conservation. After all, industry has a track record of unfettered pollution, and consumers think planned obsolescence was invented by industry to ensure growth; in fact, many people accuse marketers of creating ads that make consumers buy what they do not need.

Advocates often maintain that heavy polluters have no right to tout green initiatives, however admirable. So if you are in the petroleum, chemical, or mining industries, your green attempts, no matter how sincere, may not be viewed as such. Consider the case of the Washington Nationals' new ballpark. It opened for the 2008 season as the first major baseball stadium to earn LEED certification from the U.S. Green Building Council. This was great news for the team and their fans, but not so for the sponsor ExxonMobil. When environmentalists were quick to object to prominent Exxon billboards throughout the park, Alan Jeffers, a spokesperson for Exxon lamented, "We get criticized for not doing enough for the environment, and then get criticized when we do run an environmental campaign."[5]

To complicate matters, there are no clear-cut guidelines for environmental marketing. The U.S. Federal Trade Commission (FTC) issued "Green Guides" in 1992; however, since they were last updated in 1996, new terms such as "carbon footprint" and "carbon offsets," and "sustainable," have come into the picture. These Guides are in the process of being updated; meanwhile, without fresh guidelines even the best-intentioned green marketers risk making erroneous claims in these and other unaddressed areas.

A word of caution. The Internet is making the stakes higher now than ever before. According to the new rules, media attention to greenwashing has grown with the launch of environmental news websites such as Grist.org, Treehugger.com, Worldchanging.com – and thousands of 24/7 green bloggers and tweeters. Greenwashing even has its own website, greenwashingindex. com. Founded in 2007 by the EnviroMedia agency in collaboration with the University of Oregon, greenwashingindex.com lets visitors rate the authenticity of green marketing claims using "Greenwashing Index Scoring Criteria." Consumers can read greenwashing news and submit ads to be evaluated by others. Recent marketing campaigns spotlighted on the site include easy-Jet, who claimed that flying their airline generates less carbon dioxide than a typical airline or even driving a passenger car; Monsanto, the giant producer of genetically modified seeds, who pledged to practice sustainable agriculture; and Fiji bottled water claiming that "every drop is green," despite the fact that water is shipped thousands of miles across the sea compared to tap water which is readily available.

Tired of hearing the term "green fatigue"? It's a new phrase being used to describe consumers who feel inundated by green marketing buzzwords and a dizzying array of all things green. As a result, they have trouble separating genuine progress from just another green gimmick. The risk of greenwashing and green fatigue from the deluge of advertising claims and green PR pitches is that it can unintentionally create skeptical consumers out of a general public short on facts, and this directly impacts even the best-intentioned organizations, tangibly and intangibly. Being perceived as a greenwasher can represent a direct hit on corporate trust and credibility and ultimately hit the bottom line, either from reduced revenues or depressed market share when disillusioned customers shift their purchases to more trustworthy competitors.

Much can be done, however, to avert the risks from greenwashing. Start with well-crafted sustainable branding and marketing plans that reflect an understanding of the target audience's needs. Make sure your products and services are greened via a life-cycle approach (see Chapter 4). And engage and educate potential users to consume responsibly. Thankfully, powerful strategies exist to establish credibility and minimize the potential for backlash. The place to begin is inside one's own organization.

Five strategies for establishing credibility for sustainable branding and marketing

Follow the strategies discussed below to establish credibility for your green marketing campaign and minimize the chance of it being dubbed "greenwash."

Five strategies for establishing credibility for sustainable branding and marketing

1. Walk your talk
2. Be transparent
3. Don't mislead
4. Enlist the support of third parties
5. Promote responsible consumption

1 Walk your talk

Companies that are strongly committed to sound environmental policies need not apologize for failure to achieve perfection. Consumers understand that the greenest of cars will still pollute, the simplest of packaging eventually needs to be thrown away, and the most energy-efficient light bulbs will consume their share of coal, gas, or nuclear energy at the power plant. Thwart the most discriminating of critics by visibly making progress toward measurable and worthy goals, communicating transparently, and responding to the public's concerns and expectations. Companies that are in the vanguard of corporate greening have many of the following attributes in place, and are consequently the most able to take advantage of the many opportunities of environmental consumerism.

A visible and committed CEO

To successfully develop and market environmentally sound products and services, one must adopt a thorough approach to greening that reaches deep into corporate culture. With consumers scrutinizing products at every phase of the life-cycle, corporate greening must extend to every department – manufacturing, marketing, research and development, consumer and public affairs, and even to suppliers who provide the raw materials, components, and packaging. Only a committed chief executive with a clear vision for his or her company can add the necessary weight to the message that environmental soundness is a priority.

The need to start with – and communicate the commitment of – the CEO cannot be overstated. CEOs can forge an emotional link between a company and its customers, acting as a symbolic watchdog who supervises corporate operations and ensures environmental compliance. That's why CEOs of such environmental standouts as Interface, Patagonia, Seventh Generation, Timberland, and Tom's of Maine all maintain high profiles; Tom and Kate Chappell historically included a signed message to consumers on each their natural personal-care products. Jeffrey Hollender maintains a blog on Seventh Generation's website entitled "The Inspired Protagonist." By projecting a personal commitment to the environment, CEOs win their stakeholders' trust. Such leaders are especially believable because they are perceived as having a personal stake in the outcome.

CEOs who are not seen as watching the shop run the risk of derision by corporate watchdogs. Taking Apple to task for not doing as much as competitors to green their products and company, Greenpeace created a special "Green My Apple" campaign and website, encouraging Apple customers to voice their concerns. In May 2007, Steve Jobs, CEO of Apple, responded with a letter entitled, "A Greener Apple." In it, he detailed his company's efforts to remove toxic chemicals from its products and expand post-consumer recycling. He apologized for keeping consumers and investors in the dark regarding Apple's plans to become even greener and promised to communicate such efforts to the public in the future.[6]

Empower employees

The best-intentioned CEOs will only be as effective as their employees. Only when employees are on top of the issues and given the authority to make changes will greener products be launched and sustainable practices be put into place. Employees have many reasons to get concerned about green issues. Relying on secure jobs for their livelihoods, they have a direct stake in their company's success.

However, just like consumers, employees need to be educated about environmental issues in general, and of course about the specifics of their company's processes and brands. Many companies regularly enlist outside speakers to bring employees up to speed about trends in demographics, technology, and the economy; now, speakers, like myself, devoted to environmental specialties meet the demand for talks on climate change, clean technology, and green consumer behavior. Some companies have set up intra-company blogs or wikis to help employees identify ways to get involved, locate other colleagues with similar interests, and make a difference in their communities. Burt's Bees gives employees money to offset home energy use and Bank of America subsidizes employee purchases of hybrid vehicles.

Be proactive

Most big businesses adhere to the International Organization for Standardization (ISO)'s ISO 14001, a voluntary international framework for a holistic strategic approach to an organization's environmental policy, plans, and actions that helps an organization to (1) identify and control the environmental impact of its activities, products, or services, (2) continuously improve its environmental performance, and (3) implement a systematic approach to setting environmental targets and understanding how these will be achieved and measured. And they likely have their audits certified by an independent third party and voluntarily report results to the EPA and the public.

But the companies that project credibility go beyond what is expected from regulators and other stakeholders. So, proactively, and publicly, commit to doing your share to solve emerging environmental and social problems such as protection of rainforests or elimination of sweatshops – and discover competitive advantage in the process. Being proactive projects leadership and sends a message to investors that risks are minimized. Regulators are less likely to impose restrictions on companies whose actions transcend minimum standards. Being proactive also allows companies to help define the standards by which they will be judged and affords the greatest opportunities to find cost-effective solutions to environmental ills while beating competitors in meeting regulations and consumer expectations. Finally, proactive companies are better prepared to withstand the scrutiny that overtly "green" companies often face. In 2005 our client, HSBC, became the first major bank and member of the FTSE 100 to address climate change by becoming carbon-neutral. Its carbon management program consisted of four key steps: (1) measuring its carbon footprint, (2) reducing energy consumption through an aggressive program of energy efficiency upgrades in corporate offices and bank branches, (3) buying renewable forms of electricity to power whatever energy it could not reduce through efficiencies, and (4) offsetting whatever carbon it could not reduce via efficiency and offsets. By shooting for carbon neutrality and by initiating an industry-leading Carbon Management Plan, HSBC gained the needed credibility to launch its Effie-award-winning "There's No Small Change" U.S. retail marketing program in spring 2007, described in Chapter 6.

Be thorough

Green marketing practices have their environmental impacts, too. So look for opportunities to be environmentally efficient with marketing materials. Look for opportunities where the Internet or electronic media could work to reduce the use of paper. Be sure to use recycled paper from sustainably harvested trees and soy-based inks for printed marketing communications.

2 Be transparent

Provide the information consumers seek to evaluate your brands. These days, consumers crave even more information than most businesses are willing to disclose. Almost four out of five (79.6%) respondents in an April 2008 online survey used the Internet to conduct research on green initiatives and products, yet almost half (48%) of them found the availability of corporate information on green and environmentally safe products and services to be lacking – rating the information as fair or poor.[7] To be perceived as credible in the eyes of the consumer, provide access to the details of products and corporate practices and actively report on progress. So the public can feel good about purchasing your products, include anecdotes about exemplary community outreach efforts – digging a well, tilling a farm, or helping out at a local school.

In the future, disclosure of brand-related environmental impacts and processes may be required by law. Get a jump on competitors and regulators – and score some points with consumers – by voluntarily disclosing as much as possible about your products. In the hotly contested green cleaning-aids industry, competitors Seventh Generation, Method, and SC Johnson now disclose the ingredients (but understandably not the exact formulas) of their products. Seventh Generation even lets consumers ask "Science Man" specific questions.

Be accessible and accountable. Report the good – and the bad – about your company. Consistency in reporting such data is critical to stakeholders' ability to track progress and make comparisons. The Global Reporting Initiative (GRI) is a spin-off of the Boston-based Ceres, founders of the Ceres Principles of good corporate environmental conduct, in partnership with the United Nations Environment Programme (UNEP). It is a voluntary global standard and framework for organizations to measure, benchmark, and report on economic, environmental, and social performance. More than 1,500 companies including BP, Coca-Cola, GM, IBM, Novartis, Philips, and Unilever have adopted this de facto standard for reporting. Ben & Jerry's has gone one step further by also using a reporting standard called the Global Warming Social Footprint (GWSF), developed by the Vermont-based nonprofit Center for Sustainable Innovation, to understand if it is contributing its "proportionate share" (as measured against the performance of similar-sized companies) toward returning greenhouse gas concentrations to safer levels.

One thousand conscientious companies in 54 industries have also taken the step of joining the fast-growing ranks of B Corps (described in Chapter 3), denoting that the nonprofit B Lab has certified their companies to strict sustainable business standards, or they have benchmarked their performance to the organization's free B Impact Rating System.[8]

It's one thing to report on the good, but what about the bad? Under the new rules of green marketing, leaders communicate with "radical transparency." One pathfinder is Patagonia, the Ventura, California-based outdoor equipment manufacturer. Its Footprint Chronicles microsite at patagonia.com lets visitors trace the environmental impacts of ten Patagonia products from design through delivery, including components and where they come from, innovations used to reduce impacts on the environment, and what the company thinks it can improve on. Patagonia encourages customer comments – a move that builds loyalty – and is not hesitant to critique itself; as the company learns more, it applies this knowledge to its broad spectrum of offerings. For example, despite its reputation for using recycled fibers, Patagonia is not afraid to reveal on its site that it still uses 36% virgin polyester to make its Capilene 3 Midweight Bottoms, carefully explaining that it is needed to achieve the desired performance and durability.[9] In 2008, the Footprint Chronicles won high accolades as the People's Voice winner in the Corporate Communications category at the Webby Awards (aka "the Oscars of the Internet").[10]

Don't hide behind bad news! SIGG, the makers of popular and eco-trendy reusable aluminum bottles, learned this lesson the hard way. Thought to be BPA-free by consumers and the media, SIGG came under fire when an open letter to customers from CEO Steve Wasik in August 2009 disclosed that bottles produced prior to August 2008 contained trace amounts of BPA in the bottle's inner epoxy liner – and that the company had known about it since 2006. Although SIGG was quick to use public outreach to address consumer and retailer concerns, the damage was done. Customer trust was compromised: articles and blog posts quickly sprang up entitled "How SIGG Lost My Trust" and "Et Tu, SIGG?" written by SIGG customers who felt betrayed by the company's lack of transparency. Competitor brands such as CamelBak and Klean Kanteen were quick to capitalize on the situation by reassuring shoppers that their products were BPA-free.[11]

3 Don't mislead

Consumers may claim to know what commonly used terms such as "recyclable" and "biodegradable" mean but they can be easily mistaken, – creating risk for unsuspecting sustainable marketers. For example, products or packaging made from recycled content can be crafted from 10% recycled content or 100% recycled content. Counterintuitively, 100% recycled content is not necessarily environmentally superior to 10% if, for example, the recycled content must be shipped from far away. A package made from cornstarch may be compostable in theory, but may not break down in backyard composters; industrial composting facilities where such packages do decompose are currently limited to only about 110 communities in the United States and even these facilities may not be convenient (e.g., the closest one to San Francisco is 25 minutes away in the city of Richmond).

What about terms such as "carbon footprint," "carbon neutral," and "sustainable" which have recently come into the picture? Does a carbon footprint encompass only the emissions of a manufacturer in making a specific product or all of the organizations in the manufacturer's supply chain for that same product? Opinions abound about the best way to trace claims related to "carbon offsets" and Renewable Energy Certificates (RECs). For example, advertisers sometimes sell products for which the greenhouse gas emitted during their production and/or use is offset by funding projects such as wind farms, tree planting, or methane capture facilities that may have happened already. Advertisers also may promise that a product was produced with RECs – tradable commodities representing proof that a certain amount of electricity used in production was generated from an eligible renewal energy source, again not under their domain, so the sources may not be verifiable.

Inconsistent guidelines are further complicating the carbon-offset debate. There are currently four proposed U.S. regional greenhouse gas cap-and-trade programs, nearly 30 mandatory state regional energy portfolio standards, and voluntary REC and carbon-offset markets – all with varying, and sometimes conflicting, requirements. The FTC believes use of the term "carbon offsets" in advertising can be inherently misleading if the ad does not specify the particular manner in which reductions in carbon emissions have been obtained.[12]

Two things are clear in this debate: adopting specific standards for disclosure will indeed be tricky, and setting standards for what is a "carbon offset" and a REC will most likely take years. Since not all carbon-offset partners are legitimate, advertisers are advised to properly vet partners prior to communicating their participation. Examples of some of the most respected include *Native*Energy and TerraPass. More detail about carbon footprint labeling is included below.

Carbon labeling issues aside, the best advice for green marketers looking to stay out of trouble is to simply follow the FTC (or other appropriate government guidelines) as best you can and, if possible, to consult with lawyers who specifically address green claims. Broad guidance based on extracts from the current FTC guides can be summarized as follows:

Be specific and prominent

Marketers are liable for what consumers may incorrectly interpret as well as what they correctly take away. Prevent unintended deception with the use of simple, crystal-clear language. For example, be sure to distinguish between the packaging of a product and the product itself, like the label on the Wheaties box on your breakfast table. Emblazoned on the lid is the familiar "chasing arrows" Möbius loop symbol with the descriptive claim, "Carton made from 100 percent recycled paperboard. Minimum 35 percent post-consumer content." This claim is specific and, because it qualifies the exact amount of recycled materials, it prevents consumers from thinking the box is made of 100% materials collected at curbside, or is fully recyclable. Precision can pay off in credibility with consumers. For example, according to the 2008 Green Gap Survey conducted by Cone LLC and the Boston College Center for Corporate Citizenship, 36% of respondents found the message "environmentally friendly" credible when describing a paper product, but 60% found the message "made with 80% post-consumer recycled paper" credible.[13]

Don't play games with type size or proximity of the claim to its qualifiers. A Lexus ad in the UK made a headline claim of "High Performance. Low Emissions. No Guilt." The UK Advertising Standards Authority (ASA) deemed this to be misleading since the text of the ad clarifying the claim was not prominent enough. Plus, the claim "No Guilt" implied the car caused little or no harm to the environment.[14]

Provide complete information

Consider a product's entire life-cycle when making claims about one particular characteristic or part of the item. A washing machine advertised as "green" because of its low energy and water consumption may not have been manufactured or distributed in a green way. Advertising the washer specifically as "energy-efficient" or "water-efficient" with substantiation from, or a comparison to, existing benchmarks could help to avoid misleading customers.

In the UK, an ad for Renault unfairly compared the CO_2 emissions of a brand sold in the UK compared to one in France, with its significantly lower emissions levels due to a high percentage of nuclear in the energy mix. The ad was criticized by the ASA for misleading consumers. Accordingly, when comparing your own product's sustainability benefits to those of a competitor or a previous model, provide enough information so that consumers can stack them up fairly. Make sure the basis for comparison is sufficiently clear and is substantiated by scientific test results. A claim such as "This water bottle is 30% lighter than our previous package" is preferable to the more ambiguous "This water bottle is 30% lighter."

Do not overstate

Avoid vague, trivial, or irrelevant claims that can create a false impression of a product's or package's environmental soundness. The Colorado-based

BIOTA brand of spring water claimed to be the first company to use a biodegradable water bottle made from corn-based bioplastic. That may be true in theory, but the average consumer does not know that decomposition can take at least 75 days and only when exposed to the continuous heat and humidity found in municipal composting facilities – conditions that do not exist in backyard composters and certainly not in landfills.[15] So the company now touts itself as being "the world's first bottled water/beverage packaged in a commercially compostable plastic bottle."[16]

In August 2009, the FTC sued four manufacturers of bamboo textiles, claiming they mislabeled their products as "natural," "biodegradable," and "antimicrobial." The product, akin to rayon, is not natural and uses toxic chemicals to manufacture. In addition, the biodegradable and antibacterial properties do not make it past the manufacturing process. The companies squeaked by without a penalty but will need to label their fabrics as "viscose" or "rayon" and do away with claims of biodegradability and antimicrobial.[17] In a case very similar to the Hefty photodegradable trash bag debacle of 1990 the FTC also charged Kmart, Tender Corp, and Dyna-E International, for falsely claiming that their paper plates, wipes, and dry towels were "biodegradable" when most of these products simply wind up in landfills where they will not degrade.[18]

Broad statements such as "environmentally safe," "Earth friendly," and "eco friendly," if used at all, should be qualified so as to prevent consumer deception about the specific nature of the environmental benefit of the product asserted. Preferable alternatives include: "This wrapper is environmentally friendly because it was not bleached with chlorine, a process which has been shown to create harmful substances." Always be sure to substantiate and qualify terms such as "carbon neutral," "renewable," "recyclable," and "compostable." Answer questions such as: How have the claims been determined? For how long? By whom? Where? Compared to what?

Similar rules apply for corporate advertising. Overstating the environmental benefits of one's efforts – wrapping one's company in a green cloak – creates skepticism and invites backlash. In November 2007, the ASA in the UK ruled that a Royal Dutch Shell ad that showed an oil refinery (with environmentally preferable practices) sprouting flowers was likely to be misleading, given the environmental impacts of even the cleanest of refineries, and ordered the ad off TV. Less than a year later, the ASA ruled against another Shell ad claiming the oil sands in Canada were a "sustainable" energy source. The Canadian oil sands projects have proven controversial, as they require more energy and water than traditional extraction and refining. The ASA ruled that the ad was misleading since the claim of "sustainable" was an ambiguous term and that Shell had not shown how it was effectively managing the oil sands projects' carbon emissions.[19] Shell was not alone. In March 2008, the ASA banned a campaign by the Cotton Council International, a group committed to increasing the export of U.S. cotton, which referred to cotton as "sustainable." The ASA disagreed, maintaining that cotton is a pesticide- and energy-intensive crop that depletes groundwater.[20]

Avoid generalities or sweeping statements such as "We care about the environment" with no connection to projects you have undertaken. Quantify plans, progress, and results. For example, if you claim your company prevents pollution, explain what kind of pollution and how much. Explain the specific emissions-reduction steps taken both internally and for specific products consumers can buy. In 2005, GE launched its Ecomagination campaign which, despite GE's history of significant environmental transgressions, met with very little backlash. Why? The company was upfront about their belief that financial and environmental performance can work together. The initiative was built on ten products representing tangible investments and promising new technologies, and was supported by a pledge by GE Corporate to reduce its own carbon footprint. Finally, ecomagination.com helps businesses and consumers learn more about GE's commitment, specific goals, and how customers can reduce their own "footprint."

Tell the whole story

Decide for yourself: should advertising conducted by the U.S. Council on Energy Awareness touting the clean air benefits of nuclear energy mention the radioactive waste it generates? Should the Chevrolet Division of General Motors have run ads for cars (e.g., the Chevy electric Volt) that weren't in production yet? Does a household paper product made from partial recycled content and bleached by a chlorine-containing compound deserved to be called "Scott Naturals"? To be certain your marketing and environmental communications do not confuse or mislead the consumer, test all green messages among your audience – and in your conscience.

4 Enlist the support of third parties

As depicted in Figure 2.7 on page 34, manufacturers and retailers have lower credibility than NGOs and government when communicating on environmental matters. Fortunately, there are many ways that businesses can bolster their own credibility, among them: let stakeholders in on the steps the organization is taking, educate the public on what they can do, and, importantly, align positively with third parties that perform independent life-cycle inventories and certify claims and award eco-seals. Once having shunned relationships with industry, many nonprofit organizations now welcome associations with industry as a way to work positively toward market-based solutions. This extends their influence within society, and helps to raise money for their groups. Third-party support can take many forms. Cause-related marketing, awards, and endorsements are all possibilities. When launching the Prius, Toyota proudly touted in supplemental ads targeted at deep-green drivers the fact that the Sierra Club, the National Wildlife Federation, and the United Nations had each bestowed some type of award or endorsement on the car.

Logos, trademarks, and symbols for greener product labels and certifications seem to be everywhere: on product packaging, marketing, and advertising communications, on websites, and at trade shows. In fact, more than 400 different eco-labels or green certification systems have been found in over 207 countries. These span the gamut of industries, but are predominant in consumer products such as paper and packaging, forest products, food, cleaning products, and household appliances. Some are government-run or -sponsored, while others are run by private corporations, trade associations, or NGOs. The labels vary in the level of rigor applied to the criteria and the rules around verification; some require independent third-party certification and stakeholder review, while others allow manufacturers to self-verify. At last count, 27 countries around the globe, including China and the European Union, have active multi-attribute eco-labeling programs that require third-party certification (see Fig. 7.1).[21] More certifications and labels are expected as governments, environmental groups, NGOs, trade associations, retailers, and even manufacturers create labels and advertising symbols for products that promise environmental and social benefits.

Independent seals of approval have much to recommend them, but they are not without risk. They can lend credibility to environmental messages, – 28% of consumers look to certification seals or labels on product packaging to tell whether a product is or does what it claims[22] – and they can open the door to conversations with distributors and retailers. Markets that are especially receptive to eco-seals and independent claim certification include government agencies and their contractors looking to procure environmentally conscious goods, and retailers who are anxious to stock green goods but lack the ability to screen for "green" existing product lines and a constant stream of new product introductions. However, despite their apparent proliferation, eco-labels do not exist for all product categories or environmental or social attributes. For example, there is no label for mattresses or flatware. And, as seen in Figure 7.2, only a handful of eco-labels – the chasing arrows recycled logo (Möbius loop) (93%), ENERGY STAR (93%), and USDA's Certi-

Figure 7.1 **Worldwide eco-labels**

fied Organic (75%) among them – have broken through the clutter to gain awareness and, more importantly, purchase influence.

Also, labels and certifications can be expensive. Many seal programs require manufacturers to test their products via third parties, and some independent organizations, such as the GreenGuard seal for indoor air quality or the C2C (Cradle to Cradle) logo, require manufacturers to pay what can amount to hefty licensing fees. What's more, international governments will often require that a product be tested in one of their own country's labs, creating redundancy and exorbitant extra costs for multinational marketers.

What type of criteria should be used in selecting an eco-label? It varies. Some eco-labels focus on a single product attribute (e.g., recycled content), which keeps things simple, but can potentially mislead consumers into thinking the product is greener overall. Other labels look at several characteristics of a product, or even a product's entire life-cycle; such multi-attribute

Figure 7.2 **Which eco-labels work best?**
% U.S. adults

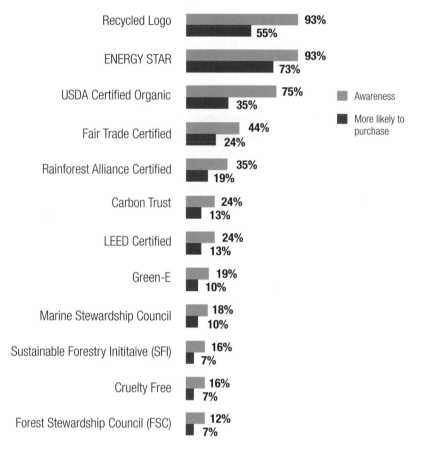

Source: © Natural Marketing Institute (NMI), 2009 LOHAS Consumer Trends Database®

certifications may raise questions about the credibility of a single-attribute certified product while also preventing easy comparisons.

Be prepared for dueling logos that fight for your consumer's attention and your pocketbook. In the forest products industry, for instance, the FSC label denoting sustainable wood harvesting, the product of a consortium of environmental advocates, progressive timber companies, and groups that support indigenous and workers' rights interests, competes with SFI-certified, the product of a not-for-profit spin-off of the American Forest and Paper Association and Canada's Forest Products Association with standards that are perceived as less strenuous.[23]

Are there too many eco-labels? Which ones are better at helping consumers decide if a product is really "greener" than another? Should more than one label exist in a product category? Should eco-labels be single- or multi-attribute? These are all questions that are on green marketers' minds, but may not be fully addressed even when the FTC releases their anticipated Green Guide updates. For businesses that can navigate the thicket of such challenges, enlisting a third party to attest to a product's green bona fides provides a powerful indicator of business integrity.

Finally, for businesses for whom third-party certification does not work, the opportunity exists to create one's own eco-label, or "self-declaration." Independent claims and standards setting and verification exists as another alternative. Consider the following as you choose the certifications that will provide the most value to your own sustainable branding efforts:

Single-attribute labels

These labels focus on a single environmental issue, e.g., energy efficiency or sustainable wood harvesting. Before certification, an independent third-party auditor provides validation that the product meets a publicly available standard. As suggested by Figure 7.2, there are many single-attribute seals available. Many of these are sponsored by industry associations looking to defend or capture new markets, or by environmental groups or other NGOs that want to protect a natural resource or further a cause.

Two single-attribute labels with a global presence include the FSC label (used for this book) and Fair Trade Certified. The FSC label ensures the sustainable harvesting of wood and paper sources. The Fair Trade Certified label, a service of Fairtrade Labelling Organizations, a global not-for-profit group, works with local bodies such as TransFair USA to guarantee strict economic, social, and environmental criteria were met in the production and trade of a range of mostly agricultural products including coffee, tea, chocolate, herbs, fresh fruit, flowers, sugar, rice, and vanilla.

Multi-attribute labels

As their name suggests, multi-attribute labels examine two or more environmental impacts through the entire product life-cycle. Wal-Mart's Sustainability Consortium promises to eventually deliver multi-attribute guidance in the form of a Sustainable Product Index, and several multi-attribute labels exist, primarily for specific categories such as EPEAT in electronics, and Global Organic Textile Standards, among them. Others address specific areas of concern: for instance, the Carbon Trust's Carbon Reduction label, and the C2C label with its emphasis on material chemistry.

Figure 7.3 **FSC and Fair Trade labels**

Reprinted with permission from the Forest Stewardship Council and TransFair

One of the oldest and most credible multi-attribute labels in the U.S. is the Washington DC-based Green Seal (Greenseal.org), founded in 1989 by a coalition of environmentalists and other interested parties. They provide a seal of approval for products that meet specific criteria within categories where they have created standards. Companies pay a fee to have their products evaluated and annually monitored. Products that meet or exceed the standards are authorized to display the Green Seal certification mark on the product and promotional material. All products or services in a category are eligible to apply for the Green Seal. The group has finalized standards spanning a wide range of commercial and consumer products and services including cleaners and cleaning services, floor-care products, food-service packaging, lodging properties, paints and coatings, papers and newsprints, and windows and doors. Wausau Paper, Anderson Windows, Clorox, Kimberly Clark, Hilton, and Service Master Cleaning franchises are just a few of the organizations whose products now bear the Green Seal certification mark – a blue globe with a snappy green check.

A de facto multi-attribute label, the Carbon Reduction label ensures that a product's carbon footprint has been measured and is being reduced.

Figure 7.4 **Green Seal certification mark**

Reprinted with permission from Green Seal

The intention is that in a low-carbon economy, global climate-change-related information will ultimately become as important and visible on product labels as price and nutritional content. Introduced in 2007 by the Carbon Trust, a UK-based not-for-profit company, the label has already been adopted by more than 65 leading brands and can be found on over 3,500 individual products with annual sales worth £2.9 billion (around $4.4 billion in mid-2010).

In April 2008, UK-based retailer Tesco commenced a test of the label on its own brand of orange juice, potatoes, energy-efficient light bulbs, and laundry detergent. Working with the Carbon Trust, Tesco seeks to accurately measure the amount of CO_2 equivalent put into the atmosphere by each product's raw materials, production, manufacture, distribution, use and eventual disposal. The label features a carbon footprint logo. Brands can also choose to indicate the amount of life-cycle-based CO_2 and other greenhouse gases on its labels.

The Carbon Reduction label is expanding its global presence. Since 2007, Tesco has opened 125 Fresh and Easy stores in Southern California, Las Vegas, and Phoenix, so it is possible their carbon-labeled products may be making an appearance soon in the U.S. Working with Planet Ark; products bearing the Carbon Reduction Label were introduced into Australia in 2010.[24]

Figure 7.5 **The Carbon Reduction label**

reducing with
the Carbon Trust

CO2

We have committed to
reduce the carbon footprint
of this product

carbon-label.com

Voluntary government labels

Unlike some countries, including Canada, Japan, and Korea, the U.S. government has opted for voluntary single-attribute, rather than multi-attribute labels. (The private sector and not-for-profit groups hold sway in the area of multi-attribute eco-labeling.) Outside of those associated with independent testing, the government-backed labels don't require any fees.

The most visible voluntary labeling program is ENERGY STAR (whom we at J. Ottman Consulting were proud to advise over many years). Launched in 1992, this joint program of the EPA and the U.S. Department of Energy identifies and promotes energy efficiency in more than 60 product categories including major appliances, lighting, and electronics used within homes and offices, and commercial buildings and homes. Nearly 3,000 product manufacturers now feature the ENERGY STAR label on their products. According to the Natural Marketing Institute, by 2009, 93% of the American public claimed to recognize the ENERGY STAR label, and 73% said it influenced their purchase (see Fig. 7.1).

Other EPA labels include WaterSense, to identify water-efficient toilets, faucets, showerheads, and other products and practices; Design for Environment (DfE), to acknowledge safer chemical formulations in cleaning products; and SmartWay, for fuel-efficient and low-emission passenger cars and

Figure 7.6 **Voluntary labels of the U.S. Environmental Protection Agency**

light trucks, as well as heavy-duty tractors and trailers and other forms of transportation used in distribution and delivery operations.

Labels or standards signifying that food and non-food products are organically grown exist throughout the globe, for example, in Europe (EU 834/2007), Japan (Japan Agricultural Standards), and Canada (Canada Organic Regime) and in the U.S. (USDA National Organic Program). Launched in 2002, the USDA Organic label now appears on a wide range of over 25,000 products from 10,000 companies including food, T-shirts, and shampoo. Stonyfield Farm, Earthbound Farm, and Horizon Organic are just a few of the popular consumer brands that bear the USDA organic seal on packages, advertisements, and other marketing communications, signifying that their products do not contain or were not processed with synthetic fertilizers, pesticides, radiation, antibiotics, hormones, or GMOs (genetically modified organisms); and they monitor other long-term processes such as soil management and animal conditions.[25]

Figure 7.7 **USDA Organic label**

Reprinted with permission from the USDA

Since 2002, the USDA has been running the BioPreferred program encouraging federal procurement officials to give preferential treatment to a list of 5,000 products in 50 product categories, and growing. Sensing mainstream consumer demand for biobased products – defined by the USDA as non-edible consumer and commercial products that are based on agricultural, marine, or forestry-based raw materials – Congress has authorized the USDA to ready a new label to help consumers identify biobased products. Expected to be launched in 2011, the new label (with which we at J. Ottman Consulting are pleased to be assisting), will appear on products and packaging ranging from compostable gardening bags made from cornstarch, to lip balms made from soybeans, even towels and bed sheets made with eucalyptus fiber.

Self-certification programs

Issued by manufacturers to denote their own environmental and social achievements, self-certification programs do not carry endorsements or the credibility of an impartial third party. However, they do provide distinct advantages in controlling costs and providing flexibility in the types and amounts of information that is provided to consumers. Some self-certification systems showcase government or third-party labeling.

Several large companies have attempted to put forth their own self-certifications; examples include: SC Johnson (GreenList), NEC (Eco Products), Sony Ericsson (GreenHeart), GE (Ecomagination), Timberland's Green Index, to be discussed in Chapter 9, and Hewlett-Packard (HP). Building from a history of environmental focus, HP's Eco Highlights label, introduced in 2008, spotlights key environmental attributes and certifications on the packages of select HP products. The easy-to-read rectangular label (see Fig. 7.8), which now appears on more than 160 HP products, allows consumers who purchase selected printing, computing, and server products to learn more about features such as power consumption compared to previous models, ENERGY STAR compliance, and percentage of recycled material used in the product. It also includes specifics on the recyclability of the packaging and the product, and updates on HP's overall recycling goals.[26]

Figure 7.8 **HP Eco Highlights label**

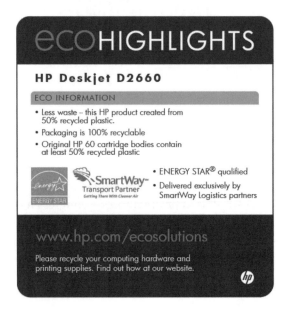

Independent claim verification

Independent for-profit organizations, including Scientific Certification Systems of Oakland, California and UL Environment of Northbrook, Illinois, will, for a fee, verify specific claims and develop standards in industries where none exists. They will also certify products against standards developed by other organizations. For example, they will certify commercial furniture to the new BIFMA (Business and Institutional Furniture Manufacturers Association) e3 multi-attribute, life-cycle-based standard (levelcertified.org) which was developed in line with the American National Standards Institute (ANSI) standards development protocols.

Environmental product declaration

ISO standards describe three types of eco-label, two of which are described above: Type I: Environmental Labels, Type II: Environmental Claims and Self Declarations, and Type III: Environmental Product Declarations (EPDs). More often used in Europe and Asia than the U.S., EPDs provide detailed explanations of the full life-cycle impacts of a given product. An excellent example is the EPD issued per ISO 14025 by Steelcase for its Think Chair, designed to fit the needs of consumers around the world. Displayed at the company's website, Steelcase.com, the EPD shares the results of three life-cycle assessments (needed to accurately assess impacts in North America, Europe, and Asia), and describes the various certifications it has received from different countries around the globe.

Considering an eco-seal endorsement or independent claim certification for your brand? Maximize its potential value and avoid backlash by sticking to these four rules of thumb:

Choose wisely

Ensure that the organization behind the seal and its methodologies are credible. Look in particular to see that their standards have been developed in accordance with such standards-writing organizations as ISO and local bodies such as the American National Standards Institute or the British Standards Institute. Labels should be consistent with expected amendments to the FTC Green Guides as well as other appropriate national environmental guidelines.

Be relevant

With so many available, it is possible that your brand may qualify for more than one eco-label, and for more than one product attribute, e.g., ingredients, packaging, manufacturing, etc. Therefore, aim to certify those attributes that are most relevant to your brand. Also, integrate your eco-labels into existing brand platforms. GE's Ecomagination (and more recent Healthy Imagination) designations extend from the company's longstanding "Imagination at Work" brand platform.

Educate

Let consumers know about the specific criteria upon which your eco-seal is based. With single-attribute labels, take care to communicate that only the specific product attribute is being certified and do not imply that the entire product is "greener" as a result. For credibility's sake, if appropriate, communicate attempts to extend the greening process to other product attributes. Products bearing self-declarations are advised to identify their label as having been issued by their own organization to avoid misleading consumers otherwise. For added credibility, products with self-declarations can consider third-party certification. Share additional details on a corporate website.

Promote your eco-label

Considering that many eco-labels are not widely recognized, help to create demand for your eco-label via marketing communications consistent with your seal's own guidelines. The ENERGY STAR label enjoys strong awareness thanks largely to the promotional efforts of the many manufacturers whose products bear the label, coupled with pro bono advertising. Be sure to look for opportunities to distinguish your commitment to your selected eco-label from competitors using the same label. Earning and promoting ENERGY STAR "Partner of the Year" status is one good route.

5 Promote responsible consumption

Are Frito's SunChips's bags truly "compostable" if consumers drop them in the trash rather than a composting bin? Is an ENERGY STAR-rated light bulb really green if it remains on after everyone leaves the room? It is one thing to design a product (and its system) to be greener, but impacts throughout the total product life-cycle cannot be minimized unless people use (and dispose) of it more responsibly. "Responsible consumption" – what I consider to be the high road of green marketing and product development – is about conserving resources associated with using products, including encouraging consumers to use only what is needed, and consciously reduce waste. Sustainability leaders are striving for the ideal goals of zero waste and zero energy, but we will never get to zero until consumers learn to responsibly consume and properly dispose of the products they buy.

As discussed in Chapter 4, consumer usage can represent a significant portion of a product's total environmental impacts, especially when it comes to those that consume resources such as energy or water. Products can be designed to make it easier for consumers to minimize resource use, like a duplex printing feature on a printer, or a dual-flush toilet. Real-time information, like Toyota's dashboard and the new crop of energy meters and monitoring services help, too.

Representing what is now an unwritten rule of green marketing – but one that will undoubtedly be writ large in the not-too-distant future – enlisting consumer support for responsible consumption is a sure-fire way to build credibility and reduce risk. Consumers intuitively understand that it is not possible to spend our way out of the environmental crisis. At the micro level, simply switching one supermarket cartful of "brown" products with "green" ones will not cure environmental ills. Creating a sustainable society requires, among other things, that every one of us use only what we need and that we help to recapture resources for successive uses through recycling and composting. When markets fail to address environmental ills, governments are sure to intervene. (Witness mandated shifts to energy-, fuel- and water-efficient appliances, light bulbs, and cars. Will cold-water laundry detergents, organic cotton, and leather-free shoes be next?) Another issue industry needs to be mindful of "the rebound effect" – whereby consumers will buy or use more of a product if it costs less to use due to enhanced efficiency. The classic case is fuel-efficient cars that are driven more miles than less-efficient vehicles.

As we learned when advising HSBC, a key to the credibility of their There's No Small Change campaign was empowering individuals and businesses to reduce their carbon footprint, in line with the bank's own efforts. In other words, we weren't asking HSBC's customers to do anything the bank hadn't already done itself. Cognizant of the risk associated with promoting a compostable bag that might only get thrown away, Frito-Lay emblazons a "compostable" message on its SunChips bags and supports additional education through a television campaign and website. Below are examples of ways that businesses are winning their stakeholders' respect by communicating the need to consume responsibly especially in the area of energy use.

HP earned the #1 spot on *Newsweek*'s list of the top green companies of 2009 by pledging to reduce product emissions and energy usage 40% from 2005 levels by 2011. Realizing it needs to partner with consumers to reach that goal, the company has launched its Power to Change campaign, encouraging users to turn off their computers and printers when they do not need them. Users can download software that reminds them to turn off their computers at night and tracks actions to calculate energy and carbon impact.

Levi Strauss and Co. has teamed up with Goodwill to educate consumers on how to lower the life-cycle impacts of blue jeans. The company's A Care Tag For The Planet campaign uses online and in-store messaging and a new care tag on jeans to encourage owners to wash in cold water, line dry when possible and, at the end of their useful life, to donate their jeans to Goodwill thrift stores. The company estimates that such steps taken by responsible consumers can reduce the life-cycle climate-change impacts by 50%. Relatedly, in Europe, Procter & Gamble's Ariel runs a Turn to 30 (degrees centigrade) campaign to encourage consumers to wash at lower temperatures, and spurred by the threat of regulation, the laundry detergent industry as a whole has united to promote responsible washing. And an industry-wide Washright campaign (washright.com), launched in 1998 by the Brussels-based International Association for Soaps, Detergents and Maintenance Products (AISE), reached 70% of European households with tips on how to wash laundry in environmentally preferable ways.[27]

A final example: the Sacramento Municipal Utility District now knows that peer pressure is an excellent strategy for promoting responsible consumption – and may be even more motivating than saving money. In a test that began in April 2008, 35,000 randomly selected customers were told via "happy" or "sad" faces printed on their monthly utility bills how their energy use compared with their neighbors' and with that of the most efficient energy users in the district. Customers who received the information cut their electricity use by 2% compared to flat usage by counterparts who did not receive messages. The utility expanded the program to 50,000 households in August 2009.[28]

Operating by the new rules of green marketing requires new strategies for engagement with the vast panoply of stakeholders who are motivated to help businesses green their products, develop effective communications, and engage consumers in exciting new ways – the subject of the next chapter.

As we go to press . . . The FTC issued proposed revisions for their Green Guides, which were last revised in 1996. The proposed Guides can be located at ftc. gov/opa/2010/10/greenguide.shtm. After the requisite rule-making process including comment period, the revised guides will be finalized, likely in the spring of 2011. The content of the proposed revisions are consistent with much of the guidance in this book. Please visit the author's website, www. greenmarketing.com, for continuing updates and her analysis.

The *New Rules* Checklist

Ask the following questions to help ensure credibility for your green marketing claims and communications.

- Are we walking our talk? Does our CEO openly support sustainability? Do our stakeholders know it?

- Are our green marketing claims consistent with our corporate actions? (i.e., are we making claims that are true?)

- Are we following official guidelines for environmental marketing claims? Are we keeping up with the dialogue on the use of newer environmental marketing terms? Does our state and/or our company's legal department have its own guidelines for the use of environmental marketing claims?

- Have we thoroughly considered all that can go wrong so as to minimize the chances of backlash from greenwash and enjoy the full benefits of positive publicity? Do we have a process for monitoring our online reputation?

- Are our brand-related sustainability claims meaningful, specific, complete, and without exaggeration? Have we tested their believability among consumers?

- Are we being transparent about the pollution our products represent as well as their environmental benefits?

- Are we being environmentally efficient with our marketing materials? Have we identified where the Internet or electronic media could work to reduce our use of paper? Are we using recycled and/or sustainably harvested paper and vegetable-based inks for our marketing communications?

- Are we taking advantage of third parties to underscore credibility? Are we considering our own self-declaration or the use of third-party verifiers?

- Do consumers know how to use and dispose of our products responsibly? In what ways might we make it easier for consumers to practice responsible consumption of our products and packages?

785266 000297

Partnering for success

Historically, the only groups with a direct interest in a company's products or operations were investors, employees, customers and end consumers, suppliers, and the press. However, with increased awareness of industry's impact on our water, land, and air, new eyes from practically every corner of society now scrutinize a firm's environmental and social impact, writing new rules for the ways business is conducted and brands are marketed. Today, a host of new corporate environmental and social stakeholders are now on the list, including the general public, citizen journalists and bloggers, educators, environmental and social activists, government bodies, community groups, church leaders and other religious groups, and even children and future generations who will feel the effects of today's corporate activities in decades to come (see Fig. 8.1).

With potential influence on such diverse activities as how businesses procure raw materials, design their products, and produce and promote them, some groups monitor corporate polluters: boycotting, conducting negative media campaigns, and lobbying for stiff new laws are tools in their arsenal. Other groups engage companies one-on-one in positive efforts, and there is much to gain from collaborating with them. Representing a myriad of capabilities and resources that can help solve complex environmental and social problems, diverse stakeholder groups can help improve understanding of how your company is perceived in the world at large. They can help identify issues to address and evaluate stakeholder satisfaction.

Figure 8.1 **The new corporate environmental and social stakeholders**

Traditional stakeholders	New stakeholders
Retailers and end consumers	General public
Employees	Children and future generations
Plant neighbors	Educators
The press	Environmental and social activists
Suppliers	Civic and religious leaders
Financial institutions	Citizen journalists
Regulators	Other government groups

Source: J. Ottman Consulting, Inc.

Forming constructive partnerships or coalitions with various stakeholders provides many advantages, including uncovering ways to cut costs, improving the value of existing products and creating new products, bolstering credibility for greener products and communications, and enhancing public image. In order to drive sustainable progress and capitalize on valuable green marketing opportunities, marketers need to follow new rules. Characterized by transparency and cooperations, these new rules call for engaging with stakeholders in frank, open discussion. They also involve the need to disclose once closely held information on product ingredients and how products are produced and workers are treated, so listen carefully to the stakeholders who take a broad view of your industry.

The general public

The power of the general public – defined as consumers and those who influence them – is on the rise. As described in Chapter 2, consumers' perceptions of the environmental impacts of products and companies now factor into their decisions of what, where, and how often they purchase. Fueled by the many opinions now broadcast over the Internet, newly uncovered learning (correct or incorrect) can upend an industry, seemingly overnight. The draft report released in 2008 from a small study on the chemical compound BPA, forcing Nalge Nunc International to quickly reformulate its polycarbonate bottles in order to prevent a complete collapse in demand for its products, is just one example.[1]

Bottlers of water are still reeling from the numerous environmental offenses being heaped on the industry – some deserved, some not. First, there's the perception of mountains of unrecyclable and unrecycled plastic bottles that clog landfills, and contribute to the Great Pacific Garbage Patch. That's compounded by the environmental impact of the millions of barrels of oil used to make the bottles, the multiple pints of water needed to fill each bottle, and the greenhouse gases associated with shipping all this water from Evian, France, and islands as far away as Fiji.[2] Finally, there's water sourcing, a favorite of the press. Nestlé Waters (Poland Spring, Perrier) and other bottlers are being accused by local residents of draining precious water supplies, while others such as Coke (Dasani) and Pepsi (Aquafina) are being condemned for simply filtering municipal supplies and failing to label it as such. (Pepsi has since come around but, as of this writing, Coke has not, preferring the more euphemistic water-process descriptors of "Pure, Fresh Taste" and "Reverse Osmosis.") Once considered hip, bottled water is now banned from government offices from Fayetteville, Arkansas to Seattle, Washington. New York City is testing a program of using filtered tap water in water coolers and it is encouraging city workers to use their own reusable water bottles.[3] Aided by nascent green marketing efforts by Nalgene and Brita (Chapter 6), consumers are increasingly turning to tap water and new, trendy reusable bottles.

The bottled water industry is especially vulnerable with its strategy of bottling water that is comparable in many instances to what's available from the kitchen tap. But it need not be in such a pickle – many consumers prefer the taste of bottled waters, and some fear chlorine in municipal water supplies. The industry could have done a better job of protecting its business and reputation: for instance, by first taking a life-cycle approach to its products – using recycled and recyclable packaging, promoting refills of its own water, tapping into local as opposed to foreign water supplies, and better ensuring the sustainability of its water sources. They also could have educated the public about the health and refreshment (beyond the convenience) benefits of their products, and publicized efforts to reduce (or offset) their environment impacts, not to mention underscoring legitimate health claims.

Strategy for educating the general public

Conduct media campaigns that can engage the general public in
relevant environmental issues

The beleaguered bottled-water industry and individual players are now
mobilizing to help clarify misguided criticism and reduce risks going forward.
In the summer of 2007, the International Bottled Water Association (IBWA)
launched a fact-based campaign consisting of full-page advertisements in
key media outlets and in the *New York Times* and the *San Francisco Chronicle*. The goal: to demonstrate the industry's commitment to environmental
stewardship and underscore its support of recycling and bottled water regulation and safety, especially in targeted markets. Realizing that bottled water
was taking the heat while soft drinks slipped under the radar, the campaign
also noted the benefits of water compared to other more widely consumed
beverages in plastic bottles.[4]

Leading the charge was Coca-Cola, Nestlé Waters, and PepsiCo, which
make up the bulk of bottled water sales. Each has made strides to reduce
its own environmental footprint, primarily via the use of "eco-shape" bottles that helped Coke reduced the weight of its Dasani bottles by 30% and
PepsiCo reduce the weight of its Aquafina bottles nearly 40%.[5] Nestlé also
went so far as to reduce the size of the paper labels on Poland Spring, Deer
Park, and Arrowhead water bottles by 30%.[6] Recognizing the need to engage
his company's entire supply chain to take more meaningful step, in 2008 in
a keynote speech to a sustainable business conference, Kim Jeffrey, CEO of
Nestlé Waters North America, acknowledged the negative impact the electronic media can have on one's business and challenged corporations to put
sustainability at the core of their businesses. Among other steps, he reached
out to suppliers and other stakeholders to increase the percentage of recycled PET in their bottles to 25% and to work to increase recycling rates of PET
containers to 60% by 2013.[7]

Children

In their learning years from preschool through college, young people find
their identity, develop their values, and discover their passions. Slowly but
surely, children become empowered to act on environmental issues through
their own purchasing and consumption habits, suggesting a key opportunity to shape their consciousness while their sustainability-related values
are forming.

Children and young adults are important industry stakeholders because of their own buying power and their ability to influence the purchases of their family – especially when it comes to a topic they are ardent about: the environment. In fact, more than half of kids between the ages of six and eight are reported to encourage their parents to buy greener products.[8] Armed with simple environmental slogans such as "Reduce, Reuse, and Recycle" (which all too often translates to "recycle, recycle, recycle"), four-foot-tall "eco-cops" can dictate behavior at home that can be misguided. Meanwhile, their college-bound elder brothers and sisters – the bright minds and future leaders of the next generation – are forming their own brand preferences for such products as laundry detergents, snacks, cars, and clothing that will often stick with them for life.

Strategies for educating children

Empower educators to teach the facts about environmental issues and how to consume responsibly

Environmental topics fit well with the full range of curricula, from science and math to the arts and social studies. For teachers, the environment and ecology are topics with a "hands-on" appeal that can liven up an otherwise dry math class or civics lesson. Teachers and administrators are willing partners when they sense an opportunity to impart legitimate information that educates students – and helps to extend tight budgets.

Supply educators with fact-based teaching materials and curriculum. Partner with a not-for-profit for added impact and credibility. During the 2004 back-to-school shopping season, the Staples Foundation for Learning, a nonprofit division of Staples, the stationery products giant, partnered with Earth Force (an international education program that involves young people in hands-on education, conservation, and restoration projects) to outfit schools with environmental educational curriculum and program materials. Representing a win–win for both organizations, the Staples Foundation has donated $1 million annually since 2004, helping Earth Force to equip more than 20,000 students each year with the skills, knowledge, and hands-on opportunity to better understand the causes and impacts of many environmental issues and do something about it![9] Taking the program up a notch, in 2007, the partnership launched the Staples Earth Force Award to recognize local student groups' environmental achievements. Award recipient Robinson Elementary School in Tampa, Florida, worked to eliminate invasive species and reintroduce native species in a local area nature preserve,[10] while the Holland Middle School students in Pennsylvania focused on the energy and cost savings that resulted from instituting a 'dark school' day when the whole community reduced their lighting and air conditioning usage.[11]

A cautionary note: when developing industry-sponsored eco-efforts for schools, be careful to avoid suggestions of bias, self-promotion, or anything that hints of greenwashing. This can backfire and mar your organization's reputation.

Find hands-on ways to engage youth in reducing their own and their family's impacts

Organize collection programs that involve students in recycling or reuse of otherwise valuable waste items. TerraCycle, the New Jersey company founded by Princeton University dropout Tom Szaky, first made headlines in 2006 by selling fertilizer made from worm poop to the Home Depot and other major retailers. They now put non-recyclable items such as food wrappers to work as raw material for tote bags and other fashion items. "Brigades" enlisted within hundreds of schools collect packaging of sponsors including Capri Sun, Kool-Aid, Oreo cookies, and Stonyfield Farm yogurt. Each used pack collected earns the school a one- or two-cent rebate to help build a garden or buy school supplies. And educators jump at the opportunity to encourage kids to recycle, to earn extra money for schools, and to repurpose what would otherwise be "trash" into new products. The Islesboro Central School in Maine lost no time in putting the monies raised by their students to work at building composting bins and supporting the Rainforest Network's efforts to buy rainforest land for restoration.[12]

Sponsor eco-oriented programming for children, teens, and families

In partnership with Boys & Girls Clubs of America, the Natural Resources Defense Council, the National Wildlife Federation (NWF), the NFL (National Football League), the NEA Foundation (National Education Association, a public entity that supports public education), and the Girl Scouts of America, the popular cable network Nickelodeon launched a section on its website entitled, "The Big Green Help," giving more than two million kids practical tips on how to be greener through online games and opportunities to participate in local activities. Nickelodeon also founded the Big Green Help Public Education Grants program,[13] awarding $200,000 in grants to support sustainability projects in schools, furthering their effort to empower kids to improve the environment.[14]

Encourage college students, faculty, and staff to collaborate on exciting educational initiatives

Beyond simply funding projects, consider ways to extend your sponsorship dollars by providing access to your products and employees. Biannually since 2002, BP Solar (part of BP's alternative energy business) has partnered with the U.S. Green Building Council and the U.S. Department of Energy to sponsor the Solar Decathlon, an international biennial competition where teams from 20 universities work together over two years to design and build solar-powered homes. In addition to funding, BP equips the teams with discounted solar materials and technical advice. The resulting homes are exhibited on the National Mall in Washington, DC. According to a 2007 winner, "The house is a wonderful example of how energy efficiency, energy generation, and good design can all work together to create spaces for living. I hope more sustainable projects take a cue from this project."[15]

The NWF runs an annual Chill Out program to raise awareness and seek practical solutions for global warming by reaching out to colleges and universities. Students and faculty from universities across the United States submit projects that help solve or mitigate the impact of global warming associated with their campuses. The schools that implement the most creative solutions are featured in a video webcast posted on the NWF website.[16] Since 2006 the Chill Out contest has engaged students on over 500 campuses and recognized the efforts of more than 20 schools.[17] Sponsors of the Chill Out program include brands with an incentive to deepen their connection with this key student target and tap their brainpower to find innovative solutions to climate change: Stonyfield Farm, ClimateCounts.org (a nonprofit organization funded by Stonyfield), Kaplan Test Prep and Admissions, and Discovery Channel's Planet Green.

Finally, DoSomething.org, a nonprofit based in New York City that inspires and empowers teenagers to get involved in topics including health, poverty, and the environment, organized a nationwide Increase Your Green competition in the fall of 2008. Open to all middle and high school students in the United States, the competition called on participants to carry out eight-week projects that reduced the environmental impact of their school and involved and/or impacted as many people as possible. All projects were designed and led by the students, whether as a class, extracurricular club, or even an entire school. Projects were judged by a panel at DoSomething.org and an outside panel of green experts, who looked at the number of hours of energy saved, the number of people involved and/or impacted, and the amount of waste recycled.

Two winners received a $1,500 grant for their school, funded by the National Grid Foundation; one winning team from Scituate High School, Massachusetts, built a biodiesel production tank. Overall, 75,000 students participated in the competition, with projects ranging from starting recycling programs and composting projects to planting community gardens.[18]

The *New Rules* Checklist

Ask the following questions to uncover opportunities for enlisting the support of the general public and youth for your company's environment-related initiatives.

○ How sensitive to and knowledgeable are our consumers about the environmental issues that affect our industry, company, and products?

○ Which types of messages do we need to be getting to consumers about the issues?

○ What do consumers need to know in order to safely and responsibly use, recycle, and dispose of our products and packaging?

○ What role do children and teens play in influencing the purchase of our brands?

○ What opportunities exist to develop environmental education programs or curricula?

○ What types of programs and events might we sponsor to reach the next generation with our messages? Community projects? Environmental clubs? Children's media? Teen initiatives? College and university programs?

○ In what ways might we leverage social media – texting, Facebook, Twitter, etc. – to reach youth?

○ Who might be appropriate and willing partners in helping us to extend our reach, enhance credibility, and share costs?

Employees

Employees wear many stakeholder hats. Relying on secure jobs, they have a direct stake in their company's success. They also have a personal stake in their employer's reputation – who wants to tell their kids they are working for a polluter that lacks a social or environmental conscience? Educated employees can recommend ways to green up the workplace, brainstorm ideas for new eco-sensitive products, build bridges to their brand's consumers, and enhance their company's image. The 2008 Society for Human Resource Management *Green Workplace Survey* found that employee morale (44%) is a top benefit in implementing environmental responsibility programs. In companies that have not already launched sustainability plans, nearly three out of four employees say they want their employers to "go green."[19] Potentially ardent consumers of a firm's products or services, workers can be a crucial link in forging good relations and building trust between the organization and the communities in which they live, as well as between their brands and consumers.

Strategy for empowering employees

Create initiatives that encourage employees to make a positive impact on their communities and brands

Many businesses now have programs for employees and even their children on Earth Day, but the environment needs to be an *everyday* priority. Eco-programs that create internal awareness and celebrate successes should be ongoing for greatest impact and credibility.

Since 2006, Alcoa has declared October as a "Month of Service," highlighting the company's dedication to sustainability and its employees' commitment to community service. Alcoa staffers around the world are encouraged to volunteer with local community groups to plant trees, rehabilitate local parks and rivers, recycle, and find solutions to climate change. In 2007, Alcoa employees clocked 634,000 hours of voluntary service aiding 187 schools, delivering over 2,300 meals, building Habitat for Humanity homes, planting 12,000 trees, and saving over 1,700 tons of CO_2.[20]

Before attempting to green its operations, Wal-Mart opted to green the people who could make it happen. Starting in 2007, the 1.3 million employees of Wal-Mart and Sam's Club were encouraged to take on a Personal Sustainability Project (PSP) aimed at achieving an attainable goal related to improving their personal health or the welfare of their family, community, or planet. Whatever worked for them made the grade, whether eating healthy meals and shedding pounds, using eco-friendly household cleaning products, recycling at home, or carpooling or riding bicycles to work. Wal-Mart claims this award-winning effort made its employees healthier, increased work satisfaction and productivity, and reduced turnover, increasing revenue and decreasing costs. It also sent a message that personal and environmental sustainability can be achieved by all workers – even those with hectic schedules, long working hours, and stretched family budgets.[21]

The Home Depot's employees know a lot about building things, and this can come in handy in the many communities in which they live and work. In January 2009, the Home Depot teamed up with KaBOOM!, a national non-profit organization committed to building playgrounds within walking distance of every child in America. In addition to financial support, tools, and raw material provided by the Home Depot, more than 100,000 Home Depot employees have volunteered their time to build or refurbish more than 1,000 play spaces. Looking to minimize the environmental impact of each playground and to maximize the opportunity to educate the community, KaBOOM! seeks to reuse and recycle materials at each site and has introduced composting bins, tree planting, and rainwater collection systems. The Home Depot employees benefit from this partnership as well: according to one employee in the Midwest, "The partnership . . . allows us to demonstrate our core value of giving back to the community and we feel great after every build when a couple days later the kids come back and play on the new playground. It's just a great experience."[22] No doubt these efforts resulted in more aware salespeople, able to guide customers to greener purchases once inside the stores.

The *New Rules* Checklist

Ask the following questions to assess opportunities for enlisting employees in your company's environment-related initiatives.

- ○ Are our employees aware of our environmental and social commitments?
- ○ What environmental and social issues are of most concern to our employees?
- ○ What do employees know about the environmental issues that affect our business? What gaps in education need filling in?
- ○ Are employees engaged in reducing their own environmental impacts and those of the organization?
- ○ In what ways might we educate employees and their families to live more sustainable lives overall?
- ○ What opportunities exist to engage our employees in our local communities?

Retailers

Fueled by health concerns, pesticide-free foods and organically grown cotton now top many a "Naturalist's" or "Health Fanatic's" shopping list. However, the environmental benefits of such products are not always so clear. For instance, many people believe that organically grown cotton clothing is healthier to wear, but do not actually know that organic growing methods are significantly less hazardous to soil and farm workers than those for traditionally grown cotton, which is extremely pesticide-intensive. Retailers can help shoppers see the links between your products and a more sustainable lifestyle.

With unique opportunities to educate the public at the point of sale, retailers are a key ally in the effort to enlighten shoppers. Often queried by the millions of now ardent green consumers about the environmental aspects of the products they stock, they need credible, cost-effective ways of responding to their customers about eco issues in general, as well as the specifics about the products they stock. Despite their desire to fill their shelves with the greener alternatives today's consumers seek, retailers fall short verifying vendor options as "green."

With IKEA, Trader Joe's, Wal-Mart, and Whole Foods Market in the lead in the U.S. and Marks & Spencer and Tesco in the UK, many retail chains have created their own lines of eco-branded products. Some are promoting the use of specific labels storewide; examples include Home Depot's Eco Options program, and Tesco's support for the Carbon Trust's Carbon Reduction Label, discussed in Chapter 7. Sensing opportunities to lead the way to all things green, Best Buy electronics retailer launched a Greener Together program to teach its 165,000 employees how to help customers make smarter shopping decisions. Their focus: how to use electronics more efficiently to save energy, and how to recycle, reuse, or trade in products at the end of their useful lives.[23]

In 2009, Wal-Mart announced a multi-stakeholder Sustainability Consortium tasked with creating a supplier index or score that will first measure the sustainability performance of suppliers, and eventually, the impacts of individual consumer products. Ratings that will likely influence which products make it to Wal-Mart's shelves, and in what quantities, will take into consideration such things as carbon footprint, material efficiency, use of natural resources, and social issues. Its goal is to influence the next generation of sustainable products, materials, and technologies. To do the job correctly Wal-Mart has enlisted the support of leading manufacturers, NGOs, government regulators, and academia. Partnering with eco-minded retailers is not just enticing; with the market quickly skewing toward greener goods, it is essential.

Strategy for partnering with retailers

Help retailers train staff, promote more sustainable products, or conduct special media outreach

Companies that partner with retailers can strengthen vendor relations and secure increased merchandising support for their brands in weekly circulars and newspaper ads, enhanced in-store signage, couponing, and sampling.

Responding to Wal-Mart's interest in greener goods, in 2005 Sun Products created a triple win for consumers, retailers, and the environment when they launched "All small & mighty," the triple-strength laundry detergent concentrate mentioned in Chapter 4. Representing myriad benefits for consumers and the environment, for retailers it could optimize space on their shelves, reduce shelf-stocking costs, and reduce customer disappointment from out-of-stock products. No wonder All small & mighty became a poster child of then Wal-Mart CEO Lee Scott with all the resulting PR benefits for the All brand.

 **Addressing
the New Rules**

Partnering with ENERGY STAR

Since its inception in 1992, the U.S. Environmental Protection Agency has leveraged retail partnerships to promote its ENERGY STAR brand and to assist both its manufacturer and retail partners to sell more energy-efficient products. Today, more than ever, with the increased demand for greener products among consumers, Jill Vohr, Marketing Manager for ENERGY STAR Products Labeling, recognizes the corresponding increase in opportunities to partner with retailers on promoting ENERGY STAR qualified products ranging from electronics to lighting, to appliances. According to Ms. Vohr, the key to leveraging these trends successfully through retail partnerships depends on where your retail customers sit on this issue. Here are three examples she provides:

1. If your retail customers have taken the initiative to develop consumer-facing platforms promoting green to their consumers, such as the Home Depot's Eco Options label, then the best course of action for you as the manufacturer is to do your homework and find out how the retailer identifies products for its green line – for the Home Depot it would be Scientific Certification Systems (SCS) – and demonstrate that your product meets these criteria.

The ENERGY STAR program supports the Home Depot by providing not just products, but also educational content and, of course, government-backed credibility to the energy-efficient pillar of the Home Depot's Eco Options. The result: ENERGY STAR is not only a feature in many of the Home Depot's Eco Options promotional activities, but manufacturer partners reap the rewards of favorable positioning for Home Depot product line reviews.

In addition to the Home Depot, there are a number of other retailers that have developed environmental marketing platforms, such as Ace Hardware's Helpful Earth Choices, Staples' EcoEasy, and JCPenney's Simply Green. Many more have programs in the works to meet consumer demand for more sustainable alternatives.

2. If the retailer has internal programs supporting greener initiatives, such as Best Buy's Greener Together platform and Wal-Mart's work with the Sustainability Consortium, manufacturers of green products should get to know others at the organization – beyond their respective merchants – who manage these programs (more often than not, the director of sustainability or environmental affairs) and identify shared interests in promoting green brands to consumers. Being proactive and taking the initiative may translate into a first-mover advantage for your brand and priority placements featuring effective environmental messages.

ENERGY STAR works with both Wal-Mart and the Sustainability Consortium to help them define and implement optimal energy-efficiency criteria for their products. For Best Buy, the ENERGY STAR program not only provides general support for promoting ENERGY STAR-labeled products within their stores, it also provides strategic guidance for where they take Greener Together and forms the basis for the energy-saving component of the Greener Together platform.

3. A final set of retailers are those that characterize their consumers as less interested in green or are taking a wait-and-see approach to green marketing and thus have held off on green marketing initiatives. These retailers are still more likely than not to be keen on green. This is simply because for retailers, even those with "browner" consumers, playing a role in the green movement adds value to their image, and this image value corresponds with enhanced loyalty and increased sales overall. Moreover, few consum-

ers would view effective green marketing negatively. If anything, they shop based on other criteria, but still recognize that the retailer cares and that counts for a lot.

So for retailers that do not seem to be engaged at all, it still might be strategically advantageous for manufacturers to educate them about the green consumer and encourage them to consider how carrying green products might be a good first step towards doing the right thing. This, in turn, may lead to an ongoing relationship with a retailer that translates into an eventual flagship role for your brand in a new green marketing effort.

For ENERGY STAR, not all retailers are gung ho about green marketing. For those retail partners that shy away from the green marketing movement for whatever reason, Ms. Vohr finds that there are still opportunities to increase ENERGY STAR penetration both for products and messaging simply because the retailers appreciate guidance they can get from partners: in this case, EPA. Similarly, manufacturers who have a handle on what's green and the benefits of green can leverage partnerships with hold-out retailers to help them navigate this new space, thus increasing the likelihood of brand favorability in the future.[24]

The *New Rules* Checklist

Ask the following questions to assess opportunities for enlisting retailer support for your company's environment-related initiatives.

- What are the most important environmental issues facing our key retailers in their trading areas?

- To what extent are our retailers aware of our environmental initiatives and the environmentally sound attributes of our products and packaging?

- What types of education and training do buyers and sales personnel require about environmental issues for our brand/category?

- Which retailers have in-store eco-labeling programs and other eco-initiatives that we have an opportunity to get involved with?

- What are the opportunities for our brand to get enhanced sales by building in-store support among less aware retailers?

Suppliers

Today's complex global supply chains often cloud visibility into raw material sourcing and product manufacturing and shipping as products wend their way over increased distances and circuitous routes. With heightened interest in sustainability specifics throughout a product's entire life-cycle, suppliers, with their intimate knowledge of their own materials, components, or technologies can offer critical support in reducing environmental impacts and bringing new product and service innovations on board.

Wal-Mart's manufacturer vendors have a big incentive to work with their own suppliers to go green. In 2006, as part of their global effort to meet consumer environmental demand and likely to help shore up an image tarnished by labor issues, Wal-Mart introduced a green rating system designed to push their 60,000 worldwide manufacturer vendors to reduce the amount of packaging they use by 5%, to use more renewable materials, and to slash energy use. Requiring unprecedented knowledge of their suppliers' own operations, Wal-Mart's vendors are being asked such questions as: What are your corporate greenhouse emissions? What is total water use of the facilities that produce for Wal-Mart? What is the location of all the facilities that supply your products? Companies that achieve high rankings are named "preferred suppliers," while those with low rankings risk losing coveted real estate on Wal-Mart's shelves.[25]

Working with suppliers to meet consumer and retailer environmental and social demands is challenging. First, many suppliers are loath to disclose trade secrets. Your supply chain can consist of several entities, stretched out long distances around the globe. Some suppliers are way upstream and are unknown to manufacturers of finished products. Suppliers may be new to environmental and social management, so may not be prepared to answer your tough questions, much less pay hefty fees for sophisticated analyses of their materials, ingredients, and processes. Taking the time to educate and work with suppliers while protecting their trade secrets can result in new products and packaging and greened-up life-cycles that can establish competitive advantage.

Strategies for partnering with suppliers

Identify chemicals in your products to ensure they are safe

SC Johnson's GreenList system, which it licenses to other manufacturers, evaluates and rates chemicals in its products. HP is collecting data from suppliers of 240 chemicals of "emerging concern," while Nike maintains a restricted substances list in an effort to identify and evaluate chemicals contained in their products.

Work with suppliers on innovative materials

Squeezed by rising energy costs and looking to reduce waste, in summer 2009 KLM, the national Dutch airline turned to its supplier, Moonen Packaging, for a new idea in on-board coffee and tea cups. Working with Nature-Works, Moonen created a paper cup coated with Ingeo brand plastic made from cornstarch. KLM's new Bio-Cups not only provide environmental benefits, they are also lighter and they pack and store better than the traditional foam cups used in-flight.[26]

Encourage suppliers to provide solutions to packaging and waste challenges

Guided by the Environmental Defense Fund, a leading environmental group, in 1990 McDonald's worked with James River Corp. to replace foam clamshells with source-reduced "quiltwraps" as an alternative to recycling polystyrene clamshells. This groundbreaking alliance was the exception then, but today it's the rule for suppliers of all stripes to actively work with retailers and manufacturers to reformulate products and packaging with green in mind, because nearly 20 years later packaging is still on the hot seat.

A number of packaging-related coalitions have since sprung up to deal with the many challenges of reducing packaging while protecting contents until they fulfill their intended purpose. The Sustainable Packaging Coalition of Charlottesville, Virginia, brings together end-product manufacturers with packaging suppliers to share best practices and designs, support innovation, and provide education, resources, and tools that can lead to environmentally and economically robust packaging. The Paperboard Packaging Alliance and the Corrugated Packaging Alliance have teamed up to raise awareness for the benefits of using renewable raw materials and for recycling at high rates through a Responsible Packaging Campaign. One of the 2009 Greener Package Awards went to Green Toys and its packaging supplier, Unisource, for using 100% recyclable corrugated box packaging for its tea sets, sandbox play sets and other toys made from recycled plastics.[27]

Encourage suppliers to provide innovative solutions to energy and carbon challenges

With the cost of a barrel of crude oil steadily increasing during 2007 (before hitting all-time highs during the summer of 2008) and the prospect of government restrictions on carbon emissions looming in the not-too-distant future,

Continental Airlines is just one of many airlines looking to tread lightly in the skies. In March 2008, they announced their intention to work with General Electric and Boeing to identify and test more sustainable fuel sources.

The *New Rules* Checklist

Ask the following questions to assess opportunities for enlisting the support of suppliers for your company's sustainable product and packaging initiatives.

- Do we know the sources of all of our product ingredients?

- Do our suppliers understand our environmental goals?

- How much do we know about our suppliers' environmental commitments and initiatives?

- How can we partner with our manufacturing suppliers to "green" our entire supply chain?

- Do we have a forum for regular and ongoing communication with our suppliers about green issues?

- Do we have a supplier scorecard to effectively assess and measure each supplier's eco-credentials?

- Do we know the new materials and technologies our suppliers are testing and developing that we can incorporate into our own new product and packaging design?

Government

Governments have a direct stake in eliminating and preventing the pollution created by consumer products and services. Federal, state, and local governments develop environmental policy, laws, and regulations that can impact directly or indirectly on the products and services of suppliers and end-product manufacturers. Government has the power to subsidize, tax, regulate, or otherwise heavily influence industry processes and product design based on their sustainability or their external cost to the environment. But not all government officials have a background in business, much less the technical aspects of product design and service delivery, and this can result in misguided policies that can unnecessarily hurt industry. Working *with* lawmakers instead of *against* them can help corporations prepare for and reduce the risks associated with legal challenges such as bans on chemicals with a negative perception or laws that might add costs to an already expensive process. By working together with government representatives, industry can take part in the dialogue to ensure new regulations are well informed and that new laws are balanced.

Government also has the ability to allocate financial support to projects and businesses that can stimulate the economy; of late, financial stimulus money has been earmarked in large measure to green businesses and technologies. So it behooves green marketers to check out available funding.

Strategies for partnering with the government

Participate in voluntary programs

Since the early 1990s, federal, state, and local governments have discovered that working with industry can yield better results than wielding the traditional "command and control" sledgehammer. So they have crafted a number of voluntary programs that benefit both industry and the environment.

These voluntary programs can extend an unbeatable package of incentives for businesses looking to control their environmental destinies. Business partners enjoy increased flexibility in meeting existing laws and regulations and can gain access to expertise and technical resources that can lead to competitive advantage, new marketing opportunities, and enhanced credibility and public recognition for their efforts. By participating in these programs, chances of being caught off guard when new regulatory laws go into effect are minimized. Voluntary participation is recognized by the government and this can lend credibility to member companies. Labeling programs such as ENERGY STAR and the USDA's Organic seal have been discussed earlier in this book. Other voluntary programs help businesses make environmental improvements cost-effectively. Examples include the EPA's WasteWise and WaterWise programs that help businesses to reduce and recycle municipal solid waste or conserve water. Many of these programs have awards components that can build recognition for one's participation and achievements. ENERGY STAR Partner of the Year is a good example.

Lobby for stricter regulations

Sometimes businesses can gain competitive advantage by lobbying for strict government regulations they are prepared to accommodate, reflectively positively on an organization and its brands. For instance, in 2006 Philips, the global lighting and consumer products giant, was struggling to get people to pay the hefty premiums required for its Halogena-IR energy-sipping light bulbs that last approximately four times longer than traditional incandescents. So Philips initiated a lobbying effort to increase light bulb efficiency standards and was rewarded when Congress passed a new energy bill, the Energy Independence and Security Act of 2007 (set to take effect in 2012) which will increase energy efficiency standards enough to eventually phase out traditional incandescent light bulbs. It is slated to save the United States an estimated $18 billion per year in energy costs – and guarantees Philips a future market for its energy-efficient bulbs without attracting the negative attention that usually comes with lobbying for self-serving regulations.[28] GE's CEO Jeffrey Immelt is now imploring government to regulate greenhouse gas emissions. His motivation? The certainty that companies need to make multi-billion-dollar bets on the types of cleaner energy technologies that his company stands ready to sell.

Partner on new product ideas

Do you have a new product idea and need the seed money to get it from bench to market? Partner with government agencies that can provide a ready source of new product technologies, funding, and expertise for meeting your goals. Numerous government organizations provide financial and technical support for environmental innovations, among them, the U.S. Department of Housing and Urban Development's Sustainable Housing and Communities Program, which offers local communities technical and financial support for sustainability projects including green commercial buildings, water-conservation initiatives, and local public transportation initiatives.[29]

The U.S. Department of Agriculture is looking to support the development of biobased products as a way to help boost the farm economy and reduce carbon emissions. Among many companies that have received support, Metabolix of Cambridge, Massachusetts received a $350,000 grant to develop biobased, biodegradable resins suitable for blow-molding into bottles. According to the American Plastics Council, more than two million tons of high-density polyethylene (HDPE) plastics are used annually for blow-molded bottles, containers, and other types of packaging, so shifting to biobased resins could make a big difference.[30]

In addition to awarding the DfE eco-label described in Chapter 7, the EPA's Design for the Environment (DfE) Partnership for Safer Chemistry works with industry to help develop safer alternatives to a wide range of products including automotive refinishing, chemical formulators, detergents, furniture and printed circuit board flame retardancy, nail polish, and wire and cable.

The *New Rules* Checklist

Ask the following questions to assess opportunities for enlisting the support of government stakeholders.

- ○ What legislation is in effect or under way at the federal, state, and local levels that will affect our brands and company?

- ○ What steps can we take to promote self-regulation and avoid mandatory regulations?

- ○ What opportunities might exist to gain competitive advantage by lobbying for stiff regulations?

- ○ What voluntary programs being conducted by governments can we join to help to preempt legislation, gain recognition and advantage, and set standards in our industry?

Environmental groups

Everyone's heard of the National Audubon Society and the Nature Conservancy, but there are actually more than 12,000 environmental organizations in the U.S. alone,[31] and of many different kinds. Some address a specific cause such as lobbying for pure air, cleaning up the Great Lakes, protecting spotted owls, or expanding their city's municipal recycling program. Others conduct research, influence policy, provide technical support, raise awareness, or meet a short-term goal. Ranging from local organizations of two or more people to global groups with 10,000-plus members, environmental groups are typically membership-based nonprofit organizations relying on fundraising and financial contributions from members and donors to achieve their mission.

Once scorned as extremists, the mainstreaming of green has made it acceptable practice for environmental groups to help businesses and governments improve their environmental sustainability. Many environmental groups now realize that, since business and government control many of the resources and yield much of the power in a market-based economy, joining together in a market-focused approach is the most effective way to clean up the environment and pave the way for a more sustainable society. While some extremist groups still adopt an antagonistic approach to working with industry, and may even be the first to encourage a boycott of products, a growing number of environmental groups actively cooperate with business leaders to effect change by acting as a sounding board, helping them improve their environmental policies and practices, and even assisting in the development and promotion of their brands.

Strategies for partnering with environmental groups

In working with environmental groups, one naturally thinks of cause-related marketing as discussed in Chapter 6. But other constructive partnership opportunities exist, starting with leveraging special expertise, working positively to protect supplies of new materials and create markets for worthy products, and strategic corporate philanthropy.

Leverage the special expertise of specific environmental groups

For-profit companies, expert in creating economic value, have much to learn from nonprofits that excel in creating and measuring environmental and social value. Happily, under the new rules, many environmental groups are now willing to share their unique expertise with well-intentioned businesses. Some nonprofits, for example, know how to best protect endangered species or nurture the forests and this can translate into innovative ways to improve a company's sustainability performance. Constructive partnerships can add credibility to a brand's image and provide businesses with important protection from environmental groups with opposing perspectives and media attacks that can mar a company's reputation.

In 2002, McDonald's, the world's largest food-service retailer, enlisted Conservation International (CI) as a partner to help develop ways to incorporate sustainability into their massive supply chain. CI developed an "environmental scorecard" for the international suppliers of McDonald's to measure and rate their use of water and energy, solid waste, and air emissions.[32]

Sometimes even former environmental foes can turn into allies. In August 2009, Kimberly-Clark, the makers of Cottonelle, Kleenex, and Scott, announced a partnership with Greenpeace to meet a lofty goal to obtain 100% of the company's wood fiber for tissue products from environmentally responsible sources. Officially ending their longstanding Kleercut campaign against the company, Greenpeace will assist Kimberly-Clark in promoting forest conservation and sourcing sustainably harvested and recycled FSC-certified fibers for its beloved brands. In the words of Scott Paul, Green-peace's USA Forest Campaign Director, "These revised standards are proof that when responsible companies and Greenpeace come together, the results can be good for business and great for the planet. Kimberly-Clark's efforts are a challenge to competitors. I hope other companies pay close attention."[33]

Protect supplies of raw materials and create new markets for sustainable products

Former owners of the Gorton's brands, Unilever, who saw the stocks of many of its most popular fish species in decline, partnered with the World Wildlife Fund (WWF, now its name outside North America) in 1995 to cre-ate the Marine Stewardship Council (MSC) and help develop sustainable fishing practices. An increasing number of grocery stores in both the U.S. (A&P, Lunds & Byerly's, Target, Wal-Mart, Wegmans, Whole Foods Market, and more) and the UK (Marks & Spencer, Sainsbury's, Waitrose, and others) now use the blue MSC eco-label on fish products to help customers identity seafood from fisheries that meet their strict environmental standards. The MSC also operates Chain of Custody certification that ensures that every company in a particular supply chain that takes ownership of MSC-certi-fied fish, from the dock onward, does not mix certified with uncertified fish. In late 2008, the University of Notre Dame in Indiana became the first U.S. university to obtain Chain of Custody certification for all fish served in on-campus dining facilities.[34]

For the most part, publishers print books on paper that is largely com-posed of virgin forest fibers because paper containing recycled content is not widely available in either book grade or bulk quantity. In 2001, sensing an opportunity to create a new market by meeting the needs of the indus-try, Canopy, a Canadian nonprofit dedicated to protecting forests by work-ing with businesses to create sustainable supply chains, collaborated with San Francisco-based New Leaf Paper company to develop environmentally sustainable paper stock for book publishing. In 2001, author Alice Munro became the first "big name" author to use New Leaf Paper's 100% post-con-sumer recycled, chlorine-free paper for the Canadian edition of her book *Hateship, Friendship, Courtship, Loveship, Marriage*. The Canadian edition of J.K. Rowling's bestselling *Harry Potter and the Order of the Phoenix* also used this new environmentally sustainable paper, proving to the publishing industry that high-quality recycled paper stock could be both mass-produced and reliably developed while remaining cost-effective. Since then, New Leaf Paper and Canopy have worked together to shift the paper-hungry book, magazine, and newspaper publishing sectors in Canada and the U.S. away from endangered forests and chlorine-bleached paper to focus on incorporating forest protection and sustainability into the paper supply chain.[35]

Leverage corporate philanthropy strategically on behalf of the environment

Corporate philanthropy, consisting of deductible gifts made through a foundation arm or at least noted as such by a corporation in IRS filings, has historically been an effective marketing and public relations tool. Donations to charities and the arts, for example, have long helped such major corporations as ExxonMobil, IBM, and Altria (formally Philip Morris) burnish their leadership images and make friends with society's influentials. Although it can be criticized as a form of propaganda, environmental giving can help companies strategically, by contributing to solution finding on issues that affect their businesses while creating more favorable impressions for a company overall – with employees, financial institutions, and consumers. According to the IEG Sponsorship Report, almost all Fortune 500 companies make charitable donations, with 25% of these committing to community service and social betterment in their mission statements. In 2005, U.S. corporations donated more than $12 billion to nonprofits, and invested $1.6 billion in cause-related marketing programs with nonprofits.[36] These donations provide not only a tax deduction, but also an opportunity to strategically align with environmental and social causes based on employee and customer interests. And, even with the expected decrease of funding in the aftermath of the 2008–2010 recession, corporate commitment to sustainability and environmental sponsorship is expected to remain a part of these organizations' core values.

One example of strategic corporate philanthropy is Bank of America's sponsorship of the Climate Change exhibit at the American Museum of Natural History in New York City in 2008,[37] which reinforces the bank's overall initiatives to reduce the impacts of climate change associated with their massive real estate holdings around the world. (Buildings create more global warming emissions than cars.) Cargill's financial support of the Nature Conservancy, Wildlife Conservation Society, Conservation International, and World Wildlife Fund, among others[38] – all credible groups that can help protect the environment where their grain grows – supports preservation of biodiversity in addition to initiatives that create bioplastics out of corn.

Representing another example, in 2002 the Home Depot, the world's largest seller of wood products, announced it would donate $1 million over five years to the Nature Conservancy to assist in the fight against illegal logging and promotion of sustainable timber programs in Indonesia. The donation was part of the retailer's push to identify the sources of all wood products sold on its shelves. The Nature Conservancy used these funds to launch a pilot sustainable forestry and timber certification program. Since announcing its donation to the Nature Conservancy, the Home Depot has reduced its imports of Indonesian wood products by 70%, and now less than 1% of the wood sold in its stores is from Indonesia.[39]

This chapter concludes our discussion of the new ways that today's consumer demands are changing the rules of green marketing, and the seven strategies for successful green marketing laid out in Chapter 3. While it may seem a tall order to address all the new rules successfully, some companies are doing a most laudable job of integrating green into the life-cycles of their products, instilling a green culture into their companies, and communicating their sustainable brands with credibility and impact. Two such sustainable brand leaders, Starbucks and Timberland, are profiled in depth in the next chapter.

The *New Rules* Checklist

Use the following checklist to assess opportunities for enlisting the support of environmental group stakeholders.

- ○ Which environmental groups can lead us to sustainable approaches to running our business? Help underscore our credibility? Protect supplies? Help foster new markets for sustainable products?

- ○ Which environmental groups have special expertise that can help us develop or refine products with minimal eco-impact?

- ○ What opportunities exist to conduct strategic corporate philanthropy with environmental groups?

785266 000297

Two sustainability leaders that superbly address the new rules

The new rules for addressing the demands of today's sustainability-minded consumers not only represent a seismic shift in communication strategy but also now require a thorough, life-cycle approach to product development and the ability to forge constructive coalitions with a wide array of new corporate stakeholders. While most businesses are still learning the new rules and trying to adapt accordingly, some business are leading the way, pioneering new strategies, and enjoying the myriad benefits. While many companies, large and small, fit into this category, two have been chosen to be profiled in depth in this chapter: Starbucks and Timberland.

Of course, no company can be considered 100% sustainable – and these companies have their eco-shortcomings, too – but I believe that the progress made by these two firms can represent a model for others who follow in their steps and, I hope, a platform from which to build on even these leaders' efforts. Consumer loyalty to these companies and their offerings proves that new sustainable branding strategies can form the basis of an enduring business and provide leverage in the face of formidable competition. They superbly demonstrate how new strategies of green marketing can create jobs, build brand loyalty, and return hefty profits, all the while contributing to a more sustainable society.

**Addressing
the New Rules**

The Timberland Company

In 2009, Timberland had over $1.3 billion in sales, more than 200 stores in 15 countries – and an environmental consciousness that reflects the aspirations of customers who appreciate the high quality of the company's footwear and apparel. And it all starts with CEO Jeffrey Swartz. Now leading the company his grandfather acquired in 1952, Swartz actively and strategically imprints his environmental and social values on the company. Passionate and visible within the environmental business community, his position on the environment is perhaps best summed up in the philosophy behind Timberland's Mountain Athletics® shoe line: "Enjoying the outdoors to the fullest, and leaving it the way you found it." Swartz believes that he has a responsibility to be proactive in minimizing his company's environmental impact and maximizing its benefit to the community. So Timberland does the right thing in order that its customers (who have good reason to care about the environment and their communities) will be educated accordingly – and will reward Swartz by choosing his company's products over those of his competitors.

Swartz's philosophy that "doing well and doing good are inextricably linked" demonstrates that Timberland is about more than just profit and exemplifies his company's strategy at a time when consumer purchases and trust in business are low. He believes that the current economic recession will strengthen his company and provide an opportunity for the brand to reinforce its status as an environmental leader in its industry.

An emphasis on cutting carbon

From its offices to its manufacturing plants to its retail stores, all of Timberland's operations are conducted with an eye toward minimizing environmental impact, along with the goal of achieving carbon neutrality in Timberland facilities and employee travel by 2010. The company uses multiple, leading-edge strategies to reduce its overall carbon footprint.

First, Timberland aims to reduce overall energy demand (which in turn yields savings). At their Stratham, New Hampshire global headquarters and the European distribution center in the Netherlands, activities such as installing skylights and replacing the outdated lighting system with energy-efficient alternatives saved 460,000 kWh of energy in its first year. An innovative new roof was installed at the New Hampshire headquarters to make it easier and cheaper to cool the building.

Second, Timberland has been able to transfer over 12% of its energy to renewable sources. Wind and other renewable sources provide 100% of the electricity needed to run Timberland's European distribution center. A $3.5 million, 400 kW solar array at Timberland's distribution center in Ontario, California provides about half of the facility's electricity – with the added bonus of preventing hundreds of thousands of pounds of greenhouse gas. In a 2006 press release announcing the Ontario solar array project Jeffrey Swartz said, "We are fully committed to reducing our environmental impact and decreasing dependency on non-renewable resources by finding alternative ways to produce energy."

Timberland enlisted the support of the Business for Social Responsibility (BSR) Clean Cargo initiative to develop tools for tracking carbon emissions. Timberland applies these tools to evaluate carrier and transportation choices for transporting products from factories to its distribution centers. These efforts to reduce its own carbon footprint have led Timberland to consider the footprint of its employees, specifically emissions associated with employee commuting. Timberland created prime reserved parking spaces at its corporate headquarters for employees who drive fuel-efficient vehicles or carpool. To further assist in the reduction of the carbon footprint associated with its employees' activities, in 2008 the New Hampshire headquarters began a "Victory Garden" from which employees purchase vegetables. Employees are able to get fresh produce without the food miles and all proceeds from the sale go to a local food bank.

Timberland's industry-leading carbon reduction strategies have not only significantly reduced its environmental impact (between 2006 and 2009 emissions reduced by 36%) but have also returned hefty financial savings; combined energy savings and reductions in business travel are helping the company save over a million dollars per year.

A social conscience, too

Timberland's environmental activities are complemented by a strong social conscience, embodied in numerous programs that engage its youthful target audience while providing opportunities for employees to develop their leadership skills and appreciate the natural environment.

First, as a global brand and a global citizen, Timberland recognizes that they have a responsibility to ensure that their products are produced in an ethical way. Their Code of Conduct helps them ensure fair, safe and non-discriminatory workplaces for their 175,000 workers in 290+ factories in 35 countries, and they aim to create positive change in communities where their products are made.

For more than 20 years, Timberland employees have been given paid time off and "service sabbaticals" to perform community service, usually associated with the outdoors. Community service "challenges [the] employees' potential, builds strong teams and galvanizes [the] company's greatest resource as a united force for change."[1] Employee volunteer time has benefited over 200 community organizations in 30 countries. By the end of 2009, more than 600,000 hours of meaningful change had been "clocked" by Timberland employees in the service of local communities and the environment.

Timberland's programs support a wide variety of social and environmental initiatives, creating goodwill in local communities and reflecting positively on the brand. For example, since 1989 Timberland has supported City Year, a Boston-based nonprofit that unites young people of all backgrounds for a year of full-time service, giving them skills and opportunities to change the world. Jeff Swartz served as chair of the group's board of trustees between 1994 and 2002, and for 20 years Timberland has provided uniforms for City Year's corps members.

The majority of Timberland's cash and product donations currently reinforces the company's Earthkeeping agenda. Current partners include Yele Haiti and Trees for the Future, which create and maintain sustainable fruit tree nurseries in the outskirts of Gonaives as part of a broader effort to reforest Haiti. Timberland also works with World Wildlife Fund's tree planting program in Nepal and Green Net, a Japan-based NGO focused on stopping the desertification of China's Horqin Desert. Since 2005, Timberland has supported Green Net and has sent volunteers to China to help plant trees and restore the formerly rich grasslands in that area.

Other company-wide programs serve as morale-boosters and leadership opportunities for employees. For example, Serv-a-palooza is an annual daylong service event that takes place at Timberland locations around the globe and focuses on improving community green spaces. Over a hundred projects get carried out in upwards of 20 countries, and include cleaning up public spaces in Lawrence, Massachusetts, to planting trees in an urban forest in Bangkok, Thailand. Outreach programs such as these not only signify positive social change, but also translate into happy employees; Timberland is consistently listed by magazines such as *Fortune* and *Working Mother* as one of the best places in America to work.

Products with minimal impact

Timberland's products combine an outdoor aesthetic, quality, and functionality characterized by their durability and ability to withstand the elements,
and are made with the environment in mind.

Timberland seeks to reduce its environmental impact at different stages
of its products' life-cycle, starting with concerted efforts to reduce the
impact of leather – a key ingredient in the company's signature boots. That's
why, in 2005, Timberland banded together with the UK-based BLC Leather
Technology Centre to convene a cross-brand organization called the Leather
Working Group (LWG), whose members work together toward the common
goal of better environmental performance of tanneries. Timberland's Earth-
keepers™ product line is specially designed to represent its environmental
values in actions. The products feature organic, recycled, and renewable
materials. Starting in the fall of 2009, Earthkeepers outsoles incorporate
Green Rubber™, a recycled, devulcanized rubber made from waste material
by Malaysia-based Green Rubber Inc., using a new proprietary technology.
Timberland estimates that the fall 2009 Earthkeepers collection will use 50
tons of Green Rubber material – cutting down on the need to use some 42
tons of virgin rubber. The company launched a Design for Disassembly boot
and boat shoe that can be returned to any Timberland store for recycling at
the end of their life.

Aside from shoes and boots, the Earthkeepers line-up includes clothing, outerwear, hats, and bags – some of which incorporate organic, recycled,
and/or renewable materials. Recycled PET plastic is used to create the nylon
for Earthkeepers backpacks and messenger bags, as well as the majority of
Earthkeepers knit scarves and hats. Organic cotton is used in the scarves,
knitted hats, T-shirts, and baseball caps; the wool jackets incorporate 50%
recycled wool; and the belt even uses small recycled leather panels.

Although Timberland products have in the past transcended the boundaries of their traditional market and emerged prominently in the "hip hop"
fashion realm, Timberland's marketing strategy is aimed at a loyal base of
16–35-year-old consumers who appreciate its functional products and the
company's values. Timberland recognizes two types of customers: the genuine outdoorsy types and working-class people who appreciate the functionality of their products – and those who wish they were, or simply want to look
the part.

Timberland's retail stores (the newest of which are LEED-certified) have
an outdoorsy feel – think exposed timber and earth tones. The use of virgin
products and toxic materials is creatively minimized: existing concrete floors
are polished, wood fixturing is made from recycled or FSC lumber, and wall
paints and floor finishes contain very low or no volatile organic compounds.

Store décor is customized to their locality: a New York City store, for instance, sports an entire wall devoted to depicting green spaces in the five boroughs.

Communicating green

Timberland's Earthkeeper advertising campaign capitalizes on its target clientele's outdoorsy yet fashionable aspirations, while challenging them to take responsibility for the environment. The company's ad campaign, launched in 2008, draws in consumers with emotional, visual representations of Timberland's slogan, "Take it all on™." Ads promoting new Earthkeepers products underscore the connection with nature with such promises as: "Wear new Earthkeepers™ [footwear] made with recycled materials or nature might get you back" and "Wear new Earthkeepers™ [footwear] made with recycled materials and nature might return the favor."

In addition to having an informative website, Timberland uses the younger generation's connectivity through a corporate presence in every social media arena, from Facebook pages to YouTube channels, to spread messages of social change. 2,400 customers now follow Jeff Swartz on Twitter. The company's environment blog covers topics such as green book reviews, green legislation, and updates on how Timberland is becoming greener. Entries are written by various members of the Timberland team, including CEO Jeff Swartz.

Cause-related marketing is an important part of Timberland's strategy, too. In one partnership, Timberland teamed up with actor Don Cheadle (of *Hotel Rwanda* fame) to create limited-edition boots, boot tags, and shirts with "Not on My Watch" and "Save Darfur" messages to raise awareness and inspire action to help stop genocide in Sudan, with profits going to AmeriCares.

Transparency

Timberland is a pioneer in transparent communications, setting standards that have become a model for others inside and outside the industry. Most notably, in the fall of 2006, Timberland pioneered the use of nutrition-type environmental labels, placing them on over 30 million shoeboxes. In the spring of 2007, to supplement the "nutrition" label, it rolled out its Green Index® rating system for select footwear, which calculates product-specific environmental impacts for each pair of Timberland shoes (see Fig. 9.1).

OUR FOOTPRINT *NOTRE EMPREINTE*

Climate Impact *Incidences sur le climat*	
Use of renewable energy	
Utilisation d'énergie renouvelable	11.63%
Chemicals Used *Produits chimiques utilisés*	
PVC-free *Sans PVC*	85.5%
Resource Consumption *Consommation de ressources*	
Eco-conscious materials	
Matériaux écologiques	26.5%
Recycled content of shoebox	
Contenu en matières recyclées de la boîte de chaussures	100%
Trees planted through 2009	
Nombre d'arbres plantés en 2009	1,118,538

PRODUCT FOOTPRINT
EMPREINTE DU PRODUIT

Green Index® Rating *Classification de L'Indice vert^{MD}*

Lower Impact	Higher Impact
Peu d'Impact	Impact élevé

0	**6**	10

For more information visit www.timberland.com/footprint
Pour plus d'information : www. timberland.com/footprint

TIM-NGI6

Figure 9.1 **Timberland's Green Index® label**

Reprinted with permission of Timberland

The label comprises two sections: "Our Footprint" delineates corporate-related impacts including climate impact (denoted by the amount of renewable energy used by Timberland footwear overall); chemicals used (the percentage of Timberland footwear that is PVC-free); resource consumption (the percentage of Timberland footwear that uses "eco-conscious materials," as well as the percentage of recycled content of the shoebox itself); and the number of trees Timberland has planted to date. The second section, "Product Footprint," provides product specific environmental information including, where available, the Green Index® rating.

The company plans to expand the use of the Green Index rating to all of its footwear in 2012, and to adapt these labels for use on its apparel and other products in the future, with the goal of increasing transparency on the environmental impacts of its products. It is also partnering with the Outdoor Industry Association to develop standard environmental metrics for outdoor industry products.

Results

Timberland's attention to quality, passion for the environment and society, and transparency has earned it a strong customer following willing to pay its premiums, even through the current economic recession, and allow it to be poised for continued long-term growth. The company has also reaped benefits in terms of its positive reputation and goodwill in the communities where employees work and serve through their volunteer projects. For instance, according to Michael Brown, the CEO and founder of City Year, a national service organization which engages young people as tutors and mentors, and long-time Timberland partner:

> Every one of the 1,550 diverse young people in service with City Year across America annually is a testament to Timberland's sup-

port for City Year. Timberland provides each young leader with a signature red jacket and a pair of boots that are a symbol of hope and help to tens of thousands of urban students in high-poverty schools, and to communities nationwide. Timberland has been essential to building every aspect of City Year for 20 years. Its people have joined us in service around the globe, our partnership has been highlighted by the Harvard Business School and we seek to redefine what a company and nonprofit can do to change the world together.[2]

Timberland has also received numerous awards and recognitions. In 2009 the Cause Marketing Forum granted Timberland a Golden Halo award for its goal of being carbon-neutral by 2010 and its policy of encouraging employee volunteerism. *Fortune* magazine rated Timberland number 78 of the "100 Best Companies to Work For" in 2007, and it has been in the top 100 ever since the list's inception in 1998. Timberland was also a 2007 recipient of the EPA's Green Power Leadership Award for its voluntary use of green power. And, in 2010, Timberland was named one of *Outside* magazine's "Best Places to Work."

Perhaps the greatest indicator of success comes straight from Jeffrey Swartz, who says,

With passion, innovation and a sense of purpose, Timberland has sought to improve our communities, our environment and the condition of those beside whom we live and work. We have improved as a company and as a community of individuals through the wisdom, humility and strong sense of justice we have gained . . . and continue to gain every step in our journey.[3]

Addressing
the New Rules

Starbucks

Starbucks proves that a global company can turn a proactive approach to sustainability into a strategic and profitable part of its brand. Key to its successful strategy is to actively listen to, interact with, and act on the expectations of its customers, who possess a strong environmental and social conscience, and to constantly demonstrate reductions in the environmental footprint of its operations. In the words of Ben Packard, Vice President, Global Sustainability, at Starbucks:

> Consumer brands, while they may not be heavily regulated or political, are on the front lines. We see over 50,000,000 customers in our stores each week, and interact with even more of them online. They give us great ideas about what we should be doing to reduce our environmental impact. We need to take that passion and mobilize it, because consumers are increasingly committed to spending their money with companies that support the global issues that they care about.

Starbucks is that medium and that company. Here's their sustainability story.

With over 16,000 stores in over 50 countries on six continents, Starbucks has many reasons to be oriented toward sustainability. Volume-wise, coffee is the second most traded commodity in the world (behind oil) and living conditions for coffee workers tend to be below par. Starbucks consumes millions of disposable cups, coffee grounds, and packaging each day along with the water used in making coffee, not to mention the 37 gallons of water embedded in the production of each cup of coffee (52.83 gallons for each latte) and in their operations. It all adds up to a significant environmental footprint, and all because of an innocuous-looking little cup of coffee!

Company: Addressing environmental and social considerations

Starbucks' history of environmental and corporate social responsibility (CSR) stretches a long way. Acknowledging a need to contribute to the communities where their coffee is produced, in 1991 Starbucks began contributing to CARE, an international development and relief organization that supports coffee-producing communities. By 1995 Starbucks became one of CARE's largest donors, and they are still in partnership today.

In 1992 Starbucks wrote an environmental mission statement and created an environmental affairs department that was charged with developing environmentally responsible corporate policies and minimizing the company's footprint. The department was also active in educating partners through the company's Green Team initiatives and using environmental purchasing guidelines. One of the department's first initiatives consisted of using recycled paper sleeves instead of double cupping. In 1999 Starbucks named its first senior vice president of its newly created CSR department, which grew from one person to fourteen in its first two years.

In 2008, the company launched its Starbucks™ Shared Planet™ initiative, integrating its social and environmental commitments to doing things that are good for the people and the planet. From the way it purchases coffee, to minimizing the company's environmental footprint, to being involved in local communities, it is a recommitment to core values, about using its global size for good, and getting its consumers and employees educated, involved, and excited about giving back. Starbucks' Shared Planet platform divides its environmental and social initiatives into three categories with specific measurable goals within each area: (1) ethical sourcing, (2) environmental stewardship, and (3) community involvement.

Environment

Since Starbucks relies on agricultural products for most of its raw materials and supplies, it makes good business sense for them to steward the environment. Under the environmental section of its Shared Planet platform, Starbucks includes products, operations, and buildings. In 2008, Starbucks outlined a series of environmental targets it is committed to reaching by 2015. Its goals are outlined as follows:

Products

- 100% of cups will be reusable or recyclable by 2015
- A 100%-recyclable cup will be developed by 2012.

Operations

- 25% of cups in its stores will be reusable
- Recycling will be available in all of its stores
- 50% of the energy used in company-owned stores will be derived from renewable resources by 2010.

- Greenhouse gas emissions will be reduced by making company-owned stores 25% more energy-efficient by 2010

- It will accomplish a significant reduction in water usage

- It will champion tropical rainforest protection as a solution to climate change.

Buildings

- All new construction will be LEED-certified and locally sourced by 2010.

Social

Starbucks is pioneering the way toward ethically sourced coffee. There may be smaller brands in the marketplace with higher percentages of fair trade coffee within their portfolios, but no company has bought more ethically sourced coffee or done more to help promote it than Starbucks.

One of Starbucks' core beliefs is that a better cup of coffee is one that also helps create a better future for farmers and a more stable climate for the planet. In this spirit, Starbucks began purchasing fair trade coffee in 2000 and became the largest buyer in 2009 when it doubled its purchases to 40 million pounds of certified coffee. At the same time, Starbucks continued to build on its own Coffee and Farmer Equity (C.A.F.E.) Practices, developed with Conservation International, the global environmental group, in 2003. C.A.F.E. Practices is a set of stringent guidelines to ensure that Starbucks' coffee purchases are ethically sourced by monitoring hiring practices. These include ensuring biological pest and disease control, and protecting water sources and minimizing water consumption of coffee suppliers, among other things.

Starbucks bought 385 million pounds of coffee in 2008, 77% of which was sourced through C.A.F.E. Practices. Starbucks' goal is to have 100% of its coffee responsibly grown and ethically traded by 2015. Its other goals in this area are:

- To invest in a better future for farmers and their communities by increasing loans to farmers by 60%, from $12.5 to $20 million

- To combat climate change by offering farmers incentives to prevent deforestation, starting with pilot programs in Sumatra, Indonesia, and Chiapas, Mexico.

To help ensure long-term supplies of its products, Starbucks has also committed to improving the lives of people in coffee-growing communities. Accordingly, it has set up the Small Farmer Sustainability Initiative (SFSI) by partnering with the Fairtrade Labelling Organizations (FLO) and TransFair USA to create a small-scale coffee farmer loan program. These loans help farmers survive the current global economic crisis and emerge as stronger business partners. Starbucks has already invested $12.5 million which small-scale coffee farmers have access to, but it has pledged to expand the fund to $20 million by 2015.

Starbucks has also developed Farmer Support Centers in Latin American and Africa. There are currently two support centers: one opened in Costa Rica in 2004, and a second in Rwanda in 2009. The Farmer Support Centers provide a team of experts in soil management and field-crop production to enhance the quality of coffee and improve farmer yields. Through the centers Starbucks has also committed to support women coffee growers (and help reduce extreme poverty) through continued training and professional development.

Empowered employees

Employees have always been at the center of Starbucks' commitment to sustainability; founder Howard Schultz's philosophy is to "treat people like family, and they will be loyal and give their all." Among its many industry-leading employee initiatives is a generous benefits package for both full- and part-time employees. Eligible employees, or "partners," receive full health benefits and a share in the company's growth through the "Bean Stock" stock option plan that allows them to buy shares of Starbucks common stock at 85% of the market value.

Starbucks also makes an effort to include its employees in its CSR initiatives. For example, two years after Hurricane Katrina hit New Orleans, when public and media attention on the city had long since dissipated, Starbucks flew 10,000 partners into the area and committed 50,000 hours, the largest amount committed by any single company. Later it was in front of the same group that Howard Schultz announced Starbucks' Shared Planet targets and new initiatives.

Sustainably innovative products

In order to keep up with its Shared Planet commitments and to stay ahead of the curve, Starbucks sells its ethically sourced drinks in containers meant to be as environmentally responsible as possible. In 2004, Starbucks put itself on the recycling scene by launching the first-ever hot cup approved by the U.S. Food and Drug Administration (FDA). The hot cup is made with 10% recycled material. Although 10% sounds small, the numbers add up quickly with volume as high as Starbucks: this cup eliminates 5 million pounds of solid waste, 11,300 tons of wood, 58 billion British Thermal Units (BTUs) of energy, and 47 million gallons of waste-water a year.

To help plan for the 100% recyclable cup scheduled to launch in 2012, in May 2009, Starbucks convened a Cup Summit, attended by 30 cup, cup-stock, and coating manufacturers, recyclers, and waste managers and an equal number of Starbucks partners. In September 2009, the company launched a pilot program in seven New York stores which examined the possibility of collecting and recycling coffee cups in the same waste stream as corrugated cardboard; its goal is to enable the recycling of all sorts of other paper food packaging, making Starbucks the leader and standard-setter in this industry.

Starbucks is also looking to make the plastic cups in which they sell more than one billion cold beverages per year more environmentally sound. In 2008, Starbucks commissioned a group of life-cycle-analysis scientists to study the environmental impact of the plastic cups. They found that changing the cups from polyethylene terephthalate (PET) to polypropylene (PP) would use 15% less plastic overall and emit 45% less greenhouse gases in production, so in 2008, Starbucks began the changeover to PP with the launch of its new Vivanno smoothie cups.

With an eye to reducing waste in its stores, Starbucks is relaunching an aggressive campaign to get customers to bring in reusable cups by providing a 10-cent discount off their drink. The company is also restocking reusable mugs. With Starbucks' new iPhone application, which customers can use to pay for drinks by scanning a digital barcode, the company gets one step closer to eliminating plastic in its stores altogether. And Starbucks has also found a way to reduce the 7 million tons of coffee grounds headed for landfills each year by creating the Grounds for your Garden program which offers customers and others spent coffee grounds for use in their gardens.

Green marketing and communications focused on consumers and transparency

Starbucks' marketing integrates sustainability initiatives with communications that specifically focus on interacting with consumers and transparency, in line with the needs of its Millennial and Generation X customers and partner (employee) expectations that the businesses they patronize and work for embrace sustainability and social responsibility. Starbucks' response is embodied in a website and two high-profile campaigns directed at its very global, very mainstream audiences.

Starbucks makes customers feel a part of the brand through a highly informative and interactive website where they can learn about and participate in five CSR efforts. The (Product) RED page explains what Starbucks is doing to support people living with AIDS in Africa. A separate Shared Planet site details Starbucks' commitments to ethical sourcing, environmental stewardship, and community involvement, with informative videos and opportunities to get involved. There is also a link to a report on progress of Starbucks' Shared Planet initiative,[4] written in line with guidelines provided by the Global Reporting Initiative. Finally, a My Starbucks Idea site, allows customers and partners to give suggestions about what they would like to see done in a variety of areas such as products and CSR. Starbucks responds on its Ideas in Action page, where it reports the ideas it has launched or is currently considering.

In addition, a high-profile media campaign consisting of traditional paid and social media highlights the brand's values and overall quality and value. With the tagline "You and Starbucks: It's Bigger Than Coffee," it draws a clear connection between consumers and Starbucks' CSR activities and communicates what "responsibly grown and ethically traded" means, a fundamental part of Starbucks' core brand. This connection to something larger than just the product it sells helps to increase brand loyalty by making consumers feel a stronger relationship with the company, as well as augment the impact of Starbucks CSR programs. The campaign includes such messages as "How can you help create a better future for farmers? You already are."

The campaign also redefines value as something that isn't about what is cheapest but about what is best for consumers, their families, and the world around them. In an economic time when there is less money to spend and Starbucks is facing increased competition from competitors such as McDonald's and Dunkin' Donuts, the campaign tells Starbucks' story by underscoring quality, value, and Starbucks' social and environmental values. The campaign validates for consumers, and for employees, that they are making the right choice and being conscientious consumers by choosing Starbucks.

Teaming up with stakeholders

Making all of these initiatives possible are Starbucks' partnerships with stakeholders. Starbucks enriches its social and environmental efforts and ensures their credibility and visibility by teaming up with a myriad of stakeholders who lend their expertise, credibility, and reach. They work with some of the best experts in coffee and international development on the planet.

To help them achieve their ambitious goals, Starbucks partners with Conservation International, with whom it has been working since 1998 to develop socially and environmentally responsible guidelines for coffee purchases through C.A.F.E. Practices; the African Wildlife Foundation, with whom it has worked since 2005 to protect wildlife and conserve natural resources in Africa and promote high-quality coffee, while improving farmer livelihoods; and, of course, fair trade.

It has also partnered with Earthwatch, with whom it has worked since 2001 to help partners and customers participate in expeditions to replant rainforests and learn about sustainable farming practices, and the U.S. Green Building Council which has been helping Starbucks since 2000 to design LEED-certified retail stores, plants, and offices.

Results

Starbucks is an excellent example of a company that has been able to turn sustainability and social initiatives into quantifiable returns on investment, whether they are in the form of growth and profits, brand loyalty, reputation, or employee attraction and retention.

Starting with six Seattle-based stores in 1987, Starbucks has over 16,000 units and currently commands 52% of the coffeehouse sales in the United States. Long a fixture on *Fortune*'s top 500 companies, Starbucks counts among its numerous accolades and awards for its sustainability and corporate social responsibility work being named on both *Fortune*'s "Twenty Most Admired Companies in America" and *Fortune*'s "100 Best Companies to Work For" lists. They have also been counted among the *Financial Times*' "World's Most Respected Companies," "Most Admired for HR" company by *Human Resources Magazine*, one of *Business Ethics Magazine*'s "100 Best Corporate Citizens" every year since 2000, and *First Magazine*'s "International Award for Responsible Capitalism." In 2009, Starbucks was also named one of the ten "Greenest Big Companies in America" by *Newsweek* and "Most Ethical Coffee Company in Europe" by Allegra Strategies.[5]

785266 000297

Conclusion

The maturing of greening as a consumer phenomenon, and its decided shift from the fringe into the mainstream, changes the rules of green marketing. A new green marketing paradigm now exists. It is characterized by a keen sensitivity for the total person who constitutes one's consumer and his or her new needs for brands that balance age-old benefits of performance, affordability, and convenience with minimal environmental and social impacts, and engage their consumers in meaningful dialogue. Manufacturers, retailers, and marketers looking to sustain their businesses long into the future must heed these new rules with communications that empower their consumers to act on pressing issues backed up by a proactive and demonstrated corporate commitment to conducting business in a sustainable way.

Meeting today's consumer needs won't be easy. Many challenges are associated with sustainable branding and green marketing – and many notable attempts, inadvertent or deliberate, of "greenwashing" abound.

But consumers want worthy businesses to succeed. As evidenced by growing participation on corporate-sponsored websites, Facebook pages, and the like, consumers are willing partners with favorite brands in the quest for innovative new ideas. In addition, much support is available from a plethora of new corporate stakeholders, among them voluntary government programs, environmental advocates willing to share expertise and partner in positive relationships, retailers looking for greener offerings, and even educators of our youth.

The marketplace will become greener and more socially aware in the years and decades ahead. Consumers' understanding of all things "green" and "sustainable" will grow, and with it their demands for more information about the eco and social performance of the products and services they buy. Businesses looking to build authentic, sustainable brands will start to ask the many questions outlined on the checklists provided throughout this book; businesses that are already leading the way will use those questions to refine their offerings and make their brands even more credible and relevant.

For further information

Web resources

Information, news, and commentary

AIGA Center for Sustainable Design
Provides graphic designers with case studies, interviews, resources, and discourse on sustainable business practice.
sustainability.aiga.org

Carbon Neutral Digest
Provides an up-to-date rating of U.S.-based organizations that offer solutions to help reduce or offset carbon footprints, and descriptions of their practices.
carbonneutraldigest.com

Circle of Blue Waternews
Daily go-to source for global water news and data.
www.circleofblue.org/waternews/waterviews

Clean Edge
A resource for companies, investors, governments, and nonprofits in the clean-technology sector. Market research reports, stock indexes benchmarking, cleantech events, free cleantech newsletter, and connecting cleantech job seekers, employers, and recruiters.
www.cleanedge.com

Climate Change
U.S. Environmental Protection Agency resource site with comprehensive and accessible information on climate change.
www.epa.gov/climatechange

Earthtweet
Social networking site. When twitter users put "#earthtweet" before a tweet, their environmentally related post is automatically posted to this site.
earthtweet.com

Eco Voice
Australia's environmental news website.
www.ecovoice.com.au

Ecolect
Tools and resources on sustainable materials.
ecolect.net

EcoWorld
Comprehensive information source on wide range of environmental information and opinion covering topics from animals and wildlife, to businesses and services, to water, oceans and ice. Latest headlines and photos.
www.ecoworld.com

ENDS Europe
Europe's environmental news and information source.
www.endseurope.com

Environment for Europeans
A European Commission sponsored website featuring environmental news, reports, and events.
ec.europa.eu/environment/news/efe/index_en.htm

Environmental Leader
News for environmental and sustainability executives.
www.environmentalleader.com

Global Oneness Project
Web-based film project that documents "our growing understanding of what it means to be part of one interconnected, interdependent world." Short films and interviews featuring people around the world working in sustainability, conflict resolution, spirituality, art, agriculture, economics, indigenous culture, social justice, and politics can be viewed and downloaded for free and used as an educational resource in schools and communities.
www.globalonenessproject.org

Green Energy TV
Online channel featuring videos on alternative/renewable/clean energy.
greenenergytv.com

Green Maven
Search engine and directory just for green and sustainability sites.
www.greenmaven.com

GreenBiz
Environmental information, tools and data for the mainstream business community. Includes Greenbuzz, a free weekly update, and the State of Green Business annual report.
www.greenbiz.com

The Greenwashing Index
A website produced by EnviroMedia Social Marketing and the University of Oregon, helps consumers evaluate environmental claims and rate ads.
www.greenwashingindex.com

The Green Power Network
News and information on green power markets operated and maintained by the National Renewable Energy Laboratory of the U.S. Department of Energy.
apps3.eere.energy.gov/greenpower

Grist
Environmental news and green living tips from an esteemed and wry voice in environmental journalism.
www.grist.org

Information/Inspiration
Eco-design resource created to support the design of environmentally and socially responsible products.
www.informationinspiration.org.uk

Institute for Sustainable Communication
Non profit organization dedicated to greening marketing communications. Addresses issues of digital and print media supply chains.
www.sustainablecommunication.org

Justmeans
Social media site for socially responsible businesses.
www.justmeans.com

LCA Information Hub
Information source maintained by the European Commission on life-cycle-related databases, tools, services, developers, and providers.
lca.jrc.ec.europa.eu/lcainfohub/index.vm

LCAccess
Resource site developed and maintained by the U.S. Environmental Protection Agency to educate people about life-cycle assessment (LCA) while "serving as a focal point for LCA practitioners and decision-makers to stay current with the field of LCA."
www.epa.gov/nrmrl/lcaccess

Learning About Renewable Energy
Run by the National Renewable Energy Lab, provides information and educational resources on energy efficiency and various applications of renewable energy.
www.nrel.gov/learning

LOHAS Online
Provides information and resources for businesses looking to appeal to LOHAS consumers.
www.lohas.com

Planetsave

One of many blogs produced by Green Options Media, encourages people to take environmental action and provides a place for visitors to share commentary, ideas, and solutions related to environmental challenges.

planetsave.com

Raymond Communications

Subscription, news, and reference information on recycling and environmental legislation in the United States and around the world.

www.raymond.com

RealClimate

Commentary by working climate scientists writing in their spare time for the interested public and journalists. Restricted to scientific topics, not involved in political or economic implications of the science.

www.realclimate.org

Sierra Club Compass

One of many blogs written by the Sierra Club, provides twice-monthly news, green living tips, and ways to take action on energy issues.

www.sierraclub.typepad.com/compass

Sustainable Life Media

Produces live and virtual sustainable business conferences and educational events (including the industry-leading Sustainable Brands conference) and offers targeted e-newsletters on eco-strategy, sustainable business, sustainable brands, green design, and an online community.

www.sustainablelifemedia.com

Sustainable Materials

Site of the Centre for Design at Royal Melbourne Institute of Technology with resources on sustainable materials, projects, tools, publications, training, and links.

www.cfd.rmit.edu.au/programs/sustainable_materials

SustainableBusiness.com

Targeted to new green ventures, includes daily news, reportage of sustainable stocks, and the SB newswire where businesses can post their press releases. Features links for green investing, sustainable job services, and business networking.

www.sustainablebusiness.com

Sustainablog.org

Provides information on environmental and economic sustainability, green and sustainable business, and environmental politics. Regularly features environmental leaders and experts in alternative energy and green technology.

www.sustainablog.org

Wal-Mart Canada ShareGreen
A platform which allows the public to browse and discuss the sustainable business practices of Canadian industries. Contains case studies that focus on waste, water, and energy management, sustainable solutions, and employee engagement. Initial case studies from Pepsi, Nike, and Stonyfield Farm.
sharegreen.ca

Worldchanging
This nonprofit online magazine, written by a global network of independent journalists, designers, and thinkers, features tools, models, and ideas for addressing environmental concerns related to building, transportation, communications, and quality of life.
www.worldchanging.com

Consumer-oriented and social networking websites

Amazon Green
Special section of Amazon.com's website, highlighting consumer-selected greener products.
www.amazon.com/green

Animal Fair
Lifestyle magazine for animal lovers and pet owners.
www.animalfair.com

Buygreen.com
A shopping site for consumer products ranging from bamboo clothing to solar-powered lights.
www.buygreen.com

Carbonrally.com
Assists consumers in reducing their carbon footprint.
www.carbonrally.com

Care2
Powered by Care2, a for-profit business, one of the largest online communities of people making a difference in healthy and green living, human rights and animal welfare. Includes free email, as well as shopping at the Eco-Superstore, healthy tips, eco news, petitions and alerts. Accepts advertising.
www.care2.com

Celsias.com
Helps consumers combat climate change. Users can read articles, join conversations, ask questions, commit to actions to reduce their carbon footprint, and create, join, and rate climate change projects. Companies can post information on what they are doing to reduce climate impact.
www.celsias.com

Change.org

Raises awareness about global warming, homelessness, women's rights, human trafficking, healthcare, and criminal justice. Provides information about how to take action with leading nonprofit organizations.
www.change.org

ClimateCounts.org

With the goal of bringing consumers and companies together to fight global climate change, this website rates the world's leading companies on climate impact and posts the resulting scores on the website's scorecard.
climatecounts.org

TheDailyGreen.com

Billing itself as "the consumer's guide to the green revolution," this lifestyle site owned by Hearst Communications provides news, information, and a community about going green. Accepts advertising.
www.thedailygreen.com

Do Something

Not-for-profit organization that promotes voluntarism among teens.
www.dosomething.org

Dwell

Magazine focusing on eco home design, products, and comfortable living.
www.dwell.com

E – The Environmental Magazine

Information, news, and resources for consumers concerned about the environment. Available both online and in print.
www.emagazine.com

Gaiam

Founded in Boulder, Colorado in 1988, Gaiam is a provider of information, goods, and services for people who value the environment, a sustainable economy, healthy lifestyles, alternative healthcare, and personal development.
www.gaiam.com

Global Green USA

The American arm of Green Cross International created by President Mikhail S. Gorbachev, focuses on stemming global climate change by creating green buildings and cities. The Green Building Resources center features building strategies and products that mitigate any adverse effects on the environment.
www.globalgreen.org

GoodGuide

Assigns 70,000 food, toys, personal care, and household consumer products a rating, combining health, environmental, and social performance, on a 1–10 scale. Also features articles about current environmental issues, such as buying organic and local.
www.goodguide.com

The Green Guide
A product of *National Geographic Magazine.* Comprehensive source of lifestyle green-ing, complete with green buying guides of products ranging from food and personal care, home and garden, to travel. Accepts advertising.
www.thegreenguide.com

GreenerChoices
A website of *Consumer Reports,* informs consumers of products and green ratings, hot topics, and solutions. The website features a "Toolkit" section including several differ-ent calculators and a section on toxic chemicals found in consumer products.
www.greenerchoices.org

GreenHome.com
Comprehensive online shopping site for greener products. Offers advice and infor-mation on greening one's life.
www.greenhome.com

HealthyStuff.org
Shopping tool listing test results on the chemical composition of more than 5,000 consumer products.
www.healthystuff.org

IGive.com
Up to 26% of each purchase made at this online store goes to shoppers' favorite causes. Among the 700+ stores in the network are Gap, Staples, Nordstrom, and Best Buy.
www.igive.com

Ideal Bite
Now owned by Disney, provides daily "Go Green" eco-living tips aimed at helping "light green" consumers take simple steps towards change.
family.go.com

MakeMeSustainable
Individuals, families, and businesses can join this online community to calculate their carbon footprint and learn about ways to reduce it.
makemesustainable.com

Natural Awakenings
A magazine with 2.5 million readers promoting a holistic orientation to nutrition, fit-ness, creative expression, personal growth, and sustainable living
www.naturalawakeningsmag.com

Natural Health Group
Commercial website providing information on vegetarian, vegan, and raw diets.
www.naturalhealthgroup.org

Natural Life Magazine
Website of magazine founded in 1976. Serves "thinking people around the world who want positive alternatives to high cost, high consumption lifestyles for themselves and their families."
www.naturallifemagazine.com

Organic Authority

Commercial website selling organic products and offering information promoting organic lifestyle.

www.organicauthority.com

Planet Green

One of Discovery's multi-platform channels of sustainable living ideas, energy conservation tips, freecycle information, green shopping, and more. Accepts advertising.

planetgreen.discovery.com

Skin Deep Cosmetic Safety Database

Database produced by the Environmental Working Group. Provides chemical composition and safety scores for over 50,000 cosmetic products.

www.cosmeticsdatabase.com

The Story of Stuff

Official website for this highly popular 20-minute animation of the consumerist society. Includes footnoted script, credits, blog, and resources.

www.storyofstuff.com

Treehugger.com

A Discovery Company website that allows users to get informed, interact, and take action. Features include information about green design and living, pop quizzes, and a sustainability-related job board.

www.treehugger.com

WorldCoolers

An online grassroots initiative that aims to raise public awareness of global warming. Website features a free downloadable Web browser add-on that gives updates on global warming topics.

www.worldcoolers.org

Yahoo! Green

Advertiser-sponsored mega-site for shopping and news, blogs, and tools for living green.

green.yahoo.com

Organizations

Business, government agencies, trade groups, environmental advocacy

1% for the Planet

A not-for-profit that facilitates businesses in donating at least 1% of their annual revenues to environmental organizations worldwide.

www.onepercentfortheplanet.org

Advertising Standards Authority
UK's independent regulator investigates complaints and monitors advertisements for false, offensive, or misleading information.
www.asa.org.uk

Advertising Standards Canada
Canada's independent self-regulatory nonprofit body that handles complaints on false, misleading, and harmful advertising campaigns.
www.adstandards.com

Alliance to Save Energy
Nonprofit coalition of business, government, and consumer leaders supporting energy efficiency and policies that minimize energy costs and lessen greenhouse gas emissions. The organization does research, conducts educational programs, advocates policies, designs and implements energy-efficient projects, and promotes technology development.
ase.org

American Center for Life Cycle Assessment (ACLCA)
Nonprofit membership organization, and part of the Institute for Environmental Research and Education (IERE), created to build capacity and knowledge of life-cycle assessment among industry, government, and NGOs. Developed and manages the Life Cycle Assessment Certified Professional (LCACP) Certification.
www.lcacenter.org

American Council for an Energy Efficient Economy (ACEEE)
Nonprofit organization dedicated to advancing energy efficiency as a means of promoting both economic prosperity and environmental protection. Contains extensive consumer resources on appliances, cars, lighting, etc.
www.aceee.org

American Hiking Society
A recreation-based nonprofit organization that champions conservation issues, builds partnerships between public and private stakeholders, and provides critical resources to plan, fund, and develop foot trails.
www.americanhiking.org

American Rivers
With 65,000 members, protects and restores rivers for the benefit of people, wildlife, and nature.
www.americanrivers.org

Australian Competition and Consumer Commission (ACCC)
As part of its primary responsibility to ensure that individuals and businesses comply with the Commonwealth competition, fair trading, and consumer protection laws, the ACCC publishes the Green Marketing and the Trade Practices Act which assists manufacturers, suppliers, advertisers, and others to assess the strength of any environmental claims they make and to improve the accuracy and usefulness to consumers of their labeling, packaging, and advertising.
www.accc.gov.au

B Lab Corporation

A nonprofit organization that bestows B Corporation certification ratings for businesses that meet comprehensive and transparent social and environmental standards and institutionalize stakeholder interests.
www.bcorporation.net

Beyond Pesticides

Formerly National Coalition against the Misuse of Pesticides, it seeks to eradicate pesticide use via identifying risks and promoting non-chemical and least hazardous alternatives.
www.beyondpesticides.org

Biodegradable Products Institute

A nonprofit association of key individuals and groups from government, industry, and academia that educates manufacturers, legislators, and consumers about the importance of biodegradable materials. The association also promotes the use and recovery of compostable materials through municipal and backyard composting.
www.bpiworld.org

Biomimicry Institute

Nonprofit organization that promotes the study and imitation of nature's designs.
www.biomimicryinstitute.org

Canopy

Based in Palo Alto, California, this nonprofit organization advocates for the urban forest and works to educate, inspire, and engage the community as stewards of young and mature trees.
www.canopy.org

Carbon Disclosure Project

Nonprofit organization holding the largest database of primary corporate climate change information in the world to support financial and policy decision-making. Represents institutional investors and 60 businesses including Cadbury, PepsiCo, and Wal-Mart.
www.cdproject.net

Carbon Trust

Set up by the British government, this London-based nonprofit company offers products and services geared towards saving energy, managing carbon management, and developing low-carbon technology. Featured support services include energy-efficiency loans, carbon surveys, an action plan tool, a carbon footprint calculator, and applied research grants. Offers the Carbon Reduction Label for use on consumer products.
www.carbontrust.co.uk

Center for a New American Dream

With the goal of helping Americans consume responsibly, enhance quality of life and promote social justice, this nonprofit group offers an action network, campaigns and program information, a community action guide, publications available for download, as well as sections for kids and teens.
www.newdream.org

Centre for Sustainable Design
Led by sustainability expert Martin Charter, and established in 1995 within the Faculty of Design, The Surrey Institute of Art & Design, University College, UK, this organization facilitates discussion and research on eco-design and environmental, economic, ethical, and social considerations in product and service development and design. Featured services and resources include research and training projects, an annual Sustainable Innovation conference, workshops, consultancy, and publications. The Centre also acts as an information clearinghouse and a focus for innovative thinking on sustainable products and services.
www.cfsd.org.uk

Ceres
A North American network of investors, environmental organizations, and other public interest groups working with companies and investors to address sustainability issues such as global climate change.
www.ceres.org

Choice
Formerly known as the Australian Consumer's Association, focuses on testing and ranking various consumer products in addition to reporting on false advertising.
www.choice.com.au

Conservation International
Using science, policy and fieldwork to protect our planet's resources.
www.conservation.org

Defenders of Wildlife
Founded in 1947, a nonprofit organization dedicated to protecting native plants and animals.
www.defenders.org

Department for Environment, Food and Rural Affairs (Defra)
The UK government body responsible for policy and regulations. Its priorities are to support British farming and encourage sustainable food production, help to enhance the environment and biodiversity, and support a strong and sustainable green economy, resilient to climate change.
www.defra.gov.uk

Earth Day Network
Educates the public and organizes global activism for a cleaner planet.
www.earthday.net/

Earthjustice
Formerly the Sierra Club Legal Defense Fund, this national nonprofit law firm lobbies for environmental legislation and takes legal action to stop environmental offenses by industries in the areas of climate and energy, wildlife and places, health and toxics.
www.earthjustice.org

Ecolabel Index
The largest global database of eco-labels, tracking 328 eco-labels in 207 countries and 40 industry sectors as of 2010
www.ecolabelindex.com

The Economics of Ecosystems and Biodiversity (TEEB)
International initiative created to draw attention to the global economic benefits of biodiversity and the growing costs of biodiversity loss and ecosystem degradation. It brings together expertise from the fields of science, economics, and policy.
www.teebweb.org

Electronics TakeBack Coalition
Promotes green design and responsible recycling in the electronics industry to protect the health and well-being of electronics users, workers, and the communities where electronics are produced and discarded. It urges consumer electronics manufacturers and brand owners to take full responsibility for the life-cycle of their products, through public policy requirements or enforceable agreements.
www.electronicstakeback.com

Environmental Defense Fund
A nonprofit environmental advocacy group that partners with Fortune 500 businesses, governments, and communities to advocate market-based solutions to environmental problems. Website features publications and resource tools for businesses to reduce their environmental footprint.
www.edf.org

Environmental Media Association
Mobilizes the entertainment industry to educate and inspire the public to act on environmental issues.
www.ema-online.org

Environmental Protection UK
Nonprofit organization based in the UK that focuses on environmental policy, campaigns, and innovation. Brings together industry leaders, academics, policy makers, and the public to bring about environmental change.
www.environmental-protection.org.uk

Environmental Working Group
A nonprofit environmental and consumer advocacy group providing information and promoting legislation on the human health and environmental impacts of consumer products.
www.ewg.org

European Advertising Standards Alliance
A nonprofit organization that brings together self-regulatory advertising organizations in Europe and also Australia, Brazil, Canada, Chile, India, New Zealand, and South Africa to promote ethical standards in advertising through self-regulation.
www.easa-alliance.org

European Environmental Bureau
Federation of European environmental citizens' organizations. Website has news, environmental articles, events, policy. It also lists active environmental organizations in Europe.
www.eeb.org

Federal Trade Commission
Publishes "Green Guides," Guides for the Use of Environmental Marketing Claims, general principles, and specific examples
www.ftc.gov/bcp/grnrule/guides980427.htm

Friends of the Earth
Environmental nonprofit organization with a network of grassroots organizations in 77 countries that focuses on global warming, toxic technologies, and promoting smarter, low-pollution transportation alternatives.
www.foe.org

Global Environmental Declaration Network (GEDnet)
An international nonprofit organization of Type III environmental declaration organizations and practitioners, organizing and allowing an open exchange of information on the various Type III environmental product declaration programs.
www.gednet.org

Global Footprint Network
International think-tank working to advance sustainability through use of the Ecological Footprint, a resource accounting tool and data-driven metric that allows the calculation of human pressure on the planet.
www.footprintnetwork.org

Global Reporting Initiative
Network-based organization that has developed the world's most widely used sustainability reporting framework involving business, civil society, labor, and professional institutions.
www.globalreporting.org

Green America
Formerly known as Co-op America, this national not-for-profit organization promotes sustainability and social and economic justice through strategic efforts aimed towards individuals, businesses, and communities. Resources include National Green Pages, a directory listing of thousands of businesses that have made commitments to sustainable, socially just principles, Green Business Network, an education system for environmentally responsible consumption and investing, and Green Festivals in major U.S. cities.
www.greenamericatoday.org

Green Design Institute, Carnegie Mellon University
Offers green design courses and provides a space for companies, foundations, and government agencies to discuss issues of environmental quality and economic development.
www.ce.cmu.edu/GreenDesign

GreenerChoices
Website for consumers run by Consumers Union, the nonprofit publisher of Consumer Reports. Provides in-depth information on green consumer products and practices.
www.greenerchoices.org

Greenhouse Gas Protocol Initiative
Partnership between the World Resources Institute and the World Business Council for Sustainable Development working with businesses, governments, and environmental groups worldwide "to build a new generation of credible and effective programs for tackling climate change." Developed the most widely used international accounting tool for government and business leaders to understand, quantify, and manage greenhouse gas emissions.
www.ghgprotocol.org

Greenpeace
A global campaigning organization that acts to change attitudes and behavior, to protect and conserve the environment by addressing such issues as energy, oceans, ancient forests, toxics, and sustainable agriculture. Campaigns have featured "Greening the Apple" (Apple Inc.) and "Kleercut" (Kimberly-Clark).
www.greenpeace.org

IEG
Provides consulting, valuation, measurement, research and training to the global sponsorship industry. Develops ways for companies and brands to partner with sports, arts, events, entertainment, nonprofit, and causes.
www.sponsorship.com

Impact Reporting and Investment Standards
Initiative developed by the Rockefeller Foundation, Acumen Fund, and B Lab to create a common framework for defining, tracking, and reporting the performance of impact capital that will allow comparison and communication across organizations that have social or environmental impact as a primary driver.
iris.thegiin.org

Industrial Designers Society of America
Annual IDEA awards feature environmental criteria. Resources in eco-design provided by eco-design special interest group.
www.idsa.org

International Association for Soaps, Detergents and Maintenance Products (AISE)
Dedicated to the sustainable improvement of products for hygiene, detergents and household and industrial maintenance products. Manages the Washright campaign in the European Union to promote responsible laundry care.
www.aise.eu

J. Ottman Consulting, Inc.
Founded in 1989 by green marketing expert and author Jacquelyn Ottman, advises Fortune 500, entrepreneurial firms, and government agencies on strategies for green marketing and sustainable product innovation. Ottman is the author of *The New Rules of Green Marketing.*
www.greenmarketing.com

Japan Environment Association
Founded in 1977, the JEA is concerned with Japan's environmental conservation activities. Their main areas of focus are: global warming, promoting the green marketplace, and environmental education.
www.jeas.or.jp

Japan Environmental Management Association for Industry
Established in 1962, this public organization with 1,100 member companies focuses on environmental assessments, air and water pollution, and global environmental issues. JEMAI controls the Eco-Leaf Product Environmental Aspects Declaration program.
www.jemai.or.jp

KaBOOM!
A nonprofit dedicated to create play spaces for children in the U.S.
kaboom.org

Life Cycle Initiative
International life-cycle partnership launched by the United Nations Environment Programme and the Society for Environmental Toxicology and Chemistry to put life-cycle thinking into practice and improve supporting tools through better data and indicators.
lcinitiative.unep.fr

Material Connexion
Member-based global materials consultancy and library of innovative and sustainable materials.
materialconnexion.com

National Advertising Division, Council of Better Business Bureaus
Reviews advertising for truthfulness and accuracy and makes its findings available to the public.
www.nadreview.org

National Audubon Society
A national network of community-based nature centers and chapters. Conserves and restores natural bird ecosystems.
www.audubon.org

National Geographic Society
Nonprofit scientific and educational organization that promotes the globalization of geographic knowledge while conserving the world's cultural, historical, and natural resources.
www.nationalgeographic.com

National Institute for Environmental Studies

Japanese environmental organization that focuses on environmental research. Areas of interest include health, chemicals, waste, and recycling.

www.nies.go.jp

National Wildlife Federation

Nonprofit organization with more than 4 million members, geared toward protecting wildlife and confronting global warming.

www.nwf.org

Natural Marketing Institute

Consulting, market research, and business development company specializing in the health and wellness marketplace. Authors of the *LOHAS Consumer Report*.

www.nmisolutions.com

Natural Resources Defense Council

With 1.3 million members and online activists, an environmental action group combining grassroots with scientists and other professionals aimed at safeguarding the Earth's people, plants, animals, and natural systems.

www.nrdc.org

The Natural Step

Not-for-profit organization that promotes a science-based model to help communities and businesses better understand and integrate environmental, social, and economic considerations. Working with companies, municipalities, academic institutions, and not-for-profit organizations.

www.naturalstep.org

The Nature Conservancy

Nonprofit conservation organization working to protect ecologically important lands and waters.

www.nature.org

O$_2$ Global Network

Members of this global network organize lectures, projects, workshops, and distribute newsletters and other material to promote, teach, and implement sustainable design. The O$_2$ site includes resources on sustainable design and a global listserv.

www.o2.org

Open MIC

Nonprofit using market feedback to make corporate management practices of the media industry more open and responsible.

www.openmic.org

Organic Consumers Association

Online and grassroots nonprofit dealing with issues of food safety, industrial agriculture, genetic engineering, children's health, environmental sustainability, and fair trade.

www.organicconsumers.org

Organic Exchange
A membership organization focused on increasing the production and use of organically grown fibers.
www.organicexchange.org

People for the Ethical Treatment of Animals
Nonprofit group that promotes animal rights via campaigns including ending fur and leather use, meat and dairy consumption, factory farming, circuses, and bull fighting.
www.peta.org

Planet Ark
Nonprofit organization based in Australia that aims to teach both individuals and businesses simple ways in which they can make substantial reductions to their environmental impact.
planetark.org

Project (RED)
Businesses donate 50% of the profits of (RED) products to help buy and distribute antiretroviral medicine for those dying of AIDS in Africa.
www.joinred.com

Rocky Mountain Institute
Independent, entrepreneurial nonprofit think-tank of a group of industry experts, thought leaders, and engineers engaged in research that addresses pragmatic designs, practices, and policies related to energy and resources, with a strong emphasis on market-based solutions.
www.rmi.org/rmi

Sierra Club
A nonprofit environmental advocacy organization founded in 1892 that combines legal action, information campaigns, and cooperative partnerships with industry to protect America's wild places.
www.sierraclub.org

Silicon Valley Toxics Coalition
A nonprofit organization engaged in research, advocacy, and grassroots organizing to promote human health and environmental justice related to the high-tech industry. Has advocated for electronics companies to reduce and eventually eliminate the use of toxic chemicals in the design and manufacturing of products and the implementation of extended producer responsibility at end of product life.
www.svtc.org/site/PageServer

Slow Food
With 100,000 members in 132 countries, a nonprofit member-supported organization that aims to counteract fast food and fast life and the disappearance of local food traditions, and raise awareness of how food tastes and how our food choices affect the rest of the world.
www.slowfoodusa.org

Surfrider Foundation
A nonprofit environmental organization dedicated to the protection and enjoyment of the world's waves and beaches through conservation, education, research, and activism.
www.surfrider.org

Sustainability Consortium
Stewarded by Wal-Mart, a partnership of researchers from leading global universities, NGOs, governmental agencies, and business partners, created with the goal of establishing scientific standards to measure the sustainability of consumer products and ultimately developing scientifically valid and coherent product indexes to allow retailers compare consumer products.
www.sustainabilityconsortium.org

Sustainable Investment Research Analyst Network (SIRAN)
Supportive network for analysts taking an environmental, social, or governance approach to investment studies.
www.siran.org

Sustainable Packaging Coalition
Industry working group develops educational resources and tools on sustainable packaging. Featured projects and resources include a comparative packaging assessment tool, sustainable performance indicators and metrics, design guidelines for sustainable packaging, and environmental technical briefs.
www.sustainablepackaging.org

TNS Media Intelligence
Tracks competitive media expenditures and creative ads for advertising agencies, advertisers, broadcasters, and publishers.
www.tns-mi.com/aboutIndex.htm

United Nations Environment Programme
Founded in 1972 to coordinate and manage United Nations environmental initiatives, research, and policies.
www.unep.org

Wildlife Conservation Society
Founded in 1895, this organization manages 500 conservation projects in 60 countries aimed at saving wildlife.
www.wcs.org

Women's Voices for the Earth
Nonprofit organization that researches the health impacts of consumer products, including cosmetic and household cleaning products.
www.womenandenvironment.org

World Business Council for Sustainable Development
CEO-led global association of about 200 companies from more than 35 countries and 20 major industrial sectors. Provides a platform for companies to explore sustainable development, share knowledge, experiences, and best practices, and to advocate

business positions in a variety of forums, working with governments and non-governmental and intergovernmental organizations. Four key areas include energy and climate, development, the business role, and ecosystems.
www.wbcsd.org

World Resources Institute
Environmental think-tank working with business partners, governments, and civil society, with over 50 active projects focused on global climate change, sustainable markets, ecosystem protection, and environmentally responsible governance.
www.wri.org

Worldwatch Institute
Independent research organization led by Lester Brown focused on developing and disseminating data and strategies to address challenges of climate change, resource degradation, population growth, and poverty. Priority programs include Energy & Climate, Food & Agriculture, and Green Economy.
www.worldwatch.org

Zerofootprint
Zerofootprint Software applies technology, design, and risk management to reduce the world's environmental footprint and provides clients with tailored carbon management solutions. The Zerofootprint Foundation engages government, educators, and other not-for-profits to combat climate change.
www.zerofootprint.net

Certification and eco-labeling organizations

Aquaculture Certification Council
This certification recognizes aquaculture that meets social, environmental, and food safety standards.
www.aquaculturecertification.org

ASTM International
Originally known as the American Society for Testing and Materials, one of the largest voluntary standards organizations focused on technical standards for materials, products, systems, and services. ASTM has developed sustainability standards or has expertise in areas including soil, water, air quality, and waste management.
www.astm.org

Blue Angel
The official eco-label of Germany, covering 10,000 products and services. Awards made on single attributes representing greatest areas of impact per category.
blauer-engel.de

Bluesign
A global network of representatives from the scientific and political communities, trade and industry, and consumer and environmental organizations. The Bluesign standard ensures environmental responsibility, health and safety with the production of textiles.
www.bluesign.com

Carbon Trust
Provides Carbon Reduction label intended to help consumers better understand a product's carbon footprint.
www.carbontrust.co.uk

Center for Resource Solutions
A national nonprofit focusing on research and marketing of renewable energy options. Promotes the Green-e label for renewable energy.
www.resource-solutions.org

Cradle to Cradle Certification
Assesses a product's safety to humans and the environment and design for future life-cycles in the categories of materials, material reutilization, energy, water, and social responsibility. Products can be certified at four levels: Basic, Silver, Gold, Platinum.
www.c2ccertified.com

Eco Mark
Japan's voluntary multi-attribute eco-labeling program covering a wide range of consumer products.
www.ecomark.jp

EcoLogo
A multi-attribute environmental standard and certification mark founded in Canada but now available worldwide.
www.environmentalchoice.com

EPEAT
Not-for-profit organization managed and operated by the Green Electronics Council of the International Sustainable Development Foundation. Evaluates electronic products in relation to 51 total environmental criteria, identified in IEEE 1680 standards.
www.epeat.net

EU Ecolabel
A voluntary multi-attribute scheme administered by the European Eco-labeling Board with the support of the European Commission. Covers a wide range of products and services, including cleaning products, appliances, paper products, textile and home and garden products, lubricants, and services such as tourist accommodation.
www.eco-label.com

Fairtrade Foundation
UK member organization of Fairtrade Labelling Organizations International.
www.fairtrade.org.uk

Fairtrade Labelling Organizations International (FLO)
An international network of 24 designated nonprofits that are responsible for issuing licenses to use the "FAIRTRADE" label on products (includes Transfair [U.S.] and Fairtrade Foundation [UK]).
www.fairtrade.net

Forest Stewardship Council
Internationally recognized standard of responsible forestry.
www.fsc.org

Good Environmental Choice – Australia
Australia's voluntary multi-attribute environmental labeling program covering a wide range of products.
www.geca.org.au

Global Organic Textile Standard
Worldwide standard for organic textiles based on materials and processes used throughout production.
www.global-standard.org

Green Good Housekeeping Seal
Launched by *Good Housekeeping* magazine in 2009 to help consumers recognize products that have earned high ratings based on a wide range of environmental criteria and effectiveness.
www.goodhousekeeping.com/product-testing/history/welcome-gh-seal

Green Seal
One of the oldest independent nonprofit labeling organizations, develops standards for and certifies a wide range of environmentally responsible commercial and consumer products and services including cleaning aids, building and maintenance materials, and lodging properties.
www.greenseal.org

International Organization for Standardization (ISO)
Based in Geneva, Switzerland, ISO is a non-governmental network of national standards institutes of 163 countries and the world's largest developer and publisher of voluntary international standards. The ISO Catalogue includes more than 18,000 published International Standards, including ISO 14001 for corporate environmental management and ISO 14020 for eco-labeling.
www.iso.org

Marine Stewardship Council
Fish certified by this global program are from wild capture fisheries that practice sustainable fishing and protect the local ecosystems.
www.msc.org

National Standard for Sustainable Forest Management (Canadian Standards Association)
Products with this label comply with national and international environmental standards for forest management.
www.csa-international.org/product_areas/forest_products_marking

NSF International
Nonprofit organization founded in 1944 to certify products and write standards related to public health, safety, and the environment for food, water, and consumer goods.
www.nsf.org

Programme for the Endorsement of Forest Certification
The PEFC label can be found on wood and paper products from forests that are certified by an independent member of this international nonprofit association to be sustainably managed. Sustainable Forestry Program located in the U.S. is a member.
www.pefc.org

Protected Harvest
Agricultural products with this label come from farms with rigorous environmental growing standards.
www.protectedharvest.org

Rainforest Alliance
Independent certification of forestry and agricultural products along with verification of forest and farm projects that aim to reduce carbon emissions.
www.rainforest-alliance.org

Scientific Certification Systems
Develops standards attesting to the quality and sustainable production of various agriculture, manufacturing, and energy products.
www.scscertified.com

TransFair USA
A nonprofit that is the only third-party certifier of Fair Trade products for the U.S. The Fair Trade Certified label can be applied to coffee, tea and herbs, cocoa and chocolate, fresh fruit, flowers, sugar, rice, and vanilla. Certified farms practice environmentally sustainable farming methods and follow the Fair Trade community-oriented principles of fair labor conditions for workers.
www.transfairusa.org

ULEnvironment
A division of UL; certifies environmental claims and develops standards.
www.ulenvironment.com

United States Department of Agriculture
Through the National Organic Program develops, implements, and administers national production, handling, and labeling standards for organic agricultural products, including the USDA Organic label. Also home to the USDA BioPreferred government procurement program and voluntary consumer label.
www.usda.gov

United States Department of Energy
Maintains the Energy Guide for appliances, and co-manages the ENERGY STAR label (with U.S. Environmental Protection Agency).
www.energy.gov

United States Environmental Protection Agency
U.S. government agency that maintains the Design for the Environment (**www.epa.gov/dfe**), ENERGY STAR (**energystar.gov**), SmartWay transportation (**www.epa.gov/smartway**), and WaterSense (**www.epa.gov/WaterSense**) voluntary labels.

United States Green Building Council
Maintains the LEED (Leadership for Energy and Environmental Design) rating system for sustainable building design and construction.
www.usgbc.org

Books

Business, design and sustainability

Companies on a Mission: Entrepreneurial Strategies for Growing Sustainably, Responsibly, and Profitably
Michael V. Russo (Stanford University Press, 2010)

The Clean Tech Revolution
Ron Pernik and Clint Wilder (Harper Collins Publishers, 2008)

Co-opportunity: Join Up for a Sustainable, Resilient, Prosperous World
John Grant (John Wiley & Sons, 2010)

Confessions of a Radical Industrialist: Profits, People, Purpose – Doing Business by Respecting the Earth
Ray C. Anderson (St. Martin's Press, 2009)

Driving Eco-innovation
Claude Fussler with Peter James (Pitman Publishing, 1996)

Ecological Intelligence: How Knowing the Hidden Impacts of What We Buy Can Change Everything
Daniel Goleman (Broadway Business, 2009)

The Green Marketing Manifesto
John Grant (John Wiley & Sons, 2008)

Green Recovery: Get Lean, Get Smart, and Emerge from the Downturn on Top
Andrew Winston (Harvard Business Press, 2009)

Hot, Flat, and Crowded: Why We Need a Green Revolution – and How It Can Renew America
Thomas L. Friedman (Farrar Straus & Giroux, 2008)

Life Cycle Assessment: Principles, Practice and Prospects
Ralph Horne, Tim Grant, and Karli Verghese (CSIRO Publishing, 2009)

Packaging Sustainability: Tools, Systems and Strategies for Innovative Package Design
Wendy Jedlicka (John Wiley & Sons, 2008)

Plan B 4.0: Mobilizing to Save Civilization
Lester R. Brown (Earth Policy Institute, 2009)

The Plot to Save the Planet: How Visionary Entrepreneurs and Corporate Titans are Creating Real Solutions to Global Warming
Brian Dumaine (Crown Business, 2008)

The Psychology of Climate Change Communication: A Guide for Scientists, Journalists, Educators, Political Aides, and the Interested Public
Center for Research on Environmental Decisions (Columbia University in the City of New York, 2009; free download at www.cred.columbia.edu/guide)

Strategy for Sustainability: A Business Manifesto
Adam Werbach (Harvard Business Press, 2009)

Sustainability by Design: A Subversive Strategy for Transforming Our Consumer Culture
John R. Ehrenfeld (Yale University Press, 2008)

The Sustainability Champion's Guidebook: How to Transform Your Company
Bob Willard (New Society Publishers, 2009)

Sustainable Energy – Without the Hot Air
David J.C. MacKay (UIT Cambridge Ltd., 2009; free download at www.withouthotair.com)

The Truth about Green Business
Gil Friend (FT Press, 2009)

Consumer books

50 Simple Things You Can Do to Save the Earth
John Javna, Sophie Javna, and Jesse Javna (Hyperion, 2008)

Big Green Purse: Use Your Spending Power to Create a Cleaner, Greener World
Diane MacEachern (Avery, 2008)

Generation Green: The Ultimate Teen Guide to Living an Eco-friendly Life
Linda Sivertsen and Tosh Sivertsen (Simon Pulse, 2008)

Green, Greener, Greenest: A Practical Guide to Making Eco-smart Choices a Part of Your Life
Lori Bongiorno (Perigee Trade, 2008)

Green Guide: The Complete Reference for Consuming Wisely
(National Geographic, 2008)

Gorgeously Green: 8 Simple Steps to an Earth-friendly Life
Sophie Uliano (Collins Living, 2008)

It's Easy Being Green: A Handbook for Earth Friendly Living
Crissy Trask (Gibbs Smith, 2006)

The Lazy Environmentalist: Your Guide to Easy, Stylish, Green Living
Josh Dorfman (Harry N Abrams, 2007)

Living Like Ed: A Guide to the Eco-friendly Life
Ed Begley Jr. (Clarkson N. Potter, 2008)

Ready, Set, Green: Eight Weeks to Modern Eco-living
Graham Hill and Meaghan O'Neill (Villard Books, 2008)

Simple Prosperity: Finding Real Wealth in a Sustainable Lifestyle
David Wann (St. Martin's Press, 2007)

Squeaky Green: The Method Guide to Detoxing Your Home
Eric Ryan and Adam Lowry (Chronicle Books, 2008)

Toolbox for Sustainable Living: A Do-It-Ourselves Guide
Scott Kellogg and Stacy Pettigrew (South End Press, 2008)

Worldchanging: A User's Guide for the 21st Century
Alex Steffen (Abrams, 2008)

Endnotes

Chapter 1

1 Natural Marketing Institute, *The LOHAS Report: 2009* (Harleysville, PA: NMI, 2009).

2 Focalyst, "It's Good to Be Green: Socially Conscious Shopping Behaviors among Boomers," Focalyst Insight Report; AARP Services and Focalyst, December 2007; https://www.focalyst.com/Sites/Focalyst/Media/Pdfs/en/CurrentResearchReports/698F1654.pdf; https://www.focalyst.com/Sites/Focalyst/Content/KnowledgeCenter, accessed September 16, 2010.

3 Randeep Ramesh, "Bhopal marks 25th anniversary of Union Carbide gas disaster," *The Guardian*, December 3, 2009; www.guardian.co.uk/world/2009/dec/03/bhopal-anniversary-union-carbide-gas, accessed September 16, 2010.

4 Known officially as the United Nations Conference on Environment and Development (UNCED).

5 Green Canary Sustainability Consulting, "New Research: 18- to 34-Year-Olds Key to Green Economy," Tuerff-Davis EnviroMedia; www.greencanary.net/news-item.php?id=693, accessed August 1, 2010.

6 The American College and University Presidents' Climate Commitment (ACUPCC) is about a global commitment to eliminate campuses' greenhouse gas emissions; www.presidentsclimatecommitment.org.

7 Sophia Yan, "Understanding Generation Y," *The Oberlin Review*, December 8, 2006; www.oberlin.edu/stupub/ocreview/2006/12/08/features/Understanding_Generation_Y.html, accessed August 1, 2010.

8 American Forest & Paper Association, "Facts About Paper," 2009; www.afandpa.org/FunFacts.aspx, accessed August 1, 2010.

9 Dan Shapley, "Green Election Issues 101," *The Daily Green*, August 28, 2008; www.thedailygreen.com/environmental-news/latest/green-elections-guide-47082517, accessed August 1, 2010.

10 League of Conservation Voters, "About LCV"; www.lcv.org/about-lcv, accessed August 1, 2010.

11 Beth Walton, "Volunteer Rates Hit Record Numbers," *USA Today*, July 7, 2006; www.usatoday.com/news/nation/2006-07-06-volunteers_x.htm, accessed August 1, 2010.

12 Gwynne Rogers, Natural Marketing Institute, email message to the author, March 29, 2010.

13 Tanya Irwin, "Study: Organic Products Selling Strong Despite the Economy," *MediaPost News*, May 4, 2009; www.mediapost.com/publications/?art_aid=105371&fa=Articles.showArticle, accessed August 1, 2010.

14 Sustainable Life Media, "Sales in Organics Soar Over 17% Despite Recession," May 6, 2009; www.sustainablelifemedia.com/content/story/brands/sales_in_organics_soar_over_17_percent_despite Recession, accessed August 1, 2010.

15 Jack Neff, "Why Burt's Bees CMO Won't Cut Spending in Recession," *Advertising Age*, May 13, 2009; adage.com/results?endeca=1&return=endeca& search_offset=0&search_order_by=score&x=0&y=0&search_phrase=Why+Burt%27s+Bees+CMO+Won%27t+Cut+Spending+in+Recession, accessed August 1, 2010.

16 John Murphy and Kate Linebaugh, "Honda's Hybrid Will Take On Prius," *Wall Street Journal*, October 1, 2008: B1.

17 Procter & Gamble, "Procter & Gamble Deepens Corporate Commitment to Sustainability," press release, March 26, 2009; www.pginvestor.com/phoenix.zhtml?c=104574&p=irol-newsArticle&ID=1270272, accessed September 16, 2010.

18 Procter & Gamble, "P&G Launches Initiative to Make Conservation of Natural Resources More User Friendly," press release, March 15, 2010; www.pginvestor.com/phoenix.zhtml?c=104574&p=irol-newsArticle&ID=1402138&highlight=future%20friendly, accessed September 16, 2010.

19 "Green Is The New Black," *Brandweek*, June 24, 2009; www.brandweek.com/bw/content_display/news-and-features/green-marketing/e3i772f176924f862d41-ded85b4a202121f, accessed August 1, 2010.

20 Helen K. Chang, "Business: Coming Clean," *Plenty* 22 (June–July 2008); www.plentymag.com/magazine/business_coming_clean.php, accessed August 1, 2010.

21 www.openmic.org.

22 Sustainable Life Media, "Consumers Chuck Green Debate for Environmental Action," February 11, 2009; www.sustainablelifemedia.com/content/story/brands/consumers_chuck_green_debate_for_environmental_action, accessed August 1, 2010.

23 Jeremy Lovell, "Global Warming Impact Like 'Nuclear War'," Reuters, September 12, 2007; www.reuters.com/article/environmentNews/idUSL1234809620070912, accessed August 1, 2010.

24 Bret Stephens, "Global Warming and the Poor," *Wall Street Journal*, August 4, 2009: A11.

25 U.S. Environmental Protection Agency, "Water Supply and Use in the United States," *WaterSense*, June 2008; www.epa.gov/watersense/pubs/supply.html, accessed 13 October 2009.

26 Leo Lewis, "Ecologists Warn the Planet Is Running Short of Water," *The Times*, January 22, 2009; www.timesonline.co.uk/tol/news/environment/article5562906.ece, accessed August 1, 2010.

27 Sustainable Life Media, "86 of S&P 100 Have Corporate Sustainability Websites," July 23, 2008; www.sustainablelifemedia.com/content/story/strategy/86_of_s_ and_p_100_have_corporate_sustainability_websites, accessed August 1, 2010.
28 Ibid.

Chapter 2

1 LOHAS, Naturalites, Conventionals, Drifters, and Unconcerneds are registered trademarks of the Natural Marketing Institute of Harleysville, Pennsylvania.
2 "Over Half of Consumers Factor Green Record into Buying Decisions," *Environmental Leader*, August 6, 2008; www.environmentalleader.com/2008/08/06/ over-half-of-consumers-factor-green-record-into-buying-decisions, accessed August 1, 2010.
3 Amazon Green (www.Amazon.com/Amazon-Green) and Yahoo! Green (green. yahoo.com).
4 Sustainable Life Media, "Americans Buy Green to Save Green When Shopping for Electronics," April 17, 2007; www.sustainablelifemedia.com/content/story/ brands/americans_buy_green_to_save_green, accessed August 6, 2010.
5 Daniel H. Pink, "Rise of the Neo-Greens," *Wired* 14.05 (May 2006); www.wired. com/wired/archive/14.05/neo.html, accessed August 1, 2010.

Chapter 3

1 Renewable Energy Certificates, also known as renewable energy credits, are tradable commodities representing proof that a certain amount of electricity used in production was generated from an eligible renewal energy source, again not under their domain (Source: www.epa.gov/greenpower/gpmarket/rec.htm).
2 "Certified B Corporation," B Lab; www.bcorporation.net, accessed August 11, 2010.
3 "Fighting Dirty, "an interview with the founders of Method green home-care products by Sarah van Schagen, March 14, 2008: www.grist.org/article/fighting-dirty, accessed August 15, 2010.
4 The jugs in question being the large, handled bottles that rival brands use rather than the small pump bottles of Method.
5 Katie Molinari, Method Products Inc., telephone interview, July 22, 2009.

Chapter 4

1 Several multi-attribute eco-labeling programs have been developed in various countries around the world for this purpose.
2 D. Sabaliunas, "Tide Coldwater: Energy Conservation through Residential Laundering Innovation and Commercialization," presented at the *10th Annual Green Chemistry and Engineering Conference,* Capital Hilton, Washington, DC, June 26–30, 2006; acs.confex.com/acs/green06/techprogram/P27314.HTM, accessed October 19, 2010.
3 U.S. Environmental Protection Agency, "Life-Cycle Assessment (LCA)"; www.epa. gov/nrmrl/lcaccess.

4 "PepsiCo Reveals Method for Calculating Carbon Footprint of Products," *Environmental Leader*, October 5, 2009.

5 Glenn Rifkin, "Saving Trees is Music to Guitar Makers' Ears," *New York Times*, June 7, 2007: C4.

6 Earthworks No Dirty Gold Campaign, "Dirty Gold's Impacts"; www.nodirtygold.org/dirty_golds_impacts.cfm, accessed August 1, 2010.

7 Earthworks No Dirty Gold Campaign, "Tiffany & Co. Stakes Bold Position on Mining Reform," press release, March 24, 2004; www.nodirtygold.org/stdnt_alternatives.cfm, accessed August 1, 2010.

8 Tiffany & Co., "Sources and Mining Practices: Our Views on Large-Scale Mining," 2009; www.tiffany.com/sustainability/mining.aspx, accessed August 1, 2010.

9 Tiffany & Co., "Our Environmental and Social Commitments," 2008; www.tiffany.com/sustainability, accessed August 1, 2010.

10 Cure Recycling, "Recycle Printer Cartridges," Earthtone Solutions Inc.; www.earthtonesolutions.com/recyclecartridgesinkjet.html, accessed August 1, 2010.

11 Emma Ritch, "Pumping up the Value of Recycled Plastics," Cleantech Group LLC, May 8, 2009; cleantech.com/news/4439/hp-lavergne-improve-value-recycled, accessed August 1, 2010.

12 Sustainable is Good, "Recycline Wins Forbes Boost Your Business Contest," December 17, 2007; www.sustainableisgood.com/blog/2007/12/recycline-wins.html, accessed August 1, 2010.

13 Jenny Hoponick, "Nonylphenol Ethoxylates: A Safer Alternative Exists to This Toxic Cleaning Agent," Rep. Sierra Club, Jersey Coast Anglers Association, November 2005.

14 Organic Trade Association, "U.S. Organic Sales Grow by a Whopping 17.1 Percent in 2008," press release, May 4, 2009; www.organicnewsroom.com/2009/05/us_organic_sales_grow_by_a_who.html, accessed August 1, 2010.

15 Emily B. York, "Safeway to Roll out House Brands to Grocery Stores Nationwide," *Advertising Age*, August 6, 2008; adage.com/article?article_id=130191, accessed August 1, 2010.

16 "Safeway Aims to Expand O Organics, Eating Right Lines Beyond Its Store Shelves," *Nutrition Business Journal: Strategic Information for the Nutrition Industry | Nutrition Industry Research*; nutritionbusinessjournal.com/retail/news/07-15-safeway-exapand-o-organics-eating-right-beyond-store-shelves, accessed 6 August 2010.

17 Sarah F. Gale, "Earth's Best: A Food Every Mother Could Love," *Organic Processing Magazine*, July–September 2006; www.organicprocessing.com/opjs06/opjs06enterprise.htm, accessed August 1, 2010.

18 Paulette Miniter, "Organic-Food Stocks a Natural Choice in Slowdowns," *SmartMoney*, February 28, 2008; www.smartmoney.com/investing/stocks/organic-food-stocks-a-natural-choice-in-slowdowns-22626, accessed August 1, 2010.

19 WWF, "Agriculture and Environment: Cotton. Environmental Impacts of Production on Water Use," WWF International, 2009; www.panda.org/what_we_do/footprint/agriculture/cotton/environmental_impacts/water_use, accessed August 1, 2010.

20 *Nikebiz*, "Nike Responsibility"; www.nikebiz.com/responsibility/considered_design/environmentally_preferred.html, accessed August 1, 2010.

21 Nicole Peyraud, "Mainstream Green," *Yogi Times*, September 2007: 38-39.

22 Organic Exchange, "OE 2009 Organic Market Report: Global Organic Cotton Grows 35%, Hits 4.3 Billion in 2009," press release, August 16, 2010; organicexchange.org/oecms/OE-2009-Organic-Market-Report-Global-Organic-Cotton-Grows-35-Hits-$4.3-Billion-in-2009.html, accessed October 1, 2010.

23 UNICEF, "Child Labor," March 6, 2008; www.unicef.org/protection/index_childlabour.html, accessed August 1, 2010.

24 BBC News, "Women Face Bias Worldwide – UN," April 5, 2008; news.bbc.co.uk/2/hi/europe/7331813.stm, accessed August 1, 2010.

25 Department for International Development, "Fairtrade Olive Oil Offers Economic Lifeline for Palestinian Farmers," press release, February 2009; collections.europarchive.org/tna/20100423085705/http://www.dfid.gov.uk/Media-Room/Press-releases/2009/Fairtrade-olive-oil-offers-economic-lifeline-for-Palestinian-farmers, accessed August 1, 2010.

26 Fairtrade Foundation, "Global Fairtrade Sales Increase by 22%," press release, June 8, 2009; www.fairtrade.org.uk/press_office/press_releases_and_statements/jun_2009/global_fairtrade_sales_increase_by_22.aspx, accessed August 1, 2010.

27 Ben Cooper, "The Just-Food Interview – Sophi Tranchell, Divine Chocolate," *Just-Food*, March 5, 2009; www.just-food.com/article.aspx?id=105703&d=1, accessed August 1, 2010.

28 Clearly So, "Divine Chocolate"; www.clearlyso.com/company.jsf?id=172, accessed August 1, 2010.

29 Andrew Cleary, "Cadbury Brings in Fairtrade Dairy Milk as Ethical Foods Prosper," Bloomberg.com, July 22, 2009; bloomberg.com/apps/news?pid=20601130&sid=a10orRl3z8Dw, accessed August 1, 2010.

30 TransFair USA, "Ben & Jerry's Goes Globally Nuts for Fair Trade"; www.transfairusa.org/content/about/ppr/ppr_100218.php, accessed October 1, 2010.

31 Amy Pellicane, Clarins, email to author, August 18, 2010.

32 Clarins, "Sustainable Development"; www.clarins.com.my/social_sustainabledevelopment.php, accessed October 1, 2010.

33 Ibid.

34 Ibid.

35 Clarins, "Clarins We Care"; my.clarins.com/clarins-cosmetics/about-clarins/commitment-to-beauty/clarins-we-care/178, accessed October 1, 2010.

36 Clarins, "The ClarinsMen Award"; int.clarins.com/clarins-cosmetics/about-clarins/commitment-to-beauty/environmental-protection/the-clarinsmen-award/174, accessed October 1, 2010.

37 Julia R. Barrett, "Phthalates and Baby Boys: Potential Disruption of Human Genital Development," *Environmental Health Perspectives* 113 (2005): A542.

38 Paul Brown and Keris KrennHrubec, "Phthalates and Children's Products," National Research Center for Women & Families, November 2009; www.center4research.org/2010/04/phthalates-and-childrens-products, accessed August 1, 2010.

39 Industrial Designers Society of America, "Nike Considered Boot," 2005; www.idsa.org/content/content1/nike-considered-boot, accessed August 1, 2010.

40 Reena Jana, "Nike Quietly Goes Green," *Bloomberg BusinessWeek*, June 11, 2009; www.businessweek.com/magazine/content/09_25/b4136056155092. htm?campaign_id=rss_tech, accessed August 1, 2010.

41 Susan Piperato, "Marmoleum & Green on Display," *New York House*, July 2009; www.metrogreenbusiness.com/archive/article.php?issue= 39&dept=57, accessed August 1, 2010.

42 Forbo, "Forbo Group Annual Report 2009," March 10, 2010; www.forbo.com/ default.aspx?menuId=33, accessed August 16, 2010. Currency information converted from CHF to USD using 2009 rate of 1.03 provided in Forbo report.

43 Environmental Health Association of Nova Scotia, "Guide to Less Toxic Products" (Halifax, Nova Scotia: EHANS, 2004; www.lesstoxicguide.ca/index. asp?fetch=household, accessed August 1, 2010).

44 Seventh Generation, *Spheres of Influence: 2007 Corporate Consciousness Report* (Burlington, VT: Seventh Generation, 2008; www.svg2007report.org/flash. html#/-2, accessed August 1, 2010).

45 Martin Wolf, Director of Product and Environmental Technology, Seventh Generation, telephone interview, August 13, 2008.

46 Rich Pirog and Andrew Benjamin, "Checking the Food Odometer: Comparing Food Miles for Local Versus Conventional, Produce Sales to Iowa Institutions" (Ames, IA: Leopold Center for Sustainable Agriculture, Iowa State University, July 2003; www.leopold.iastate.edu/pubs/ staff/files/food_travel072103.pdf, accessed August 1, 2010).

47 Paul Martiquet, "More to Eating Local," Vancouver Coastal Health Authority, April 16, 2008; www.nscg.ca/Services/archive.cfm?id=261, accessed July 10, 2009.

48 Natural Marketing Institute, *LOHAS Consumer Trends Database 2009* (NMI, 2010).

49 U.S. Department of Agriculture, Agricultural Marketing Service, "Farmers Markets and Local Food Marketing," USDA, Agricultural Marketing Service, October 10, 2009; www.ams.usda.gov/AMSv1.0/ams.fetchTemplate Data.do?template=T emplateS&navID=WholesaleandFarmersMarkets&leftNav=WholesaleandFarme rsMarkets&page=WFMFarmersMarketGrowth&description=Farmers%20Marke- t%20Growth&acct=frmrdirmkt, accessed August 1, 2010.

50 Wal-Mart, "Wal-Mart Commits to America's Farmers as Produce Aisles Go Local," press release, July 1, 2008; walmartstores.com/FactsNews/ NewsRoom/ 8414. aspx, accessed August 1, 2010.

51 Wal-Mart, "Locally Grown Fact Sheet," *Live Better Index*, Wal-Mart; www. livebetterindex.com/savemoreprod.html, accessed August 6, 2010.

52 Erica Erland, Maxwell PR, email message to the author, November 20, 2009.

53 Kettle Foods Inc., "Sustainability," November 13, 2009; www.kettlefoods.com/ about-us/sustainability, accessed August 1, 2010.

54 Cyrus Farivar, "Pulling the Plug on Standby Power," *The Economist*, March 9, 2006; at Global Technology Forum, globaltechforum.eiu.com/index. asp?layout=rich_story&channelid=3&categoryid=10&title=Pulling+the+plug+on +standby+power&doc_id=8293, accessed August 1, 2010.

55 Bosch, "Life is Better with Bosch," 15 July 2009: 91; www.bosch-home.com/Files/ bosch/us/us_en/literaturerequests/bosch_full_line_winter_08lr.pdf, accessed September 30, 2010.

56 Bosch, "New Bosch Washer and Dryer Line Fits Your Lifestyle, Pampers Your Clothes for the Next Wave in Laundry Care," press release, November 2003; www.bosch-press.com/tbwebdb/bosch-usa/en-US/PressText.cfm?CFID=707&C FTOKEN=714c9f97d9380b9-9964A3F4-B5A3-413F-9367-DE1036D275FA&Search=1&id=160, accessed October 1, 2010.

57 Bosch, "Life is Better with Bosch": 9.

58 Rebecca Smith and Ben Worthen, "Stimulus Funds Speed Transformation toward 'Smart Grid'," *Wall Street Journal,* September 20, 2009: Marketplace, B1.

59 World Business Council for Sustainable Development, "Reducing Mobile Phone No-load Energy Demand: Nokia," June 18, 2008; www.wbcsd.org/Plugins/ DocSearch/details.asp?DocTypeId=24&ObjectId=MzA0MTM, accessed August 1, 2010.

60 U.S. Environmental Protection Agency and U.S. Department of Energy, "Find a Car: 2010 Toyota Prius"; at Fueleconomy.gov, www.fueleconomy.gov/feg/ findacar.htm, accessed July 10, 2009.

61 Matthew Dolan, "Ford Device Stretches Gallons," *Wall Street Journal,* October 29, 2008: D10.

62 United Nations Environment Programme, *Global Environment Outlook 4 (GEO4): Environment for Development,* 2007: 148; www.unep.org/geo/geo4/ report/geo-4_report_full_en.pdf, accessed October 1, 2010.

63 Ibid.

64 Ibid.

65 American Water Works Association, "Water Use Statistics," Drinktap.org; www. drinktap.org/consumerdnn/Default.aspx?tabid=85, accessed August 1, 2010.

66 TreeHugger, "Dual Flush Toilet by Caroma," March 1, 2005; www.treehugger. com/files/2005/03/dual_flush_toil_1.php, accessed August 1, 2010.

67 Sustainable Solutions, "Thinking Bathrooms," 24 July 2009.

68 Sharon Nunes, "Smarter Water and Energy Conservation Policies," *Environmental Leader,* July 22, 2010; www.environmentalleader.com/2010/07/22/smarter-water-and-energy-conservation-policies, accessed August 26, 2010.

69 Stokke Global, "Tripp Trapp Highchair," 2009; www.stokke-highchair.com/en-us/ tripp-trapp-highchair.aspx, accessed August 1, 2010.

70 Emily Arnold and Janet Larsen, "Bottled Water: Pouring Resources Down the Drain," Earth Policy Institute, February 2, 2006; www.earthpolicy.org/ Updates/2006/Update51.htm, accessed August 1, 2010.

71 Campaign to End Bottled Water, "Bottled Water is a Serious Problem," Wellness Enterprises, July 24, 2009; www.endbottledwater.com/TheProblem.aspx, accessed August 1, 2010.

72 Arnold and Larsen, "Bottled Water: Pouring Resources Down the Drain."

73 Springwise, "Reusable Envelopes for Reply Mail," March 7, 2008; springwise. com/marketing_advertising/reusable_envelopes_for_reply_m, accessed August 1, 2010.

74 Ibid.

75 Jim McLain, "Patagonia Seeks to Recycle Used Capilene Products into New Clothing," *Environmental News Network,* August 23, 2005; www.enn.com/top_ stories/article/2402, accessed August 1, 2010.

76 Patagonia, "Capilene Baselayers are the Best Option for High-Sweat Activities and Wet Conditions"; www.patagonia.com/web/us/patagonia.go?slc=en_US&sct=US&assetid=10148, accessed October 1, 2010.

77 Toray, "Toray, Patagonia to Jointly Work on Chemical Recycle of Nylon 6," press release, December 12, 2007; www.toray.com/news/eco/nr071212b.html, accessed August 1, 2010.

78 VerTerra, "Company"; www.verterra.com/company.php, accessed October 1, 2010.

79 Michael Dwork, CEO, VerTerra, email message to the author, November 4, 2009.

80 Jeff Borden, "SunChips Lets the Sun in: How Frito-Lay Embraced Green and Grounded its Brand Identity," *Marketing News*, September 30, 2009: 10.

81 Ibid.

82 SunChips, "SunChips Bags"; www.sunchips.com/resources/pdf/sunchips_bags.pdf, accessed August 1, 2010.

83 GenPak, "Environmentally Friendly Food Packaging"; harvestcollection.genpak.com, accessed October 1, 2010.

84 Biodegradable Products Institute, "The Compostable Label"; www.bpiworld.org/BPI-Public/Program.html, accessed October 1, 2010.

85 Biodegradable Products Institute, "FAQ"; bpiworld.org/Default.aspx?pageId=190434, accessed October 1, 2010.

86 Reuters, "Dutch Government Blocks PlayStation One," *CNet News*, December 4, 2001; news.cnet.com/Dutch-government-blocks-PlayStation-One/2110-1040_3-276584.html, accessed August 1, 2010.

87 Philips Lighting Company, "Lighting the Future" (Somerset, NJ: Philips Lighting Company, 2008; www.lighting.philips.com/us_en/environmentandsustainability/downlad/sustainability_brochure.pdf, accessed August 1, 2010).

88 Philips Lighting Company, "Alto Lamp Technology" (Somerset, NJ: Philips Lighting Company, 2009; www.wescodist.com/healthcare/docs/alto_brochure.pdf, accessed August 1, 2010).

Chapter 5

1 Joyce Cohen, "Brushing Innovations, Built on Titanium," *New York Times*, November 13, 2007: F6.

2 Soladey, "How It Works"; www.soladey.com/about.htm, accessed July 15, 2010. Author's note: a life-cycle assessment is needed to understand the relative impacts of their system versus conventional brushing.

3 Tina Butler, "Taking Care of Business: Diapers Go Green," Mongabay.com, April 2, 2006; news.mongabay.com/2006/0402-tina_butler.html, accessed August 1, 2010.

4 Ibid.

5 Industrial Designers Society of America, "SIM from Tricycle," 2006; www.idsa.org/content/content1/sim-tricycle, accessed August 1, 2010.

6 Maggie Overfelt, "Product Samples that Save Money (and the Earth)," CNNMoney.com, October 24, 2006; money.cnn.com/magazines/fsb/fsb_archive/2006/10/01/8387304/index.htm, accessed August 1, 2010.

7 Industrial Designers Society of America, "SIM from Tricycle."

8 Overfelt, "Product Samples that Save Money (and the Earth)."

9 Michael Hendrix, "Waste Not," *Innovation*, Fall 2006: 94-96.

10 Katie Fehrenbacher, "Why the Kindle Is Good for the Planet," *Earth2Tech*, August 19, 2009; earth2tech.com/ 2009/08/19/why-the-kindle-is-good-for-the-planet, accessed August 1, 2010.

11 Associated Press, "Israel Gets First Plugs For All-Electric Car Network," MSNBC. com, December 8, 2008; www.msnbc.msn.com/id/28113041, accessed August 1, 2010.

12 Mara Der Hovanesian, "I Have Just One Word For You: Bioplastics," *BusinessWeek*, June 30, 2008: 44-47.

13 The Coca-Cola Company, "The Coca-Cola Company Introduces Innovative Bottle Made from Renewable, Recyclable, Plant-Based Plastic," press release, May 14, 2009; www.thecoca-colacompany.com/presscenter/nr_20090514_plantbottle.html, accessed August 16, 2010.

14 Brian Dumaine, "Feel-good Plastic that Fades Away," *Fortune*, April 29, 2010; money.cnn.com/2010/04/29/technology/feel_good_plastic.fortune/index.htm, accessed August 20, 2010.

15 Natureworks, "Many New Products Launch for the Foodservice Industry," LLC Ingeo News, June 13, 2009; www.natureworksllc.com/news-and-events/ingeonews/ingeonews-v6-issue4.aspx, accessed October 1, 2010.

16 Steve Davies, Director of Communications and Public Affairs, NatureWorks, email message to the author, November 14, 2009.

17 Anna Burroughs, "Are Biodegradable Plastics Good for the Environment?" Associated Content, August 15, 2006; www.associatedcontent.com/article/51038/are_biodegradable_plastics_good_for.html, accessed August 1, 2010.

18 NatureWorks LLC, "NatureWorks Discovers There Is No Technical Barrier for Recycling Plastic Bottles Made from Plants," press release, February 23, 2009; www.natureworksllc.com/news-and-events/press-releases/2009/02-23-09-sorting-recycling.aspx, accessed October 1, 2010.

19 Amy Westervelt, "Explosive Growth for LED Lights in Next Decade, Report Says," SolveClimate, May 13, 2010; solveclimate.com/blog/20100513/explosive-growth-led-lights-next-decade-report-says, accessed August 27, 2010.

20 "The Home Depot Sells Ecosmart LED Lamps Made by Lighting Science Group," *LEDs Magazine*, May 2010; www.ledsmagazine.com/products/22332, accessed August 27, 2010.

21 Joe Mullich, "Mainstreaming Alternative Energy," *Wall Street Journal*, May 6, 2008: A12-13.

22 Michael S. Davies, "Understanding the Cost of Solar Energy," *Green Econometrics*, August 13, 2007; greenecon.net/understanding-the-cost-of-solar-energy/energy_economics.html, accessed August 1, 2010.

23 Mullich, "Mainstreaming Alternative Energy."

24 "Solio Solar Charger Product Comparison Chart"; www.solio.com/charger/solio-charger-comparison-chart.html, accessed August 9, 2010.

25 Voltaic Systems Inc., "Voltaic Solar Bags and Solar Chargers"; www.voltaicsystems.com.

26 Reware, "Products"; www.rewarestore.com/product/beachtote.html.

27 Martin LaMonica, "Quiet Wind-turbine Comes to U.S. Homes," *CNET News*, October 28, 2008, updated with correction February 6, 2009; news.cnet.com/8301-11128_3-10075828-54.html, accessed August 1, 2010.

28 Warren McLaren, "Ventura: Human Powered Digital Watches," Treehugger.com, April 5, 2006; www.treehugger.com/files/2006/04/ventura_human_p.php, accessed August 1, 2010.

29 Collin Dunn, "AladdinPower Hand Generator," Treehugger.com, December 2, 2005; www.treehugger.com/files/2005/12/aladdinpower_ha.php, accessed October 1, 2010.

30 Tylene Levesque, "Human-Powered Gyms in Hong Kong," *Inhabitat*, March 8, 2007; www.inhabitat.com/2007/03/08/human-powered-gyms-in-hong-kong, accessed August 1, 2010.

31 Windstream Power, "Bike Power Generator"; www.windstreampower.com/Bike_Power_Generator.php, accessed August 1, 2010.

32 GM Volt, "Chevy Volt Exact Launch Date Will be Mid-November 2010, Tens of Thousands in 2011," April 20, 2009; gm-volt.com/2009/04/20/chevy-volt-exact-launch-date-will-be-mid-november-2010-tens-of-thousands-in-2011, accessed August 16, 2010.

33 Chevrolet, "Chevy Volt: The Future is Electrifying"; www.chevrolet.com/pages/open/default/fuel/electric.do?evar23=fuel_solutions_landing%20page, accessed August 1, 2010.

34 Jeff Sabatini, "Honda Sees a Hydrogen Future," *Wall Street Journal*, November 30, 2007: W7.

35 Ibid.

36 Ibid.

37 Tom Mutchler, "Commuting in a Honda FCX Clarity," ConsumerReports.org, January 26, 2009; blogs.consumerreports.org/cars/2009/01/commuting-in-honda-fcx-clarity-fuel-cell-car.html, accessed August 1, 2010.

38 Nissan Motor Company, *Nissan's Environmental Initiatives: Nissan Green Program* (Yokohama, Japan, February 2009).

39 Ibid.

40 Ibid.

41 Ibid.

42 Nissan USA, "Nissan LEAF: New Car," Nissan News: Technology, June 30, 2010; www.nissanusa.com/leaf-electric-car/news/technology#/leaf-electric-car/news/technology, accessed October 1, 2010.

43 Yoshio Takahashi, "Nissan Motor Turns Over a New Leaf, Going Electric," *Wall Street Journal*, August 3, 2009: B1.

44 Nissan Motor Company, *Nissan's Environmental Initiatives*.

45 Nissan-Global, "World First Eco Pedal Helps Reduce Fuel Consumption," August 4, 2008; www.nissan-global.com/EN/NEWS/2008/_STORY/080804-02-e.html, accessed October 1, 2010.

46 Nissan Motor Company, *Nissan's Environmental Initiatives*.

47 Ibid.

48 Ibid.

49 Shivani Vora, "Test-Driving Car-Share Services," *Wall Street Journal*, June 11, 2009: D2.

50 Zipcar, "Zipcar Announces Annual Low-Car Diet 'Call For Participants',"
Zipcar Press Overview, June 24, 2010; zipcar.mediaroom.com/index.
php?s=43&item=128, accessed August 11, 2010.

51 Zipcar, "Green Benefits"; www.zipcar.com/is-it/greenbenefits, accessed
August 9, 2010.

52 Ibid.

53 Zipcar, "Zipcar Announces Annual Low-Car Diet 'Call For Participants'."

54 Steven Erlanger, "A New Fashion Catches On in Paris: Cheap Bicycle Rentals,"
New York Times, July 13, 2008: A6.

55 Tamar Lewin, "A Leading Publisher Announces a Plan to Rent Textbooks to College Students," *New York Times,* August 14, 2009: A10.

56 REC Solar Power Company, "Commercial Financing"; www.recsolar.com/
CommercialFinancing.aspx, accessed August 1, 2010.

57 Peter Maloney, "Pay for the Power, Not the Panels," *New York Times*, March 26,
2008: H1.

58 Netflix, "Netflix Passes 10 Million Subscribers, with 600,000 Net Additions since
the First of the Year," Netflix.com, February 12, 2009; netflix.mediaroom.com/
index.php?s=43&item=307, accessed August 1, 2010.

59 Zonbu, "Zonbu's Zonbox Declared Greenest Computers for Consumers, Certified
as First Consumer Device to Win Gold-Level Certification from EPEAT," July 6,
2007; www.zonbu.com/download/EPEAT-June-07.pdf, accessed August 1, 2010.

60 BASF Corporation, "PremAir Technology Destroys Ozone," August 21, 2007;
www2.basf.us/corporate/news_2007/news_release_2007_00011.htm, accessed
August 1, 2010.

61 BASF Corporation, "Yellow Cab Transforms into Smog-Eater for Taxi 07 Exhibit at
New York Auto Show," April 4, 2007; www2.basf.us/corporate/news2007/040407_
Taxi07.htm, accessed August 1, 2010.

62 Reliance, "PUR Purifier of Water"; www.relianceproducts.info/index.html,
accessed August 1, 2010.

Chapter 6

1 Jacquelyn A. Ottman, Edwin R. Stafford, and Cathy L. Hartman, "Avoiding Green
Marketing Myopia: Ways to Improve Consumer Appeal for Environmentally Preferable Products," *Environment* 48.5 (2006): 22-36.

2 AFM Safecoat, "We Put Your Health First"; www.afmsafecoat.com, accessed October 1, 2010.

3 Rob Walker, "Sex vs. Ethics," *Fast Company*, June 2008: 74-78.

4 Ottman *et al.*, "Avoiding Green Marketing Myopia."

5 "Pepsi Cans Feature Recycling Info," *Environmental Leader*, April 27, 2008;
www.environmentalleader.com/2008/04/27/pepsi-cans-feature-recycling-info,
accessed August 1, 2010.

6 18Seconds.org; green.yahoo.com/18seconds.

7 Blue Planet Network, "Brita and Nalgene Partner to Challenge People to Make
a Difference," August 21, 2007; blueplanenetwork.org/news/brita_ nalgene,
accessed August 1, 2010.

8 Aileen Zerrudo, Director of Communications, The Clorox Company, email message to the author, August 25, 2009.

9 Netflix, "Netflix Facts"; www.netflix.com/MediaCenter?id=5379#about, accessed August 1, 2010.

10 Nicole Rousseau, VP Retail Marketing, HSBC U.S., email message to the author, September 24, 2009.

11 Stonyfield Farm, "Meet our CE-Yo and his Team"; stonyfield.com/about_us/meet_our_ceyo_and_his_team/index.jsp, accessed October 1, 2010.

12 Zipcar, "Zipcar Announces Annual Low-Car Diet 'Call For Participants'."

13 Philip W. Sawyer (ed.), "It's Not Easy Being Green: How to Improve Advertising with Environmental Themes," *Starch Tested Copy* 2.5 (1993): 5.

14 Don't Mess with Texas, "FAQs"; www.dontmesswithtexas.org/about/faq, accessed August 1, 2010.

15 Dawson M. Williams, "Car2Can Video Contest is 'Don't Mess with Texas' Campaign's Latest Anti-litter Initiative," *Dallas Morning News*, June 17, 2009; www.dallasnews.com/sharedcontent/dws/news/texassouthwest/stories/061709dnmetlittervideos.889ed007.html, accessed August 1, 2010.

16 Natural Marketing Institute, *Understanding the LOHAS Market Report* (Harleysville, PA: NMI, March 2008): 112.

17 "Reynolds Wrap Foil From 100% Recycled Aluminum," *Journal News*, June 6, 2009 (advertisement).

19 Cause Marketing Forum, "The Growth of Cause Marketing," 2010; www.causemarketingforum.com/page.asp?ID=188, accessed October 1, 2010.

20 Cone, "Cone Releases First Cause Consumer Behavior Study," October 1, 2008; www.coneinc.com/content1188, accessed July 20, 2010.

21 People, "Caught Caring: (RED), Bugaboo and Kelly Rutherford," People.com, September 14, 2009; celebritybabies.people.com/2009/09/14/caught-caring-red-bugaboo-and-kelly-rutherford, accessed August 13, 2010.

22 UNICEF, "International partnerships: IKEA Social Initiative," 11 May 2010; www.unicef.org/corporate_partners/index_42735.html, accessed August 13, 2010.

23 www.onepercentfortheplanet.org

24 Anya Kamentz, "Cleaning Solution," *Fast Company*, September 2008: 121-25.

25 "Clorox To Stop Using Chlorine," *Chemical & Engineering News*, August 16, 2010; pubs.acs.org/cen/news/87/i45/8745notw2.html, accessed October 1, 2010.

26 Andrew Adam Newman, "Tough on Crude Oil, Soft on Ducklings," *New York Times*, September 25, 2009: B6.

27 Rob Walker, "Big Gulp," *New York Times*, February 26, 2006; www.nytimes.com/2006/02/26/magazine/26wwln_consumed.html, accessed August 1, 2010.

28 Cone, "Cone Releases First Cause Consumer Behavior Study."

29 "Philips Launches 'A Simple Switch' Campaign," *Environmental Leader*, July 6, 2007; www.environmentalleader.com/2007/07/06/philips-launches-a-simple-switch-campaign, accessed August 1, 2010.

30 Emily Steel, "Taking Green Message to Great Outdoors," *Wall Street Journal*, October 2, 2007: B9.

31 United Nations Environment Programme, *Talk the Walk: Advancing Sustainable Lifestyles through Marketing and Communications* (UNEP, December 2005): 23.

32 Figures for June 30, 2010 from Internet World Stats, "World Internet Usage and Population Statistics"; www.internetworldstats.com/stats.htm, accessed August 1, 2010.

33 Jonathan Lemonnier, "Spending on Alternative Media Jumps 22%," *Advertising Age*, March 26, 2008; adage.com/digital/article?article_id=125950, accessed August 13, 2010.

34 No Sweat; www.nosweatapparel.com.

35 Beth Snyder Bulik, "What Your Favorite Social Network Says About You," *Advertising Age*, July 8, 2009; adage.com/digital/article?article_id=137792, accessed August 1, 2010.

36 "Role of Social Media in Sustainability Evolves," *Environmental Leader*, July 15, 2009; www.environmentalleader.com/2009/07/15/role-of-social-media-in-sustainability-evolves, accessed August 1, 2010.

37 Ibid.

38 Lauren Thaman, Associate Director, External Relations, Procter & Gamble, email message to the author, October 28, 2009.

Chapter 7

1 Emilia Askari, "USA: Ford CEO Says He's Green," *CorpWatch*, October 31, 2001; www.corpwatch.org/article.php?id=1453, accessed August 1, 2010.

2 As of February 24, 2010, General Motors officially announced their plans to "wind down" the Hummer business after the failure of the sale to a Chinese manufacturer. General Motors, "HUMMER Sale to Tengzhong Cannot be Completed. Wind Down of HUMMER Business to Begin," February 24, 2010; media.gm.com/content/media/us/en/news/news_detail.brand_gm.html/content/Pages/news/us/en/2010/Feb/0224_hummer, accessed August 12, 2010.

3 *Business Wire*, "Nine in 10 at U.N. Climate Change Conference Believe Greenwashing is a Problem," press release, December 9, 2007; www.businesswire.com/portal/site/google/?ndmViewId=news_view&newsId=20071209005061&newsLang=en, accessed August 1, 2010.

4 British Telecom, "Consumers Sceptical of Corporate Commitment to Sustainability," press release, January 4, 2007; www.btplc.com/News/Articles/Showarticle.cfm?ArticleID=11efc6a1-1df0-4189-a0f7-392c478a12bf, accessed September 29, 2008.

5 Bernie Becker, "Baseball Team Clashes with Environmentalist over Oil Company Advertising," *New York Times*, July 27, 2008; www.nytimes.com/2008/07/27/us/27stadium.html, accessed August 1, 2010.

6 Steve Jobs, "A Greener Apple," Apple Inc., September 14, 2008; www.apple.com/hotnews/agreenerapple, accessed August 1, 2010.

7 Burst Media, "Consumers Recall Green Ads," *Business Wire*, press release, April 14, 2008; www.businesswire.com/portal/site/google/?ndmViewId=news_view&newsId=20080414005857&newsLang=en, accessed August 1, 2010.

8 A certification rating provided by the B Lab nonprofit organization: www.bcorporation.net.

9 Patagonia, "The Footprint Chronicles"; www.patagonia.com/web/us/footprint/index.jsp?slc=en_US&sct=US, accessed October 1, 2010.

10 The Webby Awards; www.webbyawards.com/webbys/current.php?season=12, accessed October 1, 2010.

11 Natalie Zmuda, "Sigg Tries to Control Brand Damage after Admitting its Bottles Contain BPA," *Advertising Age*, August 31, 2009; adage.com/article?article_ id=138712, accessed August 1, 2010.

12 Christopher A. Cole and Linda A. Goldstein, " 'Green' is so Appealing," *New York Law Journal*, September 15, 2008; www.law.com/jsp/nylj/PubArticleNY. jsp?id=1202424493387, accessed August 1, 2010.

13 "How to Avoid a Green Marketing Backlash," *Environmental Leader*, April 15, 2008; www.environmentalleader.com/?s=HOW+TO+AVOID+A+GREEN +MARKETING+BACKLASH, accessed August 1, 2010.

14 Mark Sweney, "Lexus Ad Banned for Claiming SUV is Environmentally Friendly," *The Guardian*, May 23, 2007, and as "Lexus ad Banned for Green Claims"; www.guardian.co.uk/business/2007/may/23/advertising.media, accessed August 1, 2010.

15 Reilly Capps, "Questioning How Biota Sprung a Leak," *Telluride Daily Planet*, April 16, 2008; www.telluridenews.com/archive/x121157044, accessed October 13, 2008.

16 BIOTA; www.biotaspringwater.com.

17 Christina Binkley, "Picking Apart Bamboo Couture," *Wall Street Journal*, November 12, 2009: D1.

18 "U.S. Green Council Debated," *Environmental Leader*, June 17, 2009; www. environmentalleader.com/2009/06/17/us-green-product-council-debated, accessed August 1, 2010.

19 Tim Bradshaw, "Complaint Upheld over Shell Advert," *Financial Times*, August 13, 2008; www.ft.com/cms/s/0/d08d0a66-68c1-11dd-a4e5-0000779fd18c.html, accessed August 1, 2010.

20 Mark Sweney, "Ad for US Cotton Industry Banned by ASA over Green Claims," *The Guardian*, March 12, 2008; www.guardian.co.uk/media/2008/mar/12/asa. advertising1/print, accessed August 1, 2010.

21 Dr. Anastasia O'Rourke, Co-Founder, Ecolabel Index, email to author, August 17, 2010.

22 Eve Smith, Brand Strategist, BBMG, email message to the author, December 3, 2009.

23 Emily Crumley, Manager, Chain of Custody, FSC, email message to the author, November 23, 2009.

24 Vanessa Gibbin, Brand, Advertising and Research, The Carbon Trust, email to author, May 12, 2010.

25 Joan Schaffer, Spokeswoman, USDA, telephone interview with author about USDA Organic, December 1, 2009.

26 Shelley Zimmer, Manager of Environmental Affairs, HP, email message to the author, December 1, 2009.

27 International Association for Soaps, Detergents and Maintenance Products, *Promoting Sustainable Consumption of Household Laundry Detergents in Europe: Washright, a Unique Industry Campaign* (Brussels: AISE, November 2002; www. washright.com/documents/Washright_11-2002.qxd.pdf, accessed August 1, 2010).

28 Michael Sanserino, "Peer Pressure and Other Pitches," *Wall Street Journal*, September 14, 2009: B6.

Chapter 8

1 Ian Austen, "Bottle Maker to Stop Using Plastic Linked to Health Concerns," *New York Times*, April 18, 2008; www.nytimes.com/2008/04/18/business/18plastic. html, accessed August 1, 2010.
2 Mark Ritson, "Bottled Water Brands Beware: Tap is Back," *Branding Strategy Insider* blog, November 7, 2007; www.brandingstrategyinsider.com/2007/11/ bottled-water-b.html, accessed August 1, 2010.
3 Jennifer Lee, "City Council Shuns Bottles in Favor of Water from Tap," *New York Times*, June 17, 2008; www.nytimes.com/2008/06/17/nyregion/17water.html, accessed August 1, 2010.
4 International Bottled Water Association, "IBWA Launches Major Media Advertising Campaign," press release, August 2, 2007; www.bottledwater.org/content/ ibwa-launches-major-media-advertising-campaign, accessed August 1, 2010.
5 Emily Bryson York, "Nestle, Pepsi and Coke Face their Waterloo," *Advertising Age*, October 8, 2007; adage.com/print?article_id=120986, accessed August 1, 2010.
6 Rebecca Wilhelm, "Bottling Trends: Bottled Water Industry Makes Strides," *Water & Wastes Digest*, April 2008; www.wwdmag.com/Bottling-Trends-article9117, accessed August 1, 2010.
7 Mike Verespej, "Nestlé Exec Counsels Bottled-Water Industry," *Plastics News*, July 7, 2008: 1.
8 Sustainable Life Media, "More Marketers Targeting Green-Conscious Kids," July 25, 2008; www.sustainablelifemedia.com/content/story/brand/more_marketers_targeting_green_conscious_kids, accessed August 1, 2010.
9 Briana Curran, Public & Community Relations Program Manager, Staples, email messages to the author, May 28, 2009 and September 2, 2009.
10 Vince Meldrum, "Robinson Students Address Invasive Species," Earth Force news, March 18, 2008; www.earthforce.org/content/article/detail/2083, accessed August 1, 2010.
11 Earth Force, "Staples Award Winners"; www.earthforce.org/section/thank_you/ staples/staples_awards, accessed August 1, 2010.
12 Lynn Ascrizzi, "TerraCycle: Yogurt Cups, and More, Help Schools Raise Funds," Natural Resources Council of Maine, March 16, 2008; www.nrcm.org/news_ detail.asp?news=2249, accessed August 11, 2010.
13 www.biggreenhelp.com
14 Joanna Roses, Sr. Director Communications, Nickelodeon, email message to the author, October 26, 2009; www.neafoundation.org/pages/educators/grant-programs/nea-foundation-green-grants, accessed July 21, 2010.
15 Jonas Risen, "Solar Decathlon – Technische Universität Darmstadt," Greenline, October 17, 2007; greenlineblog.com/2007/10/solar-decathlon-technische-universitat-darmstadt, accessed August 11, 2010.
16 www.nwf.org/campusecology/chillout
17 Jen Fournelle, Campus Program Coordinator, National Wildlife Federation, email message to the author, September 1, 2009.

18 Aria Finger, Chief Marketing Officer, DoSomething, email message to the author, October 1, 2009.

19 "SHRM Survey Asks How 'Green' is the American Workplace?" Reuters, January 16, 2008; www.reuters.com/article/pressRelease/idUS188509+16-Jan-2008-+BW20080116, accessed July 21, 2010.

20 Alcoa, "2008 Alcoa Worldwide Month of Service: Alcoa Employees to Make a Difference Where they Live and Work," press release, September 30, 2008; www.alcoa.com/global/en/community/foundation/news_releases/2008_mos.asp, accessed August 1, 2010.

21 Michael Barbaro, "At Wal-Mart, Lessons in Self-Help," *New York Times*, April 5, 2007; www.nytimes.com/2007/04/05/business/05improve.html, accessed August 1, 2010.

22 KaBOOM!, "KaBOOM Partner: The Home Depot," Kaboom.org, 2009; kaboom.org/about_kaboom/supporting_partners/meet_our_partners/partner_spotlight_home_depot, accessed 24 July 2009.

23 Erin Gunderson, Best Buy PR, email message to the author, September 2, 2009.

24 Jill Vohr, Marketing Manager, U.S. Environmental Protection Agency, email message to the author, December 8, 2009.

25 Ahmed El Amin, "Wal-Mart Unveils 'Green' Packaging Rating System," FoodProductionDaily.com, November 2, 2006; www.foodproductiondaily.com/content/view/print/104013, accessed August 1, 2010.

26 NatureWorks LLC, "KLM, the First Airline to Introduce the Environmentally Friendly Ingeo-Lined Cup," press release, June 16, 2009, updated November 11, 2009; www.natureworksllc.com/news-and-events/press-releases/2009/06-16-09-klm-cup.aspx, accessed August 1, 2010.

27 "Paper, Cardboard Packagers Launches 'Responsible Package' Initiative," *Environmental Leader*, October 8, 2009; www.environmentalleader.com/ 2009/10/08/paper-cardboard-packagers-launch-responsible-package-initiative, accessed August 1. 2010.

28 Brian M. Carney, "Bye Bye, Light Bulb," *Wall Street Journal*, January 2, 2008: A10.

29 Sustainable Housing Communities/U.S. Department of Housing and Urban Development (HUD), "Sustainable Housing and Communities," hud.gov, 2010; portal.hud.gov/portal/page/portal/HUD/program_offices/sustainable_housing_communities, accessed August 8, 2010.

30 Doris De Guzman, "Metabolix Targets Bioplastic Bottle," ICIS.com, October 8, 2009; www.icis.com/blogs/green-chemicals/2009/10/metabolix-targets-bioplastic-b.html, accessed August 11, 2010.

31 The National Environmental Directory, July 22, 2009; eelink.net/gaindirectories.html.

32 Conservation International, "McDonald's," 2009; www.conservation.org/discover/partnership/corporate/Pages/mcdonalds.aspx, accessed August 11, 2010.

33 Kimberly-Clark, "Kimberly-Clark Sets the Bar Higher for Tissue Products with Stronger Global Forest Policy," press release, August 5, 2009; investor.kimberly-clark.com/releasedetail.cfm?ReleaseID=401321, accessed August 1, 2010.

34 Lisa Bailey, Communications Manager, Americas, Marine Stewardship Council, email message to the author, August 27, 2009.

35 Rahul Raj, VP of Marketing, New Leaf Paper, email message to the author, September 2, 2009. Nicole Rycroft, Executive Director, Canopy, telephone interview with the author, July 30, 2009.

36 James E. Austin, Roberto Gutierrez, E. Ogliastri, and E. Reficco, "Capitalizing on Convergence," *Stanford Social Innovation Review* 5.4 (Winter 2007): 24-31.

37 American Museum of Natural History, "Climate Change"; www.amnh.org/exhibitions/climatechange, accessed August 1, 2010.

38 Cargill, "Cargill: Corporate Responsibility – Partnerships"; www.cargill.com/corporate-responsibility/partnerships/index.jsp, accessed August 12, 2010.

39 The Nature Conservancy, "The Home Depot"; www.nature.org/joinanddonate/corporatepartnerships/partnership/homedepot.html, accessed August 1, 2010.

Chapter 9

1 Timberland, "Creating Sustainable Change," March 5, 2009; www.timberland.com/corp/index.jsp?page=csr_civic_change, accessed August 8, 2010.

2 Alison Franklin, City Year, email to the author, June 28, 2010.

3 This case study was prepared by Jacquelyn Ottman using secondary sources and approved for publication by Cara Vanderbeck, Timberland, by email, August 2010.

4 Starbucks Coffee Company, "Starbucks Shared Planet Goals & Progress 2009"; www.starbucks.com/responsibility/learn-more/goals-and-progress, accessed August 12, 2010.

5 This case study was prepared by Jacquie Ottman using secondary sources and approved for publication by Ben Packard, Vice President, Global Responsibility, Starbucks, by email, March 18, 2010.

About the author

At age four, her siblings called her "Junkie Jacquie" when she dragged home treasures from the neighbor's trash. At age thirty-four, Jacquie pioneered green marketing by founding J. Ottman Consulting, Inc. Her mission: apply her in-depth consumer packaged goods expertise, with a creative bent for dreaming up new products and her finely honed strategic instincts, to help businesses develop and market the next generation of products designed with sustainability in mind.

With a client roster that includes over 60 of the Fortune 500, the USDA's BioPreferred and other U.S. government labeling programs, Ottman is a sought-after keynoter for conferences and corporate forums around the globe. She is a founding co-chair of the Sustainable Business Committee of the Columbia Business School Alumni Club of New York. She is also the former co-chair of the NYC chapter of O2, the global network of green designers, and was founding jury chair for the American Marketing Association's Special Edison Awards for Environmental Achievement in New Products.

In 2004, she spearheaded the IDSA-endorsed Design:Green educational initiative with the goal of jumpstarting eco-design education in the U.S. Underwritten with an Innovation Grant from the U.S. Environmental Protection Agency, Design:Green now continues as a course in the online Certificate in Sustainable Design program of the Minneapolis College of Art and Design.

The author of hundreds of articles on green marketing topics, she blogs at Jacquie Ottman's Green Marketing Blog (www.greenmarketing.com/blog), as well as for the *Harvard Business Review* and other websites.

Her three previous books on green marketing have been translated into five languages.

Ottman is a graduate of Smith College and lives in New York City. The widow of Geoffrey S. Southworth, an industrial recycler, she is the proud stepmother of his three children and two grandchildren.

Index

Page numbers in *italic figures* refer to illustrations